Preventing Harmful Substance Use

Preventing Harmful Substance Use

THE EVIDENCE BASE FOR POLICY AND PRACTICE

Edited by

TIM STOCKWELL
Centre for Addictions Research of BC, University of Victoria, Canada

PAUL J. GRUENEWALD
Prevention Research Center, Pacific Institute for Research and Evaluation, Berkeley, CA, USA

JOHN W. TOUMBOUROU
*Centre for Adolescent Health, Department of Paediatrics, University of Melbourne and
Murdoch Children's Research Institute, Australia*

WENDY LOXLEY
National Drug Research Institute, Perth, Australia

John Wiley & Sons, Ltd

Copyright © 2005   John Wiley & Sons Ltd, The Atrium, Southern Gate, Chichester,
West Sussex PO19 8SQ, England

Telephone (+44) 1243 779777

Email (for orders and customer service enquiries): cs-books@wiley.co.uk
Visit our Home Page on www.wileyeurope.com or www.wiley.com

Reprinted October 2005

Other Wiley Editorial Offices

John Wiley & Sons Inc., 111 River Street, Hoboken, NJ 07030, USA

Jossey-Bass, 989 Market Street, San Francisco, CA 94103-1741, USA

Wiley-VCH Verlag GmbH, Boschstr. 12, D-69469 Weinheim, Germany

John Wiley & Sons Australia Ltd, 33 Park Road, Milton, Queensland 4064, Australia

John Wiley & Sons (Asia) Pte Ltd, 2 Clementi Loop #02-01, Jin Xing Distripark, Singapore 129809

John Wiley & Sons Canada Ltd, 22 Worcester Road, Etobicoke, Ontario, Canada M9W 1L1

Wiley also publishes its books in a variety of electronic formats. Some content that
appears in print may not be available in electronic books.

Library of Congress Cataloging-in-Publication Data

Preventing harmful substance use : the evidence base for policy and practice / edited
    by Tim Stockwell... [etal.].
        p. cm.
        Includes index.
        ISBN 0-470-09227-0 – ISBN 0-470-09228-9
        1. Substance abuse—Prevention. 2. Substanceabuse—Prevention—Evaluation.
    I. Stockwell, Tim. II. Title.
    HV4998.P73 2005
    362.29'17–dc22   2004019931

British Library Cataloguing in Publication Data

A catalogue record for this book is available from the British Library

ISBN 10: 0-470-09228-9 (P/B)   ISBN 13: 978-0-470-09228-6 (P/B)
ISBN 10: 0-470-09227-0 (H/B)   ISBN 13: 978-0-470-09227-9 (H /B)

Typeset in 10/12 pt Times and Sans Serif by TechBooks, New DelhiIndia
Printed and bound in Great Britain by Antony Rowe Ltd, Chippenham, Wiltshire
This book is printed on acid-free paper responsibly manufactured from sustainable forestry
in which at least two trees are planted for each one used for paper production.

Contents

About the Editors

Paul J. Gruenewald is a Senior Research Scientist and Scientific Director of Prevention Research Center (PRC) in Berkeley, California, a division of the US-based Pacific Institute for Research and Evaluation (PIRE). Research at PIRE is funded by grants and contracts from the National Institutes of Health, National Institutes of Justice, Office of Juvenile Justice and Delinquency Prevention, the Center for Substance Abuse Prevention, and other national, state, local and private funding agencies. Dr Gruenewald is Principal Investigator of a Center grant funded by the National Institute on Alcohol Abuse and Alcoholism to study "Environmental Approaches to Prevention" (P60-AA906282) and a Merit award recipient for his studies of "Alcohol Outlets and Violence" (R37-AA912927). He is currently also Director of the PIRE-based Spatial Systems Group, a group that focuses on ecological studies of alcohol- and drug-related problems. He has published widely in the areas of alcohol policy and community prevention. He is well known for his application of rigorous mathematical and statistical approaches to the analysis of community level problems related to alcohol use, drugs and crime.

Wendy Loxley is an Associate Professor at the National Drug Research Institute, at Curtin University of Technology in Perth, Western Australia, where she has been employed for fifteen years. Much of her early research career was concerned with addressing the risk of blood-borne viruses to Australian injecting drug users, and she has been involved in a number of large quantitative and smaller qualitative studies exploring this issue. Other research experiences include monitoring illicit drug use among police detainees, the evaluation of community-based approaches to drug law enforcement, and the use of testing and vaccination to prevent hepatitis C and other blood-borne viruses among injectors. She was selected by the Australian Government Department of Health and Ageing to lead the evaluation of the Community Partnerships Initiative which was aimed at the development of community-based approaches to primary prevention of illicit drug use in young people. More recently, she was the first principal investigator on a commission for the Australian Government Department of Health and Ageing which undertook a major literature review of the evidence relating to the prevention of drug use, risk and harm in Australia. She is the first author of the two volumes—Monograph and Summary—which have recently been published from this work.

Tim Stockwell is currently Director of the Centre for Addictions Research of BC, Canada, and, until mid-2004, was Director of Australia's National Drug Research Institute based at Curtin University in Western Australia. He recently co-edited the critically acclaimed Wiley book *International Handbook of Alcohol Dependence and Problems* with Nick Heather and Tim Peters. He has published widely in the field of addiction studies and has particular expertise in the areas of alcohol and other drug epidemiology and prevention policy. He was Regional Editor for Australasia of the international journal *Addiction* for six years. He was until recently a member of Australia's National Expert Advisory Committee on Alcohol, a Director of Australia's Alcohol Education and Rehabilitation Foundation and member of the World Health Organization's Alcohol Policy and Strategy Advisory Committee. He obtained his first degree in Psychology and Philosophy at Oxford University, a Master's degree in Clinical Psychology from the University of Surrey and a doctorate at the Institute of Psychiatry, the University of London.

John Winston Toumbourou is Associate Professor at the Department of Paediatrics, University of Melbourne, and a Senior Researcher at the Center for Adolescent Health, within the Murdoch Children's Research Institute. John is a founding member and the past Chair of the College of Health Psychologists within the Australian Psychological Society. He is a Principal Investigator on a number of studies investigating healthy youth development, including the Australian Temperament Project (investigating the role of childhood temperament and behaviour in the prediction of adolescent substance use, delinquency and depression), and the International Youth Development study (a collaborative longitudinal study with the Social Development Research Group at the University of Washington). John has been involved in the development of a number of youth health promotion programmes including the Chronic Illness Peer Support Program (Victorian Public Health Award 1999), the Behaviour Exchange Systems Training Program (targeting families experiencing youth substance abuse), Program for Parents (a national youth suicide prevention programme demonstrating success in reducing early youth delinquency and substance use) and Communities That Care (a community mobilisation programme targeting crime prevention and substance abuse prevention). John has been prominent in developing literature reviews and policy recommendations relevant to developmental prevention through the Victorian Premier's Drug Prevention Council Drug Info Clearinghouse and within the consortium that produced the recent Prevention Monograph summarising the evidence base for the Australian Commonwealth Government's Prevention Agenda.

Contributors

Steve Allsop, Acting Executive Director, Western Australian Drug and Alcohol Office, PO Box 126, Mt Lawley, WA 6929, Australia

Sven Andréasson, Department of Public Health, Karolinska Institute, Crafoords väg 6, Stockholm 113 24, Sweden

James C. Anthony, Bloomberg School of Public Health, Johns Hopkins University, 624 North Broadway LCID@893, Baltimore, MD 21205, USA

Ron Borland, Nigel Gray Fellow, VicHealth Centre for Tobacco Control, The Cancer Council of Victoria, 1 Rathdowne Street, Carlton, Vic 3053, Australia

Suzanne Briscoe, Research Fellow, NSW Bureau of Crime Statistics and Research, NSW Attorney General's Department, GPO Box 6, Sydney, NSW 2001, Australia

Christopher Canty, Knowledge Manager, Department of Justice, Crime Prevention, Victoria, Australia

Susan Carruthers, National Drug Research Institute, GPO Box U1987, Perth, WA 6845, Australia

Richard F. Catalano, Social Development Research Group, University of Washington, 9725 3rd Ave NE, Suite 401, Seattle, WA 98115, USA

Jonathan P. Caulkins, H. John Heinz III School of Public Policy and Management, Carnegie Mellon University, 5000 Forbes Avenue, Pittsburgh, PA 15213-3890, USA and RAND Drug Policy Research Center, 201 North Craig St, Suite 102, Pittsburgh, PA 15213, USA

Louisa Degenhardt, National Drug and Alcohol Research Centre, University of NSW, Sydney, NSW 2052, Australia

Neil Donnelly, Research Manager, NSW Bureau of Crime Statistics and Research, NSW Attorney General's Department, GPO Box 6, Sydney, NSW 2001, Australia

Mark E. Feinberg, Prevention Research Center, Health and Human Development, Pennsylvania State University, S-109 Henderson Bldg South, University Park, PA 16802, USA

Bridget Freisthler, Department of Social Welfare, UCLA School of Public Affairs, 3250 Public Policy Building, Los Angeles, CA90095, USA

Brendan J. Gomez, 402 Marion Building, 135E Nittany Avenue, State College, PA 16801, USA

Kathryn Graham, Social Factors and Prevention Initiatives, Centre for Addiction and Mental Health, The Gordon J. Mogenson Building, 100 Collip Circle, Suite 200, London, Ontario N6G 4X8, Canada

Dennis Gray, National Drug Research Institute, GPO Box U1987, Perth, WA 6845, Australia

Mark T. Greenberg, Bennett Chair of Prevention Research, Director, Prevention Research Center, Associate Director, Child, Youth and Families Consortium, HDFS—Henderson Building South, Room 109, Penn State University, University Park, PA 16802, USA

Joel W. Grube, Pacific Institute for Research and Evaluation, Center for Child and Adolescent Health Research, Prevention Research Center, 1995 University Avenue, Suite 450, Berkeley, CA 94704, USA

Paul J. Gruenewald, Pacific Institute for Research and Evaluation, Prevention Research Center, 1995 University Avenue, Suite 450, Berkeley, CA 94704, USA

Ben Haines, Research Fellow, National Drug Research Institute, GPO Box U1987, Perth, WA 6845, Australia

Wayne Hall, Office of Public Policy and Ethics, Institute for Molecular Bioscience, University of Queensland, St Lucia, Qld 4072, Australia

Delia Hendrie, School of Population Health, University of Western Australia, Nedlands, WA 6907, Australia

David Hill, Centre for Behavioural Research in Cancer, 1 Rathdowne Street, Carlton South, Vic 3053, Australia

Harold D. Holder, Pacific Institute for Research and Evaluation, Prevention Research Center, 1995 University Avenue, Suite 450, Berkeley, CA 94704, USA

Stephen James, Department of Criminology, University of Melbourne, Parkville, Vic 3010, Australia

Elizabeth LaScala, Pacific Institute for Research and Evaluation, Prevention Research Center, 1995 University Avenue, Suite 450, Berkeley, CA 94704, USA

Juliet P. Lee, Pacific Institute for Research and Evaluation, Prevention Research Center, 1995 University Avenue, Suite 450, Berkeley, CA 94704, USA

Simon Lenton, National Drug Research Institute, GPO Box U1987, Perth, WA 6845, Australia

David Levy, Pacific Institute for Research and Evaluation, Public Services Research Institute, Chapel Hill Center, Calverton Office Park, 11710 Beltsville Drive, Suite 300, Calverton, MD 20705-3102, USA

Jonathan Liberman, VicHealth Centre for Tobacco Control, The Cancer Council of Victoria, 1 Rathdowne Street, Carlton, Vic 3053, Australia

Wendy Loxley, National Drug Research Institute, GPO Box U1987, Perth, WA 6845, Australia

Michael Lynskey, Department of Psychiatry, Washington University School of Medicine, 40 N. Kingshighway, Suite One, St Louis, MO 63108, USA

Nyanda McBride, National Drug Research Institute, GPO Box U1987, Perth, WA 6845, Australia

Richard Midford, National Drug Research Institute, GPO Box U1987, Perth, WA 6845, Australia

Ted R. Miller, Pacific Institute for Research and Evaluation, 11710 Beltsville Drive, Suite 300, Calverton, MD 20705, USA

David Moore, National Drug Research Institute, GPO Box U1987, Perth, WA 6845, Australia

Peter Nygaard, Centre for Alcohol and Drug Research, Jens Baggesensvej 43–45, 8200 AArhus N, Denmark, and Pacific Institute for Research and Evaluation, Prevention Research Center, 1995 University Avenue, Suite 450, Berkeley, CA 94704, USA

D. Wayne Osgood, Liberal Arts, Department of Sociology, Pennsylvania State University, 0211 Oswald Tower, University Park, PA 16802, USA

George Patton, Centre for Adolescent Health, 2 Gatehouse Street, Parkville, Vic 3052, Australia

Jürgen Rehm, Public Health and Regulatory Policy, Centre for Addictions and Mental Health (CAMH), Room 2035, 33 Russell Street, Toronto, ON M5S 2S1, Canada and Institute of Addiction Research, Zurich, Switzerland and Public Health Sciences, University of Toronto, Canada

Lillian G. Remer, Pacific Institute for Research and Evaluation, Prevention Research Center, 1995 University Avenue, Suite 450, Berkeley, CA 94704, USA

Robin Room, Centre for Social Research on Alcohol and Drugs (SoRAD), Stockholm University, Sveaplan, S-106 91, Stockholm, Sweden

Marcia Russell, Pacific Institute for Research and Evaluation, Prevention Research Center, 1995 University Avenue, Suite 450, Berkeley, CA 94704, USA

Sherry Saggers, School of Social and Cultural Studies, Edith Cowan University, Joondalup Drive, Joondalup, WA 6027, USA

Robert F. Saltz, Pacific Institute for Research and Evaluation, Prevention Research Center, 1995 University Avenue, Suite 450, Berkeley, CA 94704, USA

Michelle Scollo, The Cancer Council Victoria, 100 Drummond Street, Carlton, Vic 3053, Australia

Tim Stockwell, Centre for Addictions Research of BC, PO Box 1700 STN CSC, Victoria, BC V8W 2Y2, Canada

Adam Sutton, Criminology Department, University of Melbourne, 234 Queensbury Street, Carlton, Vic 3053, Australia

Maree Teesson, National Drug and Alcohol Research Centre, University of New South Wales, PO Box 21, Randwick, NSW 2031, Australia

John W. Toumbourou, Centre for Adolescent Health, Department of Paediatrics, University of Melbourne and Murdoch Children's Research Institute, Royal Children's Hospital, 2 Gatehouse Street, Parkville, Vic 3052, Australia

Andrew Treno, Pacific Institute for Research and Evaluation, Prevention Research Center, 1995 University Avenue, Suite 450, Berkeley, CA 94704, USA

Eva Wallin, STAD-project, Karolinska Institute, Crafoords väg 6, 113 24 Stockholm, Sweden

Elizabeth Waters, Centre for Community Child Health, University of Melbourne, Flemington Road, Parkville, Vic 3052, Australia

Fredrik Welander, National Institute for Working Life Sweden and Centre for International Health, Curtin University of Technology, GPO Box 1987, Perth, WA 6845, Australia

Jo Williams, Centre for Adolescent Health, 2 Gatehouse Street, Parkville, Vic 3052, Australia

Sandra Younie, Health Economics Unit, Monash University, Vic 3800, Australia

Preface

In many countries today there is great concern about the use of psychoactive substances and their effects on people's lives, especially on young people. Governments in economically developed countries in particular are spending increasing amounts on the prevention of drug-related problems, in some cases as part of a broad-based prevention programme designed to tackle a range of adolescent mental health and behavioural problems. This book is concerned with what has so far been learned from rigorous research and evaluation regarding "best bets" for investment in prevention policies and programmes. The evidence for an array of prevention approaches is presented ranging from early-years prevention and environmental interventions through to harm reduction strategies. Unfortunately, as will be shown in this book, there is often a stark contrast between actual patterns of government investment and the implications of the new knowledge that is being developed in this field. Examples of mismatches between government policy and knowledge include:

- substantial investment in the prevention of substance use patterns associated with the least harms;
- investment in ineffective and even counter-productive strategies;
- poor implementation of potentially effective strategies;
- governments not being prepared to test the public's willingness to allow effective regulation and enforcement of laws regarding sale and supply of legal drugs;
- governments not being willing to lead public opinion and implement policies that will prevent harm to people who continue to use illegal drugs.

We have prepared the present text in the hope that having a clear summary of the evidence for effective prevention in one volume will contribute to correcting some of the above disparities and lead to an overall reduction in the serious harms caused by both legal and illegal drugs in many modern societies.

This book is the result of a number of collaborations between different research centres and individuals concerned with the prevention of substance use problems. These collaborations have developed both formally while working on specific projects and also informally through exchanges at scientific meetings over a number of years. More than 50 prevention specialists have contributed to this project. The scope of the subject matter, covering a wide range of problems associated with the use of legal and illegal drugs and concerning a range of interventions from education to regulation and legislation, has required contributions from a broad range of disciplines and areas of expertise.

We thank our immediate colleagues at the National Drug Research Institute in Perth, Western Australia, which is funded by the Australian Government Department of Health and Ageing, colleagues at the Prevention Research Center of the US-based Pacific Institute for Research and Evaluation, California, and the Centre for Adolescent Health at the University of Melbourne and Murdoch Children's Research Institute, Victoria, for sharing their knowledge of this far-ranging field of study. We also thank other colleagues from Australia, North America and Europe who helped us to fill some major gaps in our treatment of this complex topic. The result is not just a set of expert reviews of the best available evidence for what are "best buys" for government and non-government agencies, but also a set of insightful discussions drawn, collectively, from years of experience with the evaluation and implementation of many different kinds of prevention policy and programmes. Some of the settings examined are those usually associated with prevention such as schools, workplaces, local communities and licensed drinking venues. Others involve policy and regulatory frameworks that can impact on patterns of substance use and associated harms experienced at different life stages across whole populations. Several traditions in research and practice are drawn together and an attempt is made to synthesize a broad model of prevention that incorporates education, community action, regulation, harm reduction and law enforcement. The chapters are not intended to be encyclopedic but rather are intended to provide readers with state-of-the art summaries and useful directions to the core literature.

Major challenges for the future are (i) the dissemination of this new knowledge to community leaders and policy-makers; (ii) for researchers to work more closely with those who will implement their findings so that better outcomes can be achieved for the whole community; and (iii) for governments to have the courage to lead community opinion and support the implementation of evidence-based prevention policies for both legal and illegal drugs.

Tim Stockwell, Paul J. Gruenewald,
John W. Toumbourou and Wendy Loxley
1 August 2004

Acknowledgements

We would like to warmly thank the many people who helped with the production of this large book. First, Lesley Valerio and her colleagues at John Wiley & Sons for their encouragement and guidance throughout the project. Second, Sue Wilson who has organised, formatted and kept track of all the chapters as they developed, changed and flew around the world. She has spent many hours getting them into good shape with enormous skill and care. In a similar way, we would like to thank the scientists and staff at the Prevention Research Center, Berkeley, California, who contributed their time and effort toward editing and improving many of the chapters contributed to this book, especially Ms Barbara Nygaard and Dr Elizabeth A. LaScala who devoted substantial time and effort to editing the chapters presented in Sections 4 and 6.

We also would like to thank all the authors for sharing their wisdom and being so generous with their time. We hope they feel as we do that the end product has been worth the hard work. We would like to thank the Australian Government Department of Health and Ageing, the Western Australian Drug and Alcohol Office and the World Health Organization for sponsoring a meeting attended by many of the authors held in Fremantle, Western Australia, in 2003, under the auspices of the Kettil Bruun Society for Social and Epidemiological Studies on Alcohol. The Pacific Institute for Research and Evaluation, Calverton, Maryland, graciously contributed travel support for many US investigators. Tim Stockwell and Wendy Loxley were funded by the National Drug Strategy Branch of the Australian Government Department of Health and Ageing while working on this book, Paul J. Gruenewald was funded by grants from the US National Institutes of Health, National Institute on Alcohol Abuse and Alcoholism (Research Center Grant P60-AA06282 and Merit Award R37-AA12927). John Toumbourou was supported by a variety of grants to the Centre for Adolescent Health at the Department of Paediatrics, University of Melbourne, and the Murdoch Children's Research Institute, Royal Children's Hospital Melbourne. These included a grant from the US National Institute of Health, National Institute on Drug Abuse (ROIDA 12140).

Section 1   INTRODUCTION

EDITED BY TIM STOCKWELL, PAUL J. GRUENEWALD, JOHN W. TOUMBOUROU AND WENDY LOXLEY

1.1 Preventing Risky Drug Use and Related Harms: The Need for a Synthesis of New Knowledge

TIM STOCKWELL*
Centre for Addictions Research of BC, Victoria, Canada

PAUL J. GRUENEWALD
Prevention Research Center, Berkeley, CA, USA

JOHN W. TOUMBOUROU
Centre for Adolescent Health, Vic, Australia

WENDY LOXLEY
National Drug Research Institute, Perth, WA, Australia

SUMMARY

This book is about how to prevent the harmful use of tobacco, alcohol and other psychoactive substances such as cannabis, heroin and amphetamines. Harmful substance use is responsible for millions of preventable deaths each year across the globe, as well as many more non-fatal injuries, illnesses and social problems, all at great economic cost. Governments are increasingly investing in the prevention of these and other harms and require better evidence upon which to determine how best to make these investments. The first aim of this book is to provide expert reviews and discussion of the empirical evidence for what works and what are best buys in prevention in the domains of supply reduction, demand reduction and harm reduction. The second aim is to provide a broad framework within which new research findings can be harnessed to enable progress towards the prevention of premature loss of life and quality of life due to harmful substance use. This opening chapter describes some of the main features of such a framework, including:

* During editorship of this book Tim Stockwell was Director of the National Drug Research Institute, Curtin University, Perth, WA, Australia.

Preventing Harmful Substance Use: The Evidence Base for Policy and Practice.
Edited by T. Stockwell, P. J. Gruenewald, J. W. Toumbourou and W. Loxley.
© 2005 John Wiley & Sons, Ltd. ISBN 0-470-09227-0 (hbk) 0-470-09228-9 (pbk).

i. a broad population health focus in which the relative merits of alternative approaches are evaluated principally in terms of impact on population-levels of risky substance use and related harms;

ii. an impartial evaluation of the evidence for prevention priorities without censorship or distortion by vested interest groups, whether in government or the commercial sectors;

iii. a balanced approach which addresses fundamental social and economic circumstances that predispose towards harmful substance use as well as the more immediate antecedents of harm such as substance use patterns and settings;

iv. the need for powerful new research methodologies capable of evaluating impacts of policy changes on whole communities;

v. the need for legislative and regulatory structures which enable effective community responses.

A rationale for considering all psychoactive drugs in one volume is provided, noting (1) overlapping patterns of use and also markets for different drugs; (2) significant pharmacological interactions between different drugs; and (3) the value of contrasting the health, social and economic costs associated with different substances using common criteria when determining priorities for prevention.

SETTING THE SCENE

No society on Earth does not in some way celebrate, depend on, profit from, enjoy and also suffer from the use of psychoactive substances. Most developed and developing societies have well established relationships with and legally sanction the use of older psychoactive substances such as ethanol and nicotine. Large multinational companies manufacture, advertise and sell these products for substantial profit to millions of eager consumers while governments usually reap a rich harvest from tax revenues.

The past 100 years has also seen an upsurge in the cultivation, manufacture and trade of other psychoactive substances, some quite ancient and others new. Some of these have been developed from pharmaceutical products made initially for treating pain, mental health or other problems (e.g., heroin, barbiturates, benzodiazepines), others have been made in laboratories for recreational purposes (e.g., methamphetamine), while others, notably cannabis, are made from plants or seeds that have been cultivated and traded to new and much larger markets. In most countries legal sanctions supported by international treaties have been established to attempt to control the manufacture, trade and consumption of these products, though their use continues in varying degrees.

Around each of these drug types, with their different effects on human behaviour and emotion, have grown cultures and rituals regarding their use for particular purposes. For almost all areas of human activity there are psychoactive substances that are used with the intention of facilitating that activity in some way: religious ceremonies, physical exercise, battle, eating, sex, study, work, dancing, public performances and socializing make up a list indicative of the range. Unfortunately, as is well known, the wrong drug or perhaps just the wrong dose of a drug at the wrong time and administered the wrong way not only can impair performance in any of these areas but can also lead to serious harm. The difference between the enhancement of human performance in some spheres as opposed to its impairment is not just a function of the type of drug used (e.g., a stimulant or a central nervous system depressant) but often also a function of the dose taken, the manner of its administration and the setting in which use occurs. Adverse consequences include a host of social problems as well as injury, illness and even death. These consequences are borne not only by the user but often also by those around them in the wider community.

In this book we attempt to pull together some of the knowledge that has accumulated from efforts in different countries to prevent or reduce the serious harms that can be associated with the use of psychoactive substances. The prevention of harm usually requires the modification or elimination of patterns of drug use as a prerequisite. A number of powerful "harm reduction" strategies also seek to modify the environment in which use occurs (for example, training staff of liquor outlets to prevent violence) or the manner of drug administration (e.g., the use of shatterproof glassware). Much of the explosion of new research into "what works" in the broad field of substance misuse prevention is summarised in these pages. The contributing chapters are by prevention specialists from North America, Europe and Australasia, with backgrounds spanning many disciplines including criminology, epidemiology, psychology, sociology, anthropology, public health, education, law and health promotion. Many of these authors are renowned internationally for contributions they have made to this field. Many also work in national research centres dedicated to the study and prevention of substance use problems. They have been invited to write their contributions in readily accessible language and to make clear recommendations for future policy and practice.

Governments in North America, Europe and Australasia are beginning to make significant investments in prevention policies to reduce health care costs. Policy-makers need authoritative advice on the evidence base for prevention. In the past five decades, many of the recommendations that have been offered policy-makers have focused upon regulating access to drugs and the enforcement of drug control laws. However, there has been a significant increase in investment in the "early years" following evidence that adverse early life experiences can increase risk of many costly problems in later life (e.g., McCain and Mustard, 1999; National Crime Prevention, Attorney-General's Department, 1999; Karoly et al., 1998). In this book we will review this evidence critically and later sections will also underline the importance of interventions that affect the adult world in which children grow up. Focusing on the early childhood years has popular appeal and a degree of supporting evidence but some far more challenging areas for governments and societies to confront exist that will yield still greater results in directly reducing drug-related harm. Influences which help maintain harmful patterns of tobacco and alcohol use in particular persist throughout adulthood and contribute greatly to serious illness and premature deaths. We will attempt to summarize the extent of the support for a comprehensive range of prevention measures across the human life-span and independent of government or vested interests in the prevailing regulatory models.

With so many drugs to consider, so many potential harms to be prevented and so many different disciplines to provide perspectives and evidence for a way forward, the editorial group has attempted to provide some integration across this large literature and also a vision for future responses to drug problems. Integration is essential not only to understanding the nature of substance use problems but also implementing responses with reasonable consistency across the entire community of legislators, educators, finance departments, police, liquor licensees, parents, local councils, health authorities and treatment agencies.

In the remainder of this introductory chapter we will outline the full scope of what we believe needs to be incorporated into a broad and comprehensive approach to the prevention of risky substance use and harm.

WHAT HARMS AND COSTS ARE ASSOCIATED WITH RISKY SUBSTANCE USE?

Effective prevention requires effective targeting. Given the wide range of drug types, patterns of use and harmful consequences it is essential that otherwise effective strategies are prioritised in accordance with the burden of harm in health, social and economic terms caused by different patterns of drug use.

In Table 1.1.1 we provide a matrix illustrating some of the harm domains associated with different patterns of drug use. Some harms are caused entirely by the manner of administration or exposure to the drug (e.g., deaths from burning due to discarding or dropping lit cigarettes), others from the acute effects on judgement and coordination from a single drug administration (e.g., road deaths), others from the long-term toxic effects due to prolonged use over many years (e.g., liver disease, lung cancer) and still others as a consequence of developing dependence on a substance (e.g., neglecting family and parenting responsibilities). Within each cell there are many other possible examples.

The full impact of psychoactive substance use on the quality of life of individuals, families and communities (both positive and negative consequences) is sometimes hard to measure. However, the scientific basis for estimating the harmful consequences of drug use continues to steadily advance. International guidelines have recently been established for making estimates of national economic costs of substance use problems (Single et al., 2002). Table 1.1.2 summarises estimates of overall economic costs made for different economically developed countries for tobacco, alcohol and illicit drugs, expressed in terms of the local currency. While the methods employed and assumptions used varied significantly between these different studies, there are some common conclusions. For example, the health costs and costs due to lost productivity are estimated to be far greater for alcohol and tobacco than they are for illicit drugs.

The most recent and state-of-the-art estimates from Collins and Lapsley (2002) suggest the great bulk of these costs are those from lost productivity both in the workplace (16% of total costs) and the home (22%). The costs of crime (13%), road crashes (7%) and health care (4%) are also significant (Collins and Lapsley, 2002).

The important World Health Organization (WHO) Global Burden of Disease 2000 project (discussed in Chapter 2.2) contrasted estimates of death and disability for tobacco, alcohol and a broad category of "illicit drugs" for all regions of the world. An estimated 129 million "disability-adjusted" life-years (DALYs) worldwide were lost in 2000 from substance misuse, with tobacco the leading cause in both the developed and developing world (slightly ahead of alcohol) and alcohol misuse the leading cause in the countries "in transition" towards economic development. That figure includes almost 7 million preventable deaths world-wide, mostly of middle-aged and older people from diseases caused by tobacco and/or alcohol dependence but also many younger people from the acute effects of alcohol and illicit drug misuse (WHO, 2003).

Table 1.1.1 A matrix of risky drug use patterns and examples of associated harms to early development, health, safety and well-being

Category of harm	Drug administration	Intoxication, acute effects	Regular use, chronic effects	Dependence
Developmental harm examples	Use in pregnancy, environmental tobacco smoke and children	Family conflict, impaired parenting	Early and regular use by children. Parental modelling	Child abuse and neglect
Physical health examples	Injecting associated with spread of blood-borne viruses. Smoking poses risk of respiratory diseases	Acute medical conditions e.g., poisoning, overdose	Cancers, strokes, liver and heart disease	Withdrawal symptoms, seizures
Personal safety examples	Death from burning due to discarded cigarettes	Intentional and unintentional injuries to self and others	Increased risk of injury due to loss of tolerance due to liver disease	Risk-taking to protect supply
Mental health examples	Increased risk of dependence from quick action methods (e.g., smoking, injecting)	Psychosis, reckless behaviour	Cognitive deficits	Mood disorders
Social well-being examples	Stigma associated with injecting drug use and criminal record	Legal problems, unwanted pregnancy	Financial problems	Financial, work and relationship problems

Source: Adapted from Loxley, Toumbourou, Stockwell, et al. (2004).

Table 1.1.2   Comparison of estimates of the direct and indirect economic costs associated with use
of tobacco, alcohol and illicit drugs for various countries

Country and study	Year of data	Substance	Original Total Cost Estimate (millions)
Canada			
Single et al. (1998)	1992	Tobacco	CAN$9,560
		Alcohol	CAN$7,522
		Illicit drugs	CAN$1,371
USA			
Harwood et al. (1999)	1992	Alcohol	US$148,000
		Illicit drugs	US$98,000
France			
Kopp and Fénoglio (1999)	1997	Tobacco	F89,256
		Alcohol	F115,420
		Illicit drugs	F13,350
Australia			
Collins and Lapsley (2002)	1998/99	Tobacco	AU$21,063
		Alcohol	AU$7,560
		Illicit drugs	AU$6,075

Taking account of the available economic and epidemiological estimates, a recent analysis of the most prevalent patterns of drug-related harm in Australia concluded that prevention resources should be allocated, in order, towards the following priorities (Loxley et al., 2004):

1.   Long-term, dependent use of smoked tobacco.
2.   Short-term heavy use of alcohol (drinking to intoxication).
3.   Long-term, regular use of alcohol above low risk levels of consumption.
4.   Administration of illicit drugs by injection.
5.   Risky patterns of use of legal drugs in early adolescence.

These priorities reflect the present burden of harm in most economically developed countries though the priority order of the first two would be reversed in societies in transition to a modern economically developed economy.

A BROAD VIEW OF PREVENTION

Not Just the Prevention of Drug Use

Efforts to deter young people from experimenting with potentially harmful drugs (legal or illegal) should form just one part of a comprehensive population-based approach to preventing drug-related harms from conception to old age. As will be apparent from the contributions to this book, the diverse nature of risky drug use and related harm creates many opportunities for intervention within the social, physical and legal environments within which drug use occurs, as well as in altering the manner in which drugs are consumed.

Attempts to dissuade high-risk individuals from potentially harmful drug use have Value only alongside more powerful environmental prevention strategies that affect the whole community.

Harm Reduction as Well as Use Reduction

Both harm reduction and use reduction strategies can reduce levels of serious harms to the whole community. By "harm reduction" we refer here to strategies which may reduce the serious consequences of substance use without *necessarily* reducing use itself. The best-known examples of harm reduction involve preventing the spread of blood-borne viruses from injecting drug use, principally through alternative forms of drug use (e.g, methadone instead of heroin) and/or the provision of sterile injecting equipment. Harm reduction approaches to legal drugs are also discussed in this book, in particular Chapter 4.3 for alcohol and Chapter 5.2 for tobacco. Regardless of the category of drug being considered, harm reduction and use reduction should not be seen as black or white alternatives. Strategies designed to reduce the harm among continuing drug users should be seen as complementary to strategies to persuade drug users to use at a lower risk level or abstain altogether. Furthermore, such harm reduction strategies should not detract from efforts to discourage the uptake of risky drug use among non-drug users. From a broad perspective, the major concern is the collective impact of *all* these strategies on population levels of drug-related harm, both in the present and the future.

Shared Developmental and Social Determinants of Problem Behaviours

The fields of public health, mental health and crime prevention have recently found common cause with growing evidence of shared developmental and social risk and protective factors influencing psychosocial adjustment in young people. As will be discussed in Section 3 of this book, these factors have been identified through longitudinal and intervention research at various stages of infancy, childhood and adolescence (Williams et al., 2000; Loxley et al., 2004). These factors mostly reflect the quality of engagement at these early stages of development with family, peers, school and the wider community. Longitudinal research has found these factors predictive of a range of problem and risk behaviours in adolescence and young adulthood including truancy, delinquency, unprotected sex and mood disorders as well as substance use problems (see Chapters 2.4 and 3.2). While longitudinal research does not necessarily tell us about underlying causal processes, It is indicative of causality and as a basis for developing principles to test in intervention studies to prevent later problems. While the perspective of shared risk factors among a diverse range of human problems has emerged from the study of the early years, a broader perspective of healthy and safe communities for people of all ages needs to be included in a comprehensive agenda for prevention. As young people mature into adults, they also take on adult forms of substance use and begin to experience adult patterns of use-related harms. Among adults, substance use and related problems are very context-specific and amenable to a broader variety of preventive measures.

Community Systems and Multiple Levels of Intervention

Adults live within communities of social and economic relationships, at work, at home or at play. No longer confined to the domains of family, school and peers, adult activities and interactions span the full range of social and economic contacts entailed by work and domestic life. Adults are, in truth, engaged in multiple community systems, including those aspects of communities that shape everyday life (e.g., transportation systems), and provide access to legal and illegal drugs (e.g., alcohol, tobacco and illicit substances).

These systems are often regulated, and the regulations are enforced at several levels. Another contribution of this book will be to present the multiple levels of intervention that can contribute to reducing drug-related harms. Legislative and regulatory approaches regarding the legal status of different drugs, the enforcement of civil and criminal sanctions, local efforts to reduce the availability of legal drugs and also taxation strategies will be reviewed. The jurisdictions in which these apply can vary in scale from shire or town councils, through regional, provincial and national governments and up to the international level. Trade in tobacco and illicit drugs is the subject of international treaties though alcohol at the present time is not. Figure 1.1.1 illustrates these multiple levels of intervention (from Lenton, 1996), as well as still smaller-scale interventions that focus on specific settings (e.g., licensed premises, workplaces and schools), on families, on individuals and on the pharmacological action of drugs. Holder (1997) first drew attention to the importance of considering multiple levels of

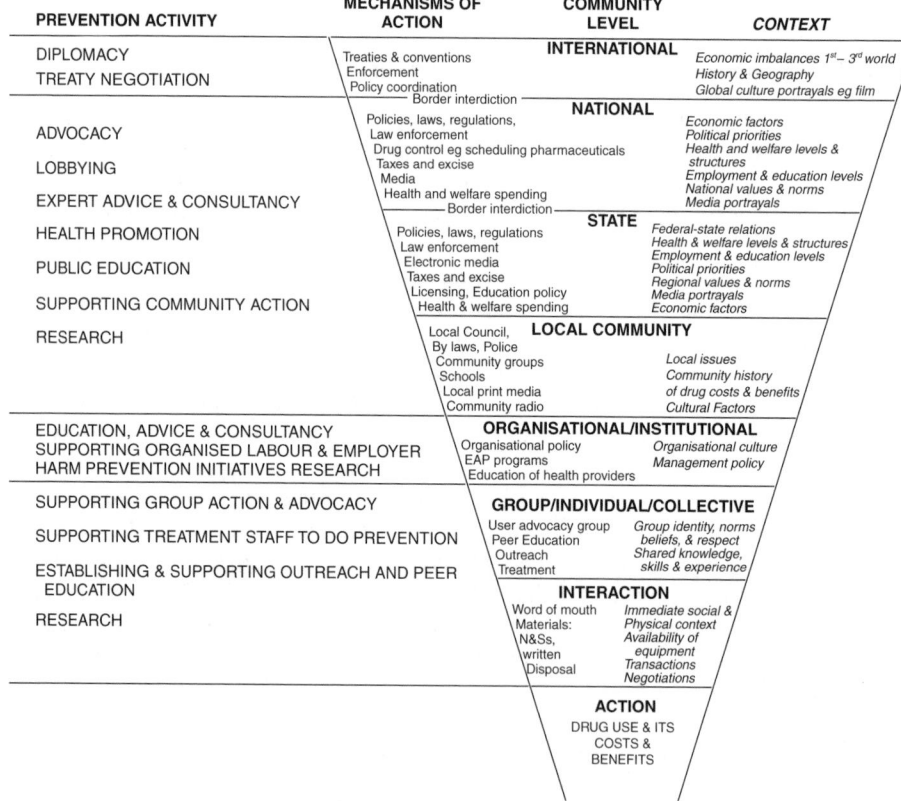

Figure 1.1.1   A public health systems model for the prevention of alcohol and other drug problems
Source: Reproduced from Lenton (1996)

influences on levels of alcohol-related harm in his Community Systems model of prevention. This model has inspired a generation of prevention research and has been applied in several significant community intervention studies. Holder and colleagues will outline the latest developments and applications of this important model in Chapter 4.2. In Chapter 2.5, Gruenewald and colleagues describe how local community systems can be studied to reveal the social and economic forces that produce problems with alcohol and illicit drug use—and can give clues to problem prevention.

Considerable interest in the idea of there being social or structural determinants of substance use problems also exists. For example, some reports (Spooner et al., 2001) have examined the influence of social and economic disadvantage on smoking, drinking and other drug use. Together, these two significant aspects of disadvantage have encouraged policy-makers and some practitioners to focus more on what some perceive to be fundamental underlying social and developmental influences rather than specific patterns of substance use *per se*. This view will be explored further in Section 3 where it will be shown that more immediate and environmental influences often overcome adverse early social and developmental risk factors. A broad perspective on prevention needs to include macro-social and economic circumstances, adverse developmental factors and also the more immediate environmental and drug use pattern factors.

A Broad View of the Required Evidence for Effective Policy and Practice

Perhaps to a greater extent than any other field of human inquiry, the prevention of substance use problems requires knowledge and expertise from many disciplines. Too often when different disciplines work on the same subject there is competition as to which perspective or method of analysis provides the single best understanding or solution. For example, is the phenomenon of drug dependence primarily a social, psychological, pharmacological or biological problem? Or, by way of a further example, does developmental psychology, economics, sociology, criminology or political science offer the most effective solutions to preventing adolescents engaging in risky drug use? In this book we will attempt to move beyond interdisciplinary rivalry and seek out complementary approaches and contributions. The challenge of integrating policies and programmes is an important new horizon for prevention efforts and the local community emerges as an important site for linking different prevention approaches and discipline perspectives.

There are a number of core questions that should be addressed collectively by these many disciplines if effective prevention of drug problems at the population level is to occur:

1. *What patterns of drug use cause the most harm?* In relation to direct health effects, this question is best answered in terms of simple quantity, frequency and variability in the amounts of drugs used over a particular time period. Linking patterns of use with health outcomes can require collaboration, for example, between psychologists with expertise in survey design and epidemiologists with expertise in documenting prevalence of death, injury and illness. To answer this question in relation to more complex social harms (e.g., to relationships, employment, mental health and child development) and to injuries caused by intoxication in high-risk settings, requires the input of many more disciplines: anthropology, ethnography, sociology, social psychology, physiology and psychiatry having particular contributions to make. To quantify complex social harms, it is not sufficient to merely describe patterns of drug use over time but also to understand the social context in which drug use occurs, individual tolerance to drug effects and

other situational and contextual factors. Quantifying drug use and related harms in this way, taking these facets of use into account, we can learn which users are most at risk in what contexts, and better target prevention programmes.

2. *What scientific principles can inform an effective prevention response?* A variety of scientific and theoretical understandings of the nature of drug-related problems can suggest potentially effective interventions. This is not the same as saying that these interventions are certain to be effective when implemented. Some simple examples can be given here of a scientifically based rationale for intervention. Social Learning Theory (Bandura, 1977) informs the circumstances under which efforts to deter high-risk behaviours (e.g., driving after drinking alcohol) will be effective, namely when a strong expectation is created that an unwanted consequence will ensue (e.g., detection and fine). Laboratory studies have shown that alcohol consumption after a full meal can result in blood alcohol levels that are two to three times lower than when the same amount is consumed on an empty stomach (Eckardt et al., 1998). It follows that providing food at social gatherings may reduce the risk of problems associated with intoxication. Pharmacological studies of the development of tolerance to drug effects show that tolerance can be rapidly acquired with continued use and subsequently lost or greatly reduced following a period of abstinence. This knowledge is consistent with the increased risk of drug overdose when formerly dependent drug users relapse shortly after leaving a treatment or correctional facility (Darke et al., 1996). Moore provides several other examples in Chapter 7.4 from ethnographic and anthropological research. The main point here is that fundamental and theoretically driven research from many disciplines can help with the design of potentially effective preventive measures.

3. *What kinds of prevention have been shown to work in well-controlled studies?* A recently published review of the evidence base for 159 intervention strategies designed to reduce problems with alcohol, tobacco and illicit drugs found markedly different levels of scientific support (Loxley et al., 2004). Particularly in relation to interventions for problems with illicit drugs, there were many commonly used educational and regulatory strategies for which no research evidence was available. In a few cases, the evidence was actually negative, suggesting the intervention did more harm than good (e.g., extending liquor outlet trading hours as a means of slowing down the rate of alcohol consumption). In many other cases, there was positive research support varying in strength from a small number of promising pilot studies, through a series of well-controlled studies to population-wide implementation and further published evidence of effectiveness. The chosen settings for this particular selection of interventions were diverse and included schools, workplaces, whole communities, prisons, courts, licensed premises, treatment facilities, general practice and the arenas where the legality of the use of different drugs is established and levels of taxation set. Most of the pages of the present book will focus upon what has been learned from efforts to prevent drug-related harm from occurring in these various settings. It has become necessary to develop a more rigorous approach to distilling what can be learned from the large relevant literatures and several examples of "systematic review" of specific areas will be provided in this book (e.g. Chapters 3.3 and 3.4 on school and youth interventions). Clearly, the return from investment of the prevention pound, dollar or euro will depend upon the selection of the most effective strategies for preferential funding. Section 7 will include two discussions from leading economists of how governments should best invest in "portfolios" of effective prevention strategies (Chapters 7.2 and 7.3).

4. *How well are current prevention strategies being implemented?* In many areas further
    investment in evaluation research has the potential to make important contributions to
    efforts to prevent drug-related harm. However, given the growing scientific basis for
    prevention, there is less and less reason to require evaluation of drug use and harm
    outcomes for a very routinely delivered prevention measure. In the field of medicine,
    for example, the effectiveness of different medications is first established in carefully
    conducted controlled clinical trials. For those medications with proven efficacy and
    acceptable levels of side-effects it is sufficient to merely adhere to recommended pro-
    tocols and monitor the appropriateness of the conditions for which they are prescribed.
    While the individual monitoring of patient's health is part of sound medical practice,
    this is not the same as a scientific demonstration of effectiveness. In the same way,
    the question posed above about whether current prevention practice is effective should
    be addressed partly by simply ascertaining whether the interventions being delivered
    have an established scientific track record of effectiveness. Beyond that, the question
    becomes one of quality assurance and whether best practice principles are being fol-
    lowed. One example of such monitoring is the assessment by Wagenaar (2000) of the
    extent to which each of the US states has implemented best practice in drink driving
    law enforcement, alcohol taxation and controls on alcohol availability. The other side
    to such monitoring of how well the whole national prevention effort is faring is the
    epidemiological monitoring of levels and trends in drug-related harms. Many countries
    conduct such monitoring through national surveys of self-reported use and harm (e.g.,
    WHO 2000a, 2000b). Some also supplement survey data with the use of regular reviews
    of official statistics that bear upon both patterns of use and related harms (e.g., Chikritzhs
    et al., 2003; Topp and Mcketin, 2003). This brings us back full circle to point 1 above
    regarding the importance of accurate epidemiological assessments and underlines the
    iterative nature required of efforts to develop and continuously improve community-
    wide and inter-disciplinary responses to drug problems as illustrated in Figure 1.1.2.
    Chapter 7.4 by David Moore will add the further dimension of how prevention strategies
    delivered with the best of intentions actually affect the daily lives of high-risk individuals
    for drug-related harm.

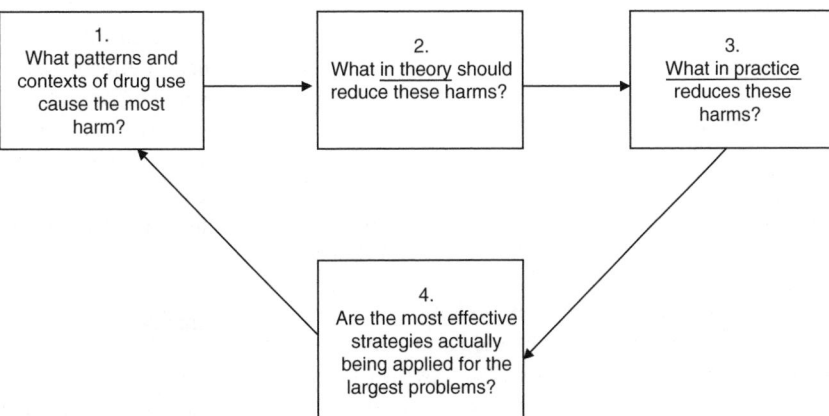

Figure 1.1.2   Core questions for interdisciplinary research into the prevention of harmful substance
use

While a matter for debate and controversy, it has become apparent to these authors that to answer the hard practical questions posed above, we need powerful new methodologies that, in some cases, will depart from traditional evaluation science. In order to evaluate community- and population-level interventions, it is necessary to move beyond the usual presumed scientific standard of the randomised controlled trial with many years follow-up. This issue will be addressed in detail by Saltz in Chapter 6.2 and also illustrated by several other contributions. For example in Chapter 2.5, Paul Gruenewald and colleagues promote the use of "ecological models" for understanding the behaviour of whole populations interacting in community systems. Traditional scientific designs appropriate for the hard sciences and laboratory work may not be appropriate where the prevention research field attempts to answer questions relevant to policies and programmes applied to large population aggregates across states and nations. However, there is also a range of rigorous and well-controlled methods that will be described in this book which can be used for evaluating interventions at the community and whole population levels.

Why Consider All Psychoactive Drugs in One Book?

While it is more usual to consider prevention and treatment responses to one particular class of drugs in one book (e.g., tobacco, alcohol or illicit drugs), there are a number of reasons why we have chosen the ambitious task of considering *all* psychoactive drugs here. The principal reason is that this can illustrate how inconsistent most societies are in their treatment of one class of drugs versus another. Our familiarity with more freely available legal drugs can blind us individually and collectively to their dangers. Conversely, fear of less familiar and illegal drugs can sometimes lead to excessively punitive responses to individual users (such as the death penalty in some countries for simple possession of cannabis). Further, individual drug users typically use many classes of drugs, often at the same time. Drug interactions, common pharmacological processes of dependence and tolerance, the often observed substitution of one class of drug by another depending on availability and apparent developmental stages in substance use preferences also provide reasons for a common approach. Finally, we consider evidence for developmental and social risk and protection factors common to other problem behaviours in the realms of crime, mental health and risk-taking.

OVERVIEW OF THE BOOK

The remaining five Sections will each start with a concise overview followed by chapters covering the extent of substance use and related health, economic and social costs from an international perspective (Section 2), the effectiveness of early life stage interventions from conception to adolescence (Section 3), the effectiveness of complementary community interventions with illustrations from well-evaluated case studies (Section 4), complementary regulatory approaches to reducing harm with examples from each of the major drug types (Section 5), broader perspectives provided by major reviews of the evidence base for each of the main substance categories and one on strategies for Indigenous peoples (Section 6), plus perspectives on the nature and use of research evidence. The final Section will take up the challenging question of how to build a comprehensive, system-wide and population-based approach to reducing harmful substance use in which both progress and unintended consequences are continuously reviewed.

Above all else we wish to provide a contemporary summary of the evidence base for prevention of the harms associated with substance use, a clear set of policy recommendations determined only by the available evidence and a vision of how we hope knowledge and practice will be continuously improved in the years ahead.

REFERENCES

Bandura, A. (1977) *Social Learning Theory*. Englewood Cliffs, NJ: Prentice Hall.

Chikritzhs, T., Catalano, P., Stockwell, T.R., Donath, S., Ngo, H.T., Young, D.J. and Matthews, S. (2003) *Australian Alcohol Indicators, 1990–2001: Patterns of Alcohol Use and Related Harms for Australian States and Territories*. Perth, Western Australia: National Drug Research Institute and Turning Point Alcohol and Drug Centre Inc. National Drug Research Institute.

Collins, D. and Lapsley, H. (2002) *Counting the Cost: Estimates of the Social Costs of Drug Abuse in Australia in 1998–9*. Monograph 49. Canberra: Australian Government Department of Health and Ageing.

Darke, S., Ross, J. and Hall, W. (1996) Overdose among heroin users in Sydney, Australia. I. Prevalence and correlates of non-fatal overdose. *Addiction*, **91**, 3, 405–412.

Eckardt, M.J., File, S.E., Gessa, G.L., Grant, K.A., Guerri, C., Hoffman, P.L., Kalant, H., Koop, G.F., Li, T.K. and Tabakoff, B. (1998) Effects of moderate alcohol consumption on the central nervous system. *Alcoholism, Clinical and Experimental Research*, **22**, 998–1040.

Harwood, J.H., Fountain, D. and Livermore, G. (1999) Economic cost of alcohol and drug abuse in the United States, 1992: a report. *Addiction*, **94**, 5, 631–634.

Holder, H.D. (1997) *A Community Systems Approach to Alcohol Problem Prevention*. Cambridge: Cambridge University Press.

Karoly, L.A., Greenwood, P.W., Everingham, S.S., Hoube, J., Kilburn, M.R., Sanders, M., et al. (1998) *Investing in Our Children: What We Know and Don't Know About the Costs and Benefits of Early Childhood Interventions*. Santa Monica: RAND Corporation.

Kopp, P. and Fénoglio, P. (1999) Le coût social des drogues licites (alcool et tabac) et illicites. Unpublished Report, L'Université de Panthéon-Sorbonne (Paris I), France.

Lenton, S. (1996) The essence of prevention. In C. Wilkinson and B. Saunders (eds), *Perspectives on Addiction: Making Sense of the Issues*. Perth: William Montgomery, pp. 73–80.

Loxley, W., Toumbourou, J., Stockwell, T.R., Haines, B., Scott, K., Godfrey, C., Waters, E. and Patton, G. (2004) *The Prevention of Substance Use, Risk and Harm in Australia: A Review of the Evidence*. Canberra: Australian Government Department of Health and Ageing.

McCain, M.N. and Mustard, J. F. (1999) *Early Years Report: Reversing the Real Brain Drain. Final Report*. Ontario: The Canadian Institute for Advanced Research.

National Crime Prevention, Attorney-General's Department (1999) *Pathways to Prevention: Developmental and Early Intervention Approaches to Crime in Australia. Full Report*. Canberra: National Crime Prevention, Attorney-General's Department.

Single, E., Collins, D., Easton, B., Harwood, H., Lapsley, H., Kopp, P. and Wilson, E. (2002) *International Guidelines for Estimating the Costs of Substance Abuse*. 2nd edn. Ontario: Canadian Centre on Substance Abuse.

Single, E., Robson, L., Xie, X. and Rehm, J. (1998) The economic costs of alcohol, tobacco and illicit drugs in Canada, 1992. *Addiction*, **93**, 991–1006.

Spooner, C., Hall, W. and Lynskey, M. (2001) *Structural Determinants of Youth Drug Use*. Canberra: Australian National Council on Drugs.

Topp, L. and McKetin, R. (2003) Supporting evidence-based policy-making: a case study of the Illicit Drug Reporting System in Australia. In *Bulletin on Narcotics Volume LV, Nos 1 and 2, 2003. The Practice of Drug Abuse Epidemiology.* Vienna: United Nations Office on Drugs and Crime.

Wagenaar, A.C. (2000) *Alcohol Policies in the United States: Highlights from the 50 States.* Cambridge, MA: University of Minnesota, School of Public Health.

Williams, B., Sanson, A., Toumbourou, J.W. and Smart, D. (2000) *Patterns and Predictors of Teenagers' Use of Licit and Illicit Substances in the Australian Temperament Project Cohort.* Melbourne: University of Melbourne.

World Health Organization (2000a) *Guide to Drug Abuse Epidemiology.* Geneva: World Health Organization, Division of Mental Health and Prevention of Substance Abuse.

World Health Organization (2000b) *International Guide for Monitoring Alcohol Consumption and Related Harm.* Geneva: World Health Organization.

World Health Organization (2003) *The World Health Report.* Geneva: World Health Organization.

Section 2   PATTERNS OF RISK AND RELATED HARMS

EDITED BY TIM STOCKWELL

2.1 Introduction

TIM STOCKWELL[*]

Centre for Addictions Research of BC, Vic, Canada

THE BOTTOM-LINE FOR DRUG PREVENTION: THE LEVEL OF DRUG-RELATED HARM IN THE COMMUNITY

Levels and patterns of risky substance use and related harms are both the beginning and end points of the prevention enterprise. Accurate measurement and monitoring of patterns of use and harm also provide essential signposts indicating whether progress is being made along the way. We start this book, therefore, with several detailed explorations of the distribution of patterns of risk by regions of the world (Chapter 2.2), over time among individuals with different risk profiles (Chapters 2.3 and 2.4) and according to the dynamics of systems that generate problem outcomes for communities (Chapter 2.5).

One reliable route to effective prevention in this controversial arena of fields with different interest groups competing for the prevention dollar is to invest in strict accordance with the levels of measurable harm associated with use of different types of drug. We are fortunate to be able to start this exploration with the global perspective provided by the World Health Organization's 2000 Global Burden of Disease study (WHO, 2003) contrasting estimates of mortality, morbidity and overall disability for different regions of the world by major categories of psychoactive substance: tobacco, alcohol and the main illicit drugs (Chapter 2.2). This is a courageous exercise employing many assumptions mixed with hard data, where available, and the best estimates current expert opinion can provide. The precise numbers produced by this exercise are less important than their obvious scale. By any reckoning, the 2000 Global Burden of Disease study demonstrates that the extent of death and disability associated with these types of drug is hugely costly in terms of loss of both life and quality of life. Beyond that, a few broad conclusions are possible that give strong indications of where the priorities for prevention effort should lie, even if these do not reflect the funding priorities of many governments:

- The health impacts of tobacco and alcohol dwarf those from the illegal drugs.
- The health impacts for younger adults are greatest for heavy sessional use of alcohol.
- The health impacts for older men and women in countries with longer life expectancy are mainly from long-term tobacco use.

[*] During editorship of book Tim Stockwell was Director of the National Drug Research Institute, Curtin University, Perth, WA, Australia.

Preventing Harmful Substance Use: The Evidence Base for Policy and Practice.
Edited by T. Stockwell, P. J. Gruenewald, J.W. Toumbourou and W. Loxley.
© 2005 John Wiley & Sons, Ltd. ISBN 0-470-09227-0 (hbk) 0-470-09228-9 (pbk).

- For older men the long-term health effects of risky alcohol use are also significant.
- The net health costs from all drugs combined fall primarily on men although women have been narrowing the gap in economically developed countries.

These data need to be considered within a broader context of wider economic and social costs though these are not always easy to estimate. It was noted in Chapter 1.1 that the inclusion of criminal justice and law-enforcement costs substantially increases estimates associated with the use of illegal drugs and, to a lesser degree, with alcohol. An overall recommendation at this stage is that reducing the substantial criminal justice and law-enforcement costs associated with drug use should be given some priority along with the important work of preventing disability and premature loss of life from risky drug use.

LONGITUDINAL RELATIONSHIPS BETWEEN SUBSTANCE USE AND MENTAL HEALTH PROBLEMS

The assessment of patterns of substance use and their relationship to adverse health and social outcomes is by no means straightforward. Substantial texts have been developed, for example, for the World Health Organization, providing guidelines to member countries for the monitoring of patterns of use and related harms for tobacco (WHO, 1998), and alcohol (WHO, 2000a) and illicit drugs (WHO, 2000b). Demonstrating relationships between patterns of use at one point in time and later harms in terms of physical or mental health is particularly demanding. In relation to longer-term adverse outcomes for physical health, careful and substantial reviews have been conducted and demanding criteria for accepting causal associations have been applied (see especially English et al., 1995). The contributions of patterns of risky substance use to longer-term adverse mental health outcomes, however, are less well established, largely because possible underlying causal mechanisms are not well understood.

The mental health consequences of different patterns of substance use have been the subject of much recent longitudinal research which is summarised in the chapter by Teesson and colleagues (Chapter 2.3). The difficulty of separating out cause from effect in longitudinal studies is illustrated by their discussion of how some studies apparently linking smoking with mental health outcomes, on closer analysis, appear to have shared but independent causes located in personal socio-economic circumstances. As a consequence, the distinguished cast of authors treat the strengthening evidence for a link between adolescent cannabis use and later mental health problems with a degree of caution and recommend further explanation of independent socio-economic factors responsible for both kinds of morbidity.

Chapter 2.4 also explores the longitudinal relationship between drug use and mental health with a particular focus on children and adolescents. Longitudinal studies suggestive of later mental health outcomes following risky patterns of use of other drugs are reported. Earlier reviews have also noted evidence of two-way causal relationships between alcohol use and anxiety-related disorders, including phobic anxiety states (Stockwell and Bolderston, 1987). Most estimates of morbidity associated with drug use do not include the broader array of mental health outcomes. We recommend that further research is conducted to investigate the different possible causal relationships that can occur for different patterns of substance use and different mental health outcomes. Understanding the consequences of different patterns of drug use for both mental as well as physical health is a central issue for societies attempting to determine appropriate legal and regulatory structures for different drugs. Estimates of adverse impacts on mental health from substance use need to be conducted and considered alongside the more accepted consequences for physical health.

RISK AND PROTECTION FACTORS FOR RISKY SUBSTANCE USE: WHAT DO THEY MEAN?

Toumbourou and Catalano provide a broad overview in Chapter 2.4 of social and developmental factors that appear to alter the risk of later substance use as identified by longitudinal research. They summarise evidence for the predictive power of these factors which basically concern the extent to which adolescents are positively engaged with their families, their peers, their schools and wider communities. Adverse indicators in these domains have been shown to be especially predictive of the later use of illicit drugs but much less so for tobacco and alcohol use (Stockwell et al., 2004). Multiple risk factors, especially in the absence of protection factors, are highly predictive of a broad range of problem behaviours, including risky substance use. The authors recommend further investment in interventions which target these high risk groups while noting that these are a relatively small proportion of the population of adolescents who engage in the more prevalent risky use of legal drugs.

Longitudinal research on its own can only provide indications of causal relationships between variables of interest—and hypotheses to test with other research methodologies. It is often possible to offer competing explanations for a significant association demonstrated in longitudinal research. One example concerns the different interpretations given to the observed relationship between parental divorce and adolescent substance use provided by the respective authors of Chapters 2.3 and 2.4. In the former, Mitchell et al. (2001) point to the fact that this relationship has been found to disappear when economic circumstances are controlled for. In Chapter 2.4, Toumbourou and Catalano describe evidence that parental divorce can result in children being raised in neighbourhoods with a lower socio-economic status and where illicit drug use is more probable. Clearly, the argument can be run both ways and more in-depth investigations with different methodologies are required to confirm or disconfirm such causal hypotheses.

Longitudinal research, however, is one very important window through which to gain clues about the antecedents of risky drug use and harm. The evidence reviewed in these two chapters indicates robust relationships across time that demand the attention of prevention practitioners and policy-makers. For example, the work of Fergusson and Horwood (2000) has shown that use of cannabis as a teenager is associated with a more than 60-fold increase in the likelihood of using other illicit substances a few years later. The use of any substance, whether legal or illegal, early in adolescence is a reliable predictor of more intense and problematic substance use in young adulthood (see Chapter 2.4). Is this outcome a direct consequence of early substance use *per se*? Or is the latter merely a marker for profound social and economic disadvantage? In practical terms, what really matters is the point at which interventions can effectively be implemented. The deeper one delves into developmental, social and economic circumstances associated with risky substance use, sometimes the more distant and harder to influence are the contributing factors that are revealed. A balance is needed between supporting efforts to improve broad social, developmental and economic conditions of the whole community in the longer term and efforts to reduce risky drug use and harm in the shorter term through more direct means—especially when concern is directed towards legally available mainstream drugs, i.e., tobacco and alcohol. The evidence base reviewed in Section 6 will illustrate how some of the strongest support can be found for regulatory and environmental policy changes that impact on these legal drugs—and which will have immediate impacts on levels of harm in the community.

THE IMPORTANCE OF ENVIRONMENTS AND COMMUNITY SYSTEMS

LaScala and colleagues in Chapter 2.5 describe advances in understanding how individuals, social networks and drug markets evolve and generate different outcomes. They provide some important groundwork for Harold Holder's overview and updating of the Community System Approach to prevention in Chapter 4.2. Markets for illicit drugs are of necessity markedly different from legally sanctioned markets for alcohol and tobacco. The different characteristics of these markets and the circumstances under which problem outcomes are more likely are discussed in terms of a variety of criminological and sociological theories. Some common principles apply, for example the extent to which illegal behaviours are susceptible to public observation and receive attention from law enforcement agencies. For example, neighbourhoods in which petty crime is tolerated are also likely to be those in which street drug dealing occurs and in which violence is more likely to erupt around alcohol outlets. Regulatory strategies, such as those affecting the price and availability of alcohol, will "play out" quite differently in different neighbourhoods depending on how local community systems and markets adapt to new trading conditions. While longitudinal research can identify drug availability and socio-economic status to be strong predictors of substance use problems, ecological research on community systems is beginning to illuminate how these relationships occur in the first place.

While approaching the problem of substance use from quite different theoretical and methodological perspectives, community systems and the risk and protection factor approach each point to the central role of local communities—in both the genesis and prevention of substance use problems. Both provide insights into the possible causes of risky drug use and related harms as well as testable hypotheses to guide intervention research.

CONCLUSION

1. Available resources for the prevention of drug-related harms should be allocated in accordance with the prevalence of particular patterns of risky use and associated harms. Globally, long-term dependent use of tobacco and heavy sessional use of alcohol are of particular concern.
2. In setting priorities for prevention, attention should be paid to social, criminal justice and mental health costs as well as impacts on physical health. Further research is required to quantify these important elements.
3. Longitudinal studies provide one window onto the processes which result in risky substance use. Other methodologies such as ecological and ethnographic studies of community systems are also required to understand more fully how characteristics of

individuals, social groups, drug markets and local neighbourhoods interact dynamically to generate different outcomes. Such understandings can provide a rich source of ideas and principles to inspire more effective prevention strategies.

4. Broad social, developmental and economic circumstances are very important especially in the prediction of the use and problems with illicit drugs. This underlines the value of targeting high risk groups in order to prevent such problems. In relation to alcohol and tobacco, risky patterns of use are virtually normative among young people and a total population approach to prevention is more appropriate.

5. Theoretically driven and rigorously evaluated intervention research that identifies key change variables for effectiveness can also shed light on causal mechanisms underlying patterns of risky substance use.

REFERENCES

English, D.R., Holman, C.D.J. et al. (1995) *The Quantification of Drug-Caused Morbidity and Mortality in Australia. 1995* Canberra: Commonwealth Department of Human Services and Health.

Fergusson, D. and Horwood, L.J. (2000) Does cannabis use encourage other forms of illicit drug use? *Addiction*, **95**, 505–520.

Mitchell, P., Spooner, C., Copeland, J., Vimpani, G., Toumbourou, J.W., Howard, J. and Sanson, A. (2001) *A Literature Review of the Role of Families in the Development, Identification, Prevention and Treatment of Illicit Drug Problems*. National Health and Medical Research Council Monograph. Canberra: Commonwealth of Australia.

Stockwell, T. and Bolderston, H. (1987) Alcohol and phobias. *British Journal of Addiction*, **82**(9), 971–980.

Stockwell, T.R., Toumbourou, J., Letcher, P., Smart, D., Sanson, A. and Bond, L. (2004) Risk and protection factors for different intensities of adolescent substance use: when does the Prevention Paradox apply? *Drug and Alcohol Review*, **23**(1), 67–77.

World Health Organisation (1998) *Guidelines for Controlling and Monitoring the Tobacco Epidemic*. Geneva: World Health Organisation.

World Health Organization (2000a) *International Guide for Monitoring Alcohol Consumption and Related Harm*. Geneva: World Health Organization.

World Health Organization (2000b) *Guide to Drug Abuse Epidemiology*. Geneva: World Health Organization.

World Health Organization (2003) *The World Health Report, 2003*. Geneva: World Health Organization. Available online: www.who.int/whr/en (accessed 21 January 2004).

2.2 The Global Burden of Disease Attributable to Alcohol, Tobacco and Illicit Drugs

JÜRGEN REHM

Centre for Addiction and Mental Health, Toronto, Canada; Institute of Addiction Research, Zurich, Switzerland; and Public Health Sciences, University of Toronto, Canada

ROBIN ROOM

Centre for Social Research on Alcohol and Drugs, Stockholm University, Stockholm, Sweden

SUMMARY

The Comparative Risk Analysis conducted as part of the WHO's estimation of the Global Burden of Disease in 2000 included three categories of psychoactive substances: tobacco, alcohol and injectable illicit drugs (heroin, cocaine, amphetamines). Of the total burden of premature death or disability, measured as Disability-Adjusted Life-Years (DALYs), tobacco accounted for 4.1%, alcohol for 4.0%, and illicit drugs for 0.8%. While for all three categories the proportional burden was highest in the developed world, the burden for alcohol was also high in low-mortality developing countries. On a global basis, there is thus strong justification for continuing a strong emphasis in public health policy on tobacco control, and for substantially increasing the emphasis on alcohol control. Comparing the respective shares of the burden of disease, there is an imbalance between the resources devoted internationally to controlling illicit substances and the resources devoted to reducing problems from alcohol and tobacco. Particularly for alcohol and tobacco, a range of effective prevention strategies have been established in the research literature. For tobacco, policy attention to implementing these strategies has lagged behind the scientific knowledge, although the new Framework Convention on Tobacco Control provides a focus for increased attention. For alcohol, policy has often moved in the wrong direction, under the pressure of international trade agreements and policies which treat alcohol as a nonproblematic commodity. An equivalent of the Framework Convention is needed for alcohol to counter these trends. The proportion of the burden of disease attributable to psychoactive substances, and particularly to tobacco and alcohol, is expected to increase in the absence of effective international public health action.

Preventing Harmful Substance Use: The Evidence Base for Policy and Practice.
Edited by T. Stockwell, P. J. Gruenewald, J.W. Toumbourou and W. Loxley.
© 2005 John Wiley & Sons, Ltd. ISBN 0-470-09227-0 (hbk) 0-470-09228-9 (pbk).

INTRODUCTION

Psychoactive substance use and abuse constitute one of the major risk factors contributing to the global burden of disease. Thus, as part of the Comparative Risk Analysis (CRA) within the Global Burden of Disease (GBD) 2000 study (Mathers et al., 2002), three different types of substances were included in the list of 26 risk factors studied: alcohol, injectable illicit drugs (heroin, cocaine, amphetamines) and tobacco. The other risk factors studied were: being underweight, deficiencies of iron, vitamin A and zinc as indicators of childhood and maternal under-nutrition; high blood pressure; high cholesterol; being overweight; low fruit and vegetable intake as other diet-related risks; physical inactivity; unsafe sex and lack of contraception as sexual and reproductive health risks; unsafe water, sanitation and hygiene, urban air pollution, indoor smoke from solid fuels, lead exposure, and climate change as environmental risks; risk factors for injury; carcinogens, airborne particulates, ergonomic stressors and noise as occupational risk factors; unsafe health care injections; and childhood sexual abuse.

Six main objectives were defined for the CRA (see WHO, 2002) based on lessons learned from the previous risk factor analysis of the 1990 GBD study (Murray and Lopez, 1997, 1999):

- Developing more comparable methods for assessing different risk factors.
- Estimating the effects on burden of disease of shifting risk factor distributions towards a counterfactual distribution (the situation if the risk factor were eliminated or minimized) rather than just estimating the difference between a categorical distinction of "exposed" vs. "unexposed".
- Estimating a range of avoidable disease burden (= the proportion of burden of disease avoidable if current exposure levels are reduced to those specified by one or more counterfactual distributions) as well as attributable disease burden (= the proportion of current burden of disease due to past exposure).
- Developing more explicit and reliable methods which will have peer-reviewed semi-structured documentation for each risk factor assessment made publicly available after the review.
- Explicitly assessing causality and developing quantitative estimates of uncertainty.
- Developing appropriate estimates for the joint effects of different risk factors and the full effects of proximal risk factors via causal webs (see also Murray and Lopez, 1999; Ezzati et al., 2003).

Rehm and Gmel (2001) compiled an overview of background and methods for the CRA for alcohol and illicit drugs. In 2002 and 2003, the main comparative results were published as part of the World Health Report (WHO, 2002; see also Ezzati et al., 2002, 2003). In the fall of 2004, the full documentation for the first risk factors will be published by WHO (Ezzati et al., 2004). The present chapter will attempt to systematically review the methodology, the results and the implications of different forms of psychoactive substance use as risk factors for the global burden of disease.

METHODOLOGY AND RISK RELATIONS

Table 2.2.1 gives an overview of the methods used for estimating the global burden of disease for each of the three substance risk factors, as well as the main health risks attributable to the substances under consideration. There are similarities, as the burden for all three substances has been estimated disaggregated by sex, age and WHO regions (see Table 2.2.2) against a theoretical minimum of no exposure, and for all substances social harm and other social consequences have not been included in the estimates.

There are also some differences in the methodology and assumptions used for estimating the burden of disease, principally with respect to exposure definitions, risk relations and so-called externalities, i.e., effects on other people who themselves do not use one of the drugs of interest. Exposure to alcohol as a risk factor was modelled based on two current, directly measured dimensions of exposure: average volume of alcohol consumption and patterns of drinking (the latter a score composed of such components as rates of heavy drinking occasions, drinking with meals, drinking in public places). Average volume of alcohol consumption was assessed by means of per capita consumption figures and surveys, while patterns of drinking were assessed both by population surveys and a key informant questionnaire (see Rehm et al., 2003a, for details). For more than 90% of the world population, per capita consumption data were available, and for more than 80% of the world population, survey data were available. However, the data quality was variable, especially for patterns of drinking in developing countries (Rehm et al., 2003a).

Exposure to illicit drugs was based on data from the United Nations International Drug Control Program (UNDCP; see www.undcp.org) and the European Monitoring Centre for Drugs and Drug Addiction (EMCDDA; see www.emcdda.org). Of course, prevalence data on exposure of illicit substances was subject to high uncertainty (see Warner-Smith et al., 2001).

For tobacco, a completely different route to estimating exposure was taken. Peto et al. (1992) developed a method to estimate cumulative exposure to tobacco directly from birth and death registration data. This method takes advantage of the fact that in many regions of the world lung cancer in excess of the low rates in non-smokers is entirely attributable to exposure to tobacco. The age-specific lung cancer death rate in excess of the non-smoker lung cancer death rate can be seen as a biological assay of the cumulative past exposure to tobacco that takes into account the time lag between exposure and outcome. Based on these considerations, the smoking impact ratio is defined as a measure of overall cumulative exposure to tobacco by putting the observed lung cancer rate in a given age-group in a population in relation to the non-smoker lung cancer rate observed in a study population, for which no other influences on lung cancer are known.

The validity of this estimation is only as good as the assumption, e.g., that excess rates of lung cancer are indeed entirely or almost entirely attributable to exposure to tobacco. This has led to a separate method of estimation for China (Ezzati and Lopez, 2003), as indoor air pollution (e.g., from indoor fireplaces) contributes considerably to lung cancer there.

The health consequences of using different psychoactive substances are very different, with alcohol being related to many non-communicable and injury disease categories including some beneficial relations for certain volume-pattern combinations (most notably coronary heart disease; CHD). Table 2.2.6 gives an overview of the most important categories. Rehm and colleagues (Rehm et al., 2003b; 2004) give details on the establishment of causality between dimensions of alcohol exposure and disease outcomes, as well as on the quantification of risk-relations, usually based on meta-analyses (mainly Gutjahr et al., 2001; Ridolfo and Stevenson, 2001).

The health burden of tobacco smoking and oral tobacco use is almost entirely a matter of chronic disease (mainly lung cancer and heart disease categories; see Ezzati and Lopez, 2003). Relative risks were taken from the American Cancer Society Cancer Prevention

Table 2.2.1 Methodology for estimating substance-use related burden of disease

Risk factor	Exposure variable	Theoretical minimum	Outcomes[1]	Sources for exposure estimates	Sources for hazard estimates
Tobacco	Current levels of smoking (indirect indicator of accumulated smoking risk based on excess lung cancer mortality); oral tobacco use prevalence	No tobacco use	Lung cancer, upper aerodigestive cancer, all other cancers, chronic obstructive pulmonary disease (COPD), other respiratory diseases, all vascular diseases, and other medical causes in adults > 30; *fire injuries, maternal outcomes and perinatal conditions*	WHO GBD lung cancer mortality database based on complete (approximately 70 countries) or partial (approximately 40 countries) vital registration and International Agency for Research on Cancer (IARC) data; exposure was indirectly estimated for most countries using lung cancer mortality as an indicator of accumulated smoking (Peto et al., 1992)	American Cancer Society—Cancer Prevention Study II prospective study of risk factors for mortality in more than one million Americans (see Garfinkel, 1985; Peto et al., 1992) and retrospective study of one million deaths in 24 urban centres and 74 rural areas of China (see Liu et al., 1998)
Alcohol	Current alcohol consumption volumes and patterns	No alcohol use (specific sub-groups may have non-zero minimum)	IHD, stroke, hypertensive disease, diabetes, liver cancer, mouth and oropharynx cancer, breast cancer, oesophagus cancer, other cancers, liver cirrhosis, epilepsy, alcohol use disorders, depression, intentional and unintentional injuries; *selected other cardiovascular diseases and cancers, social consequences* Note that for some patterns and volume combinations beneficial effects were modeled	WHO Global Status Report on Alcohol (including production and trade data) on average alcohol consumption (WHO, 1999); systematic review of country surveys on abstinence and levels of alcohol consumption including contacting researchers for unpublished data; systematic review of literature and multiple regional expert consultation for unrecorded consumption; survey data as well as primary key-informant questionnaires on patterns of drinking	Published systematic reviews and meta-analyses of health effects plus statistical modelling for role of patterns on CHD and injuries (Rehm et al., 2004)
Illicit drugs	Current use of amphetamine, cocaine, heroin or other opioids and intravenous drug use	No illicit drug use	HIV/AIDS, overdose, drug use disorder, suicide, and trauma; *other neuropsychological diseases, social consequences, Hepatitis B & C*	Systematic review of literature and databases of United Nations International Drug Control Program (UNDCP; see www.undcp.org) and European Monitoring Centre for Drugs and Drug Addiction (EMCDDA; see www.emcdda.org)	Updated systematic review of literature on cause-specific and all-cause standardized mortality ratio; UNAIDS (www.unaids.com) estimates for HIV incidence among drug users (based on prevalence surveys among high-risk groups)

Source: Adapted from World Health Report (2002).
Note: [1]Outcomes in italic are those that are likely to be causal but not quantified due to lack of sufficient evidence on prevalence and/or hazard size.

Table 2.2.2 Description of 224 age, sex and region reporting categories for Comparative Risk Assessments

8 age groups:	0–4, 5–14, 15–29, 30–44, 45–59, 60–69, 70–79, 80+ yrs
2 sexes:	male, female
14 regions:	The following regional sub-groupings used were defined by WHO (World Health Report, see WHO, 2000) on the basis of high, medium or low levels of adult and of infant mortality.

Africa D	Algeria, Angola, Benin, Burkina Faso, Cameroon, Cape Verde, Chad, Comoros, Equatorial Guinea, Gabon, Gambia, Ghana, Guinea, Guinea-Bissau, Liberia, Madagascar, Mali, Mauritania, Mauritius, Niger, Nigeria, Sao Tome and Principe, Senegal, Seychelles, Sierra Leone, Togo
Africa E	Botswana, Burundi, Central African Republic, Congo, Côte d'Ivoire, Democratic Republic of the Congo, Eritrea, Ethiopia, Kenya, Lesotho, Malawi, Mozambique, Namibia, Rwanda, South Africa, Swaziland, Uganda, United Republic of Tanzania, Zambia, Zimbabwe
Americas A	Canada, Cuba, United States of America
Americas B	Antigua and Barbuda, Argentina, Bahamas, Barbados, Belize, Brazil, Chile, Colombia, Costa Rica, Dominica, Dominican Republic, El Salvador, Grenada, Guyana, Honduras, Jamaica, Mexico, Panama, Paraguay, St. Kitts and Nevis, St. Lucia, St. Vincent and the Grenadines, Suriname, Trinidad and Tobago, Uruguay, Venezuela
Americas D	Bolivia, Ecuador, Guatemala, Haiti, Nicaragua, Peru
Eastern Mediterranean B	Bahrain, Cyprus, Iran (Islamic Republic of), Jordan, Kuwait, Lebanon, Libyan Arab Jamahiriya, Oman, Qatar, Saudi Arabia, Syrian Arab Republic, Tunisia, United Arab Emirates
Eastern Mediterranean D	Afghanistan, Djibouti, Egypt, Iraq, Morocco, Pakistan, Somalia, Sudan, Yemen
Europe A	Andorra, Austria, Belgium, Croatia, Czech Republic, Denmark, Finland, France, Germany, Greece, Iceland, Ireland, Israel, Italy, Luxembourg, Malta, Monaco, Netherlands, Norway, Portugal, San Marino, Slovenia, Spain, Sweden, Switzerland, United Kingdom
Europe B	Albania, Armenia, Azerbaijan, Bosnia and Herzegovina, Bulgaria, Georgia, Kyrgyzstan, Poland, Romania, Slovakia, The Former Yugoslav Republic Of Macedonia, Tajikistan, Turkmenistan, Turkey, Uzbekistan, Yugoslavia
Europe C	Belarus, Estonia, Hungary, Kazakhstan, Latvia, Lithuania, Republic of Moldova, Russian Federation, Ukraine
South East Asia B	Indonesia, Sri Lanka, Thailand
South East Asia D	Bangladesh, Bhutan, Democratic People's Republic of Korea, India, Maldives, Myanmar, Nepal
Western Pacific A	Australia, Brunei Darussalam, Japan, New Zealand, Singapore
Western Pacific B	Cambodia, China, Cook Islands, Fiji, Kiribati, Lao People's Democratic Republic, Malaysia, Marshall Islands, Micronesia (Federated States of), Mongolia, Nauru, Niue, Palau, Papua New Guinea, Philippines, Republic of Korea, Samoa, Solomon Islands, Tonga, Tuvalu, Vanuatu, Viet Nam

Source: WHO (2000).

Note: A stands for very low child and very low adult mortality, B for low child and low adult mortality, C for low child and high adult mortality, D for high child and high adult mortality, and E for very high child and very high adult mortality.

Study, phase II (Garfinkel, 1985) and a retrospective study of one million deaths in 24 urban centres and 74 rural areas of China (Liu et al., 1998).

Illicit drug use by injection is linked to infection and injury disease categories. However, estimates of the prevalence of illicit drug use are usually more uncertain than those for alcohol and tobacco and there is also less data on the precise risk relationships between illicit drug use and disease categories. Among the reasons for this are that (i) there are different substances which are covered under the heading of illicit drug use (WHO, 2002); (ii) the main health consequences, especially HIV infection risk, are not linked to the substance itself but to the circumstances of use (e.g., the extent of sharing of needles); and (iii) an absence of data with which to quantify these socially determined risk relations in different regions in the world.

While all three categories of substances are known to have health effects on people other than the users, data limitations meant these effects could only be estimated for passive smoking, effects of maternal alcohol consumption on the foetus, and for some alcohol-related injuries (e.g., effects of drunk driving on bystanders).

RESULTS

Table 2.2.3 gives an overview of the mortality associated with different kinds of substance use (based on WHO, 2002; see also Ezzati and Lopez, 2003; Rehm et al., 2003c). It can be seen from Table 2.2.3 that tobacco caused many more deaths worldwide than alcohol and illicit drugs together, and this rank order is the same in all regions. In terms of level of development, the more developed a region, the more deaths related to substance use. This relationship is also true for a second category of substances, illicit drugs. For alcohol, there are more attributable deaths in developing countries with low mortality, mainly in the so-called threshold countries or emerging economies, than in the developed countries. This has partly to do with patterns of drinking, which are more favourable in the latter countries, thus leading to beneficial impacts on CHD and stroke (see McKee and Britton, 1998; Puddey et al., 1999; Rehm et al., 2003d).

The picture shifts when the outcome is no longer mortality but burden of disease, as measured in Disability-Adjusted Life-Years (DALYs; Murray and Lopez, 1996). This measure combines years of life lost due to premature mortality with years of life "lost" due to disability, i.e., years lived with disabling conditions (Murray et al., 2000). The latter are calculated by multiplying the time living with a disease condition by the disability weight of the condition (Murray and Lopez, 1996). Disability weights measure the degree of impact of a disease condition on disability, i.e., activity limitations and impairments. Disability weights vary between zero (no disabling effect at all) and one (death). Each disease condition was assigned one or more disability weights, dependent on the severity and progression of the disease, using a complicated procedure that involved expert estimates of the relative impact of different disease conditions (Murray and Lopez, 1996; Mathers et al., 2002). Table 2.2.4 gives an overview of resulting burden attributable to different categories of addictive substances.

As shown in Table 2.2.4, alcohol and tobacco account for about the same amount of global burden, both about five times as much as the burden attributable to illicit drug use. Again, the same relationships to economic development prevail. Why is there such a difference in comparing results across substance categories between mortality and DALYs as endpoints?

Table 2.2.3 Mortality in 2000 attributable to tobacco, alcohol and illicit drugs by development status of region and sex

	High mortality developing regions (AFR-D, AFR-E, AMR-D, EMR-D, SEAR-D)			Low mortality developing regions—emerging economies (AMR-B, EMR-B, SEAR-B, WPR-B)			Developed regions (AMR-A, EUR-A, EUR-B, EUR-C, WPR-A)			World		
	Male	**Female**	**Both**	**Male**	**Female**	**Both**	**Male**	**Female**	**Both**	**Male**	**Female**	**Both**
Deaths (000s)	13,758	12,654	26,412	8,584	7,373	15,957	6,890	6,601	13,491	29,232	26,629	55,861
Smoking and oral tobacco	7.5%	1.5%	4.6%	12.2%	2.9%	7.9%	26.3%	9.3%	18.0%	13.3%	3.8%	8.8%
Alcohol	2.6%	0.6%	1.6%	8.5%	1.6%	5.3%	8.0%	-0.3%	3.9%	5.6%	0.6%	3.2%
Illicit drugs	0.5%	0.1%	0.3%	0.6%	0.1%	0.4%	0.6%	0.3%	0.5%	0.6%	0.2%	0.4%

Source: Based on WHO (2002).

Table 2.2.4 Burden of disease in 2000 attributable to tobacco, alcohol and illicit drugs by development status of region and sex

	High mortality developing regions (AFR-D, AFR-E, AMR-D, EMR-D, SEAR-D)			Low mortality developing regions—emerging economies (AMR-B, EMR-B, SEAR-B, WPR-B)			Developed regions (AMR-A, EUR-A, EUR-B, EUR-C, WPR-A)			World		
	Male	Female	Both	Male	Female	Both	Male	Female	Both	Male	Female	Both
Total DALYs (000s)	420,711	412,052	832,763	223,181	185,316	408,497	117,670	96,543	214,213	761,562	693,911	1,455,373
Smoking and oral tobacco	3.4%	0.6%	2.0%	6.2%	1.3%	4.0%	17.1%	6.2%	12.2%	6.3%	1.6%	4.1%
Alcohol	2.6%	0.5%	1.6%	9.8%	2.0%	6.2%	14.0%	3.3%	9.2%	6.5%	1.3%	4.0%
Illicit drugs	0.8%	0.2%	0.5%	1.2%	0.3%	0.8%	2.3%	1.2%	1.8%	1.1%	0.4%	0.8%

Source: Based on WHO (2002).

Basically, tobacco is related to mortality and morbidity later in life, whereas many of the consequences of alcohol and illicit drugs occur at younger ages. Table 2.2.5 gives a summary of these findings. In terms of gender, for all four substances there is about a ratio of 4:1 (see Table 2.2.5), with men being much more affected by substances as sources of disease burden.

Table 2.2.6 gives an overview of the extent to which major categories of disease are differentially affected by tobacco, alcohol and illicit drug use. Basically, tobacco is linked to chronic diseases with high risk of mortality. Alcohol is linked to acute disease categories, e.g., intentional and unintentional injuries, and also chronic diseases, both with and without high risk of mortality (examples of high risk: liver cirrhosis, head and neck cancers; examples of low risk: depression, alcohol dependence). Illicit drug use is linked to some infectious diseases in association with injection (HIV), and to suicide and drug use disorders.

DISCUSSION AND CONCLUSION

Before we discuss content, the methodological limitations of the approaches used should be discussed. First, no estimate can be better than the underlying data and assumptions. For categories of psychoactive substance use as risk factors for the burden of disease, this means that we should examine the reliability and validity of underlying exposure data and of the exposure risk relationships. In addition, for all three categories, there will be uncertainty in the outcome, i.e., the mortality and DALY estimates.

Obviously, the reliability and validity of the exposure data will vary by substance category. The data on illicit drugs are the most problematic, as illicit drug use is an illegal behaviour and estimates on prevalence vary tremendously, even within countries (Warner-Smith et al., 2001). In addition, there are no gold standards to compare different estimates against. For alcohol, the situation is better as per capita estimates are available for most countries on a yearly basis, based on production or sales data (whether collected by a national government, by international organizations such as the Food and Agriculture Organization of the United Nations, or by the alcohol industry; see Rehm et al., 2003a). Although all these sources have their weaknesses (see Rehm et al., 2004), the overall data quality is quite good, especially in comparison to the data situation for other risk factors. However, per capita data only yield a general volume figure for the whole population, and not a sex–age distribution. This can only be derived from survey data, where also the major variables underlying the categorisation on patterns of drinking came from. As mentioned above, survey data are available for most of the more populous countries, covering more than 80% of the world's population, but with different depth and quality (see Rehm et al., 2004, for details). While all the surveys had some information on level of abstention, valid information necessary to derive the patterns of drinking score was hard to obtain for developing countries and emerging economies (Rehm et al., 2003a; 2004). Thus, the reliability and validity of data on alcohol as exposure varied between different world regions.

With respect to tobacco, no independently measured exposure variable is taken, but exposure, including past exposure, is indirectly derived from lung cancer rates. This method has been used for several years and has been discussed extensively (see e.g., comments on Peto et al., 1992). In summary, it is fair to say that the reliability and validity of the method are better for developed than for developing nations. This is also the reason why a different method has been used for China where smoke from indoor fires contributes significantly to

Table 2.2.5 Distribution of attributable mortality and DALYs by risk factor, age and sex, 2000

	Distribution of attributable deaths (%)						Distribution of attributable DALYs (%)					
	0–4 yrs	5–14 yrs	15–59 yrs	60+ yrs	Males	Females	0–4 yrs	5–14 yrs	15–59 yrs	60+ yrs	Males	Females
Smoking and oral tobacco	0	0	30	70	79	21	0	0	61	39	82	18
Alcohol	1	1	65	33	91	9		13	87	9	85	15
Illicit drugs	0	0	100	0	80	20	0	2	98	0	77	23

Source: Based on WHO (2002).

Table 2.2.6 Selected population attributable fractions, by risk factor, sex and level of development, 2000 (% DALYs for each cause)

	World		High mortality developing (AFR-D, AFR-E, AMR-D, EMR-D, SEAR-D)			Low mortality developing— emerging economies (AMR-B, EMR-B, SEAR-B, WPR-B)		Developed (AMR-A, EUR-A, EUR-B, EUR-C, WPR-A)	
	Males	Females	Both	Males	Females	Males	Females	Males	Females
Smoking and oral tobacco									
Mouth and oropharynx cancers	15	20	16	29	35	0	0	0	0
Trachea/bronchus/lung cancer	76	42	66	75	25	57	20	90	69
Other cancer	13	1	7	5	0	12	1	19	2
Chronic obstructive pulmonary disease	49	24	38	58	19	35	14	79	57
Cardiovascular disease	19	4	12	14	2	12	2	32	10
Alcohol									
Mouth and oropharynx cancers	22	9	19	11	4	28	10	41	28
Oesophagus cancer	37	15	29	17	6	42	16	46	36
Liver cancer	30	13	25	23	10	32	11	36	28
Breast cancer	n.a.	7	7	n.a.	2	n.a.	4	n.a.	11
Other neoplasms	6	3	4	2	1	5	2	11	8
Unipolar depressive disorders	3	1	2	2	0	3	0	7	2

Continued

Table 2.2.6 Selected population attributable fractions, by risk factor, sex and level of development, 2000 (% DALYs for each cause)(Continued)

Epilepsy	23	12	18	14	7	27	13	45	36
Alcohol use disorders	100	100	100	100	100	100	100	100	100
Ischaemic heart disease	4	−1	2	7	0	5	0	2	−3
Haemorrhagic stroke	18	1	10	7	2	21	2	26	0
Ischaemic stroke	3	−6	−1	1	0	3	0	5	−16
Cirrhosis of the liver	39	18	32	19	7	45	13	63	49
Motor vehicle accidents	25	8	20	19	5	25	8	45	18
Drownings	12	6	10	8	4	10	6	43	25
Falls	9	3	7	5	1	8	3	21	8
Poisonings	23	9	18	7	3	11	7	43	26
Other unintentional injuries	15	5	11	10	4	15	6	32	16
Self-inflicted injuries	15	5	11	8	2	10	5	27	12
Homicide	26	16	24	18	12	28	16	41	32
Other intentional injuries	13	7	12	7	3	20	11	32	19
Illicit drugs									
HIV/AIDS	4	1	2	0	0	28	9	43	68
Drug use disorders	100	100	100	100	100	100	100	100	100
Unintentional injuries	1	1	1	1	0	1	1	2	6
Self-inflicted injuries	5	2	4	10	2	1	0	5	9

Source: Based on WHO (2002).
Note: Categories refer to GBD categories (see Mathers et al., 2000).

lung cancer risks (see Table 2.2.1). However, there are other countries or regions of the world with significant indoor air pollution as a contributor to lung cancer risk (Ezzati and Kammen, 2002). It follows that the degree that other risk factors have an impact on lung cancer risk, the burden of tobacco smoking and oral tobacco use is over-estimated by the indirect method.

The relationships between exposure and disease are usually taken from large-scale epidemiological studies, in part by combining exposure studies in meta-analyses in the tradition of English et al. (1995). As most of these studies were undertaken in a few developed countries (especially the USA, Canada, the UK, and Australia), the generalisability will depend on the degree to which the relationships found are transferable elsewhere, and particularly to the developing world. In the light of the contemporary discussion of social determinants of health (e.g., Berkman and Kawachi, 2000), it is highly unlikely that the exposure–risk relations can be simply transferred from one country, whichever it may be, to a very different one. However, for biologically based relations, mostly involving chronic disease categories, this method provides a good first approximation, as recent results from the developing world show. Nevertheless, even for biologically based relations, transferability has its limits, when it comes to relative risk estimates. In India and China, for example, relative risks between tobacco smoking and lung cancer seem to be lower than for the developed world, whereas other disease categories have more importance (e.g., Liu et al., 1998; Gajalakshmi, 2003).

The assumption of universal risk relations cannot be made at all for more socially determined relationships (e.g., suicide, homicide, traffic injuries, but also infectious disease caused by needle sharing). This is irrelevant for estimating risks related to tobacco use, but an important problem when estimating the burden of disease both from alcohol and illicit drugs. In the CRA for alcohol, this problem has been tackled by using a different method based on multi-level time series analyses including patterns of drinking (Rehm et al., 2004; see also Gmel et al., 2001). For illicit drugs, basically standardised mortality rates have been transposed to different regions of the world. As indicated above, this introduces a lot of uncertainty, and, given the different patterns of drug use, mortality in the developing world is probably over-estimated by this method.

Overall, in the CRA uncertainty has been quantified. In the Web Annex to the World Health Report 2002 (WHO, 2002; see also www.who.int/whr/en), the following estimated ranges of uncertainty for global estimates of attributable burden were given: tobacco with a range of coefficient of variation between 0 and 4.9; alcohol with range between 5 and 9.9 and illicit drugs with a range larger than 15. Coefficients of variation are standard errors over point estimates, i.e., they denote the variability of these estimates. Overall, these numbers reflect the certainty we can have in the estimates given above. The estimates are most certain for tobacco, followed by alcohol. The variability of tobacco is comparable to the variability of the burden of disease attributable to physiological exposures such as blood pressure or cholesterol. The variability of alcohol is in the same range as the variability of risk factors such as fruit intake or body mass index. Illicit drugs are in a group of risk factors with the highest variability, along with such factors as climate change or childhood sexual abuse. These uncertainties should be taken into consideration when interpreting the data.

Alcohol, tobacco and illicit drugs are responsible for a relatively large proportion of the burden of disease. The total burden cannot easily be quantified, as the respective proportions for the individual substances cannot simply be added. The epidemiological methodology for attributable fractions of disease basically measures which portion of the disease would disappear if the exposure disappeared (Rothman and Greenland, 1998). A consequence of this methodology is that, if exposures overlap, the overlap will be counted for both exposures. Consider the case of oesophageal cancer, which is caused by the interaction of alcohol and tobacco. Clearly, if alcohol is taken away, no cancer would occur, but the same is true for the removal of tobacco. Thus, for all cancers which are caused by the interaction of alcohol and tobacco, there will be double counting, once for alcohol and again for tobacco. Since there are more diseases where substances overlap in causation, there is some double counting and the total burden of disease attributable to psychoactive substances will be less than the sum of the burdens attributed to each singly. But even with this qualification, it is safe to say that the burden of disease attributable to substance use is huge.

There are some indications that the burden of disease from psychoactive substances has increased over the past decade, at least for tobacco, where the estimates are very comparable (WHO, 2002), and for alcohol (Rehm et al., 2004). We expect this burden to increase even more in future for two main reasons: first, increased exposure, especially in the highly populated emerging economies in South-East Asia and China. Second, the relative proportion in the total burden of diseases associated with substance use—categories such as chronic diseases, injuries, HIV and hepatitis—is predicted to increase (Murray and Lopez, 1996; Lopez and Murray, 1998).

This expected increase can be halted, however, as there are effective prevention strategies, especially for alcohol and tobacco (WHO, 2002). In the case of tobacco, the effectiveness of a variety of strategies has been demonstrated, including regulatory policies such as enforced minimum purchase ages, controls on the composition and marketing of tobacco products, no-smoking policies in workplace and public environments, economic measures such as high taxation, and interventions at the individual level, such as smoking cessation and nicotine replacement therapy (Jha and Chaloupka, 2000; Rabin and Sugarman, 2001; Asma et al., 2002; see Chapter 6.4). The successful negotiation of the Framework Convention on Tobacco Control (Shibuya et al., 2003) potentially puts in place international agreements to back up effective national policies. In the case of alcohol, a wide variety of strategies have been shown to be effective (see Chapters 6.5 and 7.5), including regulatory limits on the time and place of availability, enforced minimum purchase ages, high taxation, a low blood-alcohol level for drivers and random breath-testing to enforce it, along with other drinking-driving countermeasures, training and regulation of alcohol sales staff to minimise overselling and alcohol-related violence, and brief interventions to reduce the drinking of individual problematic drinkers (Room et al., 2002; Babor et al., 2003). At present, nations largely set their own alcohol control policies; indeed, international trade agreements and disputes over them often have results which undermine the interests of public health (Grieshaber-Otto et al., 2000), pointing to the need for an equivalent for alcohol of the Framework Convention on Tobacco Control.

The well-established findings of a number of effective strategies for reducing the harm to public health from tobacco and from alcohol pose a challenge to policy and to the political process: the burden of disease attributable to alcohol, tobacco and illicit drugs is highly preventable, and it depends on health policy decisions whether the current trends continue.

ACKNOWLEDGEMENTS

The authors would like to thank all those who worked on substance-related risk factors within the CRA for their contributions. All teams and authors are listed in Ezzati et al. (2002). Furthermore, WHO, the Swiss Federal Office of Public Health (grant no. 00.001588), the

Swiss National Science Foundation, the Addiction Research Institute in Zurich, Switzerland, the Swiss Institute for the Prevention of Alcohol and Other Drug Problems, Lausanne, and the Centre for Addiction and Mental Health in Toronto, Canada, provided financial and/or technical support for the contributions of Jürgen Rehm to the alcohol calculations in the CRA and thus to this study.

REFERENCES

Asma, S., Yang, G., Samet, J., Giovino, G., Bettcher, D.W., Lopez, A.D. and Yach, D. (2002) Tobacco. In R. Detels, J. McEwen, R. Beaglehole and H. Tanaka (eds), *Oxford Textbook of Public Health*, 4th edn, Oxford: Oxford University Press, pp. 1481–1502.

Babor, T., Caetano, R., Casswell, S., Edwards, G., Giesbrecht, N., Graham, K., Grube, J., Gruenewald, P., Hill, L., Holder, H., Homel, R., Österberg, E., Rehm, J., Room, R. and Rossow, I. (2003) *Alcohol, No Ordinary Commodity: A Consumer's Guide to Public Policy*. Oxford: Oxford University Press.

Berkman, L. and Kawachi, I. (2000) *Social Epidemiology*. Oxford: Oxford University Press.

English, D.R., Holman, C.D.J., Milne, E., Winter, M.J., Hulse, G.K., Codde, G. et al. (1995) *The Quantification of Drug-Caused Morbidity and Mortality in Australia 1995*. Canberra: Commonwealth Department of Human Services and Health.

Ezzati, M. and Kammen, D.M. (2002) The health impacts of exposure to indoor air pollution from solid fuels in developing countries: knowledge, gaps, and data needs. *Environmental Health Perspectives*, **110**(11), 1057–1068.

Ezzati, M. and Lopez, A.D. (2003) Estimates of global mortality attributable to smoking in 2000. *Lancet*, **362**(9387), 847–852.

Ezzati, M., Lopez, A.D., Rodgers, A., Vander Horn, S., Murray C.J.L and the Comparative Risk Assessment Collaborating Group (2002) Selected major risk factors and global and regional burden of disease. *Lancet*, **360**, 1347–1360.

Ezzati, M., Lopez, A.D., Rogers, A. and Murray, C.J.L. (2004) *Comparative Quantification of Health Risks: Global and Regional Burden of Disease Attributable to Selected Major Risk Factors*. Vol 1. Geneva: World Health Organization.

Ezzati, M., Vander Horn, S., Rodgers, A., Lopez, A.D., Mathers, C.D., Murray, C.J.L. and the Comparative Risk Assessment Collaborating Group (2003) Estimates of global and regional potential health gains from reducing multiple major risk factors. *Lancet*, **362**, 271–280.

Gajalakshmi, V., Peto, R., Kanaka, T.S. and Jha, P. (2003) Smoking and mortality from tuberculosis and other diseases in India: retrospective study of 43000 adult male deaths and 35000 controls. *Lancet*, **362**, 507–515.

Garfinkel, L. (1985) Selection, follow-up and analysis in the American Cancer Society prospective studies. In L. Garfinkel, O. Ochs and M. Mushinkski (eds), *Selection, Follow-up and Analysis in Prospective Studies: A Workshop*. National Cancer Institute (NCI Monograph 67), Bethesda, MD.

Global Burden of Disease 2002, World Health Organization. Available online: http://www3.who.int/whosis/menu.cfm?path=whosis,burden,burden_gbd2000docs&language=English (accessed 21 January 2004).

Gmel, G., Rehm, J. and Frick, U. (2001) Methodological approaches to conducting pooled cross-sectional time series analysis: the example of the association between all-cause mortality and per capita alcohol consumption for men in 15 European states. *European Addiction Research*, **7**(3), 128–137.

Grieshaber-Otto, J., Sinclair, S. and Schacter, N. (2000) Impacts of international trade, services and investment treaties on alcohol regulation. *Addiction* **95**(suppl. 4), S491–S504.

Gutjahr, E., Gmel, G. and Rehm, J. (2001) Relation between average alcohol consumption and disease: an overview. *European Addiction Research*, **7**(3), 117–127.

Jha, P. and Chaloupka, F. (2000) *Tobacco Control in Developing Countries*. Oxford: Oxford University Press.

Liu, B.Q., Peto, R., Chen, Z.M., Boreham, J., Wu, Y.P., Li, J.Y., Campbell, T.C. and Chen, J.S. (1998) Emerging tobacco hazards in China: 1. Retrospective proportional mortality study of one million deaths. *British Medical Journal*, **317**, 1411–1422.

Lopez, A.D. and Murray, C.J. (1998) The global burden of disease, 1990–2020. *Nature Medicine*, **4**(11), 1241–1243.

Mathers, C.D., Stein, C., Ma Fat, D., Rao, C., Inoue, M., Tomijima, N., Bernard, C., Lopez, A.D. and Murray, C.J.L. (2002) *Global Burden of Disease 2000: Version 2 Methods and Results*, Geneva: World Health Organization.

McKee, M. and Britton, A. (1998) The positive relationship between alcohol and heart disease in eastern Europe: potential physiological mechanisms. *Journal of the Royal Society of Medicine*, **91**, 402–407.

Methodology of the Comparative Risk Assessment (CRA) Guidelines and Tools. Available online: http://www.ctru.auckland.ac.nz/CRA/main.html (accessed 21 January 2004).

Murray, C.J.L. and Lopez, A.D. (eds) (1996) *The Global Burden of Disease: A Comprehensive Assessment of Mortality and Disability from Diseases, Injuries and Risk Factors in 1990 and Projected to 2020*. Boston: Harvard School of Public Health on behalf of the World Health Organization and the World Bank.

Murray, C.J.L. and Lopez, A. (1997) Global mortality, disability, and the contribution of risk factors: global burden of disease study. *Lancet*, **349**, 1436–1442.

Murray, C.J.L and Lopez, A. (1999) On the comparable quantification of health risks: lessons from the Global Burden of Disease Study. *Epidemiology*, **10**, 594–605.

Murray, C.J.L., Salomon, J.A. and Mathers, C. (2000) A critical examination of summary measures of population health. *Bulletin of the World Health Organization*, **8**, 981–994.

Peto, R., Lopez, A.D., Boreham, J., Thun, M. and Heath, C.Jr. (1992) Mortality from tobacco in developed countries: indirect estimation from national vital statistics. *Lancet*, **339**, 1268–1278.

Puddey, I.B., Rakic, V., Dimmitt, S.B. and Beilin, L.J. (1999) Influence of drinking on cardiovascular disease and cardiovascular risk factors: a review. *Addiction*, **94**, 649–663.

Rabin, R.L. and Sugarman, S.D. (eds) (2001) *Regulating Tobacco*. Oxford: Oxford University Press.

Rehm, J. and Gmel, G. (2001) Alcohol, illicit drugs and the global burden of disease. Special issue. *European Addiction Research*, **12**(3), 95–157.

Rehm, J., Rehn, N., Room, R., Monteiro, M., Gmel, G., Jernigan, D. and Frick, U. (2003a) The global distribution of average volume of alcohol consumption and patterns of drinking. *European Addiction Research*, **9**, 147–156.

Rehm, J., Room, R., Graham, K., Monteiro, M., Gmel, G. and Sempos, C.T. (2003b) The relationship of average volume of alcohol consumption and patterns of drinking to burden of disease: an overview. *Addiction*, **98**(10), 1209–1228.

Rehm, J., Room, R., Monteiro, M., Gmel, G., Graham, K., Rehn, N., Sempos, C.T., Frick, U. and Jernigan, D. (2004) Alcohol. In M. Ezzati, A.D. Lopez, A. Rodgers and C.J.L. Murray (eds), *Comparative Quantification of Health Risks: Global and Regional Burden of Disease Attributable to Selected Major Risk Factors*. Vol 1 (pp 959–1108). Geneva: World Health Organization.

Rehm, J., Room, R., Monteiro, M., Gmel, G., Graham, K., Rehn, N., Sempos, C.T. and Jernigan, D. (2003c) Alcohol as a risk factor for global burden of disease. *European Addiction Research*, **9**(4), 157–164.

Rehm, J., Sempos, C.T. and Trevisan, M. (2003d) Average volume of alcohol consumption, patterns of drinking and risk of coronary heart disease: a review. *Journal of Cardiovascular Risk*, **10**(1), 15–20.

Ridolfo, B. and Stevenson, C. (2001) *The Quantification of Drug-Caused Mortality and Morbidity in Australia 1998*. Canberra: Australian Institute of Health and Welfare.

Room, R., Jernigan, D., Carlini-Marlatt, B., Gureje, O., Mäkelä, K., Marshall, M., Medina-Mora, M.E., Monteiro, M., Parry, C., Partanen, J., Riley, L. and Saxena, S. (2002) *Alcohol and Developing Societies: A Public Health Approach*. Geneva: Finnish Foundation for Alcohol Studies, Helsinki and World Health Organization.

Rothman, K.J. and Greenland, S. (1998) *Modern Epidemiology*. 2nd edn. Philadelphia. PA: Lippincott-Raven Publishers.

Shibuya, K., Ciecierski, C., Guindon, E., Bettcher, D.W., Evans, D.B. and Murray, C.J. (2003) WHO Framework Convention on Tobacco Control: development of an evidence-based global public health treaty. *British Medical Journal*, **327**(7407), 154–157.

Warner-Smith, M., Lynskey, M., Hall, W. and Monteiro, M. (2001) Challenges and first solutions of estimating mortality attributable to illicit drug use. *European Addiction Research*, **7**(3), 104–116.

World Health Organization (1999) *Global Status Report on Alcohol*. Geneva: World Health Organization.

World Health Organization (2000) *World Health Report 2000: Health Systems: Improving Performance*, Geneva: World Health Organization.

World Health Organization (2002) *World Health Report 2002: Reducing Risks, Promoting Healthy Life*. Geneva: World Health Organization.

World Health Organization (2004) *The World Health Report, 2003*, World Health Organization, Geneva. Available online. www.who.int/whr/en. (accessed 21 January, 2004).

2.3 Substance Use and Mental Health in Longitudinal Perspective

MAREE TEESSON, LOUISA DEGENHARDT
National Drug and Alcohol Research Centre, University of New South Wales, Australia

WAYNE HALL
Office of Public Policy and Ethics, Institute for Molecular Bioscience, University of Queensland, Australia

MICHAEL LYNSKEY
Washington University in St Louis, MO, USA

JOHN W. TOUMBOUROU, GEORGE PATTON
Centre for Adolescent Health, Melbourne, Australia

SUMMARY

Comorbidity between substance use disorders and other psychological disorders has emerged as a major clinical, public health and research issue over the past few decades thanks in large part to population surveys of mental disorders that have highlighted that comorbidity is common. The reasons for comorbidity are complex but longitudinal research has begun to provide insights into the underlying mechanisms. This chapter will give a brief overview of epidemiological research into comorbidity and examines the most recent longitudinal data on patterns and causal pathways of comorbidity. The chapter highlights the increasingly consistent evidence of shared risk factors for both mental disorders and substance use disorders as well as suggesting that causal relationships may operate in both directions, that is from substance use to mental disorders and vice versa. In particular, there is a causal pathway from depression to substance use in males, and from daily cannabis use to depression and anxiety in females. There is also evidence that cannabis use precipitates psychosis in persons who are vulnerable because of a personal or family history of psychosis. Externalizing behavior problems in children, particularly conduct disorder and aggressive behavior emerging prior to age 12, have been shown to predict a greater likelihood of progressing to adolescent poly-drug use and or alcohol use problems in adulthood. The effect of childhood internalizing problems such as anxiety

Preventing Harmful Substance Use: The Evidence Base for Policy and Practice.
Edited by T. Stockwell, P. J. Gruenewald, J.W. Toumbourou and W. Loxley.
© 2005 John Wiley & Sons, Ltd. ISBN 0-470-09227-0 (hbk) 0-470-09228-9 (pbk).

and depression on the subsequent development of substance use problems is less clear. Finally, the chapter addresses the implications of this information for prevention. While we should intervene to prevent or delay the onset of substance use and mental disorders during adolescence, such interventions should not focus solely on substance use or mental disorders alone. They should target a range of potentially health-threatening behaviors including substance use, sexual risk-taking and problems of personal adjustment since many of these behaviors co-occur because of shared risk factors.

HOW COMMON IS COMORBIDITY?

The first large-scale descriptive studies of comorbidity between mental and substance use disorders were undertaken in the USA in the early 1980s. The USA National Comorbidity Study (NCS) was specifically designed to examine the extent of comorbidity between substance use and mental disorder. The NCS was conducted in 1991 with approximately 8,000 respondents aged between 15 and 54 years. The prevalence of any current (12-month) diagnosis was 29.5%. Among those with a 12-month diagnosis of any substance use disorder, 36% had at least one anxiety disorder, whilst 25% had at least one affective disorder. Among those with a 12-month diagnosis of any mental disorder, 15% had at least one co-occurring substance use disorder (Kessler et al., 1996).

A more recent survey in Australia found similar results. A nationally representative sample of 10,641 Australians were surveyed (Teesson et al., 2000) in 1997 as part of the Australian National Survey of Mental Health and Wellbeing (NSMHWB). Some 18% of those surveyed (aged 18–90 years) met criteria for a DSM-IV mental disorder in the past 12 months. This rate is lower than the NCS figure of 29.5%. This difference may be due to the younger age groups covered by the NCS (which was limited to persons 45 years and under); the omission of certain disorders from the NSMHWB (in particular, Antisocial Personality Disorder and Specific Phobias); potential cross-national differences and the use of DSM-IV diagnoses in the NSMHWB and DSM-III-R in the NCS.

The Australian survey showed a considerable degree of comorbidity in substance use disorders and other mental disorders (Andrews et al., 1999). About one in four persons with an anxiety, affective or substance use disorder also had at least one other mental disorder. That is, they had two or more different classes of disorder, such as an anxiety and affective disorder, or an anxiety and a substance use disorder. A small proportion of men (0.8%) and women (0.8%) had all three types of disorder (i.e., an anxiety, affective and substance use disorder).

The patterns of comorbidity differed between men and women, reflecting the differences in prevalence within the sexes for the individual disorders. Among women, affective and anxiety disorders most often occurred together, accounting for three-quarters of women who had more than one mental disorder. Among men, comorbid disorders more often involved an anxiety or an affective disorder in combination with a substance use disorder. These combinations of disorders affected two-thirds of men who had more than one mental disorder.

The National Survey of Mental Health and Wellbeing (NSMHWB) also included a screening questionnaire for psychotic symptoms (Degenhardt and Hall, 2001). Among those under 50 years of age who screened positive for a psychotic disorder, 7.8% (N = 27) met ICD-10 criteria for cannabis dependence in the past 12 months. This was 17.2% of all persons diagnosed with cannabis dependence. A diagnosis of cannabis dependence increased the chances of reporting psychotic symptoms 1.71 times, after adjusting for age, affective and anxiety disorders, smoking status and alcohol dependence (Degenhardt and Hall, 2001). Similarly, a low prevalence study conducted as part of the NSMHWB demonstrated that drug and alcohol use disorders were highly prevalent in those with psychotic illnesses. Lifetime diagnoses of alcohol use disorders were found in 30% of the sample and cannabis use disorder in 25%.

WHAT CAN LONGITUDINAL RESEARCH TELL US ABOUT THE CAUSES OF COMORBIDITY?

Longitudinal research is crucial to our understanding of the causes of comorbidity. In order to infer that the association between substance use disorders and mental disorders reflects a causal association, we need evidence: that there is an association between substance use disorders and mental disorders; that one precedes the other; and that plausible alternative explanations of the association can be excluded.

Association requires that substance use disorders and mental disorders occur together. So that, for example, cannabis users should have higher rates of psychosis and cannabis use should occur more frequently among people with psychoses (Hall et al., in press). As indicated above, the epidemiological literature confirms an association between substance use disorders and mental disorders. It is the nature of the association which is most contentious.

There are several reasons why associations between substance use disorders and mental disorders may occur (Caron and Rutter, 1991). These can be summarized as being: (a) that there is a direct causal relationship between the two, with the presence of one disorder making another more likely to develop; and (b) that there are common factors that increase the risk of both disorders.

Given the demonstration of an association, the important questions are: does one disorder precede the other and, if so, can we rule out other causes as an explanation of the relationship? The strongest evidence for these questions comes from longitudinal population-based studies. These are discussed in more detail below with a review of the longitudinal data which supports each argument.

Direct Causal Relationship

Mental health problems cause substance use problems

The most commonly proposed hypothesis in this area holds that the relationship between substance use disorders and other mental health problems arises because persons with mental health problems use substances to reduce anxiety and stress, the "self-medication hypothesis". Thus, substances are used to alleviate symptoms and specific substances will be selected for their specific effects upon mood. Although this hypothesis is commonly proposed, the evidence for it is not strong.

There are very few studies examining causal pathways between mental health problems and later substance use problems. Henry et al. (1993) reported a prospective study of the relationship between depressive symptoms and later multiple drug use in young adults in a New Zealand birth cohort (N = 759) whose members had been assessed intensively on risk factors for mental disorders since birth. They assessed depressive symptoms at age 11 *before* onset of drug use. They also examined the specificity of the association between depression and drug use by conducting analyses of the effects of conduct problems. They found that for males, depressive symptoms at age 11 predicted multiple drug use at age 15, even after controlling for concurrent conduct problems. For females, there was no relationship between early symptomatology and later substance use but "self-medication" in females at age 15 was associated with concurrent conduct problems and depressive symptoms.

Evidence from other studies suggests that internalizing disorders such as anxiety and depression may be more important predictors for female than male alcohol problems. In Finland, high social anxiety for females at age 8 years predicted higher rates of alcohol abuse at age 26, while anxiety for boys was associated with lower alcohol abuse (Pulkkinen and Pitkanen, 1994).

In a three-year prospective study by Patton et al. (1998), depression and anxiety symptoms and peer smoking both predicted initiation of smoking. There was interaction between the two predictors in that depression and anxiety accentuated risks associated with peer smoking and predicted later experimentation only in the presence of peer smoking. Thus, in this study, depressive and anxiety symptoms raised the risk for smoking initiation and appeared to do so by increasing susceptibility to peer smoking influences.

The causal pathway linking substance use disorders and externalizing disorders has been more fully researched and documented in the literature. There exists relatively clear data suggesting that substance use problems begin with early child behavior problems, conduct problems, and attention deficit problems, high sensation seeking, and social adversity. For example, Reinherz et al. (2000) studied data from 360 respondents followed prospectively over a 17-year period to determine factors that would predict drug disorders in early adulthood. It was found that child behavior problems such as hyperactivity, poor concentration, aggression, and hostility displayed at age 6 were predictive of substance user disorders for both males and females at age 21. In addition, a study by Windle (1990) found that antisocial behavior in early adolescence predicted substance problems in late adolescence.

Substance use problems cause mental health problems

A different type of direct causal hypothesis is that substance use problems precipitate mental health problems. Patton et al. (2002) studied the association of cannabis use with symptoms of depression and anxiety in just under 2,000 young Australians over seven years from the age of 14 to 21 years. Young adult females using cannabis daily had more than five-fold higher rates of marked depressive and anxiety symptoms, after controlling for the effects of other substance use. Furthermore, weekly use as a teenager predicted a two-fold higher rate of young adult depression and anxiety in females after controlling for baseline mental health and other potential confounders. In contrast, depression and anxiety symptoms as a teenager did not significantly predict later cannabis use.

One of the most controversial areas of comorbidity is that between cannabis and psychosis. There has been considerable debate over whether cannabis use is causally related to schizophrenia (Hall et al., in press). Until recently all reviews had argued that prospective longitudinal population-based cohort studies were required to elucidate the potential causal inference of cannabis on psychosis. Four such studies have been published recently.

The first study is a 27-year follow-up of the Swedish cohort study (Zammit et al., 2002). The Swedish cohort study was a 15-year prospective study of cannabis use and schizophrenia in 50,465 Swedish conscripts (Andréasson et al., 1987). This study investigated the relationship between self-reported cannabis use at age 18 and the risk of being diagnosed with schizophrenia in the Swedish psychiatric case register during the next 15 years.

Andréasson et al. found that compared to those who had never used cannabis, those who had used cannabis 1 to 10 times were 1.5 times more likely, and those who had used 10 or more times, were 2.3 times more likely to receive a diagnosis of schizophrenia. Andréasson et al. argued that this means that cannabis use precipitates schizophrenia in vulnerable individuals. Zammit et al. found, as did Andréassen et al., that cannabis use at baseline predicted an increased risk of schizophrenia during the follow-up period.

Zammit et al.'s findings have been supported by a study conducted by Van Os and colleagues (2002). This was a three-year longitudinal study of the relationship between self-reported cannabis use and psychosis in a community sample of 4,848 people in the Netherlands. The study found that cannabis use at baseline predicted an increased risk of psychotic symptoms during the follow-up period in individuals who had not reported psychiatric symptoms at baseline. Van Os et al. estimated the attributable risk of cannabis to psychosis was 13% for psychotic symptoms and 50% for cases with psychotic disorders adjudged to need psychiatric treatment.

In another study, Arsenault et al. (2002) examined the relationship between adolescent cannabis use and psychosis in young adults in a New Zealand birth cohort (N = 759) whose members had been assessed intensively on risk factors for psychotic symptoms and disorders since birth. Arsenault et al. found a relationship between cannabis use by age 15 and an increased risk of psychotic symptoms by age 26. An interesting result and important addition to the literature was the specificity of the effects of cannabis on psychotic symptoms: there was no relationship between other drug use and psychotic disorders and no relationship between cannabis use and depression.

Most recently, Fergusson et al. (2003) have reported a longitudinal study of the relationship between cannabis dependence at age 18 and the number of psychotic symptoms reported at age 21 in the Christchurch birth cohort in New Zealand. They found that *cannabis dependence at age 18 predicted an increased risk of psychotic symptoms at age 21 years* (RR of 2.3). This association was smaller but still significant after adjustment for potential confounders (RR of 1.8).

There is now consistent evidence from longitudinal studies that cannabis use precipitates schizophrenia in persons who are vulnerable because of a personal or family history of schizophrenia but is unlikely to cause it *de novo* (Hall et al., in press). The policy implications are not so clear. It is probably clearest that young people with psychosis or a family history of psychosis are at highest risk of experiencing psychotic symptoms after using cannabis. They should be advised to avoid using cannabis. In terms of young people who use cannabis daily, they are probably at higher risk of experiencing psychosis along with a variety of other adverse outcomes (early school leaving and depression) and should be discouraged from using cannabis in this way.

While direct causal models are appealing in their simplicity, it could also be that other variables may account for some of the associations. Alternatively, common genetic factors may play some role in increasing the likelihood of both substance use and mental disorders (Tsuang et al., 1998). These possibilities are considered below.

Common Factors

Common risk factors may well explain an association between two disorders (Caron and Rutter, 1991; Kessler, 1995). If disorders are predominantly the result of a set of risk factors and these sets are the same or similar for two disorders, it may well be the case that "comorbidity" reflects the fact that the pathways by which persons develop one disorder are the same as those by which they develop another. These common factors might be biological, personality, social and environmental, or a combination of these.

There is considerable evidence that substance use disorders and mental disorders share common biological risk factors, specifically genetic risk of developing disorders (Tambs et al., 1997; True et al., 1999; Koob and Le Moa, 2001). The possibility of a common genetic vulnerability to problematic use of different substances has been examined in a sample of male twins (Tsuang et al., 1998; True et al., 1999). Twin studies have also provided some evidence that there are common genetic influences upon substance use disorders and mental disorders. For example, research has suggested that common genetic factors increase the risk of alcohol dependence, anxiety symptoms, and affective symptoms (Tambs et al., 1997).

A study of women twins also found that there were significant common genetic factors implicated in the comorbidity between major depression and tobacco smoking (Kendler et al., 1993). This study found that the heritability of liability to tobacco smoking and major depression was 55% and 48%, respectively. Analyses were conducted to examine whether there was a causal relationship between tobacco smoking in major depression, or whether common factors accounted for the association that was observed between the two. The best explanation of the co-occurrence of tobacco smoking and major depression in this sample was a *common genetic factor*. There was *no* evidence of common *environmental* factors. The correlation between smoking and major depression due to these genetic factors was estimated at r = +0.56 (Kendler et al., 1993).

The Christchurch longitudinal study has also examined this issue (Fergusson et al., 1996) while controlling for a large number of demographic variables, family background characteristics, and personal characteristics. It found that the co-occurrence of nicotine dependence and depression could be almost completely explained by common *environmental* factors, and that the most parsimonious explanation of the relationships between the two *did not* include a causal relationship.

While this may appear to be a contradiction of the Kendler findings, it raises the issue that genetic and environmental factors are *not independent*. What is clear from both of these studies is that there is *no evidence that major depression caused nicotine dependence or vice versa*.

A similar conclusion was reached by Lynskey and colleagues (1998) in an examination of liability to alcohol, tobacco and cannabis use using the same New Zealand cohort. This study found that the simplest explanation of the relationship between alcohol, tobacco and cannabis use was a "common vulnerability" model of increased liability to the use of the three substances, which could be completely explained by a large number of environmental factors included in the analyses.

Thus, while common genetic influences or individual factors are likely to play a part in explaining comorbidity, there is also a wealth of evidence from longitudinal research that a number of other factors are common to both mental disorders and substance use disorders. For example, social disadvantage is more common among persons who (a) are problematic substance users (Institute of Medicine, 1996); (b) meet the criteria for mood disorders and anxiety disorders (Weissman et al., 1991; Blazer, 1995); and (c) meet the criteria for psychotic disorders. There is evidence that this is not merely because of downwards social drift that occurs as a result of developing the disorder. For all these groups of disorders, studies have shown that there are higher rates of separation and divorce, and a lower likelihood that persons will be married or in a *de facto* relationship (Jablensky et al., 1991; Weissman et al., 1991; Blazer, 1995).

WHAT ARE THE IMPLICATIONS OF COMORBIDITY RESEARCH FOR PREVENTION?

The longitudinal and twin studies reviewed are increasing findings of shared risk factors for a wide range of "problem" behaviors including mental disorders and substance use disorders. These findings have several implications for the design and implementation of prevention programs.

First, it may be of benefit for these programs to address a wider range of potentially harmful behaviors such as sexual risk-taking and criminal offending. Broadening the topics addressed has the benefit of giving children a better picture of the full range of health-risk behaviors with which they are likely to be tempted. The reduction of these behaviors may, in turn, lead to a reduction in substance use and substance-related harm. Recognizing that much of the association between different problem behaviors arises from the influence of common risk factors, interventions should target and attempt to modify the known risk factors for substance use and mental disorders. One such study has been reported by Tremblay et al. (1995) who implemented a comprehensive intervention program for at-risk kindergarten-aged boys that included both parent training and social skills training for the boys. At follow-up in adolescence the intervention group showed significantly reduced rates of aggressive behavior and increased grade retention. Unfortunately, substance use was not assessed at follow-up and the impact of such a program on later substance use remains an interesting question.

The extent to which existing drug-prevention programs may have beneficial effects in other areas remains largely undetermined, because evaluations of these programs have typically focused solely on their effects on drug use. Thus, as the targets of school-based prevention programs are broadened to include consideration of non-drug-related behaviors, evaluations of these programs should also be expanded to measure their impacts on crime, sexual risk-taking, and other risky activities.

In summary, while we should intervene to prevent or delay the onset of substance use behaviors during adolescence, such interventions should not focus solely on substance use. They should target a range of potentially health-threatening behaviors including substance use, sexual risk-taking and problems of personal adjustment since many of these behaviors co-occur because of shared risk factors (Lynskey, 1998).

CONCLUSION

While at present there remains much that is not known about the causes of comorbidity between mental and substance use disorders, there is increasing evidence that simple causal hypotheses may not wholly explain the associations. There is growing evidence for some direct causal relationships, in particular cannabis use predisposing to psychosis in the vulnerable. There is also a broad convergence of evidence that there are many common risk factors for both problematic substance use and mental disorders and that substance use and mental disorders (mood disorders, anxiety disorders, personality disorders and psychotic disorders) share common risk factors and life pathways. A number of longitudinal cohort and twin studies have concluded that common factors explain the comorbidity between: alcohol, tobacco and cannabis use (Lynskey et al., 1998); dependence on different illicit drugs (Tsuang et al., 1998); alcohol and nicotine dependence (True et al., 1999); and nicotine dependence and major depression (Kendler et al., 1993; Fergusson et al., 1996). The implications for prevention, while promising, remain to be tested in large-scale intervention studies.

REFERENCES

Andréasson, S., Allebeck, P. and Rydberg, U. (1987) Cannabis and schizophrenia: a longitudinal study of Swedish conscripts. *Lancet*, **2**, 1483–1486.

Andrews, G., Hall, W., Teesson, M. and Henderson, S. (1999) *The Mental Health of Australians*. Canberra: Commonwealth Department of Health and Family Services.

Arseneault, L., Cannon, M., Poulton, R., Murray, R., Caspi, A. and Moffitt, T.E. (2002) Cannabis use in adolescence and risk for adult psychosis: longitudinal prospective study. *British Medical Journal*, **325**(7374), 1212–1213.

Blazer, D. (1995) Mood disorders: epidemiology. In H. Kaplan and B. Sadock (eds), *Comprehensive Textbook of Psychiatry*. Baltimore, MD: Williams and Wilkins, pp. 1079–1089.

Caron, C. and Rutter, M. (1991) Comorbidity in child psychopathology: concepts, issues and research strategies. *Journal of Child Psychology and Psychiatry*, **32**, 1063–1080.

Degenhardt, L. and Hall, W.D. (2001) The association between psychosis and problematical drug use among Australian adults: findings from the National Survey of Mental Health and Wellbeing. *Psychological Medicine*, **31**(4), 659–668.

Fergusson, D.M., Horwood, J.L. and Swain-Campbell, N.R. (2003) Cannabis dependence and psychotic symptoms in young people. *Psychological Medicine*, **33**, 15–21.

Fergusson, D.M., Lynskey, M. and Horwood, L.J. (1996) Comorbidity between depressive disorders and nicotine dependence in a cohort of 16-year-olds. *Archives of General Psychiatry*, **53**, 1043–1047.

Hall, W., Degenhardt, L. and Teesson, M. (in press) Cannabis use and psychotic disorders: an update. *Drug and Alcohol Review*.

Henry, B., Feehan, M., McGee, R., Stanton, W., Moffitt, T.E. and Silva, P. (1993) The importance of conduct problems and depressive symptoms in predicting adolescent substance use. *Journal of Abnormal Child Psychology*, **21**, 469–480.

Institute of Medicine (1996) *Pathways of Addiction*. Washington, DC: National Academy Press.

Jablensky, A., Sartorius, N. and Ernberg, G. (1991) Schizophrenia: manifestations, incidence and course in different cultures. A World Health Organization Ten-Country Study. *Psychological Medicine*, Supplement No. 20., 1–97.

Kendler, K., Neale, M., MacLean, C., Heath, A., Eaves, L. and Kessler R. (1993) Smoking and major depression: a causal analysis. *Archives of General Psychiatry*, **50**, 36–43.

Kessler, R. (1995) Epidemiology of psychiatric comorbidity. In M.T. Tsuang, M. Tohen and G.E.P. Zahner (eds), *Textbook in Psychiatric Epidemiology*. New York: Wiley and Sons, pp. 179–197.

Kessler, R., Nelson, C.B., McGonagle, K.A., Edlund, M.J., Frank, R.G. and Leaf, P.J. (1996) The epidemiology of co-occurring addictive and mental disorders: implications for prevention and service utilization. *American Journal of Orthopsychiatry*, **66**, 17–31.

Koob, G. and Le Moa, M. (2001) Drug addiction, dysregulation of reward, and allostasis. *Neuropsychopharmacology*, **24**, 97–129.

Lynskey, M. (1998) Broadening the target of drug prevention. *The FAS Drug Policy Analysis Bulletin* **5**.

Lynskey, M., Fergusson, D.M. and Horwood, L.J. (1998) The origins of the correlations between tobacco, alcohol, and cannabis use during adolescence. *Journal of Child Psychology and Psychiatry*, **39**, 995–1005.

Patton, G.C., Carlin, J.B., Coffey, C., Wolfe, R., Hibbert, M. and Bowes, G. (1998) Depression, anxiety, and smoking initiation: a prospective study over 3 years. *American Journal of Public Health*, **88**, 1518–1522.

Patton, G.C., Coffey, C., Carlin, J.B., Degenhardt, L., Lynskey, M. and Hall, W. (2002) Cannabis use and mental health in young people: cohort study. *British Medical Journal*, **325**, 1195–1198.

Pulkkinen, L. and Pitkanen, T. (1994) A prospective study of the precursors to problem drinking in young adulthood. *Journal of Studies on Alcohol*, **55**, 578–587.

Reinherz, H.Z., Giaconia, R.M., Carmola–Hauf, A.M., Wasserman, M.S. and Paradis, A.D. (2000) General and specific childhood risk factors for depression and drug disorders by early adulthood. *Journal of the American Academy of Child and Adolescent Psychiatry*, **39**(2), 223–231.

Tambs, K., Harris, J.R. and Magnus, P. (1997) Genetic and environmental contributions to the correlation between alcohol consumption and symptoms of anxiety and depression: results from a bivariate analysis of Norwegian twin data. *Behavior Genetics*, **27**, 241–250.

Teesson, M., Hall, W., Lynskey, M. and Degenhardt, L. (2000) Alcohol- and drug-use disorders in Australia: implications of the National Survey of Mental Health and Wellbeing. *Australian and New Zealand Journal of Psychiatry*, **34**, 206–213.

Tremblay, R.E., Pagani-Kurtz, L., Masse, L.C., Vitaro, F. and Pihl, R.O. (1995) A bimodal preventive intervention for disruptive kindergarten boys: its impact through mid-adolescence. *Journal of Consulting and Clinical Psychology*, **63**, 560–568.

True, W., Xian, H., Scherrer, J., et al. (1999) Common genetic vulnerability for nicotine and alcohol dependence. *Archives of General Psychiatry*, **56**, 655–661.

Tsuang, M.T., Lyons, M.J., Meyer, J.M., Doyle, T., Eisen, S.A., Goldberg, J., True, W., Lin, N., Toomey, R., and Eaves, L. (1998) Co-occurrence of abuse of different drugs in men: the role of drug-specific and shared vulnerabilities. *Archives of General Psychiatry*, **55**(11), 967–972.

Van Os, J., Bak, M., Hanssen, M., Bijl, R.V, De Graaf, R. and Verdoux, H. (2002) Cannabis use and psychosis: a longitudinal population-based study. *American Journal of Epidemiology*, **156**(4), 319–327.

Weissman, M., Livingston, B.M., Leaf, P., Florio, L. and Holzer, C. (1991) Affective disorders. In L. Robins and D. Regier (eds), *Psychiatric Disorders in America*. New York: Macmillan, pp. 53–80.

Windle, M. (1990) A longitudinal study of antisocial behaviors in early adolescence as predictors of late adolescent substance use: gender and ethnic group differences. *Journal of Abnormal Psychology*, **99**(1), 86–91.

Zammit, S., Allebeck, P., Andréasson, S., Lundberg, I. and Lewis, G. (2002) Self-reported cannabis use as a risk factor for schizophrenia in Swedish conscripts of 1969: historical cohort study. *British Medical Journal*, **325**(7374), 1199–1201.

2.4 Predicting Developmentally Harmful Substance Use

JOHN W. TOUMBOUROU

Centre for Adolescent Health, Vic, Australia

RICHARD F. CATALANO

Social Development Research Group, University of Washington, Seattle, WA, USA

SUMMARY

Longitudinal research has consistently found that the use of a specific drug at an early age increases the likelihood of subsequently experiencing harms related to that drug. Early drug use elevates harm partly due to its tendency to lead to regular and heavy patterns of drug use. The effect of early use appears broadly similar for tobacco, alcohol, cannabis, other illicit drug use and the use of multiple drug types together (poly-drug use). For some drug types, early use and regular use have also been found to increase the likelihood of progression to other types of drug use. Developmental risk factors can be defined as prospective predictors that independently increase the probability that an individual or group will engage in patterns of drug use that have been linked to drug-related harm. Developmental protective factors are those factors that mediate or moderate the influence of risk factors. Potentially modifiable risk factors have been organised within different developmental settings including communities, families, schools, peer groups, and within individuals. Knowledge of the factors that influence the development of drug use behaviour has come from follow-up research studies and a range of intervention research. Predictive associations do not equate to causal explanations, hence the future challenge is to identify the developmental processes that underlie the probabilistic relationships established through longitudinal research. In addition to their independent influence on behaviour, existing studies have found that the cumulative number of risk factors across the course of development can additively or even exponentially impact on substance use and related harms. There is some evidence of the cascading effects of risk factors across development. For example, exposure to maternal drug use can cause developmental delays that increase exposure to subsequent risk factors such as poor school adjustment. Due to the potential for early developmental risk factors to create cascading effects leading to early drug use, targeting infants and children with high risk factors may be especially important. Others develop alcohol and tobacco use in adolescence.

Preventing Harmful Substance Use: The Evidence Base for Policy and Practice.
Edited by T. Stockwell, P. J. Gruenewald, J.W. Toumbourou and W. Loxley.
© 2005 John Wiley & Sons, Ltd. ISBN 0-470-09227-0 (hbk) 0-470-09228-9 (pbk).

These youth appear to have family and community antecedents operating in late child-hood and adolescence and may be amenable to later approaches to risk reduction.

INTRODUCTION

Developmental prevention programmes aim to improve the conditions for the healthy de-velopment of children and young people by directing evidence-based investment to modify the early developmental determinants that lead to later problems. Such programmes play a potentially important role in efforts to prevent drug-related harm. The developmental pre-vention approach has emerged through the synthesis of a range of scientific endeavour, but draws in important ways on life course development research, community epidemiology, and preventive intervention trials (e.g., Coie et al., 1993). The approach is related to the risk-focused approach to prevention developed to reduce health problems such as cancer and heart disease within the fields of public health and epidemiology (Arthur and Blitz, 2000). Information gained through developmental research can inform the design and testing of preventative interventions, in turn informing knowledge of underlying causal processes.

DEFINING DEVELOPMENTALLY HARMFUL DRUG USE

Borrowing similar techniques to those that have been used to study the predictors of heart disease, researchers over the past three decades have investigated the risk and protective factors that lead to a range of behavioural outcomes including youth drug use. Risk factors for the development of problematic drug use can be defined as prospective predictors that independently increase the probability that an individual or group will eventually engage in patterns of drug use that have high health and social costs. Protective factors are those factors that mediate or moderate the influence of risk factors (Hawkins 1992).

A number of literature reviews have examined the risk and protective factors influencing youth drug use and drug-related harm (e.g., Hawkins et al., 1992; Newcomb and Felix-Ortiz, 1992; Loxley et al., 2004). The review paper by Hawkins et al. (1992) organised risk and protective factors for youth alcohol and drug problems according to their influence in socialisation settings including communities, families, schools, peer groups, and within individuals. Hawkins and colleagues (1992) also organised what was known of protective factors arguing that they fell into three basic categories. These consisted of individual char-acteristics (a positive social orientation, high intelligence, and a resilient temperament), social bonding (warm, positive relationships and commitment to conventional lines of ac-tion) and healthy beliefs and clear standards for behaviour.

More recent literature reviews have examined risk and protective factors for develop-mentally harmful drug use by examining research completed over the 1990s (e.g., Loxley et al., 2004). As a first step in attempting to define developmentally harmful drug use Loxley et al. examined follow-up studies that had investigated the consequences of early drug use exposures. This review revealed consistent patterns across different cohorts internationally demonstrating that early exposure to substance use leads to progression in substance use behaviour. The major findings are summarised below:

- Early developmental harm and subsequent developmental pathways to drug use prob-lems can be traced to exposure to maternal substance use prior to birth, through environmental tobacco smoke in childhood or due to disrupted parenting associated with substance abuse within families (e.g., Fergusson et al., 1994).

- Early age use of a specific substance is associated with the subsequent development of more frequent use of that substance and such patterns of use generally increase the risk of problems with that substance later in life. Similar patterns have been documented in follow-up research examining tobacco (e.g., Costello et al., 1999), alcohol (e.g., Fergusson et al., 1995), cannabis (e.g., Coffey et al., 2000) and poly drug use (e.g., Newcomb and McGee, 1991). These findings come not just from cohorts in the United States but also from Scandinavian, New Zealand and Australian studies. In each of these studies findings persisted after adjusting for other underlying factors known to increase the risk of drug use problems.

- In some cases youth exposure to early or more frequent use of a specific substance has been shown to increase the risk of subsequently progressing to another type of substance use. After controlling for other risk factors, more frequent tobacco use or higher levels of alcohol use at age 14 or 15 increased the risk of progressing to frequent cannabis use (Coffey et al., 2000; McGee et al, 2000). Cannabis use at age 16 (Johnson et al., 1995) or frequent cannabis use at age 15 (Fergusson and Horwood, 2000) strongly predicted subsequent involvement in other forms of illicit drug use.

Follow-up research has also revealed patterns of substance use in childhood or adolescence that hold consequences for subsequent developmental harms and are summarised below:

- In addition to its well-documented physical health impacts, there is recent evidence associating frequent adolescent (age 15 or 16) tobacco use with the subsequent development of mental health problems. In the Dunedin cohort in New Zealand frequent tobacco use at age 15 increased the risk of age 18 mental health problems after controlling for the influence of age 15 mental health disorders, cannabis use, alcohol use, and low parental attachments (McGee et al., 2000). In a US cohort frequent tobacco use at age 16 increased the risk of major depression and antisocial personality disorder at age 22 after controlling for age, gender and prior psychiatric status (Brook et al., 1998). Newcomb and McGee (1991) have previously reported impacts on mental health symptoms using structural equation modelling to analyse trends in their Californian youth cohort.

- Apart from its well-documented association with acute harms (e.g., accidents and injuries), follow-up studies have associated adolescent alcohol use with developmental progression to crime and delinquency. After controlling for a range of family and individual predictors, higher quantity and frequency of alcohol use at age 15 predicted progression to crime at age 16 in the Christchurch cohort (Fergusson et al., 1996). Using structural equation modelling to adjust for other risk factors, Newcomb and McGee (1991) demonstrated that frequent alcohol co-occurring with tobacco use at age 18 predicted progression to general deviancy at age 22.

- There is growing evidence to implicate mid to late adolescent cannabis use as a risk factor for early adult mental health problems. Follow-up of a cohort in New York State demonstrated that after controlling for initial mental health, heavier cannabis use at age 16 predicted personality disorder at age 22 (Brook et al., 1998). In New Zealand cannabis use at age 18 increased the risk of mental disorder at 21 after adjustment for earlier mental health symptoms and other substance use (McGee et al., 2000). Frequent cannabis use in middle adolescence predicted later major depression after adjusting for earlier mental health, other substance use and a range of developmental risk factors

(Fergusson and Horwood, 1997). Evidence summarised in Chapter 2.3 of the present volume also suggests that adolescent cannabis use may increase the risk of young people subsequently developing psychotic symptoms.

- Early and frequent adolescent cannabis use has been associated with problems in social development. After adjusting for a range of influences including parents' education, family breakdown and school grades at age 15, earlier age cannabis use predicted school dropout in a US cohort (Bray et al., 2000). In the Christchurch New Zealand cohort (Fergusson and Horwood, 1997) more frequent cannabis use at 15 to 16 independently predicted school drop-out (Fergusson et al, 1996), entry to unemployment and offending (Fergusson and Horwood, 1997).

- The tendency to use different substances on the same or a different occasion is known as poly drug use. Early involvement in poly drug use is a marker of risk for later substance use problems. At age 13 approximately 9% of an Australian cohort were engaged in poly drug use and this pattern was predictive of more serious substance use at age 15 (Williams et al., 2000). Williams et al. noted that "taking any particular drug [by 15] significantly increases the likelihood of taking another type of drug" (p. 26). Structural equation modelling approaches have found early adolescent poly drug use (ages 13/14) to be an important and unique predictor of drug use problems and other adjustment difficulties in early adulthood (e.g., Guy et al., 1993). Poly drug use in early adolescence (age 13/14) tends to remain either stable or to escalate through to mid-adolescence (age 15/16) (Krohn et al., 1996; Williams et al., 2000). Adolescent poly drug use tends to be an important and unique predictor of adult poly drug use (Newcomb and Felix-Ortiz, 1992; Guy et al., 1994).

Future studies should aim to establish whether these predictive associations are maintained after controlling for a wider range of known risk factors and should attempt to identify and test underlying mechanisms explaining how early substance use might lead to developmental harms.

Identifying Risk and Protective Factors for Developmentally Harmful Drug Use

From the above summary it is possible to more clearly identify adolescent substance use behaviours that might form targets in prevention efforts aimed at reducing developmentally harmful drug use. In defining prevention targets it is important to recognise that risk is contextually defined. For example, behaviours such as moderate alcohol use may have benefits for some adult populations but even moderate use may present net developmental risks when initiated in childhood or adolescence. In the review by Loxley et al. (2004), risk factors were defined on the basis of their tendency to independently predict involvement in developmentally harmful drug use (defined as early age drug use, frequent adolescent drug use, high quantity alcohol use or poly drug use). Protective factors were defined as influences that modify the effect of risk factors while not directly predicting developmentally harmful drug use. In the Loxley et al. review, some of the major risk and protective factors influencing developmentally harmful drug use over the life course were identified (Table 2.4.1).

Inherited vulnerability (for males), maternal smoking and alcohol use, extreme social disadvantage, family breakdown (e.g., Ferguson et al., 1994) and child abuse and neglect (e.g., Ferguson and Horwood, 1997) were among the earliest risk factors that increased the likelihood that children would develop behavioural and adjustment problems and subsequently become involved in harmful drug use.

Table 2.4.1 Risk and protective factors for the development of harmful drug use

Developmental stage	Risk factors	Protective factors
Prior to birth	Extreme family economic deprivation[a] Born or raised in a sole parent household Paternal genetic risk for alcoholism[a] Maternal drug use in pregnancy	
Infancy and pre-school	Environmental tobacco smoke Child neglect and abuse	Easy temperament[a]
Primary school period (4–11)	Early school failure[a] Conduct disorder[a] Aggression[a]	Social and emotional competence[a] Shy and cautious temperament
Secondary school period (12–17)	Low involvement in activities with adults[a] Perceived and actual levels of community drug use[a] Community disadvantage and disorganisation[a] Availability of drugs within the community[a] Positive media portrayal of drug use[a] Parent-adolescent conflict[a] Favourable parental attitudes to drug use[a] Parental alcohol and drug problems[a] Parental rules permissive of drug use[a] Peer drug use[a] Delinquency[a] Sensation seeking and adventurous personality[a] Favourable attitudes to drug use[a]	Religious involvement[a] Family attachment[a] Low parental conflict (parental harmony)[a] Parent–adolescent communication[a]
Young adulthood (18–24)	Frequent drug use around late high school period	A well-managed community environment for alcohol use Marriage in early adulthood

Source: Loxley et al. (2004).
Note: [a] Similar factors were identified in the review by Hawkins et al. (1992).

From the age of school entry, early school failure, childhood conduct disorder (e.g, McGee et al., 2000), aggression and favourable parental attitudes to drug use all appeared to be risk factors for harmful drug use. From adolescence, low involvement in activities with adults (e.g, Williams et al., 2000), the perceived and actual level of community drug use, availability of drugs in the community, parent–adolescent conflict (e.g., Toumbourou and Gregg, 2002), parental alcohol and drug problems (e.g., Costello et al., 1999), poor family management, school failure, deviant peer associations (e.g., Coffey et al., 2000), delinquency, and favourable attitudes to drugs were all identified as risk factors for harmful drug use. Community disadvantage and disorganisation, and positive media portrayals of drug use, were further factors strongly associated with harmful drug use. The evidence was unclear as to whether childhood attention deficit hyperactivity disorder, intelligence, anxiety and depressive symptoms directly predicted harmful drug use.

Early age protective factors included having an easy temperament, social and emotional competence, and a shy and cautious temperament (e.g., Williams et al., 2000). Protective factors in adolescence included family attachment (e.g., Fergusson and Horwood, 1997), parental harmony, and religious involvement.

The findings summarised in Table 2.4.1 tended to confirm many of the factors that were previously identified in the literature reviews relevant to the research completed until the end of the 1980s (Hawkins et al., 1992). The review completed by Hawkins et al. also covered community intervention studies identifying a range of community protective factors including alcohol taxation, higher drinking age laws, alcohol sales restrictions and programmes aimed at enhancing school commitment and achievement.

The severity of substance abuse problems appears to be associated with the extent of developmental problems. For youth with the most severe problems, pathways to substance abuse can often be traced to the earliest years of life. Williams et al. (2000) noted that temperament risk factors in infancy and early childhood emerged only when analyses focused on the 9% of youth with the highest frequency of age 15 poly drug use (use of four or more substances). Research by Fergusson et al. (1994) examining the New Zealand Christchurch birth cohort demonstrated that when the focus narrowed on the 2.7% of youth experiencing the most severe behaviour problems, early childhood development was characterised by maternal smoking and drinking during pregnancy, birth complications, problems in infant care (low breast feeding, low infant care, poor parenting), and social instability through childhood (family breakdown and parental changes). The family backgrounds of these children were characterised by high levels of social disadvantage (teenage parents, low education, low income, sole parents) and social disconnection (low rates of church attendance, parent mobility).

THE AGGREGATE INFLUENCE OF RISK FACTORS

An understanding of risk relationships does not equate with a theoretical understanding of the underlying processes that link risk exposures to undesirable outcomes. Bearing in mind this caution, the overview that follows provides a simplified outline of risk process concepts that have been utilised to guide and interpret preventative interventions.

The current state of the science of prevention suggests that risk factors influence the course of development through their cumulative impact across time. This means that there is no single risk factor that lies at the heart of developmental problems. Rather, these problems can be regarded as having complex causes or multi-determination. The more risk factors that persist over longer periods of time, the greater the subsequent developmental impact (e.g., Newcomb and Felix-Ortiz, 1992).

In one view, the cumulative effect of developmental risk factors operates somewhat like a snowball. According to this view, risk factor exposure early in life can impair the course of development and lead to a snowball effect with risk factors in subsequent developmental stages tending to adhere and accumulate as a consequence of the earlier problems. So, for example, a mother's tobacco smoking may impede foetal and early childhood development resulting in cognitive deficits that then lead to poor school adjustment. Poor school adjustment and school behaviour problems may lead on to social aggregation with other poor school-achieving youth. Evidence from studies in Australia suggests that children with a high number of childhood risk factors explain the great majority of children who subsequently progress to illicit drug use (Stockwell et al., 2004).

From this perspective one direction for prevention efforts is to attempt to check the snowball of risk by intervening at the earliest point around the initiation of developmental problems. However, there may also be possibilities to intervene and slow the progression of problems later in life. Children with multiple risk factors have been shown to demonstrate particular improvements in outcomes where negative social interactions are reduced among school peers (Toumbourou and Gregg, 2002), through efforts to improve the early school environment (Hawkins et al., 2001; Catalano et al., 2003) or where broader community changes are implemented that reduce the risk of substance misuse translating to drug-related harms (Loxley, 2000).

For children who do not have early life risk exposures, the cumulative effect of risk may be more analogous to a "snowstorm". Just as a child may survive extreme weather for a brief period, so too a child with few early developmental risks may withstand drug use in the peer group and community for a period. However, if exposure to such influence is maintained over time and across settings, the chances of the child becoming involved in drug use increase. The protective benefits of positive relationships with adults, observed even for children with damaged developmental pathways, are again suggestive of the potential to protect health in bad environments by providing protection (analagous to providing shelter in a stormy environment). From this perspective solutions lie in improving social environments (reducing risk factors and drug use prevalence) through the course of development, strengthening the child's capacity to survive risky environments, and enhancing protective factors to reduce the impact of risk. Catalano and Hawkins (1996) have argued that social environments continue to positively influence behavioural development throughout childhood and into adolescence by enhancing positive social bonding. According to these authors, prosocial bonds are themselves influenced by establishing opportunities and skills for prosocial interaction and by recognising and rewarding prosocial behaviour.

Many problems associated with alcohol and tobacco use appear to be common in adolescents with a moderate level of developmental risk factors (Stockwell et al., 2004). This evidence suggests that in order to address these issues, prevention approaches need to address influences at the "whole-population" or "universal" levels. The adolescent risk factors identified in Table 2.4.1 may be influenced by broader ecological and legislative interventions as well as individual interventions. An example of the influence of broader interventions comes from a US experience with increasing the minimum age for alcohol use. In a study in New York State increasing the legal age for alcohol use was found to reduce youth alcohol use partly by encouraging less favourable parental attitudes to youth alcohol use (Yu, 1998), leading in turn to less permissive parental rules for youth alcohol use and an older age for the first introduction to alcohol use. Community efforts to discourage adults from drinking at levels that lead to acute and chronic harms are likely to have flow-on benefits in improving developmental pathways for children and young people. For example, a lower prevalence of alcohol misuse at the population level may lead to reductions in risk factors such as maternal alcohol use in pregnancy, less child neglect and abuse while also decreasing adolescent perceptions that alcohol misuse is common. Changing school environments so that teachers provide instruction in ways that benefit all children in their classrooms, better manage their classes and provide motivation to learn increases school adjustment, improves commitment to school and academic performance and reduces aggressiveness that forms an important set of risk and protective factors for later drug problems (Hawkins et al., 2001).

Developmental Risk and Protective Factors in a Community Context

Much of the data that underlies current knowledge of the risk factors for harmful drug use has been based on studies that have followed up individuals over time. The question is raised as to how individual-level risk factors may influence and be influenced by broader structural and social determinants. A number of studies have investigated these issues.

The influence of developmental risk and protective factors appears to remain relatively stable across different social and cultural contexts. For example, predictive relationships appear broadly similar in countries with different cultural and policy approaches to youth substance use to those adopted in the US. Beyers et al. (2004) used data from a survey instrument measuring developmental risk and protective factors to compare state-wide student samples in the US. states of Oregon and Maine with the state of Victoria in Australia. Differences noted included markedly higher levels of youth alcohol and tobacco use in Australia and slightly higher marijuana and other illicit drug use among youth in the USA. Focusing on risk and protective factor levels and associations with substance use in the two countries, more cross-national similarities than differences were noted. Where differences were observed in either the level of risk factors or in the strength of their association with substance use, youth in Australia tended to be more at risk due to tolerant attitudes and norms while youth in the USA tended to be more at risk due to social alienation measured by individual factors such as rebelliousness, academic failure and low social skills. Findings were interpreted according to the policy differences in the two countries, with Australian harm minimisation policies associated with greater acceptance of experimentation with drug use and US abstinence policies associated with punishment of use. Differences in rates of alcohol use between the two countries may also have reflected the younger legal age for purchase and use of alcohol in Australian states relative to states in the USA.

There is a small but growing body of research relevant to the relationship between community-level social environmental changes and individual changes in attitudes and behaviours. The evaluation of developmental interventions suggests that these areas have complex reciprocal effects. In some cases modifications to developmental social environments have been shown to lead to changes in individual characteristics. In other cases changes in individual characteristics have been shown to have flow-on benefits in changing social environments.

The Seattle Social Development Project (SSDP) provides an example of a social environmental intervention that led to changes in individual characteristics. The SSDP focused on improving early school social environments through interventions aimed at modifying classroom instruction and management practices and parent management and involvement. Results of observations in classrooms suggested that teachers changed the way they taught and managed their classrooms and students reported that they also perceived these changes. Students also demonstrated less aggression in teacher reports as well as greater commitment to school and achievement. The children exposed to the intervention demonstrated improved outcomes in early adulthood in a number of areas, including lower rates of substance misuse and delinquency. By providing a positive early educational experience, the children came to feel committed to completing their schooling. Although the intervention was not maintained after primary school, the children brought skills and expectations into their new school environments that enabled them to maintain better academic achievement relative to their peers in the control conditions (Hawkins et al., 2001).

In other cases changes in individual characteristics have been shown to have flow-on benefits in changing social environments. Toumbourou and Gregg (2002) examined three-month impacts following a parent education group intervention and noted that benefits extended more widely to students beyond the 10% of families where parents had directly participated in intervention activities offered in the first year of high school. This was explained by evidence that the parent education groups had attracted high-risk families (sole parents whose children reported higher initial levels of poly drug use) and that these families demonstrated differential reductions in parent–child conflict and child behaviour problems. Modelling of best-friend social networks in this project suggested that by improving the behaviour of high-risk children, the intervention had reduced negative peer influences within schools and thereby led to reductions in drug use and delinquency across the intervention schools (Toumbourou and Gregg, 2002).

Historical Trends in Developmental Influences and Projections for the Future

Western nations and some developing nations have experienced a number of changes to the family in the past 50 years. Increases in numbers of families in which both parents are working have resulted in children's needs and behaviour being less monitored in two-parent working families compared to families in which one parent stays at home. Coupled with this rise in working parents has been an increase in divorce also exacerbating the ability of parents to monitor their children's needs and activities (Mitchell et al., 2001). Improved outcomes for these children will require that their early developmental needs and activities are carefully monitored to ensure healthy realisation of their physical, social and cognitive potential. Social support will be required to enhance positive child development in the face of these changes.

Modernisation and advances in technology have led to the requirement for young people to engage for longer periods in education. These changes have meant that prolonged periods are spent through young adulthood with few legitimate responsibilities and greater periods of exposure to youth culture. Community efforts to ensure developmental pathways that actively involve and engage young people will become increasingly important as these trends progress. In the global context modernisation is likely to lead to similar trends in developing nations.

Public health advances now provide the technical capacity to address a wide variety of diseases, introducing new challenges where further application of the health sciences will be contingent on successfully modifying social conditions, lifestyles and behaviours. Important scientific breakthroughs can be expected in coming years that will improve our understanding of the influence of social trends on health. There is evidence that in recent decades poverty has become increasingly clustered around geographic locations in a number of free-market economies (e.g., Mitchell et al., 2001). Dual income families have been upwardly mobile, moving into higher-priced suburbs. Family separation has been linked to the movement of sole parents with children to communities with less expensive housing costs. Differential wealth also leads to choices in schooling, with parents who have the means selecting to pay for independent or supplementary schooling for their children. Policy planners need to monitor these trends in order to avoid the prospect that children from disadvantaged families will be aggregated into schools and communities that have few resources to promote healthy development.

As knowledge from developmental science advances, society has increased potential to ensure the conditions to promote healthy development. The diversity in families, schools and community environments introduces the importance of monitoring developmental environments in ways that can contribute to ameliorating risky aspects of these environments while promoting protective factors. Assessment systems are emerging that have been used to monitor developmental needs and provide information in formats that can be used for community policy and planning (e.g., Arthur and Blitz, 2000).

Communities are characterised by different pathways to the development of harmful drug use. Early snowballs of risk aggregation characterise pathways in many disadvantaged communities. In other communities, many young people with few risk factors in childhood become involved in developmentally harmful drug use in adolescence due to community and family pressures and due to peer influences operating in schools and communities. The reality of community differences in the risk processes that operate to adversely influence child and adolescent development leads logically to the need to carefully assess developmental risk and protective factors at the community level in order to tailor appropriate developmental prevention strategies (e.g., Hawkins et al., 1992; Arthur and Blitz, 2000; Bond et al., in press).

RECOMMENDATIONS FOR FUTURE RESEARCH AND PREVENTION POLICY AND PRACTICE

An important implication of the research examining risk and protective factors is that many of the same factors influencing the development of harmful youth drug use also predict other youth problems, including delinquency, homelessness, sexual risk-taking and mental health problems (e.g., Bond et al., in press). These findings have led to the view that many prevention strategies that have relevance in preventing harmful youth drug use may also be relevant to preventing problems in other areas. These conclusions have led to an increased attraction to undertaking developmental prevention monitoring as a co-operative activity across different government departments and other community agents. Building community coalitions to monitor and address healthy youth development has the advantage of providing a basis for coordinating money and resources from the drug and alcohol prevention sector with resources from crime prevention, mental health promotion, welfare, education and health.

Developmental research has been largely based on follow-up studies that have tracked individuals across time. The knowledge gained from these studies has led to interventions aiming to improve developmental trajectories by reshaping the social environments where young people are raised. The next phase of effectiveness trials where effective interventions are mounted on a large scale within communities allows for analyses of the change processes underlying this intervention work. Such studies can help clarify how community-level and individual-level risk processes are interrelated and can increase understanding of underlying causal processes.

Knowledge gained from developmental research provides important insights for intervention research. The cumulative effect of risk factors suggests that there are important advantages for early intervention strategies to be creatively integrated and coordinated across time. Programmes that target more than one risk factor (e.g., parental bonding and peer interaction) and coordinate intervention activities across different developmental periods and settings increase the likelihood of an effect and hence result in more consistent impacts (e.g., Arthur and Blitz, 2000). These considerations suggest that investment in prevention activities should aim to maintain a coordinated set of activities through childhood and adolescence tied to community priorities indicated by developmental levels of risk and protective factors. Activities should be coordinated to create a coherent set of intervention components applied consistently during childhood and adolescence.

There are prospects for a greater synthesis between research investigating developmental interventions and the findings from environmental interventions aimed at reducing drug-related harm at the population level. To date, these areas of work have proceeded independently with little cross-fertilisation. Protective factors have been identified from developmental research on the basis of their contribution in buffering contexts where risk factors may be high. From this perspective harm minimisation strategies such as training bar staff to avoid selling alcohol to intoxicated patrons or programmes that discourage pregnant women from excessive alcohol consumption operate as protective factors, reducing the prospects of substance use translating to developmental harms (Loxley et al., 2004). Future research should investigate the potential benefits of combining developmental prevention with broader environmental interventions.

ACKNOWLEDGEMENTS

The Victorian Drug Info Clearinghouse located within the Australian Drug Foundation published an early version of this chapter (Prevention Report 2, 2002).

REFERENCES

Arthur, M.W. and Blitz, C. (2000) Bridging the gap between science and practice in drug abuse prevention through needs assessment and strategic community planning. *Journal of Community Psychology*, **28**(3), 241–255.

Beyers, J.M., Toumbourou, J.W., Catalano, R.F., Arthur, M. and Hawkins, J.D. (2004) A cross-national comparison of risk and protective factors for adolescent substance use: the United States and Australia. *Journal of Adolescent Health*, **35**(1), 3–16.

Bond, L., Toumbourou, J.W., Thomas, L., Catalano, R. and Patton, G. (in press) Individual, family, school and community risk and protective factors for depressive symptoms in adolescents. *Prevention Science*.

Bray, J.W., Zarkin, G.A., Ringwalt, C. and Junfeng, Q. (2000) The relationship between marijuana initiation and dropping out of high school. *Health Economics*, **9**, 9–18.

Brook, J.S., Cohen, P. and Brook, D.W. (1998) Longitudinal study of co-occurring psychiatric disorders and substance use. *Journal of the American Academy of Child and Adolescent Psychiatry*, **37**, 322–330.

Catalano, R.F and Hawkins, J.D. (1996) The social development model: a theory of antisocial behavior. In J.D Hawkins (ed.), *Delinquency and Crime: Current Theories*. New York: Cambridge University Press, pp. 149–197.

Catalano, R.F., Mazza, J.J., Harachi, T.W., Abbott, R.D., Haggerty, K.P. and Fleming, C.B. (2003) Raising healthy children through enhancing social development is elementary school; results after 1.5 years. *Journal of School Psychology*, **41**, 143–164.

Coffey, C., Lynskey, M., Wolfe, R. and Patton, G. (2000) Initiation and progression of cannabis use in a population-based Australian adolescent longitudinal study. *Addiction*, **95**, 1679–1690.

Coie, J.D., Watt, N.F., West, S.G., Hawkins, J.D., Asarnow, J.R., Markman, H.J., Ramey, S.L., Shure, M.B. and Long, B. (1993) The science of prevention: a conceptual framework and some directions for a national research program. *American Psychologist*, **48**(10), 1013–1022.

Costello, E.J., Erkanli, A., Federman, E. and Angold, A. (1999) Development of psychiatric comorbidity with substance abuse in adolescents: effects of timing and sex. *Journal of Clinical Child Psychology*, **28**, 298–311.

Fergusson, D.M. and Horwood, L.J. (1997) Early onset cannabis use and psychosocial adjustment in young adults. *Addiction*, **92**, 279–296.

Fergusson, D.M. and Horwood, L.J. (2000) Does cannabis use encourage other forms of illicit drug use? *Addiction*, **95**, 505–520.

Fergusson, D.M., Horwood, L.J. and Lynskey, M. (1994) The childhoods of multiple problem adolescents: a 15-year longitudinal study. *Journal of Child Psychology and Psychiatry*, **35**, 1123–1140.

Fergusson, D.M., Horwood, L.J., and Lynskey, M.T. (1995) The prevalence and risk factors associated with abusive or hazardous alcohol consumption in 16-year-olds. *Addiction*, **90**, 935–946.

Fergusson, D.M., Lynskey, M.T. and Horwood, L.J. (1996) The short-term consequences of early onset cannabis use. *Journal of Abnormal Child Psychology*, **24**, 499–512.

Guy, S.M., Smith, G.M. and Bentler, P.M. (1993) Adolescent socialization and use of licit and illicit substances: impact on adult health. *Psychology and Health*, **8**, 463–487.

Guy, S.M., Smith, G.M. and Bentler, P.M. (1994) Consequences of adolescent drug use and personality factors on adult drug use. *Journal of Drug Education*, **24**(2), 109–132.

Hawkins, J.D., Catalano, R.F. and Miller, J.Y. (1992) Risk and protective factors for alcohol and other drug problems in adolescence and early adulthood: implications for substance abuse prevention. *Psychological Bulletin*, **112**, 64–105.

Hawkins, J.D., Guo, J., Hill, K., Battin-Pearson, S. and Abbott, R. (2001) Long term effects of the Seattle Social Development intervention on school bonding trajectories. In J. Maggs and J. Schulenberg (eds), *Applied Developmental Science: Special issue: Prevention as Altering the Course of Development*, **5**(4), 225–236.

Johnson, E.O., Schutz, C.G., Anthony, J.C., and Ensminger, M.E. (1995) Inhalants to heroin: a prospective analysis from adolescence to adulthood. *Drug and Alcohol Dependence*, **40**, 159–164.

Krohn, M.D., Lizotte, A.J., Thornberry, T.P., Smith, C. and McDowall, D. (1996) Reciprocal causal relationships among drug use, peers, and beliefs: a five-wave panel model. *Journal of Drug Issues*, **26**, 405–428.

Loxley, W. (2000) Doing the possible: harm reduction, injecting drug use and blood-borne viral infections in Australia. *International Journal of Drug Policy*, **11**, 407–416.

Loxley, W., Toumbourou, J.W., Stockwell, T., Haines, B., Scott, K., Godfrey, C. et al. (2004) *The Prevention of Substance Use, Risk and Harm in Australia: A Review of the Evidence*. Canberra: Population Health Division, Australian Government Department of Health and Ageing.

McGee, R., Williams, S., Poulton, R. and Moffitt, T. (2000) A longitudinal study of cannabis use and mental health from adolescence to early adulthood. *Addiction*, **95**, 491–503.

Mitchell, P., Spooner, C., Copeland, J., Vimpani, G., Toumbourou, J.W., Howard, J. and Sanson, A. (2001) *A Literature Review of the Role of Families in the Development, Identification, Prevention and Treatment of Illicit Drug Problems*. National Health and Medical Research Council Monograph. Canberra: Commonwealth of Australia.

Newcomb, M.D. and Felix-Ortiz, M. (1992) Multiple protective and risk factors for drug use and abuse: cross-sectional and prospective findings. *Journal of Personality and Social Psychology*, **63**, 280–296.

Newcomb, M.D. and McGee, L. (1991) Influence of sensation seeking on general deviance and specific problem behaviors from adolescence to young adulthood. *Journal of Personality and Social Psychology*, **61**, 614–628.

Stockwell, T., Toumbourou, J.W., Letcher, P., Smart, D., Sanson, A. and Bond, L. (2004) Risk and protection factors for different intensities of adolescent substance use: when does the prevention paradox apply? *Drug and Alcohol Review*, **23**(1), 67–77.

Toumbourou, J.W. and Gregg, M.E. (2002) Impact of an empowerment-based parent education program on the reduction of youth suicide risk factors. *Journal of Adolescent Health*, **31**(3), 279–287.

Williams, B., Sanson, A., Toumbourou, J.W. and Smart, D. (2000) *Patterns and Predictors of Teenagers' Use of Licit and Illicit Substances in the Australian Temperament Project Cohort.* Melbourne: Department of Behavioural Science, University of Melbourne Report prepared for the Ross Trust.

Yu, J. (1998) Perceived parental/peer attitudes and alcohol-related behaviors: an analysis of the impact of the drinking age law. *Substance Use and Misuse*, **33**(14), 2687–2702.

2.5 Population Ecologies of Drug Use, Drinking and Related Problems

ELIZABETH LASCALA, BRIDGET FREISTHLER
AND PAUL J. GRUENEWALD
Prevention Research Center, Berkeley, CA, USA

SUMMARY

This chapter summarizes recent advances in ecological studies of community systems related to the demographic, geographic and social factors that underlie alcohol and other drug-related crime. The community systems perspective states that alcohol and other drug problems are related to the interaction of social and institutional features of communities. For example, there is an interactive relationship between assaults and numbers of young males in the population, the availability of alcohol and guardianship provided by the police. The ecological perspective states that drug-related problems are the result of specific social and person–environment interactions. For example, assaults will be most prevalent in places where people likely to commit violence interact: near bars that attract young males and are poorly patrolled by police. A review of the ecological literature on alcohol and drug-related problems shows how the integration of ecological and systems perspectives is a natural extension of current research; the approach goes beyond these literatures and has strong implications for future research.

This chapter reviews the theoretical literature that discusses neighborhood contexts and population characteristics that affect alcohol and drug problems. Since many drug and alcohol problems are, in fact, criminal behaviors (e.g., driving under the influence of alcohol), this review includes much of the important theoretical literature in criminology that bears upon these outcomes. The second section reviews the empirical findings of studies that address the social theories, models and mechanisms reviewed in the first section. This discussion shows how investigators have framed questions and interpreted results in terms of the most important theoretical orientations applicable to the ecology of community drug problems. The third section presents new perspectives on the development and operation of drug markets with particular attention to ecological approaches that may unite some of the diverse, and sometimes conflicting, findings in the research literature. The integration of ecological and systems approaches in contemporary studies will lead to improved methods of assessing and controlling drug-related problems in community settings.

Preventing Harmful Substance Use: The Evidence Base for Policy and Practice.
Edited by T. Stockwell, P. J. Gruenewald, J.W. Toumbourou and W. Loxley.
© 2005 John Wiley & Sons, Ltd. ISBN 0-470-09227-0 (hbk) 0-470-09228-9 (pbk).

INTRODUCTION

A reasonable question that many residents of troubled communities often ask is, "Why are there so many alcohol and other drug problems in my neighborhood?" The answers that researchers have given to this question are many and varied, but all make one point clear: they suggest that characteristics of persons or places in an area encourage problems. Alcohol and other drug-related troubles may arise because specific populations are prone to these outcomes (e.g., drinking among young males), certain population characteristics encourage participation in substance abuse activities (e.g., poverty related to drug sales), or places in a neighborhood serve as foci for problems (e.g., bars). When asked, "What can we do about these problems?" two answers are usually given: "Change the people who create these problems" or "Change the places where these negative activities occur." There is little mystery to these observations. The mystery arises when one wants to determine what characteristics of people, places and their interactions lead to problems in the first place.

Scientific endeavor has illuminated some aspects of the person and place connections that underlie drug-related problems. Community ecologies that study the interaction between people and places as they produce problems have developed in parallel to community systems models of problem outcomes (see Chapter 4.2), models that partition communities into functional parts (e.g., regulatory, economic and enforcement) and examine their interactions as predictors of problems. These approaches have been most fully developed in alcohol research through studies of the community systems and ecologies that underlie drunken driving, motor vehicle crashes, pedestrian injury collisions, violence, youth access to alcohol (see summaries in Holder, 1998b; Stockwell and Gruenewald, 2004). The aim of the current chapter is to extend these approaches to the study of problems related to the use of illegal drugs.

THEORETICAL ORIENTATIONS

Although much of the alcohol and drug literature focuses upon individual characteristics associated with substance abuse (Lettieri et al., 1980), the past 50 years have witnessed the development of substantial research into those features of environments that constrain or facilitate ills associated with drug abuse. In the alcohol literature, this interest has been sparked by the desire to ameliorate the large number of community problems associated with access to alcohol through retail outlets (e.g., drunken driving, motor vehicle crashes, violence). In the illegal drug literature, this attention has been generated by a similar need to reduce health and social harms related to use (e.g., child abuse, accidental injuries and overdoses) and control the crime and violence tied to illegal drug markets. Fundamental differences between these commodities change the environmental focus of these two approaches. As a legally marketed commodity, the distribution of alcohol can be regulated. Consequently, much of the "environment" that has been studied by alcohol researchers includes the human as well as the regulatory and enforcement environments (e.g., underage drinking, numbers and types of alcohol outlets, beverage taxes, enforcement of drunken driving laws; Babor et al., 2003). In the United States, illicit drugs are proscribed. Thus, much of the "environment" that has been studied focuses on the human and enforcement (as contrasted to regulatory) environments (e.g., population characteristics of users, law enforcement programs; Davis et al., 1993).

As both approaches share an emphasis on human and enforcement environments, community development has been viewed as a means to combat problems; this has encouraged sociologists and criminologists to consider the theoretical roots of community-based alcohol and other drug problems for clues to prevention. While these studies have particular relevance to the community-based literature in alcohol studies (Gorman et al., 2001), it is essential to recognize the valuable theoretical contribution that has emerged from the consideration of how illegal markets are formed and sustained within communities. Also, important work on the roots of crime has led to a deepened understanding of crime outcomes related to drug and alcohol abuse and related problems such as violence.

Invisible Markets and the Character of Neighborhoods

In obvious distinction to the alcohol market, drug markets are proscribed; hence participants at all levels are motivated to keep their activities essentially invisible. Nevertheless, like the alcohol market, wholesale and retail activities sustain illegal drug markets as functioning parts of community systems: illegal drugs must be imported or produced and domestically distributed; retailers must find consumers to buy their drugs; and illegal drug marketers must develop local neighborhood resources to accomplish these objectives. For example, a narcotics distributor must secure social and physical networks in which connections can be made between buyers and sellers that minimize detection. Consequently, explanations for illegal drug activities have evolved to focus on the role played by environments that promote and sustain the sale and use of illicit substances (Parker, 1989; Sampson and Groves, 1989; Davis et al., 1993; Holder, 1998a).

Dating back to the early ecological studies at the University of Chicago, social disorganization theorists recognized the significance of urban socio-economic conditions to crime (Shaw and McKay, 1942). Present-day social organization theorists focus chiefly upon population characteristics associated with crime such as ethnic heterogeneity and residential instability (Sampson and Wilson, 1995). One main assertion of this approach is that the effect of person characteristics is mediated through socio-structural factors, such as impoverishment.

While social disorganization theorists assert that the effect of a population's ethnic/racial composition is mediated through structural indicators, the social conflict perspective asserts that a community's formal surveillance system responds with increased enforcement when racial heterogeneity rises (Liska et al., 1985). These theorists predict that ethnic/racial composition will have an independent, positive effect on drug arrest rates, independent of socio-structural indicators.

Distinct from theoretical approaches that emphasize the role of person characteristics to crime, routine activity theory primarily focuses upon the characteristics of places associated with criminal activity. This view affirms that the routine activities of everyday life can bring together three critical elements for crime to occur: motivated offenders, suitable targets or opportunities for crime, and reduced guardianship against crime (Cohen and Felson, 1979). Persons must be motivated to commit crimes, have the opportunity to exhibit criminal conduct, and do so without the surveillance that might prevent these behaviors. Thus, variations in the distributions of motivated offenders, opportunities to offend, and policing activities will differentially shape the distribution of various criminal activities. Applied to drug crimes, motivated offenders will be both dealers and buyers. Opportunities will be determined by the ways in which sellers and users make contacts (private contacts versus public exchanges of money for drugs). Finally, certain place characteristics must be present to protect these marketing activities from detection (residential exchanges, low guardianship).

The dividing line between people and place characteristics is, of course, somewhat arbitrary and so most researchers incorporate both features of neighborhoods in their explanations of criminal activities. Crime potential theory describes the way in which people and place characteristics are integrated across neighborhoods and result in varying rates of crime in different community settings. Fundamental to this approach is the concept of "crime potentials"; the likelihood that crime will be exhibited as a function of people or place characteristics (Brantingham and Brantingham, 1993, 1999). According to this perspective, individuals are ultimately responsible for criminal behavior; in the absence of a population with suitable characteristics that enable crime, no crime will be observed. Place characteristics also facilitate crime by focusing human activities in places where social interactions that lead to crime are more likely and where social controls are weak.

Spatial Interactions and Formation of Drug Markets

In addition to the contributions of person and place features to crime, crime potential theory emphasizes important spatial components of interactions between them. Places where crime rates are high are often at the edges of neighborhoods, along the boundary lines between one neighborhood and another or at retail and business areas between neighborhoods where few people live but many people visit in the course of their daily activities (Brantingham and Brantingham, 1993). Thus, an important aspect of crime potential theory is its claim that unique spatial dynamics underlie the geographic distributions of different types of crime across neighborhood areas. For example, social conflicts may arise at the racially heterogeneous boundaries of racially homogeneous neighborhoods.

One notable application of crime potential theory that makes explicit the spatial interactions that support criminal activities is the model of the geography of illicit retail markets advanced by Eck (1995). Participants in illegal markets must balance access to potential buyers and sources of drugs with at least two security risks: risks stemming from law enforcement activities, and risks stemming from physical violence from competitors and other users. The combined need for secure markets and access to buyers and sellers forms the basis for the development of two distinct marketing approaches that may result in distinctly different geographical patterns of marketplace activities. The first works through social networks and the other capitalizes upon patterns of routine activities. The social network strategy accomplishes drug transactions through friend and acquaintanceship networks. Security is obtained through the lessened accessibility of these networks to police; access is assured through the structure of these social networks. The routine activities approach accomplishes drug transactions through interactions of strangers near places where people naturally congregate for legitimate reasons. Security is assured through familiarity with local routine activities (e.g., street corners as meeting places) and policing patterns; access is accomplished by the public nature of the market.

Neighborhood Mechanisms

Despite widespread recognition of the relationship between problems and neighborhood characteristics, the social processes that explain such relationships have remained unclear (Sampson et al., 1997). This has led to an increased level of interest in neighborhood mechanisms thought to account for community variation in problem outcomes. Scientific understanding of these processes is critical to the effectiveness of many types of community-based programs. Sampson et al. (2002) summarized four classes of mechanisms:

1. *Social ties/interaction*: This is the concept of social capital, which is generally viewed as a resource that develops through social relationships. The construct has been measured in various ways including level of social ties among neighbors, frequency of social interactions and patterns associated with neighborly ties (Coleman, 1988).
2. *Norms and collective efficacy*: This concept refers to conditions indicative of mutual trust and a shared willingness and/or expectation to intervene for the common good (Shaw and McKay, 1942).
3. *Institutional resources*: These resources refer to the quality, quantity and diversity of community-based agencies and organizations that address the needs of youth and families (e.g., libraries, medical care facilities, child care availability). These resources are measured in terms of their presence rather than their utility to the communities they serve (Coulton et al., 1999).
4. *Routine activities*: This notion refers to how land use patterns and ecological distributions of daily routine activities bear on the well-being of community residents (Cohen and Felson, 1979).

SOME EMPIRICAL FINDINGS

Researchers interested in drug activity have most frequently addressed questions related to individual characteristics and community demographics. For example, using individual survey data, researchers have found that both abstinence and heavy use of alcohol and other drugs occur at high rates among African Americans (Kandel, 1991; Warner et al., 1995) and Hispanics (Barnes and Welte, 1986). Moreover, while African-Americans are less likely than the general population to initiate substance abuse in adolescence, those who do begin use in their early years are more likely to progress to heavy use (Kandel and Davies, 1991). This is consistent with the finding that African-Americans have lower than average rates of lifetime use but high rates of recent use (Ensminger et al., 1997; NHSDA, 1998). Ethnographic studies uniformly report that middle-class Whites travel to African-Americans communities to purchase illicit drugs (Williams, 1992; Riley, 1997). Thus it would seem that impoverished minority neighborhoods are often hubs for the distribution of drugs to both residents of these neighborhoods and outsiders.

Questions of place quickly come to the forefront in any consideration of drug markets. Social contacts between drug retailers and purchasers are prerequisite to drug exchanges in community settings and require the construction of complex social arrangements. What places and situations are conducive to these social arrangements are questions of great importance to understanding, and ultimately controlling the distribution and use of illegal substances. The following are examples of efforts to address these questions that point to new directions for research.

Substance Use Systems

Kadushin et al. (1998) used survey data from inner-city neighborhoods in the United States to explore interdependencies of drug use within the context of a hypothetical substance use system. The authors found that African Americans were most likely to live in neighborhoods where drug use and sales were more common, independent of income and education. In addition, indications of drug dependency were most common in "supportive" neighborhood and interpersonal environments, that is in places where drug activity was most public and social networks for drug use surrounded those most likely to use. Although weakened methodologically by sole reliance upon individual reports of neighborhood drug activities, this work indicated that systems of interpersonal and neighborhood relations were significant correlates of substance use and dependency and provided one feasible strategy for disentangling multi-level influences on drug activities.

Drug Market Dynamics

Contrary to the widely held belief that drug use is primarily a problem in impoverished communities, many who live in disadvantaged areas see drug sales as the most pressing problem. Saxe et al. (2001) carried out multivariate analyses using 1990 Census data and survey measures to test the assumption that drug use and the visibility of drug sales predominate in neighborhoods that are most disadvantaged, have the highest concentration of minority residents and have the greatest population density. They found that neighborhoods with these characteristics reported much higher levels of visible drug sales but only slightly higher levels of drug use, and no difference in levels of drug dependency.

Freisthler et al. (in press) examined self-reported drug activities and neighborhood characteristics derived from 2000 Census data to examine how neighborhood disorganization was related to individual exposure to drug sales. Surrogates for drug activities have been documented in the growing literature relating neighborhood characteristics to crime (Morenoff et al., 2001). Chief among these surrogate measures are indices of neighborhood disorganization (e.g., poverty) and residential instability. The results of this study showed that variables representing these aspects of neighborhood structure influenced rates of self-reported exposure to drug activities. At the aggregate level, poverty was directly related to higher rates of drug activity; residential instability moderated reports of drug activity among African Americans and young people.

One conclusion to be drawn from these studies is that drug sales serve a large catchment area of users, some of whom live within, but many of whom live outside, neighborhoods where drug markets are located. Another conclusion is that spatial interactions of populations and places underlie the distribution of drug use and crime in community settings.

Spiral of Decay

LaGrange (1999) applied concepts from routine activities and research on the spatial distribution of crime to the study of minor criminal activities such as property damage. The interest was in assessing the spatial relationships between minor crimes and characteristics of people and places in neighborhoods. Specific focus was upon the association of these crimes with schools and shopping malls, places that may contribute to an increased concentration of offenders and victims and suffer from inadequate place management. The presence of schools and shopping malls in a neighborhood consistently predicted increased damage of all types in the surrounding areas, after controlling for demographic and socio-structural differences. The author argued that the geographic spread of these minor crimes through neighborhoods may lead to a "spiral of decay" and signify places where criminal behavior is less likely to be observed, reported or result in an effective police response. An increase in these types of crimes may be associated with a corresponding increase in place characteristics that support more serious crime.

Racial Conflict

Mosher (2001) used principles of social disorganization and conflict theories to examine drug possession and trafficking arrests. Mosher found that, in a sample of US cities, racial composition was the strongest predictor of drug arrests. This study employed no scale of general deprivation that considered differences between racial groups; consequently, the effects attributable to African-Americans and Hispanic arrest rates may be due to differences in deprivation between neighborhoods. However, as this argument makes clear, the fact that greater numbers of drug arrests occur in one area rather than another may reflect the operation of social structures different than those directly related to the etiology of drug use and crime (e.g., varying levels of enforcement across different neighborhoods).

NEW PERSPECTIVES

The tradition of theory accounting for alcohol and other drug use and misuse has been focused on the individual and centered on individual risk and protective factors such as self-esteem and resistance skills (Petraitis et al., 1995). However, it is increasingly acknowledged that, to the extent that these factors are operable, their effects are expressed within the context of broader social and physical conditions. From this fundamental observation, four recommendations for future research arise.

1. *Develop and test theoretical models of multi-level ecological relationships*
   The simplest recommendation to make regarding understanding drug use and crime is to introduce multi-level influences into individual-level models of drug use. This has been accomplished by working out the characteristics of neighborhoods related to drug use and crime and introducing these neighbourhood characteristics into individual models of use and crime. This empirical strategy has led to the idea of "risk factor theory", the notion that observations of negative and positive influences on measured levels of drug use can be compiled into a balance sheet of risk and protective influences (Hawkins et al., 1992). From a theoretical perspective this actuarial approach suffers significant limitations. Communities are dynamical systems and risk factors vary in nature and effect across neighborhoods. For example, if relatively wealthy and geo-graphically proximal consumers form part of the demand for drugs in an impoverished area, one "risk factor" for drug crimes in this area will be the population of affluent in-dividuals living in a nearby neighborhood. Yet this same factor, proportion of wealthier households, might be protective in other neighborhoods. While it is clear that multiple and interactive influences must be included in theoretical models, the critical question is how best to accomplish this.

2. *Identify spatial interactions between populations and places that support drug activities*
   The theoretical foundations for spatial interactions essential to an explanation of crime patterns across community areas must go beyond individual level differences and identify and address the spatial interdependencies that exist between populations and neighborhoods that support drug activities. The predisposing characteristics that may lead persons to use drugs are enabled in different social and physical contexts, and these vary by area and change over time as communities develop new formal and informal social and institutional structures. The contact processes that underlie interactions between buyers and sellers, retailers and wholesalers, companies of users, and the activities of police need to be identified in order to provide a basis upon which to develop effective policies and build successful community prevention programs. These require acknowledgement of the social dynamics that enable these problem behaviors, identification of community components that support drug activities in some areas, but not others, and recognition of the differing and interacting roles of the demand for drugs and social controls that regulate drug supply. Drug markets must continuously develop and change to maintain contact with a supply of new users and to avoid detection by law enforcement. They evolve over time, rely upon social contacts to develop and maintain connections between buyers and sellers, and spread to public venues when guardianship is low (see Caulkins, 2000). With these considerations in mind, one can ask, what person and place characteristics might predict an increased concentration of drug crimes? What are the necessary elements that must converge in time and space to enhance drug transactions? Do these elements differ based on type of drug? How do conditions surrounding drug use differ from conditions needed for sale and distribution of illicit substances? What kinds of relationships among various community sectors are associated with dangerous patterns of use (e.g., needle sharing)?

3. *Assess the contingent relationships of drug sales and use to ecological conditions*
   A pertinent question to ask about illegal drug markets is whether, as often supposed, all such markets thrive in socially disorganized neighborhoods. Or is there a continuum of mechanisms from informal (social network) to formal (public retailing) that are used depending on circumstances (e.g., levels of guardianship, population density, traffic flow)? Organized neighborhoods with higher levels of residential population densities, sufficient guardianship and more disposable income may enable reliance upon informal social networks that are less likely to be disrupted; disorganized neighborhoods with weak social controls, and higher population densities during business hours may enable reliance upon more formal retailing activities, independent of the characteristics of the local population. And, perhaps, importing, production and wholesaling activities take place more diffusely across urban centers near hubs of transportation. It is likely that multiple markets exist serving various demands using a variety of different distribution channels.

   A common finding in criminology, that areas characterized by proportionally larger minority populations have higher drug possession and trafficking arrest rates, might serve as an example of the contingent relationships of sales and use to ecological conditions. Arrests might be easier to make and decoy operations and stings may be easier to accomplish in poor inner-city areas where there are more public, stranger-to-stranger drug transactions than in neighborhoods where such activities are more covert. One conclusion to draw from this example is that public retailing markets are more likely to form in disorganized neighborhoods and the public nature of these markets make them more likely targets of enforcement. This would provide an alternative explanation to the racial conflict perspective (described above).

4. *Explain drug use and the ecological succession of crime*

One of the central problems in the study of alcohol and other drugs is how to assess and understand change in community systems and ecological relationships as they influence patterns of use and problems. The previous three recommendations point toward studies of relationships between ecologies of places and people behaviors. What is missing is a dynamic conceptualization that begins to explain why drug markets emerge in certain community environments.

One way to view the development of drug markets that has some theoretical and empirical support is to see drug sales and use as part of a "succession" of illegal activities that people participate in over the course of many years and decades as rural, suburban and urban environments grow and expand. Minor crimes such as vandalism that occur in all communities may be more common in areas where social controls are weakened (for whatever reasons). These offenses may be significant indicators that guide the subsequent growth of more serious crime, through processes described as "broken windows" or "spiral of decay" (Skogan 1990: 40; Kelling and Coles, 1996; Felson 1998). This perspective asserts that an excess of minor crimes in a neighborhood signals an increase in place characteristics that encourage potential offenders and provides new venues for more serious crimes, like drug marketeering, and related problems such as violence. Gruenewald and colleagues (2003) assert that both characteristics of people and places and their interactions are related to violence. In terms of person characteristics, illegal drugs are commonly used by individuals who are already more likely to be involved in violent interactions (e.g., young males). In terms of place, violence is assumed to occur more often in and around drug market locations because violence is often used as a strategy for regulation and enforcement of drug market activities (Goldstein, 1998). In addition, illegal substances are proscribed and hence use take place in areas already more conducive to violence because guardianship is low. These more serious crimes further degrade the organization of neighborhoods by reducing social supports that might otherwise act as stabilizing influences (e.g., community recreational and social services).

IMPLICATIONS FOR PREVENTION EFFORTS

It would seem from the foregoing discussion that the primary problem for scientists who study community alcohol problems and illegal drug markets is how to integrate person and place characteristics and their interactions within a spatial context to better predict where and what types of problem activities are likely to occur. It is noteworthy that the first two categories of neighborhood mechanisms (see discussion above) refer to characteristics of people (social ties, collective efficacy), and the second two focus on place characteristics (institutional resources, routine activities). When viewed geographically, neighborhoods may be composed of different combinations of these mechanisms because they consist of relatively more people (residential areas) or more places (business areas) and these compositions vary temporally (day versus night). Thus the interactions between person and place characteristics may create social and physical climates that facilitate one type of drug market or another. For example, drug markets may adapt to the relative degree of social organization and stability exhibited by different neighborhoods, adaptations suited for maximizing returns, while minimizing exposure to enforcement.

The community systems and ecological approaches suggest that it is essential to assess the responsiveness of alcohol and drug problems to regulatory and enforcement efforts and make adjustments that serve community-specific policy and program objectives. For example, particular interventions may work best alone, synergistically or not at all to reduce drug-related problems in community settings. These might include reductions in alcohol access (e.g., by regulating outlet densities, hours and days of sale), improved place management around establishments that enable drug contacts (e.g., discourage loitering, keeping storefronts clean), community development to ameliorate neighborhood conditions that support local drug markets (e.g., improved public housing, childcare and educational programs), and community policing guided by more complete and accurate problem surveillance.

Different approaches to problem surveillance and resulting enforcement and prevention activities can benefit from the systems and ecological approaches reviewed in this chapter. For example, the US enforcement sector is committed to disrupting illicit drug markets with the ultimate goal of eradication. A much different approach to drug law enforcement has been adopted in the Netherlands, where supply reduction represents just one of a number of sectors (health and social services being examples of others) involved in the management of drug markets and minimization of drug-related harms (Canty et al., 2000). International reviews (MacCoun and Reuter, 1998) indicate that most Western countries appear to be pursuing a middle-of-the-road course between these two perspectives—a modified supply reduction model that reflects an attempt by police to maintain a supply reduction focus while trying to ensure that their efforts do not impede the harm minimization work performed by health and social welfare sectors (e.g., needle exchange programs). Clearly, from an international perspective, a more comprehensive view of the ecological development of drug activities and related problems, the roles of these activities in communities' lives, and an open perspective on the full range of prevention interventions available is necessary to stem the tide of drug problems that are arising with the continued urbanization of the world's population.

ACKNOWLEDGEMENTS

Research for and preparation of this manuscript were supported by NIAAA Research Center Grant P60-AA006282 and NIAAA Grant No. R37-AA012927.

REFERENCES

Babor, T., Caetano, R., Casswell, S., Edwards, G., Giesbrecht, N., Graham, K., Grube, J., Gruenewald, P., Hill, L., Holder, H., Homel, R., Österberg, E., Rehm, J., Room, R. and Rossow, I. (2003) *Alcohol, No Ordinary Commodity: A Consumer's Guide to Research and Public Policy*. Oxford: Oxford University Press.

Barnes, G.M. and Welte, J.W. (1986) Patterns and predictors of alcohol use among 7–12th grade students in New York State. *Journal of Alcohol Studies*, **47**, 53–62.

Brantingham, P.L. and Brantingham, P.J. (1993) Nodes, paths and edges: considerations on the complexity of crime and the physical environment. *Journal of Environmental Psychology*, **13**, 3–28.

Brantingham, P.L. and Brantingham, P.J. (1999) A theoretical model of crime hot spot generation. *Studies on Crime and Crime Prevention*, **8**, 7–26.

Canty, C., Sutton, A. and James, S. (2000) Models of community-based drug law enforcement. *Police Practice and Research*, **2**, 171–187.

Caulkins, J.P. (2000) The evolution of drug initiation: from social networks to public markets. In *Optimization, Dynamics, and Economic Analysis: Essays in Honor of Gustav Feichtinger*. New York: Physica-Verlag, pp. 353–367.

Cohen, L.E. and Felson, M. (1979) Social change and crime rate trends: a routine activity approach. *American Sociological Review*, **44**(4), 588–608.

Coleman, J.S. (1988) Social capital in the creation of human capital. *American Journal of Sociology*, **94**, 95–120.

Coulton, C.J., Korbin, J.E. and Su, M. (1999) Neighborhoods and child maltreatment: a multi-level study. *Child Abuse and Neglect*, **23**, 1019–1040.

Davis, R.C., Lurigio, A.J. and Rosenbaum, D.P. (1993) *Drugs and the Community: Involving Community Residents in Combating the Sale of Illegal Drugs*. Springfield, IL: Charles C. Thomas.

Eck, J.E. (1995) A general model of the geography of illicit retail marketplaces. In J.E. Eck and D. Weisburd (eds), *Crime and Place: Crime Prevention Studies*, vol. 4. Washington, DC: Police Executive Research Forum.

Ensminger, M.E., Anthony, J.C. and McCord, J. (1997) The inner city and drug use: initial findings from an epidemiological study. *Drug and Alcohol Dependency*, **48**, 175–184.

Felson, M. (1998) *Crime and Everyday Life*, 2nd edn. Thousand Oaks, CA: Pine Forge Press.

Freisthler, B.F., LaScala, E.A., Gruenewald, P.J. and Treno, A.J. (in press) An examination of drug activity: effects of neighborhood social organization on the development of drug distribution systems. *Substance Use and Misuse*, **40**.

Goldstein, P.J. (1998) Drugs, violence, and federal funding: a research odyssey. *Substance Use and Misuse*, **33**, 1915–1936.

Gorman, D., Speer, P.W., Gruenewald, P.J. and Labouvie, E.W. (2001) Spatial dynamics of alcohol availability, neighborhood structure and violent crime. *Journal of Studies on Alcohol*, **62**, 628–636.

Gruenewald, P.J., Freisthler, B., Remer, L., LaScala, E. and Treno, A. (2003) Ecological models of alcohol, drugs and violent crime: crime potentials, crime mapping, and geospatial analysis. Paper presented at the International Research Symposium, Perth, Western Australia—Preventing Substance Use, Risky Use and Harm: What is Evidence Based Policy? 24–27 February.

Hawkins, J.D., Catalano, R.F. and Miller, J.Y. (1992) Risk and protective factors for alcohol and other drug problems in adolescence and early adulthood: implications for substance abuse prevention. *Psychological Bulletin*, **112**, 64–105.

Holder, H.D. (1998a) *Alcohol and the Community: A Systems Approach to Prevention*. New York: Cambridge University Press.

Holder, H.D. (1998b) Planning for alcohol-problem prevention through complex systems modeling: results from *SimCom*. *Substance Use and Misuse*, **33**(3), 669–692.

Kadushin, C., Reber, E., Saxe, L. and Livert, D. (1998) The substance use system: social and neighborhood environments associated with substance use and misuse. *Substance Use and Misuse*, **33**(8), 1681–1710.

Kandel, D.B. (1991) The social demography of drug use. *Milbank Quarterly*, **69**: 365–414.

Kandel, D.B. and Davies, M. (1991) Cocaine use in a national sample of US youth (NLSY): ethnic patterns, progression, and predictors. In S. Schober and C. Schade (eds), *The Epidemiology of Cocaine Use and Abuse*. Rockville, MD: National Institute on Drug Abuse, pp. 151–188.

Kelling, G.L. and Coles, C. (1996) *Fixing Broken Windows: Restoring Order and Reducing Crime in Our Communities*. New York: Free Press.

LaGrange, T.C. (1999) The impact of neighborhoods, schools, and malls on the spatial distribution of property damage. *Journal of Crime and Delinquency*, **36**(4), 393–422.

Lettieri, D.J., Sayes, M. and Pearson, H.W. (1980) *Theories on Drug Abuse: Selected Contemporary Perspectives* (Research Monograph 30). Rockville, MD: National Institute on Drug Abuse.

Liska, A., Chamlin, M., and Reed, M. (1985) Testing the economic production and conflict models of crime control. *Social Forces*, **64**, 119–138.

MacCoun, R. and Reuter, P. (1998) Drug control. In M. Tonry (ed.), *The Handbook of Crime and Punishment*. Oxford: Oxford University Press.

Morenoff, J.D., Sampson, R.J. and Raudenbush, S.W. (2001) Neighborhood inequality, collective efficacy, and the spatial dynamics of homicide. *Criminology*, **39**(3), 517–559.

Mosher, C. (2001) Predicting drug arrest rates: conflict and social disorganization perspectives. *Crime and Delinquency*, **47**, 84–104.

National Household Survey on Drug Abuse (1998) Rockville, MD: Substance Abuse and Mental Health Services Administration.

Parker, R.N. (1989) Poverty, subculture of violence, and type of homicide. *Social Forces*, **67**, 983–1007.

Petraitis, J., Flay, B.R. and Miller, T.Q. (1995) Reviewing theories of adolescent substance use: organizing pieces in the puzzle. *Psychological Bulletin*, **117**, 67–86.

Riley K.J. (1997) *Crack, Powder Cocaine, and Heroin: Drug Purchase and Use Patterns in Six US Cities*. Washington, DC: National Institute of Justice and Office of National Drug Control Policy.

Sampson, R.J. and Groves, W.B. (1989) Community structure and crime: testing social-disorganization theory. *American Journal of Sociology*, **94**, 774–802.

Sampson, R.J. and Wilson, W.J. (1995) Toward a theory of race, crime, and urban inequality. In J. Hagan and R. Peterson (eds), *Crime and Inequality*. Stanford, CA: Stanford University Press.

Sampson, R.J., Morenoff, J.D. and Gannon-Rowley, T. (2002) Assessing neighborhood effects: social processes and new directions in research. *Annual Review of Sociology*, **28**, 443–478.

Sampson, R.J., Raudenbush, S.W. and Earls, F. (1997) Neighborhoods and violent crime: a multilevel study of collective efficacy. *Science*, **277**, 918–924.

Saxe, L., Kadushin, C., Beveridge, A., Livert, D., Tighe, E., Rindskopf, D., Ford, J., and Brodsky, A. (2001) The visibility of illicit drugs: implications for community-based drug control strategies. *American Journal of Public Health*, **91**(12), 1987–1994.

Shaw, C. and McKay, H.D. (1942) *Juvenile Delinquency and Urban Areas*. Chicago: University of Chicago Press.

Skogan, W.G. (1990) *Disorder and Decline; Crime and the Spiral of Decay in American Neighborhoods*. New York: Free Press.

Stockwell, T. and Gruenewald, P.J. (2004) Controls on the physical availability of alcohol. In N. Heather and T. Stockwell (eds), *The Essential Handbook of Treatment and Prevention of Alcohol Problems*. New York: John Wiley, pp. 199–212.

Warner, L.A., Kessler R.C., Hughes, M., Anthony, J.C. and Nelson, C. (1995) Prevalence and correlates of drug use and dependence in the United States: results from the National Comorbidity Survey. *Archives of General Psychiatry*, **52**, 219–229.

Williams. T. (1992) *Crackhouse: Notes from the End of the Line*. New York: Penguin Books.

Section 3 INTERVENTIONS FOR CHILDREN AND ADOLESCENTS

EDITED BY JOHN W. TOUMBOUROU

3.1 Introduction

JOHN W. TOUMBOUROU

University of Melbourne, Vic, Australia

SUMMARY

One important emphasis in efforts to reduce the harm associated with alcohol, tobacco and other drug use involves developing and implementing effective policies and programmes that can reduce substance use and misuse among children and adolescents. The findings in this section have clear implications for practitioners and policy-makers and emphasise the opportunities for effective and well-integrated interventions operating at different levels. In efforts to reduce alcohol-related harm, there is evidence for the effectiveness of a number of national and state-level policies. These include taxation or other interventions to increase the price of alcohol, laws that increase the minimum drinking age, and stricter laws for new drivers that forbid even low blood alcohol concentrations. To be effective, policies must be carefully implemented and enforced and this often requires community support. This emphasis on working at the community-level is also reflected in other aspects of prevention research. Evidence from a number of longitudinal studies demonstrates that experiences growing up from infancy, on through early childhood, into the school years and into adolescence each contribute to the likelihood of substance misuse and harm emerging in subsequent years. For this reason protecting the healthy development of children and young people requires a well-coordinated series of programmes ranging from early family interventions for parents with infants, through to programmes for school age youth, and on to programmes to support adults. As is well evidenced by the extensive research examining school drug education, to succeed, each of these areas must be well supported through training and assistance. Coalitions are increasingly being formed and encouraged to implement and maintain an appropriate range of policies and programmes within a specific community. An evaluation of the functioning of community coalitions suggested that they were more effective when a better standard of both initial training and ongoing technical assistance were provided, enabling coalition members to develop a solid understanding of the prevention strategy being developed and implemented in their community. The chapters in this section emphasise the need to pursue a range of directions in investing in prevention, including healthy policies and well-planned prevention programmes intervening at different stages in the life course.

Preventing Harmful Substance Use: The Evidence Base for Policy and Practice.
Edited by T. Stockwell, P. J. Gruenewald, J. W. Toumbourou and W. Loxley.
© 2005 John Wiley & Sons, Ltd. ISBN 0-470-09227-0 (hbk) 0-470-09228-9 (pbk).

INTERVENTIONS FOR CHILDREN AND ADOLESCENTS

Levels of substance use rise steadily in the adolescent years and tend to have strong continuity with the subsequent development of drug-related harm in adulthood. The four chapters in this section start to answer questions as to where prevention investment should focus in order to effectively reduce these problems. On one hand, there appears to be good evidence, as presented in Chapter 3.4, that policies must be an important consideration. Increasing the age at which alcohol can be legally purchased and used, increasing the price of alcohol and applying laws that require lower blood alcohol levels for young drivers provide evidence of universal impacts in reducing alcohol use and related harms. On the other hand, evidence presented in both Chapters 3.2 and 3.3 demonstrates that interventions in childhood and adolescence can also reduce the development of early age and regular youth substance use and thereby contribute to reducing subsequent harms.

There is evidence that introducing policy interventions may be complementary to efforts to encourage conditions for healthy development. For example, one study (Yu and Shacket, 1998) revealed that when New York State mandated an older age for alcohol use, parents' attitudes against youth alcohol use steadily toughened. Such attitudes tend to translate into family rules and practices that make it more difficult for youth to obtain and use alcohol, perhaps explaining one mechanism underlying the common observation of lower rates of youth alcohol use following the introduction of older age laws for youth alcohol purchase and use.

Policy changes can also impact adult behaviours and such changes can have important implications for children and young people. For example, wider community patterns of alcohol and drug misuse can influence maternal drug use and this can directly impact the development of babies and children through behaviours such as maternal tobacco and alcohol use. Alcohol and drug use can also reduce the adequacy of parental practices and has been associated with violence, neglect and abuse (Mitchell et al., 2001). Hence, there is potential for policies that reduce overall rates of substance misuse within a specific population to also benefit children and young people (Loxley et al., 2004).

Policy planners need to be aware that there are many points in the development of children where interventions may be beneficial. This introduces the requirement to think in the long term and to carefully consider each community's specific context in planning developmental prevention initiatives. In disadvantaged communities, efforts to support economically impoverished and vulnerable mothers may be warranted (Olds et al., 1997). Although starting prevention at an early age has obvious appeal, there is evidence that prevention can also be beneficial at later ages such as in the pre-school years (Schweinhart and Weikart, 1993), in the school years (Kellam and Anthony, 1998) and in adolescence and beyond (Loxley et al., 2004).

Although the scientific basis for developmental prevention is maturing, Chapter 3.2 lists a number of areas where future research will be required. Currently the evidence is largely derived from small efficacy trials that have followed individuals over time. It remains to be demonstrated whether programme impacts can translate into evidence for effectiveness in large aggregate populations. The current efficacy evidence is encouraging in that there has been some demonstrations that underlying process theories can explain the behavioural changes that are observed following participation in prevention programmes (Kosterman et al., 2001). Understanding underlying change processes augers well for efforts to achieve effectiveness in wider dissemination projects in the future.

A great deal of investment has been directed at the area of school-based drug education. Chapter 3.3 presents directions for improving research and practice in school-based
drug education, emphasising as one component the need to continue with a programme of
basic research investigating programme content. An interactive approach to building programme content that includes consultation with stakeholders and careful study of the factors
influencing the emergence of youth behaviour is recommended. Such recommendations appear particularly pertinent from an international perspective, but may introduce a different
direction to the US literature where the focus has been more on the need for schools
to implement existing evaluated programmes with fidelity (e.g., Hansen and McNeal,
1999).

The importance of work at the community level in achieving well-coordinated prevention
is reflected in a number of the contributions to this section. The existing evidence from
Chapter 3.2 suggests that developmental prevention programmes operating at different
points in the life-course and in different settings can be beneficial. This evidence suggests
that a sequence of programmes that aim to achieve a cumulative developmental impact
is likely to be particularly useful. Such findings emphasise the importance of continuing
interventions across the course of development and into different developmental settings.
A similar sentiment is echoed in recommendations for school drug education (Chapter 3.3)
where the design and selection of school programmes are considered to be best facilitated
through research and consultation at the school level. Making effective programmes readily
available to schools and training school staff in the implementation of programmes is one
important element in this endeavour. The focus on the local community is also evident in
the consideration of alcohol policies (Chapter 3.4). It is clear that policy changes may be
optimally effective where they are accompanied by educational efforts to ensure community
awareness, in turn creating motivation for local enforcement.

The expectation that different influences may operate in different communities suggests
the importance of tailoring interventions for specific communities. Community coalitions
have been proposed as a model for investigating and addressing the developmental influences impacting young people (Hawkins and Catalano, 1992) and have also been proposed
as a method of encouraging the coordinated enforcement of both community laws and
policies impacting young people (Holder et al., 1997). There may be opportunities in building workable coalitions to coordinate prevention activities using funding from different
jurisdictions (e.g., crime prevention, health promotion, mental health, education, substance
abuse prevention).

In Chapter 3.5 a model of coalition functioning is proposed and evaluated based on
observation of the implementation of the Communities That Care (CTC) programme in
Pennsylvania. According to these observations, the prevention knowledge of coalition members, the quality of functioning of coalitions, and their fidelity to a logical prevention plan
were each influential in predicting the community coalitions that sustained their activities
beyond their initial start-up periods. Although impacts on substance use were not examined, coalitions that functioned more effectively showed greater reductions in rates of youth
delinquent behaviour within their communities.

Taken collectively, the findings in this section have clear implications for practitioners
and policy-makers and suggest that effective approaches may require a marriage between
various levels of government and the local community. As is outlined in Table 3.1.1, there
are interrelated objectives for prevention that have the potential to coordinate different jurisdictions in a common effort to reduce drug-related harm. The possibility of achieving a

strong coalition within a specific community may increase where communities have some level of existing organisation and knowledge of prevention approaches. To encourage an evidence-based approach to service delivery focused on local community needs, national and state policies could provide resources to implement training for local coalitions. Positive outcomes in addressing adolescent problem behaviours are more likely to be achieved when a critical mass of people within a community have an agreed understanding of how to develop, manage and sustain an effective mixture of policies and programmes. The diverse range of programmes evaluated in this section suggests the need for future research to explore the potential for synergistic benefits in communities where developmental prevention strategies have been creatively integrated with interventions aiming to more directly reduce harms related to alcohol and drug use.

Table 3.1.1   Objectives for different policy jurisdictions and operational settings within a comprehensive approach to prevention

Setting	Supply control	Demand reduction / social improvement	Reduction of harm
National and state objectives	Coordinated policies and strategies for supply control. Integrated operation of border control, drug control (policies, laws and regulation), taxes and excise, social marketing and media controls	Effective and coordinated policies and strategies for reduction of demand and social improvement. Integrated expenditure on health, mental health, welfare, education, prevention	Effective and coordinated policies and strategies to reduce harm. Including police training (eg., drink–drive programmes), treatment programmes (methadone), courts (diversion), prisons
Local community objectives	Effectively planned and locally coordinated supply reduction programmes	Well-planned and coordinated strategy for investment in social improvement and prevention. Reduction of local risk factors, enhancement of protective factors	Effective and coordinated local strategy for reducing drug-related harms
Local community activities	Licensing and enforcement, policing, distribution (alcohol, tobacco, other drugs)	Targeted early childhood programmes. Parent education. Schools drug-education and organisation. Social opportunities and employment	Driver breath testing by police, alcohol server training, keg registration, needle exchange programmes
Objectives for families and adults	The availability and price of drugs reflect evidence for their harms	Enhanced social connection. Patterns of drug use within public health guidelines	Reduction in risky drug use and harm
Objectives for children and young people	Drugs are unfashionable and difficult to access	Healthy social development	Less drug use, delayed age of first drug use, less frequent and more moderate drug use

Source: Developed from Loxley et al., (2004).

REFERENCES

Hansen, W.B. and McNeal, R.B. Jr. (1999) Drug education practice: results of an observational study. *Health Education Research,* **14**(1), 85–97.

Hawkins, J.D. and Catalano, R.F. et al., (1992) *Communities That Care: Action for Drug Abuse Prevention.* San Francisco: Jossey-Bass.

Holder, H.D., Saltz, R.F., Grube, J.W., Voas, R.B., Gruenewald, P.J. and Treno, A.J. (1997) A community prevention trial to reduce alcohol-involved accidental injury and death: overview. *Addiction,* **92**(Suppl. 2), S155–S171.

Kellam, S.G. and Anthony, J.C. (1998) Targeting early antecedents to prevent tobacco smoking: findings from an epidemiologically based randomized field trial. *American Journal of Public Health,* **88**, 1490–1495.

Kosterman, R., Hawkins, D.J., Haggerty, K.P., Spoth, R. and Redmond, C. (2001) Preparing for the drug-free years: session-specific effects of a universal parent training intervention with rural families. *Journal of Drug Education,* **31**(1), 47–68.

Loxley, W., Toumbourou, J.W, Stockwell, T., Haines, B., Scott, K., Godfrey, C., Waters, E., Patton, G., Fordham, R., Gray, D., Marshall, J., Ryder, D., Saggers, S., Sanci, L. and Williams, J. (2004) *The Prevention of Substance Use, Risk and Harm in Australia: A Review of the Evidence.* Canberra: Population Health Division, Australian Government Department of Health and Ageing.

Mitchell, P., Spooner, C., Copeland, J., Vimpani, G., Toumbourou, J.W., Howard, J. and Sanson, A. (2001) *A Literature Review of the Role of Families in the Development, Identification, Prevention and Treatment of Illicit Drug Problems.* National Health and Medical Research Council Monograph. Canberra: Commonwealth of Australia.

Olds, D.L., Eckenrode, J., Henderson, Jr. C.R., Kitzman, H., Powers, J., Cole, R., Sidora, K., Morris, P., Pettitt, L.M. and Luckey, D. (1997) Long-term effects of home visitation on maternal life course and child abuse and neglect: 15-year follow-up of a randomised trial. *Journal of the American Medical Association,* **278**, 637–643.

Schweinhart, L.J. and Weikart, D.P. (1993) Success by empowerment: the high/scope Perry preschool study through age 27. *Young Children,* **49**, 54–58.

Yu, J. and Shacket, R.W. (1998) Long-term change in underage drinking and impaired driving after the establishment of drinking age laws in New York State. *Alcohol Clinical and Experimental Research,* **22**(7), 1443–1449.

3.2 What Do We Know about Preventing Drug-Related Harm through Social Developmental Intervention with Children and Young People?

JOHN W. TOUMBOUROU, JO WILLIAMS, GEORGE PATTON

Centre for Adolescent Health, University of Melbourne, Vic, Australia

ELIZABETH WATERS

Centre for Community Child Health, University of Melbourne, Vic, Australia

SUMMARY

This chapter examines the evidence for the effectiveness of interventions aiming to reduce drug-related harm by improving conditions for healthy development in the earliest years through to adolescence. Of the interventions beginning prior to birth, there is efficacy evidence that family home visitation is a feasible strategy for implementation with disadvantaged families and can reduce risk factors for early developmental deficits and thereby improve childhood development outcomes. There is efficacy evidence for strategies such as parent education and school preparation through the pre-school age period. Some of the strongest evidence for efficacy in reducing developmental pathways to drug-related harm comes from interventions delivered through the early school years to improve educational environments. Of the interventions targeting the high school age period, school drug education has been the most commonly evaluated. The evidence suggests that short-term reduction in both drug use and progression to frequent drug use may be achievable through this strategy, but the prospects for longer-term and population-level behaviour change are still unclear. In overview, a range of prevention strategies have been developed and evaluated. Most of the existing evidence is restricted to efficacy studies and there are future challenges to progress evaluation through to studies of effectiveness. In general, prevention programmes appear more successful where they maintain intervention activities over a number of years and incorporate more than one strategy. Much of the existing research has been based in North America and evaluates discrete programmes. Future research should test effects in other countries, in different social contexts and seek to better understand the interrelated effects of combining

Preventing Harmful Substance Use: The Evidence Base for Policy and Practice.
Edited by T. Stockwell, P. J. Gruenewald, J. W. Toumbourou and W. Loxley.
© 2005 John Wiley & Sons, Ltd. ISBN 0-470-09227-0 (hbk) 0-470-09228-9 (pbk).

interventions within a community. Developmental prevention programmes target different age periods and social settings, hence communities have the challenge of coordinating a mixture of programmes that address the local conditions that adversely influence child and youth development. There are opportunities in this work to coordinate prevention activities using funding from different jurisdictions (e.g., crime prevention, health promotion, mental health, education, substance abuse prevention).

INTRODUCTION

As children grow and develop, their experiences in settings such as the family, the local community, schools and peer groups and their own attitudes and behaviour are important in influencing whether or not they will subsequently become involved in heavy and harmful drug use. As a wide range of contexts will be influential, many different intervention strategies are relevant. This chapter contains evidence for a variety of prevention strategies and has been organised to focus on opportunities for coordinated strategies across the course of development in different settings. Due to limited space, this review is not comprehensive but seeks rather to present model programmes and evaluations and to document evidence for intervention impacts on developmental risk and protective factors.

Table 3.2.1 provides definitions for a range of prevention strategies. The organisation of strategies in Table 3.2.1 emphasises the grouping of prevention activities according to the workforce requirements for the coordinated delivery of interventions and the settings where children are exposed to developmental influences.

The wide range of strategies in Table 3.2.1 highlights the complex task faced by service planners in deciding between alternative service options. In what follows we evaluate the evidence for the effectiveness of preventative interventions accumulated from well-controlled evaluation studies (see Table 3.2.2). By well-controlled we refer to quality design features such as implementation description, randomisation to control conditions, adequate sample power and longitudinal follow up. In organising the evidence, we present in Table 3.2.2 a simplified evaluation rating-scheme that has been designed to encourage programme developers to advance prevention strategies to higher levels of evidence.

At the initial stage service developers have the challenge of organising interventions that can impact underlying developmental processes into coherent programmes that can be understood and implemented by others. Programmes can initially be evaluated for theoretical coherence, practical feasibility for delivery in specific settings, and consumer approval within different populations. Strategies that have a theoretical basis for intervention development within a specific setting and population but have not yet achieved an agreed programme format we have flagged as "warranting further research" (⏃).

Where programmes have been clearly documented and their delivery steps have proved to be feasible, evaluation evidence is sought that short-term impacts are consistent with programme process theories. In such cases evidence might demonstrate that delivered intervention elements impacted targeted developmental risk and protective factors and led to early changes in behaviours. In this chapter different programmes have been grouped according to commonalities in their underlying prevention strategies (the developmental stage and setting they address). Strategies that have consistently achieved evidence for programme impacts in at least two well-controlled evaluation studies we have rated as having achieved "evidence for impacts" (★). In cases where two or more well-controlled programme

Table 3.2.1 Definition of prevention strategies

Prevention strategies (*Settings*)	Definitions
Family setting—family services	
Preventing and delaying pregnancy in young and vulnerable mothers	The use of a broad range of programmes designed to prevent pregnancy amongst teenagers and vulnerable mothers. Strategies include delaying the initiation of sexual activity, encouraging the use of contraception, reducing risky sexual behaviour and providing access to pregnancy termination.
Family home visiting	A professional such as a nurse developing a relationship with a vulnerable family over a period of time in the context of offering, support, information and advice on pregnancy, infant health, maternal health, and advocacy for service access.
Parent education	One or more parents (or carers) receiving information and/or engaging in a course of instruction aimed at encouraging healthy child development.
Family intervention	One or more parents (or carers), children and other family members receiving information, engaging in a course of instruction and/or obtaining therapeutic assistance together aimed at encouraging healthy family development.
School setting—school services	
School preparation programmes	Programmes aimed at better preparing children for the transition to school.
School organisation and behaviour management	Includes interventions to maximise learning opportunities, encourage positive interpersonal relationships at school, and policies and procedures to ensure effective discipline.
School drug education (curricula)	Delivery of a structured social health education curriculum within the school usually by classroom teachers, but in some cases by visiting outside professionals.
Peer settings—Typically coordinated by schools, non-government organisations or local government	
Peer intervention and peer education	Youth peers of common identity provide support or deliver a health message.
Youth sport and recreation programmes	Provision or utilisation of recreational opportunities outside the school setting to promote the positive development of children and young people.
Mentorship	Strategies to develop prosocial relationships between youth and positively functioning adults within the community.
Community setting—Locally, Regionally or State coordinated programmes	
Community-based drug education	Adolescent drug education curricula or information delivered in a community setting other than in schools.
Preventative case-management	Coordinated delivery of more intensive services tailored to meet a range of developmental needs. Generally targeted to children and adolescents with multiple risk factors.
Community mobilisation	Campaigns to initiate or strengthen an explicit strategy of coordinated community action aiming to advance community conditions for healthy development in children and young people.
Health service reorientation	Includes reorientation of existing health services to enhance service access for vulnerable families and to modify factors that can otherwise disrupt healthy development.
Employment and training	Includes provision of pre-employment assistance, employment experience, training or intervention in a post-school training setting, with the aim of ensuring developmental outcomes.
Law, regulation, policing and enforcement	Modification to and enforcement of legislation or regulations, policing strategies and procedures for dealing with offenders aimed at reducing access to substances and preventing initiation or escalation of youth behaviour problems.
Social marketing	Use of the mass media to promote a health message.

Source: Based on Toumbourou et al. (2000).

Table 3.2.2 Effectiveness of prevention strategies aiming to prevent the development of drug-related harm

Developmental period	Intervention strategies/settings	Strength of evidence	Comments
Prior to birth	Preventing and delaying pregnancy in young and vulnerable mothers, health service reorientation	⚑	Few studies have examined drug use impacts
	Family home visiting	★★	Small samples. Effects for selected population groups only
Infancy and early childhood (0–4)	Parent education, school preparation programmes	★★	Generally small studies with short-term follow-up. Some notable long-term findings for school preparation
Primary (elementary) school age (5–10)	Family intervention, parent education	★★	Some strong designs. Mostly small studies. Some adolescent outcomes
	Early school drug education	★	Need process studies. Social influences appear critical
	School organisation and behaviour management	★★	Some strong designs. Adolescent follow-ups are being reported
Adolescence (11–24)	School organisation and behaviour management, peer intervention and peer education, youth sport and recreation programmes, mentorship	⚑	Some interventions such as peer education have the potential for negative outcomes
	Parent education, family intervention, social marketing, preventative case management	★	Family interventions appear useful as selective interventions
	High school drug education, law, regulation and policing, community mobilisation	★★	Drug education has been less clearly effective in preventing alcohol use

Notes:
⚑ Warrants further research.
★ Evidence for implementation.
★★ Evidence for outcome efficacy.
★★★ Evidence for effective dissemination.

evaluations have demonstrated behaviour change maintained to at least one year of follow-up, we have designated programmes to have evidence of "outcome efficacy" (★★). The challenge beyond this level of evidence is for programmes to consistently demonstrate long-term effectiveness (three years or longer) in real-world conditions across large population aggregates. To date, no developmental prevention strategy is rated as having progressed to this level of evidence.

Our ratings summarised in Table 3.2.2 demonstrate that there are a number of prevention strategies within which carefully designed and implemented programmes have achieved evidence for outcome efficacy in modifying developmental pathways leading to drug-related harm. Evidence supports the relevance of a variety of strategies and intervention targets.

Prior to Birth

Prior to birth programmes have been developed to address a number of intervention targets including preventing teenage pregnancy, reducing foetal exposure to harmful drug use and encouraging the healthy development of mother and baby.

Preventing and delaying pregnancy in young and vulnerable mothers

Although there is evidence for the successful implementation of these strategies, their outcome in preventing pre-birth exposure to drug use and drug use problems in future generations has not yet been demonstrated. There is evidence that in some cases these programmes may reduce drug use for vulnerable young women (Toumbourou et al., 2000).

Health service reorientation (antenatal)

Small studies have provided preliminary evidence addressing the feasibility of implementing screening and assessment interventions for pregnant women. Overall results show some level of acceptance for these services, but designs do not yet enable behavioural outcomes to be clearly established (Loxley et al., 2004).

Family home visiting   ★★

Relevant programme targets include reducing foetal and infant exposures to harmful drug use, the family's harmful drug use and reduction of early developmental risk factors for the child's later involvement in drug abuse. Olds and colleagues evaluated a programme involving regular home visiting by a nurse from late pregnancy until the child's second birthday for low-income, unmarried and adolescent women having their first babies. The programme focused upon supporting the mother, promoting positive attachment with the child and teaching parenting skills. Follow-up of mothers randomly assigned to receive differing levels of programme exposure was completed when the children reached their 15th birthday. For the sub-sample of mothers who were unmarried and poor, significantly lower rates of subsequent births, longer periods between children, less welfare dependence, less alcohol and drug impairment and fewer arrests were observed. Relative to the controls, the children reported fewer instances of running away from home, fewer convictions and probation violations, fewer lifetime sexual partners, fewer cigarettes smoked per day, and fewer days consuming alcohol over the previous six months. Replications have been reported in two sites (Olds et al., 1999).

Savings and returns to government have been estimated at around $5 for every $1 spent on the programme over the first 15 years of the child's life. Intensive home visitation has been shown to be most cost-effective when provided as a selective intervention to women at increased risk by virtue of factors such as young age, poverty, lack of partner support and drug abuse. There is evidence that this strategy may not demonstrate benefits where it is applied more universally to include low-risk mothers (Mitchell et al., 2001).

Infancy and Early Childhood (0–4 Years)

Major prevention targets from birth through the pre-school years include child developmental needs for sustenance, nurture and stimulation, and parenting competence.

Health service reorientation   ♭

Service models have been developed to reduce the impact of maternal smoking and to assist families to reduce problems associated with alcohol and drug use. There has been little research evaluating the impact of these strategies on either maternal drug use or child development (Loxley et al., 2004).

Parent education   ★★

Parent education remains an important prevention strategy from the period immediately following birth through into adolescence. In the period surrounding birth, the focus is on developing a strong bond between the mother and newborn infant and on ensuring the parent is competent to meet the child's developmental needs. Interventions have been based on cognitive, behavioural and social learning theories. A number of small efficacy studies have supported parent education from the first year for mothers in specific contexts including maternal depression; parents with intellectual disability; and early child behaviour problems. Small evaluation trials incorporating randomised assignment to a control condition have shown evidence for efficacy in short-term follow-ups of up to one year (Loxley et al., 2004).

Systematic reviews of the available efficacy evidence suggest that behavioural parent education programmes tend to have moderate effect sizes with improvements at short-term follow-up observed for around two-thirds of participants. Interventions are successful in enrolling around two-thirds of parents seeking assistance for child behaviour problems. Improvements have been shown to deteriorate with time (Mitchell et al., 2001).

School preparation programmes   ★★

An important developmental pathway for adjustment difficulties begins with the transition to primary school. Better preparing children for primary school is a practical strategy for improving the transition for vulnerable families. Evidence from a number of small efficacy trials of pre-school programmes has revealed positive impacts in areas including child intelligence and academic readiness and parental educational participation.

The Perry Preschool project carried out in Ypsilanti (Michigan) offered four half-days of structured pre-school experience combined with weekly home visits over one or two years for disadvantaged 3 and 4-year-olds. The aim of the programme was to provide intellectual stimulation, to increase cognitive abilities, and to increase later school achievement. A small evaluation study where 127 disadvantaged African-American children were randomly allocated to the intervention or a control condition found several long-term programme advantages for the intervention group maintained to age 27. These included a lower incidence of drug use and teenage pregnancy, lower risk of high-school drop out, increased likelihood of employment and reduced reliance on welfare compared to non-intervention controls. Women suffered substantially less from mental health problems compared to those who did not participate and males from the programme had considerably fewer arrests relative to the controls (Schweinhart and Weikart, 1993).

Findings supportive of school preparation have also been reported by evaluations of ten other similar programmes followed up by the Consortium for Longitudinal Studies (1983) and the evaluation of the Carolina Abercedarian pre-school project (Campbell and Ramey, 1994). The combined findings suggest that pre-school preparation programmes can have long-term benefits on school success.

There have been a series of cost benefit analyses of the 27-year Perry Preschool Program study. The estimates of government savings appear better than a $2 savings for every dollar invested in the programme (Mitchell et al., 2001).

Primary School Age (5–10)

From the entry to primary school, children are increasingly exposed to a broader range of influences. Relationships with teachers and other children increasingly shape development.

Family intervention (primary school-aged populations) ★★

As the child's capacity for social interaction develops, interventions aiming to build skills for healthy child and family relationships become relevant. Targets for these programmes include child social and emotional competence, family rules and rituals, parenting skills and family social support networks.

The Iowa Strengthening Family Program (ISFP) developed out of successful experience running Professor Karol Kumpfer's Strengthening America's Families Program with high-risk populations in drug treatment and disadvantaged community settings. The ISFP was targeted to all families in rural Iowa schools in late childhood. Group interventions involved seven two-hour sessions and encouraged harmonious family relationships by developing communication skills and family management strategies for adolescents and parents in separated groups with reinforcement in combined sessions. An experimental trial following 300 families randomly assigned to receive the intervention suggested initially that the programme was about as successful as parent education alone in discouraging youth alcohol use. However, four-year follow-up data have suggested that benefits may have extended to reductions in youth hostile and aggressive behaviour. Returns of just over $9 for every $1 invested in the program have been estimated (Spoth, et al., 2002).

Improvements in parent and child outcomes have also been observed in short-term evaluations where intensive family intervention programmes have been delivered to parents in drug treatment settings (Catalano et al., 1999).

Parent education (primary school-aged populations) ★★

Information relevant to the delivery of parent education programmes for primary school-aged children was summarised above. In overview, these programmes continue to demonstrate enhanced parenting skills, improved parental functioning, improvements in parent–child relationships and reductions in child behaviour problems when delivered in late childhood.

A five-session, professionally led, parent-education programme aimed to enhance positive parent–child interactions and improve family management. Relative to controls, 100 young people whose families were randomly assigned to the intervention showed increased family bonding and reduced alcohol use two years after the intervention. Recent estimates suggest a return of just over $5 for every $1 invested in the programme (Spoth et al., 2002).

The Australian Triple-P programme has emerged as a popular model for providing a multi-tiered approach to service delivery, graded according to the severity of child behaviour problems and parental difficulties. Evidence has associated exposure to this programme with improvements in child behaviour for follow-ups in small samples of up to one year (Sanders et al., 2000). Larger state level evaluations of effectiveness are underway.

Early school drug education ★

The evaluation of school drug education programmes suggests they are feasible for delivery in settings such as primary schools. In the early years of school drug education, targets include building relationships and social-emotional skills rather than discouraging drug use specifically. Future investment could examine process factors more carefully (including relationships, skills and intentions) as a preliminary to long-term follow-up. Evaluation findings suggest that primary school drug education programmes that focus on knowledge, attitudes and values alone may be of limited benefit (Godfrey et al., 2002).

School organisation and behaviour management ★★

Efforts to enhance teacher–student relationships and reduce negative school peer interactions appear to be important in reducing the translation of early developmental risk into pathways of social marginalisation. The Fast Track programme in the USA has included intensive individual and group components to enhance competencies in the early school years for children with a high number of developmental risk factors. An experimental trial randomised 900 children to intervention or control groups, finding moderate improvements in children's educational and social progress by Grade 3 (Conduct Problems Prevention Research Group, 2002).

The Linking the Interests of Families and Teachers (LIFT) programme supplemented classroom social competence training and parent components with monitoring of playground behaviour to reinforce social skills. Students received individual rewards for positive social behaviours but an additional group reward was withheld if negative behaviours were not reduced. An experimental trial randomising 670 students to intervention or control conditions revealed reductions in school playground aggressive behaviour, with effects particularly pronounced for the children who were most aggressive at baseline. Grade 5 students showed lower rates of delinquent peer involvement, lower arrests and less initiation of alcohol and marijuana use after three years. Larger developmental benefits were also evident for younger cohorts (Eddy et al., 2000).

The Seattle Social Development Project (SSDP) combined teacher training in effective classroom management and instruction with student social competence and parent education components. A quasi-experimental trial assigning 800 children from high crime neighbourhoods into comparison or intervention classrooms revealed early increases in school retention and bonding, with effects also evident for low-achieving students. Long-term follow-up into early adulthood revealed moderate reductions in school failure, substance abuse and delinquency. The programme appeared to offer differential improvements for the most vulnerable students from low SES backgrounds (Hawkins et al., 2001).

Adolescence (11–24)

Increasing independence and mobility through adolescence introduce a greater range of social influences into the young person's life. Social changes including technological advances and free market competition mean that many adolescents face a higher educational threshold in order to enter employment. These changes underlie the current social trend for adolescents to spend more years in education and to delay into the late twenties their entry into independent living responsibilities.

School organisation and behaviour management, peer intervention and peer education, youth sport and recreation programmes, mentorship

There are a number of promising strategies in the adolescent period that are still maturing with respect to their potential for programme evaluation. Evaluations using randomisation to a control group have linked exposure to the Big Brother/Big Sister mentorship programme with longer-term behaviour change. This programme incorporates good design features that include careful matching of mentors to clients, training, ongoing support and evaluation. In Australia the Good Sports programme operated by the Australian Drug Foundation provides evidence that a process of accreditation can be feasibly implemented as a method of reducing the risk that young people will be introduced to alcohol or smoking through sports participation. Some interventions such as peer education have the potential for negative outcomes where they aggregate youth with behaviour problems (Loxley et al., 2004).

Parent education (adolescent age period) ⋆

Through the adolescent phase parent education focuses on parent skills for communication, reducing conflict and healthy relationship boundaries. An Australian parent education programme used adult learning principles to improve parents' skills for relating to adolescents. Six hundred parents and early high school students completed surveys in 14 schools targeted for intervention, with procedures matched in 14 control schools. Although only 10% of parents were recruited into the parent education groups, post-intervention findings demonstrated that benefits extended more broadly across families in the intervention schools. At the 12-week follow-up parents and adolescents reported a reduction in family conflict. Adolescents reported increased maternal care, less delinquency, and less substance use. Evaluation suggested that the substance use of respondents was influenced by their best friend's substance use. Improvements in troubled family relationships appeared to impact a wide group of families linked through peer-friendship networks (Toumbourou and Gregg, 2002).

Recruiting and engaging relevant families remain an important challenge for parent education programmes. In a recent US project addressing youth tobacco use, households were screened by phone to identify families with children in the age range 12 to 14. Of the 2,400 families identified, 55% of parents and adolescents participated in a baseline phone survey and then half the parents were randomly assigned to participate in a programme called Family Matters. The programme involved mailing a sequence of four booklets to parents, with discussion with a phone counsellor after each mailing. Parents and adolescents were re-interviewed at the completion of the three-month programme and again 12- months later. Relative to the controls, smoking onset was reduced by 16.4% for the youth in the families exposed to the intervention. The programme had no impact on the initiation of alcohol use (Bauman et al., 2001).

Family intervention (adolescent age period) ⋆

Family intervention programmes have been based on a variety of theoretical frameworks including family systems theories and social learning approaches. An important focus in their application in families with adolescent children is the transition to respectful adult-to-adult relationships.

A number of brief family therapy approaches have been evaluated for their effects on youth substance misuse (Mitchell et al., 2001). The Functional Family Therapy approach has evidence as a strategy for reducing re-offending among voluntary and court-mandated adolescent offenders and has also been demonstrated to prevent offending among the younger siblings of targeted offenders. Economic evaluation estimated the net economic crime prevention benefit at around $4 for each $1 invested (Aos et al., 1998). Process evaluation (Robbins et al., 1996) has suggested a critical programme component may involve reducing family out-group tendencies by reframing problem attribution away from individual blame (e.g., bad son) to focus on the concept of a mismatch in adolescent and parent needs.

Preventative case management

For young people who have entered maladjusted developmental trajectories in childhood, adolescence can be a developmental period that provides new opportunities to intervene through settings such as educational counselling, and policing. Given early developmental deficits can result in complex and multifaceted problems, treatment approaches have focused on coordinating a range of evidence-based interventions. The Multisystemic Treatment programme targeted court referred serious juvenile offenders. Treatment objectives were set in consultation with the offender and their family. Clinicians trained in evidence-based therapies were rewarded for attaining agreed outcomes relevant to family relationships, individual competencies, peer relationships, work, education, health and mental health. The programme was effective in engaging families with complex problems and small well-controlled evaluations have shown reductions in crime and delinquency maintained after one to two years (Cunningham and Henggeler, 1999). The net economic crime prevention benefit is around $5 for each $1 invested (Aos et al., 1998). A similar strategy for students with evidence of poor school performance and substance misuse involved school counsellor assistance to achieve improvements in behaviour and academic goals. A small experimental trial revealed lower substance use after two years (Bry et al., 1998).

Social marketing

The mass media can be used to widely disseminate information about alcohol and other drugs and in some cases can influence attitudes and perceived norms (Carroll et al., 2000). The role these programmes can play in preventing substance use initiation is unclear, although there is some evidence to suggest the potential to encourage less harmful substance use behaviours (Loxley et al., 2004).

School-based drug education ★★

Future challenges confronting high school drug education programmes are summarised in Chapter 3.3. There appears to be evidence for at least short-term behavioural impacts following high school drug education that have been developed on theoretical principles and delivered with fidelity. The prospects for longer-term and population-level behaviour change are still unclear.

Law, regulation and policing ★★

Evidence that policy interventions can reduce youth alcohol use is summarised in Chapter 3.4. There is some evidence that policy interventions can also reduce youth tobacco use. For example, evidence from studies that have randomised communities to policy interventions discouraging retailers from selling cigarettes to underage youth have reported reductions in youth tobacco use (Forster et al., 1998; Toumbourou et al., 2000). Evidence relevant to legislative and law enforcement efforts aimed at reducing illegal drug use and harms is summarised in other sections of the present volume.

Community mobilisation ★★

Community mobilisation programmes focusing on the adolescent period have been developed that aim to reduce perceived favourable community norms and access to licit and illicit drugs. Programme strategies combining school and parent components with community mobilisation to reduce the availability of alcohol and drugs have shown some small reductions over one to three years in tobacco and marijuana initiation (Johnson et al., 1990), escalation to regular marijuana use (Stevens et al., 1996) and alcohol initiation while also reducing estimates of peer drug use (Perry et al., 1996).

There is evidence that community mobilisation programmes can effectively draw together coalitions, assess local conditions influencing drug-related harms, plan and implement the coordinated delivery of programmes and monitor and evaluate intervention delivery. Such integrated community programmes have demonstrated effectiveness in reducing harms associated with alcohol use (Holder et al., 1997). Further work will be required to establish that community mobilisation programmes can be effectively disseminated outside of the context of research demonstration programmes.

COORDINATING INTERVENTION PROGRAMMES

Although most people agree with the principle of early investment to prevent later problems, there are a number of important barriers that must be overcome in order to establish an effective prevention framework. It is sometimes said that the long-term focus of prevention does not fit the short-term requirement for political priorities. Evidence for effectiveness in preventing harms associated with substance use and in reducing related social problems provides the basis for quantifying the economic benefit achievable through preventative investment and such information can then be used to encourage the political resolve to move service systems toward effective prevention investments.

The early history of prevention efforts reveals a number of programmes that were based on intuitive and "common-sense" principles that were subsequently found to be ineffective.

As a consequence of this experience, programmes have increasingly been developed out of careful consideration of the theoretical and empirical evidence for behaviour change. A major challenge facing the successful dissemination of evidence-based programmes is that they are often poorly implemented in settings such as schools and communities. To overcome these difficulties prevention programmes need to be accompanied by adequate resources for training and technical support (Hallfors and Godette, 2002).

In general, prevention programmes appear more successful where they maintain intervention activities over a number of years through childhood and into adolescence and incorporate strategies that intervene in different socialisation domains (e.g., family, school, community, and peer groups). Developmental prevention programmes target different age periods and social settings, hence communities have the challenge of coordinating a mixture of programmes that address the local conditions that adversely influence child and youth development. A practical approach to improving the local targeting of community prevention plans has involved the use of local assessments of social developmental risk and protective factors. One successful approach encourages assessments to be conducted by local coalitions who then use the information to plan and implement prevention plans incorporating an integrated range of evidence-based strategies (Arthur and Blitz, 2000).

Childhood and adolescent prevention programmes address developmental influences that influence not just substance use but also a range of other health and social outcomes. For this reason efficiencies can be achieved by coordinating and delivering local prevention activities using funding that bridges different jurisdictions (e.g., crime prevention, health promotion, mental health, education, substance abuse prevention). By emphasising the local community's role in planning and service delivery, important gains may be possible in prevention planning and coordination across the range of funding jurisdictions (Arthur and Blitz, 2000).

CONCLUSION

There is a growing evidence base for developmentally based preventative interventions. Large investments will be required in coming years to disseminate programmes that have evidence for efficacy in dissemination trials that will enable effectiveness to be evaluated (Pentz, 2003).

Existing evidence supports the view that strategies such as early home visitation can be implemented with at-risk families and, when well implemented, this strategy can result in a variety of relevant early intervention outcomes. In many countries there are opportunities for drug treatment services to cooperate with other service providers to ensure quality programmes are targeted to all mothers experiencing drug use and mental health problems.

There are demonstrations that investment in the years prior to school entry may be important for ensuring healthy development and the fuller realisation of learning potential. Efforts to reform early school environments in the LIFT programme and the Seattle Social Development Project raise the interesting prospect that outcomes for the most disadvantaged children are greatly influenced by broader support and understanding within the school environment. Future research should investigate the possibility that programmes of this type might contribute to population-level improvements in child development outcomes when delivered on a large scale outside the research context.

Considerable progress has been made in the past decade in the identification and evaluation of strategies that can successfully prevent patterns of adolescent drug use associated with later harms. Research in future years should continue to focus on both innovations to expand the range of strategies and also evaluation to advance the level of evidence for existing strategies.

ACKNOWLEDGEMENTS

This chapter is based on a previous report (Loxley et al., 2004).

REFERENCES

Aos, S., Barnoski, R. and Lee, R. (1998) Preventive programs for young offenders: effective and cost-effective. *Overcrowded Times*, **9**(2), 1–11.

Arthur, M.W. and Blitz, C. (2000) Bridging the gap between science and practice in drug abuse prevention through needs assessment and strategic community planning. *Journal of Community Psychology*, **28**(3), 241–255.

Bauman, K.E., Foshee, V.A., Ennett, S.T., Pemberton, M., Hicks, K.A., King, T.S., and Koch, G.G. (2001) The influence of a family program on adolescent tobacco and alcohol use. *American Journal of Public Health*, **91**(4), 604–610.

Bry, B.H., Catalano, R.F., Kumpfer, K., Lochman, J.E., and Szapocznik, J. (1998) Scientific findings from family prevention intervention research. In R.S. Ashery, E.B. Robertson, and K.L. Kumpfer (eds), *Drug Abuse Prevention through Family Interventions*. Rockville, MD: US Department of Human Services, National Institute on Drug Abuse, pp. 103–129.

Campbell, F. and Ramey, C. (1994) Effects of early intervention on intellectual and academic achievement: a follow-up study of children from low-income families. *Child Development*, **65**, 684–698.

Carroll, T., Lum, M., Taylor, J. and Travia, J. (2000) *Evaluation of the Launch Phase of the National Alcohol Campaign. Sydney*: Commonwealth Department of Health and Aged Care.

Catalano, R.F., Gainey, R.R., Fleming, C.B., Haggerty, K.P. and Johnson, N.O. (1999) An experimental intervention with families of substance abusers: one-year follow-up of the focus on families project. *Addiction*, **94**, 241–254.

Conduct Problems Prevention Research Group (2002) Evaluation of the first three years of the Fast Track prevention trial with children at high-risk for adolescent conduct problems. *Journal of Abnormal Child Psychology*, **30**(1), 19–35.

Consortium for Longitudinal Studies (1983) *As the Twig is Bent: Lasting Effects of Pre-school Programmes*. Hillsdale: NJ: Erlbaum.

Cunningham, P.B. and Henggeler, S.W. (1999) Engaging multiproblem families in treatment: lessons learned throughout the development of Multisystemic Therapy. *Family Process*, **38**, 265–281.

Eddy, J.M., Reid, J.B. and Fetrow, R.A. (2000) An elementary school-based prevention program targeting modifiable antecedents of youth delinquency and violence: linking the interests of families and teachers (LIFT). *Journal of Emotional and Behavioral Disorders*, **8**(3), 165–176.

Forster, J.L., Murray, D.M., Wolfson, M., Blaine, T.M., Wagenaar, A.C. and Hennrikus, D.J. (1998) The effects of community policies to reduce youth access to tobacco. *American Journal of Public Health*, **88**, 1193–1198.

Godfrey, C., Toumbourou, J.W., Rowland, B., Hemphill, S. and Munro, G. (2002) *Drug Education Approaches in Primary Schools*. Technical Report 4. South Melbourne: Australian Drug Foundation, Drug Info Clearinghouse. pp. 1–14.

Hallfors, D. and Godette, D. (2002) Will the "principles of effectiveness" improve prevention practice? Early findings from a diffusion study. *Health Education Research*, **17**(4), 461–470.

Hawkins, J.D., Guo, J., Hill, K., Battin-Pearson, S. and Abbott, R. (2001) Long term effects of the Seattle Social Development intervention on school bonding trajectories. In J. Maggs and J. Schulenberg (eds), *Applied Developmental Science*. Special issue: *Prevention as Altering the Course of Development*, **5**(4), 225–236.

Holder, H.D., Saltz, R.F., Grube, J.W., Treno, A.J., Reynolds, R.I., Voas, R.B. and Gruenewald, P.J. (1997) Summing up: lessons from a comprehensive community prevention trial. *Addiction*, **92**(2), 293–301.

Johnson, C.A., Pentz, M.A., Weber, M.D., Dwyer, J.H., Baer, N., MacKinnon, D.P., Hansen, W.B. and Flay, B.R. (1990) Relative effectiveness of comprehensive community programming for drug abuse prevention with high-risk and low-risk adolescents. *Journal of Consulting and Clinical Psychology*, **58**(4), 447–456.

Loxley, W., Toumbourou, J.W., Stockwell, T., Haines, B., Scott, K., Godfrey, C., Waters, E., Patton, G., Fordham, R., Gray, D., Marshall, J., Ryder, D., Saggers, S., Sanci, L. and Williams, J. (2004) *The Prevention of Substance Use, Risk and Harm in Australia: A Review of the Evidence*. Perth, WA: National Drug Research Institute and the Centre for Adolescent Health.

Mitchell, P., Spooner, C., Copeland, J., Vimpani, G., Toumbourou, J.W., Howard, J., and Sanson, A. (2001) *A Literature Review of the Role of Families in the Development, Identification, Prevention and Treatment of Illicit Drug Problems*. Melbourne: Commonwealth of Australia.

Olds, D.L., Henderson, C.R., Kitzman, H.J., Eckenrode, J.J., Cole, R.E. and Tatelbaum, R.C. (1999) Prenatal and infancy home visitation by nurses: recent findings. *The Future of Children*, **9**(1), 44–65.

Pentz, M.A. (2003) Evidence-based prevention: characteristics, impact, and future direction. *Journal of Psychoactive Drugs*, **35**(Suppl, no. 1), 143–152.

Perry, C.L., Williams, C.L., Veblen-Mortenson, S., Toomey, T.L., Komro, K.A., Anstine, P.S., Mc-Govern, P.G., Finnegan, J.R., Forster, J.L., Wagenaar, A.C., and Wolfson, M. (1996) Project Northland: outcomes of a communitywide alcohol use prevention program during early adolescence. *American Journal of Public Health*, **86**(7), 956–965.

Robbins, M.S., Alexander, J.F., Newell, R.M. and Turner, C.W. (1996) The immediate effect of reframing on client attitude in family therapy. *Journal of Family Psychology*, **10**(1), 28–34.

Sanders, M.R., Markie-Dadds, C., Tully, L. and Bor, W. (2000) The Triple P-Positive Parenting program: a comparison of enhanced standard, and self directed behavioral family intervention. *Journal of Consulting and Clinical Psychology*, **68**(4), 624–640.

Schweinhart, L.J. and Weikart, D.P. (1993) Success by empowerment: the high/scope Perry preschool study through age 27. *Young Children*, **49**, 54–58.

Spoth, R.L., Guyll, M. and Day, S.X. (2002) Universal family-focused interventions in alcohol-use disorder prevention: cost-effectiveness and cost-benefit analyses of two interventions. *Journal of Studies on Alcohol*, **63**(2), 219–228.

Stevens, M.M., Freeman, D.H., Mott, L. and Youells, F. (1996) Three-year results of prevention programs on marijuana use: the New Hampshire study. *Journal of Drug Education*, **26**(3), 257–273.

Toumbourou, J.W. and Gregg, M.E. (2002) Impact of an empowerment-based parent education program on the reduction of youth suicide risk factors. *Journal of Adolescent Health*, **31**(3), 279–287.

Toumbourou, J.W., Patton, G., Sawyer, S., Olsson, C., Web-Pullman, J., Catalano, R. and Godfrey, C. (2000) *Evidence-Based Interventions for Promoting Adolescent Health*. Melbourne: Centre for Adolescent Health.

3.3 The Evidence Base for School Drug Education Interventions

NYANDA McBRIDE

National Drug Research Institute, Curtin University of Technology, Australia

SUMMARY

In this chapter, school drug education refers to the use of a sequenced health curriculum delivered in classrooms with the specific aim of reducing levels of student drug use and/or related harm. School drug education is a developing field and this chapter outlines methods for improving practice and research. Results of school drug education studies, with a behavioural orientation, report success in the short to medium term; however, these findings are limited to a small number of the total research studies conducted. There is an extensive amount of drug education activity that occurs in the school setting, but unfortunately much of this activity remains unevaluated and therefore contributes little to development of the field. Findings from a recent systematic review have identified several essential ingredients for future programmes to enhance behavioural effectiveness as well as identifying areas for further research. In summary, programmes can be improved by: adopting adequate research design; encouraging programme planners to adopt a formative phase of development that involves talking to young people and testing the intervention with young people and teachers; providing the programme at relevant periods in young people's development; ensuring programmes are interactive and based on skill development; setting behaviour change goals that are relevant and inclusive of all young people; including booster sessions in later years; including information that is of immediate practical use to young people; including appropriate teacher training for interactive delivery of the programme; making effective programmes widely available; and adopting marketing strategies that increase the exposure of effective programmes. These improvements to school drug education research and programme development cannot occur in isolation to the practical implementation of programmes at the school level. Identification of barriers and strategies that lead to effective drug education are important. Evidence-based implementation and practice research will enhance this development and reinforce school drug education as an important strategy in a community approach for dealing with youth drug issues. Public investment in school drug education should be accompanied by both research expenditure to improve practice and by adequate training to ensure quality standards are met.

Preventing Harmful Substance Use: The Evidence Base for Policy and Practice.
Edited by T. Stockwell, P. J. Gruenewald, J. W. Toumbourou and W. Loxley.
© 2005 John Wiley & Sons, Ltd. ISBN 0-470-09227-0 (hbk) 0-470-09228-9 (pbk).

INTRODUCTION

In this chapter, school drug education refers to the use of a sequenced health curriculum delivered in classrooms with the specific aim of reducing levels of student drug use or related problems. School drug education can be a controversial field, arousing debate as to its underlying goals and potential benefits. Health professionals typically identify school drug education as a means of encouraging behaviour change in young people. In contrast, education practitioners often conceptualise drug education as an aspect of the school curriculum that aims to academically advance students while enhancing personal development. While these different philosophies need not be mutually exclusive, neither stance on its own captures the full complexity of school drug education.

This chapter provides a summary of recommendations for practice based on the best evidence from past research. Research is considered essential to identify critical components that can contribute to successful implementation, and to increase the prospects of achieving student development and behaviour change goals. Some of the key research and practice issues that may impact on meeting current recommendations are then discussed along with other issues that may assist in the future development of the drug education field.

SYSTEMATIC LITERATURE REVIEW OF SCHOOL DRUG EDUCATION

This section summarises the methodology and findings from a recent systematic review of school drug education research literature adopting a behavioural or health orientation (McBride, 2002). This systematic review involved a review of previous reviews (1990–June 2001) and a review of recent primary studies (1997–June 2001) to ensure that historical and recent findings of the field were represented.

There were several criteria for accepting past reviews: such that a review was comprehensive with clear search strategies, selection, inclusion and appraisal criteria; a review encompassed the school setting and student group as a primary focus; a review included classroom drug education; it was published in 1990 or later; and it provided appropriate guidelines determining inclusion of studies.

Details from accepted reviews were systematically recorded to assess quality and content. The reference lists of review articles were also systematically searched for any further publications/reports that were not identified through the electronic databases. These documents were then accessed and the above criteria applied.

Recent primary studies were assessed for inclusion based on the following criteria: the study was inclusive of school-aged students in a school setting; it encompassed a classroom intervention; it included drug-related behavioural measures; it had a positive impact on students' drug-related behaviours; and it adopted adequate study design and methodology. A cut-off date of 1997 was selected for these types of publications, as the most recent comprehensive review of school drug education effectiveness included studies to 1997. As with the reviews, reference lists of the primary studies were systematically searched for any further publications or reports that were not previously accessed and could be included in the systematic review.

A combination of key words were used to identify appropriate publications and searches were undertaken in 18 databases (McBride, 2002).

Reviews—1990 to June 2001

Based on the selection criteria, a total of 165 review articles were critically analysed, and 19 were accepted. Eleven of these publications met all selection criteria and were defined as first-level reviews, the remaining second-level reviews were of good quality, met most of the selection criteria but focused on studies with one topic or from one jurisdiction. Second-level reviews were only accepted if they had a publication date on or after 1995. Reviews accepted for the systematic literature list appear in the reference list of this chapter and are indicated by an asterisk (* = first-level review, ** = second-level review).

Nine of the first-level reviews concluded that school drug education can have a consistent positive impact on behaviour (Hansen, 1992; Tobler, 1992; Bruvold, 1993; Stead et al., 1996; Tobler, 1997; Tobler and Stratton, 1997; White and Pitts, 1997; White and Pitts, 1998; Tobler et al., 1999). The other two first-level reviews resulted in mixed findings (Sharp, 1994, Foxcroft et al., 1997).

Three of the second-level reviews concluded that school drug education can have a positive impact on behaviour (Dusenbury and Falco, 1995; Dusenbury et al., 1997; Paglia and Room, 1998). Two second-level reviews concluded that school drug education had a mixed impact on behaviour (positive or nil effect) (Lloyd et al., 2000; Stothard and Ashton, 2000). Three other second-level reviews, all of which assessed a specific approach to school drug education, found limited effect (Gorman, 1995; Gorman, 1996; Flay, 2000).

Primary studies—1997 to June 2001

The total number of recent primary study publications revealed during electronic data base searches, and the scanning of reference lists of previously accessed papers, totalled 69 papers representing 65 programmes. The total number of primary studies accepted into this review based on the above mentioned criteria was five (7.7%), two of which were of the same programme. There were multiple reasons for the rejection of the remaining 60 studies (McBride, 2002). Primary studies accepted for this systematic literature review are documented in the reference list and indicated by a cross (× = main group or whole population effect, ×× = sub-group effect e.g., effect for higher risk youth only).

Three primary studies reported main group effects and each required intervention over a number of years. Two of these programmes were classroom-based and one was a comprehensive school/community programme. One of the classroom programmes demonstrated main effects for three behavioural domains including level of alcohol consumption, level of harmful and hazardous consumption, and harm associated with own use of alcohol (McBride et al., 2000). This Australian study had an explicit goal of harm minimisation. The other classroom programme adopted an abstinence goal but also measured alcohol-related misuse in addition to use and delayed use. This programme, conducted in the USA, demonstrated a main effect on an alcohol misuse scale (Maggs and Schulenberg, 1998). The comprehensive programme demonstrated a main effect for the measurement items of past month and past week alcohol use (Williams et al., 1999). This USA programme had a general drug focus and also adopted an abstinence goal.

Two classroom-based studies demonstrated sub-group effects (for example, the programme was effective with males, high-risk groups, etc. rather than the whole study group). Both programmes were drug-specific, classroom-based, and focused on prevention. The project conducted in the Netherlands focused on preventing smoking (Dijkstra et al., 1999) and the other from the USA focused on preventing alcohol use (Shope et al., 2001).

RECOMMENDATIONS FOR DRUG EDUCATION PRACTICE FLOWING FROM THIS REVIEW

To fully understand the background and intention associated with the following summarised list of recommendations, readers should review the complete text of this systematic review (McBride, 2002).

Dissemination

Many programmes marketed and available to schools have no proven behavioural effectiveness. Generally, efficacious programmes, often generated within research organisations, are either not readily available or are not widely advertised to education practitioners. Researchers of effective programmes need to be skilled in dissemination and marketing techniques, while funding and policies need to ensure that effective programmes are easily transferred from researchers to practitioners. Efforts to encourage a greater interchange between research and practitioners could help to ensure the inclusion and evaluation of components likely to be efficacious in culturally adapted drug education programmes. Curriculum planners should be provided with the skills to assess the quality of available programmes and question effectiveness when this information is not provided. Where there is evidence that programmes are efficacious, programme funding should include requirements for quality assurance to ensure effective programme components are delivered well.

Timing and Programming Considerations

Information about timing and programming issues suggests several areas for attention which can be summarised in two general categories. First, it is clear that programmes are more likely to succeed if they take into account student experiences and needs (Dusenbury and Falco, 1995; White and Pitts, 1998; Tobler et al., 1999; Williams et al., 1999; McBride et al., 2004). In particular, programme content should be based on the drug use experiences of the students, assessed using local prevalence data, and should capture young people's interests by incorporating their experiences in the goals, content and scenarios of the programme. These recommendations require information to be provided prior to curriculum planning and pilot testing with formative evaluation prior to full programme implementation. Second, the review finds that drug education is best taught within the health component of the school curriculum, with emphasis on classroom programmes, reinforced at critical times over several years. This recommendation requires teachers or health education curriculum managers to critically analyse the sequencing of programmes in curriculum planning. Further research is needed to establish whether there are benefits in extending drug education beyond classroom curriculum to incorporate additional areas such as parental and policy components.

Content and Delivery

The content and delivery area would benefit from more research due to the extensive but largely ineffective use of methods and foci developed from the US experience (Stothard and Ashton, 2000). There are some content and delivery factors from the dominating Life Skills Training programme and Social Influence approaches that have added value to programmes such as the use of normative components, interaction between peers, and teacher training. However, the evaluations of these programmes have revealed conflicting results and problems in research methodologies that weaken any claim for delivering these programmes in their entirety (McBride, 2002). Research is also required to clarify the contribution that resistance skills training can make to school drug education programmes. Other issues are becoming clear as research progresses, including the benefits of encouraging a high level of interaction between students and the use of utility knowledge (i.e., knowledge that is directly related to skill development or performance) (Tobler, 1997; Tobler and Stratton, 1997; Maggs and Schulenberg, 1998; Dijkstra et al., 1999; Tobler et al., 1999; Williams et al., 1999; Shope et al., 2001; McBride et al., 2004). Skill development will become even more important as alternatives to abstinence, such as harm minimisation, are further developed. Other content and delivery factors need more research to identify the importance of their role in drug education. For example, there is debate as to whether using peer leaders in classroom drug education increases effectiveness. Additionally, evidence points to multi-drug or general drug education programmes during primary school years with single content programmes in secondary school (Tobler et al., 1999); however, this placement should be guided by local prevalence data (White and Pitts, 1997; Maggs and Schulenberg, 1998; Shope et al., 2001; McBride et al., 2004).

Teacher Training/Skills of Teacher/Facilitator

Teacher training is critical to the successful delivery of school drug education (Sharp, 1994; Dusenbury and Falco, 1995; Tobler and Stratton, 1997; Maggs and Schulenberg, 1998; Dijkstra et al., 1999; Tobler et al., 1999; Williams et al., 1999; Shope et al., 2001; McBride et al., 2004). Training should encourage interactive classroom teaching and should be reinforced in later years. There may be advantages in interactively modelling activities to enable teachers to participate in and review the activity to ensure effective transfer to the classroom. Other areas of teacher training require further research to clarify the effectiveness, for example, the impact of general pre-service training in drug education skills and methodologies.

CONTEXTUAL AND PRACTICAL ISSUES THAT MAY IMPACT ON EFFECTIVE SCHOOL DRUG EDUCATION

There are numerous contextual and practical issues which impinge on drug education research and practice. These issues go above and beyond those identified in the above systematic review, and can have an important impact on the effectiveness of school drug education. The following section attempts to capture some of these issues and the nuances associated with them.

Drug Education Research

There is debate, particularly within research circles, about the value of school drug education as a public health/health education strategy. However, results from a limited number of school drug education studies with a behavioural orientation report implementation success and student behaviour change in the short to medium term. Well-controlled studies have demonstrated that school drug education has the potential to delay the age at which students initiate drug use, to reduce the number who progress to frequent or high amounts of use and to reduce associated harms (Maggs and Schulenberg, 1998; Dijkstra et al., 1999; McBride et al., 2004). The capacity of studies to demonstrate behaviour change has been particularly true where programmes have been evidence-based, delivered as part of a research project, and where most of the components were delivered as intended. However, such studies are limited to a small proportion of the total research that has been conducted. There are several reasons for this, with three key reasons including: (1) problems with design and methodology that raise uncertainties about results; (2) limited inclusion of behavioural measures; and (3) when behavioural measures have been included, only a limited range of behaviours have been measured. These three dimensions of school drug education research are discussed in more detail below. Each of these limitations, however, can be rectified in future drug education research and should be seen as potential areas for improvement to increase knowledge and a greater likelihood of achieving successful behaviour change.

Design and methodology problems

In the present review only 7.7% of all primary studies conducted between 1997 and June 2001 were accepted (McBride, 2002). This low acceptance rate was largely due to limitations in research and evaluation design and methodology. Other systematic reviews have reported similar low rates of acceptance for similar reasons (Foxcroft et al., 1997). However, the problem seems to be slowly resolving. A recent systematic review by Foxcroft and colleagues of alcohol misuse in young people (many of which were school-based programmes) indicated that there was an increase of 40% in studies with acceptable evaluation, compared to their previous review conducted five years earlier (Foxcroft et al., 2003). Although this is a promising finding, most accepted studies on which current knowledge is based are from research institutions, and the vast number of other evaluations conducted in school settings continue to provide limited value for the development of the field due to evaluation weaknesses.

Limited behavioural assessment

On a similar note, most evaluations of programmes conducted by outside research organisations do not include measures of behavioural impact. Between 1978 and 1990 only 36% of all research and evaluation included measures of behaviour (Tobler and Stratton, 1997). More recently, between 1998 to 2001, 41.5% of evaluations included behaviour change (McBride, 2002). This small increase over time continues to limit the field, for in health terms, it is only by increasing our understandings about how components of school drug education can contribute to behaviour change that the field can continue to develop.

Limited behavioural measures

The third issue concerns the limited range of behaviours generally measured by studies incorporating behavioural assessment. Research from the USA has dominated the field with approximately 84% of all acceptable behavioural studies drawn from the American experience (Foxcroft et al., 2003). The USA has a national drug policy of non-use and delayed use for young people, and research funded from this policy has limited scope to measure alternative drug-related behaviours such as reducing the level or pattern of use and reducing alcohol-related harms. In effect, only a limited range of the potential behaviour change targets have been investigated within the school drug education field. Other countries are more flexible in their policies and in some cases have adopted a harm minimisation philosophy.

This increases the potential number of behavioural measures that can be assessed, thereby increasing the potential to identify success. However, countries with a more flexible approach have generally invested little in behavioural research. The expansion of research to include other drug-related behaviours, such as the reduction of severity of drug use or related harm, is still in its infancy, although early studies are promising. For example, a recent harm minimisation alcohol education programme reported similar consumption and delayed use effects to well-considered abstinence-based programmes, but with the added advantage of medium to long term (17 months post-programme) harm reduction effects (McBride et al., 2004). Such programmes need to be replicated to assist in refining our focus and in developing the field.

Behavioural expectations for school drug education

In the past, research has frequently identified that delayed use and non-use effects decay once implementation is complete. This leads us to consider appropriate and acceptable expectations of the field. The presumption that school drug education should or could have a continued effect after young people leave school, or even after the immediate delivery of a programme, needs to be questioned. Reviewers such as Foxcroft et al., (2003) cite quality drug education studies where outcomes were maintained as long as three years following drug education programme exposure. This evidence demonstrates that drug education has the capacity for longer-term impacts. However, do drug education programmes really need to be tested on this criterion to justify their value? As young people leave school they are generally exposed to less parental influence, have more disposable income, are drawn to public venues for social activity, and in terms of alcohol, are starting to reach legal age. Logically, then, the impact of school drug education programmes should be expected to decrease once young people are no longer exposed to school programmes. Other strategies are required to maintain behaviour change effects as young people leave school and are exposed to a new context and range of new experiences. This does not reduce the usefulness of school drug education as a prevention strategy, but rather acknowledges that it can provide a period of impact, which may reduce use and problems, at a time when use and experimentation are high. Recent evidence also suggests that level of alcohol use during secondary school is one predictor of level of use as young people reach their twenties, suggesting some possible, but as yet unmeasured, continuation of effects over time (Toumbourou et al., 2004). School drug education is probably best seen as one strategy within a whole community response to drugs and young people. Singularly, it is unlikely to hold all the answers and logic tells us that frameworks such as Holder's (1989) model for prevention of drug-related problems, which target several settings and types of intervention over the lifetime, are much more likely to reduce problems and benefit the community. We therefore may need to refine our expectations of school drug education to take into account the progression and transition of adolescents to young adults, their changing context and its relationship to drug use, while keeping in mind appropriate frameworks, and evidence-based programmes for dealing with drug-related issues over an extended period. Schools are just one part of this process.

Improvements in practice and implications for research

As the use of effective drug education programmes proliferates within schools, drug education research is faced with increasing difficulty in establishing appropriate comparison groups. Researchers generally contrast intervention groups against comparison groups of students who participate in existing programmes, many of which are considered best practice by education practitioners. As programmes improve and become widely available, more education practitioners are likely to use evidence-based resources. The difference between these and newly developed research programmes will be less distinct, perhaps comparing small changes within similar programmes. Comparisons between these programmes may have advantages in helping to clarify the contribution of specific components, but may also find it more difficult to demonstrate significant differences. Researchers should assess and report drug education activities in control conditions when analysing and reporting findings to enrich the comparisons that can be made between interventions. Additionally, this issue will need to be taken into consideration when interpreting and discussing the potential impact and value of school drug education as a strategy within a community response to drug issues.

Drug Education Practice

There is an extensive amount of drug education activity that occurs in the school setting; however, much of this activity remains unevaluated and therefore contributes little to the development of the field. There are several reasons for a lack of impact evaluation but often this issue is constrained by the education philosophy of school drug education. Generally, the education sector views school drug education as contributing to the development of the individual by enhancing the connection that young people have to education and the community, and by reinforcing messages from parents and the wider community (Commonwealth Department of Education, Science and Training, 1999) rather than on specific drug-related behavioural outcomes.

There is often little evaluation evidence that these educational objectives can be achieved, and if evaluation is undertaken it is likely to be process-oriented, providing limited information on success in meeting the stated educational aims, and with no information about health impact. The barriers to introducing effective evaluation are several including limited financial resources to undertake effective evaluations, lack of evaluation skills among staff, limited time, and poor linkages with organisations which can assist in conducting effective evaluations. Providing the means to encourage and assist in impact evaluation of programmes would certainly benefit the field by providing information from a wider range of programmes to inform future directions.

In addition to the ideology and evaluation debate, the practical application of drug education in schools needs to be given some consideration. In particular, there are challenges to determine the extensiveness of school drug education required to ensure effectiveness, the types of programmes that should be available to schools, and strategies to address the low status of health/drug education in the education sector. Each of these issues is considered below.

The extensiveness of school drug education

In recent years there has been a trend towards school programmes that involve more than the classroom component. Other components may include policy, staff development, school environment, parental involvement, and local community involvement. To date, there is little behavioural evidence to indicate whether this broad approach is successful. However, the curriculum component is widely acknowledged as critical to success largely because it involves direct interaction with students. Inherent to this success is staff training. There is also some evidence supportive of parental involvement. Education organisations and schools currently face the challenge of deciding whether or not to implement broad school programmes. As was argued above, it would be useful to base decisions in this area on components that are critical to behavioural success. However, it would also be necessary to consider costs, available expertise and time constraints which would determine a school's ability to effectively implement broader components. For example, research suggests that schools often find it hard to attract parents or have a limited core group of parents who are involved in school activity. As such, alternative settings may offer better opportunities to attract and maintain a higher level of parental involvement. An extensive amount of research is still required to provide clarity on the range of activities schools can undertake towards reducing youth drug use problems.

Types of programmes available to schools

Schools continually have demands placed on them to include additional programmes and subjects within an already crowded curriculum. This issue is one that cannot be ignored if effective drug education programmes are to be implemented. Practical difficulties arise when findings from the drug education research literature promote, for example, the use of drug specific programmes for secondary school-aged students. This means that to be effective across a number of drug types, schools need to provide several programmes and this is unlikely to be practical or possible. As was argued above, one solution may involve schools basing their selection of programmes on behavioural surveys of their student population and focusing content on those drugs which have a high level of prevalence and harm. A research programme which looks at generic harm reduction skills may also be a future area of focus that goes some way to answering timetabling demands. Whatever the future of drug education research and practice, it is important to base work on evidence and balance that with the practicalities of implementing programmes in schools.

Recently, there have been some moves by education authorities to adopt evidence-based principles for school drug education. These principles tend to provide guidelines for general programming and implementation rather than providing or promoting specific evidence based programmes. Inherent to, and a strength of this approach, is the provision of information on how to select evidence-based programmes while ensuring schools have the flexibility to make choices that best suit their circumstances and students. Unfortunately, the weakness in evidence-based principles for school drug education is that the underlying evidence is often modified with non-evidence-based material supportive of educational philosophy, reducing clarity of focus and potentially undermining effectiveness. The process towards evidence-based practice is beneficial to the field in that it provides a starting point from which further awareness is generated and action can be taken. However, ensuring that the evidence-based guidelines incorporate education philosophy without loss of effectiveness is critical to their success.

The low status of school drug education

A further challenge for efforts to enhance school drug education is the low status of health education, the subject under which drug education usually resides. This low status often sees drug/health education classes allocated to inappropriate classrooms, untrained and or unwilling teachers required to teach the subject, and limited timetable flexibility. These and other factors reduce the potential impact of school drug education and can only be addressed through a comprehensive programme of change. Recently in Australia, drug education information sessions with administrators and teachers resulted in schools adopting drug education as a priority issue for the school. When a subject is a priority issue, it receives whole school attention and the barriers associated with low status are removed. Strategies to provide such sessions may be one of the practical considerations generated to overcome the low status barrier. This and other practicalities of providing drug education in a school setting need to be adequately addressed before drug education can be widely promoted as a meaningful part of a school programme.

CONCLUSION

There are several considerations that result from this analysis of school drug education. First, the different philosophies adopted by the education and health sectors have been a barrier to the field. The conflict between behaviourally effective programmes promoted by health and research academics and the cognitive and social skills approaches prevailing in the education sector can be overcome, and there are examples of this occurring. However, an extensive amount of work, at several levels, will need to be undertaken before change is likely to occur on a large scale. Proactive interchanges need to be formalised and developed. Perhaps the most effective starting point is to bring together decision-makers from education and health settings to generate effective strategies for integrating research and educational practice. Ultimately, however, the focus should be on what is of most benefit for young people. If a programme with educational goals can also positively impact on a disruptive social behaviour and reduce negative outcomes for young people, then a disservice may be done when such programmes are not provided.

Second, while earlier systematic examinations of school drug education programmes have reported mixed success and even negative results, there are now a number of rigorously conducted and evaluated programmes with meaningful behavioural effects that can lead the way for the future. Regular updates of systematic reviews ensuring that new information is readily available for incorporation will be critical as new effective programmes are developed. However, these improvements to school drug education research and programme development cannot occur in isolation to the practical implementation of programmes at the school level. Identification of implementation barriers and strategies to overcome these barriers to effective drug education in schools are just as important as testing and making such programmes readily available to schools.

Finally, it is clear that school drug education is a developing field and that continued modification and refinement are required for it to reach its full potential. Evidence-based implementation and research will enhance this development, and as is already occurring, will reinforce school drug education as an important strategy in a community approach to dealing with youth drug issues. The development of new understandings about school drug education can only assist in ensuring that the field contributes at an optimal level to a community response to drug issues and young people.

ACKNOWLEDGEMENTS

Many thanks to Susan Carruthers for her comments and suggestions on earlier drafts of this chapter.

REFERENCES

Note: *, **, × and ×× indicate that the review was used in the literature review. See text for details.

Bruvold, W. (1993) A meta-analysis of adolescent smoking prevention programs. *American Journal of Public Health*, **83**(6), 872–880.*

Commonwealth Department of Education, Science and Training (1999) *National School Drug Education Strategy.* Available online: http://www.detya.gov.au/archive/schools/publications/1999/strategy.htm (accessed October 2003).

Dijkstra, M., Mesters, I., De Vries, H., Van Breukelen, G. and Parcel, G. (1999) Effectiveness of a social influence approach and boosters to smoking prevention. *Health Education Research*, **14**(6), 791–802.××

Dusenbury, L. and Falco, M. (1995) Eleven components of effective drug abuse prevention curricula. *Journal of School Health*, **65**(10), 420–431.**

Dusenbury, L., Falco, M. and Lake, A. (1997) A review of the evaluation of 47 drug abuse prevention curricula available nationally. *Journal of School Health*, **67**(4), 127–131.**

Flay, B. (2000) Approaches to substance use prevention utilising school curriculum plus social environment change. *Addictive Behaviours*, **25**(6) 861–886.**

Foxcroft, D., Ireland, D., Lister-Sharp, D., Lowe, G. and Breen R. (2003) Longer-term primary prevention for alcohol misuse in young people: a systematic review. Paper presented at International Research Symposium. Preventing substance use, risky use and harm: What is evidence based policy? 24–27 February, Fremantle, Western Australia.

Foxcroft, D., Lister-Sharp, D. and Lowe, G. (1997) Alcohol misuse prevention for young people: a systematic review reveals methodological concerns and lack of reliable evidence of effectiveness. *Addiction*, **92**(5), 531–538.*

Gorman, D. (1995) Are school based resistant skills training programs effective in preventing alcohol misuse? *Journal of Alcohol and Drug Education*, **41**(1), 74–98.**

Gorman, D. (1996) Do school-based social skills training programs prevent alcohol use among young people? *Addiction Research*, **4**(2), 191–210.*

Hansen, B. (1992) School based substance abuse prevention: a review of the state of the art in curriculum, 1980–1990. *Health Education Research: Theory and Practice*, **7**(3), 403–430.*

Holder, H. (1989) Prevention of alcohol related problems. *Alcohol Health and Research World*, **14**(4), 339–342.

Lloyd, C., Joyce, R., Hurry, J. and Ashton, M. (2000) The effectiveness of primary school drug education. *Drugs, Education, Prevention and Policy*, **7**(2), 109–126.**

Maggs, J. and Schulenberg, J. (1998) Reasons to drink and not to drink: altering trajectories of drinking through an alcohol misuse prevention program. *Applied Developmental Science*, **2**(1), 48–60.×

McBride, N. (2002) *Systematic Literature Review of the School Drug Education.* Monograph No 5. Perth, Western Australia: National Drug Research Institute.

McBride, N., Farringdon, F., Midford, R., Meuleners, L. and Phillips, M. (2004) Harm minimisation in schools: final results of the School Health and Alcohol Harm Reduction Project (SHAHRP). *Addiction*, **99**, 278–291.

McBride, N., Midford, R., Farringdon, F., Phillips, M. (2000) Early results from a school alcohol harm minimisation study: the School Health and Alcohol Harm Reduction Project. *Addiction*, **95**(7), 1021–1042.×

Paglia, A. and Room, R. (1998) *Preventing Substance Use Problems among Youth: Literature Review and Recommendations.* Ontario: Addiction Research Foundation and Addiction and Mental Health Services Corporation.**

Sharp, C. (1994) *Alcohol Education for Young People: A Review of the Literature from 1983–1992.* National Foundation for Education Research.*

Shope, J., Elliott, M., Raghunathan, T. and Waller, P. (2001) Long term follow-up of a high school Alcohol Misuse Prevention Program's effect on students subsequent driving. *Alcoholism: Clinical and Experimental Research*, **25**(3), 403–410.××

Stead, M., Hastings, G. and Tudor-Smith, C. (1996) Preventing adolescent smoking: a review of options. *Health Education Journal*, **55**, 31–54.*

Stothard, B. and Ashton, M. (2000) Education's uncertain saviour. *Drug and Alcohol Findings*, **3**(4–7), 16–20.**

Tobler, N. (1992) Drug prevention programs can work: research findings. *Journal of Addictive Diseases*, **11**(3), 1–28.*

Tobler, N. (1997) Meta analysis of adolescent drug prevention programs: results of the 1993 meta analysis. In W. Bukoski (ed.), *Meta Analysis of Drug Abuse Prevention Programs*. Rockville MD: NIDA.*

Tobler, N. and Stratton, H. (1997) Effectiveness of school based drug prevention programs: a meta-analysis of the research. *Journal of Primary Prevention*, **18**(1), 71–128.*

Tobler, N., Lessard, T., Marshall, D., Ochshorn, P. and Roona, M. (1999) Effectiveness of school-based drug prevention programs for marijuana use. *School Psychology International*, **20**(1), 105–137.*

Toumbourou, J., Williams, I., White, V., Snow, P., Munro, G. and Schofield, R. (2004) Prediction of alcohol-related harm from controlled drinking strategies and alcohol consumption trajectories. *Addiction*, **99**(4), 498–508.

White, D. and Pitts, M. (1997) *Health Promotion with Young People for the Prevention of Substance Misuse*. University of York, York: NHS Centre for Reviews and Dissemination.*

White, D. and Pitts, M. (1998) Educating young people about drugs: a systematic review. *Addiction*, **93**(10), 1475–1487.*

Williams, C., Perry, C., Farbakhsh, K. and Veblen-Mortenson, S. (1999) Project Northlands: comprehensive alcohol use prevention for young adolescents, their parents, schools, peers and communities. *Journal of Studies on Alcohol*, **13**, 112–124.×

3.4 Alcohol Policy and Youth Drinking: Overview of Effective Interventions for Young People

JOEL W. GRUBE AND PETER NYGAARD

Prevention Research Center, Berkeley, CA, USA

SUMMARY

Alcohol policy refers to (1) formal legal and regulatory mechanisms, rules, and procedures for reducing the consumption of alcohol or risky drinking behaviors; and (2) enforcement of these measures. Policy approaches to preventing and reducing drinking and drinking problems among youth have traditionally focused on limiting access to alcohol or on direct deterrence of young drinkers or those who supply alcohol to them. The aim of such policies is to increase the "full price" of alcohol to young people by increasing resources necessary for them to obtain it or the potential costs for possessing or consuming it. More recently, policies have begun to focus on harm reduction. Harm reduction policies attempt to prevent or reduce alcohol problems by targeting heavy drinking, drinking in risky situations, or by moderating the relationship between drinking and problem outcomes, without necessarily affecting overall consumption.

Based on the available evidence, the most effective policies appear to be: (1) taxation or price increases; (2) increases in the minimum drinking age; (3) zero tolerance; and (4) graduated licensing. Random breath testing, sobriety check points, and dram shop liability appear promising for reducing drinking and drinking problems based on studies with the general population, although there is less evidence for their effectiveness specifically with young people. The evidence is growing for the effects of license restrictions (e.g., limiting outlet density or hours of sale). There is some support for responsible beverage service programs, particularly those that are mandated or motivated by reduction of liability. The evidence on advertising restrictions is conflicting. Evidence that designated driver and safe rides programs, warning labels, social host liability, and keg registration are effective strategies for preventing drinking or drinking problems among young people is lacking.

Overall, there is insufficient research to evaluate the effects of many alcohol policies on alcohol consumption or problems among young people. Such research should be conducted to inform policy and evaluate policies as they are implemented. Finally, it is

Preventing Harmful Substance Use: The Evidence Base for Policy and Practice.
Edited by T. Stockwell, P. J. Gruenewald, J. W. Toumbourou and W. Loxley.
© 2005 John Wiley & Sons, Ltd. ISBN 0-470-09227-0 (hbk) 0-470-09228-9 (pbk).

clear from the available research that policies cannot be effective unless accompanied by enforcement and by awareness on the part of the intended targets of the policy and enforcement efforts.

ALCOHOL POLICY AND YOUTH DRINKING: OVERVIEW OF EFFECTIVE INTERVENTIONS FOR YOUNG PEOPLE

Policy approaches to prevention have considerable promise for addressing the problems associated with drinking among young people. In general, two policy orientations to preventing and reducing alcohol-related problems among youth are commonly advocated: (1) the public health approach; and (2) the harm reduction approach. Based on the distribution of consumption model, *public health policies* attempt to reduce alcohol-related problems by targeting overall consumption in the population. The public health approach assumes that decreases in overall consumption lead to reductions in heavy consumption and in alcohol-related problems. Most public health policy approaches to reducing drinking among youth have focused on limiting access to alcohol and on deterring either young drinkers themselves or those who provide alcohol to them. The purpose of such policies is to increase the "full price" of alcohol to young people by increasing the resources necessary to obtain it or the potential costs for possessing or consuming it (Laixuthai and Chaloupka, 1993). Other public health policies rely on persuasion or education and attempt to increase perceptions of the negative consequences of possessing or consuming alcohol. Public health policies may also communicate norms to young people about the unacceptability of their drinking and to adults about the unacceptability of providing alcohol to them.

Harm reduction policies attempt to prevent alcohol problems by targeting heavy drinking, drinking in risky situations, or by moderating the relationship between drinking and problem outcomes, without necessarily affecting overall consumption. Some harm reduction policies rely on deterrence, but the focus of the deterrence is on specific problematic drinking behaviors (e.g., drinking and driving; intoxication). Other harm reduction policies attempt to provide the means for young people to avoid risky drinking situations (e.g., safe rides programs).

Although they are often presented as two distinct approaches to reducing and preventing youth alcohol problems, clearly distinguishing between public health and harm reduction policies is often difficult. Some public health policies may reduce heavy drinking or drinking in risky situations. Similarly, harm reduction policies may also lead to a decrease in overall consumption. In attempting to place policies into this typology, it is necessary to focus on the *primary* target of a specific policy. Hence, for the purpose of this chapter, focusing on youth, policies implemented to reduce availability of alcohol to young people or deter young people from drinking in order to reduce overall consumption are considered public health approaches. Policies specifically targeting risky drinking, drinking in risky situations, or drinking-related risky behaviors are considered harm reduction approaches.

Table 3.4.1 shows a list of selected alcohol policies that have been used to target youth drinking and drinking problems. This list is not inclusive of all such alcohol policies, but rather represents those that are commonly used or advocated or that have been evaluated. These policy interventions are organized in Table 3.4.1 according to whether they are

Table 3.4.1 Typology of alcohol policy measures targeting drinking and drinking problems among youth

Policy	Overall consumption	Heavy drinking	Risky situations
Public health policies			
Minimum legal drinking age (MLDA)	X		
Taxation (price)	X		
Monopoly	X		
Outlet density restrictions	X		
Hours of sale	X		
Alcohol advertising restrictions	X		
Harm reduction policies			
Zero tolerance			X
Graduated driver licensing (GDL)			X
Random breath testing (RBT)			X
Sobriety checkpoints			
Responsible beverage service (RBS)	X	X	[X]
Designated driver/safe rides programs			X
Dram shop liability	[X]	X	[X]
Social host liability	[X]	X	[X]
Warning labels			X
Keg registration	[X]	X	

Note: Xs in brackets denote secondary targets of policies.

primarily public health or harm reduction oriented. Table 3.4.1 also indicates whether each policy targets overall consumption, heavy (risky) consumption, or drinking in risky situations.

In addition to problems of distinguishing between public health and harm reduction policies, there is no consensus as to what constitutes alcohol policy. In this chapter, alcohol policy is used only to refer to (a) formal legal and regulatory mechanisms, rules, and procedures for reducing the consumption of alcohol or risky drinking behaviors; and (b) enforcement of these measures.

ALCOHOL POLICIES FOR REDUCING YOUTH DRINKING

This chapter reviews the literature on alcohol policies and alcohol consumption and problems among young people. Citations are limited to a few representative references in each policy area. Where possible, previous reviews are referenced. Otherwise, priority is given to intervention studies investigating effects of changes in policy using experimental, quasi-experimental, or time series designs. In a few cases where there is limited evidence, cross-sectional comparisons and descriptive studies are cited. Although numerous studies have investigated the effects of alcohol policies on drinking and drinking problems, considerably fewer focus on drinking and drinking problems among youth. Often the effectiveness of a policy for youth drinking is inferred from its impact on the general population. That is, it is assumed that a policy affecting the general population will produce similar effects among young people. This assumption may or may not hold. In some cases young people may be more susceptible to policy changes and in other cases they may be less susceptible. Table 3.4.2 summarizes the research evidence for the effectiveness of commonly advocated policy strategies aimed at youth.

PUBLIC HEALTH POLICIES

Minimum Legal Drinking Age

The available evidence strongly indicates that a higher minimum legal drinking age (MLDA) is associated with lower levels of drinking and drinking problems among young people. A recent review of 241 studies on MLDA in the United States concludes that higher drinking ages are associated with lower rates of drinking and driving (DUI), traffic crashes, and other mortality and morbidity (Wagenaar and Toomey, 2002). It has been estimated that raising MLDA age to 21 years in the USA reduced single vehicle night-time crashes involving young drivers by 11% to 16% at all levels of crash severity (e.g., Dee, 1999) and reduced alcohol-related crashes by as much as 19% (Voas et al., 2003). The existing studies on MLDA are predominantly from North America, most notably the USA. However, one review suggests that the relationship between legal drinking age and drinking and driving among youth may apply to other countries. This systematic review of 33 evaluations of minimum legal drinking age laws in the United States, Canada, and Australia reported a median decline of 16% in crash-related outcomes for the targeted age groups following passage of laws to increase the MLDA (Shults et al., 2001).

Taxation/Price

Numerous studies have focused on the impact of taxation or price on alcohol consumption and related problems. It has been estimated that increasing taxation on alcohol in the USA to keep pace with inflation would lead to a 19% reduction in heavy drinking by youth and a 6% reduction in high-risk drinking (Laixuthai and Chaloupka, 1993). International research confirms that alcohol price is related to consumption and alcohol-related problems among young people. Thus, for example, increases in price were found to reduce alcohol-related crashes in Canada (Adrian, Ferguson and Her, 2001). In contrast to these studies, however, recent research using longer time series, more contemporaneous data, and controlling for potentially confounding differences among states in the USA has found no evidence for the effects of taxation and price on alcohol consumption and alcohol-related traffic fatalities, either among youth or in the general population (Dee, 1999; Young and Likens, 2000).

Although taxation and price increases may be effective prevention strategies, price elasticities are not attributes of commodities and are moderated by social, environmental, and economic factors. As a result, the price sensitivity of alcohol may vary considerably across time, states, and countries, depending on drinking patterns and attitudes and on the presence of other alcohol policies. More recent studies, for example, suggest that the relations between taxes on alcohol and alcohol consumption and problems may have weakened in recent years in the USA, possibly because of the implementation of the age 21 MLDA and other alcohol policies (Young and Likens, 2000). In addition, price increases may lead to changes in patterns of consumption such as switching to less expensive beverages or purchasing

Table 3.4.2 Effectiveness of policies to reduce drinking and drinking problems among youth

Policy	Evidence for effectiveness	Generalizability
Public Health Policies		
Minimum drinking age	Strong evidence that increases in the minimum drinking age can have substantial effects reducing drinking and involvement in alcohol-related crashes among young people. Enforcement of underage sales and drinking laws is key to this policy option.	Evidence primarily from one country.
Taxation/price	Strong evidence that price increases are substantially related to reductions in youth drinking and drinking problems.	Evidence primarily from one country.
Monopoly	Weak evidence that removing state monopolies increases sales to and consumption by young people. Moderately strong evidence that removing monopolies increases consumption in the general population.	Evidence from a few countries.
Outlet density restrictions	Moderately strong evidence that increased outlet density increases drinking problems (DUI) among young people. Mixed evidence that increased outlet density is related to increased drinking and drinking problems in the overall population.	Evidence limited to one country (USA).
Hours of sale	Mixed evidence that changes in hours of service can impact drinking and drinking problems among young drinkers.	Evidence from a few countries
Advertising restrictions	Inconclusive (primarily negative) evidence that advertising bans or restrictions reduce drinking or drinking problems among youth.	Evidence from several countries.
Harm Reduction Policies		
Zero tolerance	Strong evidence that zero tolerance laws can reduce underage drinking, drinking and driving, and traffic crashes, if they are enforced.	Evidence from several countries.
Graduated driver licensing	Strong evidence that graduated driver licensing can decrease drinking and driving among youth.	Evidence from a few countries.
Random breath testing	Limited evidence that RBT can reduce drinking by young people. Strong evidence of effects on the general population.	Evidence from a few countries.

(Continued)

Table 3.4.2 Effectiveness of policies to reduce drinking and drinking problems among youth (*Continued*)

Policy	Evidence for effectiveness	Generalizability
Sobriety check points	Limited evidence that sobriety checkpoints can reduce drinking by young people. Strong evidence of effects on the general population.	Evidence limited to one country.
Responsible beverage service (RBS)	Some evidence that clerk training decreases sales to minors. Moderately strong evidence that mandated RBS (especially outlet policy) can reduce intoxication and related problems in the general population.	Evidence from a few countries.
Designated driver	Some evidence that drinkers use designated drivers. No evidence that designated driver programs reduce drinking and driving. Some evidence that they may increase consumption among non-designated drivers. May be a poor understanding among designated drivers should not drink.	Evidence limited to one country.
Safe rides	Some evidence that heavy drinkers occasionally use safe rides programs. No evidence that they affect drinking and driving.	Evidence limited to one country.
Dram shop liability	Some evidence that dram shop liability laws can reduce consumption, traffic crashes, and fatalities among young people and in the general population.	Evidence limited to one country.
Warning labels	Negative evidence that warning labels reduce drinking either among young people or the general population.	Evidence limited to one country
Keg registration	Little available evidence for effectiveness or ineffectiveness.	Evidence limited to one country.

and drinking alcohol in less expensive venues without reducing overall consumption. As a result of these complexities, it is difficult to estimate the effects of tax increases in any specific case.

Licensing Restrictions

Licensing has been used in various ways including granting/denying licenses to sell alcohol, restricting hours of sales, restricting the number or density of outlets in a given area, and restricting the types of beverages or container sizes that can be sold. Research evidence for the effectiveness of any of these strategies in reducing drinking by young people is scarce.

Monopoly/privatization

Studies examining policy movements from state monopolization of alcohol sales to privatization generally find an increase in overall consumption following privatization (Wagenaar and Holder 1995), but rarely report on consumption by young people. In one of the few studies focusing on youth, Valli (1998) describes the effects on drinking among 13- to 17-year-olds in a Finnish township, when medium-strength beer was made available in grocery stores as opposed to being available only in state monopoly stores. The results show that age limits were observed less strictly and that the beverage of choice among girls changed from wine to medium-strength beer.

Outlet density restrictions

Studies find significant relations between outlet densities and alcohol consumption, violence, drinking and driving, and car crashes (e.g., Gruenewald, et al., 2002). In one of the few studies focusing on youth (Treno et al., 2003), on- and off-license outlet density was positively related to frequency of driving after drinking and riding with drinking drivers among 16- to 20-year-old youth. Outlet density surrounding college campuses has also been found to correlate with heavy drinking, frequent drinking, and drinking-related problems among students (Weitzman et al., 2003). All the available studies are cross-sectional, however, and the causal nature of the relations between outlet density and alcohol consumption and problems among youth is an open question.

Hours of sale

Restricting the days and hours that alcohol sales are allowed is a common policy strategy that is promoted for reducing drinking and drinking-related problems. Generally, greater restrictions have been associated with decreases in drinking and drinking problems, although the findings are mixed. Thus, some studies have failed to find changes in consumption or alcohol-related problems following changes in hours of sale (McLaughlin and Harrison-Stewart, 1992). Other studies report increases in traffic crashes and assaults following extensions of trading hours (Chikritzhs and Stockwell, 2002). Although the evidence is mixed, it appears that in some contexts changes in hours of service may be associated with drinking and drinking-related problems among young people.

Advertising Restrictions

Only a few studies have considered the effects of alcohol advertising restrictions on alcohol consumption or problems. Saffer (1991) investigated the effects of restrictions on broadcast alcohol advertising on alcohol consumption and alcohol problems (liver cirrhosis mortality, motor vehicle fatalities) in 17 countries including Europe and North America. He found that countries with partial restrictions on alcohol advertising had lower alcohol consumption and fewer problems than countries with no restrictions. Countries with complete bans had lower rates than countries with partial restrictions. A reanalysis, however, suggested that there was reverse causation, with those countries experiencing low rates of alcohol problems being more likely to adopt alcohol advertising bans than were countries with high rates of alcohol problems (Young, 1993). More recently, a study of alcohol advertising restrictions in 20 countries over 26 years found that moving from no restrictions to partial restrictions or from partial restrictions to total bans reduced alcohol consumption between 5 and 8% (Saffer and Dave, 2002). Other recent studies have found no effects of advertising bans (Nelson and Young, 2001). Apparently no studies have investigated the specific effects of advertising restrictions on drinking or drinking problems among young people. The effect of advertising restrictions on young people's drinking is best considered an open question.

HARM REDUCTION POLICIES

Zero Tolerance

Zero tolerance laws are a special case of minimum drinking age laws that apply a lower legal blood alcohol content (BAC) to drivers under the legal drinking age. These laws have been found to be very effective in reducing underage drinking and related problems. In one study, zero tolerance laws were associated with a 19% reduction in self-reported driving after any drinking and a 24% reduction in reported driving after five or more drinks using survey data from 30 states across the USA (Wagenaar et al., 2001). Similarly, it has been estimated that the implementation of zero tolerance laws in the USA reduced alcohol-related fatal crashes among young drivers by as much as 24% (Voas et al., 2003). Effective enforcement and awareness of the laws among young people have been identified as key factors in the success of zero tolerance laws (Voas et al., 1998; Ferguson et al., 2000). Impediments to the enforcement of these laws include: (a) requiring that zero tolerance citations be supported by evidential BAC testing; (b) undue costs to police (e.g., paperwork, time, court appearances); and (c) lack of behavioral cues for stopping young drivers at very low BACs. It has been suggested that the most effective zero tolerance laws include passive breath testing, are implemented in combination with DUI checkpoints or random breath testing, and involve streamlined administrative procedures (Ferguson et al., 2000). Using media to increase young people's awareness of reduced BAC limits and of enforcement efforts may also increase the effectiveness of zero tolerance laws.

Graduated Driver Licensing (GDL)

Graduated driver licensing (GDL) laws place restrictions on the circumstances under which young or novice drivers are allowed to drive, such as prohibiting driving during certain hours or driving with other young people in the vehicle. Some GDL laws contain zero tolerance provisions. Studies of GDL routinely show that it is associated with reductions in drinking, motor vehicle crashes, and alcohol-related crashes among young people (e.g., Shope and Molnar, 2003). GDL also may be an important adjunct to zero tolerance laws. For example, GDL violations might provide cause for stopping young drivers at night who may be drinking at very low levels that otherwise would not be detected.

Random Breath Testing (RBT)

In Random Breath Testing (RBT) programs, motorists can be stopped without reason and required to take a breath test to establish BAC levels. In Australia, RBT programs have been found to result in substantial reductions in crashes (Armstrong and Howell 1988). Enforcement and public awareness seem to be key to the success of RBT programs (McCaul and McLean 1990). There is some evidence, however, that drinking drivers may change their driving patterns and use minor and relatively less safe roads when enforcement of RBT is intense and publicity is high, thus increasing their chances of a crash. Although there are no studies specifically focusing on the impact of RBT on young drivers, there is reason to believe that when enforced, the efficacy of this approach also applies to young people.

Sobriety Checkpoints

Random breath testing cannot be undertaken in some countries, most notably the USA, because of legal or constitutional barriers. *Sobriety checkpoints*, however, can be implemented in the USA under proscribed circumstances as determined by state laws, often involving pre-notification about when and where they will be established. Breath tests at such checkpoints can be given only if there is probable cause to suspect that a driver has been drinking. Even under these restricted circumstances there is evidence that sobriety checkpoints reduce drinking and driving and related traffic crashes. An evaluation of one checkpoint program (Lacey et al., 1999) found a 20% decrease in alcohol-related fatal crashes and a 6% reduction in single vehicle night-time crashes that were sustained up to 21 months after implementation of the program. A recent review of American and Australian studies (Peek-Asa, 1999) concludes that the available evidence consistently indicates that both RBT and sobriety checkpoints reduce alcohol-related crashes, injuries, and fatalities. No studies, however, appear to have addressed the effects of these programs on young drivers. Nonetheless, sobriety checkpoints appear to be a promising approach.

Responsible Beverage Service (RBS)

Responsible beverage service (RBS) consists of the implementation of a combination of outlet policies (e.g., requiring clerks or servers to check identification for all customers appearing to be under the age of 30 years) and training (e.g., teaching clerks and servers to recognize altered or false identification). RBS can be implemented at both on-license and off-license establishments. Such programs have been shown to be effective in some circumstances. Thus, RBS has been found to reduce (a) the number of intoxicated patrons leaving a bar; (b) car crashes; (c) sales to intoxicated patrons; (d) sales to minors; and (e) incidents of violence surrounding outlets (e.g., Wallin et al., 2003). Voluntary programs appear to be less effective than mandatory programs or programs using incentives such as reduced liability. Few studies, however, have evaluated the effects of RBS programs on underage drinking. In one study of off-license RBS, voluntary clerk and manager training were found to have a negligible effect on sales to minors above and beyond the effects of increased enforcement of underage sales laws (Grube, 1997). Similarly, a study in Australia found that, even after training, age identification was rarely checked in bars, although decreases in the number of intoxicated patrons were observed (Lang et al., 1998).

How RBS is implemented and what elements are included in a particular program may be an important determinant of its effectiveness. Policy development and implementation within outlets may be more important than server training in determining RBS effectiveness.

Research indicates that establishments with firm and clear policies (e.g., checking ID for all patrons who appear under the age of 30) and a system for monitoring staff compliance are less likely to sell alcohol to minors (Wolfson et al., 1996). In addition to problems in implementing RBS, evaluation of the effectiveness of RBS is difficult because of the great variation in the quality and focus of available programs.

Designated Driver

Designated driver programs are a popular strategy to reduce drinking and driving. Designated driver programs encourage groups of drinkers to select a group member who is not to drink and who can then drive safely. Although designated driver programs are being strongly promoted, there is little available evidence of their effectiveness. There is some evidence that those who serve as designated drivers are heavier drinkers and more likely to report drinking and driving and riding with drinking drivers than are drinkers who never serve as designated drivers (e.g., Caudill et al., 2000a). Unfortunately, some data indicate that young people do not have a good idea of what constitutes a safe designated driver. Young people report that the designated driver is often the person in their group who had consumed the least alcohol, even though that may have been a significant amount (Stevenson et al., 2001; Nygaard et al., 2003).

Safe Rides

Safe rides programs offer drinkers low cost or free transportation as an alternative to driving themselves. As with designated driver programs, there is little available research on their effectiveness. Some evidence indicates that safe rides programs are used relatively infrequently by drinkers (e.g., Caudill et al., 2000b). Such programs cannot be recommended without further evaluation to establish their effectiveness with young drinkers.

Dram Shop (Civil) Liability

Dram shop liability laws allow individuals injured by a minor who had been drinking or by an intoxicated adult to recover damages from the alcohol retailer who served or sold alcohol to the person causing the injury. Owners and licensees can be held liable for their employees' actions under most or all dram shop liability laws. Many dram shop liability statutes include a Responsible Business Practices Defense. This provision allows retailers to avoid liability if they can establish that they took reasonable steps to avoid serving minors and obviously intoxicated adults. Key to the defense is evidence that RBS training procedures and policies were fully implemented at the time of the illegal sale or service. Research suggests that implementation of dram shop liability may lead to significant increases in checking age identification and greater care in service practices. Overall, dram shop liability has been estimated to reduce alcohol-related traffic fatalities among underage drivers by 3–4% (Chaloupka et al., 1993).

Social Host (Civil) Liability

Under social host liability laws, adults who provide alcohol to a minor or serve intoxicated adults in social settings can be sued, through civil action, for damages or injury caused by that minor or intoxicated adult. There is very little research on the effectiveness of social host liability laws and what evidence exists is conflicting. In one study in the USA, social host liability laws were associated with decreases in alcohol-related traffic fatalities among adults, but not among minors (Whetten-Goldstein et al., 2000). Social host statutes were not related to single vehicle night-time crashes for either group. In a second study social host liability laws were associated with decreases in reported heavy drinking and in decreases in drinking and driving by lighter drinkers (Stout et al., 2000). They had no effect on drinking and driving by heavier drinkers. The conflicting findings may reflect the lack of a comprehensive program that insures that social hosts are aware of their potential liability. Although social host liability may send a powerful message, that message must be effectively disseminated before it can have a deterrent effect.

Warning Labels

Warning labels on beverage containers constitute another strategy for targeting risky drinking. An early evaluation of warning labels on alcohol beverage containers in the USA found that about one-fifth of respondents to a national survey remembered seeing the warnings six months after their introduction (Kaskutas and Greenfield, 1992). A study of US adolescents found that there were increases in awareness, exposure to, and memory of the labels after they were implemented, but there were no changes in alcohol use or beliefs about the risks targeted by the warning (MacKinnon et al., 1993). Overall, there is no evidence that alcohol beverage warning labels have any discernible effect on drinking or drinking problems among young people.

Keg Registration

Keg registration laws require the name of a purchaser of a keg of beer be linked to that keg. Keg registration is seen primarily as a tool for prosecuting adults who supply alcohol to young people at parties or for prosecuting retailers who sell kegs to minors. Keg registration laws have become increasingly popular in the USA. There is apparently only a single published study on the effectiveness of these laws. In that study of 97 US communities, it was found that requiring keg registration was significantly and negatively correlated with traffic fatality rates (Cohen et al., 2001). The evidence for the effectiveness of keg registration is best considered inconclusive.

Enforcement

Some alcohol policies, such as increases in excise taxes or alcohol warning labels, can be implemented without significant enforcement effort. For deterrent policy strategies, however, enforcement appears to be a key determinant of effectiveness. The deterrent effect of alcohol policies is affected by their severity, the probability of their imposition, and the swiftness with which they are imposed. The probability of being detected and having penalties imposed may be particularly important. Some research suggests that policies that increase the probability of detection and arrest for drinking and driving infractions, for example, have greater effects on alcohol-related traffic fatalities than do policies that increase penalties (Benson et al., 1999).

Enforcement against Youth

Although often severe, penalties for many alcohol offenses by youth are seldom enforced and therefore can have only a modest deterrent effect. Arrests of minors for possession of alcohol, for example, are rare, in part, because of the burden of prosecuting them and reluctance on the part of law enforcement and courts to enforce criminal penalties in such cases (Wagenaar and Wolfson, 1994). Moreover, because criminal proceedings are often lengthy and removed in time from the infraction, the punishment is seldom swift or certain. Less severe sanctions (e.g., fines, community service, loss of drivers license) may be more likely to be enforced and thus to generate a deterrent effect than would under-enforced criminal penalties. Deterrence may also be increased if penalties are imposed administratively through citations issued at the time of apprehension, without requiring court appearances. The size of the fines and length of community service should be sufficiently substantial, however, to register social disapproval and to generate a meaningful deterrent effect.

Enforcement against Retailers

Minimum drinking age limits notwithstanding, minors can often purchase alcohol with little difficulty. Increasing enforcement against retailers who sell to minors, however, can have a substantial impact. Grube (1997) found that enforcement of sales laws coupled with media coverage produced a net reduction in sales to minors of 30–35%. In a study in New Orleans, enforcement of underage sales laws increased compliance with alcohol sales laws from 11% to 39% (Scribner and Cohen, 2001). The greatest gains in compliance occurred among those retailers who had been cited (51%), but substantial gains were also seen for those not cited (35%). The extent to which such reductions in sales translate into decreases in underage drinking, however, is unknown. Young drinkers may be particularly adept at identifying outlets that continue to sell to minors despite enforcement efforts or may shift to alternative social sources for alcohol. Support for the importance of reducing retail access to alcohol can be obtained from the literature on tobacco control. Most notably, a recent randomized community trial suggests that increasing retailer compliance with age identification for underage tobacco sales not only reduced tobacco sales to minors and youth smoking, but also underage drinking (Biglan et al., 2000). Enforcement of laws prohibiting sales to intoxicated patrons can also be effective. Thus, McKnight and Streff (1994) found a rise in refusals of service to "pseudo-patrons" simulating intoxication, and a decline in the percentage of drunk drivers coming from bars and restaurants following increased enforcement of laws prohibiting sales to intoxicated patrons.

CONCLUSION

Generally, drinking by young people is normative in most Western countries. A majority of young people have tried drinking and substantial numbers are current drinkers. In addition, alcohol consumption by youth is often typified by a pattern of heavy episodic or binge drinking, which is associated with considerable costs both to the individual and to society. It is thus imperative to develop strategies to reduce drinking by youth and the risks associated with it.

Based on the available evidence, the most effective policies appear to be: (a) taxation or price increases; (b) increases in the minimum drinking age; (c) zero tolerance; and (d) graduated licensing. Of these policies, two target overall consumption among young people and two target risk behaviors. Random breath testing, sobriety check points, and dram shop liability also appear promising for reducing drinking and drinking-related problems based on studies with the general population, although there is less evidence for their effectiveness specifically with young people. The evidence is growing for the effects of outlet license restrictions (e.g., outlet density, hours of sale). There is some empirical support for responsible beverage service programs, particularly those that are mandated or motivated by reduction of liability. The evidence on advertising restrictions is conflicting with some studies showing reductions in consumption and problems, and others showing no effects of such policies. Evidence that designated driver and safe rides programs, warning labels, social host liability, and keg registration are effective strategies for preventing drinking or drinking problems among young people is largely lacking. For many policy strategies there is not sufficient research to evaluate their effects on drinking by young people. Such research should be conducted to inform policy or at least to evaluate policies as they are implemented.

No policy can be effective unless it is adequately implemented, it is enforced, and there is awareness of both the policy and enforcement efforts on the part of the intended targets (e.g., Voas et al., 1998). Awareness and knowledge of policies on the part of those charged with enforcement and public support can each be important for effective implementation. Law enforcement officers and community leaders may often perceive little popular support for such policies or their enforcement (Wagenaar and Wolfson, 1994). The difficulty of implementing effective policies in the face of public opposition may be considerable. Public support may, in fact, be greater for those policies that are least effective in reducing drinking and drinking problems among youth. Surveys in Canada and the USA, for example, indicate that public support may be strongest for interventions such as reducing service to intoxicated patrons and treatment. There is also considerable public support for policies targeting promotion such as providing warning labels and banning or restricting alcohol advertising. There is less support for more demonstrably effective policies targeting access such as increasing the drinking age or increasing taxes. The strategic use of media, however, can help overcome such resistance and elicit public support for effective policy interventions.

ACKNOWLEDGEMENT

A preliminary version of this chapter was presented at the International Symposium on Preventing Substance Use, Risky Use, and Harm: What is Evidence-Based Policy? Fremantle, Western Australia, 24–27 February 2003. Preparation of this chapter was supported, in part, by National Institute on Alcohol Abuse and Alcoholism grants AA12136 and AA06282.

REFERENCES

Adrian, M., Ferguson, B.S., and Her, M. (2001) Can alcohol price policies be used to reduce drink driving? Evidence from Canada. *Substance Use and Misuse*, **36**, 1923–1957.

Armstrong, B.K. and Howell, C.M. (1988) Trends in injury and death in motor vehicle accidents in Australia in relation to the introduction of random breath testing. *Australian Drug and Alcohol Review*, **7**, 251–259.

Benson, B.L., Rasmussen, D.W. and Mast, B.D. (1999) Deterring drunk driving fatalities: an economics of crime perspective. *International Review of Law Economics*, **19**, 205–225.

Biglan, A., Ary, D.V., Smolkowski, K., Duncan, T. and Black, C. (2000) A randomised controlled trial of a community intervention to prevent adolescent tobacco use. *Tobacco Control*, **9**, 24–32.

Caudill, B.D., Harding, W.M. and Moore, B.A. (2000a) DWI prevention: profiles of drinkers who serve as designated drivers. *Psychology of Addictive Behaviors*, **14**, 143–150.

Caudill, B.D., Harding, W.M. and Moore, B.A. (2000b) At-risk drinkers use safe ride services to avoid drinking and driving. *Journal of Substance Use*, **11**, 149–159.

Chaloupka, F.J., Saffer, H. and Grossman, M. (1993) Alcohol control policies and motor vehicle fatalities. *Journal of Legal Studies*, **22**, 161–186.

Chikritzhs, T. and Stockwell, T. (2002) The impact of later trading hours for Australian public houses (hotels) on levels of violence. *Journal of Studies on Alcohol*, **63**, 591–599.

Cohen, D.A., Mason, K. and Scribner, R.A. (2001) The population consumption model, alcohol control practices, and alcohol-related traffic fatalities. *Preventive Medicine*, **34**, 187–197.

Dee, T.S. (1999) State alcohol policies, teen drinking, and traffic fatalities. *Journal of Public Economics*, **72**, 289–315.

Ferguson, S.A., Fields, M. and Voas, R.B. (2000) Enforcement of zero tolerance laws in the United States. Paper presented at the 15th International Conference on Alcohol, Drugs, and Traffic Safety, Stockholm, Sweden, 21–26 May.

Grube, J.W. (1997) Preventing sales of alcohol to minors: results from a community trial. *Addiction*, **92** (suppl. 2), S251–S260.

Gruenewald, P.J., Johnson, F.W. and Treno, A.J. (2002) Outlets, drinking and driving: a multilevel analysis of availability. *Journal of Studies on Alcohol*, **63**, 460–468.

Kaskutas, L. and Greenfield, T.K. (1992) First effects of warning labels on alcoholic beverage containers. *Drug and Alcohol Dependence*, **31**, 1–14.

Lacey, J.H., Jones, R.K. and Smith, R.G. (1999) Evaluation of *Checkpoint Tennessee: Tennessee's Statewide Sobriety Checkpoint Program*. Washington, DC: National Highway Traffic Safety Administration.

Laixuthai, A. and Chaloupka, F.J. (1993) Youth alcohol use and public policy. *Contemporary Policy Issues*, **11**, 70–81.

Lang, E., Stockwell, T., Rydon, P. and Beel, A. (1998) Can training bar staff in responsible serving practices reduce alcohol-related harm? *Drug and Alcohol Review*, **17**, 39–50.

MacKinnon, D.P., Pentz, M.A., and Stacy, A.W. (1993) Alcohol warning labels and adolescents: the first year. *American Journal of Public Health*, **83**, 585–587.

McCaul, K.A. and McLean, A.J. (1990) Publicity, police resources and the effectiveness of random breath testing. *Medical Journal of Australia*, **152**, 284–286.

McKnight, A.J. and Streff, F.M. (1994) Effect of enforcement upon service of alcohol to intoxicated patrons of bars and restaurants. *Accident Analysis and Prevention*, **26**, 79–88.

McLaughlin, K.L. and Harrison-Stewart, A.J. (1992) Effect of a temporary period of relaxed licensing laws on the alcohol consumption of young male drinkers. *International Journal of the Addictions*, **27**, 409–423.

Nelson, J.P. and Young, D.J. (2001) Do advertising bans work? An international comparison. *International Journal of Advertising*, **20**, 273–296.

Nygaard, P., Waiters, E.D., Grube, J.W. and Keefe, D. (2003) Why do they do it? A qualitative study of adolescent drinking and driving. *Substance Use and Misuse*, **38**, 835–863.

Peek-Asa, C. (1999) The effect of random alcohol screening in reducing motor vehicle crash injuries. *American Journal of Preventive Medicine*, **16**, 57–67.

Saffer, H. (1991) Alcohol advertising bans and alcohol abuse: an international perspective. *Journal of Health Economics*, **10**, 65–79.

Saffer, H. and Dave, D. (2002) Alcohol consumption and alcohol advertising bans. *Applied Economics*, **5**, 1325–1334.

Scribner, R.A. and Cohen, D.A. (2001) The effect of enforcement on merchant compliance with the minimum legal drinking age law. *Journal of Drug Issues*, **31**, 857–866.

Shope, J.T. and Molnar, L.J. (2003) Graduated driver licensing in the United States: evaluation of results from early programs. *Journal of Safety Research*, **34**, 63–69.

Shults R.A., Elder R.W., Sleet D.A. et al. (2001) Reviews of evidence regarding interventions to reduce alcohol-impaired driving. *American Journal of Preventive Medicine*, **21**(suppl.1), 66–88.

Stevenson, M., Palamara, P., Rooke, M., Richardson, K., Baker, M. and Baumwol, J. (2001) Drink and drug driving among university students: what's the skipper to do? *Australian and New Zealand Journal of Public Health*, **2**, 511–513.

Stout, E.M., Sloan, F.A., Liang, L. and Davies, H.H. (2000) Reducing harmful alcohol-related behaviors: effective regulatory methods. *Journal of Studies on Alcohol*, **61**, 402–412.

Treno, A.J., Grube, J.W., and Martin, S. (2003) Alcohol outlet density as a predictor of youth drinking and driving: a hierarchical analysis. *Alcoholism: Clinical and Experimental Research*, **27**, 835–840.

Valli, R. (1998) Forandringar i ungdomarnas alkoholvanor nar mellanolet slapptes fritt: Fallet Jakobstad (Changes in young people's alcohol consumption with improved availability of medium strength beer: the case of Pietarsaari). *Nordisk Alkohol- and Narkotikatidskrift (Nordic Alcohol and Drug Studies)*, **15**, 168–175.

Voas, R.B., Lange, J.E. and Tippetts, A.E. (1998) Enforcement of the zero tolerance law in California: a missed opportunity? *In 42nd Annual Proceedings of the Association for the Advancement of Automotive Medicine*. Des Plaines, IL: Association for the Advancement of Automotive Medicine, pp. 369–383.

Voas, R.B., Tippetts, A.S. and Fell, J.C. (2003) Assessing the effectiveness of minimum legal drinking age and zero tolerance laws in the United States. *Accident Analysis and Prevention*, **35**, 579–587.

Wagenaar, A.C. and Holder, H.D. (1995) Changes in alcohol consumption resulting from the elimination of retail wine monopolies: results from five US states. *Journal of Studies on Alcohol*, **56**, 566–572.

Wagenaar, A.C. and Toomey, T.L. (2002) Effects of minimum drinking age laws: review and analyses of the literature from 1960 to 2000. *Journal of Studies on Alcohol*, Suppl. **14**, 206–225.

Wagenaar, A.C. and Wolfson, M. (1994) Enforcement of the legal minimum drinking age in the United States. *Journal of Public Health Policy*, **15**, 37–53.

Wagenaar, A.C., O'Malley, P.M. and LaFond, C. (2001) Very low legal BAC limits for young drivers: effects on drinking, driving, and driving-after-drinking behaviors in 30 states. *American Journal of Public Health*, **91**, 801–804.

Wallin, E., Norstrom, T. and Andréasson, S. (2003) Alcohol prevention targeting licensed premises: a study of effects on violence. *Journal of Studies on Alcohol*, **64**, 270–277.

Weitzman, E.R., Folkman, A., Folkman, K.L. and Wechsler, H. (2003) Relationship of alcohol outlet density to heavy and frequent drinking and drinking-related problems among college students at eight universities. *Health and Place*, **9**, 1–6.

Whetten-Goldstein, K., Sloan, F.A., Stout, E. and Liang, L. (2000) Civil liability, criminal law, and other policies and alcohol-related motor vehicle fatalities in the United States: 1984–1995. *Accident Analysis and Prevention*, **32**, 723–733.

Wolfson, M., Toomey, T.L., Murray, D.M., Forster, J.L., Short, B.J. and Wagenaar, A.C. (1996) Alcohol outlet policies and practices concerning sales to underage people. *Addiction*, **91**, 589–602.

Young, D.J. (1993) Alcohol advertising bans and alcohol abuse: comment. *Journal of Health Economics*, **12**, 213–228.

Young, D.J. and Likens T.W. (2000) Alcohol regulation and auto fatalities. *International Review of Law and Economics*, **20**, 107–126.

3.5 Testing a Community Prevention Focused Model of Coalition Functioning and Sustainability: A Comprehensive Study of Communities That Care in Pennsylvania

MARK T. GREENBERG, MARK E. FEINBERG, BRENDAN J. GOMEZ
Prevention Research Center, Pennsylvania State University, PA, USA

D. WAYNE OSGOOD
Department of Sociology, Pennsylvania State University, PA, USA

SUMMARY

There is evidence that community action approaches can reduce problems related to alcohol use and youth substance use. However, to date there has been little attention to the processes underlying successful community approaches. Coalitions and partnerships have become a popular vehicle for community action to reduce adolescent substance abuse and promote positive youth development. This chapter provides a broad overview of results of a detailed study of the Communities That Care (CTC) initiative in the state of Pennsylvania. CTC is a systematic approach to community action that includes the formation and training of a local coalition to identify factors underlying child and youth development in order to redress adverse influences through empirically supported programs. Findings emphasize the importance of community organizational and motivational readiness, initial training and ongoing technical assistance (TA) for the effective functioning of coalitions. Further, the prevention knowledge of coalition members, the quality of coalition functioning, and their fidelity to the CTC model all are predictive of sustainability of effort. Finally, coalitions that function more effectively showed greater changes in the rate of youth delinquency in their communities. Data on youth substance abuse changes were not available. These findings have clear implications for practitioners and policy-makers who can focus resources and attention early in the coalition lifecycle. Important areas of focus include adequate early training of key leaders and

Preventing Harmful Substance Use: The Evidence Base for Policy and Practice.
Edited by T. Stockwell, P. J. Gruenewald, J. W. Toumbourou and W. Loxley.
© 2005 John Wiley & Sons, Ltd. ISBN 0-470-09227-0 (hbk) 0-470-09228-9 (pbk).

ongoing, high quality TA that helps the coalition's local committee (board) maintain fidelity to the model and effective internal board functioning. Maintaining a critical mass of knowledgeable board members is crucial and this requires orientation for new board members as well as ongoing TA to help community leaders sustain a sense of direction. Finally, it is important to note that while coalitions in themselves do not ensure positive outcomes in addressing adolescent problem behaviors, such outcomes are more likely to be achieved when communities are better poised for effectively developing, managing and sustaining coalition preventive efforts.

INTRODUCTION

In the past few decades, communities in many countries have struggled to reduce their levels of both adolescent substance abuse and related problem behaviors, including delinquency, violence, and school failure. In the United States of America both federal and state policies have promoted the idea that local coalitions that bring together diverse constituencies to conduct public advocacy, decision-making and program and policy changes at the local level should be a central part of the solution for reducing problem behaviors in communities. Although the long-term effects of such coalitions are still unclear, these ideas have substantial political appeal and public support, as many believe that investing in and empowering local communities to make better and more coordinated decisions is a useful strategy.

Communities That Care (CTC; Hawkins and Catalano, 1992; Hawkins et al., 2002) is a new and quickly growing model of "community empowerment" based on central tenets of prevention science (e.g., risk and protective factors are to be identified and targeted by empirically supported programs). This chapter discusses findings of a study that examined the coalition processes and outcomes in a substantial initiative in the state of Pennsylvania. The goals of the chapter are to provide a brief rationale for such collaboratives, to review current research on collaborative approaches, to present both a conceptual model and empirical data on the activities of coalitions, and to make recommendations for improving their effectiveness.

THE MOVEMENT TO COMMUNITY COALITIONS

Community-based, comprehensive prevention approaches implemented through locally based coalitions have become increasingly popular in recent years (Butterfoss et al., 1993; Kumpfer et al., 1993). This approach was originally developed within the agent/host/environment public health model to address cardiovascular disease (e.g., Puska et al., 1985), but has been extended to other health problems as diverse as cancer, HIV infection, lead poisoning, low birth weight, and injury, as well as behavioral health problems such as violence, alcohol and substance abuse, and teenage pregnancy (Roussos and Fawcett, 2000). In part, these shifts reflect disenchantment with categorical funding, isolated and poorly coordinated social service agencies, and high-cost and at times ineffective treatment.

The growing popularity of a comprehensive community approach is due to developments in both theory and practice. Theorists and researchers have come to recognize the several layers of overlapping contextual and structural influences on individual behavior problems (e.g., Pollard et al., 1999). Individual behaviors include risky sexual behaviors, violence, and substance abuse, which may be influenced by family structure and interaction, the quality and nature of school systems, health care systems, the faith community, etc. These factors in turn depend on community norms, attitudes, laws and enforcement. Further, policy-makers recognize that while individual prevention programs can have significant effects on behavior, reducing community-level rates of problem behaviors demands coordination of strategies across a range of community actors; discrete programs are rarely sufficient (Butterfoss et al., 1993). Such coordinated strategies might include systematic evidence-based programs and policies to alter behavior and attitudes/norms both for individual adolescents and their families as well as for the entire community environment.

Research on Community Collaboration

As a result of the explosion of community prevention/promotion coalitions in the past two decades, there has been greater opportunity and interest in studying the dynamics and outcomes of coalitions. Most studies in this area have been qualitative case studies of one or at most a handful of coalitions (e.g., Farquhar, 1978; Rindskopf and Saxe, 1998). Recently however, several studies have been conducted with a sample size of ten or more community coalitions (Kumpfer et al., 1993; COMMIT, 1995; Butterfoss et al., 1996; Saxe et al., 1997; Yin et al., 1997; Kegler et al., 1998). Aguirre-Molina and Gorman (1996) in their review reported a number of studies that had demonstrated positive findings through well-organized, community-based, drug prevention programs.

The limited evaluation of coalition outcomes, in part, reflects the difficulty of evaluating comprehensive, community-based prevention and health promotion initiatives. Many researchers have noted the complexity of the task (Farquhar, 1978; Altman, 1986; Hollister and Hill, 1995). For example, as the community is the unit of analysis, a high level of resources is needed to have sufficient sample size, and thus power to detect effects. As community-level randomization is frequently not feasible, matching communities is an option, but this strategy limits the conclusiveness of findings (Hollister and Hill, 1995). Furthermore, evaluating community-based prevention coalitions requires delineating specific long-term outcomes (e.g., adolescent delinquency or arrest), intermediate outcomes (e.g., increased school bonding or enhanced family relations), and immediate outcomes of programs (e.g., program attendance). More importantly, though, because communities are empowered to make their own decisions in such models, each community may select different short and long-term outcomes to target, prioritize different risk factors, and select a different array of programs (Klitzner, 1993). Thus, comparing long-term, intermediate, or immediate outcomes across communities is often quite difficult.

Recently, Hallfors and colleagues (Hallfors et al., 2002) have examined the effectiveness of the Fighting Back Against Substance Abuse coalitions funded by the Robert Wood Johnson Foundation. Using a quasi-experimental design with comparison sites, the study examined alcohol and other drug use outcomes and attitudes in 14 intervention and comparison communities. These coalitions were developed at the grassroots, attempted to bring diverse stakeholders together for decision-making, included community education and awareness, prevention, and treatment for both children and youth and used schools, community agencies and police to alter a variety of policies, norms and behaviors. There were no positive effects of the coalitions on the outcome of youth substance abuse, and for coalitions that primarily targeted adults there were mild negative effects. The authors derive a number of tentative conclusions for the discouraging findings, including: (1) too many competing agendas may have paralyzed the process and reduced efficiency and quality; (2) there were no requirements for coalitions to use evidence-based programs and thus programs that were run may have had no impact; and (3) the coalitions may have been poorly implemented. They suggest that coalitions should have limited and clearly focused goals, outcomes, and benchmarks. These indicators should be well defined and use effective pre-intervention as well as ongoing measurement to assess outcome. In addition, communities should be strongly encouraged to use evidence-based programs and policies and should carefully monitor dosage and quality of implementation of programs. To do so would also require ongoing technical assistance (TA) in evaluation, program choice, and program implementation. Although this evaluation was not a randomized trial, it was well constructed with the use of appropriate counterfactuals. The findings clearly call into question the general efficacy of broad coalitions that use grassroots models in which there is little TA or use of current evidence in the field of substance abuse prevention.

Despite obstacles in coalition evaluation, we believe that much can be gained through high-quality evaluative research (Altman, 1986). The findings herein derive from an action research project in which aspects of training, TA, and coalition functioning were examined in order to understand how these and other factors influenced perceived coalition efficacy, and outcomes, including sustainability. We believe its results have important implications for the structure and processes necessary for effective coalition activity.

THE COMMUNITIES THAT CARE MODEL (CTC)

The goal of CTC is to reduce adolescent problem behaviors (e.g., substance abuse, delinquency, pregnancy) through a set of well-planned stages. In Stage 1 key leaders are mobilized in a community and form a prevention board. These leaders then receive training in both the public health model that focuses on the influence of risk and protective factors as well as board operations. A second session of training focuses on the tasks of undertaking a multimethod assessment of the community's risk and protective factors. After assessment (Stage 2), the coalition prioritizes which risk and protective factors should be addressed (Stage 3), selects and implements evidence-based prevention programs to address the prioritized risk factors (Stage 4), and then provides ongoing monitoring of outcomes to reassess and improve programming (Stage 5). CTC uses well-designed curriculum materials to implement a specific and clear training model. Despite the success of the CTC model in terms of dissemination and acceptance, little high-quality, generalizable evaluation research has been conducted on this approach (Harachi et al., 1996).

The examination of CTC sites in Pennsylvania represented an important opportunity to further develop the knowledge base in this field. CTC has been promoted nationally and abroad as an example of comprehensive community-based models of prevention. The US Office of Juvenile Justice and Delinquency Prevention has incorporated CTC's general model in its national program and has provided funding for implementing CTC (Title V). CTC is also being implemented overseas, for example in Britain with funding from the Rowntree Foundation. There also are ongoing efforts to implement and evaluate CTC in Scotland, The Netherlands, and Australia.

Pennsylvania Evaluation of CTC: Questions and a Model

Pennsylvania was an early adopter of CTC, and has offered training, TA, and funding to over 100 communities to date. Given this supportive context, CTC dissemination and implementation in Pennsylvania reflect a reasonable approximation of the potential for such strategies given current knowledge and best practices.

Fundamental questions of coalition functioning

To introduce our proposed model of community coalition functioning requires addressing some fundamental questions regarding community collaboratives. First, does community readiness foster more effective prevention coalitions? In some views, a key determinant of success is the organizational and motivational "readiness" of the community in terms of leadership capacity, organizational resources and networks, and public and local leadership attitudes. When communities are not "ready", some suggest that pre-intervention readiness development should be undertaken. However, others have argued that the processes leading to coalition success are frequently unpredictable and idiosyncratic (Klitzner, 1993). For example, an especially skilled leader or a particular political conflict may create or destroy a successful coalition when readiness indicators would suggest otherwise.

Second, does participation in training influence participants' attitudes and knowledge of prevention as well as their evaluation of the functioning and perceived efficacy of their coalition? Few reports have evaluated the success of training community leaders in risk/protective factor-focused prevention methods (Arthur et al., 2003). Harachi et al., (1996) examined the effects of training in 35 communities in Oregon. One year after training, about half the respondents showed at least a moderate understanding of protective factors, and two-thirds had at least a moderate understanding of risk factors. We hypothesize that training is linked to higher levels of project functioning, greater influence on other sectors of the community, and, consequently, a higher level of overall effectiveness.

A third issue is how the internal functioning of the coalition is related to a coalition's effectiveness. Much of the available research indicates that factors such as participation, leadership, complexity, task-focus, cohesion and identity are related to indicators of success (Florin et al., 2000). However, it is conceivable that smooth, integrated coalition functioning may not be necessary for the coalition to be effective. In many coalitions, only a small number of members may undertake the majority of the actual work. It may be work undertaken by a few competent and effective individuals that leads to success, rather than the smooth functioning of the coalition as an integrated, consensus-driven, cohesive body of community leaders.

Finally, does ongoing TA really make much of a difference in coalition outcomes? Although initial training is essential, there is some consensus that ongoing TA plays an important role (Florin et al., 1993; Roberts and Wasik, 1996). For example, Kegler et al., (1998) found that high quality TA from state-level staff facilitated implementation of community tobacco coalitions.

Model of coalition functioning

Figure 3.5.1 provides a conceptual model of coalition functioning. In this model, the initial level of community readiness influences the functioning of the coalition directly. The training and TA received by the coalition are expected to contribute to coalition functioning, in part through participants' positive attitudes and knowledge regarding prevention. The

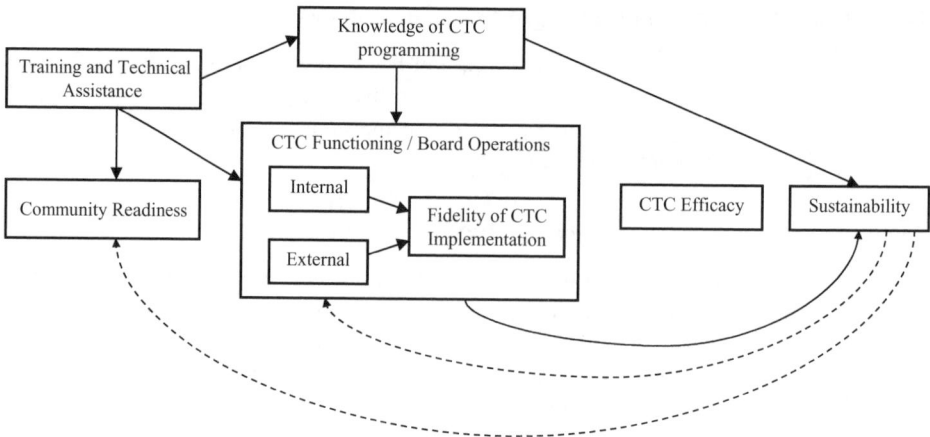

Figure 3.5.1   Theoretical model of coalition functioning and sustainability
Note: Boxes in bold indicate constructs examined in this study.

functioning of the coalition is reciprocally related to community readiness (recursive relationships are represented by dashed lines in the figure), as a well-functioning coalition may
have a positive effect on a community. In addition, a high level of coalition effectiveness is
expected to enhance positive attitudes towards prevention, and thus a dashed line is shown
leading to attitudes/knowledge. Effectiveness of the coalition is assumed to be associated
with positive outcomes regarding the targeted problem behaviors at the community level.
These positive outcomes are also shown as influencing community readiness: the experience of achieving positive outcomes should improve the community willingness to support
collaboration.

Study sample

The central purpose of our evaluation was to assess CTC implementation in the first 21
communities (ranging from entire counties to single neighborhoods) that participated in the
CTC training process. Pennsylvania's CTC program began in 1994, when key leaders from
seven counties responded to the state's announcement of support for CTC. In 1996, another
cycle of six counties entered the CTC process, with eight more the following year. One
county actually contained two separate CTC projects in two different areas; we evaluated
each area separately and thus the sample size was 21. Communities whose applications for
the CTC program were successful received a one-year planning grant of about $15,000.
Activities during this planning year included attendance of key community leaders at three,
multi-day training sessions. It should be noted unlike many community-based coalition
studies, CTC was not undertaken with a predominantly urban sample. Only three of the 21
sites were located in major metropolitan areas; almost half the sites were largely rural or
semi-rural. This sample represents a cross-section of the kinds of communities in which
coalition prevention takes place.

   The primary participants in the research were 203 members of the 21 local CTC collaborative boards which included program directors and key leaders. The participants had a
mean age of 48.0 (sd = 9.1). Some 106 participants were men, 97 were women; 73% of
the sample identified themselves as Caucasian; 15% African-American; 2% Hispanic; and

10% as multi-ethnic or other. Participants were generally highly educated; only 16% of the sample did not have a Bachelor's degree; 33% had a Bachelor's degree only; and 51% had an advanced degree.

Recognizing the need for a multi-method approach, the study assesses the perceptions of multiple raters including the 203 local leaders, state TA staff, and the research team. Data included interviews with leaders and mobilizers, ratings of these interviews by research staff, review of archival records and administrative reports, and independent ratings by TA coordinators hired by the state (see Feinberg et al., 2002; Feinberg et al., 2004a; 2004b, for specification of measures). Measures assessed the perceptions of key leaders, TA coordinators, and research staff regarding central constructs such as community readiness, internal and external functioning of the coalitions, and fidelity to the CTC model. Note that analyses conducted at the level of individuals—the 203 local leaders—may demonstrate different patterns than analyses where the community is the level of analysis. In some cases, we conducted multi-level models to model both individual and community level factors.

Ready or Not?

Results indicate that key leaders, perceptions of community readiness were strongly associated both with internal functioning and perceived effectiveness of the coalition (Feinberg et al., in press a). This finding points to the importance of community readiness, yet it is rarely assessed as a determinant of the *kinds* of strategies appropriate for a community. For communities low in readiness, alternative approaches (e.g., the development of local institutional and leadership infrastructure) might be more effective than directly funding complex coalition efforts.

What is the Influence of Training?

The training of community board members is an integral part of community-based health promotion models and central to the CTC model. We examined whether participation in CTC training influenced participants' attitudes and knowledge of prevention as well as their evaluation of the internal and external functioning of their coalition, and its perceived efficacy (Feinberg et al., 2002). Activities during this planning year included attendance of key community leaders involved in the effort at three multi-day training sessions. The state contracted with Developmental Research Programs (in Seattle) to provide the CTC training available at that time. It should be noted that since 2000 the CTC program has been operated by the Channing-Bete Company and some components have been updated. The first training session was the Key Leader Orientation which presented an overview of prevention concepts and the CTC model. Key leaders also received guidance in creating a collaborative planning committee and effective administrative structure. The second training session on Risk/Resource Analysis reviewed the risk and protective factors associated with problem behaviors and issues regarding collection of survey, archival, and other data in a community. The last training session, "Promising Approaches", reviewed existing prevention programs that have demonstrated efficacy and that are matched to specific community risk factors. Between the second and third training sessions, the local community CTC coalitions undertook a risk and resource analysis of their target area, prioritized risk factors, and developed a comprehensive plan to implement or enhance prevention programs to address those risk factors. The communities then submitted these plans to the state for three-year funding of specific prevention programs.

The average number of participants per county per training was 5.2 (ranging from 3 to 9). We examined the extent to which greater training participation was linked to individual attitudes and knowledge, as well as coalition project functioning. Although few findings were significant at the level of individual CTC leaders, significant findings occurred at the community level. Having more leaders from a community attend the Key Leader training was associated with greater perceived community readiness, external and internal CTC functioning, and perceptions of efficacy and sustainability. Higher attendance at the Promising Approaches training was linked to a more accurate understanding of risk factors. Greater attendance at the Risk/Resource training at the community level was associated with higher community readiness, but related to a lower sense of direction and perceived efficacy of the CTC leadership.

These findings suggest that the long-term influence of training may be especially important at the project or community level. That is, when a larger number of key leaders attend training, the prevention science framework may more easily take hold and continue to influence members' thinking years later. Thus, we recommend that prevention coalitions devote time and energy to training new board members and participants. Because substantial turnover occurs in such contexts, maintaining a critical mass of knowledgeable members to provide collective reinforcement of attitudes and knowledge may be important to prevent program drift.

We also found that training was positively associated with research staff's ratings of local CTC projects' clarity of goals and roles, fidelity to the risk factor model, and board structure and stability. Thus, the evidence suggests that attendance at training improved the quality, nature, and clarity of the internal organization of the CTC coalition. This is a particularly important finding because other scholars have reported that effective internal board operation and dynamics are key features of effective, sustainable coalitions (Florin et al., 2000).

However, not all training experiences were positive; the Risk/Resource training was negatively associated with sense of direction within the project. This specific training imparts to key leaders a framework and method for undertaking the intensive and time-consuming task of data collection and analysis regarding community risk and resources. Qualitative information suggests that some participants felt overwhelmed by aspects of the analysis task. It is understandable that the training at this stage may have left participants feeling thus, especially because the CTC Youth Survey (a succinct tool facilitating the measurement of multiple community-wide risk and protective factors [Pollard et al., 1999]) was not available at that time. The findings suggest that CTC training, and other similar models, may do well to help community leaders re-create a sense of direction at the *end* of this stage of the training process.

Is Technical Assistance (TA) Necessary?

We asked all interviewees about their CTC project's need for further technical assistance (TA) in eight specific areas: leadership development; coalition building; diversity/cultural awareness; fund-raising/development; effective prevention approaches; program evaluation and monitoring; program implementation; and risk/protective factor focused prevention framework.

Our results indicated that communities with greater readiness, knowledge, and CTC internal functioning reported a lower overall level of need for TA (Feinberg et al., 2004 b). In addition, those individuals who attended the Key Leader training reported less need for TA on coalition building, program implementation, and understanding the prevention framework.

Our community field experience indicates that even when CTC boards were operating relatively effectively, TA was still needed to link assessment of risk to evidence-based program selection and implementation (Hallfors et al., 2002). The complexity of managing these tasks within a coalition framework should not be underestimated (Kreuter et al., 2000). The importance of greater TA for quality implementation became clear as we found that the issues CTC coalitions were struggling with could not easily be addressed via an occasional phone call with a consultant. Partly in response to our recommendation, Pennsylvania (PA) expanded its cadre of CTC technical assistants from two to five consultants distributed through regions of the state.

THE IMPORTANCE OF COALITION PROCESSES

As discussed above, training and technical assistance were related to the domains of attitudes and knowledge, and functioning of the coalition. To further test aspects of the model in Figure 3.5.1, we examined the relations among constructs in the center of the figure (Feinberg et al., 2004a). Results indicated that internal functioning was highly related to perceived effectiveness. Internal functioning and management of external relations were moderately related, but there was little association between external linkages and other aspects of the model. The implication is that internal functioning and external linkages are distinct domains and that some coalitions may succeed at one and do poorly in the other area (Manger et al., 1992). As we hypothesized, key leaders' attitudes and knowledge regarding prevention were directly related to internal functioning. One interpretation of this finding is that more positive attitudes and greater knowledge of prevention-related issues were linked to more directed and purposeful coalition functioning.

Our findings indicated that both community readiness and internal functioning of the coalition were related to perceived effectiveness. Using a mediational analysis, we examined whether readiness directly affected effectiveness, or whether it did so indirectly; better readiness leads to better internal function which then leads to perceived effectiveness. Results indicated that most of the relationship between readiness and perceived effectiveness was the result of the quality of internal board functioning. Thus, while community readiness is important at the outset of coalition development, training and TA also impact internal functioning—and it is how that board functions that influences its perceived effectiveness.

A final observation centers on the role of turnover in coalitions' memberships. Our research supported findings from previous studies of community coalitions suggesting that the expected rate of turnover of coalition members is fairly high (Fawcett et al., 1997; Lasker et al., 2000), and that turnover is problematic (Gottlieb et al., 1993). High rates of turnover may be one reason for poor coalition functioning, as turnover affects the stability of knowledge and vision. Turnover may also be a consequence of poor functioning.

INVESTIGATING COALITION OUTCOMES

Finally, we note that *perceived* coalition effectiveness is a necessary but not sufficient goal. Two other outcomes are important. The first is obtaining changes in community level rates of problem behaviors. At present, there is little evidence for the effectiveness of coalitions for reducing communities' rates of delinquency and substance abuse, and one study has shown the potential for negative effects (Hallfors et al., 2002). The second important outcome is achieving sustainability of coalition activities and funding over long periods of time. Coalitions typically have difficulty *sustaining* positive initiatives over time.

Community Level Changes in Risk Behaviors

Because CTC primarily focuses on reducing the rates of youth delinquency and other problem behaviors, we examined whether counties utilizing the CTC model would show decreasing rates of delinquency relative to other communities (unfortunately no standard-ized data on youth substance use was available in these communities). Delinquency was defined as the total number of Uniform Crime Report Part I offenses (Federal Bureau of Investigation, 2001) for juveniles under the age of 18 and included murder, rape, robbery, aggravated assault, burglary, larceny and auto theft. Given the relatively small amount of funds provided for the CTC process in each county, it was *not* expected that CTC would have a marked effect on the rates of major problem behaviors during the first years of operation.

To assess counties with and without CTC sites that were comparable in other ways, we identified five risk factors (measured in 1994) that differentiated CTC and non-CTC counties. The variables were: (1) population size of the county; (2) the homeless assistance rate; (3) rate of welfare receipt; (4) teen birth rate; and (5) an ethnic heterogeneity index. These factors were utilized in a propensity analysis to assess the likelihood of each PA county becoming a CTC county, and we eliminated those counties (5 CTC and 14 non-CTC) where scores fell outside the range of the other group.

As a result, the analysis compared 15 CTC counties to 33 non-CTC counties (out of 67 total counties in PA) between 1992 and 1998. The statistical model focused on changes in delinquency rates within counties over this period, gauging the effectiveness of CTC by whether the rates in CTC counties improved relative to the trends for rates in the other coun-ties. The exponentiated coefficients for the model indicate that upon the start of CTC, there was a 1.8% increase in delinquency compared to other counties (perhaps an initial reporting effect as community leaders and institutions brought greater focus to delinquency issues) followed by a 1.5% decrease for each following year. These changes, while promising, were modest in size and did not reach conventional levels of statistical significance.

A second set of analyses examined how the degree of change in rates of delinquency across time was related to the *quality* of the coalition processes. We created a delinquency change score that was equal to the delinquency rate for the three years of CTC operation minus the rate for the five prior years for each county. This rate was adjusted for trends in non-CTC counties. Removed from this analysis were two Pittsburgh sites and the Philadelphia site because data were not available separated for the selected CTC neighborhoods in these large counties and the Dauphin County site because it was a significant outlier with a dramatic drop in delinquency rate. We then examined which CTC site factors were related to the rate of change in delinquency. Communities with greater declines in rate of delinquency were those communities whose coalitions had greater community readiness, greater fidelity to the CTC model, and had CTC leaders who had greater influence in the community.

Sustainability

Despite the popularity of the coalition model, there is little qualitative research on what factors lead local coalitions to retain sufficient commitment and enthusiasm to continue their activities over longer periods of time. In Pennsylvania, CTC coalitions were funded through state support for three years and then funding was terminated. As a result, sustainability of CTC is defined here as the extent to which the structure and initiatives of coalitions continue past the external funding period (Paine-Andrews et al., 2000).

To assess the sustainability of the CTC process, we longitudinally assessed 20 sites approximately a year after their three-year funding from the state was discontinued (Gomez et al., in press). Phone interviews with community mobilizers indicated whether the coalition was still meeting regularly, if it conducted ongoing assessment of risk and protective factors, and whether new prevention funds had been obtained. Approximately 33% of coalitions were defined as continuing with both board operations and new funding.

We hypothesized that sustainability would be more likely when coalition functioning during the initial funding period was successful. Thus, our model of the factors that led to sustainability included community readiness, knowledge of CTC programming, and effective internal and external board functioning.

Three findings emerged. First, coalition members' knowledge of prevention was associated with continuation of coalition board activity, suggesting that board members, knowledge of prevention is an important factor in sustainability. Knowledge of risk factors and program selection may be a powerful driving force for system maintenance. Second, self-reported internal functioning predicted sustained board activity. Third, both the research team's rating of the fidelity of CTC implementation and the technical assistant ratings of the quality of implementation predicted sustained board activity, indicating that the quality of implementation contributes to coalition sustainability. The greater the adherence of the coalition to the prescribed intervention model, the more likely it was to be sustained.

CONCLUSION

In general, the findings above lend support to our proposed model of coalition functioning and sustainability. However, given our sample size, it is not possible to test a complete quantitative model of influence. It would be valuable, for example, to know whether coalition knowledge influences sustainability directly, through coalition functioning, or both. Although we are not able to fully explore a sequential, mediational model of coalition development, we have established links between training and TA and both board knowledge and internal functioning. Second, community readiness also predicted board functioning, but board functioning, rather than readiness, predicted both perceived efficacy and sustainability. Third, board knowledge was related to fidelity of implementation of the CTC model and both fidelity and positive board functioning predicted sustainability. Finally, community readiness, fidelity to the model, and the external influence of the board predicted declining rates of delinquency.

The current findings indicate that prevention knowledge of coalition members, coalition functioning, and fidelity to the CTC model were predictive of sustained efforts in community-wide prevention through the continuing activities of the coalition board. These findings have clear implications for practitioners and policy-makers who can focus resources and attention early in the coalition lifecycle to promote sustainability. Important areas of focus include adequate early training of key leaders so that they are knowledgeable about the logic model that underlies the coalition's purpose and actions (Feinberg et. al., 2002), and ongoing, high quality TA that helps the board maintain fidelity to the model and creates effective internal board functioning (e.g., high cohesion, task orientation and performance [Feinberg et al., 2004a]). Maintaining a critical mass of knowledgeable board members is crucial and this requires orientation for new board members as well as ongoing TA to help community leaders sustain a sense of direction.

Understanding the factors that influence both the functioning and outcomes of community coalitions is essential for developing effective community-wide delivery systems for prevention activities. The study of CTC in Pennsylvania indicates some important factors in the early development and evolution of coalitions that have implications for both research and community planning. It is important to note that while coalitions in themselves do not ensure positive outcomes in addressing adolescent problem behaviors, such outcomes are more likely to be achieved when communities are better poised to effectively develop, manage and sustain coalition preventive efforts. Well-designed trials are necessary that can provide further findings on the short- and long-term effects of coalitions such as CTC in reducing youth substance abuse and promoting youth development.

REFERENCES

Aguirre-Molina, M. and Gorman, D.M. (1996) Community-based approaches for the prevention of alcohol, tobacco, and other drug use. *Annual Review of Public Health*, **17**, 337–358.

Altman, D.G. (1986) A framework for evaluating community-based heart disease prevention programs. *Social Science Medicine*, **22**(4), 479–487.

Arthur, M.W., Ayers, C.D., Graham, K.A. and Hawkins, D.J. (2003) Mobilizing communities to reduce risks for drug abuse: a comparison of two strategies. In W.J. Bukoski and Z. Sloboda (eds), *Handbook of Drug Abuse Prevention: Theory, Science and Practice*. New York: Kluwer Academic/Plenum Publishers, pp. 129–144.

Butterfoss, F.D., Goodman, R.M. and Wandersman, A. (1993) Community coalitions for prevention and health promotion. *Health Education Research*, **8**(3), 315–330.

Butterfoss, F.D., Goodman, R.M. and Wandersman, A. (1996) Community coalitions for prevention and health promotion: factors predicting satisfaction, participation, and planning. *Health Education Quarterly*, **23**(1), 65–79.

COMMIT (1995) Community intervention trial for smoking cessation (COMMIT): I. Cohort results from a four-year community intervention. American Journal of Public Health, **85**(2), 183–192.

Farquhar, J.W. (1978) The community-based model of life style intervention trials. *American Journal of Epidemiology*, **108**(2), 103–111.

Fawcett, S.B., Lewis, R.K., Paine-Andrews, A., Francisco, V.T., Richter, K.P., Williams, E.L. and Copple, B. (1997) Evaluating community coalitions for prevention of substance abuse: the case of project freedom. *Health Education and Behavior*, **24**(6), 812–828.

Federal Bureau of Investigation, U.S. Department of Justice (2001) *Crime in the United States*, 2000. Washington, DC: United States Government Printing Office.

Feinberg, M.E., Greenberg, M.T. and Osgood, D.W. (2004a). Readiness, functioning, and perceived effectiveness in community prevention coalitions: A study of Communities That Care. *American Journal of Community Psychology*, **33**(3–4),163–176.

Feinberg, M.E., Greenberg, M.T. and Osgood, D.W. (2004b) Technical assistance correlates of perceived need in Communities That Care. *Evaluation and Program Planning*, **27**(3), 263–274.

Feinberg, M.E., Greenberg, M.T., Osgood, D.W., Anderson, A. and Babinski, L. (2002) The effects of training community leaders in prevention science: Communities That Care in Pennsylvania. *Evaluation and Program Planning*, **25**, 245–259.

Florin, P., Mitchell, R. and Stevenson, J. (1993) Identifying training and technical assistance needs in community coalitions: a developmental approach. *Health Education Research*, **8**(3), 417–432.

Florin, P., Mitchell, R. Stevenson, J. and Klein, I. (2000) Predicting intermediate outcomes for prevention coalitions: a developmental perspective. *Evaluation and Program Planning*, **23**, 341–346.

Gomez, B.J., Greenberg, M.T. and Feinberg, M.E. (in press) Sustainability of community coalitions: an evaluation of Communities That Care Prevention Science.

Gottlieb, N.H., Brink, S.G. and Gingiss, P.L. (1993) Correlates of coalition effectiveness: The Smoke Free Class of 2000 Program. *Health Education Research*, **8**(3), 375–384.

Hallfors, D., Cho, H., Livert, D. and Kadushin, C. (2002) Fighting back against substance use: are community coalitions winning? *American Journal of Preventive Medicine*, **23**, 237–245.

Harachi, T.W., Ayers, C.D., Hawkins, J.D., Catalano, R.F. and Cushing, J. (1996) Empowering communities to prevent adolescent substance abuse: process evaluation results from a risk- and protection-focused community mobilization effort. *The Journal of Primary Prevention*, **16**(3), 234–254.

Hawkins, J.D. and Catalano, R.F. (1992) *Communities That Care: Action for Drug Abuse Prevention*. San Francisco, CA: Jossey-Bass.

Hawkins, J.D., Catalano, R.F. and Arthur, M.W. (2002) Promoting science-based prevention in communities. *Addictive Behaviors*, **27**, 951–976.

Hollister, R.G., and Hill, J. (1995) Problems in the evaluation of community-wide initiatives. In J.P. Connell, A.C. Kubisch, L.B. Schorr and C.H. Weiss (eds), *New Approaches to Evaluating Community Initiatives: Concepts, Methods, and Contexts*. Washington, DC: The Aspen Institute, pp. 127–172.

Kegler, M.C., Steckler, A., Malek, S.H. and McLeroy, K. (1998) A multiple case study of implementation in 10 local Project ASSIST coalitions in North Carolina. *Health Education Research*, **13**(2), 225–238.

Klitzner, M. (1993) A public health/dynamic systems approach to community-wide alcohol and other drug initiatives. In R.C. Davis, A.J. Lurigio and D.P. Rosenbaum (eds), *Drugs and the Community*. Springfield, IL: Charles C. Thomas, pp. 201–224.

Kreuter, M.W., Lezin, N.A. and Young, L.A. (2000) Evaluating community-based collaborative mechanisms: implications for practitioners. *Health Promotion Practice*, **1**(1), 49–63.

Kumpfer, K.L., Turner, C., Hopkins, R. and Librett, J. (1993) Leadership and team effectiveness in community coalitions for the prevention of alcohol and other drug abuse. *Health Education Research*, **8**(3), 359–374.

Lasker, R.D., Weiss, E.S. and Miller, R. (2000) *Promoting Collaborations that Improve Health*. New York: Center for the Advancement of Collaborative Strategies in Health.

Manger, T.H., Hawkins, J.D., Haggerty, K.P. and Catalano, R.F. (1992) Mobilizing communities to reduce risks for drug abuse: lessons on using research to guide prevention practice. *The Journal of Primary Prevention*, **13**(1), 3–22.

Paine-Andrews, A., Fisher, J.L., Campuzano, M.K., Fawcett, S.B., and Berkley-Patton, J. (2000) Promoting sustainability of community health initiatives: an empirical case study. *Health Promotion Practice*, **1**(3), 248–258.

Pollard, J.A., Hawkins, J.D. and Arthur, M.W. (1999) Risk and protection: are both necessary to understand diverse behavioral outcomes in adolescence? *Social Work Research*, **23**(3), 145–158.

Puska, P., Nissinen, A., Tuomilehto, J., Salonen, J.T., Koskela, K., McAlister, A., Kottke, T.E., Maccoby, N. and Farquhar, J.W. (1985) The community-based strategy to prevent coronary heart disease: conclusions from the Ten Years of the North Karelia Project. *Annual Review of Public Health*, **6**, 147–193.

Rindskopf, D. and Saxe, L. (1998) Zero effects in substance abuse programs: Avoiding false positives and false negatives in the evaluation of community-based programs. *Evaluation Review*, **22**(1), 78–94.

Roberts, R.N. and Wasik, B.H. (1996) Evaluating the 1992 and 1993 Community Integrated Service System Projects. *New Directions for Evaluation*, **69**, 35–49.

Roussos, S.T. and Fawcett, S.B. (2000) A review of collaborative partnerships as a strategy for improving community health. *American Review of Public Health*, **21**, 369–402.

Saxe, L., Reber, E., Hallfors, D., Kadushin, C., Jones, D., Rindskopf, D. and Beveridge, A. (1997) Think globally, act locally: assessing the impact of community-based substance abuse prevention. *Evaluation and Program Planning*, **20**(3), 357–366.

Yin, R.K., Kaftarian, S.J., Yu, P. and Jansen, M.A. (1997) Outcomes from CSAP's community partnership program: findings from the national cross-site evaluation. *Evaluation and Program Planning*, **20**(3), 345–355.

Section 4 INTERVENTIONS IN THE COMMUNITY: ILLUSTRATIVE CASE STUDIES

EDITED BY PAUL J. GRUENEWALD

4.1 Introduction

PAUL J. GRUENEWALD

Prevention Research Center, Berkeley, CA, USA

The multi-level nature of the social processes that support drug use and related harms requires preventive interventions that address these problems at each unique level, from individual choices to use to national choices to tax use. Thus efforts to prevent harmful substance use may take place on many levels, from efforts to individually educate young people to resist drug use (Chapter 3.2: building resilience among children) to efforts to change national policies with regard to drug distribution (Chapter 6.5: taxes to increase the costs of drugs). Ultimately, effective preventive interventions will be optimized to reduce use with some combination of prevention strategies at these multiple scales (Chapters 7.2 and 7.3: optimal prevention portfolios and strategies).

In the past century, it has become clear that prevention research and intervention at the community level are one of the appropriate levels at which to work: community-based prevention research provides ready access to moderate-sized populations and systems that can feasibly be measured to detect changing patterns of social process (Chapter 2.5: drug use systems). Communities, loosely defined to be small cities and towns of several hundred thousand people or less, can also be treated as units in experimental and quasi-experimental tests of the effectiveness of prevention programs to reduce substance use (Holder and Howard, 1992). The community has been a test bench for preventive interventions throughout the world (Babor et al., 2003) and a particular focus of study with regard to the prevention of alcohol problems (Holder, 1998) and drug abuse (Davis et al., 1993). The chapters in this section contribute to this tradition, providing the reader with guides to what works best in theory, research and practice.

One of the primary emphases of community-based programs is their focus on populations rather than individuals. Rather than focus upon changing individual behaviors with regard to substance use, community-based programs attempt to change behaviors of populations. This difference is of substantive importance when viewed from the perspective of community-based preventive interventions. Most community-based preventive interventions attempt to change the social processes that underlie use, affecting large numbers of users, with individual change being one of the consequences, but with the identification of the particular individuals that do change as irrelevant. This perspective is particularly pertinent to substance use problems that are very broadly represented in populations (e.g., most alcohol problems), or that involve complex social systems for distribution and use (e.g., illegal drug sales and use). In these circumstances, case finding is very costly, and the reduction of substance use problems in the population of users is beneficial to a broad

Preventing Harmful Substance Use: The Evidence Base for Policy and Practice.
Edited by T. Stockwell, P. J. Gruenewald, J.W. Toumbourou and W. Loxley.
© 2005 John Wiley & Sons, Ltd. ISBN 0-470-09227-0 (hbk) 0-470-09228-9 (pbk).

number of social institutions (e.g., policing and emergency medical systems). The chapters in this section also present examples of applications of community-based preventive interventions to different populations and sub-populations of users.

Chapter 4.2, "Community Systems and Ecologies of Drug and Alcohol Problems" (H. Holder et al.), presents an overview of the theoretical bases of the "systems" approach that typically underlies community-based prevention programs. Communities are viewed as multiple systems of agents (e.g., the police) with functions that are designed to achieve some end (e.g., reduction of illegal drug sales). These systems interact with one another. So, for example, distribution systems for illegal drugs both shape and respond to police activity, and are supported by larger economic and social constraints of communities (see also Fagan, 1993). As Holder et al. argue, the interactions of these systems matter a great deal since efforts to intervene in these systems can have unexpected consequences. The ecologies of these systems may also provide support for the maintenance of a number of substance use problems in different community settings.

Chapter 4.3, "Violence Prevention in Licensed Premises" (Haines and Graham), provides one example of a preventive intervention directed at a specific social context (i.e., bars and taverns) that is intended to affect behaviors in a specific sub-population (i.e., patrons of bars and taverns). Efforts to prevent violence in bar settings are directed toward intervening in the system of alcohol distribution and use by, among other things, reorganizing a second community system (i.e., police enforcement practices) in order to reinforce prevention efforts.

Chapter 4.4, "Application of Evidence-Based Approaches to Community Interventions" (Treno et al.), provides an overview of international community-based prevention efforts to reduce alcohol problems, and provides an example of a local neighborhood-based preventive intervention to reduce alcohol-related violence among young people. This approach is unique because it demonstrates how to mix approaches at multiple scales of the community, neighborhood, and local community-based organizations.

Chapter 4.5, "Preventing Alcohol and Other Drug Problems in the Workplace" (Midford et al.), provides yet another illustration of an important domain for community preventive interventions, the workplace. The authors provide an outline of the costs of drug use to work productivity, examine the mechanisms by which substance use affects work performance, and discuss the contentious issues regarding the effectiveness and utility of workplace drug testing.

Chapter 4.6, "Effects of a Community Action Program on Problems Related to Alcohol Consumption at Licensed Premises" (Wallin and Andréasson), provides an example of a community-based approach to policing alcohol outlets for the purpose of preventing access to alcohol among young people, and to prevent service to intoxicated patrons. The results of this preventive intervention highlight the importance of having the cooperation and support of law enforcement agencies and alcohol distributors in efforts to reduce problems related to alcohol. In the best of circumstances, collective action of this sort leads to rapid reductions in problems.

Chapter 4.7, "Strategies for Community-Based Drug Law Enforcement: From Prohibition to Harm Reduction" (Canty et al.), continues the discussion of the role of law enforcement in local problems related to illegal drug sales and use. The prevention of illegal drug sales and use at the community level is both an essential activity of law enforcement and a social problem of great complexity. The authors argue that enforcement for the purposes of drug prohibition may not be the best strategy as direct impacts on drug distribution systems (e.g., disrupted drug markets) may reinforce the underground drug economy and increase rather than decrease other problems related to use (e.g., needle sharing, sexually transmitted diseases). The secondary costs of successful enforcement may outweigh the benefits. This argument returns us to Chapter 4.2 where it is emphasized, and should be emphasized once again, that interventions in community systems can have secondary consequences of great, and sometimes unrecognized, importance. Community-based research and prevention efforts should be conducted with these aspects of community systems in mind.

REFERENCES

Babor, T., Caetano, R., Casswell, S., Edwards, G., Giesbrecht, N., Graham, K., Grube, J., Gruenewald, P., Hill, L., Holder, H., Homel, R., Osterberg, E., Rehm, J., Room, R. and Rossow, I. (2003) *Alcohol, No Ordinary Commodity: Research and Public Policy.* Oxford: Oxford University Press.

Davis, R.C., Lurigio, A.J. and Rosenbaum, D.P. (1993) *Drugs and the Community: Involving Community Residents in Combating the Sale of Illegal Drugs.* New York: Thomas.

Fagan, J. (1993) The political economy of drug dealing among urban gangs. In R.C. Davis, A.J. Lurigio and D.P. Rosenbaum (eds), *Drugs and the Community: Involving Community Residents in Combating the Sale of Illegal Drugs.* New York: Thomas, pp. 19–54.

Holder, H.D. (1998) *Alcohol and the Community: A Systems Approach to Prevention.* Cambridge: Cambridge University Press.

Holder, H.D. and Howard, J.M. (1992) *Community Prevention Trials for Alcohol Problems.* New York: Praeger.

4.2 Community Systems and Ecologies of Drug and Alcohol Problems

HAROLD D. HOLDER, ANDREW TRENO
Prevention Research Center, Berkeley, CA, USA

DAVID LEVY
Public Services Research Institute, Calverton, MD, USA

SUMMARY

This chapter outlines the theoretical bases underlying the "community systems approach" to alcohol and other substance-related problems. It begins by contrasting this approach with more individual-based approaches and argues for its application to these problems on both practical and theoretical grounds. It then presents an illustration of how this approach may be applied using "computer systems modeling" as an illustration. It is argued that such modeling reflects the complexity of the use/abuse system, provides a means to integrate existing prevention and epidemiological studies, can be used to assist prevention planning by projecting potential outcomes for various prevention strategies, and ultimately provides a prevention planning tool that can be utilized in a variety of settings. Three simulation programs (i.e., SimCom, SimSmoke and SimPot) are presented. Finally, the chapter discusses two types of modeling strategies which fit within this broader approach: (1) the mean field approach; and (2) the network approach. While the former attempts to reduce complex ecological interactions to their root dynamics, the latter creates a higher-resolution, graph-based model that describes spatial and temporal interactions between individuals and community systems. Thus, while the former provides the advantage of characterizing complex problems simply, the latter more accurately captures the dynamics underlying them. It is argued that both techniques should be used in parallel, and with reference to statistical assessment of goodness-of-fit to available data that will provide measures of optimal performance at various scales. It is concluded that the effective prevention of alcohol, tobacco, and drug problems must be based upon an approach that provides the greatest possible potential return for research and prevention interventions.

Preventing Harmful Substance Use: The Evidence Base for Policy and Practice.
Edited by T. Stockwell, P. J. Gruenewald, J.W. Toumbourou and W. Loxley.
© 2005 John Wiley & Sons, Ltd. ISBN 0-470-09227-0 (hbk) 0-470-09228-9 (pbk).

INTRODUCTION

The development of effective community-level alcohol and other drug (AOD) interventions requires that prevention planners and policy-makers understand how various aspects of communities influence AOD use and subsequent problems. The community is more than a mere collection of individuals living in physical and social proximity. A broader and more appropriate perspective on community substance use research and action suggests that we are all participants in a total community system: a dynamic, self-adaptive social, economic, and spatially distributed system of actors and organizations including licensed establishments selling alcohol, police responsible for enforcing laws regulating substance use, and parents monitoring youth activities. In this approach the community can provide strategic levers to improve its members' health and well-being, establish appropriate standards for consumption and set formal and informal controls on the abuse of alcohol and other substances.

This community systems perspective on the prevention of AOD problems suggests that effective prevention efforts must influence the relationships between individuals and their drug and alcohol use environments. As examples, alcohol sales and service practices at retail outlets, enforcement activities targeting alcohol sales to minors, and zoning regulations addressing alcohol outlet densities are all seen as aspects of the alcohol environment that, when manipulated, can change individual drinking behaviors and subsequent problems. Indeed, even environmental factors not typically considered a part of the alcohol environment (e.g., highway placement patterns, lighting of streets in commercial districts) could be conducive to prevention efforts. Thus, the community systems perspective indicates the value of combining efforts to change individual substance use decisions and behaviors with relevant environmental change (Holder, 1998a, 1998b). From this perspective community drug and alcohol problems are not simply attributable to the actions of a set of definable high-risk individuals but are rather the cumulative result of the structure and flow of complex social, cultural, and economic factors within the community system.

Individual vs. Environmental Prevention

Many prevention programs are aimed at individuals in specific settings (e.g., children in the classroom or employees in the workplace). Such individual programs, however, may be more effective if incorporated into a comprehensive set of strategies that also address community systems and the ecologies of drug use. The potential drug user/abuser plays a range of life roles (e.g., student, employee, co-worker, spouse, parent, friend, and neighbor) within a variety of settings, each with its own unique code of behavior regarding substance use. Accordingly, the effects from single-component preventive interventions (e.g., school-based education or educational programs in the workplace) stand a good chance of being neutralized by the multiplicity of counter-forces operating in the individual's life (e.g., ready availability of drugs through social networks). A natural extension of this logic is that prevention strategies may be most effective when focused on the total system rather than on specific individuals-at-risk. Individuals often return to environments that reinforce precisely those problem behaviors that person-centered programs attempt to prevent.

Practically speaking, it is not possible to permanently "inoculate" a community population against alcohol and other drug-related problems. The community, acting as a dynamic system, changes as new members enter and others leave, as alcoholic beverage marketing and promotion evolve, as social and economic conditions change, and as drug availability increases or decreases. For example, adolescent use of AOD might be combated with strategies aimed at increasing pre-adolescents' resistance skills against peer pressure to drink, after-school activities and school-based alcohol education programs. However, such an approach would not affect the behaviors of community members not directly involved with these adolescents, retail sales of alcohol nor the availability of social sources of AOD. In any case the population of young people will be constantly renewed, requiring re-administration of the program at regular intervals, a costly re-application of prevention resources.

Despite these limitations, the individual risk approach is still commonly used in health problem prevention. It follows a straightforward logic, similar to a case finding method to disease prevention: find the persons at risk, then educate, serve or treat them in an appropriate manner to reduce the individual risk to each person identified. A central problem of this approach for AOD use is that risks for these behaviors are pandemic; all youth are at risk and the vectors for transmission are global, including such entities as television media, retail advertising, adult role models, and others. Thus, while conceptually more complex, the community systems perspective is clearly more appropriate to these problems. In this approach, AOD problems are viewed as the outcomes of processes driven and sustained by the community-at-large. The intention is to reduce the collective risk to populations through appropriate interventions affecting these processes.

COMPLEX SYSTEMS AND PREVENTION

The community systems where people live and prevention programs are embedded are complex arrangements with many parts that interact over time (dynamic systems). Forrester's (1969) study of complex networks serves as the support for community systems research; he cautioned policy-makers about unintended consequences that quick and easy "solutions" to social problems may yield. He describes urban areas as having a number of separate social, physical, and economic states representing levels of crime, housing, population, economic stability, health, revenue, welfare, social services, natural resources, energy, and so on. Due to the large number of interacting components required to explain an urban area, this "high-order" system contains both positive feedback loops (i.e., systems processes by which growth generates further action and thus further growth) and negative feedback loops (i.e., systems processes by which growth is regulated toward some goal or constrained). To illustrate the former, as populations increase, housing supply, retail development, and highway construction follow, as do some additional problem behaviors such as elevated rates of crime. In contrast, negative feedback loops regulate the community system toward some objective: for example, crime that increases as population increases can be regulated by policing efforts. However, within these complex systems, regulations intended to achieve one goal (e.g., restricting alcohol outlets to retail areas) may have unintended consequences for others (e.g., increasing concentrations of crime) or be disproportional to the original intent of regulation.

This type of "systems thinking" has supported current community-based foci for prevention. The influences of environment and lifestyle on increased risk of cardiovascular disease and cancer were fully recognized in the mid-1970s by the public health profession (Margolis et al., 1974). Community-wide interventions were developed to reduce these risks. In like manner, community-based prevention strategies are now being developed to modify the environments and contexts within which substance use occurs in order to reduce the harmful effects of such use. These approaches were developed on the basis of two essential premises: (1) prevention strategies are most effective when focused on the community-at-large rather than on specific high-risk individuals; and (2) no single prevention program, no matter how effective for its specific target population, can sustain its impact, particularly if system-level changes are not accomplished (Holder, 1998a, b; Holder and Wallack, 1986). To make changes in the community system or the economic, physical, and social environments of the community, public policies are needed. For example, local alcohol policies can include making a priority of drinking and driving enforcement by police; mandating server training for bars, pubs, and restaurants; setting a written policy for responsible alcoholic beverage service by a retail licensed establishment; and/or allocating enforcement resources to prevent alcohol sales to underage persons. While environmental preventive interventions for the amelioration of problems related to illegal drugs are still in their nascent stage, environmental strategies are evolving to address these issues (e.g., local place management around retail shops).

COMPUTER SYSTEMS MODELS AS TOOLS FOR PREVENTION RESEARCH AND PLANNING

A fundamental problem with AOD problem prevention is the gap between the pressing need to address these ills and the lack of the scientific base required to support the adoption and implementation of prevention policies and programs. Effective public policy to reduce drug-related problems is best formulated when decision-makers are aware of existing prevention alternatives and the potential effect of each alternative within a cost containment framework.

A computer systems model is a mathematical structure (or theory) in which one can interrelate and interpret research observations and findings. A model can be defined as a set of well-defined variables expressed quantitatively with specific and well-defined relationships between variables. Computer models are representations of reality; because they are approximations, models can only reflect the best available data and experiences and are subject to alteration as new information becomes available. This methodological approach holds promise for addressing challenges associated with community-based AOD problem prevention, and takes into account the multiple components of prevention strategies. Such models are designed to replicate the historical patterns and dynamics of target communities with regard to substance availability and use, and then simulate future patterns and dynamics under alternative assumptions and interventions.

Computer systems models for AOD problem prevention (as will be described below) have the following objectives: (1) to develop a conceptual model which reflects the complexity of the use/abuse system; (2) to provide a means to integrate existing prevention and epidemiological studies; (3) to develop and validate a tool which could be used to assist prevention planning by projecting potential outcomes for various prevention strategies; and (4) to provide a prevention planning tool that can be loaded and utilized in multiple locations. Such a model can be thought of as having two parts: structure and data. The structure describes the elements and relationships that compose the system and is generic enough to be used in diverse situations. The data enable the model to take on the unique character of the specific situation (e.g., community) to be modeled. The structure is expressed both conceptually in flow charts and diagrams and also in the computer program code. This program is loaded with specific data to conduct a simulation.

Via simulation the state of the system at subsequent points in time is estimated by the model itself from the prior states, the equations, parameters, etc. internal to the model itself. If the conceptualization of model relationships is correct (i.e., in accord with the real world), and the quantitative specification of that conceptualization is accurate, model estimates of system behavior by simulation should provide sufficiently accurate approximations of actual system behavior. Thus, a critical component of the development of each model is a systematic examination of its behavior to assess its internal and external validity. Internal validity is determined by testing whether the model performs in the expected manner and makes sensible forecasts. External validity is determined by testing whether the model's predictions are consistent with findings in the published literature.

Examples of Computer Systems Models of Substance Abuse

SimCom

The most advanced application of computer simulation technology applied to substance abuse planning is a fourth-generation computer model of alcohol use and abuse, SimCom (SIMulated COMmunity). SimCom is a dynamic computer model developed to simulate alcohol use and its consequences and to assess interventions for reducing alcohol-involved problems. The model was developed at the Prevention Research Center (PRC) in Berkeley, California. It is a tool designed for policy-makers concerned with alcohol-related deaths, injuries, and diseases and their costs to society (Holder, 1998a,1998b).

SimCom replicates historical patterns and forecasts future "business as usual" dynamics of alcohol-related problems. It also simulates future potential changes in specific alcohol-involved problems that may be realistically expected from well-defined programs and/or policies. SimCom simulates the complexity and dynamics of a real community (such as a city, county or state) when loaded with appropriate local data. It shows the dynamics of alcohol consumption patterns, retail activity, drinking and driving behavior, mortality and morbidity, social norms, regulatory behavior, and economic consequences among the population in a community. These components of community systems are represented by seven *subsystems* in the model. Each subsystem is composed of many factors, variables, and parameters. An example is shown in Figure 4.2.1.

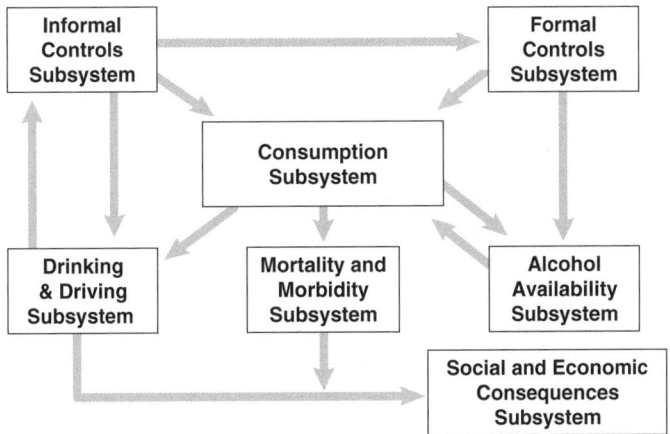

Figure 4.2.1   Model subsystems

The heart of the model is the Consumption Subsystem that subdivides the community population into 14 age and gender subgroups. The total consumption for the community is calculated based on the distribution of the population in these subgroups for each model year. In the Informal Controls Subsystem, social, ethnic and other cultural norms influence levels of alcohol consumption through means that increase or decrease acceptance of alcohol use. This subsystem also simulates the influence of the news media, levels of advertising and promotion of alcohol, and youth norms about drinking. Interventions can occur through education, mass communications, and restrictions on marketing. The Formal Controls Subsystem simulates the effects of interventions introduced by state or local regulatory agencies to influence access to alcohol and availability of alcohol through retail sales or the consumption of alcohol during a specific time period. Licensing, enforcement, penalties or zoning might be exercised to affect consumption. The Alcohol Availability Subsystem focuses on the availability of alcohol for on-premise or off-site consumption. Population growth and economic indicators explain and predict the number and types of outlets with permits to sell alcoholic beverages. In the Drinking and Driving Subsystem, driving events at varying blood alcohol concentration (BAC) levels are computed for the community's population subgroups and are mapped into numbers of driver fatal and injury crashes. This subsystem reflects the effects of driving under the influence (DUI) arrest rates, enforcement, legal BAC limits, severity of sanctions, etc. on injury and fatal crashes. The Mortality and Morbidity Subsystem uses group-specific risk rates linked to levels of alcohol consumption to convert numbers of persons in each age/gender subgroup into annual cases of alcohol-associated deaths, illnesses and non-traffic injuries. Finally, the Social and Economic Consequences Subsystem computes the direct costs of traffic and non-traffic fatalities and injuries to the community.

The data inputs to SimCom are compiled from syntheses of the best available published scientific knowledge from research findings and survey data about alcohol-involved problems. The structure of the simulation is represented by organized sets of mathematical formulae and algorithms that relate the alcohol consumption and other subsystems described above. Using local data inputs, consumption levels in the community are estimated annually for age/gender subgroups in relation to: (1) historical patterns and dynamics; (2) changes in factors such as income, price, and legal minimum drinking age; and (3) model-generated changes in retail availability, social norms and/or enforcement of regulations. The model then applies risk rates for each subgroup to derive numbers of DUI arrests and convictions, driver fatalities and injuries, alcohol-related mortality and morbidity, non-traffic accidental injuries and deaths, and total direct costs to the community.

Ultimately SimCom simulates changes in consumption and related drinking behaviors brought about by the effects of interventions (programs and policies) on factors called *intermediate variables*. These often consist of structural features of community systems that can be manipulated to ameliorate problems, such as operating hours of alcohol outlets and police enforcement patterns. The model accomodates changes in these variables on a yearly basis, calculates the long-term effect and compares the results to "business as usual". This feature allows policy-makers to conduct experiments to determine the effects of well-defined programs and/or policies (interventions) on specific alcohol-involved problems (target outcomes) in their community. For example, as shown in outline in Figure 4.2.2, intermediate variables X, Y, and Z are identified as effective in reducing alcohol-involved driver fatalities (target outcome). These are the perceived risk of punishment for DUI (X), the DUI arrest rate (Y), and the level of DUI enforcement (Z). Effects can then be estimated

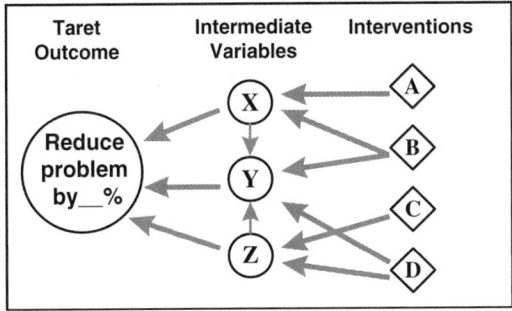

Figure 4.2.2   Effect of intermediate variables on target outcome

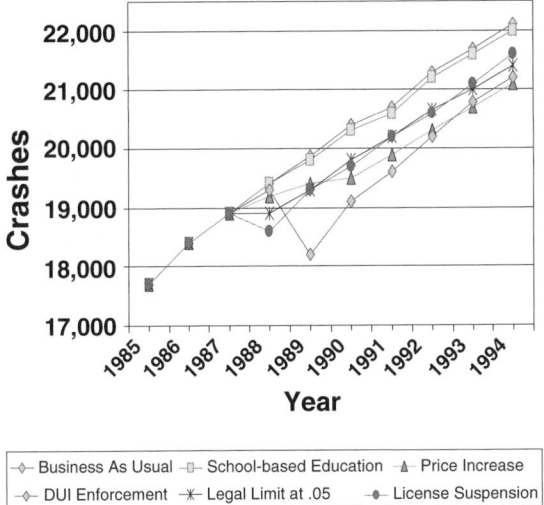

Figure 4.2.3   Motor vehicle injury crashes San Diego, CA

using SimCom for a single intervention such as increasing media coverage of DUI (A). Or, effects can be determined for a prevention strategy that combines several intervention actions, such as policies or programs that increase the perceived risk of punishment (X) and the DUI arrest rate (Y) such as officer training (B), and that increase DUI enforcement (Z) through special patrols (C) and random breath testing (D).

Figure 4.2.3 illustrates the utility of the use of SimCom in terms of the effects of various changes in five alcohol interventions compared to "business as usual". Specifically, DUI enforcement, school-based education, lower BAC limits, price increases, and policies regarding license suspension were considered. Using the procedures discussed above, it was determined that the highest levels of motor vehicle crashes would occur under the "business as usual" condition or when only school-based educational programs were implemented. Enforcement, policy, and economic interventions returned more substantial returns in terms of reduced injury crashes (Holder, 1998a).

Using SimCom, policy-makers can assess the potential success of policy or programmatic actions for reaching the community's goals prior to the commitment of available resources.

Once congruence has been established, a series of alcohol-involved problem prevention interventions can be posited and their likely effects simulated over a 10 to 20-year period. The general procedure for any state or locality is: (1) to begin with a congruent model (the generic model is loaded with local or state data and benchmarks tested); (2) to alter policy-sensitive variables for the future to represent potential prevention program or policy interventions; (3) to run the model with these changes; and (4) to compare the model outcomes generated using different values for the policy change variables.

SimSmoke

SimSmoke is a similarly structured dynamic model designed to estimate the prevalence and incidence of smoking in a general population, the long-term consequences of smoking in terms of mortality from various causes related to chronic exposure to cigarette smoke, and the relationship of price, retail and social availability, and social marketing to the patterns of smoking. The transition from alcohol to tobacco is enabled by the fact that tobacco, like alcohol, is a legal commodity with a long tradition of prevention research (Levy et al., 2000; Levy et al., 2003). In SimSmoke, the effects of youth access policies influence youth smoking through its effect on retail tobacco availability. The availability of cigarettes to youth is defined within a geographical area, e.g., a neighborhood, community, county, state, or nation. Cigarettes are generally acquired from retail establishments, including food shops, drug stores, restaurants, bars, independent vending machines, and gasoline stations. Retail availability encompasses the number and location of stores (which affects the distance traveled and the ability to find a store selling to minors), the number and location of vending machines, and the prevalence of self-service displays (which affects the likelihood of being able to purchase). There is no assumption of a licensing requirement, only that the establishment is operated for profit. SimSmoke accounts for, or simulates, the alternative sources of cigarettes to youth over time in response to policy changes. Cigarette availability to youth is an economically stimulated response to demand for cigarettes in general and to youth demand in particular.

For each module a similar approach was followed. First, the conceptual model was developed. While extant literature shaped this development, the goal was to provide a conceptually coherent model that often went beyond the literature. Then the research was examined to ensure that the model was consistent with the existing evidence and to provide guidance in the choice of parameters for the model. Next, the coherent model was tested. Once coherency of the model was established, sensitivity testing was conducted to examine the internal validity of each module. The ranges of the policy variables were inspected to determine whether the results implied reasonable parameters for each of the equations. Once the model appeared to be internally valid, benchmark testing was conducted. Values for policy variables from well-designed empirical studies were loaded into the program, and the effects of the model were compared to the results of the studies. This last step served as an additional check to determine that the module yielded consistent, valid results.

Results showed that large potential gains could be realized from the implementation of a comprehensive tobacco control policy package. The Arizona SimSmoke model estimated that tobacco control policies implemented across the state substantially reduced smoking rates in Arizona by over 20%. This confirmed previous work that attributed reductions in smoking prevalence to comprehensive tobacco control policies. Much of the reduction, almost 70%, was attributed to price increases between the years 1994 and 2000. The model

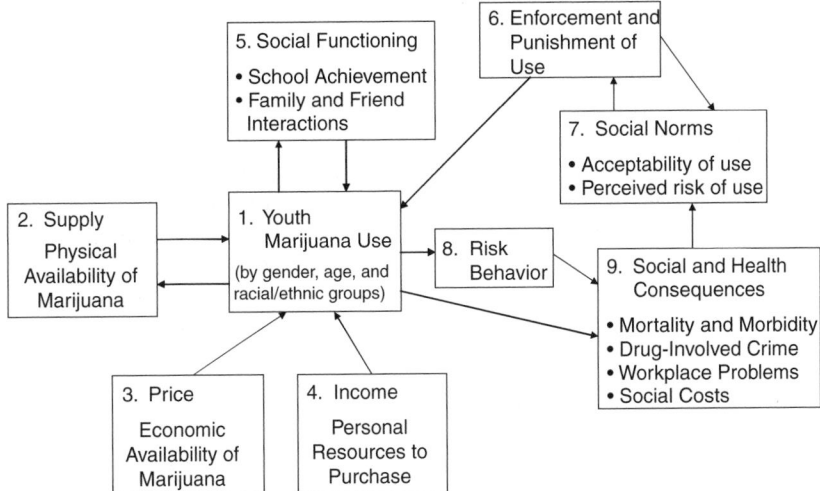

Figure 4.2.4   Basic outline of a computer model of youth marijuana use: SimPot

also attributed over 20% of the overall effect to media/cessation policies. Finally, the model estimated that only a small percentage of the smoking reductions could be credited to clean air laws and youth access policies. The model estimated that before the comprehensive tobacco control policies were implemented, about 5,000 people died annually from smoking. After these tobacco control policies were enacted, smoking prevalence diminished. The SimSmoke model projected these factors into the future and provided a prediction on how many lives would be saved. The model predicted that over 25,000 lives would be saved over the next 40 years.

Similar programs have been developed at the Prevention Research Center (Sim Pot) for marijuana and cocaine following the conceptual model outlined in Figure 4.2.4. As with SimCom the heart of the model is consumption, which is conceptualized as both an input and output process operating within a broader systems model. Price, income, and enforcement regarding use are seen as impacting use, which in turn affects risk behavior and social and health consequences directly and unidirectionally. Other model variables which operate bidirectionally include social functioning and supply. Social norms surrounding use are influenced by social and health consequences and enforcement. As with SimCom, the further development of this model will involve a series of steps by which it tested and evaluated relative to its predictive capacity given empirical data.

Ecological Models and Computer Systems Models: The Next Wave

Although computer simulation models of alcohol and drug problems have come a long way in helping us explain the influences of regulation and enforcement on AOD problems, they suffer three significant shortcomings. First, the level of complexity of these models may obscure the relevant dynamics for specific problems; and the numbers of parameters estimated as inputs to these models often number in the hundreds. Another challenge is that the stable equilibria and boundary conditions for these models are not easy to ascertain; the sheer complexity of these models makes them unsuitable for classical systems analysis. Another shortcoming is the fact that many of the ecological processes implied by these models are spatially distributed (e.g., DUI arrests occur at specific locations) and imply spatial dynamics not addressed by these models (e.g., interactions with patterns of enforcement). In an important sense, the current round of simulations is either too complex (for further mathematical analysis) or not complex enough (to address important spatial interactions related to alcohol and drug use, Gorman et al., 2004).

While keeping within the broader systems approach, recent work has begun to consider two complementary alternative modeling strategies: (1) mean field approaches; and (2) network approaches. Mean field approaches attempt to reduce complex ecological interactions to their root dynamics, the essential causes of system complexity. Network approaches address explicit spatial components and interactions for the purposes of defining the spatial patterns of problems.

Mean field approach

The mean field approach to computer modeling consists of replacing observed and randomly fluctuating quantities with their long-term averages. This approach is often used as a compromise between the complexities of data structures within systems and the need to develop simplified representations of them. Hence, it is not surprising to see literatures associated with the dynamics of populations in complex systems dominated by simplicity (see, for example, Anderson and May 1991).

Simplified approaches have had a positive influence on research activity in fields ruled by complexity such as immunology, epidemiology and ecology. In the early twentieth century, the work of Lotka (1925) and Volterra (1926) helped define mutualistic and competitive interactions in biological systems. Similarly, the work of physicians Sir Ronald Ross on malaria and Kermack and Mackendrick on the dynamics of communicable disease helped define and relate the concepts of basic reproductive number (the number of secondary infections generated by an "average" infectious individual in a population of susceptibles), threshold, invasion and epidemic (see Krebs, 1994; Brauer and Castillo-Chavez, 2001). More recently, Perelson et al. (1997) using aggregate models helped redefine HIV infections and have altered views on treatment. These research endeavors, developed with the aid of aggregated models, have been the key to the evaluation of public health policies that include treatment, vaccination, quarantine, isolation, education and other forms of control. These research endeavors have spurred an interest in the development of aggregated modeling approaches in alcohol problem research. In many fields threshold definitions are defined by averages—average predation rate, average contact rate, average life span—that do not reflect the variability inherent at the individual level. Drinking levels may also be defined in terms of averages—such as the average number of drinks consumed in a specific time period (Dufour, 1999). Fine grain variations in these behaviors over time can reduce expendable complexity, while allowing researchers to examine drinking outcomes and related problems.

Network approach

The alternative or "network approach" creates a higher-resolution, graph-based model that describes spatial and temporal interactions between individuals in the community system. Instead of modeling aggregate behaviors and relating these to overall rates of problem outcomes across communities (the "mean field" approach), network approach models disaggregate behavioral interactions, represent these interactions as networks of relationships, and then study the emergence of aggregate phenomena over time (Durrett and Levin, 1994;

Keeling, 1999). For example, as applied to alcohol-related violence, the disaggregate behaviors of interest are the flows of individuals to-and-from alcohol outlets and/or other retail or residential spaces across community neighborhoods. The network of interactions consists of those social interactions that may result in alcohol-related violence (e.g., obtaining and using alcohol in different locations and interacting with others who are potentially violent). The emergent phenomena of interest are the development and change in geographic distributions of alcohol-related violence, with an emphasis upon the surfacing of violence "hot spots". In this application, an important goal of network approaches would be to understand how aggregate interactions result in nonlinear phenomena that characterize development and change in violence rates. These models provide much higher spatial resolution than mean field models and introduce explicit local spatial dimensions representing neighborhood topology (e.g., proximity of alcohol outlets to residential areas).

One of the most valuable attributes of network models is that they evolve over time and space. Given the state of the system at every node today, one can infer the state of the system tomorrow by updating each node attribute and each edge weight according to the current values of the node attributes, edge weights and output variables (feedback). An important feature of this updating process is that it is a function of any positive or negative feedback loops in the model. Mathematically, this updating process defines a Markov chain that can be analyzed either computationally or theoretically. These models are, however, also computationally intensive and require more detailed knowledge of the disaggregated behaviors and interactions on which they are based, thus making the model more prone to uncertainty. Both types of models (mean field and network) should be analyzed in parallel, and with reference to statistical assessment of goodness-of-fit to available data that will provide measures of optimal performance at various scales.

CONCLUSION

Computer systems modeling on substances of abuse provides rich opportunities for technology transfer; for example, the previously discussed alcohol model can be transferred to illegal drugs. The model is composed of eight interacting subsystems; these same subsystems exist in any social, cultural and economic system in which illicit substances are used. There is consumption (use of drugs), retail (illicit suppliers, distributors, and outlets for drugs), formal regulation and control (laws and enforcement of possession, use, and sale of drugs), social norms and public pressure (values and social rules in support of and against drug use and drug sales), etc. Clearly these models will need to consider the specifics of drug epidemiology and prevention research as applied to illegal drugs as they will provide essential knowledge on which to base any computer model of drug use and drug problems. Experimental and expert knowledge from drug program and prevention specialists, state and local prevention policy-makers, drug enforcement personnel, and informants would be used in addition to ethnographic observations. These valuable sources of knowledge and experience would add essential richness and realism to the model. A validated drug systems model could provide estimates of future drug activities under various economic and cultural assumptions. These data could provide key information for validating supply computer models, thus offering state prevention coordinators much-needed information for drug and alcohol prevention program planning and evaluation, appropriate to the limits and mandates of a civilian agency.

Effective prevention of alcohol, tobacco, and drug problems must be based upon an approach that provides the greatest possible potential return for research and prevention interventions. The systems perspective described in this chapter and operationalized in a series of computer-based models used for simulation of alternative prevention strategies provides such a potential. While traditional experimental design with specifically targeted individuals offers a time-honored means to test specific and well-defined prevention programs, these targeted strategies alone lack the potency to address pervasive public health problems at the community level. A more comprehensive and realistic approach will be needed in the twenty-first century.

ACKNOWLEDGEMENT

Research for and preparation of this manuscript were supported by Grant Number R01-AA011968 from the National Institute on Alcohol Abuse and Alcoholism, National Institutes of Health.

REFERENCES

Anderson, R.M. and May, R.M. (1991) *Infectious Diseases of Humans: Dynamics and Control*. New York: Oxford University Press.

Brauer, F. and Castillo-Chavez, C. (2001) *Mathematical Models in Population Biology and Epidemiology*. New York: Springer-Verlag.

Dufour, M.C. (1999) What is moderate drinking? Defining "drinks" and drinking levels. *Alcohol Research and Health*, **23**, 5–14.

Durrett, R. and Levin, S. (1994) Stochastic spatial models: a user's guide to ecological applications. *Philosophical Transactions of the Royal Society of London B*, **343**, 329–350.

Forrester, J.W. (1969) *Urban Dynamics*. Cambridge, MA: MIT Press.

Gorman, D.M., Gruenewald, P.J., Hanlon, P.J., Mezic, I., Waller, L.A., Castillo-Chavez, C., Bradley, E., and Mezic, J. (2004) Implications of systems dynamic models and control theory for environmental approaches to the prevention of alcohol- and other drug use-related problems. *Substance Use and Misuse*, **39**(12): 1713–1750.

Holder, H.D. (1998a) *Alcohol and the Community: A Systems Approach to Prevention*. Cambridge: Cambridge University Press.

Holder, H.D. (1998b) Planning for alcohol-problem prevention through complex systems modeling: results from SimCom. *Substance Use and Misuse*, **33**(3), 669–692.

Holder, H.D. and Wallack, L. (1986) Contemporary perspectives for preventing alcohol problems: an empirically-derived model. *Journal of Public Health Policy*, **7**(3), 324–339.

Keeling, M.J. (1999) Spatial models of Interacting populations. In J. McGlade, *Advanced Ecological Theory*. Oxford: Blackwell Science, pp. 64–99.

Krebs, C.J. (1994) *Ecology: The Experimental Analysis of Distribution and Abundance*, 4th edn. New York: Addison-Wesley.

Levy, D.T., Friend, K. and Holder, H.A. (2000) *Computer Simulation Model of Smoking Rates, Public Policies and Smoking-Attributed Deaths*. Working paper, Berkeley, CA: Pacific Institute for Research and Evaluation.

Levy, D., Mumford, E. and Pesin, B. (2003) Tobacco control policies, and reductions in smoking rates and smoking-related deaths: Results from the SimSmoke model. *Expert Review of Pharmacoeconomics and Outcomes Research*, **3**, 4.

Lotka, A.J. (1925) *Elements of Physical Biology*. Baltimore, MD: Williams and Wilkins Co.

Margolis, J.R., Gillum, R.F., Feinleib, M., Brasch, R.C. and Fabsitz, R. (1974) Community surveillance for coronary heart disease: the Framingham Cardiovascular Disease Survey. Methods and preliminary results. *American Journal of Epidemiology*, **100**, 425–436.

Perelson, A.S., Essunger, P. and Ho, D.D. (1997) Dynamics of HIV-1 and CD4+ lymphocytes in vivo. *AIDS*, **11**, S17–S24.

Volterra, V. (1926) Variazioni e fluttuazioni del numero d'individui in specie animali conviventi. *Memorie dell'Accademia dei Lincei*. Ser. VI, vol. 2.

4.3 Violence Prevention in Licensed Premises

BEN HAINES

National Drug Research Institute, Curtin University of Technology, Australia

KATHRYN GRAHAM

Centre for Addiction and Mental Health, Ontario, Canada

SUMMARY

Licensed premises are associated with a significantly increased risk of aggression and violence. Risk factors for violence in licensed premises include high levels of intoxication, environmental sources of frustration or irritation, socially permissive environments, aggressive patrons, and inexperienced or violent staff. Interventions to reduce alcohol-related violence in licensed premises have included broad-based community interventions, Responsible Beverage Service programmes, local accords or agreements on appropriate industry practices, programs to train staff in techniques for better managing aggression and other problem behaviour, interventions to reduce environmental risks, changes to industry regulations, and targeted policing approaches. Many of these interventions, especially broad-based community interventions, have shown significant reductions in violence. However, rigorous evaluations have been rare, and a wide range of strategies showing promising results are worthy of further study. These include targeted policing strategies, training programs for staff, especially security staff, and multi-component strategies targeting a range of known risk factors for violence.

Bars, nightclubs and pubs fill a special role in modern western society. They provide gathering places for people, especially young adults, to socialize and meet potential romantic partners. However, these are also places that carry a certain amount of risk for violence due to: the increase in aggression associated with alcohol intoxication (Bushman, 1997); social interactions among persons who are all feeling the effects of alcohol (Graham et al., 2000); the nature of some bar-room activities, e.g., slam or mosh dancing (Graham et al., 2000), expectations among some cultures and subcultures that violence is more acceptable in the bar context or while intoxicated (Graham and Homel, 1997), competitive games such as pool (Graham et al., 1980; Homel and Clark, 1994), and the fact that the locations are frequented by young males who are generally higher risk than other segments of the adult population for aggression (Graham and

Preventing Harmful Substance Use: The Evidence Base for Policy and Practice.
Edited by T. Stockwell, P. J. Gruenewald, J.W. Toumbourou and W. Loxley.
© 2005 John Wiley & Sons, Ltd. ISBN 0-470-09227-0 (hbk) 0-470-09228-9 (pbk).

West, 2001), especially young males drinking in groups (Pernanen, 1991; Homel and Clark, 1994). As noted by Indermaur (1999), the sheer predictability of violence in bars argues for violence prevention interventions targeted at licensed premises. However, the literature on effective interventions to reduce violence in licensed premises is sparse. In this chapter, we first describe the link between alcohol and aggression generally, and the literature on the environmental determinants of alcohol-related aggression in the bar context. We then describe existing interventions to reduce bar violence and review the evidence of their effectiveness.

THE LINK BETWEEN ALCOHOL AND AGGRESSION AND THE INFLUENCE OF THE ENVIRONMENT IN WHICH ALCOHOL IS CONSUMED

A substantial proportion of violent crime involves offenders and/or victims who have been drinking (Graham and West 2001; Pernanen et al., 2002). Although the causal role of alcohol in aggression has been disputed for decades (see Room and Collins, 1981), and while differing disciplines of academic study have markedly different views on the causality of intoxication in violence (Lynskey, 2001), a recent meta-analysis of experimental research mostly from the USA found that the effects of alcohol intoxication do indeed play a causal contributing role in aggression (Bushman, 1997). However, this relationship is clearly intertwined with expectations and experience with the effects of alcohol (Lipsey et al., 1997) as well as a variety of environmental factors such as permissive drinking settings (Graham et al., 1980; Homel and Clark, 1994; Graham et al., 2000), and sources of frustration and irritation in the bar environment such as overcrowding (Graham et al., 1980; Homel and Clark, 1994, Macintyre and Homel, 1997).

Several physiological mechanisms have been proposed to link the effects of alcohol on the brain with aggressive behaviour (see Pihl and Hoaken, 2001). These include mechanisms such as a reduction in fear, anxiety and sensitivity to threat mediated by the effects of alcohol on the GABA neurotransmitter as well as reduced problem-solving ability linked to alcohol's effects on the frontal cortex. The moderating role of the social and physical environment on the relationship between alcohol and aggression has been demonstrated both in the laboratory and in studies of naturally occurring aggression (see reviews by Ito et al., 1996; Chermack and Giancola, 1997; Graham and Homel, 1997). This relationship indicates a complex interaction with a range of environmental factors including rewards for aggression (Hoaken et al., 1998), permissive attitudes toward alcohol-related aggression (Graham et al., 2000), and the presence of threats or provocations (see discussion by Graham and Wells, 2003).

There are also individual differences in whether alcohol is associated with increased aggression. Most people do not become more aggressive when they drink, and even those who do become aggressive do not necessarily do so every time they drink. A number of studies have found that heavy drinking, especially a pattern of drinking to intoxication or drinking large amounts of alcohol per occasion, is associated with high risk of aggression (Dawson, 1997; Wells et al., 2000; Rossow, 2001; Wells and Graham, 2003). In addition, it appears that alcohol has a greater effect on male aggression than on female aggression (Giancola et al., 2002; see also meta-analysis by Bushman, 1997).

Of those who have experienced alcohol-related aggression, one of the most likely locations for the aggression to have occurred was a bar or club (Pernanen 1991; Archer et al., 1995; Graham et al., 2002; Leonard et al., 2002). As noted above, many risk factors come together in bars, such as, the effects of alcohol on not one but on many people (Leonard 1984; Homel and Clark, 1994), patronage by high risk groups, namely young males (Martin, et al., 1992; Lang et al., 1995), permissive environments and competitive or provocative activities (Graham et al., 1980). The risks, however, are only one side of the picture. In general, the atmosphere in bars tends to be jovial and pleasant (Pernanen, 2001) and aggression in most bars is very infrequent (Graham et al., 1980; Homel and Clark, 1994; Graham et al., 2004). For one thing, alcohol has positive as well as negative effects on social interactions (Baum-Baicker, 1985; Heath, 2000; Mäakelä and Mustonen, 2000); in fact, some of the same physiological effects linked to aggression can also be linked to positive interactions such as decreased social anxiety and increased group bonding (see Graham, 2003).

The distribution of violence across licensed premises is also important. Violence is neither normally nor evenly distributed across licensed premises but, rather, a small proportion of venues account for the vast majority of violence (Graham et al., 1980; Homel and Clark, 1994; Macintyre and Homel, 1997; Briscoe and Donnelly, 2001). For example, detailed mapping of assault locations in New South Wales, Australia, reported that in Sydney 12% of venues account for 60% of assaults, and in Newcastle 8% of venues accounted for 80% of assaults (Briscoe and Donnelly, 2001). The same study also found that 38% of bars in Sydney had zero assaults in the two-year study period.

There is a small literature suggesting that specific characteristics of licensed premises are associated with increased or decreased risk of violence and aggression (for reviews see Graham and Homel, 1997; Homel et al., 2001; Graham and West, 2001). First, the characteristics of those who frequent the establishment are associated with the likelihood of aggression. Research in Australia identified the presence of large groups of heavy-drinking young men as one of the most significant risk factors (Homel et al., 1991). Similarly, the importance of a "macho" value set emphasising power and status concerns, honour, retribution, and face-saving has also been implicated in bar-room aggression in North America (Burns, 1980; Graham and Wells, 2003).

As might be expected, given the link between alcohol and aggression, intoxication is also a major risk factor for bar-room aggression (Graham et al., 1980; Homel and Clark, 1994). Cheap drink promotions, which act to encourage rapid alcohol consumption and intoxication, are also highly associated with the risk of violence and aggression (Homel et al., 1991; Homel and Clark, 1994). The serving of food is associated with a reduced risk of violence (Graham, 1985; Homel and Clark, 1994), and venues failing to serve food have been linked to increased violence (Homel et al., 1991). This may be because venues serving food attract a different clientele, but it may also be due to the fact that alcohol is absorbed more slowly when a person eats before or during drinking, thus reducing the level of blood alcohol concentration (BAC) obtained with a specific number of drinks.

A very permissive social atmosphere in which the usual constraints on behaviour are lowered or absent appears to be one of the more significant factors associated with the risk of aggression and violence (Graham et al., 1980; Graham, 1985; Homel and Clark, 1994). Such highly permissive environments feature unrestrained swearing, overt sexual activity, overt drug dealing, male rowdiness, and so forth. Permissive environments have been associated with poor standards of décor and venue maintenance, which in itself may create expectations among patrons about the types of behaviour that are likely or acceptable in that bar. In addition to general permissiveness, a number of environmental factors associated with causing frustration or irritation on the part of patrons have been linked with elevated rates of violence. Such factors include overcrowding and bumping (Macintyre and Homel, 1997), smokiness (Graham et al., 1980; Homel et al., 1991; Homel and Clark, 1994), bad and loud music (Homel and Clark, 1994), and competitive games such as pool (Graham et al., 1980).

The contribution of illicit drug use to violence on licensed premises is not clear. Although permissive atmospheres including tolerance for illicit drugs have been linked to violence (Graham et al., 1980; Homel and Clark, 1994), studies from the UK have reported that patrons of licensed premises believe that ecstasy (MDMA), and to a lesser extent cannabis, are far less likely to be associated with violence than is alcohol (Engineer et al., 2003), and that patrons feel safer in drug-oriented nightclubs than in drinking-oriented nightclubs (Richardson and Budd, 2003). Informal observations from a study of Toronto nightclubs (Purcell et al., 2003) were consistent with the findings of Engineer et al. that nightclubs characterized by use of drugs such as ecstasy and marijuana and low use of alcohol appeared to have much less violence compared with nightclubs where most patrons consumed high quantities of alcohol.

Perhaps one of the most important aspects of the bar setting that distinguishes it from other drinking settings is the role of bar staff, especially security staff, as guardians. Bar staff play a critical role not only in whether aggression occurs but in preventing or increasing the escalation of aggression (Graham et al., 1980; Graves et al., 1981; Homel and Clark 1994; Wells et al., 1998). Moreover, working in a bar is also one of the most high risk occupations for experiencing violence (Warchol, 1998). Refusal of service to intoxicated patrons has sometimes precipitated incidences of violence (Felson et al., 1986) and aggressive security staff have been reported as a problem in some instances (Graham et al., 1980; Homel & Clark, 1994); however, recent research on bars frequented by young people found that refusal of service accounted for a small proportion of incidents of aggression (Graham and Wells, 2001).The role of bar staff as guardians and the impact of the bar-room environment offer an important opportunity for prevention interventions to focus on other aspects of the alcohol–aggression link besides the drinker.

Another important aspect of preventing aggression related to licensed premises is the broader social context in which licensed premises exist, such as policies limiting outlet density. As will be described below, a number of interventions with licensed premises (e.g., Surfers Paradise–Homel et al., 1997; Geelong Accord–Felson et al., 1997) were precipitated by problems related largely to the high density of licensed premises within a specific area. These studies demonstrated that intervening at the level of the licensed premises as well as focusing on the broader context of local policies and policing has achieved considerable reductions in violence. They suggest that links between these different levels of prevention efforts are important and may reinforce one another. At the population level, communities may intervene to reduce over-concentrations of outlets and moderate rates of associated alcohol problems (see Chapters 4.2 and 6.5). These effects appear to be achieved through reductions in risky social contacts involving the use of intoxicating substances (e.g., drinking at bars). Within this context, interventions at the level of licensed premises may be particularly effective, acting in a context in which broader population pressures are already in mitigation.

Interventions to Reduce Bar-room Violence

Licensed premises have been the focus of a variety of interventions, including training and licensing of bar staff, risk assessments and development of house policies, enhanced and focused enforcement and community policing, regulations related to hours of sale and other operating functions, local accords or agreements regarding policies and practices, designated driver and ride service programmes, and community approaches that combine several interventions (see Graham, 2000). To a large extent, most of the research in this area has been directed toward evaluating the effectiveness of interventions on serving to intoxication and on drink driving. More recently, however, interventions have been developed that focus directly on preventing violence in and around licensed premises. The following describes the major initiatives in this area.

The Surfers Paradise project

The Surfers Paradise Safety Action project (Homel et al., 1997), and its later replications (Hauritz et al., 1998), was a broad-based intervention, featuring Responsible Beverage Service (RBS) training, extensive education and training for security staff (including ethics training, recruitment processes, conflict resolution skills, incident reporting, and local legal issues), restrictions on eligibility to practise as security staff, extensive community involvement in policies and regulations related to licensed premises, including policies prohibiting cheap drink promotions, reductions in permitted trading hours, and an industry code of practice. Evaluation demonstrated significant reductions in violence as assessed by a range of outcome measures including a reduction in incidents of aggression documented by unobtrusive observers in licensed premises as well as police and crime statistics and reports by security companies indicating a significant drop in assaults, serious assaults, and disorderly conduct (Homel et al., 1997). Risk assessments of licensed venues also demonstrated positive changes in management practices (Homel et al., 1997). Subsequent replications of the Surfers Paradise model in regional Australian towns (Hauritz et al., 1998), quite different in nature to Surfers Paradise, also demonstrated impressive reductions in violence (56% reduction in aggressive incidents, 75% reduction in total physical assaults). Despite the initial success in Surfers Paradise, in subsequent years sustainability became an issue, and violence levels in Surfers Paradise eventually reverted to previous norms (Hauritz et al., 1998). Nevertheless, the results of the project strongly suggest that modification of the various factors associated with the risk of violence in the licensed environment can lead to at least temporary reductions in violence.

The Safer Bars programme

The Safer Bars programme was developed using research knowledge about risk factors and the nature of bar-room aggression. The programme includes a risk assessment workbook (Graham, 1999) for the owner/manager to identify and reduce environmental risks for aggression and a three-hour training programme for bar staff and managers in managing problem behaviour (Braun et al., 2000). The risk assessment identifies environmental risks related to aggression and violence and suggests ways to reduce these risks. Topics covered include: entering the bar; creating a social and physical atmosphere that decreases provocation and triggers; setting and maintaining policies and rules; screening, hiring and supervising staff; and special issues around closing time. The training uses group discussion and role play to address: the escalation of aggression; intervening early; teamwork; planning a coordinated response; controlling anger; nonverbal and verbal techniques; dealing with intoxicated persons; and legal liability.

Safer Bars was evaluated using a randomised control design with large capacity (capacity greater than 300) bars and clubs in Toronto, Canada. Hierarchical Linear Modelling (HLM) was used to evaluate the change in the 18 experimental bars compared to the 12 control bars. These analyses indicated a significant reduction in moderate to severe physical aggression by patrons in the experimental bars compared to control bars which actually showed an increase in aggression (Graham et al., 2004). The effect on experimental bars was moderated, however, by turnover of managers and doorstaff, with higher turnover associated with higher post-intervention aggression. The results support the conclusion that training of bar staff can reduce physical aggression. However, the results should be interpreted with caution because of the generally low rate of physical aggression in the study.

The STAD project

The STAD project in Stockholm involved an extensive intervention including RBS training, community mobilisation, and legal sanctions. The project demonstrated significant reductions in violence following the programme, during a time period where the national crime rate was rising (Wallin et al., 2003). This project is described in more detail in Chapter 4.6 by Wallin and Andréasson (this volume).

Ansvarlig Vertskap/Responsible Host

The first Ansvarlig Vertskap/Responsible Host project was developed in Norway to prevent and reduce alcohol-related violence in licensed premises. The intervention includes a two-day training course for "key-persons" (leaders) on alcohol law, signs of intoxication, conflict resolution and cooperation with the police, as well as a shorter but similar course for servers and security staff, along with a broad patron education campaign. A skills-based competency testing system for staff has also been developed for use with the programme.

The pilot project, conducted in Kristiansand, Norway, in 1997–98, was so successful that a larger project was initiated in Bergen in 2000. The project in Bergen began with a study which mapped experiences and proposals from the licensed premises. The study found that around 90% of Bergen bar owners agreed that over-serving damages their reputation and that high alcohol intake increases the risk of violence (Virtannen, personal communication). Owners of licensed premises reported substantial problems with violence, and the study found considerable support for an intervention focused on serving and violence.

The evaluation of this programme is currently ongoing, with plans to extend the project to Oslo and Trondheim in the coming year. Impact evaluations are not yet available. The project is very well supported by the local community, and very high bar participation rates indicate strong industry support.

Policing/Enforcement Approaches

A number of the community approaches described above included enforcement as a key component (e.g., Homel et al., 1997; Wallin et al., 2003; see also Graham, 2000; Homel et al., 2001). There have also been interventions focused specifically on policing and enforcement.

A key early study of the impact on policing in the UK (Jeffs and Saunders, 1983) found that high-visibility uniformed policing of licensed premises led to a significant reduction in arrests for assaults. A similar intervention to this in Australia (Burns et al., 1995) reported a decrease in assault-related injuries. The Geelong community accord in Australia (Felson et al., 1997; Rumbold et al., 1998; Lang and Rumbold, 1997) is a further example of an effective police-driven strategy. In this accord, the police, liquor licensing, and the alcohol industry agreed on an approach that was mainly targeted at bar-hopping, heavy consumption, and underage drinking. A number of compulsory elements were introduced, including a cover (entry) charge after 11p.m. disallowing free re-entry if patrons left the bar, a uniform minimum price for the various beverages, and more rigorous ID checking. Various local community stakeholders noted a significant reduction in bar-hopping, street disorder, and assault rates. Similarly, police data were suggestive of a significant reduction in rates of serious assaults, although the lack of an appropriate comparison condition did not allow firm conclusions to be drawn in terms of the effectiveness of the accord.

More recently, the TASC (Tackling Alcohol-Related Street Crime) project was completed in Cardiff, Wales (Maguire et al., 2003). The TASC project was a very broad, multi-faceted intervention, driven and implemented largely by the police. It included highly targeted policing operations aimed at specific high-risk licensed premises, RBS training for bar staff, improving dialogue between police and proprietors, restrictions on who could practise as bar security, improved public transport provision, publicity campaigns, increased use of closed circuit television, the provision of cognitive behavioural therapy to repeat violent offenders, training and education for security staff, and support for victims of assault. There is some evidence that rates of assault in the project area dropped slightly, while rates in surrounding areas increased substantially. There were also anecdotal reports from police that the highly targeted operations on specific premises produced dramatic reductions in violence at the relevant premises. However, the impact evaluation was not very rigorous and it is difficult to assess the extent that the results of the study can be generalised. In sum, although none of the policing efforts have included controlled outcome studies, the overall direction of results indicates that a targeted policing approach is likely to be an effective approach to reducing bar-related violence.

Regulating, Licensing and Training Security Staff

Security staff (also known as doorstaff or "bouncers") play a crucial role in alcohol-related violence in larger clubs and bars. They are normally the first line of response to violent or potentially violent incidents and act as the main means of "policing" conduct within licensed premises. Moreover, at least some assaults in bars are perpetrated by security staff themselves (Homel and Clark, 1994; Homel et al., 1994; Wells et al., 1998), and a proportion of assaults are perpetrated against them (Maguire et al., 2003). Given their central and primary role in managing violent or potentially violent incidents, a variety of interventions, including most of the interventions described above, have attempted to modify security staff behaviour, and/or restrict eligibility to work as security staff (Homel et al., 1997; Maguire et al., 2003). In general, the results of training programmes have shown positive results (Homel et al., 1997; Wallin et al., 2003; Graham et al., 2004); however, in all cases, training has been embedded in a larger programme of interventions such that it is not possible to separate the effects of the training from the effects of other interventions such as policy changes.

In Australia, and elsewhere, there are a wide variety of regulatory approaches attempting to define who can work as security staff (Rydon, 1995). These approaches tend to involve screening out those with past criminal records, particularly for crimes of violence. No direct evidence has been found, however, regarding the impact of these programmes on rates of violence and/or aggression in licensed premises.

It is clear that at least some violence is associated with the characteristics of certain bar patrons (Graham et al., 1980; Homel and Clark, 1994; Tomsen, 1997), and security staff screening of patrons in order to exclude undesirable customers is a normal part of security work (Winlow et al., 2001). Studies using focus groups in the UK found that security staff make decisions based largely on appearance as to someone's likelihood of causing violence (Engineer et al., 2003). However, no research has been identified regarding the impact of various patron screening approaches on the likelihood of violence or on the accuracy of security staff judgements on patron propensity to violence. Similarly, licensed premises make substantial use of changes in décor, pricing, entry limitations, and so forth, in order to attract the "right" type of clientele and to subtly discourage undesirables (Hollands, 2003). These two approaches (screening of clientele and the targeting of certain "types" of clientele) are therefore two of the main methods used by licensed premises to reduce problems. As yet, however, there is no evidence on their impact or effectiveness.

Hours of Operation

There is some evidence that increasing permitted trading hours (usually in regard to closing times) increases violence (d'Abbs et al., 1994; Chikritzhs et al., 1997; Chikritzhs and Stockwell, 2003); however, the evidence is unclear as to whether a decrease in trading hours will reduce violence. For example, when licensing hours in Darwin, Australia returned to 4 a.m. from a temporary change to 6 a.m., along with implementation of a $5.00 cover charge in all venues to reduce "club-hopping" and an increase in public transport availability, there was a significant reduction in public disorder and public intoxication in the area, but a significant increase in assaults (d'Abbs and Forner, 1995). The increase in assaults was almost solely accounted for by the 2–4 a.m. time period, immediately preceding the new closing time. A recent review of the topic reported that shifts in trading hours are associated with a shift in the peak occurrence of violence (and drink driving) in line with the shift in trading hours (Stockwell and Gruenewald, 2001), however the evidence on levels of harm and consumption is less clear. In sum, there is scant and sometimes contradictory evidence on the impact of closing hours on rates of violence. While it is clear that the timing of violence is affected by closing hours, the impact on overall rates of violence remains uncertain.

Responsible Beverage Service (RBS)

RBS programmes are the most well-researched type of intervention in licensed premises (see Graham, 2000). While outcome evaluations relating to RBS programmes have had mixed results, it appears that RBS programmes tend to have a small but positive effect on reducing practices linked to high levels of drunkenness. Homel has argued that it is likely that reductions in intoxication will be a necessary but not sufficient component of interventions aiming to reduce violence in licensed premises (Homel et al., 2001). Certainly, RBS programmes are frequently included in broad-based interventions that have shown reductions in violence, such as the Surfers Paradise study (Homel et al., 1997), the STAD project (Wallin et al., 2003; see also this volume), the Geelong Accord (Felson et al., 1997), the Rhode Island Community Alcohol Abuse/Injury Prevention Project (Putnam et al., 1993), and the TASC study (Maguire et al., 2003). As yet, however, there is no evidence of the direct effect of RBS programmes, *per se*, on reducing violence.

Other Approaches

Liquor licensing regulations

Liquor laws are the main means of managing alcohol-related harm in licensed premises; however, there is very little research or evaluation conducted on their effects on this aspect of patron behaviour (Stockwell, 1994; Doherty and Roche, 2003).

Interventions focused on public transportation

Various studies using a variety of methodologies have identified public transport availability as a key issue (Homel et al., 1991; Marsh and Kibby, 1992; d'Abbs et al., 1994; Homel et al., 1997; Engineer et al., 2003) moderating the incidence of alcohol-related violence around licensed premises. Where there is a high concentration of licensed premises, a lack of public transport has the effect of retaining large groups of intoxicated and frustrated people in a small area. No direct evaluations of the impact of strategies to improve transport have been identified, although such interventions have been part of larger multi-component interventions that demonstrated reductions in violence (Homel et al., 1997; Hauritz et al., 1998) as well as interventions that did not show a reduction in violence (d'Abbs and Forner, 1995).

Safer drink containers

It is well established that intentional and unintentional injuries from broken drinking vessels are relatively common in licensed premises (Shepherd, 1998). This relationship led to the logical suggestion that replacing conventional glass vessels with tempered glass should reduce injuries. However, a randomised controlled trial comparing conventional glassware with tempered (toughened) glassware (Warburton and Shepherd, 2000) reported *increased* injuries to staff from accidental breakage of tempered glassware. As yet, there is no research on the impact of tempered glass on intentional injuries to patrons; however, given the increased risk of accidental injury from tempered glass to staff, it may be more important to explore the potential for reductions in injuries using plastic cups and beer tins and avoiding glassware altogether.

CONCLUSION

Prevention at the level of licensed premises appears a promising addition to the variety of effective prevention tools available. A variety of strategies are available, each with corresponding strengths and weaknesses in the practical context. Community approaches such as the Surfers Paradise study and the STAD project tend to produce the largest and most significant effects. However, community interventions are much more expensive and all have shown difficulties with sustainability (Homel et al., 2001). They also require a local political climate that is conducive to their implementation. On the other hand, small-scale harm reduction approaches such as Safer Bars may offer a more financially attractive option to individual bar owners, given the lack of focus on reducing alcohol consumption.

Given the highly uneven distribution of alcohol-related violence, most of which occurs at a small number of violent premises, and the clear contribution that various characteristics of the venue, particularly staff behaviour and management policies, appear to make to the likelihood of violence, it seems likely that targeted interventions with high-risk premises would be the most effective violence reduction strategy. However, the body of research on effectiveness of interventions to prevent violence in licensed premises is relatively small. Moreover, the majority of strategies that are actually used in practice to reduce harm are largely unevaluated. This includes the wide range of regulatory requirements implemented by governments, as well as the informal systems, such as patron screening and targeting certain clientele, that have gained widespread acceptance among premise managers.

It is likely that interventions specifically directed toward reduced alcohol sales will only be implemented by licensed premises if there is some form of regulatory impetus (Homel et al., 2001). Policing interventions in particular occupy a unique place on the prevention spectrum due to their ability to exert sanctions against non-complying venue operators. The TASC project (Maguire et al., 2003) was an entirely police-based intervention, which unfortunately was not accompanied by a comprehensive evaluation. Nonetheless, it gave positive indications that it may have had an impact on reducing alcohol-related crime.

Preventing alcohol-related violence in licensed premises is clearly a difficult issue. The most promising approaches to date have included community-focused interventions, interventions to improve the effectiveness of bar staff and approaches that include increased policing. However, there are many gaps in the literature, and it seems that situational prevention of violence in licensed premises remains an area of prevention policy that is in its infancy.

REFERENCES

Archer, J., Holloway, R. and McLoughlin, K. (1995) Self-reported physical aggression among young men. *Aggressive Behavior*, **21**, 325–342.

Baum-Baicker, C. (1985) The psychological benefits of moderate alcohol consumption: a review of the literature. *Drug and Alcohol Dependence*, **15**, 305–322.

Braun, K., Graham, K., Bois, C., Tessier, C., Hughes, S. and Prentice, L. (2000) *Safer Bars Trainer's Guide*. Toronto: Centre for Addiction and Mental Health.

Briscoe, S. and Donnelly, N. (2001) Assaults on licensed premises in inner-urban areas. *Alcohol Studies Bulletin, 2*, NSW Bureau of Crime Statistics and Research.

Burns, L., Flaherty, F., Ireland, S. and Frances, M. (1995) Policing pubs: what happens to crime? *Drug and Alcohol Review*, **14**, 369–375.

Burns, T.F. (1980) Getting rowdy with the boys. *Journal of Drug Issues*, **10**, 273–286.

Bushman, B.J. (1997) Effects of alcohol on human aggression: validity of proposed mechanisms. In M. Galanter (ed.), *Recent Developments in Alcoholism*, Vol. 13: *Alcohol and Violence*. New York: Plenum Press, pp. 227–244.

Chermack, S.T. and Giancola, P.R. (1997) The relation between alcohol and aggression: an integrated biopsychosocial conceptualization. *Clinical Psychology Review*, **17**, 621–649.

Chikritzhs, T. and Stockwell, T. (2003) The impact of later trading hours for Australian public houses (hotels) on levels of violence. *Journal of Studies on Alcohol*, **63**, 591–599.

Chikritzhs, T., Stockwell, T. and Masters, L. (1997) *Evaluation of the Public Health and Safety Impact of Extended Trading Permits for Perth Hotels and Night-clubs*. Technical Report. Perth: National Drug Research Institute.

d'Abbs, P. and Forner, J. (1995) *An Evaluation of Measures Designed to Reduce Nightclub-Related Violence and Disorder in Darwin*. Darwin: Menzies School of Health Research.

d'Abbs, P., Forner, J. and Thomsen, P. (1994) *Darwin Nightclubs: A Review of Trading Hours and Related Issues*. Darwin: Menzies School of Health Research.

Dawson, D.A. (1997) Alcohol, drugs, fighting and suicide attempt/ideation. *Addiction Research*, **5**(6), 451–472.

Doherty, S.J. and Roche, A.M. (2003) *Alcohol and Licensed Premises: Best Practice in Policing*. Adelaide: Australasian Centre for Policing Research.

Engineer, R., Phillips, A., Thompson, J. and Nicholls, J. (2003) *Drunk and Disorderly: A Qualitative Study of Binge Drinking among 18 to 24 Yr Olds*. London: Home Office Research Studies.

Felson, R.B., Baccaglini, W. and Gmelch, G. (1986) Bar-room brawls: aggression and violence in Irish and American bars. In A. Campbell and J.J. Gibbs (eds), *Violent Transactions: The Limits of Personality*. New York: Basil Blackwell, pp. 153–166.

Felson, M., Berends, R., Richardson, B. and Veno, A. (1997) Reducing pub hopping and related crime. In R. Homel (ed.), *Policing for Prevention: Reducing Crime, Public Intoxication, and Injury*, Crime Prevention Studies 7. New York: Criminal Justice Press.

Giancola, P.R., Helton, E.L., Osborne, A.B., Terry, M.K., Fuss, A.M. and Westerfield, J.A. (2002) The effects of alcohol and provocation on aggressive behavior in men and women. *Journal of Studies on Alcohol*, **63**(January), 64–73.

Graham, K. (1985) Determinants of heavy drinking and drinking problems: the contribution of the bar environment. In E. Single and T. Storm (eds), *Public Drinking and Public Policy*. Toronto: Addiction Research Foundation.

Graham, K. (1999) *Safer Bars: Assessing and Reducing Risks of Violence*. Toronto: Centre for Addiction and Mental Health.

Graham, K. (2000) Preventive interventions for on-premise drinking: a promising but under-researched area of prevention. *Contemporary Drug Problems*, **27**, 593–668.

Graham, K. (2003) The Yin and Yang of alcohol intoxication: implications for research on the social consequences of drinking. *Addiction*, **98**, 1021–1023.

Graham, K. and Homel, R. (1997) Creating safer bars. In M. Plant, E. Single and T. Stockwell (eds), *Alcohol: Minimising the Harm*. London: Free Association Press, pp. 171–192.

Graham, K. and Wells, S. (2001) Aggression among young adults in the social context of the bar. *Addiction Research*, **9**, 193–219.

Graham, K. and Wells, S. (2003) "Somebody's Gonna Get Their Head Kicked in Tonight!" Aggression among young males in bars—A question of values? *British Journal of Criminology*, **43**, 546–566.

Graham, K. and West, P. (2001) Alcohol and crime: examining the link. In N. Heather, T.J. Peters and T. Stockwell (eds), *International Handbook of Alcohol Dependence and Alcohol-Related Problems*. Chichester: John Wiley & Sons, pp. 439–470.

Graham, K., LaRoque, L., Yetman, R., Ross, T.J. and Guistra, E. (1980) Aggression and barroom environments. *Journal of Studies on Alcohol*, **41**, 277–292.

Graham, K., Osgood, D.W., Zibrowski, E., Purcell, J., Gliksman, L., Leonard, K., Pernanen, K., Saltz, R.F. and Toomey, T.L. (2004) The effect of the *Safer Bars* program on physical aggression in bars: results of a randomized control trial. *Drug and Alcohol Review*, **23**, 31–41.

Graham, K., Wells, S. and Jelley, J. (2002) The social context of physical aggression among adults. *The Journal of Interpersonal Violence*, **17**, 64–83.

Graham, K., West, P. and Wells, S. (2000) Evaluating theories of alcohol-related aggression using observations of young adults in bars. *Addiction*, **95**, 847–873.

Graves, T.D., Graves, N.B., Semu, V.N. and Sam, I.A. (1981) The social context of drinking and violence in New Zealand's multi-ethnic pub settings. In T.C. Hanford and L.S. Gaines (eds), *Social Drinking Contexts*. Rockville, MD: NIAAA, pp. 103–120.

Hauritz, M., Homel, R., McIlwain, G., Burrows, T. and Townsley, M. (1998) Reducing violence in licensed venues through community safety action projects: the Queensland experience. *Contemporary Drug Problems*, **25**(3), 511–551.

Heath, D.B. (2000) *Drinking Occasions: Comparative Perspectives on Alcohol and Culture*. Philadelphia, PA: Brunner/Mazel.

Hoaken, P.N.S., Assaad, J.M. and Pihl, R.O. (1998) Cognitive functioning and the inhibition of alcohol-induced aggression. *Journal of Studies on Alcohol*, **59**, 599–607.

Hollands, R. (2003) Producing nightlife in the new urban entertainment economy: corporatization, branding, and market segmentation. *International Journal of Urban and Regional Research*, **27**(2), 361–385.

Homel, R. and Clark, J. (1994) The prediction and prevention of violence in pubs and clubs. *Crime Prevention Studies*, **3**, 1–46.

Homel, R., McIlwain, G. and Carvolth, R. (2001) Creating safer drinking environments. In N. Heather, T. Peters and T. Stockwell (eds), *International Handbook of Alcohol Dependence and Problems*, Chichester: John Wiley & Sons, Ltd.

Homel, R., Tomsen, S. and Thommeny, J. (1991) The problem of violence on licensed premises: The Sydney Study. In T. Stockwell, P. Rydon and E. Lang (eds), *The Licensed Drinking Environment: Current Research in Australia and New Zealand*. Perth: National Centre for Research into Prevention of Drug Abuse.

Homel, R., Hauritz, M., Wortley, R., Clark, J. and Carvolth, R. (1994) *The Impact of the Surfers Paradise Safety Action Project*. Brisbane: Griffith University, Centre for Crime Policy and Public Safety.

Homel, R., Hauritz, M., Wortley, R., McIlwain, G. and Carvolth, R. (1997) Preventing alcohol-related crime through community action: the Surfers Paradise Safety Action Project. In R. Homel (ed.), *Policing for Prevention: Reducing Crime, Public Intoxication, and Injury*. New York: Criminal Justice Press.

Indermaur, D. (1999) Situational prevention of violent crime: theory and practice in Australia. *Studies on Crime and Crime Prevention*, **8**(2).

Ito, T.A., Miller, N. and Pollock, V.E. (1996) Alcohol and aggression: a meta-analysis on the moderating effects of inhibitory cues, triggering events, and self-focused attention. *Psychological Bulletin*, **120**, 60–82.

Jeffs, B.W. and Saunders, W.M. (1983) Minimising alcohol related offences by enforcement of the existing licensing legislation. *British Journal of Addiction*, **78**, 67–77.

Lang, E. and Rumbold, G. (1997) The effectiveness of community-based interventions to reduce violence in and around licensed premises: a comparison of three Australian models. *Contemporary Drug Problems*, **24**, 805–826.

Lang, E., Stockwell, T., Rydon, P. and Lockwood, A. (1995) Drinking settings and problems of intoxication. *Addiction Research*, **3**, 141–149.

Leonard, K.E. (1984) Alcohol consumption and escalatory aggression in intoxicated and sober dyads. *Journal of Studies on Alcohol*, **45**, 75–80.

Leonard, K.E., Quigley, B.M. and Collins, R.L. (2002) Physical aggression in the lives of young adults: prevalence, location, and severity among college and community samples. *Journal of Interpersonal Violence*, **17**(5), 533–550.

Lipsey, M.W., Wilson, D.B., Cohen, M.A. and Derzon, J.H. (1997) Is there a causal relationship between alcohol use and violence? A synthesis of evidence. In M. Galanter (ed.), *Recent Developments in Alcoholism*, Vol. **13**. New York: Plenum Press, pp. 245–282.

Lynskey, M.T. (2001) Alcohol use and violent behaviour among youth: results from a longitudinal study. In P. Williams (ed.), *Alcohol, Young Persons and Violence*. Canberra ACT: Australian Institute of Criminology: pp. 163–181.

Mäakelä, K. and Mustonen, H. (2000) Relationships of drinking behaviour, gender and age with reported negative and positive experiences related to drinking. *Addiction*, **95**, 727–736.

MacIntyre, S. and Homel, R. (1997) Danger on the dance floor: a study of interior design, crowding and aggression in nightclubs. In R. Homel (ed.), *Policing for Prevention: Reducing Crime, Public Intoxication and Injury.* Monsey, New York: Criminal Justice Press.

Maguire, M., Nettleton, H., Rix, A. and Raybould, S. (2003) *Reducing Alcohol Related Violence and Disorder: An Evaluation of the 'TASC' Project.* London: Home Office Research, Development and Statistics Directorate.

Marsh, P. and Kibby, K. (1992) *Drinking and Public Disorder.* London: Portman Group.

Martin, C., Wyllie, A. and Casswell, S. (1992) Types of New Zealand drinkers and their associated alcohol-related problems. *Journal of Drug Issues*, **22**, 773–796.

Pernanen, K. (1991) *Alcohol in Human Violence.* New York: The Guilford Press.

Pernanen, K. (2001) Consequences of drinking to friends and the close environment. In H. Klingemann and G. Gmel (eds), *Mapping the Social Consequences of Alcohol Consumption.* Dordrecht: Kluwer Academic Publishers.

Pernanen, K., Cousineau, M.M., Brochu, S. and Sun, F. (2002) *Proportions of Crimes Associated with Alcohol and Other Drugs in Canada.* Canadian Centre on Substance Abuse.

Pihl, R.O. and Hoaken, P.N.S. (2001) Biological bases of addiction and aggression in close relationships. In C. Wekerle and A. Wall (eds), *The Violence and Addiction Equation: Theoretical and Clinical Issues in Substance Abuse and Relationship Violence.* New York: Brunner-Routledge.

Purcell, J., Graham, K., Gliksman, L., Tessier, C. and Jelley, J. (2003) Redesign on the fly: *Safer Bars* and the Toronto experience. *Nordisk Alkohol and Narkotikatidskrift*, **20**, (English Supplement), 155–160.

Putnam, S.L., Rockett, I.R.H. and Campbell, M.K. (1993) Methodological issues in community-based alcohol related injury prevention projects: attribution of project effects. In T.K. Greenfield and R. Zimmermann (eds), *Experiences with Community Action Projects: New Research in the Prevention of Alcohol and Other Drug Problems.* Rockville, MD: Center for Substance Abuse Prevention.

Richardson, A. and Budd, T. (2003) *Alcohol, Crime and Disorder: A Study of Young Adults.* London: Home Office Research, Development and Statistic Directorate.

Room, R. and Collins, G. (1981) Alcohol and disinhibition: Nature and meaning of the link. In *Proceedings of a conference, 11–13 February, 1981, Berkeley/Oakland, California*, Rockville, MD: National Institute on Alcohol Abuse and Alcoholism.

Rossow, I. (2001) Alcohol and homicide: a cross-cultural comparison of the relationship in 14 European countries. *Addiction*, **96**(Suppl. 1), S77–S92.

Rumbold, G., Malpass, A., Lang, E., Cvekovski, S. and Kelly, W. (1998) *An Evaluation of the Geelong Local Industry Accord.* Melbourne: Turning Point Alcohol and Drug Centre Inc.

Rydon, P. (1995) Alcohol industry practices relating to liquor licensing regulations. In T. Stockwell (ed.), *An Examination of the Appropriateness and Efficacy of Liquor Licensing Laws across Australia.* Vol. 5. Canberra: Australian Government Publishing Service.

Shepherd, J. (1998) Editorial: the circumstances and prevention of bar-glass injury. *Addiction*, **93**(1), 5–7.

Stockwell, T. (1994) *An Examination of the Appropriateness and Efficacy of Liquor Licensing Laws across Australia.* Vol. 5. Canberra: Government Publishing Services.

Stockwell, T. and Gruenewald, P. (2001) Controls on the physical availability of alcohol. In N. Heather, T.J. Peters and T. Stockwell (eds.), *International Handbook of Alcohol Dependence and Problems.* Chichester: John Wiley & Sons.

Tomsen, S. (1997) A top night: social protest, masculinity and the culture of drinking violence. *British Journal of Criminology*, **37**(1), 90–103.

Virtannen, M. personal communication to Kathryn Graham, 2003.

Wallin, E., Norstrom, T. and Andréasson, S. (2003) Alcohol prevention targeting licensed premises: a study of effects on violence. *Journal of Studies on Alcohol*, **64**, 271–277.

Warburton, A.L. and Shepherd, J. (2000) Effectiveness of toughened glassware in terms of reducing injury in bars: a randomised controlled trial. *Injury Prevention*, **6**, 36–40.

Warchol, G. (1998) *Workplace Violence, 1992–96* (NCJ168634) Washington, DC: US Department of Justice, Office of Justice Programs, Bureau of Justice Statistics.

Wells, S. and Graham, K. (2003) Aggression involving alcohol: relationship to drinking patterns and social context, *Addiction*, **98**, 33–42.

Wells, S. Graham, K. and West, P. (1998) "The good, the bad, and the ugly": responses by security staff to aggressive incidents in public drinking settings. *Journal of Drug Issues*, **28**(4), 817–836.

Wells, S., Graham, K. and West, P. (2000) Alcohol-related aggression in the general population. *Journal of Studies on Alcohol*, **61**(4), 626–632.

Winlow, S., Hobbs, D., Lister, S. and Hadfield, P. (2001) Get ready to duck: bouncers and the realities of ethnographic research on violent groups. *British Journal of Criminology*, **41**, 536–548.

4.4 Application of Evidence-Based Approaches to Community Interventions

ANDREW J. TRENO, JULIET P. LEE, BRIDGET FREISTHLER,
LILLIAN G. REMER, AND PAUL J. GRUENEWALD
Prevention Research Center, Berkeley, CA, USA

SUMMARY

The development of evidence-based approaches to combating alcohol-related problems lies at the heart of prevention science as both an area of scientific inquiry and practice. This chapter reviews the current state of this evidence base within the context of reviewing the international literature on community preventive interventions from a community systems perspective and introduces the Sacramento Neighborhood Alcohol Prevention Project (SNAPP) as an example of the implementation process for environmental preventive interventions as applied to specific populations in small areas. SNAPP is a multi-component environmentally based community prevention project designed to reduce alcohol access, drinking and alcohol-related problems among youth and young adults in two economically and ethnically diverse neighborhoods with substantial minority and low-income representation through a series of interventions targeted at the neighborhood level. Preliminary analyses indicate a substantial reduction in youth access to alcohol as a result of project activities. The project provides support for the view, suggested by prior research conducted in various countries, that targeting interventions to the neighborhood level is appropriate to the implementation of alcohol-related preventive interventions.

INTRODUCTION

Drinking alcohol has been consistently linked to injury in the general population (Cherpitel, 1995; Treno et al., 1997). In fact, each year alcohol is related to 16,000 fatal (National Highway Traffic Safety Administration, 1998) and over 1,000,000 nonfatal (Blincoe, 1996) traffic-related injuries. Additionally, alcohol has been related to an estimated 2,700,000 violent crime victimizations (Greenfield, 1998). Overall, it has been estimated that alcohol accounts for 5% of all deaths in the United States and almost half of those involving injuries

Preventing Harmful Substance Use: The Evidence Base for Policy and Practice.
Edited by T. Stockwell, P. J. Gruenewald, J.W. Toumbourou and W. Loxley.
© 2005 John Wiley & Sons, Ltd. ISBN 0-470-09227-0 (hbk) 0-470-09228-9 (pbk).

(Vinson et al., 1995). Moreover, increased severity of injury has been linked to drinking in studies of specific types of injuries including intimate partner violence (Stets, 1990; Martin and Bachman, 1997; Leonard and Quigley, 1999) and falls (Hingson and Howland, 1987). In general, a number of studies have found alcohol to be predictive of an injury involving violence (Cherpitel, 1994; Treno et al., 1994).

Given the general recognition that alcohol is responsible for significant numbers of injuries and deaths, much recent attention has been directed toward the implementation and evaluation of environmental strategies to reduce alcohol-related problems. While only a few such programs have included rigorous evaluations with well-defined outcomes (e.g. Saving Lives, Community Mobilizing for Change on Alcohol, and Community Trials), these programs have generally proven effective in reducing alcohol access to youth, problematic drinking patterns, vehicular and nonvehicular unintentional injuries, and assaultive violence (Hingson et al., 1996; Holder et al., 1997; Holder et al., 2000; Wagenaar et al., 2000). Typically, however, environmentally focused prevention programs have been designed to be universally applicable and implemented at the community level with demonstrated effects consisting of overall reductions of problem rates community-wide. Little attention has been directed toward the implementation of environmental strategies at the neighborhood level where many alcohol-related problems tend to occur.

An increase in attention to neighborhood programs could yield benefits, in terms of the development of the evidence base underlying alcohol prevention efforts, for a number of reasons. First, a smaller unit of analysis below the level of the community may allow for an investigation of program effects among special populations such as ethnic minority groups. Second, while some problems like drunk driving are clearly community-wide problems, other problems such as public drinking or violence concentrated around alcohol outlets may be more local in nature and so more effectively targeted at the neighborhood level (local bars). Here the geographic specificity of the problem is the important focus (i.e., whether it is experienced community-wide or more localized). Third, many neighborhoods are characterized by their own agencies and organizations, particularly ethnically oriented community-based organizations (CBOs); these CBOs may offer significant resources uniquely suited to the development and implementation of culturally specific interventions. In order to benefit from these advantages the SNAPP project was developed and is currently implemented in two low-income, predominantly ethnic minority neighborhoods in Sacramento, California. The project was designed to evaluate the efficacy of a multi-component program of environmental interventions designed to reduce youth access to alcohol, drinking and subsequent alcohol-related problems in these neighborhoods.

REVIEW OF COMMUNITY PREVENTION INTERVENTIONS

Characteristically, community prevention trials that emphasize environmental prevention are community wide, do not target high-risk groups, seek to bring about community system level change, use media to target key community leaders in the pursuit of policy change, and seek to mobilize the entire community in the pursuit of such change.

A number of community prevention studies have been conducted primarily in New Zealand, Australia and Finland. One early New Zealand study, the Community Action Project (CAP), targeted support for public policies limiting alcohol consumption and supportive of moderate alcohol use (Casswell and Gilmore, 1989). A media campaign was designed to influence drinking among young males and to promote support for restrictions on alcohol advertising and availability through community organization (Stewart and Casswell, 1993). Work with the police and the licensing authorities attempted to restrict alcohol availability via the licensing process. Issues pertaining to alcohol were negotiated with local city councils, including the use of bylaws and placing conditions on leased property such as sports grounds. The media advocacy component capitalized on the inevitable publicized controversies that these issues ignited. Norms about target social behaviors were significantly changed in communities exposed to both media and community organization compared with the other two conditions including those concerned with alcohol's effect on fitness and the provision of alcoholic drinks when entertaining (Casswell and Gilmore, 1989).

Another New Zealand study, the Waikato Rural Drink Driving Project, reduced drink driving crashes in the Te Awamutu Police District by increasing police enforcement of drink driving in the district through Compulsive Breath Testing and mobile patrols. The results of this local action project included: a reduction in fatal traffic crashes from 22% to 14%, a sixfold reduction in alcohol positive breath test results by the police, a 23% increase in prosecutions for drink driving, and a rise in local news coverage of drink driving enforcement activities.

Two Australian studies were similarly targeted. The COMPARI Project focused on the general context of alcohol use in the community. While the analysis failed to demonstrate an impact, the project was highly valued by the community. After completion of the university-managed demonstration project, the project was transferred to local control (Midford et al., 1999). Another Australian study, the Surfers Paradise project, sought to reduce violence associated with the concentration of licensed establishments in a resort town (Homel et al., 1997). The project focused on increasing safety in and around licensed establishments by creating a community forum, developing and implementing risk assessments and improving the external regulation of licensed premises by police and liquor licensing inspectors. The Surfers Paradise project and its replications in three North Queensland cities (Hauritz et al., 1998) resulted in significant improvements in police effectiveness (Homel et al., 1997).

A final study conducted in Finland, the Lahti Project, was designed to decrease alcohol-related harm by increasing awareness of alcohol consequences and lowering high-risk drinking (Holmila, 1995, 1997). The evaluation found that the project had increased local newspaper attention to alcohol issues, public perception of alcohol as a social problem, and knowledge of alcohol content and the limits for risky drinking while decreasing heavy drinking (Holmila, 1997).

Similar community trials studies have been conducted in the United States. The Rhode Island Community Alcohol Abuse/Injury Prevention Project (Putnam et al., 1993) was directed toward reducing alcohol-related injuries. The intervention resulted in a 27% increase in alcohol-related assault arrest rates (reflecting increased enforcement) while emergency room visits declined 9% for injury, 21% for assault, and 10% for motor vehicle crashes with no comparable decline in the control community. However, long-term follow-up indicated that these effects were not maintained after the project ended (Stout et al., 1993).

The Saving Lives Project was conducted in six communities in Massachusetts and was designed to reduce alcohol-impaired driving and related problems such as speeding (Hingson et al., 1996). Results of the evaluation indicated that during the five years that the program was in operation, cities that received the Saving Lives intervention experienced a

25% greater decline in fatal crashes than the rest of Massachusetts. This general statistic reflected a 42% reduction in fatal auto crashes within the experimental communities and a 47% reduction in the number of fatally injured drivers who tested positive for alcohol. In addition, the experimental communities showed an overall 5% decline in visible crash injuries and an 8% decline in crash injuries among 16–25-year-olds. In addition, there was a decline in self-reported driving after drinking (specifically among youth) as well as speeding.

The Communities Mobilizing for Change on Alcohol (CMCA) was designed to reduce the accessibility of alcohol to youth under the legal drinking age of 21. Interventions included decoy operations with alcohol outlets (police typically have underage buyers purchase alcohol at selected outlets), citizen monitoring of outlets selling to youth, keg registration (which requires purchasers of kegs of alcohol to provide identifying information, thus establishing liability for resulting problems at parties where minors may be drinking), alcohol-free events for youth, shortened hours of sale for alcohol, responsible beverage service training, and educational programs for youth and adults. Merchant survey and underage decoy data revealed that checking for age identification increased while the likelihood of sales to minors decreased. Also, merchants reported more care in controlling sales to youth (Wagenaar et al., 1996). The telephone survey of 18–20-year-olds indicated that they were less likely to consume alcohol themselves and less likely to provide it to other underage persons. Finally, the project found a statistically significant net decline (intervention compared to control communities) in drinking and driving arrests among 18–20-year-olds and disorderly conduct violations among 15–17-year-olds (Wagenaar et al., 2000a,b).

The Community Trials project (Holder et al. 1997; Holder et al., 2000) was a five-component community-level intervention conducted in three experimental communities, which were matched with three comparison sites. Broadly defined, the goal of the project was to reduce alcohol-related harm among all residents of the three experimental communities via intervention components such as: media and community mobilization, responsible beverage service training, strategies to reduce underage sales of alcohol, increased enforcement of drinking and driving laws, and reductions in access to alcohol through alcohol outlets. Post-intervention analysis demonstrated several important improvements in the experimental communities versus the comparison communities, including reductions in injury traffic crashes, alcohol-involved traffic crashes, and assault injuries (Holder et al. 1997; Holder et al. 2000).

The Sacramento Neighborhood Alcohol Prevention Project (SNAPP)

While some community prevention projects in general, and the Community Trials project in particular, have demonstrated both the efficacy and cost-effectiveness of environmentally-based alcohol prevention projects implemented at the community level, a number of questions remain unanswered. First, could these strategies be tailored to the unique needs of economically and ethnically diverse populations? Second, could they also address the problem of intentional injuries (i.e., assaultive violence) in the context of more economically and ethnically diverse settings? Finally, could these interventions be implemented at the neighborhood level?

SNAPP set as its goals the reduction of alcohol access, drinking, and related problems in two low-income, predominantly ethnic minority neighborhoods, focusing on individuals between the ages 15 and 29, a group identified with high rates of alcohol-involved problems

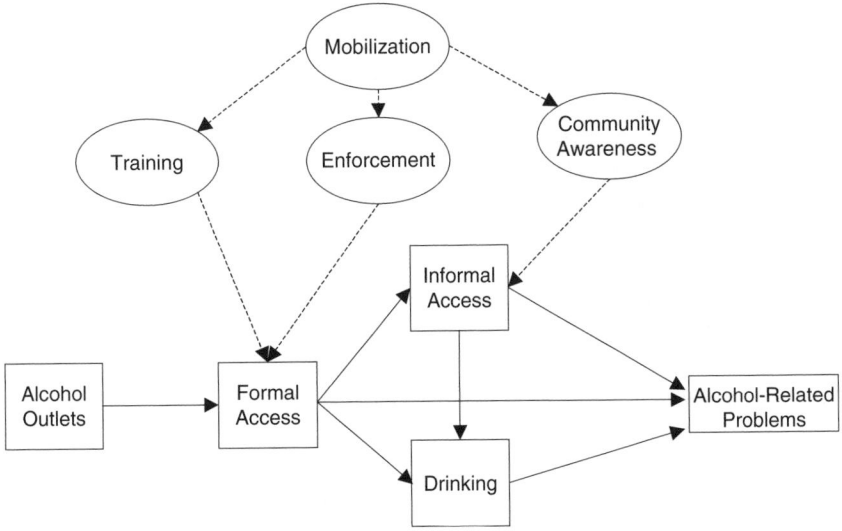

Figure 4.4.1 Project logic model

that greatly concerned local community stakeholders. Two neighborhoods in Sacramento, identified here as the South and North sites, were selected to be the intervention sites because they were economically and ethnically diverse and had high rates of crime, gang activity, domestic abuse and other drinking-related problems. Importantly, these neighborhoods also had local community-based organizations (CBOs) sympathetic to, but inexperienced in, environmental prevention. These CBOs served as liaisons to other community agencies and organizations to facilitate community mobilization efforts around project goals while providing the local knowledge and energy for program implementation.

Project logic model

Figure 4.4.1 presents a simplified logic model indicating the relationship between alcohol outlets and alcohol problems, and the manner in which the SNAPP project components intervened. As indicated by the solid lines, alcohol outlets lead directly to formal access (i.e., purchases made directly from outlets). Formal access may lead to problems directly, as purchasers consume what they purchase, or indirectly by increasing informal access (i.e., alcohol availability in the social environment). This distinction is important to emphasize, particularly in the youth prevention field. Environmental prevention efforts may fail by focusing exclusively on underage sales and ignoring social or informal sources for alcohol, which have been identified as critical sources for underage youth (Harrison et al., 2000). The model also notes that formal access may directly contribute to alcohol-involved problems. For example, alcohol outlets might serve as "magnets" that attract large numbers of individuals predisposed to engage in problem behaviors. As a general observation it is important to note that neighborhoods with high levels of formal access (i.e., high densities of alcohol outlets) are often characterized by alcohol-related problems such as violence (Gorman et al., 2001; Lipton and Gruenewald, 2002) and driving after drinking (Gruenewald et al., 1996; Gruenewald et al., 2002).

While most alcohol prevention projects focus solely on changing individual drinking behaviors to reduce alcohol-related problems, SNAPP aimed to decrease alcohol-related problems by using environmental interventions to decrease both formal and informal access to alcohol. As indicated by the broken lines in Figure 4.4.1, the project interventions (indicated in circles) played three different and critical roles in the reduction of overall alcohol access. The combined enforcement and merchant training activities targeted the reduction of alcohol sales and beverage service. In contrast, the community awareness activities targeted the reduction of informal access. The community mobilization activities operated in support of the other project interventions by engaging the formal sectors of the community (enforcement and licensing) with the informal sectors (CBOs and voluntary residents groups). Following the logic of the project conceptual model, it was anticipated that program interventions would reduce both formal and informal access to alcohol that were likely to result in drinking and related problem outcomes.

Study design

The quasi-experimental design of the study took a "phased" approach to program implementation and statistical examination of outcome data. In both North and South sites as well as the community at large there was a baseline data collection phase. In the first year, while interventions were applied in the South neighborhood, the North neighborhood served as a no-treatment comparison site. Subsequently, application of the same interventions in the North neighborhood served as a replication test of intervention effectiveness, and data from the South neighborhood served to test for long-term impacts of the interventions. Data collected from Sacramento at large served to control for historical conditions affecting outcomes at both sites.

Project interventions

There were a total of five project interventions including community awareness, responsible beverage service, an underage access component, an enforcement component and a mobilization effort to marshal neighborhood support for the overall project.

1. *Community awareness*: This component's purpose was to heighten awareness of the problem of youth and young adult drinking and to inform the public and alcohol retailers about increased enforcement of underage possession and sales laws, as well as laws regarding sales to intoxicated patrons. The specific objectives of the component were: (a) to increase public and parental knowledge of the problem of underage youth and young adult drinking and drinking problems as well as to garner support for the intervention programs; (b) to motivate parents of youth and young adults to participate in activities to reduce underage drinking and to curb problematic drinking among young adults; and (c) to alter youth perceptions of community norms about drinking in general and drinking in high-risk situations in particular.
2. *Responsible Beverage Service (RBS)*: The RBS program was designed to help retailers develop policies and train staff to reduce alcohol sales to minors and intoxicated persons. The RBS training focused on: (a) raising awareness of the problems of youthful drinking and sales of alcohol to minors and intoxicated persons; (b) raising awareness of community norms against the sale of alcohol to minors and intoxicated persons; (c) training in methods of age identification, estimation of intoxification levels and customer interaction; (d) providing information about laws and associated penalties

for sales to minors and intoxicated persons; and (e) assisting owners and managers to review existing policies and providing new policy options to reduce sales to minors and intoxicated persons.

3. *Underage access*: This component focused on increasing actual and perceived enforcement of laws prohibiting sales and provision of alcohol to minors and was accomplished by working with neighborhood police to increase the number of off-license decoy operations.

4. *Enforcement component*: Enforcement efforts targeting on-premise establishments were designed to parallel those of the off-premise intervention. These activities took the form of business compliance checks where police visited establishments subsequent to informing the business by mail about increased enforcement of beverage service laws.

5. *Community mobilization effort*: To mobilize the neighborhoods in support of the overall project goals and interventions, project lead agencies worked with a Collaborative Advisory Committee with members drawn from each of the two geographical areas that worked to ensure intervention implementation and fidelity to project design. Research staff at the Prevention Research Center worked through this committee to implement project interventions and to collect local data for the evaluation. The intervention strategies though generic in nature were tailored to take advantage of existing conditions and to more specifically address unique neighborhood problems.

Data collection and evaluation design

Data were collected from various sources for the purposes of documenting project history and intervention dosage, demonstrating intervention effectiveness, and ultimately establishing the basis for the overall evaluation. First, process data was collected using a Management Information System (MIS) to record both the history of the project and the dosage of implementation. Second, Apparent Minor and Pseudo-Intoxicated Patron surveys were conducted to determine the effectiveness of project activities in altering patterns in formal access to alcohol at the neighborhood level. The Apparent Minor survey documented the frequency of sales of alcohol to study-trained young women who were over the age of 21 years, but judged by an independent panel to appear younger. The Pseudo-Intoxicated Patron survey documented the frequency of service of alcohol to study-trained individuals who acted as though they were intoxicated while frequenting on-premise sales outlets. Third, using a telephone survey and archival data, the project collected both intervening and outcome measures. Table 4.4.1 shows the different sources of data, the evaluative purpose for each data source, and the measures collected.

One contribution of the current project to the evaluation of community-based interventions is the opportunity to apply geostatistical techniques to evaluate neighborhood-level outcomes. This approach views neighborhoods, and ultimately individuals and individual events nested within neighborhoods, as the units of analysis, each having specific geographic (i.e., spatial) relationships to one another. From this perspective one could think of the geostatistical portion of the study as addressing the question of whether data from South and North Census blocks (N = 37) change with respect to those from all other blocks in Sacramento (N = 243).

Table 4.4.2 indicates the differences in assault rates, socio-demographics and alcohol outlets by study area. These data begin to detail the types of information that is used in the geographic evaluation. As can be seen in Table 4.4.2, both the North and South study

Table 4.4.1 Type and content of evaluation information from archival data sources

Data collection source	Evaluative purpose	Intervention/ outcome type	measures
Management Information System	Process information Dosage of interventions	Mobilization	# of contacts with law enforcement and community leaders # of Sub-Advisory Committee meetings # of RBS task force meetings # of Presentations to Neighborhood Organizations
		Awareness	# of brochures passed out to community members # of in-home presentations # of meetings with parents and school officials
		Responsible Beverage Service training	# of trainings Types of establishments trained (on- or off-premise)
		Underage enforcement	# and outcome of sting operations # and type of premise violations # of letters sent to establishments on the outcome of sting operations
		Enforcement	# and type of premise violations
Apparent Minor survey	Effectiveness of intervention implementation	Responsible Beverage Service training	# and type of outlets that sell alcohol to apparent minors
		Underage enforcement	# and type of outlets that sell alcohol to apparent minors
Pseudo-Intoxicated Patron Survey	Effectiveness of intervention implementation	Responsible Beverage Service training	# and type of outlets that sell alcohol to pseudo-intoxicated patrons
Telephone survey	Project outcomes	Alcohol use	frequency quantity variances of use
		Drinking activities	frequencies of drinking in different social and physical places
		Alcohol access	frequencies of obtaining alcohol from different venues frequencies of obtaining alcohol from friends or strangers
		Drinking problems	self-reported criminal victimization drinking and driving injury involvement
Archival data	Project outcomes	Violent crime	assaults homicide robbery
		Crashes	alcohol-involved crashes
		Public disorder	public drunkenness loitering
		Injuries	motor vehicle injuries pedestrian injuries bicycle injuries falls

Table 4.4.2   Descriptive information for dependent and independent measures by study area

	Variable	At large	South	North
Assaults	Crime incidents (per 1,000 population)	8.46	9.77	12.58
	Emergency medical service events (per 1,000 population)	3.28	5.10	6.47
Socio-demographics	%African American	17.2	17.4	19.5
	% Hispanic	20.8	39.3	31.0
	% Persons in living in poverty	18.3	35.6	33.0
Alcohol outlets*	Bars/roadway mile	.029	.057	.052
	Restaurants/roadway mile	.231	.216	.187
	Off-premise/roadway mile	.133	.362	.245

Note: *Outlets per roadway mile include those within a 1/2 mile buffer zone for the North and South study areas.

sites have higher rates of assaults (per 1,000 population) as recorded by both the police and Emergency Medical Service technicians than the at-large area. Additionally, 2000 Census data show that 39% and 31% of the population in the South and North study sites, respectively, is Hispanic compared to only about 21% in the at-large area. Similarly, about one-third of residents in both study sites live in poverty (35.6% for South, 33.0% for North) compared to less than 20% of the population of the at-large area. In addition, data from the California Alcohol Beverage Control Agency shows that the two study areas have higher concentrations of both bars and off-premise alcohol outlets per roadway mile.

Assessment of project implementation

Data from the MIS and Apparent Minor and Pseudo-Intoxicated Patron surveys can be used to assess the effectiveness of the program interventions on alcohol access to youth and intoxicated patrons resulting from activities in the South site relative to both the North site and Sacramento at large. However, as measures of intervention strength it is useful to consider the separate intervention components in terms of their sequencing and intensity. Not surprisingly, mobilization activities preceded other program activities, occurring primarily during the first 18 months of the project. This timing was consistent with the general intervention design that assumed that mobilization of critical neighborhood and community leaders was a prerequisite for the fine-tuning and implementation of other project interventions. This was followed by community awareness followed by RBS and enforcement activities in the South over the next two years. Activities in the North were similarly patterned though over a shorter period of time.

While the documentation of program activities discussed above provided important information for the project evaluation, an additional critical issue concerns the effects of these activities on project intermediary measures, notably sales to minors and service to intoxicated patrons, as measured by our Apparent Minor and Pseudo-Intoxicated Patron surveys. Table 4.4.3 presents the result of our Apparent Minor and Pseudo-Intoxicated Patron surveys. Notably, we found a one-third reduction in sales to apparent minors in the South site relative to baseline compared to increases of 205% in the North and 23.7% in the at-large area. Between waves 2 and 3 we found decreases of 28.1%, 59.0% and 76.6%. In contrast, we found increases in service to pseudo-intoxicated patrons in the South, North, and at-large areas of 26.5%, 8.8%, and 46.0% between waves 1 and 2 and decreases of 3.4%, 5.7% and 17.4% between waves 2 and 3.

Table 4.4.3 Purchase/service rates for waves 1, 2 and 3 of apparent minor and pseudo-intoxicated patron surveys

	Apparent Minor survey				Pseudo-Intoxicated Patron survey			
	Pre	Post 1	Post 2	Post–Pre	Pre	Post 1	Post 2	Post–Pre
South	0.49	0.32	0.23	−0.26	0.68	0.86	0.83	0.15
North	0.20	0.61	0.25	0.05	0.8	0.87	0.82	0.02
At large	0.38	0.47	0.11	−0.27	0.63	0.92	0.76	0.13

Interestingly, there were declines in sales to apparent minors in the final project year across all conditions. Taken together, these findings suggest that project activities were successful in reducing sales to minors in both the South and North neighborhoods, along with in the control area. The effect noted in the control may be due to contamination. Specifically, the Sacramento Police Department, having determined the effectiveness of the project, implemented underage decoy operations city-wide. Unfortunately, efforts to reduce intoxicated patron service appear to have been less successful.

CONCLUSION

To what extent and how does our experience with SNAPP contribute to the current evidence base underlying prevention science? SNAPP is the first project of its kind to assess the efficacy of access-oriented environmental prevention strategies in the context of economically and ethnically diverse populations at the neighborhood level. The specific environmental strategies were derived from a logic model linking outlets and access to drinking and subsequent problems. In addition, the evaluation plan incorporated data used to index major elements from the underlying logic model. This is important since many studies have been conducted without careful assessment of either project activities or effects on intermediary measures. Typically, the focus in project interventions evaluation has been on assessment of outcomes, with program implementation and fidelity to protocols assumed rather than directly assessed.

To date, SNAPP's project evaluation has been able to track and assess intervention implementation levels and the success of those interventions. The decrease in sales to apparent minors in the South site compared to the North and at-large suggests the potential success of combining training and enforcement of underage sales laws to reduce underage access to alcohol. Whether either of these strategies alone would have sufficed is impossible to determine, given the study design. The threat of the upcoming enforcement activities may well have served to increase participation in the training program. Notably, the local police were instrumental in assisting in recruiting off-premise establishments for RBS trainings. There was, however, no comparable enforcement of laws regarding service to intoxicated patrons. Yet the absence of a parallel reduction in service to pseudo-intoxicated patrons lends support to the hypothesis that training alone is unlikely to bring about desired changes at least in this critical area.

A number of conclusions and recommendations may be drawn concerning the project's overall design, implementation and data collection activities. First, the project began with a logic model of the processes underlying the production of problem outcomes related to alcohol. The development of such a model would appear to be a prerequisite to the implementation and evaluation of any project to reduce alcohol-related problems regardless of its underlying theoretical assumptions. Most, if not all, prevention programs have an implicit conceptual model. Such models need to be explicitly incorporated into the evaluation design for empirical and conceptual soundness and clarity. Second, SNAPP's interventions were designed to address the specific elements in the conceptual model. For example, an enforcement component was designed and implemented because the proposed logic model hypothesized, based on prior work, that formal access played a critical role in increasing drinking and alcohol-related problems. It would seem that project interventions would flow directly from rationale(s) provided in the logic model. Third, our measures of program implementation, intermediary measures, and outcomes were selected to provide indices of changes in the levels of model elements over the course of the project relative to baseline and comparison measures. In sum, the lesson provided by SNAPP, at least in its early phase, points to the need for neighborhood prevention projects to provide integrative models that link elements at the community and neighborhood level to program activities and measures provided by a comprehensive evaluation component.

ACKNOWLEDGEMENTS

Research for and preparation of this chapter were supported by the National Institute on Alcohol Abuse and Alcoholism (NIAAA) Grant No. ROI AA11968 Additional program funds were provided by Grant No. 6KD1-SP08636-03-1 from the Center for Substance Abuse Prevention (CSAP) and Grant no. 1999/257 from The California Endowment.

REFERENCES

Blincoe, J.L. (1996) *The Economic Cost of Motor Vehicle Crashes, 1994, DOT HS 808 424*. Washington, DC: National Highway Traffic Safety Administration.

Casswell, S. and Gilmore, L. (1989) An evaluated community action project on alcohol. *Journal of Studies on Alcohol*, **50**, 339–346.

Cherpitel, C.J. (1994) Alcohol and injuries resulting from violence: a review of emergency room studies. *Addiction*, **89**, 157–165.

Cherpitel, C.J. (1995) Alcohol and casualties: comparison of county-wide emergency room data with the country general population. *Addiction*, **90**, 343–350.

Gorman, D.M., Speer, P.W., Gruenewald, P.J. and Labouvie, E.W. (2001) Spatial dynamics of alcohol availability, neighborhood structure and violent crime. *Journal of Studies on Alcohol*, **62**, 628–636.

Greenfield, L.A. (1998) *Alcohol and Crime: An Analysis of National Data on the Prevalence of Alcohol Involvement in Crime. Report prepared for Assistant Attorney General's National Symposium on Alcohol Abuse and Crime*. Washington, D.C: US Department of Justice.

Gruenewald, P.J., Johnson, F.W. and Treno, A.J. (2002) Outlets, drinking and driving: a multilevel analysis of availability. *Journal of Studies on Alcohol*, **63**(4), 460–468.

Gruenewald, P.J., Millar, A.B., Treno, A.J., Yang, Z., Ponicki, W.R. and Roeper, P. (1996) The geography of availability and driving after drinking. *Addiction*, **91**(7), 967–983.

Harrison, P.A., Fulkerson, J.A. and Park, E. (2000) The relative importance of social versus commercial sources in youth access to tobacco, alcohol, and other drugs. *Preventive Medicine*, **31**(1), 39–48.

Hauritz, M., Homel, R., McIlwain, G., Burrows, T. and Townsley, M. (1998) Reducing violence in licensed venues through community safety action projects: the Queensland experience. *Contemporary Drug Problems*, **25**, 511–551.

Hingson, R. and Howland, J. (1987) Alcohol as a risk factor for injury or death resulting from accidental falls: a review of the literature. *Journal of Studies on Alcohol*, **48**, 212–219.

Hingson, R., McGovern, T., Howland, J., Heeren, T., Winter, M. and Zakocs, R. (1996) Reducing alcohol-impaired driving in Massachusetts: the Saving Lives Program. *American Journal of Public Health*, **86**, 791–797.

Holder, H.D., Gruenewald, P.J., Ponicki, W.R., Treno, A.J., Grube, J.W., Saltz, R.F., Voas, R.B., Reynolds, R., Davis, J., Sanchez, L., Gaumont, G. and Roeper, P. (2000) Effect of community-based interventions on high-risk drinking and alcohol-related injuries. *Journal of the American Medical Association*, **284**, 2341–2347.

Holder, H.D., Saltz, R.F. and Grube, J.W. (1997) A community prevention trial to reduce alcohol-involved accidental injury and death: overview. *Addiction*, **92**(S), S155–171.

Holmila, M. (1995) Community action on alcohol: experiences of the Lahti Project in Finland. *Health Promotion International*, **10**, 283–291.

Holmila, M. (1997) *Community Prevention of Alcohol Problems*. London: Macmillan Press, Ltd.

Homel, R., Hauritz, M., Wortley, R., McIlwain, G. and Carvolth, R. (1997) Preventing alcohol-related crime through community action: the Surfers Paradise Safety Action Project. In R. Homel (ed.), *Policing for Prevention: Reducing Crime, Public Intoxication, and Injury*. Monsey, NY: Criminal Justice Press.

Leonard, K.E. and Quigley, B.M. (1999) Drinking and marital aggression in newlyweds: an event-based analysis of drinking and the occurrence of husband marital aggression. *Journal of Studies on Alcohol*, **60**(4), 537–545.

Lipton, R.I. and Gruenewald, P.J. (2002) The spatial dynamics of violence and alcohol outlets. *Journal of Studies on Alcohol*, **63**(2), 187–195.

Martin, S.E. and Bachman, R. (1997) The relationship of alcohol to injury in assault cases. In M. Galanter (ed.), *Recent Developments in Alcoholism*. New York: Plenum Press, pp. 41–56.

Midford, R., Boots, K., Masters, L. and Chikritzhs, T. (1999) Time series analysis of outcome measures from a community alcohol harm reduction project in Australia. In Casswell, S., Holder, H., Holmila, M., Larsson, S., Midford, R., Barnes, H., Nygaard, P. and Stewart, L. Kettil Bruun Society Thematic Meeting Fourth Symposium on Community Action Research and the Prevention of Alcohol and Other Drug Problems. (pp. 278–290). Auckland: University of Auckland.

National Highway Traffic Safety Administration (1998) *Traffic Safety Facts 1997: Alcohol DOT HS 808 764*. National Highway Traffic Safety Administration, Washington, DC: National Center for Statistics and Analysis.

Partnerships Project, New Zealand Police (1999) Doing Something about Rural Drink Drive: The Waikato Experience. Project report funded by the Alcohol Advisory Council of New Zealand. ISBN 0-477-02947-7.

Putnam, S.L., Rockett, I.R.H. and Campbell, M.K. (1993) Methodological issues in community-based alcohol-related injury prevention projects: attribution of program effects. In T.K. Greenfield and R. Zimmerman (eds.), *Experiences with Community Action Projects: New Research in the Prevention of Alcohol and Other Drug Problems*. Rockville, MD: Center for Substance Abuse Prevention.

Stets, J.E. (1990) Verbal and physical aggression in marriage. *Journal of Marriage and Family*, **43**, 721–732.

Stewart, L. and Casswell, S. (1993) Media advocacy for alcohol policy support: results from the New Zealand Community Action Project. *Health Promotion International*, **8**, 167–175.

Stout, R.L., Rose, J.S., Speare, M.C., Buka, S.L., Laforge, R.G., Campbell, M.K. and Waters, W.J. (1993) Sustaining interventions in communities: the Rhode Island community-based prevention trial. In T.K. Greenfield and R. Zimmerman (eds), *Experiences with Community Action Projects:*

New Research in the Prevention of Alcohol and Other Drug Problems, Rockville, MD: Center for Substance Abuse Prevention, pp. 253–261.

Treno, A.J., Cooper, K. and Roeper, P. (1994) Estimating alcohol involvement in trauma patients: the search for a surrogate. *Alcoholism: Clinical and Experimental Research*, **18**(6), 1306–1311.

Treno, A.J., Gruenewald, P.J. and Ponicki, W.R. (1997) The contribution of drinking patterns to the relative risk of injury in six communities: a self-report based probability approach. *Journal of Studies on Alcohol*, **58**(4), 372–381.

Vinson, D.C., Mabe, N., Luralie, L.L., Alexander, J., Becker, J., Boyer, J. and Moll, J. (1995) Alcohol and injury: a case-crossover study. *Archives of Family Medicine*, **4**, 505–511.

Wagenaar, A.C., Murray, D.M. and Toomey, T.L. (2000a) Communities mobilizing for change on alcohol: effects of a randomized trial on arrests and traffic crashes. *Addiction*, **95**(2), 209–217.

Wagenaar, A.C., Murray, D.M., Gehan, J.P., Wolfson, M., Forster, J.L., Toomey, T.L., Oerry, C.L. and Jones-Webb, R. (2000b) Communities mobilizing for change on alcohol: outcomes for a randomized community trial, *Journal of Studies on Alcohol*, **61**, 85–94.

Wagenaar, A.C., Toomey, T.L. Murray, D.M., Short, B.J., Wolfson, M. and Jones-Webb. R. (1996) Sources of alcohol for underage drinkers. *Journal of Studies on Alcohol*, **57**(3), 325–333.

4.5 Preventing Alcohol and Other Drug Problems in the Workplace

RICHARD MIDFORD

National Drug Research Institute, Curtin University of Technology, Australia

FREDRIK WELANDER

National Institute for Working Life, Sweden; the Centre for International Health, Curtin University of Technology, Australia

STEVE ALLSOP

Western Australian Drug and Alcohol Office; the Centre for International Health, Curtin University of Technology, Australia

SUMMARY

Alcohol is the most commonly used drug in industrialised societies and is likely to cause the most problems in the workplace. Apart from cannabis, illicit drug use is very low and poses much less of a problem in the workplace. Occupational groups often influence alcohol and other drug (AOD) use. Men most at risk work in male-dominated blue-collar occupational groups and in the hospitality industry. Women, at greatest risk, work in competitive occupations. There are a number of individual and environmental predictors of problematic alcohol use. The highest risk category of employee is a young male with low self-esteem and an arrest history, who has family and friends with AOD problems. A stressful work environment, poor supervision and easy availability also contribute to problematic use. Alcohol has been implicated in transportation crashes, but the evidence for involvement in other workplace accidents is less clear. The main productivity loss due to AOD use is absenteeism, although job performance also suffers. The cost of AOD use to business is consistently high, which suggests that effective interventions will produce substantial cost benefit.

Interventions to reduce the risk posed by AOD use fall into the following five broad categories:

- Policy development, which provides the basis for further interventions.
- Information and education programmes, which explain why AOD use can be a problem in the workplace.

Preventing Harmful Substance Use: The Evidence Base for Policy and Practice.
Edited by T. Stockwell, P. J. Gruenewald, J.W. Toumbourou and W. Loxley.
© 2005 John Wiley & Sons, Ltd. ISBN 0-470-09227-0 (hbk) 0-470-09228-9 (pbk).

- Health promotion programmes, which change health environments and teach participants how to improve their health, including unhealthy AOD use.
- Regulation of use and compliance drug testing, which bans specific AOD use and measures exposure to the banned drugs by chemical analysis, thus providing objective evidence of transgression.
- Assistance and treatment, which commonly involves referring employees with an identified AOD problem to an Employee Assistance Programme (EAP).

The less structured and more demanding working life of the twenty-first century is putting greater stress on workers and this is likely to have ramifications for AOD use and related work problems. Optimum outcomes are likely to be obtained by tailoring responses to the workplace, where location, size, history, culture, workforce and type of the work are all factors that need to be considered. Performance management, with well-articulated occupational health and safety objectives, is likely to provide the best basis for an effective workplace AOD program.

HISTORICAL OVERVIEW

In pre-industrial societies, work time was not demarcated as it is today and because drug use was part of social activity, it also formed part of work activity. In the nineteenth century the Industrial Revolution changed the nature of work. Work became more specialised and occurred in specific places, such as factories and offices, between particular hours and on particular days. This reduced worker flexibility and increased demands on their performance. This greater regulation of the workplace brought with it a need to moderate the influence of alcohol on work performance, and the Industrial Revolution is often identified as a catalyst in the establishment of widespread drinking controls (Normand et al., 1994).

The Industrial Revolution also saw the evolution of the roles of employer and employee. In the early part of the nineteenth century it was the norm to view the workforce as a resource to be exploited for maximum profit. However, more enlightened approaches demonstrated that investing in the care of the workforce actually created a more productive workplace. In both models the employee has an obligation to provide a "fair day's work for a fair day's pay". However, the enlightened approach imposed a reciprocal obligation on the employer to provide more comprehensive care for their employees. Accompanying this evolution of management practice was an increasing number of legal and safety requirements, which prescribed the behaviour of both groups. In addition, this period saw the rise of the union movement, which has been a strong force in the collective protection of employee rights.

It is important to understand these historical developments, because the way contemporary Western workplaces respond to problems associated with alcohol and other drug (AOD) use is shaped by these experiences and concepts. Clearly where work is safety sensitive and/or complex, such as in piloting an aeroplane, there is a compelling argument for the employee to be unaffected by alcohol or other drugs. However, what else justifies regulating employees' AOD use? What level of intrusion is acceptable as part of the monitoring process? How should an employer respond to problematic AOD use? What are the obligations of employees to their fellow workers and their employers in terms of work performance? This chapter examines the issues that need to be considered when making decisions about how to prevent

AOD problems in the workplace and presents strategies that evidence indicates are likely to achieve better outcomes.

LEVELS OF AOD USE AND HARM IN WESTERN INDUSTRIALISED SOCIETIES

Alcohol is the most commonly used drug in Western industrialised societies. The other licit drug, tobacco, comes a distant second. Cannabis generally ranks third and is the most widely consumed illicit drug. Lifetime alcohol use typically ranges from 80–90% in adult Western populations (Abraham et al., 1999; Maxwell, 2003). In Sweden approximately 90% of men and 70% of women drink alcohol: of these, 18% and 12% respectively consume at a level that increases the probability of sustaining physical and/or mental harm (Leifman, 2002).

Tobacco use has been steadily declining in most Western countries, particularly those with comprehensive control policies. Lifetime use of tobacco in Australia and the USA in 2001 was respectively 49% and 69% (Maxwell, 2003). The lifetime prevalence rate for the Netherlands was 68% in 1997 (Abraham et al., 1999). Prevalence rates of recent smoking are much lower. There is, however, a striking gap in smoking rates between the lowest and highest socio-economic groups. In some countries, the poorest smoke three times more than the richest (World Health Organization, Regional Office for Europe, 2002).

The level and type of illicit drug use vary from country to country, because of cultural differences, availability, changing fashions in use and economic circumstances. However, use tends to occur predominantly among young adults in major urban centres, and cannabis consistently ranks as the most used illicit drug (United Nations Office on Drugs and Crime, 2003). Lifetime use of cannabis has remained essentially steady in Australia from 1995 (31%) to 2001 (33%), but has risen slightly in the USA over the same period from 32% to 38% (Maxwell, 2003). In the Netherlands in 1997, 29% of the population had ever used cannabis during their lifetime (Abraham et al., 1999). One exception to the number one ranking of cannabis is Sweden. Here cannabis ranks after benzodiazepines (United Nations Office on Drugs and Crime, 2003). Illicit drug use in Sweden is generally low by Western standards, with approximately 12% of the population having used at least once. There are approximately 26,000 regular users in a population of nine million, with men comprising about 75% of those involved in heavy and/or regular drug use (Guttormsson, 2002).

These population AOD use statistics from around the world indicate that patterns of use in communities are associated with culture, sex and age. Accordingly any attempt to understand the nature of alcohol and other drug problems in a particular workplace needs to look at the socio-demographic profile of the workforce and the prevalence of use in the community from which the workforce is drawn. Clearly alcohol is the drug most likely to cause problems in the workplace. Not only is it used by a large percentage of the population, but it impairs many behaviours which are crucial to effective work performance. Illicit drug use often causes considerable concern in the community, but apart from cannabis, use is very low. This suggests that illicit drug use poses much less of a problem in the workplace, although because use is often associated with particular age groups, cultures, and regions, certain workplaces may experience a disproportionate level of risk.

Levels of AOD Use in the Workforce

An occupational group often sets normative AOD consumption practices by within group socialisation and transmission of group culture. Plant (1979) conducted one of the early studies of the relationship between occupational group and AOD use. He looked at drinking patterns of Scottish workers producing alcohol and determined that occupation was an influential factor in determining an individual's drinking patterns and consequent alcohol-related problems. In the USA, a random survey of 43,809 people in employment measured alcohol dependency/abuse, according to well-established criteria, and found that problems occurred in more than 35% of workers in some occupations and in less than 1% in others (Stinson et al., 1992). Hagen et al. (1992) found substantial differences in the level of drinking between different industries and occupational groups in the Australian workforce. Women employees generally drank in a less risky manner than their male counterparts. However, women in particular employment categories, such as sales, management and business, were at greater risk than their male colleagues. They were also heavy consumers of sleeping medication. Generally women in competitive occupations engaged in more risky drinking. In the male workforce risky drinkers were over-represented in male-dominated, blue-collar occupational groups and in the hospitality industry. These findings are supported by American and European studies (e.g., Kjærheim et al, 1995; Ames and Rebhun, 1996).

There has been little research on work-related illicit drug use. Normand et al. (1994) analysed workplace drug use trends for 18–28-year-olds from follow-up components of the US High School Senior surveys. Cannabis use was most prevalent in the 1991 survey, with 5% of men and 1% of women reporting use at work over the past 12 months. Use of other illicit drugs was reported by less than 1% of each gender sample. Gleason et al. (1991) analysed the 1984 US National Longitudinal Survey of Youth and found that 7% of 19–27-year-olds reported using illicit drugs at work. Reported illicit drug use was higher among men than women, among blue-collar workers than white-collar workers and among younger workers. Drug use was most common among young workers in the entertainment/recreation and construction industries, and least common among those in professional services and public administration industries. Interestingly, data showed a relatively high rate of illicit drug use (13%) by transportation industry operatives. The use of AODs by workers in safety-sensitive positions is a particular concern and, because of this, prevalence in the transport industry has been studied in some detail. Williamson et al. (1992) found that 30% of the Australian long-distance truck drivers they surveyed reported using drugs to stay awake. An American study, involving voluntary drug testing of 317 male drivers of tractor-trailers (articulated trucks), found that 29% tested positive for alcohol, cannabis, cocaine, or stimulants. Alcohol was found in less than 1% of the drivers, but 15% had used cannabis and 12% had used non-prescription stimulants (National Institute on Drug Abuse, 1989).

Risk Factors for Workplace AOD Problems

A number of studies have identified predictors of problematic drinking in the working population. Lehman et al. (1995) examined the relationship of individual and environmental factors to problematic AOD in a sample of municipal workers. They found that each domain significantly predicted drug use at and away from work, although the best fit was provided by a model including both domains. The profile of the employee most likely to be a problematic user was a young male with low self-esteem and an arrest history, who came from a family with AOD problems, and who associated with AOD-using peers. The employee with problematic AOD use was also likely to be estranged from work and to work under risky

Table 4.5.1   Indicators of AOD use

Individual predictors	Work environment predictors
Young and male	Long working hours and some types of shift work
Single, separated or divorced	High risk of injury at work
Low educational and skill level	High physical demands
More than usual recent stressful events	Monotonous work
Low self-esteem	Tight deadlines
Depressed	Job insecurity
	Poor supervision

job conditions. Table 4.5.1 lists those predictors of on the job and other problematic use of AODs that have been consistently identified in different studies (Plant, 1979; Mensch and Kandel, 1988; Newcomb, 1988; Ames et al., 2000).

AOD Availability and Normative Use

The workplace is also part of the broader community and will be affected by patterns of use and harm at the community level. Social and cultural factors are important here and a worker's socialisation experiences within the family and community are determining factors in the pattern of AOD problems that emerge at work. The level of alcohol problems in a factory in Malaysia that employs a predominantly Muslim workforce is likely to be low, because of the proscription of alcohol in that culture. Conversely, a mine situated in the Pilbara region of Western Australia is likely to have a high level of alcohol problems, because consumption in the community from which it draws its workforce is very high (Midford et al., 1998).

Nature of AOD Harm in Workplace

A considerable number of studies have investigated the relationship between employees' use of AODs and job outcomes, which can be broadly categorised as relating to accident and injury, and productivity. According to Normand et al. (1994) most do not control well for extraneous variables and identify associations rather than causal relationships. However, the studies do consistently identify a small negative relationship between AOD use and work-related outcomes.

Accidents and injury

It is well known that alcohol impairs performance: it affects balance and coordination; it impairs reflexes; it reduces caution. Performance also remains affected during the hangover phase when alcohol has been eliminated from the bloodstream. There is a considerable amount of evidence on the link between alcohol and traffic crashes. Alcohol is also involved in a range of other injuries such as drowning, burns, falls, fires and aviation crashes (Gossop, 2000). However, the evidence linking alcohol with work injuries is mixed.

There is good evidence linking alcohol, and to a lesser extent other drug use, with transportation accidents. A number of American studies have identified alcohol, cannabis, cocaine and stimulants as the drugs most commonly found in commercial vehicle drivers killed in traffic crashes. Studies of American railroad crashes similarly identified the presence of alcohol and cannabis in a high percentage of workers involved. It should be noted though that impairment caused by cannabis is likely to be relatively minor, because a person can test positive many days after actual use (Normand et al., 1994).

The evidence for involvement of AOD use in other workplace accidents and injuries is less well documented. Working under the influence does not seem to be widespread and even when it occurs, employees develop strategies to compensate for their impairment. One such strategy seems to be not coming to work, given the evidence of higher absenteeism among workers with high AOD use. Some employees have the opportunity to structure their work tasks so as to reduce risk when impaired. Some jobs, such as office work, offer little opportunity for accident and injury, no matter how impaired the worker. Research reviews indicate that alcohol may be a factor in up to 10% of workplace injuries (Phillips, 2001; Zwerling, 1993). In the case of illicit drugs the evidence base is weaker and the estimates much lower.

Productivity

The best-documented productivity-related outcome of employee AOD use is higher absenteeism. Studies commonly report that problem drinkers are away from work two to three times as often as their non-problem-drinking peers and there is a correlation between drinking habits and long-term sickness absence and early retirement (Martin et al., 1994; Upmark et al., 1999). Studies on the association between absenteeism and use of drugs other than alcohol are less numerous, but again time off work was consistently a greater problem for the drug-using workers (Normand et al. 1990).

Job turnover is another measure of productivity, because of the cost involved in recruiting and training new staff. Research indicates that there is a clear relationship between illicit drug use and job turnover. However, the relationship between alcohol use and turnover is less clear. Male problem drinkers seem to stay in the same job, but there is greater turnover of female problem drinkers. Where there is turnover of workers with problematic AOD use, it is more likely to be a job loss rather than a job change (Martin et al., 1994; Normand, et al., 1994).

The job performance of problematic AOD users has been measured in a few studies, which consistently indicate poorer performance across a number of domains (Martin et al., 1994). Specific productivity problems were:

- procrastination
- inconsistent performance
- neglect of detail
- poorer quality work
- less quantity of work
- more mistakes.

In addition to direct measures of output, Blum et al. (1992) found that heavier drinking also affected:

- self-direction
- conflict avoidance
- interpersonal relationships.

These deficits are likely to contribute in a global manner to a less productive workplace.

The Cost to the Workplace and Society

A number of researchers have estimated the dollar cost of AOD use to various sectors of the community. An Australian study looked at the social cost of alcohol, tobacco and illicit drug use borne respectively by different sectors, including the workplace: in 1998/99 tobacco cost Australian workplaces A$2.5 billion; alcohol A$1.9 billion and illicit drugs A$1 billion (Collins and Lapsley, 2002). Maynard et al. (1987) conducted a study in England and Wales and estimated that the annual social cost related to alcohol problems was £2 billion, of which sickness and absenteeism accounted for over £800 million. A German study (Brecht et al., 1996) found that 74% of workplace AOD cost was indirect and related to premature death (52%), absenteeism (26%) and early retirement (22%). These are costs that in part are borne by the employer, but also by the entire community.

This research clearly indicates that AOD use is a large cost to business. What is lacking is specificity, which makes it difficult to present clear advice on how best to respond. Measuring the costs associated with AOD use does not indicate the degree to which those costs can be decreased by particular policies or programmes. The figures do, however, suggest that employers are likely to gain substantial cost benefit from effective interventions.

RESPONDING TO WORKPLACE AOD PROBLEMS

In recent years many employers have developed formal and informal policies and practices to limit AOD use and harm in the workplace. These initiatives have generally formed part of a broader occupational health and safety protocol for the workplace, which in itself is driven by a legal duty to provide a safe workplace and the common law obligation of due care. In Australia, each state has occupational health and safety legislation, which imposes substantial compliance liability on employers (Midford, 2003). The onus is on the employer to be proactive in dealing with occupational health and safety risks, including those linked to AOD use.

A similar situation exists in many Western industrialised nations. In Sweden, for example, every employer is bound by law to provide a safe work environment. They are also required to develop a written policy regarding the use of alcohol and other drugs. Employees have to be involved in the development of the policy, which has to specify procedures for responding to related problems (Prop. 2000/01: 20, 2000; SFS 1977: 1160, 1977).

SPECIFIC INTERVENTION STRATEGIES

Reviews of the literature suggest that interventions to deal with workplace AOD problems fit into five broad categories (Allsop et al., 1997):

- policy development
- information and education programmes
- health promotion programmes
- regulation of use and compliance drug testing
- assistance and treatment.

Developing a Workplace AOD Policy

Simply developing and implementing a written policy on how the workplace views and will respond to AOD problems is an effective strategy in itself and provides a good foundation for further interventions. An effective policy should address the following development and content issues (Duffy and Ask, 2001):

- consultation with the workforce during development;
- universal application;
- tailored to suit the organisation;
- comprehensive coverage of and specific procedures for responding to drug use in the workplace;
- publicise the policy to maximise awareness;
- education and training on implementation of the new AOD policy;
- pace implementation to maximise acceptance;
- evaluation in terms of stated objectives.

Information and Education Programmes

There is a long history of providing education about AODs as a strategy to prevent use and harm, the rationale being that people will make better decisions if they are better informed. Unfortunately, the research evidence as to its effectiveness is inconsistent: some programmes achieved change in the short term, but this was not sustained (Roman and Blum, 2002). This does not mean that education should be abandoned; rather, it should be undertaken regularly as part of a broader approach. Education is best used to give employees an understanding of why AOD use can be a problem in the workplace. This understanding provides a foundation and rationale for more targeted programs, such as health promotion to enhance well-being, specific prevention measures such as drug testing or counselling for high-risk employees.

Health Promotion Programmes

Health Promotion programmes are designed primarily to enhance well-being, with a secondary aim of preventing health-related problems (Shain, 1994). Programmes seek to make environments more supportive of health and teach participants how to improve or maintain their health. The most common targets for health promotion programmes are smoking cessation, exercise, weight loss and stress management. This type of intervention has only recently been tried in the workplace and there is no substantial body of research to indicate whether it is effective in this setting. It has, however, been useful at the community level. The following key elements should be incorporated into the design of any workplace health promotion programme to optimise its effectiveness:

- provide participants with a greater sense of control over their own health in general or in relation to a particular health practice such as reducing alcohol consumption;
- attend to the interdependent nature of health practices, such that alcohol consumption is linked to weight loss, sleeping and stress management;
- provide personal follow-up and support to maintain changed behaviour.

Regulation of Use and Compliance Drug Testing

A body of literature on regulation of use without associated drug testing really only exists in relation to smoking. Australian investigations of workplace smoking bans suggest that they can influence attitudes towards smoking, which in turn can assist smokers to reduce use (Borland et al., 1991). Smoking bans also have good worker support and because breaches are quite public, few smokers are prepared to risk social disapproval, irrespective of the likely company response (Borland et al., 1990).

Many workplaces also have bans on other types of drug use. These may be absolute bans (e.g., no use of any illegal drug), conditional (e.g., use of medications must be reported), or with limits (e.g., blood alcohol levels over 0.05 mg% will not be tolerated). However, compliance checking is usually conducted through drug testing and this has created technical, ethical, legal and industrial relation challenges. In Sweden, for example, there is concern that testing may breach the European Constitution's law on protection of the individual's human rights and fundamental freedom (Eriksson and Olsson, 2001). This concern has been echoed in Canada, because drug testing may be unreasonable and discriminatory and thus conflict with the Canadian Charter of Rights and Freedoms (Pinsonneault, 1994). The contention arises primarily because of the invasiveness of the procedure, which except for alcohol testing, involves the employee providing a urine sample. The research literature is not a counterbalancing source of support for the measure. Some studies have indicated that testing programmes reduced drug use and increased productivity, but their methodology was weak and the findings need to be interpreted with caution (Normand et al., 1994). Zwerling and colleagues, whose work is often cited as key evidential support in favour of drug testing, stated that "many of the claims cited to justify preemployment drug screening have been exaggerated" (Zwerling et al., 1990, p. 2643).

An individual's exposure to drugs can be measured through the analysis of hair, blood, saliva, exhaled breath and urine. Drug testing can be categorised into four main types:

- pre-employment screening (screening job applicants)
- screening with probable cause (e.g., after an accident)
- mass screening (testing the whole workforce)
- random screening (equal chance of each employee being tested without cause or notice).

Testing for alcohol is usually conducted through breath analysis. Detection of other drugs is most commonly via urine testing, usually employing immunoassay and gas chromatography/mass spectrometry (GCMS).

Breath testing employees for alcohol is less intrusive than giving a sample of urine. Good research evidence allows nomination of a blood alcohol concentration that is associated with degree of impairment (commonly 0.05 mg% for non-safety-critical positions and 0.00 mg% for safety-critical positions) (McLean et al., 1980). This is not possible with urine screening for other drugs. Also, breath analysis is logistically easier and cheaper than urine drug testing, with the sample of breath being analysed immediately and on site. Nevertheless, accurate breath testing relies on using quality machines that are regularly calibrated. It is also important to note that impairment can be high in individuals with a low blood alcohol level, if they have low tolerance. Even individuals with a zero blood alcohol level may be impaired as a result of a hangover.

The immunoassay urine test is sensitive to most of the drugs likely to be encountered. It is a relatively low cost screening method. However, it does not identify specific drugs (i.e., it can identify a metabolite as being related to amphetamine type stimulants, but not identify which specific drug). Immunoassay tests are not 100% reliable and interpretation of results may confuse licit substances with illicit ones. A positive immunoassay test result should be confirmed by another method, such as GCMS, which is more accurate and can distinguish different types of drugs. However, GCMS is more expensive than immunoassay, and its sensitivity means that some metabolites may show positive days after the individual was exposed to the drugs. A number of countries have developed standards for the process of gathering (e.g., ensuring chain of custody) and interpreting urine test results. These include minimum detection levels of metabolites to determine a "positive" result. Adherence to these guidelines will result in negligible levels of false positives. Non-adherence will result in flaws and invitation to successful legal and industrial challenges.

As indicated, urine testing measures the presence of metabolites, not the drugs themselves. Some of these metabolites can be identified several days after the individual was exposed to the drug, but there is no evidence that links the presence of drug metabolites with performance. The *Journal of the American Medical Association* has stated: "Drug testing does not provide any information about patterns of drug use, about abuse of or dependence on drugs, or about mental or physical impairments that may result from drug use" (Council on Scientific Affairs 1987, p. 3114). In short, it is important to recognise that urine testing measures exposure to drugs, not pattern of drug use, intoxication or impairment. For example, an individual who has a positive test (using Australian Standards) for cannabinoids has used cannabis in the recent past. This may be the past few hours, in which case they are likely to be intoxicated, or the last few days, in which case they have engaged in an illegal activity, but will not be intoxicated.

Recently there has been an increased focus on saliva testing. Saliva testing is attractive, because it is likely to be perceived as less invasive. It can also detect the direct presence of a drug, rather than the presence of metabolites. In other words, if the result is positive, the individual will have the active drug in their system and they are effectively "intoxicated". A positive result will not directly determine level of impairment. However, current intoxication, rather than past exposure (as inferred by a positive urine test) is a better assessment of immediate risk. Currently there are no accepted national standards on conducting and interpreting saliva test results and there are some weaknesses in the method, especially in detecting cannabis use. Nevertheless, this is a rapidly advancing area of research and method of detection.

One criticism of any form of drug testing is that the methods focus on the individual user, with little if any attention to other factors. Structural issues that can underpin hazardous and harmful drug use are often ignored when drug testing programmes are implemented. For example, concern has been expressed about the impact of amphetamine use on long-distance drivers. However, tight schedules may require drivers to drive for overly long periods. Reducing amphetamine use through a drug-testing programme may actually increase accidents if more drivers fall asleep at the wheel. Effective prevention will involve strategies that address the structural factors that encourage drivers to stay at the wheel for excessive periods.

Other methods of identifying long-term problematic drinking have been researched. A study by Hermansson et al. (2000) investigated combining biological markers such as GGT (glutamyltransferase) and CDT (carbohydrate-deficient transferrin) with the AUDIT

(Alcohol Use Disorders Identification Test) pen and paper screening tool. They found that combining GGT with the AUDIT was optimal in a routine workplace health examination since each detects a different group with alcohol-related problem.

Assistance and Treatment

Referral to an Employee Assistance Programme (EAP) has been the most common way of responding to an employee with an identified AOD problem, although the EAP has a much broader role than AOD counselling (Calogero et al., 2001; Roman and Blum, 2002). An EAP is typically operated by an external provider and the services most frequently offered include AOD awareness and education, supervisor training in problem recognition and referral, employee assessment, treatment, and follow-up support. The great majority of EAP clients self-refer and on average about 5% of employees will use the service in a 12-month period (Blum et al., 1995). In other cases the client is referred by the supervisor, because of performance problems or as part of a disciplinary response. In providing a service to the workplace, EAPs have to balance the needs of the employee and employer, which in many circumstances do not coincide. This conflict of interest is particularly salient on issues of productivity, safety, and drug testing. If EAPs are to be seen by workers as not simply another means of control, they need to manage their responsibility boundaries carefully.

Various studies do indicate that treating AOD problems through EAPs results in a decline in health-care costs; a decline in accidents; lower levels of worker compensation claims; reduced absenteeism; and increased productivity. However, the research that produced these findings was of poor quality (Allsop et al., 1997; Roman and Blum, 2002). What can be claimed with greater confidence is that some EAP components produce useful outcomes. Studies found that constructive confrontation and referral by supervisors improved job performance; EAP involvement and initial intense treatment for workers with AOD problems produced better outcomes than self-help strategies; long-term follow-up and support by EAP staff reduced AOD disability, relapse rates and treatment costs. While research support for the effectiveness of EAPs is patchy, it is clear that the approach is strongly supported by employers, employees and unions. This has meant that EAPs are well accepted as a way of dealing with AOD problems in the workplace (Calogero et al., 2001).

THE NEW WORKING LIFE

The great majority of research on AOD use and the workplace has been done in traditional, discrete work settings. However, Western society is facing dramatic change to working life that has been labelled the third industrial revolution by some commentators. Many countries around the world are becoming post-industrial societies, where work is no longer confined to a physical location, because of information and communication technology (Magnusson and Ottosson, 2003). Large numbers of predominantly white-collar workers are affected by this change, with many also expected to work longer and be available out of hours. Compensation comes in the form of working on stimulating tasks and having more influence over their work situation. The story for workers with lower educational levels is different: they are facing less control over their work situation due to short-term employment contracts. It is also likely that this group will face increased psychological demands, but because they are on short-term contracts developing supportive social relationships with colleagues is more difficult. This could result in, what Theorell (1997) calls "iso-strain" which occurs when individuals become more isolated, while simultaneously facing excessive demands and little latitude in decision-making.

The new working life also puts new demands on how we approach alcohol and drugs in the workplace. One reason for this relates to the increase in project and other forms of temporary employment. At the beginning of the 1990s Aasland and Riise (1990) noted that the workplace has many qualities that make it a particularly suitable setting for AOD prevention. The workplace can be a positive environment where everyone has a valued role; where workers provide mutual support and where different work areas are clearly defined. The question is, what happens when this starts to deteriorate? During the 1990s there was an increase in temporary employment in Sweden, primarily in care settings (Theorell, 1997; Magnusson and Ottosson, 2003). During the same period there was an increase in absenteeism due to illness, which in turn was related to deteriorating psychosocial work conditions (Wikman and Marklund, 2003).

The twenty-first-century workplace is in many ways a new environment where the individual has to find her/his position. It is an environment that demands a new set of skills from the individual. Historically, it was enough if an individual could produce a certain amount of goods within a certain timeframe. The new working life is characterised by globalisation, service-centred industries and customer accessibility. Here flexibility and responsiveness are of utmost importance. It has also become more common for work and leisure time to overlap as more people work from home. The result is less demarcation between work and family life. Working at a distance can also result in a more isolated working situation, because of less supervision and support (Docherty and Huzzard, 2003). These are all factors that could have a negative impact on AOD use, while at the same time making detection of problems more difficult.

CONCLUSION

This chapter has outlined the issues that need to be considered when dealing with AOD problems in the workplace and has presented a range of intervention approaches. It is important to look beyond the "alcoholic" and "drug addict" as the source of AOD problems in the workplace. Optimum outcomes are likely to be obtained by matching a range of strategies to the nature of the problem and the characteristics of the workplace. Geographical location, workplace size, history, culture, characteristics of the workforce and nature of the work are all factors that need to be taken into consideration. Reducing AOD problems in the workplace in essence involves the application of sound management. Basic principles of performance management and occupational health and safety provide the best foundation for developing an effective workplace AOD programme.

REFERENCES

Aasland, O.G. and Riise, G. (1990) Alkohol og arbeid. *Tidskrift for Norsk Loegeforening*, **13**(110), 1697–1699.
Abraham, M.D., Cohen, P.D.A., van Til, R. and de Winter, M.A.L. (1999) *Licit and Illicit Drug Use in the Netherlands*. Amsterdam: CEDRO Centrum voor Drugsonderzoek.

Allsop, S., Bush, R., Phillips, M. et al. (1997) *Alcohol and Other Drugs in the Australian Workplace: A Critical Literature Review*, Bedford Park: National Centre for Education and Training on Addiction.

Ames, G.M. and Rebhun, L.A. (1996) Women, alcohol and work: interactions of gender, ethnicity and occupational culture. *Social Science of Medicine*, **43**(11), 1649–1663.

Ames, G.M., Grube, J.W. and Moore, R.S. (2000) Social control and workplace drinking norms: a comparison of two organisational cultures. *Journal of Studies on Alcohol*, March, 203–219.

Blum, T.C., Roman, P.M. and Harwood, E.M. (1995) Employed women with alcohol problems who seek help from Employee Assistance Programs: descriptions and comparisons. *Recent Developments in Alcoholism*, **12**, 125–156.

Blum, T.C., Roman, P.M. and Martin, J.K. (1992) Alcohol consumption and work performance. *Journal of Studies on Alcohol*, **54**, 61–70.

Borland, R., Owen, N. and Hocking, B. (1991) Changes in smoking behaviour after a total workplace smoking ban. *Australian Journal of Public Health*, **15**, 130–134.

Borland, R., Owen, N., Hill, D. and Chapman, S. (1990) Changes in acceptance of workplace smoking bans following their implementation: a prospective study. *Preventive Medicine*, **19**, 314–322.

Brecht, J.T., Poldrugo, F. and Schädlich, P.K. (1996) Alcoholism: the cost of illness in the Federal Republic of Germany. *Pharmaco-Economics*, **10**, 484–493.

Calogero, C., Midford, R. and Towers, T. (2001) Responding to drug-related harm in the workplace: the role of prevention, counselling, and assistance programs. In S. Allsop, M. Phillips and C. Calogero (eds), *Drugs and Work: Responding to Alcohol and Other Drug Problems*. Melbourne: IP Communications, pp. 60–73.

Collins, D.J. and Lapsley, H.M. (2002) *Counting the Cost: Estimates of the Social Costs of Drug Abuse in Australia in 1998–99*. Canberra: Commonwealth Department of Health and Ageing.

Council on Scientific Affairs (1987) Scientific issues in drug testing. *Journal of the American Medical Association*, **257**(22), 3110–3114.

Docherty, P. and Huzzard, T. (2003) Marknads-, management- och medarbetartrender 1985–2005. In C. von Otter (ed.), *Ute och inne i svenskt arbetsli*. Stockholm: Arbetslivsinstitutet, pp. 135–157.

Duffy, J. and Ask, A. (2001) Ten ingredients for developing and implementing a drug and alcohol policy in your workplace. In S. Allsop, M. Phillips and C. Calogero (eds.), *Drugs and Work: Responding to Alcohol and Other Drug Problems*. Melbourne: IP Communications, pp. 135–157.

Eriksson, M. and Olsson, B. (2001) Alkohol- och drogtester i svenskt arbetsliv. *Arbetsmarknad & Arbetsliv*, **7**(4), 225–238.

Gleason, P., Veum, J. and Pergamit M. (1991) Drug and alcohol use at work. *Monthly Labor Review*, **114**(8), 3–7.

Gossop, M. (2000) *Living with Drugs*. Aldershot: Ashgate.

Guttormsson, U. (ed.) (2002) *Trends in Alcohol and Other Drugs in Sweden*—Report 2002. Rapport nr. 68, Stockholm: Centralforbundet for alkohol- och narkotikaupplysning.

Hagen, R., Egan D. and Eltringham, A. (1992) *Work, Drugs and Alcohol Occupational Health and Safety Commission Enquiry into Alcohol, Drugs and the Workplace*. Melbourne: Victorian Occupational Health and Safety Commission.

Hermansson, U., Helander, A., Huss, A., Brandt, L. and Rönnberg, S. (2000) The Alcohol Use Disorders Identification Test (AUDIT) and Carbohydrate-Deficient Transferring (CDT) in a routine workplace health examination. *Alcoholism: Clinical and Experimental Research*, **24**(2), 180–187.

Kjærheim, K., Mykletun, R., Aasland, O.G., Haldorsen, T. and Andersen, A. (1995) Heavy drinking in the restaurant business: the role of social modelling and structural factors of the work-place. *Addiction*, **90**, 1487–1495.

Lehman, W.E.K., Farabee, D.J., Holcom, M.L. and Simpson, D.D. (1995) Prediction of substance use in the workplace: unique contributions of personal background and work environment variables. *Journal of Drug Issues*, **25**(2), 253–274.

Leifman, H. (2002) Konsumtionsvanor och alkoholproblem. In S. Andréasson (ed.), *Den svenska supen I det nya Europa. Nya villkor för alkoholprevention: En kunskapsöversikt* (pp. 29–64). Rapport nr. 2002 (11), Stockholm: Statens Folkhälsoinstitut.

McLean, A.J., Holubowycz, O.T. and Sandow, B.L. (1980) *Alcohol and Crashes: Identification of Relevant Factors in this Association.* Adelaide: Road Accident Research Unit, University of Adelaide.

Magnusson, L. and Ottosson, J. (2003) Den tredje industriella revolutionen och den "nya ekonomin"— mellan sken och verklighet. In C. von Otter (ed.), *Ute och innei svenskt arbetsliv.* Stockholm: Arbetslivsinstitutet, pp. 57–76.

Martin, J.K., Kraft, J.M. and Roman, P.M. (1994) Extent and impact of alcohol and drug use problems in the workplace. In S. Macdonald and P. Roman (eds), *Drug Testing in the Workplace: Research Advances in Alcohol and Drug Problems* Vol. 11. New York: Plenum Press, pp. 3–31.

Maxwell, J.C. (2003) Update: comparison of drug use in Australia and the United States as seen in the 2001 National Household Surveys. *Drug and Alcohol Review,* **22**, 347–357.

Maynard, A., Hardman, G. and Whelan, A. (1987) Data note 9: measuring the social costs of addictive substances. *British Journal of Addiction,* **82**, 701–706.

Mensch, B.S. and Kandel, D.B. (1988) Do job conditions influence the use of drugs? *Journal of Health and Social Behavior,* **29**, 169–184.

Midford, R. (2003) Alcohol and other drugs. In A. Wyatt and M. Oxenburgh (eds), *Managing Occupational Health and Safety.* Sydney: CCH Australia Ltd., pp. 64081–64115.

Midford, R., Stockwell, T., Daly, A., Phillips, M., Masters, L., Gahegan, M. and Philip, M. (1998). Alcohol consumption and injury in Western Australia: a spatial correlation analysis using geographic information systems. *Australian and New Zealand Journal of Public Health,* **22**(1), 80–85.

National Institute on Drug Abuse (1989) *Drug Use by Tractor-Trailer Drivers: Drugs in the Workplace.* Washington, DC: US Department of Health and Human Services.

Newcomb, M.D. (1988) *Drug Use in the Workplace: Risk Factors for Disruptive Substance Use among Young Adults.* Dover, MA: Auburn House.

Normand, J., Lempert, R.O. and O'Brien, C.P. (1994) *Under the Influence? Drugs and the American Work Force.* Washington, DC: National Academy Press.

Normand, J., Salyards, S.D. and Mahony, J.J. (1990) An evaluation of preemployment drug testing. *Journal of Applied Psychology,* **75**, 629–639.

Phillips, M. (2001) The prevalence of drug use and risk of drug-related harm in the workplace. In S. Allsop, M. Phillips and C. Calogero (eds), *Drugs and Work: Responding to Alcohol and Other Drug Problems.* Melbourne: IP Communications, pp. 60–73.

Pinsonneault, M. (1994) Some legal aspects of drug testing in the Canadian workplace. In S. Macdonald and P. Roman (eds), *Drug Testing in the Workplace: Research Advances in Alcohol and Drug Problems.* Vol. 11, New York: Plenum Press, pp. 165–183.

Plant, M.A. (1979) *Drinking Careers: Occupations, Drinking Habits, and Drinking Problems,* London: Tavistock.

Prop. 2000/01:20. (2000) *Nationell handlingsplan för att förebygga alkoholskador.* Stockholm.

Roman, P.M. and Blum, T.C. (2002) The workplace and alcohol problem prevention. *Alcohol Research and Health,* **26**(1), 49–57.

SFS 1977:1160. (1977) *Arbetsmiljölag. Svensk Författningssamling,* Stockholm: Näringsdepartementet.

Shain, M. (1994) Alternatives to drug testing. In S. Macdonald and P. Roman (eds), *Drug Testing in the Workplace: Research Advances in Alcohol and Drug Problems,* Vol. 11. New York: Plenum Press, pp. 257–277.

Stinson, F.S., Debakey, S.F. and Steffens, R.A. (1992) Epidemiologic Bulletin No. 30. Prevalence of DSM-III-R alcohol abuse and/or dependence among selected occupations, United States, 1988. *Alcohol Health Research World,* **16**, 165–172.

Theorell, T. (1997) How will future work life influence health?, *Scandinavian Journal of Work Environment Health*, **23**(suppl. 4), 16–22.

United Nations Office on Drugs and Crime (2003) *Global Illicit Drug Trends* 2003, Vienna: United Nations.

Upmark, M., Möller, J. and Romelsjö, A. (1999) Longitudinal, population-based study of self-reported alcohol habits, high levels of sickness absence, and disability pensions. *Journal of Epidemiological Community Health*, **53**, 223–229.

Wikman, A. and Marklund, S. (2003) Tolkningar av arbetssjuklighetens utveckling i Sverige. In C. von Otter (ed.), *Ute och inne i svenskt arbetsliv*. Stockholm: Arbetslivsinstitutet, pp. 21–56.

Williamson, A.M., Feyer. A., Coumarelos, C. and Jenkins T. (1992) *Strategies to Combat Fatigue in the Long Distance Road Transport Industry: Stage 1: The Industry Perspective*. Report CR 108, Canberra: Federal Office of Road Safety.

World Health Organization, Regional Office for Europe (2002) *The European Report on Tobacco Control Policy*. Copenhagen: WHO Regional Office for Europe.

Zwerling, C. (1993) Current practice and experience in drug and alcohol testing in the workplace. *Bulletin on Narcotics*, **XLV**(2), 155–196.

Zwerling, C., Ryan, J. and Orav, E.J. (1990) The efficacy of pre-employment drug screening for marijuana and cocaine in predicting employment outcome. *Journal of the American Medical Association*, **264**(20), 2639–2643.

4.6 Effects of a Community Action Program on Problems Related to Alcohol Consumption at Licensed Premises

EVA WALLIN AND SVEN ANDRÉASSON

Karolinska Institutet, Department of Public Health, Stockholm, Sweden

SUMMARY

In this chapter we present outcome results from a multi-component community action program on problems related to alcohol consumption at licensed premises. Alcohol consumption at licensed premises is associated with various problems, e.g., assaults and injuries. In Sweden, the number of licensed premises has increased markedly over the past 15 years. The ten-year community alcohol prevention program started in 1996 in the northern part of central Stockholm, Sweden (project area) with a control area in the southern part of central Stockholm. Main intervention components included community mobilization, training of servers in responsible beverage service, and stricter enforcement of existing alcohol laws. Actors portraying drunk patrons and young people (18 years old but looking younger according to an expert panel) have attempted to order beer from licensed premises. Police statistics on reported violent crimes for the period January 1994 to September 2000 were collected and analyzed with time-series analyses (ARIMA-models). The results show a decrease in alcohol-related problems at licensed premises. The number of licensed premises that refused alcohol service to intoxicated patrons changed from 5% in 1996 to 47% in 1999, and 70% in 2001. Refusal of alcohol service to minors changed from 55% in 1996, to 59% in 1998 and 68% in 2001. Changes in alcohol service occurred both in the project and control area. During the project period assaults decreased significantly by 29% in the project area but increased slightly in the control area. Policy initiatives were implemented by the licensing authority and by the police equally in all of Stockholm. The multi-component program seems to have successfully reduced problems related to alcohol consumption at licensed premises. The most likely explanation for this is a combination of RBS training, building of community networks and policy routines initiated by the project. The results from the effect studies support earlier findings that multi-component interventions targeting licensed premises at the community level have the potential to reduce alcohol-related problems.

Preventing Harmful Substance Use: The Evidence Base for Policy and Practice.
Edited by T. Stockwell, P. J. Gruenewald, J.W. Toumbourou and W. Loxley.
© 2005 John Wiley & Sons, Ltd. ISBN 0-470-09227-0 (hbk) 0-470-09228-9 (pbk).

INTRODUCTION

Sweden has a long tradition of strict alcohol control policies, i.e., a state-run alcohol monopoly for the retail sale of alcohol. However, during the past decade, the national alcohol policy has changed, making alcohol more accessible. This has resulted in an increased total consumption of alcohol by the Swedish population (Leifman, 2002). One example of the easier access of alcohol is the rapid increase of licensed premises in Sweden. In a recent study, Norström has shown that there is a statistically significant association between beer/liquor consumption at licensed premises in Sweden and the assault rate (Norström, 1998). Other studies have also shown associations between public violence and the number of licensed premises (Roncek and Maier; 1991; Norström, 2000).

PREVENTION STRATEGIES TO REDUCE ALCOHOL-RELATED PROBLEMS AT LICENSED PREMISES

Different approaches to interventions to reduce alcohol-related problems at licensed premises have been elaborated (Graham, 2000). Reviews of these approaches indicate various effects (see Table 4.6.1).

Responsible Beverage Service Training and House Policies

One group of licensed premise interventions have focused on encouraging responsible beverage service (RBS), mainly through training of servers and implementing stricter policies. Early efficacy studies showed mixed results. Some studies indicated that it was possible to reduce alcohol-related problems by promoting responsible beverage service (Russ and Geller, 1987; Saltz 1987; Gliksman et al., 1993). Significant effects were indicated with regard to the refusal rate of alcohol service to intoxicated patrons and, for more comprehensive programs, to reductions in patrons' BAC levels (Saltz, 1987). Another group of studies did not show any effects from serving practices (McKnight, 1991; Rydon et al., 1996). Other outcome measures for RBS programs have been alcohol-related traffic crashes or DUI arrests, as they have focused on drinking and driving. Significant effects with regard to reduction in alcohol-related traffic crashes were shown in a study of mandatory training in the State of Oregon (Holder and Wagenaar, 1994).

Based on experiences from previous research studies, minimum requirements for RBS programs have been identified. According to Mosher et al., (2002) the following five requirements can influence the effectiveness of RBS training programs:

1. *Cover all basic information with servers.* Relevant information includes physiological effects of alcohol and social problems associated with alcohol use. Legal requirements pertaining to alcohol service are considered of core importance.
2. *Use behavioral change/communication techniques.* By simply providing information, the chances of promoting behavior change or increasing the skills level are limited (Bandura, 1977; Glanz et al., 1997). As it is important that servers are taught specific skills to manage responsible service techniques (e.g., refusing alcohol sales to an intoxicated patron), role-playing or other skill-building techniques need to be used.

Table 4.6.1 Compilation of licensed premise interventions

Project	Study design	Location	Target group	Intervention	Effects
TIPS (Training for Intervention Procedures by Servers of Alcohol) (Russ and Geller, 1987) **(I)**	Pre/post Trained *vs.* untrained staff	USA	Servers at two taverns. Half the staff trained in each venue.	6 hr training for servers, (discussions, videos, role-play). Written test.	Pseudopatron evaluation: ordering drinks every 20 minutes for 2 hours. Trained servers initiated more server intervention (3.24 interventions) than did untrained staff (0.75 interventions). Mean patron BAC 0.059% (trained staff) vs. 0.103 (untrained staff).
Navy Server Study (Saltz, 1987) **(I)**	Treatment and control group	San Diego, USA	Managers and servers at one Navy club for enlisted personnel. One control site.	18 hr training + management policies.	Significant reduction in patrons over the legal limit of intoxication (0.10% BAC), from 33% to 15% in experimental bars.
(Howard-Pitney, 1991) **(I)**	Treatment and control group	Park City, Utah, USA	Servers at 26 establishments. 14 control establishments.	1 day training.	No differences in policies or practices between the treatment and control group.
The McKnight Server Training Study (McKnight, 1991) **(I)**	Treatment and control group	Eight states, USA	Servers and managers at 100 establishments. 135 control establishments.	6 hr training for managers. 3 hr for bar staff.	Significant, overall increase in observed intervention at participating establishments, not in comparison group. Increased frequency of interventions (from 14 to 27%) at trained establishments. Refusal rate of intoxicated patrons unchanged (with a rate of 5%).
(Gliksman et al., 1993) **(I)**	Treatment and control group	Thunder Bay, Ontario, Canada	Owners/managers and servers at four drinking establishments. Four control establishments	Server intervention training 4.5 hr. Development of house policy.	Trained servers responded more appropriately toward "pseudopatrons" portraying problematic scenes, than did untrained servers.

(*Continued*)

Table 4.6.1 Compilation of licensed premise interventions (*Continued*)

Project	Study design	Location	Target group	Intervention	Effects
The Rhode Island Community Alcohol Abuse and Injury Prevention Project (CAAIPP) (Buka and Birdthistle, 1999) **(I)**	Prospective study design. Randomized intervention and control group	Rhode Island, USA	Establishments in one community. Two control communities.	5 hr training.	Short-term effects (15 months after training): trainees showed significantly higher levels of desired serving behavior than non-trained servers (self-reported behavior). Persistent but diminished effects 4 years posttraining.
FREO respects you, (Lang, et al., 1998) **(I)**	Treatment and control group	Fremantle, Australia	7 "high risk" premises. Seven matched premises in neighboring area—controls.	Risk assessment and feedback for managers. Management policies. 3 hr training for managers and staff.	No changes in service refusals to drunk patrons and ID checking for young pseudopatrons. Significant reduction of number of patrons exceeding BAC 0.08%.
(Holder and Wagenaar, 1994) **(I)**	Time-series analyses	Oregon, USA	All licensed premises in the State of Oregon.	Mandated server training for all alcohol servers.	Reduction in traffic crashes.
Project ARM: Alcohol Risk Management (Toomey et al., 2001) **(I)**	Treatment and control group	Minnesota, USA	Five bars. Nine controls.	One-on-one consultation program for owners and managers.	11.5% decrease in underage sales, 46% decrease in sales to pseudo-intoxicated patrons (not statistically significant).
The Michigan Enforcement Study (McKnight and Streff, 1994) **(II)**	Treatment and control group	Washtenaw County, Michigan, USA	Two counties.	Media attention. Increased enforcement of alcohol service laws by police officers in plain clothes. Positive feedback for well managed bars, warning or fines for others.	Refusal of alcohol service to pseudopatrons simulating intoxication increased from 17.5% to 54.3%. Percentage drunk drivers from bars declined from 31.7% to 23.3%.
Community Policing for English Pubs (Jeffs and Saunders, 1983) **(II)**	Treatment and control group	England	One entertainment area. One control site.	Uniformed police officers visit pubs 2 to 3 times a week.	20% reduction in recorded public disorder offences in intervention area. No reduction in control area.

Study	Design	Location	Setting	Intervention	Results
The Sydney Policing Study (Burns et al., 1995)(**II**)	Treatment and control group	Sydney, Australia	One entertainment area. One control site.	Uniformed police visited licensed premises at high risk times on more than 1,200 occasions.	Significant *increase* in recorded assaults in comparison with control site. Slight *decrease* in emergency department admission for assault injuries for intervention area.
The Rhode Island Project, (Putnam et al., 1993) (**II**)	Treatment and control group	Rhode Island, USA	One community. One control site.	A strong liquor law enforcement component with mandated penalties. Increased police presence in bars.	*20% increase* in assault arrest rates in intervention area compared with control community. 25% *decrease* in emergency room visits for assault-related injuries in intervention area.
The Surfers Paradise Safety Action Project, (Homel et al., 1994) (**III**)	Pre-/post-intervention design	Surfers Paradise, Australia	One major tourist area with 20 nightclubs.	Community mobilization. Code of practice signed by licensees. Training of security staff. No discounting.	Halving of violent incidents observed: 9.8 to 4.7 per 100 hours observation. Rose again to 8.3 two years later.
Communities Mobilizing for Change on Alcohol, (Wagenaar et al., 1999, 2000a, 2000b) (**III**)	Randomized treatment- and control. Time-series analyses	Minnesota, USA	Seven intervention communities. Eight control communities.	Community mobilization. Changes of community policies. Server training. Enforcement (e.g. compliance checks).	Reduction in alcohol sales to underage patrons on-sale (42.6% buy rate baseline, 29.0% buy rate at follow-up). Reduction in arrest and traffic crashes for adolescents 18–20 years by 31 per 100,000/year.
Three Community Trial, (Holder et al., 2000) (**III**)	Matched treatment and control group	California, USA	Three intervention communities. Three control communities.	Community mobilization. Training in responsible beverage service. Enforcement of alcohol laws. Policy changes.	Decline in nighttime injury crashes by 56 per 100,000/year. Decline in traffic crashes with driver under the influence of alcohol by 67 per 100,000/year. Decline in assault injuries by 68 per 100,000/year.

Note: I = Training in responsible beverage service and house policies, II = Stricter enforcement of existing alcohol laws, III = Multi-component interventions combining community mobilization, RBS training, house policies and stricter enforcement

3. *Focus on both managers and servers.* Managers must also be targeted, as they are responsible for supervising the servers and therefore need to be familiar with the servers' responsibilities and skills.
4. *Include policy development for managers.* Encouraging managers to develop written house policies increases the chances of implementing RBS at the establishment. A policy signals that the establishment expects and supports the use of responsible service practices.
5. *Minimum length—four hours.* The most effective RBS programs last at least four hours.

To conclude, experiences from RBS training programs indicate some positive direct effects on alcohol problems, especially when such programs are mandatory (Graham, 2000).

Strict Enforcement of Extant Alcohol Regulations

Another strategy to be tested is increased enforcement of extant alcohol laws. A study by McKnight and Streff (1994) on stricter enforcement at licensed premises showed significant effects in terms of reduced alcohol service to intoxicated pseudopatrons and reduced drunk driving.

Multi-Component Interventions

Licensed premise interventions with a multi-component approach, combining training, house policies and enforcement, show a promising potential for reducing alcohol-related problems, primarily alcohol-related traffic crashes (Holder et al., 2000; Wagenaar et al., 2000a).

Overall, reviews of licensed premise interventions suggest an increased potential for multi-component interventions combining training of bar staff, written house policies, and stricter enforcement of extant regulations for decreasing alcohol problems at licensed premises (Graham, 2000; Homel et al., 2001).

LICENSED PREMISES IN STOCKHOLM—A NEW TARGET FOR PREVENTION

In the mid-1990s, changes in the Swedish national alcohol policy and the anticipated negative consequences that could potentially follow caused concern among leading officials in the Stockholm County Council. This resulted in the initiation of a ten-year alcohol prevention project. The project, entitled "Stockholm Prevents Alcohol and Drug Problems (STAD)" aimed to develop, implement and evaluate promising alcohol prevention methods in the local community (Andréasson et al., 1999). Stockholm City was chosen as the project area. A review of extant research literature on community alcohol prevention guided the choice of three main areas to develop for prevention: (1) prevention targeting youth (including family programs); (2) brief intervention in primary health care; and (3) prevention targeting licensed premises. There were several arguments for including intervention at licensed premises as one of the prevention strategies. As mentioned earlier, the experiences from other countries were promising.

Another argument was the increasing number of licensed premises in Sweden, and especially Stockholm, causing anticipation of an increase in intoxication and violence. Outlet density also increases the potential for alcohol-related accidents (Gruenewald et al., 2002). Moreover, opening hours had been extended. Since 1997 it has been possible for nightclubs in Stockholm to stay open until 05.00 a.m. According to an Australian study, extended opening hours resulted in a significant increase in monthly arrests for these establishments (Chikritzhs and Stockwell, 2002). A study from Iceland showed that extended hours of operation were associated with an increase in police work assignments, suspected drunk driving and admissions to emergency wards (Ragnarsdóttir et al., 2002).

During this period there were also other changes of relevance to the initiation of a community action project. In 1995, a new Swedish Alcohol Law was launched. Before 1995 the County Administration had been responsible for the licensing of premises. With the new law this responsibility was decentralized to the municipalities. Since 1995, the municipal License Board has been in charge of licensing of new premises and (together with the police) of monitoring of establishments, providing a new opportunity for prevention at the municipal level.

According to the Swedish Alcohol Law, it is illegal to serve alcohol to patrons markedly intoxicated by alcohol or to underage persons (the legal drinking age is 18 years). The server risks a fine and a prison sentence of a maximum of six months. The establishment also risks losing its license to serve alcohol.

Another requirement in the Swedish regulations is that restaurant owners must have sufficient knowledge of the alcohol law. At the time this project was started, training was offered to restaurant owners by private organizations, but there was no available training in responsible beverage service for servers.

Intervention Targeting Licensed Premises in Stockholm

The community action project targeting licensed premises was initiated in 1996. A project coordinator was employed, whose task was to inspire and mobilize important target groups in preventing problems related to alcohol consumption at licensed premises. The northern part of central Stockholm was chosen as the project area, with approximately 550 licensed premises. Inspired by other community action projects, a prevention strategy was chosen that included the following components: needs assessment, problem analyses, formation of action group, developing and implementing an action plan, creating support from key leaders, and evaluation (Holder et al., 2000; Wagenaar et al., 2000b). Each component will be described in detail below:

- *Needs assessment*: The project started by conducting interviews with 50 selected restaurant owners and representatives from authorities within the project area (the northern part of central Stockholm, approximately 550 licensed premises) on their views on responsible beverage service, e.g., the existence of problems and their interest in cooperating on these issues.
- *Problem analysis*: Baseline studies were conducted regarding the frequency of alcohol service to intoxicated patrons and underage customers in 1996 and 1997 (Rehnman et al., 1996; Andréasson et al., 2000).
- *Action group*: One part of the community mobilization involved an action group established in 1996. The group consists of representatives from the Licensing Board, the

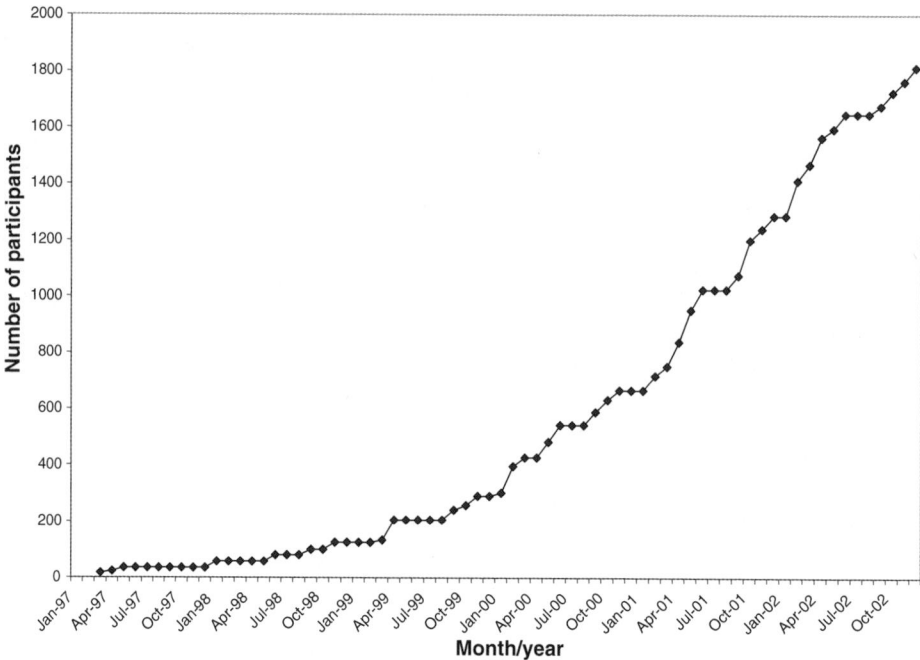

Figure 4.6.1 Number of RBS-trained participants, cumulative development, 1997–2002

Police Authority, the County Administration, the National Board of Health, the orga-
nization for restaurant owners, the trade union for restaurant staff, Stockholm County
Council, and influential restaurant owners from the most popular restaurant area in
Stockholm. This group has had regular meetings since its start (5–6 times each year).

- *Action plan*: The action group has mainly focused on RBS training and policy work. A
  two-day training in responsible beverage service for serving staff, restaurant owners and
  doormen has been developed. The training covers the Swedish Alcohol Law, medical
  effects of alcohol, restaurant-related crimes, other drugs, and conflict management. It
  also includes a written exam. If the participants pass the exam, they receive a diploma.
  In Figure 4.6.1 the cumulative development of participants during the project period
  is shown. The action group also works with policy issues. Licensed premises situated
  within the intervention area have been encouraged to develop written house alcohol and
  drug policies, both for staff and for patrons. Another important issue for the group is to
  make monitoring of alcohol service to underage and intoxicated patrons more efficient
  (see Table 4.6.2 for the cumulative development of new routines for monitoring of
  alcohol service by the Licensing Board).
- *Creating support for the program*: During the project period the group was active in
  disseminating information about the project to various target groups. Oral and written
  presentations, as well as the local media, have been used for this purpose. A result of
  this activity is that the STAD-training has become mandatory, since December 1999,
  for all serving staff at licensed premises with late opening hours (01.00 a.m. or later)
  situated in Stockholm (Wallin et al., 2002).

Table 4.6.2 Estimated intervention effect on police-reported violence

	Parameter	SE
Intervention	−.344***	.046
Control	.313***	.054
Dummy August	−.166	.106
Noise		
AR(1)	.29**	.11
SAR(1)	.15	.10
SAR(2)	.39**	.11
Constant	4.14***	.23
Diagnostics		
$Q^+(12)$	14.98, p > .24	
$Q^+(24)$	24.69, p > .42	

Notes: ***p < 0.001 **p < 0.01 *p < 0.05
$^+$Test for autocorrelated residuals

OBJECTIVES

The objective of this chapter is to study the effects of a multi-component community action program on problems related to alcohol consumption at licensed premises.

Key research questions are:

- Has alcohol service to intoxicated patrons at licensed premises in Stockholm decreased?
- Has alcohol service to underage patrons at licensed premises in Stockholm decreased?
- Has the community action program led to a reduction in violent crimes?

METHOD

Evaluation Design

The main outcome measures have been alcohol service to intoxicated patrons, alcohol service to underage patrons, and violent crimes. A quasi-experimental study design, with an intervention area (northern part of central Stockholm) and a control area (in the southern part of central Stockholm) was used for all studies. Both areas are situated in the central Stockholm, although not adjacent to each other.

Alcohol Service to Underage Youth

Young people (both boys and girls), 18 years old (legal drinking age at licensed premises in Sweden) but looking younger, according to an expert panel, visited licensed premises trying to order beer. This is a method that has been tested in other research projects (Forster et al., 1995; Wagenaar et al., 2000a). The licensed premises were selected to represent various categories: restaurants with or without a bar, bar/pubs, and nightclubs. Measures were conducted in 1996 (baseline), 1998 (follow-up I), and 2001 (follow-up II), using a repeated measure design (Wallin and Andréasson, in press). At baseline the study was conducted in both spring and autumn to investigate if there were any seasonal differences in alcohol service to the young adolescents. As no such differences were found, only one measure a year was conducted for both follow-up studies. Therefore, the number of purchase attempts were about half the size compared to the baseline, 1996. The number of orders was 600 in 1996, 252 in 1998 and 238 in 2001. The adolescents visited the licensed premises in pairs, each ordering a beer (if they were admitted by the doorman). They did not show any ID card, even if they were asked by the server. After every study visit a protocol was filled out including, for example, time of visit, if they were served beer, sex of the server, and estimated age of the member of staff who served them. The data were analyzed using the software program Log Exact for the logistic regression analysis.

Alcohol Service to Intoxicated Patrons

Studies of overserving have been conducted recurrently during the project period, 1996 baseline, 1999 (follow-up I) and 2001 (follow-up II), with a repeated measure design (Andréasson et al., 2000, Wallin et al., 2002). The licensed premises were selected to represent the following categories: regular restaurants, bar/pubs, nightclubs and hotel bars. Male actors portraying drunk behavior visited the licensed premises in pairs, and attempted to order beer. This method has also been used to evaluate other RBS programs (Gliksman et al., 1993; Rydon et al., 1996). Observers were present at all visits. After every study visit both the observers and the actors filled out a study protocol. Included in the observers' protocol were, for example, average age of the guests, crowdedness, and number of intoxicated guests. The actors' protocol focused on the alcohol-ordering outcome: served or not served. The data were analyzed with the statistical software program SAS (version 8.2), using the procedure logistic.

Violent Crimes

Police statistics on reported violent crimes for the period January 1994 to September 2000 were collected and analyzed with time-series analyses (ARIMA-models) (Box and Jenkins, 1976). The following offences were included in our violence indicator: assaults, illegal threats and harassment, violence and threats targeted at officials (including policemen and doormen). The indicator covers all such reported violent crimes committed both indoors and outdoors between 10 p.m. and 6 a.m. Since the intervention began in January 1998, the pre-intervention period comprises 48 months, and the post-intervention period 33 months. The following double logarithmic model was used to estimate the intervention effect:

$$\ln E_t = a + b_1 \ln C_t + b_2 I_t + N_t$$

where E and C denote the violence indicator in the experimental and control area, respectively. N is the noise (error term) and is allowed to have a temporal structure estimated in terms of autoregressive and/or moving average parameters. I is a dummy variable that represents the intervention (Wallin et al., 2002).

RESULTS

Alcohol Service to Underage Youth

About half of the servers, 55% ($N = 600$), refused alcohol service to the underage patrons at baseline in 1996. At the first follow-up the refusal rate was 59% ($N = 252$), and at the second follow-up in 2001 68% (N = 238) denied alcohol service (Wallin and Andréasson, in press). The increased refusal rate of 13% in 2001 as compared to 1996 was statistically significant. There were no differences between the project or control area. A factor that significantly impacted the outcome in 2001 was if the licensed premises had a doorman. The odds ratio of being served was lower, 0.18 (95% CI 0.09–0.38), on licensed premises with security personnel.

Alcohol Service to Intoxicated Patrons

At baseline 92 licensed premises were visited. Only 5% of the licensed premises in both the project and the control area denied alcohol service to the "intoxicated" patrons (Andréasson et al., 2000). The results from the follow-up study in 1999 showed a statistically significant improvement. About half, 47% of all licensed premises visited, project and control area combined (N = 103), refused alcohol service (Wallin et al., 2002). At the second follow-up in 2001 there was also a statistically significant improvement. The denial rate was 70% (N = 100) for both areas combined (Wallin and Gripenberg, 2002). There were no statistically significant changes between the project and control area in any of the follow-up studies. Figure 4.6.2 shows the cumulative developement, 1997–2002, of the number of notification letters regarding overserving.

Violent Crimes

The numbers of violent crimes in the intervention and control area are displayed in Figure 4.6.3. Based on the premise of a gradual intervention effect beginning in January 1998, a model was estimated. In the model we controlled for a major annual event (the Stockholm Water Festival), in the month of August for the years 1994–98 by including a dummy variable that was coded 1 for August 1999 and August 2000, and 0 otherwise. No filtering was necessary to achieve stationarity as the crime indicator had no strong time-trends. Therefore the estimation was performed on the raw data.

The analyses showed a significant reduction in crimes in the project area when controlling for the development in the control area (see Table 4.6.1). The change was estimated at −29% (Wallin et al., 2003).

DISCUSSION

The results based on our main outcome measures point to a decrease in problems related to alcohol consumption in Stockholm during the project period. Alcohol service to underage and intoxicated patrons decreased significantly in 2001 compared to 1996. The results from the analysis of violent crimes indicate a reduction of 29% since the intervention started, when controlling for the development in the control area.

The refusal rate of alcohol service has increased in both the project and control area. Possible explanations for this could be spillover effects, primarily of enforcement activities. This indicates that enforcement has a stronger impact on alcohol service practices than does RBS training. Our results do not support the notion that the RBS training alone has produced the changes. This is in accordance with other studies showing that training (if not mandatory) has a limited impact on alcohol service practices (Graham, 2000; Homel et al., 2001).

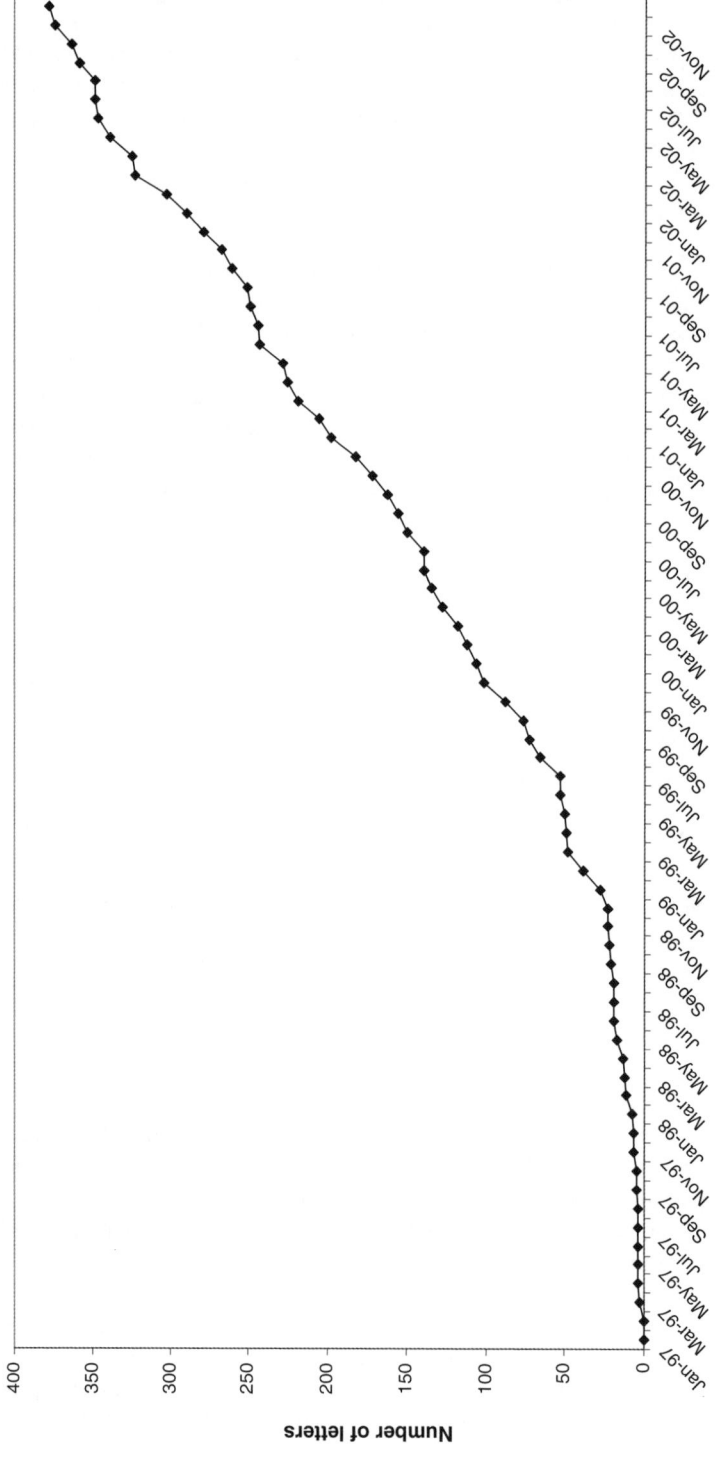

Figure 4.6.2 Number of notification letters regarding overserving; cumulative development 1997–2002

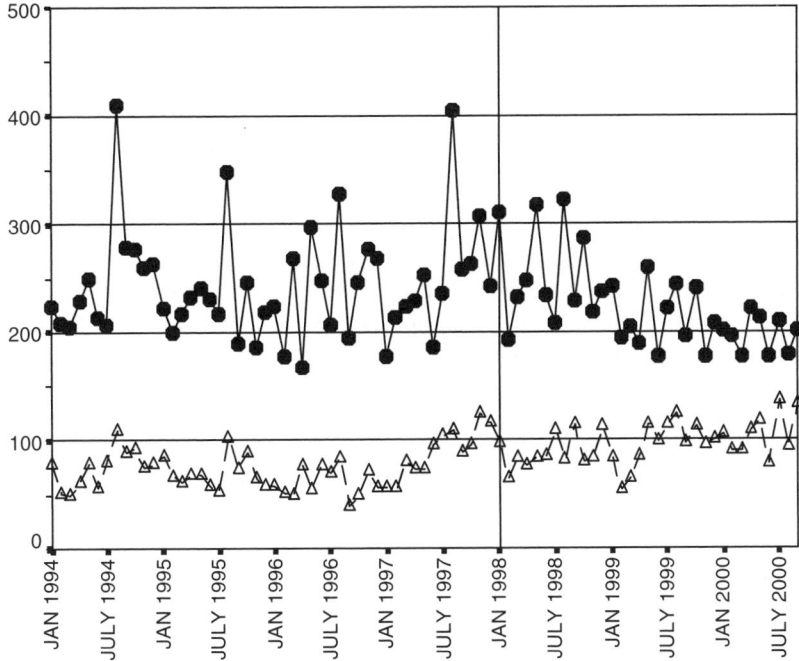

Figure 4.6.3 Police reported violence in experimental area (filled circles) and in control area (triangles), 1994–2000

However, the same pattern was not found in the violence study. Reductions in violence were only present in the project area, and not the control area. This raises the question of how to reconcile the apparently conflicting results of the effect studies. Our hypothesis of a causal chain, where an increasing refusal rate of alcohol to intoxicated patrons results in a decrease in violence, has been challenged. The research on alcohol-related aggression tells us that alcohol can contribute to aggression if combined with expectancies of drinking-related aggression (Graham et al., 2000). It is possible that it is the *combination* of community mobilization, RBS training and enforcement that has the strongest impact on violence. As the development of written house policies has been small, the contribution of this component seems to be limited. The training includes conflict management and motivates the servers and doormen to respond professionally to situations involving intoxication. Thus, increased skills in conflict management, over and above mere refusal of further service, may contribute to a decrease in violence. Another explanation for the differences may be found in the characteristics of the two study areas. Although we selected a control area that was *most* similar to the project area in outlet density and profile as an entertainment district, there are differences that have to be considered. Nightclubs have been identified as a category of licensed premises that disproportionately contribute to alcohol-related problems, e.g. violence (Stockwell et al., 1993). There are many more nightclubs in the project area compared with the control area. The numbers of guests at these premises are high, and these establishments have late opening hours (3–5a.m.) All of them have doormen, a category of restaurant staff observed to be very important in handling aggressive situations either by preventing or provoking them (Wells et al., 1998). Early on in the project, the nightclubs (especially the popular ones) were identified as an important group to approach. Restaurant owners from the nightclubs have been very active in the action group, and the majority of these premises have sent servers to training. The Licensing Board and the police have also focused much of their enforcement activities on the nightclubs, especially as they have very late opening hours and the observed incidence of problems is high in these entertainment areas. Most of the nightclubs are found within the intervention area. It is possible that the majority of violent incidents were related to the nightclubs, and that changes in the nightclub environment have had an impact on police-reported violence. A third explanation to consider is displacement of problems. The reduction in violence in the project area could partly be explained by patrons choosing licensed premises in other areas instead, such as the control area. It is possible that this could explain part of the reduction, but it seems unlikely that this should be the main explanation, given the distances between the areas. Results from the multi-component Surfers Paradise program in Australia showed some turnover of guests, but the majority stayed at their favorite premises, adapting to the new expectancies and drinking norms (Homel et al., 1994).

Although we restricted the violence indicator to night-time and to geographical areas with a high density of licensed premises, the indicator covers all violent crimes committed in those areas at night, whether restaurant-related or not. We excluded violent crimes against underage persons, although abuse targeted at women was included, a crime that most often occurs in private homes. This category is only a small proportion of the total number of cases. Therefore, it is not likely that any changes in patterns of violence against women in private homes can explain the decrease in violent crimes during the project period. However, we cannot conclude that the project activities provide the only explanation for the total reduction of 29%, but it is reasonable to assume that they have contributed significantly to the decrease.

In the Fall of 2002 the community action program was extended in full scale to the control area. Licensed premises in this area participated in RBS training and the local Police Authority were actively involved in the program. The community action program has been institutionalized and regulated in a written agreement signed by all members of the action group (Wallin and Andréasson, 2004). Each partner's responsibility for the ongoing work is specified. Both the RBS training and the policy work are included in the agreement. The transition phase took about six years from the project started to the signing of the agreement. A long time-period for community mobilization and implementation of a program is one facilitator both for achieving positive results and enabling institutionalization (Holder and Moore, 2000).

CONCLUSION

In this chapter we have presented data from three outcome studies of problems related to alcohol consumption at licensed premises. The results show a reduction in alcohol service to intoxicated and underage patrons, and a reduction in violent crimes during the project period. Some of these changes have also occurred in the control area, indicating spillover effects from the community action program. The multi-component program seems to have successfully reduced alcohol problems related to alcohol consumption at licensed premises. The most likely explanation for this is a combination of RBS training, building of community networks and policy routines initiated by the project.

ACKNOWLEDGEMENT

This chapter was originally presented at the KBS meeting: Preventing Substance Use, Risky Use and Harm: What is Evidence-based Policy? Perth, Western Australia, 24–27 February 2003.

REFERENCES

Andréasson, S., Lindewald, B. and Rehnman, C. (2000) Over-serving patrons in licensed premises in Stockholm. *Addiction*, **95**, 359–363.

Andréasson, S., Lindewald, B., Hjalmarson, K., Larsson, J., Wallin, E. and Rehnman, L. (1999) Exploring new roads to prevention of alcohol and other drug problems in Sweden: the STAD project. In S. Casswell, H. Holder, M. Holmila, S. Larsson, R. Midford, H.M. Barnes, P. Nygaard and L. Stewart, (eds), *Fourth Symposium in Community Action Research and the Prevention of Alcohol and Other Drug Problems*. Auckland: University of Auckland. Alcohol and Public Health Research Unit, pp. 314–330.

Bandura, A. (ed.), (1977) *Social Learning Theory.* Englewood-Cliffs, NJ: Prentice Hall.

Box, G.E.P. and Jenkins, G.M. (1976) *Time-Series Analysis and Control.* Oakland, CA: Holden-Day.

Buka, S.L. and Birdthistle, I.J. (1999) Long-term effects of a community-wide alcohol server training intervention. *Journal of Studies on Alcohol*, **60**, 6027–6036.

Burns, L., Flaherty, B., Ireland, S. and Frances, M. (1995) Policing pubs: what happens to crime? *Drug and Alcohol Review*, **14**, 369–376.

Chikritzhs, T. and Stockwell, T. (2002) The impact of later trading hours for Australian public houses (hotels) on levels of violence. *Journal of Studies on Alcohol*, **63**, 591–599.

Forster, J.L., Murray, D.M., Wolfson, M. and Wagenaar, A.C. (1995) Commercial availability of alcohol to young people: results of alcohol purchase attempts. *Preventive Medicine*, **24**, 342–347.

Glanz, K., Lewis, F.M. and Rimer, B.K. (eds) (1997) *Health Behavior and Health Education.* San Francisco: Jossey-Bass, Inc.

Gliksman, L., McKenzie, D., Single, E., Douglas, R., Brunet, S. and Moffatt, K. (1993) The role of alcohol providers in prevention: an evaluation of a server intervention programme. *Addiction*, **88**, 1195–1203.

Graham, K. (2000) Preventive interventions for on-premise drinking: a promising but under-researched area of prevention. *Contemporary Drug Problems*, **27**, 593–668.

Graham, K., West, P. and Wells, S. (2000) Evaluating theories of alcohol-related aggression using observations of young adults in bars. *Addiction*, **95**, 847–863.

Gruenewald, P., Johnson, F.W. and Treno, A.J. (2002) Outlets, drinking and driving: a multilevel analysis of availability. *Journal of Studies on Alcohol*, **63**, 460–468.

Holder, H.D. and Moore, R.S. (2000) Institutionalization of community action projects to reduce alcohol-use related problems: systematic facilitators. *Substance Use and Misuse*, **35**, 75–86.

Holder, H.D. and Wagenaar, A.C. (1994) Mandated server training and reduced alcohol-involved traffic crashes: a time series analysis of the Oregon experience. *Accident Analysis and Prevention*, **26**, 89–97.

Holder, H.D., Gruenewald, P.J., Ponicki, W.R., Treno, A.J., Grube, J.B., Saltz, R.F., Voas, R.B., Reynolds, R., Davis, J., Sanchez, L., Gaumont, G. and Roeper, P. (2000) Effects of community-based interventions on high-risk drinking and alcohol-related injuries. *JAMA*, **284**, 2341–2347.

Homel, R., McIlwain, G. and Carvolth, R. (2001) Creating safer drinking environments. In N.Heather, T.J. Peters, and T. Stockwell, (eds), *Handbook of Alcohol Dependence and Alcohol-Related Problems*. Chichester: John Wiley and Sons. Ltd. pp. 721–740.

Homel, R., Hauritz, M., Wortley, R., McIlwain, G. and Carvolth, R. (1994) Preventing alcohol-related crime through community action: the Surfers Paradise Safety Action Project. In R. Homel, (ed.), *Policing for Prevention: Reducing Crime, Public Intoxication and Injury*, Vol. 7. Monsey, New York: Criminal Justice Press, pp. 36–90.

Howard-Pitney, B., Johnson, M.D., Altman, D.G., Hopkins, R. and Hammond, N. (1991) Responsible alcohol service: a study of server, manager, and environmental impact. *American Journal of Public Health*, **81**, 197–199.

Jeffs, B. and Saunders, B. (1983) Minimising alcohol-related offences by enforcement of the existing licensing legislation. *British Journal of Addiction*, **78**, 67–78.

Lang, E., Stockwell, T., Rydon, P. and Beel, A. (1998) Can training bar staff in responsible serving practices reduce alcohol-related harm? *Drug and Alcohol Review*, **17**, 39–50.

Leifman, H. (2002) Alcohol consumption pattern and alcohol problems. In S. Andréasson, (ed.), *Drinking in Sweden in the Context of the European Union. New Challenges to Alcohol Prevention: A Review of the Literature*: Stockholm: Gothia, pp. 29–63 (in Swedish).

McKnight, A.J. (1991) Factors influencing the effectiveness of server-intervention education. *Journal of Studies on Alcohol*, **52**, 389–397.

McKnight, A.J. and Streff, F.M. (1994) The effect of enforcement upon service of alcohol to intoxicated patrons of bars and restaurants. *Accident Analysis and Prevention*, **26**, 19–88.

Mosher, J.F., Toomey, T.L., Good, C., Harwood, E. and Wagenaar, A.C. (2002) State laws mandating or promoting training programs for alcohol servers and establishment managers: an assessment of statutory and administrative procedures. *Journal of Public Health Policy*, **23**, 90–113.

Norström, T. (1998) Effects on criminal violence of different beverage types and private public drinking. *Addiction*, **93**, 689–699.

Norström, T. (2000) Outlet density and criminal violence in Norway, 1960–1995. *Journal of Studies on Alcohol*, **61**, 907–911.

Putnam, S.L., Rockett, I.R. and Campbell, M.L. (1993) Methodological issues in community-based alcohol-related injury prevention projects: attribution of program effects. In T.K. Greenfield and R. Zimmerman (eds), *Experiences with Community Action Projects: Research in the Prevention of Alcohol and Other Drug Problems*. CSAP Prevention Monograph-14. Rockville, MD: US Department of Health and Human Services, pp. 31–42.

Ragnarsdóttír, þ., Kjartansdóttír, Á. and Daviósdðttír, S. (2002). Effects of extended alcohol serving-hours in Reykavik. *NAD*, **42**, 145–154.

Rehnman, C., Lindewald, B. and Andréasson, S. (1996) *En stor stark tack! En studie av legitimationskontroll på restauranger i Stockholm under våren och hösten 1996*. Rapport 1. Stockholm: STAD-projektet.

Roncek, D.W. and Maier, P.A. (1991) Bars, blocks and crimes re-visited: linking the theory of routine activities to the empiricism of "Hot Spots". *Criminology*, **29**, 725–753.

Russ, N.W. and Geller, E.S. (1987) Training bar personnel to prevent drunken driving: a field evaluation. *American Journal of Public Health*, **77**, 952–954.

Rydon, P., Stockwell, T., Lang, E. and Beel, A. (1996) Pseudo-drunk-patron evaluation of bar-staff compliance with Western Australian Liquor law. *Australian and New Zealand Journal of Public Health*, **20**, 290–295.

Saltz, R.F. (1987) The roles of bars and restaurants in preventing alcohol-impaired driving: an evaluation of server intervention. *Evaluation and the Health Professions*, **10**, 5–27.

Stockwell, T., Lang, E. and Rydon, P. (1993) High risk drinking settings: the association of serving and promotional practices with harmful drinking. *Addiction*, **88**, 1519–1526.

Toomey, T., Wagenaar, A.C. and Gehan, J.P. (2001) Project ARM: alcohol risk management to prevent sales to underage and intoxicated patrons. *Health Education and Behavior*, **28**, 186–199.

Wagenaar, A.C., Murray, D.M. and Toomey, T. (2000a) Communities mobilizing for change on alcohol (CMCA): effects of a randomized trial on arrests and traffic crashes. *Addiction*, **95**, 209–217.

Wagenaar, A.C., Gehan, J.P., Jones-Webb, R.J., Toomey, T.L. and Forster, J.L. (1999) Communities mobilizing for change on alcohol: lessons and results from a 15-community randomized trial. *Journal of Community Psychology*, **27**, 315–326.

Wagenaar, A.C., Murray, D.M., Gehan, J., Wolfson, M., Forster, J.L., Toomey, T., Perry, C. and Jones-Webb, R. (2000b) Communities mobilizing for change on alcohol: outcomes from a randomized trial. *Journal of Studies on Alcohol*, **61**, 85–94.

Wallin, E. and Andréasson, S. (in press) Can I have a beer, please? A study of alcohol service to young adults on licensed premises in Stockholm. Accepted for publication in *Prevention Science*.

Wallin, E. and Andréasson, S. (2004) Institutionalization of a community action program targeting licensed premises in Stockholm, Sweden. *Evaluation Review*, **28**(5), 396–419.

Wallin, E. and Gripenberg, J. (2002) *Dags att gå hem? En uppföljande studie av servering till berusade kroggäster i Stockolm, 2001*. Rapport 21. Stockholm: STAD-projektet.

Wallin, E., Gripenberg, J. and Andréasson, S. (2002) Too drunk for a beer? A study of overserving in Stockholm. *Addiction*, **97**, 901–907.

Wallin, E., Norström, T. and Andréasson, S. (2003) Alcohol prevention targeting licensed premises: a study of effects on violence. *Journal of Studies on Alcohol*, **64**, 270–277.

Wells, S., Graham, K. and West, P. (1998) The good, the bad, and the ugly: responses by security staff to aggressive incidents in public drinking settings. *Journal of Drug Issues*, **28**, 817–836.

4.7 Strategies for Community-Based Drug Law Enforcement: From Prohibition to Harm Reduction

CHRISTOPHER CANTY*
Department of Justice, Victoria, Australia

ADAM SUTTON, STEPHEN JAMES
University of Melbourne, Australia

SUMMARY

This chapter explores challenges for police in local or "grassroots" implementation of laws relating to illicit drugs. Three "ideal" models of drug law enforcement, with marked variation in commitment to harm minimisation, are developed. The first model, "prohibitionism", involves police focusing exclusively on disrupting and suppressing drug production, distribution and use. "Modified supply reduction", the second model, incorporates police attempts to accommodate harm reduction efforts by health, welfare and other agencies. The third model, "market regulation", requires police to adopt harm minimisation as their own strategic and tactical goal. For each model, aims, methods and dilemmas facing police are explored.

INTRODUCTION

Police drug law enforcement in Australia and in many other developed countries is in somewhat of a crisis. A number of recent research-based reviews have argued that the lack of demonstrable impact by enforcement operations on street-level drug availability (e.g., Weatherburn and Lind, 1995), and corrupt dealings between some police and drug traffickers (e.g., Wood, 1997) provide reasons enough for major change (see also Sutton and James, 1996). In Australia, the most comprehensive critique, however, arose from the two-year review of drug law enforcement conducted for the then National Police Research Unit (NPRU—see Sutton and James, 1996).[1] Briefly, it found that State and Territory

---

* The views expressed are those of the author and do not necessarily reflect government policy.

[1] The unit has since been renamed the Australasian Center for Policing Research (ACPR).

Preventing Harmful Substance Use: The Evidence Base for Policy and Practice.
Edited by T. Stockwell, P. J. Gruenewald, J.W. Toumbourou and W. Loxley.
© 2005 John Wiley & Sons, Ltd. ISBN 0-470-09227-0 (hbk) 0-470-09228-9 (pbk).

Drug Squads, relevant sections of the Australian Federal Police and other specialist police dedicated to the difficult tasks of targeting and successfully prosecuting "major players" in the illicit drug industries were, by their own acknowledgement, experiencing limited success. Moreover, an important indirect consequence of these agencies' almost exclusive focus on "high level" figures was neglect of the impacts that enforcement might be having on local drug markets and users. For most specialist drug enforcement bodies in Australia, what happened to users and low-level dealers was not their concern—if anyone was to monitor these issues, it should be regional detectives or local uniformed police. However, local police generally had little specialised expertise in illicit drug issues—and often saw their role as simply to ensure that visible symptoms of use and trafficking were suppressed. The report found that at the local or "grassroots" level, drug law enforcers often had little or no capacity to account for the intended or, more importantly, unintended impacts of their work either on the availability of illicit drugs or on modes of use. The report argued that, in effect, locally-based enforcement (representing the bulk of drug law enforcement conducted Australia) appeared to be occurring in a "policy vacuum" (Sutton and James, 1996: 112–113).

Findings in the NPRU review and other reports have highlighted apparent inconsistencies between law enforcement efforts and "official" Australian philosophies of "harm minimisation". Since 1985, Federal and State Governments formally had been committed to strategies that emphasise harm minimisation, rather than the "zero tolerance" stance favoured by jurisdictions in the United States.[2] Harm minimisation acknowledges that psychoactive substances have been and continue to be used by members of society; that total eradication of drugs and/or drug use is not possible; and (most importantly for the present discussion) that attempts to eliminate specific drug availability and use may result in increased net harm for society (Rumbold and Hamilton, 1998: 135). Since the mid-1980s successive Australian national drug strategies have been based on recognition that illegal drug use and supply cannot be eliminated, but instead should be managed in ways which most effectively keep harms to a minimum. Relevant initiatives have included needle exchange programmes, which have helped ensure that the rate of spread of HIV in the heterosexual community in Australia has been lower than in comparable countries such as the United States (Rumbold and Hamilton, 1998), and methadone maintenance, which helps stabilise heroin use and reduce amounts of drug-related offending (Parker and Kirby, 1996). Officially, anti-trafficking or supply reduction efforts by police are seen as having roles in national and state drug strategies—but only to the extent that they can be shown to contribute to the overall aim of reducing harms associated with drug use (Victorian Premier's Drug Advisory Council, 1996: 59).

Many experts argue, however, that there are fundamental tensions between policies of harm minimisation and legislative frameworks which prohibit some drugs. For example, the illegality of production, distribution and consumption of a substance tends to increase the chances of overdose by consumers who have no certainty about the quality and quantities they are using (Rumbold and Hamilton, 1998). Prohibition also can award organised, often violent, criminal groups dominance over drug production and distribution networks (Parliamentary Joint Committee on the National Crime Authority, 1989). Within the context of these policy tensions, some police practices actually may increase harm (Kutin, 1998: 160). For example, research in Sydney has suggested that police "crackdowns" can result in the adoption of unsafe injecting practices by those keen to avoid police detection, and in

---

[2] The Australian Prime Minister, Mr. John Howard, in recent times has indicated his support for a shift towards policies more closely aligned with a "zero tolerance" approach. For a detailed discussion of zero tolerance policing, see Marshall (1999).

greater numbers of syringes being discarded hastily (Maher et al., 1998; Maher and Dixon, 1999). In responding to local business and other community demands to suppress visible symptoms of illicit trading and use, police may force users "underground" and away from health and other support services. Success in reducing supply of a specific drug may simply cause users to shift to more harmful substances or into more harmful modes of consumption, for example, from smoking to injecting. Thus, Hamid (1991) argues that success by New York police in disrupting the Rastafarian trade in ganja (marijuana) helped give rise to a crack-based economy. McCoy (1994: 55) points out that, in Thailand, the success of the United Nations Drug Control Program in reducing opium cultivation led to an increase in the price of opium smoking to 80 baht per day, compared to only 10 baht for heroin, thereby encouraging a shift to intravenous heroin use. Police determination to suppress street-level drug trafficking also may inadvertently help give rise to bag-snatching or other predatory crime by addicts seeking an alternative source of income (Grapendaal et al., 1995; Maher et al., 1998: 62). All this highlights what the former Victorian Chief Commissioner of Police called the "significant challenge facing police [in] the interpretation of the enforcement role in harm minimization" (Comrie, 1998: 20).

Few advocates of reform in Australia have been under the illusion that ensuring that local drug law enforcement practices become more consistent with harm minimisation philosophy is likely to be an easy task. While police agencies throughout the country have been formally committed to these philosophies for more than a decade, operational drug law enforcement cultures remain typically anchored in a "war on drugs" conception, in which supply reduction is considered the key approach. Local-level police have rarely been made aware of the implications that harm minimisation might have for their operational procedures (see Maher and Dixon, 1999). Most police still consider harm to drug users "to be the responsibility of services and agencies outside law enforcement—in particular welfare, medical and educational agencies" (James and Sutton, 1998: 220). In addition, a shift towards harm reduction would require major restructuring within law enforcement agencies themselves. Such agencies would need to become far less hierarchical and bureaucratic, far more capable of adopting flexible, problem-oriented approaches at the neighbourhood level (Eck and Spelman, 1987). Central managers would be required to encourage and reward decision-making and the exercise of discretion by local police, while at the same time providing appropriate systems of accountability and supervision (Dixon and Maher, 1999). Such changes are not easily achieved in police organisations, many of which have historically founded on paramilitary models (Brown and Sutton, 1997).

MODELS OF DRUG LAW ENFORCEMENT

Preceding paragraphs have argued that "operationalising" a formal commitment to harm minimisation is likely to present a traditional, hierarchically based police organisation with many challenges. In the course of their evaluation work on drug law enforcement, the authors have become aware of a variety of approaches that might seem to fulfil the ostensible aim of helping reduce drug-related harms at the community level. These approaches are often classified under the broad rubric of "community-based drug law enforcement". Many community-based approaches, however, stop short at modifying supply reduction in order to improve co-existence and co-operation between law enforcement and other relevant agencies. Our argument is that such co-existence models often do very little to change the dynamics of drug law enforcement, and may even help relevant agencies persist with practices which are fundamentally inconsistent with harm reduction.

To help understand why we take this view, it is helpful to step back a little and think about different models of drug law enforcement. In the next section we develop three "ideal models" (or "ideal types"—see Weber, 1949) which reflect the degree to which harm minimisation principles have become central to a police agency—and in particular to drug law enforcement at the local level. We term these models "prohibitionism", "modified supply reduction" and "market regulation" (Table 4.7.1). In the "prohibitionist" model, police are totally dedicated to supply reduction and pay little or no attention to harm reduction issues. In the "modified supply reduction" model, police still see supply reduction as their overriding goal, but acknowledge the legitimacy of harm reduction work and try not to undermine it at the local level. Finally, the "market regulation" model reflects a more far-reaching commitment to harm reduction by the police organisation itself.

Table 4.7.1   Three models of community based drug law enforcement

Prohibitionism	Modified supply reduction	Market regulation
AIM Reduce supply. Disrupt/dismantle supply networks.	AIM Reduce supply. Disrupt/dismantle supply networks. Avoid undermining harm reduction work by others.	AIM Reduce drug-related harms.
METHODS Seize drugs Arrest key drug market participants.	METHODS Seize drugs. Arrest key drug market participants. Ongoing liaison with key harm reduction groups.	METHODS Assess drug-related harms. Use law enforcement to reshape illicit drug markets and use patterns in ways that minimise harm.
INFORMATION TYPICALLY GATHERED Police-generated data (e.g., arrests, seizures). Intelligence from other agencies (e.g., Customs).	INFORMATION TYPICALLY GATHERED Police-generated data. Intelligence from other agencies. Feedback on enforcement impacts in sensitive areas.	INFORMATION TYPICALLY GATHERED Pooled data (police, health etc.) on: illicit drug availability; distribution networks; use patterns; drug-related harms (e.g., overdoses, predatory and organised crime).
PURPOSE OF INFORMATION Help law enforcers achieve objectives of: - detecting and seizing drugs; - identifying key market participants.	PURPOSE OF INFORMATION Help achieve objectives of seizing drugs and arresting key market participants. Help enforcement avoid undermining harm reduction work.	PURPOSE OF INFORMATION Help identify and prioritise illicit drug-related harms. Help achieve law enforcement objective of harm reduction.
CHALLENGES/ DILEMMAS Inconsistent with harm reduction philosophy.	CHALLENGES/ DILEMMAS Tensions between dictates of supply reduction and harm reduction.	CHALLENGES/ DILEMMAS Inconsistent with expectation that "law should be enforced".

As discussion will emphasise, each of these three approaches toward the policing of illicit drugs has its own distinctive aims, methods, ways of using information and ways of relating to other agencies at a local level. Each model also can pose its own specific challenges and dilemmas. In presenting these schemata, the authors have tried, as far as possible, to avoid being judgmental. We should acknowledge, however, that our own preference is for "market regulation", which seems most compatible with the Australian government's professed commitment to harm reduction. This chapter does not, however, attempt to re-argue the case for harm minimisation. Our objective purely is to facilitate clearer thinking about the ways agencies in Australia and elsewhere can approach the task of drug law enforcement, and can try to minimise the problems associated with illicit substances.

Model 1: Prohibitionism

"Prohibitionism" represents the extreme end of the continuum of police responses to illicit drug issues, where focus is purely on the fact that production, possession and consumption are illegal.

Aim

A strict prohibitionist stance involves unequivocal enforcement of laws against illicit drugs and unswerving commitment to disrupting the drugs markets—at all levels—in order to reduce supply. In such a system, police enforce the law without concern for any unintended impacts (such as users shifting to more harmful drugs or modes of use), even if creation of this "collateral damage" may seem inconsistent with the underlying rationales for drug laws (Brown et al., 1995: 13).

Methods

Strict prohibitionist enforcement puts emphasis on reducing the production and distribution of illicit substances and targets all those involved in relevant markets, whether as producers, suppliers or users. While in countries like Australia there has been a stated commitment to focusing arrests on higher-echelon figures ("going for the head of the beast"), practical difficulties in identifying and successfully prosecuting such individuals mean that disruption of markets at any level may be regarded as positive.[3] In this model, increases in volumes of seizures and numbers of arrests are seen as reflecting greater disruption, and hence more effective policing.[4]

Use of information

Within a prohibitionist approach, police focus upon the illegality of drug production, distribution and use. Police interest is centred not upon identifying and reducing drug-related

---

[3] See Sutton and James (1996: 156) for a detailed discussion of Australian drug law enforcement agencies' acknowledged problems in successfully targeting and prosecuting "high-level" figures. In essence, such targeting requires four things: that such figures do in fact exist; that they can readily be identified; that relevant specialist agencies have sufficient resources to be able to apprehend them; and that the relevant individuals play such critical roles in criminal organisations that they cannot readily be replaced. Current research puts all of these presumptions in doubt. From their interviews with agency representatives, Green and Purnell (1996: 25–26) conclude that, in light of these problems, and the fact that political and other performance assessments nonetheless continue to be result-driven, many investigators tended to see it as legitimate and necessary to arrest lower-level players.

[4] It is, of course, debatable whether higher volumes of drug seizures and arrests in fact reflect disruption of illicit drug markets and reduced availability at the street level (see Moore, 1990; Sutton and James, 1996; 79–82; Weatherburn and Lind, 1995).

harms *per se*, but upon breaches of the criminal law. Intelligence will be gathered from any organisation or source which can assist in the key tasks of identifying and suppressing illicit drugs and apprehending suppliers. Sources of information can be wide-ranging, from military satellite surveillance (used by US authorities to target crops in source countries) through to undercover operators and informants within illegal organisations. Information is only valued, however, if it will assist police, whose key questions are: "Who is involved in illicit drug production, distribution and/or use?"; "Which individuals or organisations should be targeted?" and "Which drugs should be intercepted and seized?" Police are not concerned about, and therefore do not seek information on, possible unintended consequences of supply reduction efforts, for example, increases in health harms to users; increased risks to the non-using community through the presence of discarded needles; increased dominance of distribution networks by violent, organised criminal groups. Indeed, they may often de-value health workers and user representatives because of a perceived unwillingness to supply police with the type of data they want.

Relations with other groups

As stated, an exclusive emphasis on supply reduction can generate tension between law enforcers and health and welfare groups. This can be exacerbated if police interactions with users and low-level dealers drive such participants underground, away from relevant services. Given acknowledged difficulties in identifying and successfully prosecuting major players, police also may shift to a strategy of attempting to arrest as many users and minor dealers as possible, hoping to cause the distribution system to collapse (see Green and Purnell, 1996). Such an approach places police in direct conflict with anyone involved in the drugs markets, from influential (though elusive) high-level distributors to (far more easily located) street-level dealers, users and user/dealers. In these contexts, it becomes difficult, if not impossible, for local police to draw on the knowledge of such groups in order to be able to monitor illicit drug availability and relevant harms.

Dilemmas for police

Experience in the United States confirms that, if the political context is supportive, prohibitionist approaches to illicit drugs can flourish. Every arrest or seizure can be cited as evidence of success, and apparent failure (e.g., the fact that illicit drugs continue to be available) simply becomes the grounds for allocating increased powers and resources (Brown et al., 1995). Conflicts between law enforcement and other agencies can be overridden, and a wide range of interests made to conform with the law enforcement objective (Green, 1996). In countries such as Australia which have acknowledged and endorsed harm minimisation principles; however, unequivocal commitment to prohibitionism has been difficult to sustain. Research both at the local and national levels can consistently highlight its negative consequences and is likely to force some attempts to accommodate alternative approaches.

Model 2: Modified Supply Reduction

"Modified supply reduction" is a model of drug law enforcement which reflects an attempt to maintain a supply reduction focus but, at the same time, accommodate concerns among health and other interest groups that illicit drug-related harms be kept to a minimum.

Aim

Within such a framework, police still put emphasis on enforcing laws and disrupting markets, however they try to ensure that their supply reduction efforts do not significantly impede the harm minimisation work performed by other agencies (for example, health or welfare).

Methods

Police still utilise traditional policing methods but can see the benefit of interagency co-operation and information exchange. Arrest and drug seizure remain the primary police strategies. However, there is willingness to accept that these may not always be the most appropriate response to a drug offence. An attempt is made to avoid overt police presence or action in situations where this would undermine the harm reduction efforts of other agencies. For example, police commanders may issue formal instructions advising local patrol officers not to make arrests near needle exchanges, acknowledging that promoting users' access to clean equipment helps to prevent the transmission of blood-borne diseases. Similarly, users apprehended by police may be referred to treatment agencies.

Use of information

In this model, police can see the value not just of traditional intelligence but also of non-tactical information from health and other sources. Police allocate representatives to engage in ongoing liaison with groups involved in harm reduction, with a view to trying to ensure that such programmes are not undermined. Information tends to be of a qualitative nature (representatives share their experiences and views on local drug markets) and its trade conducted on a one-to-one basis (that is, between specific individuals who trust each other) rather than through formal data-pooling protocols. Information in this model is used not just to answer the traditional supply reduction questions ("Who should be targeted?"; "Which drugs should be seized?") but also to monitor the impacts of enforcement on work by others ("Are our efforts detracting from harm reduction?").

Relations with other groups

Due to the two-way flow of information, and attempts by the law enforcement sector to avoid seriously impeding harm reduction work by other agencies, conflict between police and the health and welfare sectors may be reduced. However, as police essentially remain committed to supply reduction efforts to disrupt the market, potential for conflict persists. Liaison serves essentially as a "lubricant", rather than being seen as central to successful policing. Conflict with low-level market participants is reduced if, under this model, local police adopt a policy of referring users to treatment programmes, and concentrate their enforcement efforts on more dangerous, socially disruptive and violent elements.

Dilemmas for police

Increased interaction between police and groups who do not share their specific objectives carries with it the dangers both of greater frequency and increased perceived legitimacy of complaints. Attempts to meet various, sometimes competing, demands can generate stresses within a police organisation. Those who favour traditional supply reduction strategies and techniques may perceive harm minimisation as simply acceding to the goals and demands

of non-police groups. For their part, police who have been assigned responsibilities for negotiation, liaison or information exchange with other agencies may find themselves isolated
from the majority of their colleagues, who are still performing traditional police duties. Unless liaison staff are particularly senior—or well respected—they may not be able to bring
about major changes in mainstream police work. If this is the case, such police members
may feel that they are fulfilling little more than an empty public relations exercise.

In worst case scenarios, such officers may side with members of other agencies and
thereby become increasingly marginalised from their own (Pearson et al., 1992), and the
interagency interface (for example, a consultative committee) may become little more than
an arena for airing grievances. Alternatively, personnel from outside agencies such as health
may become cynical about the supposed police reform process, arguing that it is all "talk"
with no serious commitment to practical change. The solution here may be seen in educating
police members (and those outside the organisation) about the need for police to make greater
commitment to harm reduction. However, while the overriding goal (and job description)
of the police remain focused on supply reduction, this may be an uphill battle. Despite the
ongoing potential for conflicts between supply reduction and harm minimisation principles,
such tensions will not necessarily be reflected in dilemmas for operational personnel. For
the majority of police within this model, job satisfaction still is attained through arrests and
drug seizures. However, patrol and other operational officers may attain some additional
satisfaction from a belief that their work is not exacerbating problems for users, and may
be of benefit.

Model 3: Market Regulation

The third model of drug law enforcement could be termed "market regulation".

Aim

Within such an approach, there is organisational commitment by police to the philosophies
and practices of harm minimisation. It is fully recognised that law enforcement represents
just one of a number of sectors involved in the management of drug markets, and that supply
reduction is but one of a range of methods to reduce drug-related harms. The overriding
aim of policing here is not simply to reduce supplies of illicit drugs *per se* but to reduce
drug-related harms.

Methods

Within this approach, police liaise and co-operate constantly, both formally and informally,
with other agencies. Police see themselves as one of many agencies helping to reduce drug-
related harms. Police focus their enforcement resources on activities and groups assessed
as causing harm to others (for example, producers and traffickers using intimidation and
violence or actively recruiting new users; users who are committing property or violent
crimes). Police use their discretionary powers to refer some drug offenders to welfare
services. Police monitor impacts of their own work upon drug markets to ensure that they
are not inadvertently moving users from less harmful substances, modes of consumption, or
means of obtaining funds to ones which are more harmful. Police also work co-operatively
with other agencies to reshape markets and try to move users and dealers towards less
harmful practices. Within this approach, police utilise problem identification and analysis

as a means for decision-making (for example, they may decide not to break up a small network of established users who are trading in marijuana but give priority instead to disrupting a network which uses violence and intimidation to increase market dominance).

Use of information

Police are committed to a harm minimisation approach and, therefore, collection of information on drug-related harms is seen as essential to the law enforcement role. Information from health and user sources is highly valued (indeed, if it were not already being collected by others, police themselves would try to collect such data). Both qualitative and quantitative data on local drug markets are shared and pooled between agencies, not just through individual contacts but through formal protocols. Information is gathered through constant monitoring of local drug markets and is used to identify existing problems, alert agencies to possible future issues and assess the appropriateness and effectiveness of actions. Law enforcement and other agencies attempt to respond flexibly to identified drug-related problems.

Under this market regulation (or containment) model, one of the primary objectives of data collection is to assist in monitoring drug-related harms. The aim is to reduce health harms (morbidity and mortality) and drug-related crime (assaults, robberies, burglaries, etc.). Drug-related community concerns (fear, feelings of insecurity) also are monitored and addressed, for example, safe injecting facilities may be tolerated as a way to reduce disquiet and harm associated with highly visible 'street-level' use. A secondary set of measures reflects the quality of arrests based on associated harms. The aim here is to decrease the proportion of arrests of non-predatory, non-violent users/dealers. Police instead identify and arrest more dangerous, harmful operators within drug markets. Within this system, information serves a long-term, ongoing self-assessment purpose. Partnerships are needed in order to set priorities and monitor performance. For police, data gathered are used to answer many questions, among them: "How do we set our priorities?"; "How do we know what the problems are?"; "What are the local drug-related harms?"; "How should we interact with the market so as to reduce harms?"; "How do we monitor our own performance?"; and "What impacts, intended and unintended, have our actions had upon harms?"

Relations with other groups

Within the drug market regulation model, interagency partnership is seen as absolutely essential. Police declare that they cannot successfully fulfil their mandate without partners and without the information generated through such partnerships. Co-operation with health and welfare organisations is emphasised. For all local law enforcement efforts, the focus is on those users and dealers identified as most harmful.

Dilemmas for police

This model, while offering police opportunities to impact upon drug markets in a productive, rewarding and rational manner, is certainly not without challenges. Compared to strict enforcement, setting priorities within this model will be more difficult. Problem analysis and response generation, while potentially more fulfilling, always are likely to be more complex and time-consuming than patrolling an area and charging anyone dealing in illicit substances. Police managers initiating such an approach can anticipate resistance from specialist drug law enforcers and general duties police who see it either as inferior to traditional, "real" policing or as "going soft" on drugs and drug users. Apparent police inaction against users and dealers also may well elicit claims of corruption—or at least ineptitude—from local communities. Police are likely to be perceived by at least some members of their local communities as not carrying out their duty to enforce the law. These perceptions will have to be countered through education and communication—particularly at the neighbourhood level. Police command also must make unequivocal commitment to supporting the new strategies, and to protecting staff at the local level from unwarranted criticism.

CONCLUSION

We would emphasise that the three models described above are ideal types. International reviews (e.g., MacCoun and Reuter, 1998) seem to indicate that while in the majority of Western countries police appear to be pursuing variants of modified supply reduction, some US forces are close to embracing the prohibitionist model, and only the Netherlands has ensured that policing puts primary emphasis on market management. We would stress, however, that in reality no police department, whether in Australia or any other Western country, fully corresponds to any one of the models. Our main purpose has not been to classify existing practices but to help clarify the various ways in which drug law enforcement can be approached at the local level.

Readers need to make their own decisions about which model is preferable and/or capable of being achieved within their own jurisdictions. For those of us who wish to move away from demonising illicit drugs *per se* toward approaches which put emphasis on minimising associated harms, the strict prohibitionist model clearly is the most regressive. Some critics may also want to argue that modified supply reduction represents an awkward and unhelpful compromise—nonetheless experience in countries such as Sweden indicates that it can be sustained over a long period (Swedish National Institute for Public Health, 1998). This approach certainly can have popular appeal because it continues to legitimate the suppression of local drug markets, while at the same time according treatment agencies a significant role. Ultimately however, in our view, the market regulation model is the most progressive, and the most likely to facilitate effective programmes to contain problems such as drug overdose, drug addiction and drug-related offending. It is against this last model that we would assess the credentials of any community-based drug law enforcement initiative which presented itself as being concerned with harm minimisation.

ACKNOWLEDGEMENTS

This is a modified version of the paper Canty et al. (2001) and a paper delivered at the First International Conference on Drugs and Young People, Melbourne, 23 November 1998. The authors acknowledge the National Community Based Approach to Drug Law Enforcement Board of Control, Adelaide, for a 1998–1999 grant to evaluate community drug law enforcement initiatives. The chapter is reproduced by permission of Taylor & Francis, Ltd. (www.tandf.co.uk).

REFERENCES

Brown, M. and Sutton, A. (1997) Problem oriented policing and organisational form: lessons from a Victorian experiment. *Current Issues in Criminal Justice*, **9**(1), 21–33.

Brown, M., Sutton, A., James, S. and Wallace, S. (1995) *Illegal Drug Use in Victoria, Stage 1: Final Report*. Report commissioned by the Victoria Police Drug Squad. Melbourne: Victoria Police.

Comrie, N. (1998) Drug crime: what does enforcement mean? *Police Life*, **June**, 20–21.

Dixon, D. and Maher, L. (1999) Law enforcement, harm minimization, and risk management in a street-level drug market. Paper presented to the Australasian Conference on Drugs Strategy, Adelaide, 27–29 April.

Eck, J.E. and Spelman, W. (1987) *Problem-Solving: Problem-Oriented Policing in Newport News*. Police Executive Research Forum.

Grapendaal, M., Leuw, E. and Nelen, H. (1995) *A World of Opportunities: Life-Style and Economic Behavior of Heroin Addicts in Amsterdam*. Albany, NY: State University of New York Press.

Green, L. (1996) *Policing Places with Drug Problems*. Thousand Oaks, CA: Sage.

Green, P. and Purnell, I. (1996) *Measuring the Success of Law Enforcement Agencies in Australia in Targeting Major Offenders Relative to Minor Offenders*. Adelaide: National Police Research Unit.

Hamid, A. (1991) From ganja to crack: Caribbean participation in the underground economy in Brooklyn, 1976–1986. Part 1. Establishment of the marijuana economy. *The International Journal of the Addictions*, **26**(6), 615–628.

James, S. and Sutton, A. (1998) Policing drugs in the third millennium: the dilemmas of community-based philosophies. *Current Issues in Criminal Justice*, **9**(3), 217–227.

Kutin, J. (1998) Law enforcement and harm minimisation. In M., Hamilton, A. Kellehear and G. Rumbold, (eds), *Drug Use in Australia: A Harm Minimisation Approach*. Melbourne: Oxford University Press.

MacCoun, R. and Reuter, P. (1998) Drug control. In M. Tonry (ed.), *The Handbook of Crime and Punishment*. Oxford: Oxford University Press.

Maher, L. and Dixon, D. (1999) Policing and public health: law enforcement and harm minimization in a street-level drug market. *The British Journal of Criminology*, **39**(4), 488–512.

Maher, L., Dixon, D., Lynskey, M. and Hall, W. (1998) *Running the Risks: Heroin, Health and Harm in South West Sydney*. Sydney: National Drug and Alcohol Research Centre.

Marshall, J. (1999) *Zero Tolerance Policing (Information Bulletin No. 9)*. Adelaide: South Australian Office of Crime Statistics.

McCoy, A. (1994) *Historical Review of Opium and Heroin Production*. Fort Washington, DC: Office of Special Technology.

Moore, M. (1990) Supply reduction and drug law enforcement. In M. Tonry and J.Q. Wilson (eds.), *Crime and Justice: A Review of Research*, Vol. 13. Chicago: University of Chicago Press.

Parker, H. and Kirby, P. (1996) *Methadone Maintenance and Crime Reduction on Merseyside (Crime Detection and Prevention Series Paper 72)*. London: Home Office.

Parliamentary Joint Committee on the National Crime Authority (1989) *Drugs, Crime and Society*. Canberra: Australian Government Publishing Service.

Pearson, G., Blagg, H., Smith, D., Sampson, A. and Stubbs, P. (1992) Crime, community and conflict: the multi-agency approach. In D. Downes (ed.), *Unravelling Criminal Justice*. Basingstoke: Macmillan.

Rumbold, G. and Hamilton, M. (1998) Addressing drug problems: the case for harm minimisation. In M., Hamilton, A. Kellehear and G. Rumbold (eds), *Drug Use in Australia: A Harm Minimisation Approach*. Melbourne: Oxford University Press.

Sutton, A. and James, S. (1996) *Evaluation of Australian Drug Anti-Trafficking Law Enforcement*. Adelaide: National Police Research Unit.

Swedish National Institute for Public Health (1998) *A Preventive Strategy: Swedish Drug Policy in the 1990s*.

Victorian Premier's Drug Advisory Council (1996) *Drugs and Our Community*. Melbourne: Premier's Department Victoria.

Weatherburn, D. and Lind, B. (1995) *Drug Law Enforcement Policy and its Impact on the Heroin Market*. Sydney: New South Wales Bureau of Crime Statistics and Research.

Weber, M. (1949) *The Methodology of the Social Sciences*. New York: Free Press.

Wood, J. (1997) *Final Report, Royal Commission into the New South Wales Police Service*. (Vols. I–III). Sydney: New South Wales Government.

Section 5 LEGISLATIVE AND REGULATORY PERSPECTIVES ON THE PREVENTION OF RISKY DRUG USE AND HARM

EDITED BY WENDY LOXLEY

5.1 Introduction

WENDY LOXLEY

National Drug Research Institute, Curtin University of Technology, Western Australia

Recreational drugs are highly regulated. The importation, manufacture, distribution and/or use of many drugs are absolutely prohibited in most countries. Laws and regulations relating to non-prohibited or licit drugs also play a vital role in assisting in the control and limitation of harmful drug use, by prohibiting or reducing the most risky patterns of drug use and the promotion of use.

Laws and regulations have actions across a number of levels as shown in Figure 5.1.1. At the highest level are international treaties and conventions which require signatories to exercise certain controls over the import, export, manufacture, promotion and use of certain substances. Tobacco now has its own treaty, the Framework Convention on Tobacco Control, and there are others regulating narcotics and other controlled drugs. Laws and regulations operate at national and state levels to prohibit the use of substances, regulate the environments within which they are used and/or the populations who may use them, and the ways in which they can be promoted and sold. Pharmaceutical scheduling limits the availability of some recreational drugs, while licensing, retailing and advertising regulations limit the availability and/or promotion of others such as tobacco or alcohol. Other legal and regulatory mechanisms include taxes and other price controls, local council by-laws, and regulations which influence the levels and nature of law enforcement.

The chapters in this section consider a range of legislative and regulatory options. Chapters 5.2 and 5.3 deal with tobacco and alcohol by, respectively, proposing alternative regulatory frameworks for tobacco, and evaluating the efficacy of alcohol law enforcement under current frameworks. Chapters 5.4 and 5.5 consider currently illicit drugs—first, cannabis, in which the current legal framework is itself under review, and then alternatives to traditional procedures in criminal justice for illicit drug using offenders. Finally, Chapter 5.6 reminds us that communities are not all alike and that social, cultural and structural differences should be taken into consideration when determining regulatory strategies to reduce drug-related harm.

CONTROLLING THE TOBACCO INDUSTRY

Tobacco is the leading cause of premature death and hospitalisation in developed countries and increasingly inflicts its damage on the developing world although, as Rehm and Room note in Chapter 2.2, alcohol-related harms approach and even outstrip those of tobacco

Preventing Harmful Substance Use: The Evidence Base for Policy and Practice.
Edited by T. Stockwell, P. J. Gruenewald, J.W. Toumbourou and W. Loxley.
© 2005 John Wiley & Sons, Ltd. ISBN 0-470-09227-0 (hbk) 0-470-09228-9 (pbk).

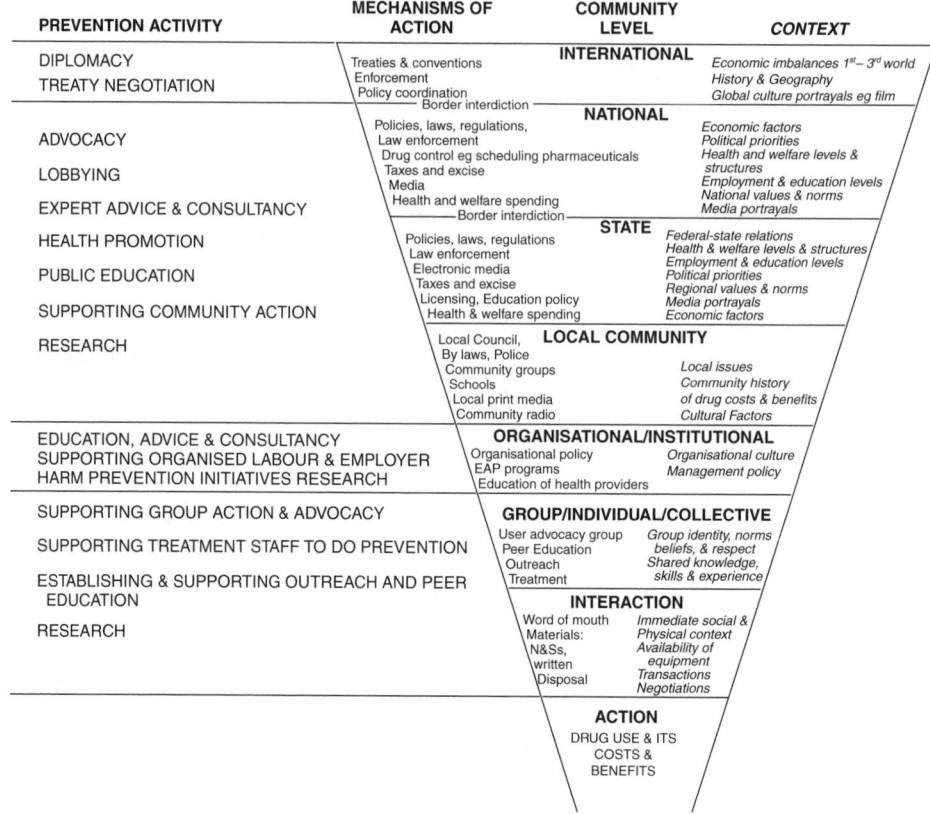

Figure 5.1.1 A public health systems model for the prevention of alcohol and other drug problems. *Source:* Reproduced from Lenton (1996).

in some developing countries By the year 2020, tobacco smoking will cause 8.4 million premature deaths annually (Murray and Lopez, 1997). The impact of regulatory controls on the price, promotion and availability of cigarettes has strong empirical support, but in some countries progress in reducing tobacco-related harm has slowed and new initiatives may be required if there is to be further progress.

Liberman and Borland (Chapter 5.2) demonstrate that, despite regulations, tobacco remains highly under-regulated in proportion to its harms and addictiveness and in comparison to other consumer products and drugs. The tobacco industry, far from seeking to minimise the harms its products cause, acts in ways that undermine sound tobacco control policy in seeking to maximise profitability. Clearly, more effective regulation is needed and Liberman and Borland describe what would be required in a comprehensive regulatory framework, and discuss two possible ways of achieving it. They believe that the tobacco industry should be subject to control by an agency that would seek to minimise the harms of tobacco to the community.

The ways in which such structures could be developed would vary from country to country and these authors, wisely, do not attempt to prescribe the detail for any given jurisdiction. Their plea, though, to "see a more rational regulatory approach to tobacco and the tobacco industry, with the necessary controls introduced, and tobacco-related mortality and morbidity minimised" will strike a chord with all those who are concerned with the health of communities in both the developed and developing worlds.

MANAGING ALCOHOL-RELATED VIOLENCE

The physical availability of alcohol has increased markedly in most economically developed countries over the past two decades. There is a clear international trend for increased risky alcohol use by adolescents and young adults (Loxley et al., 2004). Alcohol use is significantly associated with violent crime and the causal link between alcohol consumption and violence is beyond dispute. The relationship between alcohol and violent crime is a complex one and there are multiple contributory and causal mechanisms, including the characteristics of the drinker, the effects of alcohol, the drinking environment, and the cultural expectations surrounding alcohol and violence. Violent crimes are disproportionately associated with drinking in licensed premises (Briscoe and Donnelly, 2001).

Donnelly and Briscoe (Chapter 5.3) are concerned with the regulation of alcohol in licensed premises. In a Sydney study, they demonstrate that existing liquor laws, which have been shown to be effective in reducing alcohol-related problems in licensed premises, have reduced efficacy if they are not appropriately enforced. Alcohol service to intoxicated patrons is an offence against NSW liquor law, but despite observing a high prevalence of service to intoxicated patrons, Donnelly and Briscoe found that very few enforcement actions were targeted towards this problem. The majority of enforcement practice, rather, tended to be focused on patrons or minors, rather than on licensees or bar staff.

One of the essential take-home messages of this study is that effective enforcement-based approaches rely on high quality integrated information systems which allow policy-makers to appraise where the balance of enforcement activity lies, and assess where changes to that practice could be made to minimise alcohol-related harms.

ILLICIT DRUGS

Laws and regulations do more than enforce prohibition; they shape community values and opinions about drug use. Sanctions against drug users may depress drug use prevalence in the general community by expressing social norms against drug users and by dissuading people from using drugs due to fear of apprehension and punishment (deterrence). Deterrence theory asserts that undesirable behaviour can be curtailed if punishment is sufficiently certain, swift, and severe, although the perceived certainty of punishment appears to be the major driver of deterrence (MacCoun, 1993).

Specific deterrence refers to the degree to which being legally punished for a crime deters future criminal activity. This appears to be unsupported by the existing evidence and the severity of legal punishment appears to have very little impact on drug use (Manski et al., 2001; see also Chapter 6.3). There is, indeed, a considerable debate as to whether bringing illicit drug users into contact with the criminal justice system for using certain substances does more harm than good. The consequences of such contact may not only be criminal convictions, and sometimes incarceration, but also rapid and unsafe use of drugs because of the fear of apprehension. The next two chapters deal with this issue both in terms of cannabis (Chapter 5.4) and illicit drugs generally (Chapter 5.5). In both chapters, the emphasis is on alternatives to traditional criminal justice procedures.

The Legal Status of Cannabis

Lenton (Chapter 5.4) summarises the research literature on deterrence and shows that, in Australia at least, criminal penalties are not a major deterrent to cannabis use. The social impacts of receiving a criminal conviction can, however, be considerable, impacting on such areas as employment, accommodation and travel. Civil penalties for cannabis use, rather than criminal convictions, enjoy community support in Australia and are no worse at deterring cannabis use than is strict prohibition with criminal penalties schemes. Lenton concludes that the application of the criminal law to prevent cannabis use is an inefficient and ineffective use of valuable and scarce criminal justice resources. Rather, prohibition with civil penalties should maintain any general deterrent effect while reducing individual and community costs of conviction.

Illicit Drug Use and Crime

The association of illicit drug use and crime is one of the aspects of such use that is most troubling to the community. The nexus between illicit drug use and crime inevitably raises the question of which comes first—illicit drug use or crime. This is critical for policy in terms of whether crime control or drug control measures should be pursued when dealing with illicit drug use among the criminal justice population. The criminological literature tends to suggests that crime comes first but the picture is complex because drug-using criminals are not a homogeneous group. Some research supports an escalation model: drug-related offenders start committing crimes before they begin using illicit drugs; but use of such drugs becomes part of the lifestyle and can lead to dependency that increases the need to commit crimes to support their drug use (Makkai, 2002).

Loxley (Chapter 5.5) is concerned with alternatives to traditional criminal justice procedures for illicit drug-using offenders. Diversion programmes and similar schemes, including those that build drug treatment into sentencing, such as the British Drug Treatment and Testing Orders or the US and Australian drug courts, are becoming more prevalent as police, courts and judiciaries realise that imprisonment does little to reduce recidivism, and that early clinical or educational intervention with a drug-using offender may stave off a life of crime and save considerable community expense. This chapter examines what is known about the effectiveness of five such programmes: two in each of Australia and the UK and one in the USA.

In general, it is found that evaluations are limited and in some cases mainstreaming has been undertaken before effectiveness could be established; there are also methodological limitations in much of the data. It is too soon to say whether these programmes will reduce crime and illicit drug use, although there are some encouraging signs. The desire to implement such programmes, however, should not blind policy-makers to the need to do good evaluation research on pilot programmes and only implement these more widely when it can be definitively shown that they are both effective and cost-effective.

THE SOCIAL ECOLOGY OF COMMUNITIES

The final chapter in this section conveys something of a cautionary tale. The link between poor health and disadvantage is now beyond dispute and there is a clear relationship between alcohol and other drug use and social factors, such as unemployment, low income and insecure housing (Shaw et al., 1999). The local community is one of the primary levels for integrating and coordinating planning and it is critical that national and state policies, legislative models and regulations enable and empower local communities to develop effective prevention strategies. Community programmes ideally consist of a range of complementary interventions developed by a wide range of stakeholder agencies such as police, health services, drug agencies and local businesses (Loxley et al., 2004).

Freisthler and Gruenewald (Chapter 5.6) caution that finding the right mix of programmes and policies within any community requires understanding the local and global impacts of such interventions and their interaction with local social and economic conditions. They use a social ecology model to show that while some global efforts such as reducing poverty, improving education, and eliminating poor housing will generally reduce alcohol- and drug-related problems, the effects of some regulatory efforts such as reductions in alcohol outlet densities or increasing residential stability may vary from community to community, depending on their particular characteristics.

These findings should give pause to those who would assume that because a regulatory strategy works to reduce harmful drug use in one community, it will invariably do likewise in another. We should take heed of those regulations and legal frameworks that have been shown to be effective in well-designed and rigorous studies, but be aware that application of these regulations to all communities will not necessarily result in similar outcomes. To quote Freisthler and Gruenewald: "the local effects of preventive interventions will be moderated by the larger social contexts of community settings, contexts that, once recognized, may be used to enhance the effectiveness of these programs". One of the conclusions that can be drawn from this is that harnessing what is known globally at the local level and applying local level knowledge can enhance the effectiveness of regulatory and legislative interventions.

REFERENCES

Briscoe, S. and Donnelly, N. (2001) *Temporal and Regional Aspects of Alcohol-Related Violence and Disorder*. Report No. 1. New South Wales: National Drug Research Institute, Curtin University of Technology and NSW Bureau of Crime Statistics and Research.

Lenton, S. (1996) The essence of prevention. In C. Wilkinson and B. Saunders (eds), *Perspectives on Prevention*. Perth: William Montgomery Pty. Ltd., 73–80.

Loxley, W., Toumbourou, J.W., Stockwell, T., Haines, B., Scott, K., Godfrey, C. et al. (2004) *The Prevention of Substance Use, Risk and Harm in Australia: A Review of the Evidence*. Canberra: Australian Government Department of Health and Ageing.

MacCoun, R.J. (1993) Drugs and the law: a psychological analysis of drug prohibition. *Psychological Bulletin* **113**(3), 487–512.

Makkai, T. (2002) Illicit drugs and crime. In A. Graycar and P. Grabosky (eds), *Cambridge Handbook of Australian Criminology*. Cambridge: Cambridge University Press.

Manski, C.F., Pepper, J.V. and Petrie, C.V. (2001) *Informing America's Policy on Illegal Drugs: What We Don't Know Keeps Hurting Us*. Washington, DC: National Academy Press.

Murray, C. and Lopez, A. (1997) Alternative projections of mortality and disability by cause 1990–2020: global burden of disease study. *Lancet*, **349**(9064), 1498–1504.

Shaw, M., Dorling, D. and Davey Smith, G. (1999) Poverty, social exclusion, and minorities. In M. Marmot and R.G. Wilkinson (eds), *Social Determinants of Health*. Oxford: Oxford University Press.

5.2 Regulating Tobacco to Minimise Harms

JONATHAN LIBERMAN AND RON BORLAND

VicHealth Centre for Tobacco Control, the Cancer Council of Victoria, Australia

SUMMARY

Tobacco remains highly under-regulated in proportion to its harms and addictiveness, and in comparison to consumer products, food and other drugs. The areas of under-regulation fall into two main categories; marketing and product design. The tobacco industry continues to act in ways that undermine sound tobacco control policy, including: marketing products in ways designed to increase and sustain use; designing products in ways that make them more addictive; designing products in ways that make the experience of smoking more pleasant than it intrinsically is; and making no real attempts to reduce the harmfulness of its products. No jurisdiction in the world regulates what can and cannot be in, or added to, tobacco products, nor the amounts of ingredients or additives, notwithstanding that they contribute to harmfulness and addiction and that their presence in products is precisely controlled by manufacturers.

In this chapter, we elaborate on the inadequacies of the current situation, and sketch out ways in which tobacco might be better regulated. We argue that a comprehensive regulatory framework is required, dealing with: the characteristics of products; communication with consumers about products; mechanisms to encourage the development and distribution of less harmful and/or less addictive products; the control of prices as a tool to discourage use and/or shift use in less harmful directions; the control of the circumstances in which products are made available to users; and adequate monitoring of the operation of the tobacco industry and decisions made by those exercising regulatory responsibilities.

We suggest looking to models of regulation that aim to turn the current relationship between the tobacco industry and the community on its head, making the tobacco industry the servant, rather than the master, of the community through a specialist agency, which would not only reactively seek to keep the industry within limits, but also have a proactive role in shaping the market for products through control of the product itself, communication and price. We point to different models through which these aims might be achieved, and through which the potential dangers—both at the individual and population health level—of moving to "reduced risk" products might be minimised.

Preventing Harmful Substance Use: The Evidence Base for Policy and Practice.
Edited by T. Stockwell, P. J. Gruenewald, J.W. Toumbourou and W. Loxley.
© 2005 John Wiley & Sons, Ltd. ISBN 0-470-09227-0 (hbk) 0-470-09228-9 (pbk).

INTRODUCTION

The World Health Organization estimates that 4 million people die prematurely each year as a result of tobacco-related disease (World Health Organization, 1999). By the year 2020, it is estimated that tobacco will cause 8.4 million premature deaths annually (Murray and Lopez, 1997). It will kill 500 million people who are alive today (World Health Organization, 1999). While the overall burden of mortality and morbidity moves increasingly into the developing world, tobacco use remains the number one preventable cause of death and disease in developed countries. It is harmful not only to its users, but also to others who are exposed to tobacco smoke. Tobacco use typically begins in childhood. It is addictive. "[T]he pharmacological and behavioral processes that determine tobacco addiction are similar to those that determine addiction to drugs such as heroin and cocaine" (United States Department of Health and Human Services, 1988). These realities highlight the scale of the tobacco problem and the regulatory challenges it poses. In this chapter, we outline some of these regulatory challenges and suggest some ways of thinking about, and progressing, them.

THE FRAMEWORK CONVENTION ON TOBACCO CONTROL

The importance of strong action on tobacco has been recognised internationally. In May 2003, the 192 members of the World Health Organization unanimously adopted an international treaty, the Framework Convention on Tobacco Control (FCTC), aimed at reducing tobacco-related death and disease (Framework Convention on Tobacco Control, 2003). The FCTC is the first treaty that the WHO has developed. Its objective is set out in Article 3:

> The objective of this Convention and its protocols is to protect present and future generations from the devastating health, social, environmental and economic consequences of tobacco consumption and exposure to tobacco smoke by providing a framework for tobacco control measures to be implemented by the Parties at the national, regional and international levels in order to reduce continually and substantially the prevalence of tobacco use and exposure to tobacco smoke.

The treaty covers a wide range of matters that are essential to good tobacco control. These include: use of price and tax measures, which are "an effective and important means of reducing tobacco consumption by various segments of the population, in particular young persons" (Art. 6); protection against exposure to environmental tobacco smoke (Art. 8); regulation of the contents of products (Art. 9); regulation of disclosure of the contents of products and emissions that result from their use (Art. 10); regulation of packaging and labelling, including the use of health warnings (Art. 11); promotion of public awareness and education (Art. 12); regulation of tobacco advertising, promotion and sponsorship (Art. 13); promotion of tobacco cessation and tobacco dependence treatment (Art. 14); regulation of illicit trade in products (Art. 15); regulation of sales to and by minors (Art. 16); promotion of economically viable alternatives for tobacco workers, growers and sellers (Art. 17); use of liability laws (both civil and criminal) to hold the tobacco industry legally accountable for the harm it has caused and continues to cause (Art. 19); and encouragement of research, surveillance and exchange of information (Art. 20).

Domestic Implementation

Though the FCTC sets out the main matters that need to be addressed in a comprehensive approach to tobacco control, the details of how these are to be progressed effectively remain to be worked out at the domestic level by the parties who ratify it. There are many different ways in which countries can attempt to achieve the FCTC's goals; many different types of regulatory and non-regulatory strategies that can be implemented. Ultimately, the manner of proceeding to action will depend on a range of social, cultural, political, legal and constitutional considerations that exist in particular countries.

Even in countries that are often seen as leaders in tobacco regulation, the tobacco industry has enjoyed remarkable freedom from the type of regulation to which others, such as pharmaceutical companies and food producers, are subject. Not regarded as a drug like marijuana, heroin or cocaine; not a pharmaceutical; not an ordinary consumer product; not a food. So, what is it precisely? There are thus also important issues of how tobacco is seen, and how it comes to be seen in the future, in different countries. What sort of a product is it? What sort of models should those seeking to regulate it look to?

The "New" Tobacco Industry

One important element of the context in which these regulatory issues need to be addressed and progressed is that we are now dealing with a tobacco industry in the process of "re-inventing" itself. No longer claiming that evidence of the harmfulness of smoking shows just an "association" and not a causal link; or that the jury is still out; or that tobacco use is not addictive; or that, if it is, it is addictive in the way that shopping is; the major players in the tobacco industry now acknowledge the harmfulness and addictiveness of tobacco use. On British American Tobacco's website, its head of science and regulation, Dr Chris Proctor, tells visitors that: "Along with the pleasures of cigarette smoking come real risks of serious diseases, such as lung cancer, respiratory disease and heart disease" (Proctor, 2003). Philip Morris' senior Vice-President, Steven Parrish, explains that, in 2000, Philip Morris' tobacco companies updated their policy approach to the issues of addiction and disease causation in smokers "to make it clear that they agree with the consensus that cigarette smoking is addictive, and causes lung cancer and other fatal diseases" (Parrish, 2002: 114). The change in approach to these issues inevitably comes side-by-side with an acceptance of the need for regulation. Parrish explains: "[O]nce you begin actively communicating that you are selling a product that is both deadly and addictive, it is not much of a leap to come to the conclusion that there needs to be significant additional regulation" (2002: 114). Others, however, do not go as far. BAT's website declares: "We support and wish to help deliver tobacco regulation that can help to reduce the impact of tobacco on public health, while ensuring that adult consumers can continue making informed choices about consumption of a legal product" (British American Tobacco, 2003). The disjunction between "informed choices" and addiction is conveniently elided.

While the tobacco industry and the public health community might be in agreement about the need for regulation, one suspects they might have very different ideas in mind about the form that regulation should take. It is essentially ideas about what form regulation might take that we seek to explore in this chapter. Our aim is not to recommend a particular regulatory model, but to explore some of the regulatory challenges and some of the ways that we might think about addressing them. Our ideas are, of course, heavily influenced by the context in which we live—in a developed country with a particular set of social, cultural, political, legal and constitutional norms. But the ideas we explore here are explored at a level that, we hope, is general enough to have something useful to offer to those who are trying to come to grips, in quite different contexts, with the same regulatory challenges posed by tobacco.

THE OBJECTIVES OF SOUND TOBACCO CONTROL AND THE WAY THE TOBACCO INDUSTRY UNDERMINES THEM

We take as the starting point in our exploration that the central goal of sound tobacco control is to minimise tobacco-related population harms. This goal is commonly broken down into four objectives: prevention; cessation; protection from exposure to tobacco smoke; and reducing the exposure of users to the harmful consequences of use (i.e. regulation of the product itself).

Curiously, while agreement on these objectives is relatively easy to reach—though *implementation* of the fourth, i.e. regulating the product itself to reduce harm, raises particular complexities—there seems to be little questioning of the place of the tobacco industry in a world with these regulatory aims. Yet, day-by-day, the tobacco industry operates in ways that undermine them.

There are essentially four main things that the tobacco industry does—beyond simply making its products available for purchase—that run directly counter to these objectives:

1. It markets tobacco products in ways designed to increase and sustain use by making them appear more attractive than they intrinsically are, minimising the salience of the harms of use as compared to the "benefits", and making their use seem socially normative. This takes a variety of forms, such as:
   (a) advertising and sponsorship that associates tobacco products with images of glamour, fun, attractiveness, and so on. These include both more traditional forms of direct advertising and sponsorship, and new forms of advertising to which the tobacco industry is increasingly turning as avenues of promotion are being closed to it by regulation (Carter, 2003).
   (b) Having tobacco products widely available for sale, and having them prominently displayed in the venues where they are available.
   (c) Taking no steps to try to ensure that users of its products fully appreciate, in a real sense, the nature and magnitude of harms of use.
2. It designs products in ways that make them more addictive. Much evidence has emerged on this issue over the last few years, in the USA in particular. It was evidence such as this that led the US Food and Drug Administration to seek to exercise regulatory authority over tobacco products, a move that was ultimately overturned, on statutory interpretation grounds, by a majority of the US Supreme Court (Food and Drug Administration et al., v Brown & Williamson Tobacco Corp et al., 2000).
   Henningfield and Zeller write that the FDA:

   > found that cigarettes and smokeless tobacco products were highly controlled with respect to their nicotine content, their bioavailable nicotine, and the rate at which the delivered nicotine could be absorbed into the bloodstream. . . . The FDA also found that many aspects of cigarette design and manufacture, including the use of *reconstituted tobacco* [a paper-like product formed from tobacco material and other substances] and various chemical ingredients, were

routinely employed to control nicotine delivery. Its analysis suggests that cigarette design could be employed either to increase or decrease the addictive effects of cigarettes by, for example, increasing what was variously referred to as the nicotine "kick" or "impact" of cigarettes. In other words, it is evident that addictiveness is not an all-or-nothing attribute of a product. Rather, a product can apparently be engineered to become more or less addictive by controlling its physical properties. With respect to drug products, this concept is well understood, and drug manufacturers are required to design their products so as to achieve desired effects while minimizing addictive ones.

(2002: 130)

3. It manufactures products in ways that make the experience of smoking more pleasant than it intrinsically is. Through the use of additives and design features such as filter ventilation, the smoke is made to taste less harsh and unpleasant, thus masking some of the inherent signs of toxicity. Long-time Canadian tobacco control advocate, David Sweanor, has likened this to adding Kool-aid to the cyanide that killed over 900 people in Jonestown, Guyana, in 1978.
4. It makes no real attempts to reduce the harmfulness of its products except where this coincides with increased consumer acceptability or is mandated by governments. Decisions about product design are made with a focus on consumer acceptability and profits, regardless of potential harm. For example, tobacco manufacturers have tested a range of filters that markedly reduce exposures to key toxins (Institute of Medicine, 2001) but have not introduced them because they reduce the taste and acceptability of the product.

Of course, the tobacco industry does not do any of these things for no reason. It does each of them because they are rational things to do in the pursuit of profit. What else would we expect from it? The legitimacy of the current dynamic—where the tobacco industry operates in circumstances in which, subject to certain specified legislative restrictions on its conduct, the more products it is able to sell, the more people it addicts and kills, the more money it makes—is widely assumed. Yet, one can see, with just a glance, how inconsistent it is with the objectives of sound tobacco control that we set out earlier. Liberman discusses this dynamic and argues that "[i]t is hard to imagine how the problems caused by tobacco can ever be fully tackled, and tobacco adequately regulated to reduce the harms it causes, while its manufacturers are allowed to operate with their current perverse incentive" (2003).

A proper understanding of the tobacco industry's incentive to act in ways that are contrary to public health must be kept in the front of one's mind when its calls for regulation are assessed. Patently, the tobacco industry wants regulation that is in its interests. And one may assume that it wants regulation that delivers it two things: handsome, ongoing profits; and protection from legal liability for the harm it causes. While comprehensive tobacco regulation is required for all the reasons we outline, the need to get it right, in public health terms, is made even more important, and urgent, by the fact that the tobacco industry is circling now, looking, after years of brazen infliction of addiction, death and disease, to secure itself the ultimate regulatory prize: to be allowed to continue to inflict addiction, death, and disease, but to inflict it with full legal immunity.

The Regulation of Marketing and Product Design

The actions of the tobacco industry that run directly counter to public health objectives fall into two categories: marketing and product design. Regulation has, to date, gone much further in the former category than in the latter. Many jurisdictions have enacted strong legislation to deal with tobacco advertising and sponsorship, though these jurisdictions have seen the emergence of new forms of advertising as the tobacco industry seeks to navigate its way through and around legislative restrictions. Carter details a number of such new forms of advertising in Australia and describes the "creativity of the industry in circumventing marketing restrictions" (2003). One gets a sense of a never-ending cat-and-mouse game, with any new piece of legislation seen by the tobacco industry and its lawyers as posing yet another challenge to legal ingenuity: examine it carefully word-for-word, and find a way around it; and stuff the object of the legislation.

With respect to the latter category, product design, no jurisdiction in the world regulates what can and cannot be in, or added to, tobacco products, nor the amounts or levels of ingredients or additives. This is despite the fact that ingredients and additives contribute to both harmfulness and addiction, and that their presence in products is precisely controlled by manufacturers. Henningfield and Zeller provide some examples of what regulation of the product itself might be able to achieve: regulation of particle sizes if "particle size can be controlled to decrease the fraction of particles that can be absorbed in the lungs"; "if ammonia increases the addictive kick of nicotine doses, and if menthol enhances the rapid absorption of nicotine deep into the lungs and increases carcinogenicity, such compounds might be prohibited"; "if pH manipulations increase the speed of nicotine absorptions, standards might be set to diminish the rate of absorption"; "incremental reductions in cigarette toxicity through performance standards such as allowable maximums for nitrosamines, pesticide residues, arsenic, carbon monoxide, and other substances" (Henningfield and Zeller, 2002: 136).

The Promise and the Danger of Harm Reduction

In the past few years, harm reduction has emerged as the fourth plank of tobacco control policy. The three longer-standing, and less controversial, pillars—prevention, cessation, and protection of non-smokers—remain the central ones. But as the acceptance has grown that smoking will not be completely eliminated, and that regulation is preferable to prohibition, the possible benefits of a harm reduction strategy for existing users have been widely contemplated. In this context, the US Institute of Medicine of the National Academies, which provides science-based advice on matters of biomedical science, medicine and health, has concluded that "[f]or many diseases attributable to tobacco use, reducing risk of disease by reducing exposure to tobacco toxicants is feasible" (Institute of Medicine, 2001: 4).

The harm reduction debate has occurred in a context in which a new generation of potentially less harmful nicotine-delivering products have been developed by the tobacco industry and others, and are beginning to be sold, particularly in the USA. It has also occurred in a context in which the public health community now understands that smokers have been deceived by the "low-tar" experience of the past 25 years. In the 1970s, the public health community believed that low-tar cigarettes were likely to be less harmful than higher-tar cigarettes, and supported their introduction and smokers moving to these products (King et al., 2003). But the hoped-for health benefits have not eventuated, and one can only guess how many smokers may have quit rather than switch to products they thought—at great cost—to be less harmful. There is much literature that explains how the tobacco industry played the low-tar move to its advantage; encouraging smokers to switch to lower-tar products, while engineering the products to cheat the Federal Trade Commission tests and not deliver any less harm to smokers (Tobacco Control, 2001). We will not go into that literature here, but Myers explains very well the dynamic that was at work, and reminds us to be vigilant this time round:

> While the public health community was interested in newly designed products for their potential health benefit, internal tobacco industry documents indicate that the tobacco industry sold these products to keep people smoking. To accomplish this goal, the tobacco industry did not need to make products that were actually safer; it only needed to make products that would be perceived by the public as safer. According to its own documents, that is exactly what it did.
>
> (2002, 141–142)

Harm reduction thus does not come without its dangers. But even beyond the kinds of dangers mentioned above, there are broader population health effects to consider. What might be the population effects of a move to less harmful, or "risk-reduced" products? What impact might this have on prevention and cessation efforts? Could the overall population health impact be a negative one, with more users, and the overall burden of death and disease higher than it would have been with fewer users of more harmful products (Kozlowski et al., 2001)? The essential point is that harm reduction must occur within an appropriate regulatory framework, one with mechanisms for identifying and monitoring all these dangers and taking appropriate action.

WHAT IS NEEDED?

The challenges of tobacco regulation are complex. Liberman describes the central regulatory challenge as being "to construct a framework under which tobacco products can continue to be made available to people who are addicted, or otherwise wish to use them, but in circumstances where all operating forces and influences are moving, as far as possible, towards the minimisation of harm" (2003: 465). He notes that this inevitably broadens out into consideration of products that are alternatives to, and compete with, traditional tobacco products. Borland describes the aim of "controlling the tobacco market, as part of a comprehensive tobacco control strategy" as being "to minimise population harm from tobacco use by controlling the form and contents of, and information about, tobacco products in ways that minimise population exposures to tobacco related toxins" (Borland, 2003: 375).

In practical terms, an appropriate regulatory framework would be required to deal with each of the following:

- the characteristics of products, including ingredients, additives, manufacturing processes and toxic outputs;
- monitoring of actual exposures in individual smokers (i.e., what smokers actually take in when they smoke);
- communication with consumers about products, both on packs and more broadly—including the promotion and marketing of products and the provision of information about contents (including the actual performance of contents), health and cessation;
- mechanisms to encourage the development and distribution of less harmful and/or less addictive products;
- the control of prices as a tool to discourage use and/or shift use in less harmful directions;
- the control of the circumstances in which products are made available to users;
- adequate monitoring of, and access to, information about, the operation of the tobacco industry and decisions made by those exercising regulatory responsibilities.

It is clear that the powers to achieve these controls must be vested in a specialist agency, with the knowledge, expertise and resources to exercise them wisely. In the USA, legislation giving the FDA authority over tobacco has been proposed. In the UK, the Royal College of Physicians, observing that "[t]obacco products have enjoyed an unprecedented degree of freedom from the safety regulations that apply to virtually all other food or drug products available in Britain" has recommended that "[t]obacco products in Britain should therefore be regulated either by the Medicines Control Agency or by a nicotine regulatory authority similar in concept to the Food Standards Agency" (Royal College of Physicians, 2003). (The Medicines Control Agency has since been subsumed within the Medicines and Healthcare Products Regulatory Agency after its merger with the Medical Devices Agency.)

While there is much to learn from the way agencies such as these operate, there are difficulties in looking too closely to regulators of food and drugs as models for tobacco regulation. The aim of bodies such as the US FDA and the UK Medicines and Healthcare Products Regulatory Agency (and of the Australian Therapeutic Goods Administration), is essentially to ensure consumer health and safety. They deal with products that, if regulated effectively, are beneficial to consumers. But not so tobacco. In the case of tobacco, the best a regulator can try to do is minimise the harm the products cause. This is not to say that regulatory agencies such as these could not regulate tobacco, but that their authority to do so would have to be granted in a way that differed from their more familiar mandates; and this would have to be very clearly set out in the legislation conferring the power.

WHAT SORT OF AGENCY AND WITH WHAT POWERS?

That a specialist agency is needed for tobacco products does not answer vital questions of detail: What sort of agency? With what powers? How is it to be resourced? Here, we come back to our earlier comments that these questions will be answered differently in different countries; there can be no single answer to such questions. At a broad level, countries with state-owned monopolies, countries with widely disseminated industries that consist of many players including cottage industries, and those where the market is dominated by a small number of for-profit companies, will be in very different positions. And at the micro level, as we have said, within these countries, social, cultural, political, legal and constitutional considerations will dictate what approaches can be taken.

We have written papers exploring both the regulatory challenges and some of the responses that we might bring to them. Essentially, we are looking at the viability of models of regulation that turn the current relationship between the tobacco industry and the community on its head: models that make the tobacco industry the servant, rather than the master, of the community, through an agency that does much more than reactively seek to keep the industry within certain limits; models that give an agency with a statutory harm-minimisation charter a proactive role in shaping the market for products, through communication both on packaging and more broadly (being the only entity allowed to communicate about products in a commercial context) and pricing; models under which incentives are created for the development of less harmful and less addictive products, but under which the dangers of harm reduction strategies are minimised. We are looking towards models of regulation where the regulatory agency has access to all information it needs to make decisions, and where it effectively stands between the manufacturer and the consumer, making the fully-informed (as far as is possible), rational, volitional decisions that consumers cannot make both because of their incapacity to translate complex scientific data and marketing messages into personal understanding, and the effects of addiction.

Liberman has looked at the idea of an agency exercising strict controls over both manufacturers and retailers through strict licensing or contractual arrangements. In such a model, manufacturers and retailers would effectively be service-providers to the agency, allowing the agency to do what it exists to do, namely ensure that products are made available to consumers who are addicted or otherwise wish to use them, and operating only within the parameters determined by the agency. The agency would decide which products it wanted on the market, with what ingredients, in what packaging (generic, if it chose), and manufacturers and retailers would compete to meet its requirements—its manufacture and end-supply requirements, respectively. The profits of manufacturers and retailers would lie in meeting the agency's harm-minimisation objectives, rather than in growing and sustaining markets in the ordinary way. The agency would communicate with consumers about the relative harms and addictiveness of different products. It would use its powers of communication and pricing policy to encourage users towards less harmful forms of use, where it determined this to be appropriate. As the body responsible for deciding what products might be placed on the market and in what circumstances, it would have the power to create incentives for the development of less harmful products. It would use its powers to control the circumstances of end-supply—how supply outlets could be configured, what might be displayed—and to create incentives for the sale by retailers of less harmful products or of tobacco cessation products (Liberman, 2003).

Borland has explored the idea of a monopsonistic agency, i.e., an agency that is the sole purchaser of products from manufacturers and importers, to whom manufacturers and importers tender for market share, and which enters contractual arrangements with retailers to sell its products. As the sole purchaser, the agency could exercise control over product ingredients—it could ensure the reduction or elimination of additives and features that mask inherent toxicity or enhance addictiveness, and so on; it could set and revise performance and emission standards for toxic compounds and over product packaging. It could create incentives for manufacturers to innovate in product design. It could market products under its own name, marketing those that it preferred consumers to use more favourably than others. It would have no incentive to make differential claims of potential harmfulness that were not supported by the evidence (Borland, 2003).

In both models, the agency would be established by legislation and required by statute to act under a strict charter, requiring it to exercise all functions *only* according to certain criteria, such as the core goal of minimising the population harms caused by tobacco products (and their alternatives), and other sub-goals such as reducing uptake, encouraging cessation, and minimising the dangers of an illicit market. Its responsibility to ensure minimisation of the dangers of an illicit market would direct it to keep actual consumer preferences in mind as it sought to move users to less harmful products, i.e. it would not move too far and too rapidly ahead of consumer preferences. Crucially, the agency would need to be set up in such a way as to insulate it from the corrupting influence of revenue considerations. And its establishment and operation would need to draw on the literature about the dangers of regulatory capture by the regulated industry, and the ways to minimise such risks.

There is always a danger in focusing on a particular set of ideas that its context will not be fully appreciated. It is important that we stress that we do not have in mind a new world in which we see a vigorous market for tobacco products and their competitors with rates of use increasing from present levels. We have quite the opposite in mind. The only competition we envisage is in competing for the agency's favour, i.e. in being able to satisfy the agency's harm-minimisation objectives. All communication in the marketplace would be only as decided upon by the agency—in terms of content, frequency, and location. This, in our view, represents the best opportunity for balanced communication to consumers about the harms and addictiveness of products. And again, lest the fuller picture, and the place of what we are suggesting in that overall picture, be obscured, all of this would be occurring in a context where prevention and cessation efforts were continuing, and the use of less harmful products would not be advertised as a good alternative to cessation or to never commencing at all. As long as harm reduction is embraced—and the evidence suggests that, if appropriately managed, it can contribute as a fourth plank of sound tobacco control policy—the risks of higher levels of use than would otherwise be the case are inevitable. What we are trying to ensure is that this occurs in the safest, most carefully controlled, framework that we, as a community, can put in place.

CONCLUSION

The regulatory challenges posed by tobacco are far from simple, but there is much important progress to be made. For too long, tobacco products and the tobacco industry have sat outside the laws and regulations that apply to other products and industries: whether food, drug, or consumer products. All this in the face of the reality that the mortality and morbidity caused by tobacco are without compare. Hopefully, the coming years will see a more rational regulatory approach to tobacco and the tobacco industry, with the necessary controls introduced, and tobacco-related mortality and morbidity minimised. Given the size of the problem, and the many as yet unexplored opportunities for regulatory intervention, it is not a lot to ask.

REFERENCES

Borland, R.A. (2003) Strategy for controlling the marketing of tobacco products: a regulated market model. *Tobacco Control*, **12**, 374–382.

British American Tobacco (2003) British American Tobacco website. Available online: http://www .bat.com/oneweb/sites/uk_3mnfen.nsf/vwPagesWebLive/80256BF30082A32C80256D16005E1 F2A?opendocument&DTC=20031111 (accessed 26 November 2003).

Carter, S. (2003) Going below the line: creating transportable brands for Australia's dark market. *Tobacco Control*, **12**, 87iii–94.

Food and Drug Administration et al. v Brown and Williamson Tobacco Corp et al. (2000). Available online: http://caselaw.lp.findlaw.com/cgi-bin/getcase.pl?court=US&navby=case&vol=000 &invol=98-1152 (accessed 26 November 2003).

Framework Convention on Tobacco Control (2003) World Health Organisation. Available online: http://www.who.int/tobacco/fctc/text/en/fctc_en.pdf (accessed 26 November 2003).

Henningfield, J. and Zeller, M. (2002) Could science-based regulation make tobacco products less addictive? *Yale Journal of Health Policy, Law, and Ethics*, **III**(1), 127.

Institute of Medicine (2001) *Clearing the Smoke: Assessing the Science Base for Tobacco Harm Reduction*. Washington, DC: National Academy Press.

King, W., Carter, S., Borland, R., Chapman, S. and Gray, N. (2003) The Australian tar derby: the origins and failure of a harm reduction program. *Tobacco Control*, **12**(Suppl. III), iii61–iii70.

Kozlowski, L.T., Strasser, A.A., Giovino, G.A., Erickson, P.A. and Terza, J.V. (2001) Applying the risk/use equilibrium: use medicinal nicotine now for harm reduction. *Tobacco Control*, **10**, 201–203.

Liberman, J. (2003) Where to for tobacco regulation: time for new approaches? *Drug and Alcohol Review*, **22**, 461–469.

Murray, C., and Lopez, A. (1997) Alternative projections of mortality and disability by cause 1990–2020: global burden of disease study. *Lancet*, **349**(9064), 1498–1504.

Myers, M. (2002) Could product regulation result in less hazardous tobacco products? *Yale Journal of Health Policy, Law, and Ethics*, **III**(1), 139.

Parrish, S. (2002) Bridging the divide: a shared interest in a coherent national tobacco policy. *Yale Journal of Health Policy, Law, and Ethics*, **III**:(1), 109.

Proctor, C. (2003) British American Tobacco Website. Available online: http://www.bat.com/oneweb/sites/uk_3mnfen.nsf/vwPagesWebLive/ED9E7B3E9270D92880256BF40003317F?opendocument&DTC=20031121 (accessed 26 November 2003).

Royal College of Physicians (2003) Nicotine addiction in Britain: a report of the Tobacco Advisory Group of the Royal College of Physicians. Available online: http://www.rcplondon.ac.uk/pubs/books/nicotine/9-summary.htm (accessed 27 November 2003).

Tobacco Control (2001) Special Supplement. Debunking myths around "light" cigarettes and implications for "reduced risk" products. *Tobacco Control*, **10**(Suppl. I), i1–i47.

United States Department of Health and Human Services (1988) *The Health Consequences of Smoking: Nicotine Addiction*. Rockville, MD: Surgeon General's Office.

World Health Organization (1999) Tobacco—Health Facts, Fact Sheet No 221. Available online: http://www.who.int/inf-fs/en/fact221.html (accessed 27 November 2003).

5.3 Intelligence-Led Regulation of Licensed Premises

NEIL DONNELLY

NSW Bureau of Crime Statistics and Research; Curtin University of Technology, WA, Australia

SUZANNE BRISCOE

NSW Bureau of Crime Statistics and Research, NSW, Australia

SUMMARY

The potential for levels of alcohol-related crime to be minimised through improved and better integrated law enforcement and liquor licensing information systems is critically examined. Licensed premises have been clearly identified as an important situational risk factor for alcohol-related problems with a minority of more problematic premises accounting for a large percentage of problems. Training bar staff to serve alcohol responsibly has been promoted as one strategy to address problems arising from patron intoxication; however, evidence for the effectiveness of this strategy has been mixed. Enforcement of existing liquor laws has been shown to be an effective strategy in reducing alcohol-related problems associated with licensed premises, though the specific form such enforcement takes may need to vary across different settings or cultures. A prerequisite for any effective enforcement-based approach, however, is that there be in place high-quality, integrated information systems which facilitate the allocation of limited resources toward dealing with more problematic licensed premises. Such systems would also allow policy-makers to readily appraise where the balance of enforcement activity lies and assess where changes to that practice could be made to minimise alcohol-related harms.

A study which entailed a comprehensive analysis of patterns of enforcement actions in licensed premises in one Australian jurisdiction, New South Wales (NSW), is described. This study involved combining data from four separate sources, including court data and law enforcement penalty notice data. Despite evidence clearly showing a high prevalence of service to intoxicated patrons, it was found that only around 3% of enforcement actions were targeted towards this problem. The majority of enforcement practice tended to be focused on patrons or minors, rather than on licensees or bar staff. This study found that currently the various enforcement information systems in NSW are poorly integrated

Preventing Harmful Substance Use: The Evidence Base for Policy and Practice.
Edited by T. Stockwell, P. J. Gruenewald, J.W. Toumbourou and W. Loxley.
© 2005 John Wiley & Sons, Ltd. ISBN 0-470-09227-0 (hbk) 0-470-09228-9 (pbk).

and do not readily enable the identification of those premises repeatedly found to be in breach of the liquor licensing laws. Suggestions are made as to how these information systems could be better integrated, with the goal being to minimise alcohol-related harms. These include physical linkage across different enforcement information systems, standardisation of offence coding protocols and the inclusion of mandatory fields in penalty notices to record the details of the particular licensed premises in which the breach of the law took place.

INTRODUCTION

In this chapter we examine the potential for levels of alcohol-related crime to be minimised through improved and better integrated law enforcement and liquor licensing information systems. In the first section of this chapter, we provide a brief overview of research identifying licensed premises as an important risk setting for alcohol-related crime, as well as evidence showing that some premises are at much greater risk of alcohol-related problems than others. Second, we review evidence concerning the role of enforcement in improving compliance with those aspects of the liquor laws most likely to impact on problems arising from intoxication among patrons. We also consider the limitations of server training programmes in isolation from enforcement-driven activity.

Finally, we examine the extent to which current information systems in New South Wales (NSW), Australia, allow for the efficient identification of problematic licensed premises which are repeatedly in breach of the liquor laws. We describe a recent investigation in which liquor licensing enforcement data, from a number of sources including court proceedings and infringement/penalty notices, were combined. As well as identifying the strengths and limitations of each of these data sources, we provide a critical discussion of the potentials and challenges of integrating these to enable better focusing of harm minimisation initiatives.

LICENSED PREMISES AS A SITUATIONAL RISK FACTOR FOR ALCOHOL-RELATED PROBLEMS

It is well established that alcohol-related problems tend to be concentrated at particular times and localities rather than being randomly distributed. As an example, in NSW, Australia, crime incidents such as assault and offensive behaviour, which are known to be associated with alcohol misuse, are more likely to occur late at night and on weekends and to have an over-representation of younger male perpetrators (Briscoe and Donnelly, 2001). The concentration of alcohol-related problems at particular times and places has obvious implications for efficiently targeting limited law enforcement and crime prevention resources.

There are a number of lines of evidence that show licensed premises to be an important situational risk factor for alcohol-related problems in the general community. Research from North America has demonstrated that geographical areas with higher concentrations of liquor outlets (i.e., higher outlet density) also have higher rates of violent crime, with some variation across different licence types (Scribner et al., 1995; Gorman et al., 2001; Lipton and Gruenewald, 2002). In Australia, Stevenson et al. (1999) found that local government areas in NSW with higher levels of outlet density and alcohol sales also had higher rates of assault, offensive behaviour and malicious damage to property, even after controlling for the effects of various socio-demographic factors.

Evidence from the most recent Australian survey of victims of crime (the Australian Bureau of Statistics Crime and Safety survey) shows that 12% of all assault victims (approx. 80,000 persons) reported that their most recent assault occurred at a pub or club. For males alone, 18% of assault victims reported being assaulted at pubs or clubs (approx. 60,000 persons; Australian Bureau of Statistics, 1999). While these data comprise the location of assault for assault victims, victimisation at licensed venues increases considerably when only alcohol-related violence is considered. For example, a secondary analysis of the 1998 Australian National Drug Strategy Household survey (NDSH) data found that more persons report being assaulted by an intoxicated person in pubs and clubs than in any other location, with 37% of victims of alcohol-related violence having been assaulted at a pub or club (Teece and Williams, 2000).

In areas that have many licensed venues attracting a large number of people, the proportion of assaults occurring on licensed premises increases substantially. Previous research from the NSW Bureau of Crime Statistics and Research (BOCSAR) mapped all recorded incidents of assault in the inner Sydney area in order to identify "hotspots" associated with violent crime. Overall, 17% of assaults in five of these hotspots occurred on licensed premises and in one particular "hotspot", up to one-third of all assaults occurred at licensed venues. Furthermore, it was apparent from the crime maps that many of the assaults that occurred outdoors also took place within very close proximity of licensed premises. These recorded crime data were supplemented with surveys of assault victims presenting both to police and to a large hospital emergency department in the vicinity of these hotpots. From these reports it was found that over 42% of respondents had been assaulted just outside or inside hotels, pubs, clubs or nightclubs (Jochelson, 1997).

While licensed premises are generally a risk setting for alcohol-related problems in communities, it is also the case that some licensed premises are associated with a dispro-portionate amount of harm. Stockwell (1997) described variation in terms of "risk" within one particular at-risk licence type, namely hotels. This analysis classified 84 hotels located in Perth, Australia, as either high or low-risk based on the number of traffic accidents and drink-driving offences linked to each premises by police. A highly skewed distribution of risk across these hotels was revealed, whereby only a small percentage of the premises were classified as at relatively higher risk for alcohol-related traffic accidents and driving offences. This finding is consistent with other evidence from the USA and Australia. Exam-ining incidents of violent crime in the Milwaukee area between 1986 and 1989, Sherman et al. (1991; cited in Sherman, 1992) showed that only 12% of all taverns produced over half of the 2,019 violent offences reported to police, while 40% of taverns had no violent incidents over the same four-year period. Similar skewed distributions of assaults at licensed premises were also found in the inner Sydney, Newcastle and Wollongong areas of NSW using recorded crime information (Briscoe and Donnelly, 2003a).

Direct observational studies conducted in licensed premises have also confirmed this highly skewed pattern of violence at licensed venues (Homel and Clark, 1994). Further-more, this type of research design has been able to provide valuable insight into some of the characteristics of licensed premises which place them at higher risk for alcohol-related problems. Characteristics of problematic licensed premises identified by these studies in-clude irresponsible alcohol promotions, such as cheap or free drinks; over-crowding; low comfort; poor entertainment; aggressive bouncers or security staff and the service of alcohol to obviously intoxicated patrons (Graham et al., 1980; Homel and Clark, 1994).

Another important risk factor for alcohol-related problems, in the Australian context at least, is that of extended or late trading. From our study of on-premises assaults in inner Sydney, Newcastle and Wollongong, we found that assaults at licensed premises were much more likely to occur during the extended trading period, with the most frequent time being midnight to 3 a.m. (Briscoe and Donnelly, 2003a). Further, when we compared the number of police recorded assaults at Sydney hotels with the extended trading status of these hotels, we found that nearly three-quarters of the most problematic hotels were ones which could trade 24-hours a day. An evaluation of a policy allowing for an extra hour of late night trading at Perth hotels provides further evidence for extended trading being a risk factor for violence. Compared to similar premises that did not adopt late trading, hotels that opened for the extra hour had twice the level of assaults in and around their premises, as well as an increase of almost 40% in alcohol-related road crashes involving their customers (Chikritzhs et al., 1997).

Importantly, however, the increased problems associated with the late trading venues found in the Perth study appear to result from increased alcohol consumption rather than increased opportunity for crime to occur, since there was no apparent difference between the two groups after alcohol sales were controlled for. Subsequent analyses from this research have also shown that the blood alcohol levels (BALs) of drivers in road crashes, who had been drinking at the extended trading premises, were significantly higher than those drinking at the control premises (Chikritzhs and Stockwell, 2002). This evidence, in conjunction with the findings emanating from observational studies, confirms that levels of patron intoxication are an important risk factor for alcohol-related problems associated with licensed venues.

Enforcement of Liquor Laws as a Pivotal Harm Reduction Strategy

While clearly showing that licensed premises are an important setting for alcohol-related crime, the above research also highlights the fact that some venues account for a dispropor-tionate amount of these alcohol-related problems. As discussed above, a factor identified in the alcohol literature as pivotal to this increased risk is patron intoxication. As a conse-quence, initiatives such as the Responsible Service of Alcohol (RSA) have been developed and implemented to minimise harmful outcomes such as aggression, violence and drink-driving. These initiatives aim to reduce the levels of intoxication among patrons of licensed premises through a number of strategies, including avoidance of irresponsible alcohol pro-motions like discounted drinks; training of bar staff to recognise signs of intoxication among patrons; and, importantly, imparting staff with the necessary skills to prevent intoxication or refuse service to patrons if they are already intoxicated (Saltz, 1986).

However, in practice, it is unclear to what extent RSA approaches succeed in achieving their goals. In a review of RSA programmes, Stockwell (2001) reported that initial demon-stration projects conducted in the United States and Canada during the 1980s showed promising results. Attempts to implement such projects at a broader community level, both overseas and in Australia, however, have not resulted in the same level of success, partic-ularly in terms of service refusal to intoxicated persons. Stockwell (2001) argued that one reason for the lack of success in replicating successful RSA outcomes was that there has been less uniform management commitment to RSA in the general community, compared to establishments involved in demonstration projects.

A further factor important to the success of RSA initiatives at the community level is that they need to be supported by effective and visible enforcement of the prevailing liquor laws (Saltz and Stanghetta, 1997). Criminological research has provided a large amount of evidence that increasing the perceived risk of apprehension for an offence can deter individuals from future violations of the law (e.g., Homel, 1988; Nagin, 1998; Sherman et al., 1998). Focusing efforts on enforcement of the liquor laws, particularly those associated with intoxication, thus has the potential to improve compliance of licensed premises staff and, perhaps, increase the commitment of management to RSA-type initiatives. While there have been relatively few studies to date examining the effect of varying levels of enforcement on alcohol-related problems at and around licensed premises, those that have been undertaken present encouraging findings.

Jeffs and Saunders (1983) report the results of a law enforcement initiative at an English seaside resort town in which uniformed police officers visited all licensed premises on a regular basis to overtly check for either underage drinking or acute intoxication among patrons. During the enforcement campaign, public order offences declined by 21% in the intervention town, with no change in arrest rates in the control site. Once the visits were stopped, however, arrest rates for these offences returned to previous levels. Further evidence for the potential role of enforcement in promoting the responsible service of alcohol at licensed premises was provided by an evaluation of a police enforcement initiative in Washtenaw County, Michigan (McKnight and Streff, 1994). This initiative involved plain-clothes officers visiting licensed premises and detecting and breaching bar staff who served obviously intoxicated persons. Although there were relatively few citations and warnings, the percentage of pseudo-drunk patrons who were refused alcohol increased from 18% at baseline to 54% at three-month follow-up (though this fell to 41% by 12-month follow-up). Additionally, the experimental county experienced a marked reduction in the number of persons arrested for drink-driving (from 32% to 23% attributed to licensed premises). A further deterrence-based initiative, which involved feedback from police to licensees about alcohol-related incidents linked to their premises, has recently been trialled in a regional area of NSW, Australia. While the final results from this evaluation have yet to be published, the interim results from this research do appear encouraging (Wiggers, 2003).

Although these studies suggest that there is a clear role for an enforcement component in reducing levels of alcohol-related harm associated with licensed premises, the optimal amount of enforcement activity and the nature of this enforcement still need to be explored. An attempt to replicate the Jeffs and Saunders' trial in Sydney, Australia, which failed to find a positive effect for increased enforcement, highlights the challenges researchers face in experimentally testing the impact of enforcement on alcohol-related harm[1] (Burns et al., 1995). While it is beyond the scope of this discussion to provide a complete overview of different modes of enforcement activity, a clear structural requirement for the development of such initiatives is that adequate and well-integrated information systems be put in place to monitor current levels of enforcement activity.

Information Requirements for Effective Enforcement Activity—Challenges in Practice

In the final section of this chapter we describe a recent investigation of liquor licensing enforcement in NSW which utilised existing information systems. As well as providing a snapshot of current levels of enforcement of the NSW liquor laws relating to intoxication

---

[1] The authors of this study identified several reasons for the nil effect of the intervention, including contamination in the control sites.

among patrons of licensed premises (summarised briefly below), this study has identified a number of critical data quality issues pertaining to enforcement-based information systems in this jurisdiction.

Motivation for this research grew from a previous study we conducted which investigated the extent to which laws prohibiting intoxication at licensed premises in NSW were being adhered to by licensees and bar staff. In this study we surveyed 1,090 18–39-year-olds throughout NSW in order to estimate the prevalence of intoxication among patrons drinking at licensed premises (Donnelly and Briscoe, 2003). Almost 70% of the total sample reported that they had exceeded the Australian national guideline for acute alcohol-related harm at least once during the previous 12 months (60 grams per day for males and 40 grams per day for females). Over 50% of these drinkers reported that the last occasion of such "at-risk" drinking had occurred at a licensed premises. This sub-group of respondents were then asked if they had showed each of the following five signs of intoxication the last time they were drinking at a licensed premises: (1) slurred speech; (2) loud or quarrelsome behaviour; (3) spilling drinks; (4) staggering or falling over and (5) loss of coordination. Crucially, it was found that over half of those respondents whose last occasion of at-risk drinking occurred at a licensed premises reported showing at least one of the five visible signs of intoxication, while almost one in five reported showing at least three of these signs of intoxication.

In this survey, we also investigated whether responsible service of alcohol practices had occurred in response to these signs of intoxication, and found that only 10% of the "intoxicated" patrons reported experiencing responsible service from licensed premises staff on this last at-risk drinking occasion. Instead, the majority of patrons showing signs of intoxication reported that the bar staff simply continued to serve them more alcohol. The worrying levels of consumption reported in this survey are in fact likely to be conservative (rather than exaggerated over-estimates), given the finding from Stockwell et al. (2002) that in Australia, self-reported survey estimates of the amount of alcohol consumed only accounts for around one-half of total per capita alcohol consumption. Given the very high degree of concordance found in this survey between the number of standard drinks respondents reported having consumed and the number of signs of intoxication they reported showing, the intoxication estimates are also likely to be conservative, though clearly at levels of public health concern (Donnelly and Briscoe 2003). Furthermore, while this survey relied upon patrons' own reports of how servers responded to them, the low levels of responsible service provision reported are consistent with estimates obtained for other investigations which utilised the more direct pseudo-intoxicated patron methodology (Saltz and Stanghetta, 1997; Lang et al., 1998). On the basis of these findings, it appeared that compliance with the intoxication provisions of the NSW liquor laws by licensees and bar staff was poor. Thus we were interested in quantifying the extent to which these provisions were being enforced by the relevant authorities in NSW.

In order to achieve this, it was necessary to identify all relevant enforcement modalities and associated data sources in NSW and attempt to consolidate these for the first time. Liquor licensing enforcement in NSW can be distinguished in terms of those matters which are prosecuted in court and those which are dealt with by way of an administrative penalty (e.g., an infringement notice) issued by a law enforcement officer. Information on these types of enforcement action was available from four different sources: (1) the liquor licensing authority, who kept data on matters finalised in the specialist Licensing Court jurisdiction; (2) the NSW Bureau of Crime Statistics and Research (BOCSAR), who had data on matters finalised in more generalised magistrates' courts (Local Courts); (3) the police, who held data on infringement notices issued by their officers; and (4) the compliance division of the liquor licensing authority, who had data on infringement and compliance notices issued by their licensing inspectors (Briscoe and Donnelly, 2003b).

Combining these data, we found that, overall, 4,619 enforcement actions were pursued under the NSW liquor laws in 2001, with police infringement notices comprising over half of these. Offences prosecuted in the courts were the next most frequent type of enforcement action (975 matters), together with penalty and compliance notices issued by the liquor licensing authority (955). However, examining the types of offences pursued under the liquor laws, we found that much enforcement activity was focused on breaches committed by patrons or minors. Over one-quarter of all recorded breaches were against a patron for failing to leave a licensed venue, while a further 14% (681) were against minors. Action taken against licensees and vendors was primarily for breaches of legislative requirements associated with liquor licences. Some 11% of breaches recorded by enforcement agencies were associated with the operation of licences or licensed venues, and the vast majority of these were for failure of licensed premises to display their licence or other required signs.

By contrast, only a very small proportion of enforcement activity was concentrated on licensees or vendors who were in breach of the intoxication provisions of the liquor laws. Only around 3% of all recorded breaches in 2001 were for these conduct offences (Briscoe and Donnelly, 2003b). Furthermore, we found some evidence that when licensees and vendors were prosecuted for liquor offences, the penalties imposed by the courts were minimal. For example, in around one-quarter of all offences proven in the specialised Licensing Court jurisdiction, the defendant was dismissed with no conviction recorded against them. Where fines were imposed on licensees by the Licensing Court, they were on average substantially less in monetary value than would have been the case if a penalty notice had been issued for the offence in lieu of prosecution.

This investigation, in conjunction with our earlier survey work, demonstrates that there exists a relatively low risk of formal action being taken against licensed premises for breaches of the intoxication provisions. Furthermore, where action is successful for intoxication-related offences, minor penalties often ensue. Given that high levels of intoxication are predictive of harmful outcomes associated with licensed premises, this finding in itself is of some concern.

However, what is perhaps more apparent from our research in this area is the disparate nature of the available data on enforcement actions that are initiated under the NSW liquor laws. This would undoubtedly hinder any attempts by enforcement agencies to monitor liquor licensing enforcement activity on a regular basis, as well as prevent the tracking of offenders who are repeatedly in breach of the liquor laws. For regulation of licensed premises to be intelligence-driven in this jurisdiction, a number of data quality issues would need to be addressed. First, for the current information systems to inform enforcement practice, integration of the various databases would need to occur. As well as the obvious lack of any physical link between these systems, a major limitation is the absence of standardised coding for offences. Each of the four data sources we accessed utilised different offence coding systems and it was necessary to undertake major recoding of the data in order to provide a comparable breakdown of where the balance of enforcement practice currently lies. For queries on the levels of total law enforcement practice to be undertaken quickly, and in real time, by enforcement agencies, an online system would need to be developed which integrated the four data sources and employed a standardised set of offence codes.

Second, within the current information systems there is no means, other than manually, to readily identify those licensed premises which are repeatedly found to be in breach of the liquor laws. This limitation is particularly pertinent with respect to police infringement notice data, given that there is no field on these penalty notices for recording the licence number of premises where the breach occurred. These notices contain the personal details of the offender only and not any uniquely identifying information related to the licensed premises. This makes it difficult to identify those premises which have received numerous infringement notices for repeatedly breaching the liquor laws. In addition to aiding enforcement agencies, an information system which enabled the ready identification of such problematic premises would be extremely useful for judicial officers when considering the degree of appropriate sanctioning.

CONCLUSION

There is a body of research showing that licensed premises are an important situational risk factor for alcohol-related crime, and that some licensed premises, in particular, are at much higher risk than others. Research also indicates that a strong enforcement component is necessary to improve compliance with liquor laws, particularly those relating to patron intoxication. The clear implication of these findings is that limited law enforcement and crime prevention initiatives can be strategically targeted to those times and places which are at much greater risk for alcohol-related crime. Such targeting can be greatly facilitated by having in place well integrated and comprehensive information systems which enable the identification of those licensed premises which are repeatedly in breach of the liquor licensing laws.

In NSW a number of distinct sources of such data have been identified. Our descriptive analyses of these have identified that there is an acute need to better integrate these information systems for the purposes of targeting harm minimisation initiatives. Potential for improvements include establishing physical links between these systems, standardising offence codes and specifically coding for the licensed premises where an infringement notice has been issued. Such integration would necessarily require high levels of inter-sectoral cooperation and coordination across the various enforcement and judicial agencies in this jurisdiction.

ACKNOWLEDGEMENTS

The authors would like to gratefully acknowledge the Drug Programs Bureau, NSW Health for providing funding for the collaborative research venture into alcohol-related crime between the NSW Bureau of Crime Statistics and Research (BOCSAR) and the National Drug Research Institute (NDRI). We would also like to acknowledge the invaluable level of support given to this Project by Dr Don Weatherburn, Director, BOCSAR and Professor Tim Stockwell, Director, NDRI.

REFERENCES

Australian Bureau of Statistics (1999) *Crime and Safety, Australia, April 1998*. ABS Catalogue No. 4509.0, Canberra: Australian Bureau of Statistics.

Briscoe, S. and Donnelly, N. (2001) Temporal and regional aspects of alcohol-related violence and disorder. *Alcohol Studies Bulletin*, No. 1, Sydney: NSW Bureau of Crime Statistics and Research.

Briscoe, S. and Donnelly, N. (2003a) Problematic licensed premises for assaults in inner Sydney, Newcastle and Wollongong. *Australian and New Zealand Journal of Criminology*, **36**, 18–33.

Briscoe, S. and Donnelly, N. (2003b) Liquor licensing enforcement activity in New South Wales. *Alcohol Studies Bulletin*, No. 4, Sydney: NSW Bureau of Crime Statistics and Research.

Burns, L., Flaherty, B., Ireland, S. and Frances, M. (1995) Policing pubs: what happens to crime? *Drug and Alcohol Review*, **14**, 369–375.

Chikritzhs, T. and Stockwell, T.R. (2002) The impact of later trading hours for Australian public houses (hotels) on levels of violence. *Journal of Studies on Alcohol*, **63**, 591–599.

Chikritzhs, T., Stockwell, T. and Masters, L. (1997) *Evaluation of the Public Health and Safety Impact of Extended Trading Permits for Perth Hotels and Nightclubs*. Perth, WA: National Centre for Research into the Prevention of Drug Abuse, Curtin University.

Donnelly, N. and Briscoe, S. (2003) Signs of intoxication and server intervention among 18–39-year-olds drinking at licensed premises in New South Wales, Australia. *Addiction*, **98**, 1287–1295.

Gorman, D.M., Speer, P.W. and Gruenewald, P.J. (2001) Spatial dynamics of alcohol availability, neighborhood structure and violent crime. *Journal of Studies on Alcohol*, **62**, 628–636.

Graham, K., LaRoque, L., Yetman, R., Ross, T.J. and Guistra, E. (1980) Aggression and bar room environments. *Journal of Studies on Alcohol*, **41**, 277–292.

Homel, R. (1988) *Policing and Punishing the Drinking Driver: A Study of General and Specific Deterrence*. New York: Springer–Verlag.

Homel, R. and Clark, J. (1994) The prediction and prevention of violence in pubs and clubs. In R.V. Clarke (ed.), *Crime Prevention Studies*. Vol. 3. Monsey, NY: Criminal Justice Press.

Jeffs, B.W. and Saunders, W.M. (1983) Minimizing alcohol related offences by enforcement of the existing licensing legislation. *British Journal of Addiction*, **78**, 67–77.

Jochelson, R. (1997) *Crime and Place: An Analysis of Assaults and Robberies in Inner Sydney*. Sydney: NSW Bureau of Crime Statistics and Research.

Lang, E., Stockwell, T., Rydon, P. and Beel, A.C. (1998) Can training bar staff in responsible serving practices reduce alcohol-related harm? *Drug and Alcohol Review*, **17**, 39–50.

Lipton, R. and Gruenewald, P. (2002) The spatial dynamics of violence and alcohol outlets. *Journal of Studies on Alcohol*, **63**, 187–195.

McKnight, A.J. and Streff, F.M. (1994) The effect of enforcement upon service of alcohol to intoxicated patrons of bars and restaurants. *Accident Analysis and Prevention*, **26**, 79–88.

Nagin, D.S. (1998) Criminal deterrence research at the outset of the 21st century. In M. Tonry (ed.), *Crime and Justice: A Review of the Research*. Vol. 25. Chicago: University of Chicago Press, pp. 1–42.

Saltz, R.F. (1986) Server intervention: will it work? *Alcohol Health and Research World*, **10**, 13–19.

Saltz, R.F. and Stanghetta P. (1997) A community-wide Responsible Beverage Service program in three communities: early findings. *Addiction*, **92**, S237–S249.

Scribner, R., Mackinnon, D. and Dwyer, J. (1995) The risk of assaultive violence and alcohol availability in Los Angeles County. *American Journal of Public Health*, **85**, 335–340.

Sherman, L.W. (1992) Attacking crime: police and crime control. In M. Tonry and N. Morris (eds), *Modern Policing*. Chicago: University of Chicago Press.

Sherman, L.W., Gottfredson, D., MacKenzie, D., Eck, J., Reuter, P. and Bushway, S. (1998) *Preventing Crime: What Works, What Doesn't, What's Promising?* Washington, DC: National Institute of Justice.

Stevenson, R.J., Lind, B. and Weatherburn, D. (1999) The relationship between alcohol sales and assault in New South Wales, Australia. *Addiction*, **94**, 397–410.

Stockwell, T. (1997) Regulation of the licensed drinking environment: a major opportunity for crime prevention. In R. Homel (ed.), *Policing for Prevention: Reducing Crime, Public Intoxication and Injury*. Monsey, NY: Criminal Justice Press.

Stockwell, T. (2001) Responsible alcohol service: lessons from evaluations of server training and policing initiatives. *Drug and Alcohol Review*, **20**, 257–265.

Stockwell, T.R., Heale, P., Chikritzhs, T.N., Dietze, P. and Catalano, P. (2002) How much alcohol is drunk in Australia in excess of the new Australian alcohol guidelines? *Medical Journal of Australia*, **176**, 91–92.

Teece, M. and Williams, P. (2000) Alcohol-related assault: time and place. In *Trends and Issues in Crime and Criminal Justice*, no. 169, Canberra: Australian Institute of Criminology.

Wiggers, J. (2003) Problem-oriented policing: an alternative approach to reducing alcohol-related harm associated with alcohol consumption on licensed premises. Paper presented at the Kettil Bruun Society Thematic Meeting. Preventing substance use, risky use and harm: What is evidence-based policy? Fremantle, Western Australia, 24–27 February.

5.4 Deterrence Theory and the Limitations of Criminal Penalties for Cannabis Use

SIMON LENTON

National Drug Research Institute, Curtin University of Technology, Western Australia

SUMMARY

When policy-makers think about how to encourage people to adhere to the law, they often think about increasing the certainty and severity of punishment. Most criminological research on deterrence has shown that the certainty of apprehension, rather than the severity of punishment, is more likely to produce deterrence. However, the likelihood of being apprehended for a minor cannabis offence is so low that it is unlikely that variables such as certainty, celerity, or severity will have much impact on use. This chapter summarises the research literature on deterrence and employs data from Australian research on the social impacts of a conviction for a minor cannabis offence to explain why criminal penalties are not a major deterrent to cannabis use. It shows, however, that the social impacts of receiving a criminal conviction for such an offence can be considerable. A range of other variables such as public attitudes to cannabis use, the perceived fairness of the law and its enforcement, peer influences, and the utility of cannabis use are likely to far outweigh the deterrent value of a criminal conviction. In Australia, civil penalties are supported by the majority of the public, are more likely to be viewed as just by those apprehended, use fewer criminal justice resources and are no worse at deterring cannabis use than is strict prohibition with criminal penalties schemes. It concludes that the application of the criminal law to prevent cannabis use is an inefficient and ineffective use of valuable and scarce criminal justice resources. Rather, prohibition with civil penalties should maintain any general deterrent effect while reducing individual and community costs of conviction. Criminal justice savings should be directed towards accurate, balanced public education campaigns on the harms of cannabis and how these can be reduced, dissuading use, especially among the young and others most at risk of harm, and offering treatment responses attractive to cannabis users experiencing problems with their use.

Preventing Harmful Substance Use: The Evidence Base for Policy and Practice.
Edited by T. Stockwell, P. J. Gruenewald, J.W. Toumbourou and W. Loxley.
© 2005 John Wiley & Sons, Ltd. ISBN 0-470-09227-0 (hbk) 0-470-09228-9 (pbk).

INTRODUCTION

The theoretical underpinning of much of our criminal law in general, and our drug law in particular, is *classical deterrence theory* which asserts that "undesirable behaviour can be curtailed if punishment is sufficiently certain, swift, and severe" (Schneider and Ervin, 1990: 585–586). Like much traditional social theory, deterrence theory comes from an instrumental perspective in that it assumes that behaviour is motivated by rewards and punishments in the immediate external environment (Tyler, 1990).

Modern deterrence theory (e.g., Becker, 1968; Andenaes, 1974; Gibbs, 1985) is an off-shoot of the rational-choice paradigm which asserts that people choose to act rationally in ways that will maximise their expected utility (MacCoun, 1993). Punishment certainty, severity and celerity, proportionality, and specific and general deterrence, remain at the core of modern deterrence theory. Most deterrence theory research focuses on two aspects: the certainty and severity of legal punishments (MacCoun, 1993).

General and Specific Deterrence

Although criticised for their oversimplification (e.g., Stafford and Warr, 1993), two types of deterrence effects have been identified—*general* deterrence which is the prevention of criminal activity by others, and *specific* deterrence, the dissuasion of law breakers from further offending (Tyler, 1990). Deterrence can be absolute, or marginal. Marginal deterrence occurs when an offender commits a less harmful, rather than a more harmful act, because the expected punishment associated with the latter act exceeds that for the former.

According to Tyler (1990) increasing the certainty and severity of punishment for committing a crime has frequently been viewed as an effective way of reducing the rate at which the crime is committed. He notes that when policy-makers think about how to obtain compliance, they often implicitly adopt an instrumental perspective. Schneider and Ervin point out that "many citizens and public officials have an amazing faith in punishment and believe that public problems can be solved by outlawing the offending behaviour and specifying its punishment" (1990: 586). In contrast to the instrumental perspective, the normative perspective is concerned with the influence of what people regard as *just* and *moral* as opposed to what is in their *self-interest*. The normative approach also examines the connection between normative commitment to legal authorities and law-abiding behaviour (Tyler, 1990).

DETERRENCE THEORY AND DRUG LAW

The goal of law-makers and law enforcers to increase adherence to the law is no different with respect to those laws that apply to drug use. Deterrence theory is relevant to the drug law debate as it predicts that if "decriminalisation" (the application of civil rather than criminal penalties) or "legalisation" were to reduce the perceived certainty or severity of legal penalties, then drug use would become more prevalent (MacCoun, 1993). The section below summarises the literature in relation to this and related issues.

Research on Deterrence Effects

Despite the prevalence of deterrence theory in academic and popular understandings of the law in society, research and theory in criminology and sociology have called into question deterrence theory and its apparent over-dependence on legal penalties. Since the early

1970s deterrence research has employed three major methodological approaches: (1) natural experiments; (2) ecological comparisons based on available data; and (3) perception/self-report surveys of individuals. One of the major fields of enquiry has been the relationship between perceptions of the certainty and severity of penalties, and self-reported involvement in illegal activities. Although there are some inconsistencies, the general conclusion to be reported in the early literature was that individuals' perceptions of the likelihood that they would be punished for an offence, although not their expectations of punishment severity, deter further offending (Saltzman et al., 1982). However, there were significant methodological problems with this early research, the most serious of which related to the problem of causal ordering. Cross-sectional (one-wave) designs were the standard method of investigating the perceptual deterrence hypothesis that those who perceived the likelihood of being apprehended for a particular offence as *high*, would be *less likely* to commit that offence. All but a handful of these studies correlated the respondent's perceptions of sanction risk with self-reported measure of *past* criminal behaviour collected at the same time as the perceptions. But later research (e.g. Saltzman et al., 1982) confirmed that as the behaviour occurred *before* the measurement of perceptions, what the research was actually describing was an "experiential" effect. That is, rather than showing that those who thought it was likely that they would get caught were less likely to engage in illegal behaviour, it showed that those who had engaged in a high level of illegal behaviour had learned that the likelihood of getting caught was low. Thus, much of the early deterrence research that was used as evidence for one of the core tenets of classical deterrence theory, actually showed the opposite.

Reviews of Deterrence Literature

A number of reviews of the deterrence literature have been conducted. Some of these (e.g., MacCoun, 1993) have been reviews of the literature as a whole. More selective reviews have also been conducted of the perceptual deterrence literature (e.g., Williams and Hawkins, 1986), aggregate studies (e.g., Demers and Lundman, 1987), policy impact studies (e.g., Cook, 1980), specific deterrence studies (e.g., Smith and Gartin, 1989), studies of specific populations such as juvenile criminals (Schneider and Ervin, 1990) and drink-driving offenders (Homel, 1988). It should be noted that cannabis use has often been used in the literature as a model offence of study. As a consequence there is considerable research on the deterrence of cannabis.

The main findings of these reviews are as follows:

- In both macro and micro studies the effects of the severity of penalties are inconsistent and usually only small when present (Smith and Gartin, 1989; MacCoun et al., 1993).
- Macro, population-based, criminal opportunity studies have tended to find results for the certainty, but not for the severity, of punishment, but severity is more likely to matter when punishment is highly probable (MacCoun et al., 1993).
- There is considerable evidence that, as a whole, the criminal justice system prevents crime, but evidence regarding the link between intended and actual policy is limited, so it is difficult to determine whether a specific change in policy will add to any deterrent effect (Nagin, 1998).
- Most individual perceptual deterrence studies find an inverse relationship between the perceived certainty of penalty and frequency of self-reported offences, but the direction of causation is unclear (Gibbs, 1985; Williams and Hawkins, 1986; Demers and Lundman, 1987; Schneider and Ervin, 1990), consistent with the experiential hypothesis.

- With regards to cannabis, certainty and severity effects are generally small and account for less than 5% of the variance in use (MacCoun, 1993).
- Two-wave perceptual studies have shown that perceptions of the likelihood and severity of formal penalties explain little or no variance in self-reports of cannabis use (Demers and Lundman, 1987).
- Experienced offenders generally perceive penalties as less likely than the non-offending general public (MacCoun, 1993).
- Panel studies of general deterrence have consistently found that perceptions of legal penalties are unstable and considerably smaller than found in early cross-sectional studies (Williams and Hawkins, 1986). This is unsurprising as the public has little direct knowledge of the details of law and its enforcement (MacCoun, 1993).
- Research points to the significance of informal as opposed to formal controls. For example, when non-legal social sanctions such as those from peers were included in the models used, in most cases, the perceived certainty or severity of formal legal sanctions became statistically non-significant (Williams and Hawkins, 1986).
- There is also suggestive evidence about the contexts in which deterrent threats can foster defiance (Sherman and Smith, 1992) or stigmatisation (Makkai and Braithwaite, 1994) that actually increase crime (Braithwaite, 1993).
- Although the expected risks and rewards undoubtedly influence decision-making, much evidence suggests people do not combine information in the way expected utility theories assert, and that as behaviour becomes over-learned, it becomes less reasoned and more automatic (MacCoun, 1993).
- Macro studies show an overall negative correlation between the objective certainty of legal penalties and the crime rate, but it is unclear whether high certainty leads to low crime rates, or whether a high crime rate overloads the justice system and produces low certainty of apprehension (Gibbs, 1985).
- Macro studies suggest that increasing the severity of penalties can undermine the deterrence effects of penalty severity as defendants fight cases more aggressively and courts become more lenient in sentencing (Cook, 1980; MacCoun, 1993).
- Macro studies show that variations in rates of different types of crime are largely a function of changes in social disapproval of crimes and not the perceived certainty and severity of penalty (Gibbs, 1985).
- Macro policy impact studies show that more severe drink-driving laws have a deterrent effect but the effect is generally short-lived and the problem quickly returns to baseline (MacCoun, 1993).
- Drink-driving recidivism rates are largely unaffected by the type or quantity of penalty. The exception to this is licence disqualification which may be an effective deterrent, especially for non alcohol-related offences (Homel, 1988).

A review of 19 articles on deterrence of cannabis use (both specific and general deterrence) and 17 articles on specific deterrence published since 1980 led to the following conclusions:

- Severity of penalties has almost always failed to predict cannabis use.
- The certainty of penalty is not a good predictor of cannabis use.
- Evidence of specific deterrence effects is rare, and when it occurs, it is often among those who are less likely to take risks and have the most to lose such as inexperienced offenders and cannabis users, the employed, and women.

- Conversely, those who may be more entrenched in cannabis use or other offending, and may possibly benefit most from reducing crime or use, are least likely to change their behaviour after punishment.
- Extra-legal factors, such as peer attitudes, the perceived morality of the act, and sense of citizenship, have emerged as better predictors of both cannabis use and other offending.
- Cannabis use prior to punishment is the best predictor of use after punishment, highlighting the lack of deterrent effect of punishments.
- Specific deterrence effects are most likely where offenders do not have a history of offending without getting caught (i.e., punishment avoidance).

THE IMPACT OF CANNABIS "DECRIMINALISATION" ON THE GENERAL DETERRENCE OF CANNABIS USE

A handful of policy impact studies have been undertaken on "natural experiments" where minor cannabis offences have been "decriminalised". Taken as a whole, this research fails to find that removing criminal penalties for cannabis possession and use results in higher rates of cannabis use in the general community.

Eleven US States "decriminalised" cannabis during the 1970s. Four controlled studies conducted on these examples provide strong evidence for the view that those States which removed criminal penalties did not experience greater increases in cannabis use among adults or adolescents, nor more favourable attitudes towards the drug, than those States which maintained strict prohibition against cannabis possession and use (Single et al., 2000).

The Australian research on the impact of the South Australian Cannabis Expiation Notice (CEN) system concluded that the observed increase in lifetime use by South Australian adults was not likely to be due to the CEN scheme; rates of recent (weekly) use, and rates of use among young adults and school students had not increased at a greater rate in South Australia than other States which had not changed their laws (Donnelly et al., 2000). The CEN system is an example of a prohibition with civil penalties scheme. Under such schemes the possession and use of cannabis remain illegal and civil penalties such as infringement notices and fines apply. If fines are paid prior to a due date, there are no *criminal* consequences, such as acquiring a criminal record. Typically, under such schemes, large-scale cultivation and supply of cannabis remain subject to criminal sanctions.

In Europe, a cross-national comparison between the Netherlands, other European states and the USA shows that, despite the introduction of cannabis coffeeshops, the Dutch do not have higher rates of cannabis use than these other countries (MacCoun and Reuter, 1997). However, while reductions in criminal penalties in the Netherlands from 1976 to 1992 have had only limited effects on cannabis use, the increase in commercial access to cannabis in the Netherlands from 1992 to 1996 with the growth in numbers of cannabis coffeeshops has been associated with growth in the cannabis-using population, including among young people (MacCoun and Reuter, 1997, 2001a). In follow-up published correspondence these authors suggest that the use of prohibition with civil penalties, rather than partial prohibition with increasing commercialisation of the cannabis industry through a coffeeshop system, might meet the same goals with fewer risks (MacCoun and Reuter, 2001b).

SPECIFIC DETERRENCE, SOCIAL IMPACTS, AND THE ECONOMIC COSTS OF CONVICTION VERSUS INFRINGEMENT NOTICE SCHEMES

In a comparison of the social impacts of a conviction under strict cannabis prohibition in Western Australia (WA), with that of an infringement notice under the CEN system in South Australia (SA), Lenton et al. (2000) compared the experiences of 68 first offenders in each of SA and WA. There were no significant differences between the groups regarding the impact of the CEN or conviction on respondents' drug use. Neither the CEN nor the cannabis conviction appeared to have much impact on subsequent cannabis use. For example, 91% of the SA infringement notice group and 71% of the WA group said that their cannabis use was not at all affected by their apprehension one month after. Rates of post-apprehension cannabis use were highly correlated with rates of use prior to apprehension, consistent with other research.

However, there were differential impacts in terms of the social impacts on those receiving a conviction versus an infringement notice. While 32% of WA respondents identified at least one negative employment consequence related to their cannabis conviction (including failing to get a job, losing a job or ceasing to apply for jobs requiring a criminal record check), only one (2%) of the expiators identified one consequence that was related to their CEN (Lenton et al., 2000). Some 32% of the WA group compared to none of the SA group reported subsequent criminal justice consequences of their cannabis apprehension (including subsequent further attention by police, and further charges) and this did not appear to be due to possible confounders. There was a significant difference between the groups in terms of the negative relationship consequences of conviction or CEN. Only 5% of the SA expiator group identified any negative relationship consequences of their CEN, while 20% of the WA group identified at least one negative relationship event related to their cannabis conviction (including family disputes and stress in their primary relationship). None of the respondents in the SA expiator group identified any negative accommodation consequences but 16% of the WA sample did so (being forced to change accommodation and losing work-provided accommodation when they lost their job). There was no significant difference between the groups in terms of negative travel effects of conviction or CEN. None of the expiators and five of the WA sample (7%) identified at least one negative travel consequence (including unsuccessful applications for visas or being denied entry at the border), and a further 9% of the WA group were very concerned about this possibility in the future. It appeared that the time from apprehension to interview (average 38 months) may not have been long enough for travel effects to be evident in a large enough number of the convicted sample to result in a significant finding (Lenton et al., 2000).

With regards to the economic costs of a strict prohibition with criminal penalties approach against a prohibition with civil penalties model, estimates unanimously favour the latter over the former. It seems that the savings in criminal justice resources due to "decriminalisation" are greater the larger the jurisdiction. Thus California was estimated to save over $US100 million per year in state judicial resources in the ten years post-decriminalisation (Aldrich and Mikuriya, 1988) and in South Australia savings were estimated at $A1.3 million per year (Brooks et al., 1999).

CANNABIS, DETERRENCE AND THE LIKELIHOOD OF APPREHENSION

The importance of normative factors such as public acceptance of the law and a moral commitment to a particular law are likely to be more relevant in situations where the likelihood of being apprehended is low—less than about 30% according to Tittle and Rowe (1974, cited in Silberman, 1976). Based on household survey and police arrest data, it has been estimated that in 1993 some 200,000 West Australians used cannabis in that year and there were approximately 2,500 distinct persons whose most serious offence was a minor cannabis offence (2,038 possess or use cannabis and 420 implement offences) (Lenton, 2000). This means that in that year, the likelihood of a cannabis user being convicted of a minor cannabis offence in WA was approximately 1.25%) (Lenton, 2000). Given the number of episodes of use of the typical cannabis user in one year, the risk per episode of use is probably less than 0.01%. It is clear that even if Tittle and Rowe grossly over-estimated that the probability of apprehension for effective deterrence should be at least 30%, and there is no reason to believe that they did, the likelihood of apprehension for a minor cannabis offence is probably far less than this. Even taking into account that deterrence, when it occurs, is undoubtedly more about *perceptions* of sanction risk, rather than *actual* sanction risk, the actual sanction risk for minor cannabis offences is probably very low. It is hard to imagine how, without massed urine testing or placing a police officer in every living room, the likelihood of detection could be increased to a level where a deterrence effect is probable. The evidence thus points to the need to address non-legal, normative factors which impinge on the effectiveness of these cannabis laws.

NON-DETERRENCE FACTORS INFLUENCING COMPLIANCE WITH THE LAW

The research evidence suggests that, while deterrence theory is not without some empirical support, there are likely to be a range of other factors affecting the extent to which drug laws are obeyed. These include normative variables such as public attitudes to use, the perceived fairness of the law and its enforcement, peer influences, and the utility of cannabis use which are likely to far outweigh the deterrent value of a criminal conviction.

Extent to which the Illegal Behaviour is Accepted in the General Community

Sarat (1977) pointed to the importance of public opinion in understanding the application and interpretation of the law and its ability to regulate conduct. Despite the proscription of cannabis use in all Australian jurisdictions, most recent data suggests that 33% of Australians have ever used cannabis and 13% have used it in the last year (Australian Institute of Health and Welfare, 2002). Furthermore, there is now a great deal of research which shows that, in Australia, the majority of the general public do not support the application of criminal (as opposed to civil) penalties for minor cannabis offences. National and state-wide surveys of the Australian public conducted since the early 1990s suggest that while support for cannabis legalisation remains under 40% (Bowman and Sanson-Fisher, 1994;

Lenton and Ovenden, 1996; Australian Institute of Health and Welfare, 1999), more than 70% believe that civil, rather than criminal penalties should apply to minor cannabis offences (Bowman and Sanson-Fisher, 1994; Lenton and Ovenden, 1996). In sum, the widespread community support for the removal of criminal penalties for minor cannabis offences is likely to undermine adherence to the criminal law.

Social Acceptance in Referent Population (Peers)

With respect to cannabis use, a number of studies have found that peer attitudes to cannabis use were stronger determinants of use of the drug than were perceptions about the likelihood of sanction (e.g., Demers and Lundman, 1987). It is probably not surprising that peer attitudes are a powerful influence on offending behaviour; however, what is important is that most research suggests that they are far more powerful than perceptions of the risk of legal sanction. In our own research with cannabis users convicted for the first time, some 78% of the sample said that "the majority" or "all or nearly all" of their friends used cannabis in the six months prior to their offence and some 57% had family or friends who had been charged with a cannabis offence (Lenton and Heale, 2000).

Drug Use and Offending History—Punishment Avoidance

Stafford and Warr (1993) have noted that most of the time, people who commit crime do not get punished and that the avoidance of punishment is likely to affect perceptions of the certainty and severity of punishment. There is some evidence showing that punishment avoidance does more to encourage crime than punishment does to discourage it. For example Apospori et al. (1992) found that violating the law reduced the perceived risk of punishment most strongly for those who have more experience with being arrested and convicted for committing crimes. The most plausible explanation for this is that those with more extensive histories of criminal justice sanctions may also have a far more extensive history of offending without being apprehended. If punishment avoidance does indeed undermine deterrence, then the experience of convicted cannabis users would suggest that deterrence effects are unlikely. In our study of convicted cannabis users, 44% used the drug daily and 29% weekly in the four weeks prior to arrest. Despite the fact that this was only their first conviction for a cannabis, or any other, offence, the majority of the sample were an experienced, rather than a naïve cannabis using group (Lenton and Heale, 2000). Similarly, with regards to punishment avoidance, given that on average, the sample had been using cannabis for more than six years at the time of their first arrest, most had probably used the drug many hundreds, if not thousands, of times prior to their apprehension. Thus it is likely that their apprehension did little to undermine their belief that punishment risk was low.

Extent to Which the Individual's Values are Consistent with the Law

Previous research had shown that attitudes toward particular laws, and specifically cannabis laws, were the most powerful predictors of substance use (e.g., Paternoster and Piquero, 1995). Lenton et al. (2000) found no differences between the SA expiator group and WA convicted groups on their attitudes to the law in general, cannabis laws in particular, and the role of police. The majority of both groups saw themselves as largely law-abiding and had respect for the role of police as law enforcers and the rule of law in general but they also shared a lack of support for punitive drug laws, and had a high level of support for the legalisation of cannabis.

Experience of Law Enforcement when Apprehended—Justice and Respect

How an offender is treated at the point of apprehension also seems to affect subsequent compliance. According to Sherman (1993), people obey the law more when they believe that it is administered fairly than when they believe it is not. Research shows that respect for the law and future compliance with it are affected by whether the offender believes that they have been treated fairly (Tyler, 1990) and respectfully (Makkai and Braithwaite, 1994) at the point of apprehension. In our comparative study of the impact of arrest and conviction for a minor cannabis offence under strict prohibition in Western Australia with the impact of an infringement notice under the civil penalty scheme in place in South Australia (Lenton et al., 2000), we found that 49% of the WA group, compared with only 18% of the SA expiators, said that they had become less trusting of police, and 43% of the WA group, compared to 15% of the SA expiators, were more fearful of police as a result. The greater loss of trust in the WA sample appeared in part due to the greater number of that group who were apprehended in a private residence, but did not appear to be due to other possible confounders. Whether this was the result of an increased sense of violation from having police search one's home, or because more of these arrests were drug-related, rather than incidental, is unclear. There was a non-significant trend for fewer of the WA group to say police respected their rights when they were apprehended (32% vs 52%), and for more of the WA sample to say they had become less respectful of police as a result of their apprehension (40% vs 15%).

The extent to which such effects would result in more compliance with the cannabis laws under civil penalty schemes as opposed to strict prohibition is unclear, particularly given the extent to which they are *mala prohibita* (proscribed by laws but not by public mores). However, these findings suggest there are good reasons to favour a prohibition with civil penalties scheme over the prohibition with criminal penalty scheme on the basis of maintaining respect for the law and its officers.

Experience of Sentencing

As Homel (1988) has argued, there are two main factors in the experience of sentencing: sentence *severity*, and the *fairness* of the penalty. According to Tyler (1990), those facing court are more likely to be compliant with the law if they believe that the court has listened to their arguments and considered them; what he refers to as "procedural fairness". Our study of convicted cannabis offenders found 75% thought their penalty was "too harsh" and 82% saw their sentence as "unjust" although 66% thought it was customary for their kind of offence. Furthermore, while 70% of those who appeared in court were given an opportunity to speak on their own behalf, in only 16% of cases did respondents feel that their comments had been taken seriously (Lenton et al., 1999).

CONCLUSION

A review of the criminological research on deterrence suggests that policy-makers and law enforcers are being overly optimistic if they believe that applying criminal penalties for minor cannabis users will effectively deter use of the drug. However, the social impacts on those convicted and the economic costs of criminal penalty schemes can be considerable. It is not surprising that criminal penalties do little to deter cannabis use in the community generally, or among users themselves. Deterrence effects are likely to be undermined by a low likelihood of apprehension; low levels of public support for criminal penalties; attitudes of those apprehended and their peers which are very positive toward cannabis; and significant punishment avoidance effects, especially for experienced users. As it is difficult to increase classical deterrence factors (especially the likelihood of apprehension and swiftness of punishment), policy-makers, law enforcers and the judiciary should attend to legitimacy factors. Where illegality of cannabis is maintained, but civil rather than criminal penalties are applied, there is no evidence that this has resulted in increased prevalence of use. In Australia, civil penalties are supported by the majority of the public, are more likely to be viewed as just by those apprehended, use fewer criminal justice resources and are no worse at deterring cannabis use than is strict prohibition with criminal penalties schemes. Jurisdictions which maintain criminal penalties for minor cannabis offences would do well to consider the evidence which favours employing civil, rather than criminal, penalties for these offences. Criminal justice savings should be directed towards accurate, balanced public education campaigns on the harms of cannabis and how these can be reduced, dissuading use, especially among the young and others most at risk of harm, and offering treatment responses attractive to cannabis users experiencing problems with their use.

REFERENCES

Aldrich, M.R. and Mikuriya, T. (1988) Savings in California law enforcement costs attributable to the Moscone Act of 1976—a summary. *Journal of Drug Issues*, **20**, 75–81.

Andenaes, J. (1974) *Punishment and Deterrence*, Ann Arbor, MI: University of Michigan Press.

Apospori, E., Alpert, G.P. and Paternoster, R. (1992) The effect of involvement with the criminal justice system: a neglected dimension of the relationship between experience and perceptions. *Justice Quarterly*, **9**(3), 379–392.

Australian Institute of Health and Welfare (1999) *1998 National Drug Strategy Household Survey— First Results*, Canberra: AIHW.

Australian Institute of Health and Welfare (2002) *2001 National Drug Strategy Household Survey— First Results*, Canberra: AIHW.

Becker, G. (1968) Crime and punishment: an economic approach. *Journal of Political Economy*, **76**, 169–217.

Bowman, J. and Sanson-Fisher, R. (1994) *Public Perceptions of Cannabis Legislation: National Drug Strategy*. Monograph Series No. 28, Canberra: Australian Government Printing Service.

Braithwaite, J. (1993) Beyond positivism: learning from contextual integrated strategies. *Journal of Research in Crime and Delinquency*, **30**, 383–399.

Brooks, A., Stothard, C., Moss, J., Christie, P. and Ali, R. (1999) *Costs Associated with the Operation of the Cannabis Expiation Notice Scheme in South Australia*. Adelaide: Adelaide Drug and Alcohol Services Council.

Cook, P. (1980) Research in criminal deterrence: laying the groundwork for the second decade. In N. Morris and M. Tonry (eds), *Crime and Justice: An Annual Review of Research*, Vol. 2. Chicago: University of Chicago Press, pp. 201–234.

Demers, D.K. and Lundman, R.J. (1987) Perceptual deterrence research: some additional evidence for designing studies. *Journal of Quantitative Criminology*, **3**, 185–194.

Donnelly, N., Hall, W. and Christie, P. (2000) The effects of the CEN scheme on levels and patterns of cannabis use in South Australia: evidence from National Drug Strategy Household Surveys 1985–95. *Drug and Alcohol Review*, **19**, 265–269.

Gibbs, J. (1985) Deterrence theory and research. *Nebraska Symposium on Motivation*, **33**, 87–130.

Homel, R. (1988) *Policing and Punishing the Drinking Driver*. New York: Springer-Verlag.

Lenton, S. (2000) Cannabis policy and the burden of proof: is it now beyond reasonable doubt that cannabis prohibition is not working? *Drug and Alcohol Review*, **19**, 95–100.

Lenton, S. and Heale, P. (2000) Arrest, court and social impacts of conviction for a minor cannabis offence under strict prohibition. *Contemporary Drug Problems*, **27**, 805–833.

Lenton, S. and Ovenden, C. (1996) Community attitudes to cannabis use in Western Australia. *Journal of Drug Issues*, **16**, 783–804.

Lenton, S., Bennett, M. and Heale, P. (1999) *The Social Impact of a Minor Cannabis Offence Under Strict Prohibition: The Case of Western Australia*. Perth: National Centre for Research into the Prevention of Drug Abuse, Curtin University of Technology.

Lenton, S., Humeniuk, R., Heale, P. and Christie, P. (2000) Infringement versus conviction: the social impact of a minor cannabis offence in SA and WA. *Drug and Alcohol Review*, **19**, 257–264.

MacCoun, R.J. (1993) Drugs and the law: a psychological analysis of drug prohibition. *Psychological Bulletin*, **113**, 487–512.

MacCoun, R. and Reuter, P. (1997) Interpreting Dutch cannabis policy: reasoning by analogy in the legalisation debate. *Science*, **278**, 47–52.

MacCoun, R. and Reuter, P. (2001a) Evaluating alternative cannabis regimes. *British Journal of Psychiatry*, **178**, 123–128.

MacCoun, R. and Reuter, P. (2001b) Cannabis regimes: a response. *British Journal of Psychiatry*, **179**, 369–370.

MacCoun, R.J., Kahan, J.P., Gillespie, J. and Rhee, J. (1993) A content analysis of the drug legalisation debate. *Journal of Drug Issues*, **23**, 615–630.

Makkai, T. and Braithwaite, J. (1994) Reintegrative shaming and compliance with regulatory standards. *Criminology*, **32**, 361–385.

Nagin, D.S. (1998) Criminal deterrence research at the outset of the twenty-first century. *Crime and Justice: A Review of Research*, **23**, 1–42.

Paternoster, R. and Piquero, A. (1995) Reconceptualizing deterrence: an empirical test of personal and vicarious experiences. *Journal of Research in Crime and Delinquency*, **32**, 251–286.

Saltzman, L., Paternoster, R., Waldo, G.P. and Chiricos, T.G. (1982) Deterrent and experiential effects: the problem of causal order in perceptual deterrence research. *Journal of Research in Crime and Delinquency*, **19**, 172–189.

Sarat, A. (1977) Studying American legal culture: an assessment of survey evidence. *Law and Society Review*, **11**, 427–488.

Schneider, A.L. and Ervin, L. (1990) Specific deterrence, rational choice, and decision heuristics: applications in juvenile justice. *Social Science Quarterly*, **71**, 584–601.

Sherman, L.W. (1993) Defiance, deterrence, and irrelevance: a theory of the criminal sanction. *Journal of Research in Crime and Delinquency*, **30**, 445–473.

Sherman, L.W. and Smith, D.A. (1992) Crime, Punishment and stake in conformity: legal and informal control of domestic violence. *American Sociological Review*, **57**, 680–690.

Silberman, M. (1976) Toward a theory of criminal deterrence. *American Sociological Review*, **41**, 442–461.

Single, E., Christie, P. and Ali, R. (2000) The impact of cannabis decriminalisation in Australia and the United States. *Journal of Public Health Policy*, **21**, 157–186.

Smith, D.A. and Gartin, P.R. (1989) Specifying specific deterrence: the influence of arrest on future criminal activity. *American Sociological Review*, **54**, 94–105.

Stafford, M.C. and Warr, M. (1993) A rich conceptualiation of general and specific deterrence. *Journal of Research in Crime and Delinquency*, **30**, 125–135.

Tyler, T. (1990) *Why People Obey the Law*. New Haven, CT: Yale University Press.

Williams, K.R. and Hawkins, R. (1986) Perceptual research on general deterrence: a critical review. *Law and Society Review*, **20**, 545–572.

5.5 Interventions for Illicit Drug Users Within the Criminal Justice System: A Review of Some Programmes in Australia, the United Kingdom and the United States

WENDY LOXLEY

National Drug Research Institute, Curtin University of Technology, Western Australia

SUMMARY

This chapter describes procedures and programmes in criminal justice which divert illicit drug users to education or treatment. The programmes discussed include the Australian Illicit Drug Diversion Initiative (IDDI), which involves State-based pre-arrest and pre-sentence programmes diverting illicit drug users to education or treatment; the British Arrest Referral (AR) Schemes in which drug-using offenders at the point of arrest are offered referral to treatment by drug workers working in close co-operation with the police; and Australian and US drug courts and UK Drug Treatment and Testing Orders (DDTO), which give courts pre- and post-sentence powers to require drug-related offenders to undergo treatment. The extent to which these various procedures have been found to be effective and meet their stated objectives is examined.

Most of those diverted in the Australian IDDI are cannabis users, and it is concluded that civil penalties for cannabis use may be a better approach to keeping minor cannabis offenders out of the criminal justice system. It is not yet clear whether AR Schemes reduce drug use and offending, although it is clearly feasible for workers to make contact with drug users who have never been in treatment. US drug courts have been shown to be effective in reducing drug use and criminal behaviour but evaluations are plagued with methodological difficulties. Australian drug courts have been found to improve the health and well-being of participants, reduce illicit drug use and reduce recidivism and the cost is comparable to that of incarceration. Evaluators of the British DTTOs claim that the programme shows promise but is not yet proven.

It is generally too soon to say whether these programmes will reduce crime and illicit drug use, and it is of concern that most of the approaches have been mainstreamed before

Preventing Harmful Substance Use: The Evidence Base for Policy and Practice.
Edited by T. Stockwell, P. J. Gruenewald, J.W. Toumbourou and W. Loxley.
© 2005 John Wiley & Sons, Ltd. ISBN 0-470-09227-0 (hbk) 0-470-09228-9 (pbk).

good evidence of effectiveness is available. Other concerns include the need to develop programmes in consultation with ethnic and other minorities, and to extend programmes to those apprehended for, or convicted of, alcohol-related crimes.

INTRODUCTION

One of the major economic and social impacts of legal and illegal drug use on the community is crime. The causal links between alcohol consumption and violence appear to be beyond dispute (Graham and West, 2001), but the causal links between illicit drug use and crime are less clear, and the question of whether the drug use or the crime came first is inevitably raised. One persuasive view is that drug-related offenders start committing crimes before they start using illicit drugs, but use of such drugs becomes part of the lifestyle and can lead to dependence, increasing the need to commit crimes to support their drug use (Makkai, 2002a).

Many crimes against persons or property are associated with drug use, and the prevention of these crimes and their precipitating drug use are high on the list of community priorities. The community also attempts to prevent use and supply of illicit drugs, whether or not these can be shown to be associated with other criminal activity. These distinctions, although apparently trite, are useful when considering interventions in criminal justice, because the objectives and targets of interventions are not always clearly specified although they are fundamental to the nature and the effectiveness of those interventions.

INTERVENTIONS WITHIN CRIMINAL JUSTICE

Alternatives to traditional approaches for drug-related offenders have long been a feature of criminal justice (Crime Research Centre, 2003), relating to the well-established finding that criminal sanctions have little effect on recidivism (Howells and Day, 1999). Treatment programmes for alcohol and other drug problems are associated with reduced drug use and, *inter alia*, reductions in crime (Gossop et al., 1998). This is particularly true of methadone maintenance therapy, which has proven effectiveness in reducing drug use and criminal behaviour when adequate doses are given (Gowing et al., 2001).

There are at least three contemporary approaches within the criminal justice system to encouraging drug users into treatment or education. One is to target drug users early in their drug use careers in order to prevent escalation of drug use into criminal careers. A second is to target drug users at the point at which they are apprehended for drug-related crime in order to minimise the likelihood of their becoming more serious criminals. A third approach is to target serious criminals with long-term drug dependence and divert them from incarceration into treatment. Examples of each approach can be seen in programmes operating in Australia, the United Kingdom and the United States. The prevention potential of programmes such as these ranges from minimising individual drug use, crime and adverse health and social effects to lessening the adverse effects of drug use experienced by the community, including loss of amenity, petty crime, motor vehicle accidents, and heightened anxiety and disquiet. Reducing the impact of drug users on crowded courts and prison systems is a further priority.

This chapter overviews some of these programmes, considers what is known about their effectiveness and makes recommendations for research and practice based on their examples.

The Australian Illicit Drug Diversion Initiative

The Australian Illicit Drug Diversion Initiative (IDDI) is a nationally consistent approach involving diversion by police or courts of drug offenders to compulsory assessment and appropriate education or treatment. Successfully completed, diversion allows the offender to avoid incurring a criminal record. It is designed to prevent a new generation of drug users emerging in Australia and committing drug-related crime. Further aims include reducing the number of people appearing before the courts for use or possession of small quantities of illicit drugs. The IDDO is underpinned by 19 national principles, while recognising that Australian law enforcement and assessment and treatment services are jurisdictionally based. Diversion of Indigenous people is a particular priority, being consistent with the Royal Commission into Aboriginal Deaths in Custody recommendations that custodial sentences for Indigenous Australians should be avoided wherever possible (Royal Commission into Aboriginal Deaths in Custody, 1991).

The programme was initiated early in 1999. Most of the police diversion programmes relate to cautioning for minor cannabis offences, while the court diversion programmes generally require offenders to participate in drug treatment and other health and welfare services as a condition of bail (Health Outcomes International, 2002).

The British Arrest Referral Scheme

Like Australia, the UK has made considerable investment in nation-wide programmes. Arrest Referral (AR) Schemes have been in operation since the 1980s, and are now offered through all 43 British police forces. Under these Schemes, offenders arrested for drug-related crimes are offered referral to treatment by AR workers working in close co-operation with the police who provide direct access to prisoners in custody suites. Accessing treatment occurs after, and independent of, any further criminal justice procedure.

Drug Courts

Drug courts are part of an emerging trend in judicial administration towards the development of "problem-solving" or "specialised" courts which seek to address the underlying problems of individual litigants (Freiberg, 2002). Drug courts were first established in the USA in the 1970s, in the context of rising crime and drug use and continued re-offending despite tough sentencing regimes, and their development was motivated by the need to reduce court congestion (Makkai, 1998).

US courts were originally targeted at non-violent offenders whose involvement in the criminal justice system was largely a result of their drug-use, and often included small-scale drug-use offences (Makkai, 1998). More recently, however, there has been a move towards more serious offenders: in his second review of US courts Belenko found that participants were "older offenders who have fairly extensive criminal histories and numerous service needs" (2001: 51) and noted that many courts had moved from their initial function of providing diversion programmes for first time drug offenders, to dealing with more complex clients, who increasingly had criminal records that included violent crimes.

Drug courts are in operation in the USA, Canada, Ireland, Scotland and Australia. There are a wide variety of models in use around the world but the common features typically include:

- an integrated approach involving criminal justice procedures, drug treatment, and social welfare programmes;
- ongoing involvement with the court;
- frequent substance abuse testing, with sanctions for failing the tests;
- frequent contacts with health and welfare services;
- sanctions and rewards based on the offender's behaviour.

The aims of drug courts relate to both criminal justice and the therapeutic/rehabilitation process, and typically include reducing or eliminating: drug use, drug-related criminal activity, imprisonment rates, and burdens on the judicial and correctional system; and improving the health and psychosocial well-being of the participants (Freiberg, 2002; Makkai, 2002b).

In Australia, drug courts have been implemented on a pilot basis in New South Wales (NSW), Victoria, Queensland, South Australia (SA) and Western Australia (WA), with the first court in NSW commencing in February 1999. Australian drug courts generally target heavy illicit drug users with substantial criminal records who might otherwise be facing custodial sentences. They have quite marked jurisdictional characteristics which make comparing them very difficult, although their philosophies tends to be similar (Freiberg, 2002). All but one of the courts exclude alcohol dependents and violent criminals, which is a concern because many people presenting to drug courts are alcohol dependent, and alcohol plays a prominent role in public disorder and violent crime (Makkai, 2002b).

Drug Treatment and Testing Orders (England and Wales)

The Drug Treatment and Testing Orders (DTTO) operate somewhat like the US and Australian drug courts, in that courts are allowed to make orders requiring offenders to undertake treatment as part of a community sentence. For many of these offenders, the incentive to comply is, as it is in the drug court, that the order is usually an alternative to a custodial sentence (Turnbull et al., 2000), although there is a considerable range of severity of offences.

Why do England and Wales not go "all the way" and establish drug courts like those in the USA, Australia, Canada, Scotland and Eire? Bean (2002) argues that there are three characteristics of drug courts which make it unlikely that drug courts would emerge in England and Wales in the near future. One concern is judicial supervision: in the drug court model the judge (or magistrate) controls the treatment programme and this level of judicial supervision is not appropriate under current legislation. The second issue relates to the diminishment in the drug court of the traditional roles of prosecutors and defenders, whereby the adversarial system is replaced by agreements between both sides that offenders shall be assisted with the reduction of their drug problems. Bean maintains that this makes "supporters of the traditional system . . . understandably nervous" (2002: 140). Third, sanctions are applied to offenders who fail to meet the requirements of their drug court programme: in Britain this would be considered multiple sanctions and disallowed by law (Bean, 2002).

THE EFFECTIVENESS OF PROGRAMMES

Difficulties with Evaluations

Evaluating programmes in the real world is always difficult, and additional complications arise when selection bias and the motivation of offenders to succeed are confounding factors. A further consideration is the possibility of unintended negative consequences which in diversion programmes include the impact of non-custodial sentences on families, and net-widening, which occurs when a diversion initiative increases the number of people involved in the criminal justice system or offenders receive a more serious sentence that they would otherwise have received (Spooner et al., 2001).

Each of the programmes discussed above has been evaluated and operates as part of jurisdictional policy. Some are pilots, and their evaluations have been undertaken to offer guidance to governments as to whether they should be extended. Many of the evaluations were undertaken or completed before the programmes were fully operational or before much data could be collected. This is particularly true where the evaluation relied, as did the Australian IDDI evaluation, on national data sets developed for that purpose. In that case, the data set was not complete by the time the evaluation was reported, so that only "indicative" data were used. In other cases, offenders were still completing their programmes when the evaluations were undertaken so that completion rate data were incomplete.

Belenko (2002) found that there had been little rigorous empirical research on US drug courts: relatively few evaluations had used experimental designs with random assignments to the drug court so that the impact of the court on recidivism could be rigorously assessed; and there was little empirical evidence about the long-term effects of drug courts, with most evaluations having follow-up periods of no longer than a year. Poor data also limited the scope of evaluations.

Evaluation of the Australian Illicit Drug Diversion Initiative

The first independent national evaluation report of the Australian IDDI was completed in 2002 (Health Outcomes International, 2002), at which time many of the programmes had only recently been initiated. Indeed, one of the major observations of the evaluation was that the negotiation and implementation of the programs had taken longer than anticipated and, as noted, only "indicative" data were available.

The evaluation found that 90% of the almost 20,000 diverted offenders had been diverted by the police—almost all through cannabis cautioning programmes—rather than the courts. Few of these received a second diversion for a similar offence, suggesting to the evaluators that the diversion served, at least, as a deterrent. Other than among those in first offence diversion programmes, the average age was mid-20s. This pattern appeared to address the IDDI aim of reducing the number of people appearing before the courts for use or possession of small quantities of illicit drugs, but the evaluators noted that diversion programmes did not appear to be engaging illicit drug users early in their drug-taking career, and suggested that there were "clear limitations on the capacity of police to identify and engage with people early in their drug experience" (Health Outcomes International, 2002: 26). Other complementary early intervention strategies, they suggested, might also be needed.

A major aim of the IDDI is to prevent first offenders from entering the criminal justice system, but under diversion they can still receive a criminal conviction for second, third or subsequent cannabis use offences. The introduction of prohibition with civil penalties for minor cannabis offences, now legislated in half of Australian jurisdictions, is an alternative to police diversion of cannabis users. In these jurisdictions, cannabis users no longer receive a criminal record for simple and minor cannabis offences (Lenton, 2004) although they can be required to attend education sessions if they are to avoid paying a fine, or if they have committed more than three offences. Civil penalties for cannabis use may be found to be a better approach than diversion to keeping minor cannabis offenders out of the criminal justice system.

Evaluations of Arrest Referral Schemes

Researchers in the UK have defined problem drug use as "that which involves dependency, regular excessive use, or use which creates serious health risks" (Edmunds et al., 1998: iii) and it is claimed that this group represents some 3% of the illicit drug-using population. This proportion has been estimated from treatment agency data, factored up to allow for the number of problematic users not in touch with agencies. The denominator is all users of illicit drugs, regardless of drug type or frequency of use. The UK AR Schemes attempt to target the problematic proportion by accessing drug users who have been apprehended for drug-related offences; these tend to be "prolific problem drug-using offenders—opiate and crack users; injectors and prolific shoplifters" (Edmunds et al., 1998: 2).

The official AR evaluation shows that in one year almost 50,000 offenders, half of whom had never been in treatment, were screened by AR workers. Of these, half were referred to specialist drug treatment and approximately 11% took up treatment. Three investigations with different methodological approaches were used and the authors claimed that

> despite the differences in methods, the emerging data presented a consistent picture of reductions in drug use and offending (as measured by self-report and police data) among arrest referral clients. The fact that research utilising different methods have provided consistent findings suggests that these data are robust.
>
> (Sondhi et al., 2002: 36)

Despite this positivity, the findings to date are not compelling, although at the time of reporting the evaluation had not been concluded and more may have emerged in the interim. In one study a large proportion of those contacted by AR workers received custodial sentences—since the outcome variables were drug use and offending, it is not clear whether the referral or the prison sentence was responsible for an observed reduction in these variables, although the authors maintained that "incarceration did not entirely account for the observed reduction in offending behaviour" (Sondhi et al., 2002: 39). In the other two studies, methodological problems included small follow-up samples and objective (police) data which did not differentiate outcomes according to whether or not the AR was taken up, and whether or not an offender received a custodial sentence.

What is clear, is that it is feasible for AR workers to make contact with drug users who have never been in treatment before. One of the three evaluation studies, however, showed that while it was possible to attract such offenders into treatment, it was more difficult to keep them in treatment than it was with voluntary clients (Sondhi et al., 2002).

Evaluations of Drug Courts

There are two major meta-analyses of the effectiveness of US drug courts (Belenko, 1998, 2001). The first concluded that, in general, drug courts were effective in reducing drug use and criminal behaviour during the duration of the programme. The second found that recidivism was lower for participants in drug courts than in control groups. Evaluations varied widely, however, with many methodological difficulties, as noted above.

The evaluations of three Australian jurisdictional (NSW, Queensland and WA) drug courts have been completed. It is not possible to compare completion or graduation rates across courts because many drug court offenders had not completed their programmes by the time of reporting, but the proportions who were terminated from their programmes, or left voluntarily, ranged from 49% to 66%.

The NSW drug court was the first Australian drug court to be implemented and had a rigorous evaluation process which included a control group of referred offenders who were randomly allocated to the traditional court process (Makkai, 2002b). Overall, the court contributed to a significant improvement in the health and well-being of its participants, along with a reduction in illicit drug use (Freeman, 2002). The impact on criminality and recidivism was less clear-cut, with the data failing to demonstrate statistically significant reductions in recidivism and criminal re-offending (other than illicit drug use) (Lind et al., 2002).

In Queensland, post-programme recidivism was significantly reduced for those who completed the drug court programme. Five areas impacted on the likelihood of graduation: community ties; commitment to the court; the frequency of drug testing; drug use history (in particular opiate use) and a greater incentive to succeed, as measured by the length of probable sentence if the programme were terminated. Makkai and Veraar (2003) suggested that early risk assessment tools should be developed to identify offenders with a low probability of completion, so that more intensive supervision and support could be provided.

In the WA drug court evaluation, no significant differences in recidivism between those who completed the programme, those who did not and control groups were found, in part because of low numbers. Indicative data, however, suggested that completion of an order reduced recidivism and lengthened time taken to reoffend. The court was found mainly to attract white offenders, and the youth drug court attracted relatively few juvenile offenders. It was suggested that different provisions, including specifically tailored treatment agencies in the community, were required for Indigenous and juvenile offenders (Crime Research Centre, 2003).

Evaluations of Drug Treatment and Testing Orders

Like the Australian IDDI, the British DTTO started slowly, which the authors suggest is the norm for national schemes. As with drug courts, it was found that short-term reductions in drug use and offending among those on orders were relatively easy to obtain, but by six months only one in three had been successfully maintained on their programme, although those who had continued reported further reductions in drug use and offending.

Overall, the evaluators claimed that the programme is "promising but not yet proven" (Hough et al., 2003: 77). They concluded that the challenge was now to find ways to engage with, and encourage, offenders to complete their orders (Hough et al., 2003). In this, the findings are very similar to those found in drug court evaluations.

THE COST-EFFECTIVENESS OF THE PROGRAMMES

Cost-effectiveness studies in this area are thin on the ground and the cost-effectiveness evaluation of the NSW drug court (Lind et al., 2002) appears to have been the first such study of drug courts anywhere in the world (Freiberg, 2002). The NSW evaluation compared the cost of drug court participation with the cost of serving the original sentence, and found that the cost of a drug court programme was essentially comparable to the cost of incarceration. The drug court was, however, more cost-effective in reducing the rate of offending—particularly in averting opiate possession and use, where the drug court made savings of $AU19,000 for each offence (Lind et al., 2002).

In the AR national monitoring and evaluation programme, Sondhi et al. (2002) report, in the absence of specific economic data, the findings of an economic simulation of the likely impact of AR Schemes on economic outcomes. They suggest that the benefit to cost ratio of the schemes is around 7:1. The data used for the simulation, however, came from non-offending drug users in voluntary treatment and an assessment of the cost-effectiveness of the scheme with offenders awaits specific data.

There do not appear to have been, to date, any economic evaluations of the Australian IDDI or the British DTTOs.

IMPLICATIONS FOR POLICY AND PRACTICE

The programmes reviewed in this chapter are generally directed towards illicit drug users who vary across a spectrum of severity with respect to their drug use and offending. The Australian IDDI system to date has predominantly impacted on cannabis users whose use is their only offence, although court diversion programmes are available for more serious users and offenders, and drug courts generally deal with the most serious users and offenders. In the UK, AR Schemes and DTTOs are directed towards drug users with serious drug use and offending patterns, and US drug court programmes vary widely with respect to the nature of offending and drug use.

It is too soon, in most cases, to assess whether the programmes meet their objectives, and inevitably, they will meet some objectives more completely than others. Police diversion in Australia (the greatest part of the IDDI) may act as a deterrent to some users and reduce the burden of simple cannabis offences on the courts (although no court data are presented to sustain this) but the hope of engaging illicit drug users early in their drug-taking career appears not, so far, to have been realised. Perhaps, as the evaluators have suggested, other early intervention strategies are needed.

The evaluators of the UK AR Schemes, which target drug-related offenders rather than users, suggest that contact with an AR worker is associated with reductions in re-arrest, offending and drug use, although the published evidence is not compelling. More evaluation is needed to determine whether such targeting is effective in reducing dependence and criminal recidivism.

Drug courts have been shown to be effective in both the USA and Australia although further evaluations with strong research designs are still needed. Completion rates for both drug courts and the British DTTO are low, however, and the search is now on to find ways to better predict who is likely to be successful and how to better support those on the programmes. One feature of both the UK DTTO and the Australian drug courts is a willingness to promote methadone maintenance as an appropriate treatment modality: this is far less likely in the USA (Rempel and Depies Destefano, 2001), which limits use of the one treatment which has been shown to be effective in preventing crime among opiate users.

The strategic lesson to be learned from this brief survey, perhaps, is that programme investment should be made in situations where the desired outcomes are clear, and the effectiveness of programmes to meet those outcomes has been established. One of the features of almost all the programmes is that evidence of the readiness of these programmes to be "rolled out" in national schemes had hardly been established before the schemes were developed. There are at least three levels of evidence that ought to be considered:

- Evidence for *implementation*. This applies where published studies report a sound theoretical rationale, a clearly specified service delivery format, acceptance within service delivery organisations, subject recruitment on a scale adequate to assess contribution of the programme to population health, and consumer approval.
- Evidence for *outcomes*. This applies where positive outcomes are consistently published in well-controlled interventions of sufficient scale to ensure outcomes within the constraints imposed by large-scale population health frameworks.
- Evidence for *dissemination*. This requires published reports of impacts where programs are delivered on a large scale by government auspice bodies or other service delivery agents (Loxley et al., 2004).

While it might be asking too much for evidence for dissemination to be yet available—although this should surely be where the evaluation task is directed—it is apparent that in some cases there was little or no evidence for outcomes, let alone effectiveness, before the programme was brought into national play.

Moreover, evaluations have been plagued with inadequate or missing data, and poor methodological designs. Under these circumstances, perhaps the best that can be said about the area, at present, is that what promise there may be has barely been demonstrated.

RECOMMENDATIONS FOR RESEARCH AND PRACTICE

- Good, rigorous programme evaluations with appropriate research designs, adequate funding and time, and well-developed data systems are needed if this field is to progress.
- Prohibition with civil penalties may be a better approach for simple cannabis offences than diversion programmes which do not eliminate the possibility of criminal conviction.
- Many of the programmes predominantly attract white males, and minority drug users including ethnic minorities, females and juveniles are under-represented. The need to consult minority communities in the development of schemes such as these is clearly a priority.
- The extension of these programmes to those apprehended for, or convicted of, alcohol-related crimes is warranted.

Finally, if criminal justice interventions are to be used to reduce drug use and drug-related offending, it is essential that criminological literature about who offends and for what reasons is taken into consideration. Importantly, the finding that many drug-related offenders commenced their offending prior to their drug use should give pause to those who see a simple linear relationship between minor drug use, escalation of drug use, dependence and offending.

REFERENCES

Bean, P. (2002) Drug treatment courts British style: the drug user treatment court movement in Britain. In L.D. Harrison, F.R. Scarpitti, M. Amir and S. Einstein (eds), *Drug Courts: Current Issues and Future Perspectives*. Vol. 3. Huntsville, TX: The Office of Criminal Justice Center, Sam Houston State University.

Belenko, S. (1998) *Research on Drug Courts: A Critical Review*. New York: National Center on Addiction and Substance Abuse at Columbia University.

Belenko, S. (2001) *Research on Drug Courts: A Critical Review, 2001 Update*. New York: National Center on Addiction and Substance Abuse at Columbia University.

Belenko, S. (2002) The challenges of conducting research in drug user treatment court settings. In L.D. Harrison, F.R. Scarpitti, M. Amir and S. Einstein (eds), *Drug Courts: Current Issues and Future Perspectives*. Vol. 3. Huntsville, TX: The Office of Criminal Justice Center, Sam Houston State University.

Crime Research Centre (2003) *Evaluation of the Perth Drug Court Pilot Project*. Perth, WA: The University of Western Australia.

Edmunds, M., May, T., Hough, M. and Hearnden, I. (1998) *Arrest Referral: Emerging Lessons from Research*. London: Home Office, Drug Prevention Initiative.

Freeman, K. (2002) *New South Wales Drug Court Evaluation: Health, Well-Being and Participant Satisfaction*. Sydney: New South Wales Bureau of Crime Statistics and Research.

Freiberg, A. (2002) Australian drug courts: a progress report. Paper presented at 2nd Australasian Conference on Drugs Strategy, 7–9 May. Perth, WA: Western Australian Police Service.

Gossop, M., Marsden, J. and Stewart, D. (1998) *NTORS at One Year: Changes in Substance Use, Health and Criminal Behaviour One Year After Intake*. London: Department of Health.

Gowing, L.R., Proudfoot, H., Henry-Edwards, S.M. and Teesson, M. (2001) *Evidence Supporting Treatment: The Effectiveness of Interventions for Illicit Drug Use*. Woden: Australian National Council on Drugs.

Graham, K. and West, P. (2001) Alcohol and crime: examining the link. In N. Heather, T.J. Peters and T. Stockwell (eds), *International Handbook of Alcohol Dependence and Problems*. Chichester: John Wiley and Sons, Ltd, pp. 439–470.

Health Outcomes International (2002) *Evaluation of Council of Australian Governments' Initiatives on Illicit Drugs*. Kent Town, SA: Health Outcomes International Pty Ltd.

Hough, M., Clancy, A., McSweeney, T. and Turnbull, P. (2003) T*he Impact of Drug Treatment and Testing Orders on Offending: Two-Year Reconviction Results*. London: Research Development and Statistics Directorate, Home Office.

Howells, K. and Day, A. (1999) *The Rehabilitation of Offenders: International Perspectives Applied to Australian Correctional Systems* (Trends and Issues in Crime and Criminal Justice No. 112). Canberra: Australian Institute of Criminology.

Lenton, S. (2004) Deterrence theory and the limitations of criminal penalties for cannabis use. Chapter 5.4, this volume.

Lind, B., Weatherburn, D., Chen, S., Shanahan, M., Lancsar, E., Haas, M. et al. (2002) *New South Wales Drug Court Evaluation: Cost-Effectiveness*. Sydney: New South Wales Bureau of Crime Statistics and Research and Centre for Health Economics Research and Evaluation.

Loxley, W., Toumbourou, J.W., Stockwell, T., Haines, B., Scott, K., Godfrey, C. et al. (2004) *The Prevention of Substance Use, Risk and Harm in Australia: A Review of the Evidence*. Canberra: Australian Government Department of Health and Ageing.

Makkai, T. (1998) *Drugs Courts: Issues and Prospects* (Report No. 95). Canberra: Australian Institute of Criminology.

Makkai, T. (2002a) Illicit drugs and crime. In A. Graycar and P. Grabosky (eds), *Cambridge Handbook of Australian Criminology*. Cambridge: Cambridge University Press.

Makkai, T. (2002b) The emergence of drug treatment courts in Australia. *Substance Use and Misuse*, **37**(12–13), 1567–1594.

Makkai, T. and Veraar, K. (2003) *Final Report on the South East Queensland Drug Court*. Canberra: Australian Institute of Criminology.

Rempel, M. and Depies Destefano, C. (2001) Predictors of engagement in court-mandated treatment: findings at the Brooklyn Treatment Court 1996–2000. In J.J. Hennessy and N.J. Pallone (eds), *Drug Courts in Operation: Current Research*. New York: The Haworth Press.

Royal Commission into Aboriginal Deaths in Custody (1991) *Royal Commission into Aboriginal Deaths in Custody: National Report*. 5 vols. Canberra: Australian Government Publishing Service.

Sondhi, A., O'Shea, J. and Williams, T. (2002) *Arrest Referral: Emerging Lessons from the National Monitoring and Evaluation Programme*. London: Home Office.

Spooner, C., Hall, W. and Mattick, R. (2001) An overview of diversion strategies for Australian drug-related offenders. *Drug and Alcohol Review*, **20**, 281–294.

Turnbull, P., McSweeney, T., Webster, R., Edmunds, M. and Hough, M. (2000) *Drug Treatment and Testing Orders: Final Evaluation Report*. London: Home Office.

5.6 Social Ecology and the Invention of New Regulatory Strategies for Preventing Drug and Alcohol Problems

BRIDGET FREISTHLER AND PAUL J. GRUENEWALD

Prevention Research Center, Berkeley, CA, USA

SUMMARY

Community-based prevention programs are one effective means of reducing alcohol- and drug-related harm. But there is little information on how policy and regulatory change in communities interact with local conditions to moderate reductions in harm. Understanding the differential effectiveness of policies across different neighborhoods will enable focused preventive interventions to reduce alcohol and drug problems. In order to understand the impact of community-wide global policies on local neighborhood problems, prevention researchers must understand the local correlates of problem outcomes.

The current chapter uses social disorganization and routine activities theories to explain how different characteristics of neighborhoods (population and place characteristics) are related to a variety of problem outcomes (assaults, motor vehicle crashes, drug sales, drug possession, and drug overdoses). An ecological model is developed which describes how neighborhood conditions may be related to outcomes across areas of one community. An important facet of this model is that it assumes the movement of populations within and across neighborhood areas and interactions between local and neighboring populations are important components of a full explanation of the geographic distribution of alcohol and drug problems.

Results from statistical analyses of community-based data show: (1) population and place characteristics both make important contributions to problem rates; (2) spatial interactions of populations between neighborhood areas affect drug and alcohol problems; and (3) risk and protective factors are heterogeneously related to problem outcomes across community areas.

Policies that continue global efforts to reduce poverty, improve education, and eliminate poor housing will generally act to reduce alcohol- and drug-related problems. Furthermore, regulatory efforts to change rates of drug and alcohol problems using other

Preventing Harmful Substance Use: The Evidence Base for Policy and Practice.
Edited by T. Stockwell, P. J. Gruenewald, J.W. Toumbourou and W. Loxley.
© 2005 John Wiley & Sons, Ltd. ISBN 0-470-09227-0 (hbk) 0-470-09228-9 (pbk).

mechanisms (i.e., reductions in outlet densities) would benefit from some local focus. Until the mechanisms that relate these characteristics of regulation to problem outcomes are better understood, blanket regulation of these aspects of drug and alcohol markets will have to be undertaken with considerable care. Consequently, the local effects of preventive interventions will be moderated by the larger social contexts of community settings, contexts that, once recognized, may be used to enhance the effectiveness of these programs.

INTRODUCTION

Prevention researchers have long sought ways to reduce alcohol- and drug-related harm at the community level. The community systems approach is a useful framework that allows researchers to model the effects of alcohol and drug policies on local problems due to alcohol and other drug use (Holder, 1998). This approach views policy and regulatory change in community settings as dynamically interacting with local conditions to affect problem outcomes. For example, a reduction in the number of alcohol outlets will be effective only to the degree that such reductions alter the use of alcohol by relevant demographic subgroups (e.g., young males). As argued by Gruenewald, Holder and Treno (2003), the community systems approach is not complete without the recognition that communities consist of geographically dispersed and interacting subgroups that use community resources in different ways. Thus, local context matters and, sometimes, can matter a great deal. Consequently, locating alcohol outlets in low traffic flow areas produces little impact on drunken driving crashes. Locating the same outlets in high traffic flow areas adjacent to highway systems produces great impacts on drunken driving crashes (Gruenewald and Treno, 2000). And the growth of populations of drinking drivers in one area of a community affects motor vehicle crashes someplace else (i.e., high outlet density areas; Gruenewald et al., 2000).

Communities wanting to regulate the physical availability of alcohol by reducing the number and density of alcohol outlets may meet with mixed results. Reducing the number of alcohol outlets in low-income minority areas may result in fewer assaults in those areas (Gorman et al., 2001; Lipton and Gruenewald, 2002), but may lead to the development of outlets in other community areas. The degree to which the locations of those new outlets attract similar populations may displace the problem from one neighborhood area to another. Similarly, the extent to which these populations are willing to travel greater distances to obtain alcohol may increase another alcohol-related problem—motor vehicle crashes. Therefore a global policy to limit outlet densities may simultaneously increase some problems (motor vehicle crashes) and decrease others (assaults). Only through a more thorough understanding of the social ecology of these problems will policy-makers be able to develop strategies that reduce all types of alcohol- and drug-related harm.

It is suspected that similar spatial dynamic relationships underlie rates of problems related to the use of illegal drugs (see Chapter 2.5), but not much evidence has been accumulated in this regard. Illegal drugs may be marketed either in public places with greater vehicle and pedestrian traffic flow or through private social networks (Eck, 1995). Public markets will arise where there is low guardianship and considerable social disorganization. Private markets will predominate in places where there is greater guardianship and social organization. Importantly, if both of these systems (public and private) exist, then local information about population and place characteristics are needed to reveal geographic patterns related to drug use and drug markets across neighborhoods.

Currently, empirical models of alcohol- and drug-related problems are usually developed and implemented at the community level. But as these arguments suggest, neighborhoods can act as 'micro' community systems in that residents and businesses in each neighborhood area can participate to varying degrees in many system components. For example, police enforcement is a broadly distributed community system that affects neighborhoods differentially according to enforcement priorities. However, such a fragmented approach to the interaction of community systems with local neighborhood conditions brings with it many complex analytic problems. Missing from the traditional discussions of the community systems approach are descriptions of how characteristics of local populations, the movement of these populations within and across neighborhood areas, and the interactions of local populations with neighboring populations in local places can increase or decrease the level of alcohol- and drug-related problems in these areas.

The goals of this chapter are to use this approach to analyze data from one community and examine the contribution of both social disorganization and routine activities theories to the explanations of alcohol- and drug-related problems. This chapter will describe how the interaction between people and places combine to produce problems and show how local conditions can determine the effectiveness of state and national policies related to substance use and related problems.

THEORETICAL APPROACH

In order to understand these interactions between people and the places in which they live, work, and play, we developed an ecological model that examines how characteristics of populations and features of places interact to create problems. By doing this, we rely on integrating two sociological theories describing problem behaviors: social disorganization and routine activities. In a broad sense, social disorganization refers to deviant behaviors and the societal context that produces them (Shaw and McKay, 1947). Applications of this theory generally focus upon how characteristics of people at the aggregate level, such as concentrated disadvantage or residential instability, are related to some problem outcome (see Sampson et al., 1997).

Alternately, routine activities theory (Cohen and Felson, 1979; Felson, 1987) is concerned with how characteristics of places within these neighborhoods, specifically those related to low guardianship or motivated offenders, contribute to alcohol- and drug-related problems. These "place" characteristics may include such things as greater density of retail establishments or amount of vacant housing, places with low guardianship where police presence and other deterrents to crime are limited.

In reality, neither of these theories alone has been able to fully describe why and where social problems occur. These theories may not be mutually exclusive, and in fact, may be inextricably linked. Places, without the presence of people, cannot create violence, traffic crashes, or conduct drug transactions. Similarly, people who participate in or are victims of these activities must be in some location when the problem occurs. By looking at the interactions of these theoretical approaches we can develop better-informed models of how people, place, and space are related to alcohol- and drug-related problems (see also Smith et al., 2000; Rice and Smith, 2002).

The Role of Alcohol Outlets

One place where it appears that drug and alcohol problems occur more frequently is in and around locations of alcohol outlets. These problems include motor vehicle crashes (Gruenewald et al., 1996), pedestrian injury collisions (LaScala et al., 2001) and increased drinking and driving by young people (Treno et al., 2003). Areas with greater densities of bars have been found to have more assaults (Roncek and Maier, 1991; Scribner et al., 1995; Gorman et al., 2001; Lipton and Gruenewald, 2002) and higher rates of child maltreatment (Freisthler, 2004). It is argued that: (1) bars are often places that attract clientele likely to be involved in violent interactions (e.g., young males); (2) bars are often located in community areas with less guardianship (e.g., retail areas); (3) bars provide opportunities for social interactions that may lead to violence; and (4) bars provide an intoxicating substance that appears to disinhibit aggression among males (Pihl et al., 1997). Similar arguments have been put forward to support empirically observed cross-sectional relationships between rates of violence and locations of off-premise establishments (Scribner et al., 1995; Alaniz et al., 1998). These effects, however, may be related to other criminogenic aspects of the environments of off-premise outlets (e.g., illegal drug activity and prostitution, Alaniz, et al., 1998). As bars may have lower levels of guardianship, it may make them attractive locations in which to conduct drug transactions. Providing support for this claim, Cohen et al. (2003) found that drug sales occurring within bars decreased during periods of high police enforcement, indicating that increasing levels of guardianship at bars may reduce problems.

THE CURRENT STUDY

Although a great deal of work has been pursued in the research literature identifying individual correlates and predictors of illegal drug use and related harm, little is known about the ecological characteristics of people, places and their interactions that support greater incidence of alcohol and drug problems. In particular, there is no convincing study demonstrating that population (e.g., social disorganization) and place (e.g., routine activities) interactions are relevant, let alone important, to the prediction and control of these problems. To that end, we use incident-based ecological models to examine how population and place characteristics are related to five different classes of alcohol- and drug-related problems: assaults, motor-vehicle crashes (MVC), and illicit drug possessions, sales, and overdoses. Using archival data sources, we created ecological models that examined local conditions related to these outcomes in 304 census block groups for a mid-sized city in California. The data for the outcomes measured in this study refer to and are measured at locations where these events occurred. This differs from population-based ecological models where data location is based on the residence of the victim (see Gruenewald et al., 2003).

METHOD

Three different measures of assaults for the year 2000 were obtained from (1) police incident records; (2) emergency medical services records; and (3) hospital trauma center records. These sources represent a continuum of assault severity. In 2000, out of 4,130 assault incidents, 34% resulted in a call to emergency medical system (EMS), and only 16% of those appeared at trauma centers.

Motor vehicle crashes were also measured using three different data sources, also representing a continuum of severity: the Statewide Integrated Traffic Records System (SWITRS) which includes all reported fatal and injury collisions from all California roadways except those considered private property, EMS, and hospital trauma center data. For two measures (SWITRS and EMS), we make a distinction between all MVC and night-time MVC (those crashes which occur between 8 p.m. and 4 a.m.). Night-time MVC are known to include more cases in which the crash was alcohol-involved (Fell and Nash, 1989; Zador, 1989; Kennedy, et al., 1996).

Problems related to illicit drug use were measured by drug possessions and drug sales from police incident data and drug overdose events from EMS. All outcomes were geocoded to either street address or intersection for the analysis. Over 99% of the police incidents and EMS events, and 78% of the SWITRS traffic crashes and hospital trauma center events were successfully geocoded.

Indices of social disorganization have been most frequently measured at the neighborhood level using population characteristics from the US Census (Coulton et al., 1995; Sampson et al., 1997). We used the percentage of college graduates, high school graduates, poverty, female-headed households with children, unemployed, 15–29-year-olds, African American, Hispanics, foreign-born, moved within the past five years, moved within the past year, owner-occupied housing, and income greater than $75,000 and an index of concentrated extremes to create factors to represent constructs of social disorganization. Three scales were created from a principal components analysis using a covariance matrix and oblique factor rotations. They generally index neighborhood characteristics reflecting concentrated wealth (e.g., index of concentrated extremes $(+)$ and percentage poverty $(-)$), residential instability (e.g., percentage movement in past five years $(+)$ and percentage owner-occupied housing $(-)$), and lower educational attainment (e.g., percentage college graduates $(-)$ and percentage high school graduates $(-)$). These three factors account for 80% of the variance in these measures across the block groups in our study.

Surrogates for routine activities are represented by the density (per roadway mile) of bars, restaurants, off-premise alcohol outlets, non-alcohol retail establishments, and vacant housing. It is assumed that alcohol establishments are foci of retail activities associated with alcohol use, densities of non-alcohol retail establishments are foci of general retail activity (e.g., areas with high pedestrian and motor vehicle traffic flow), and densities of vacant housing represent areas of reduced guardianship. Counts of bars, restaurants, and off-premise alcohol outlets were obtained from California Alcohol Beverage Control. Data on retail establishments were obtained from the City Revenue Division and vacant housing from Census 2000. Over 99% of all alcohol outlets and 88% of retail establishments were geocoded to their street address.

Identifying Spatial Interactions between People and Places

One key feature of the archival data collected for the current study is that each outcome is identified by the location of the event. Thus, the police incident, EMS and trauma events examined in this study may be produced (1) by persons living within a neighborhood; (2) by the interaction of these persons with others living outside the neighborhood; or (3) by interactions between persons who live exclusively outside of the neighborhood. Importantly, when using incident-based data of this sort, local population demographics may have *no* bearing upon the incidence of local events. The regrettable tendency of nearly all ecological

Table 5.6.1 Guide to models found in Table 5.6.3
examining goodness of fit for each variable set

	Local	Lagged
Social Disorganization (People characteristics)	Model 4	Model 5
Routine Activities (Place characteristics)	Model 6	Model 7

analyses of incident data to assume that local populations produce the harms identified with a geographic location is belied by the fact that incidents may occur in places where no one lives (e.g., parkland). While at the level of nations, states, provinces, and cities it may be reasonable to assume a match between local populations and local problems, at the level of neighborhoods this assumption is untenable. Thus, when using incident data at the neighborhood level, it is particularly important to consider characteristics of populations living outside of areas where problems occur.

The simplest way in which to proceed to characterize spatial interactions between neighborhoods is to recognize that, at a minimum, we are interested in interactions between people and places located "here", in some target location, and "there", in some other remote location. Most simply, those other locations may be neighborhoods adjacent to the target neighborhood. Taking the simplest approach there are a minimum of four combinations of spatial interactions to consider: (1) people may remain in a neighborhood and experience a problem in that neighborhood; a "local" effect (Local Social Disorganization); (2) people from outside neighborhoods ("there") may travel to some target neighborhood ("here") and cause problems, either with others from "there" or those living "here" (Lagged Social Disorganization); (3) people from "here" may go to *places* in their local neighborhoods and experience a problem (e.g., while visiting a bar; Local Routine Activities); and (4) people from outside a neighborhood ("there") may go to *places* in local neighborhoods ("here") and experience problems. Again this can occur with others from "here" or "there" (Lagged Routine Activities).[1] The distinction between the different models in the current study occurs by examining differences in those population characteristics (either "here" or "there") contributing to these problems or in specific places within these neighborhoods from populations living "here" or "there". Thus, both "local" and "lagged" effects can be related to people and places. Keeping the level of complexity of these possible relationships to a minimum, we focus only upon neighborhoods identified with Census block groups and the relationships of person and place characteristics between target neighborhoods ("here") and adjacent neighborhoods ("there"). Table 5.6.1 depicts these four relationships and the subsequent statistical models of the analyses testing these effects. This allows us to ask the simple question as to whether local and lagged people and place characteristics are associated with drug and alcohol problems.[2]

In addition to local and lagged people and place effects, a further differentiation of effects can be discerned. Local populations may "mix" with distal (lagged) populations to produce

---

[1] Of course, an endless number of other people and place combinations may matter, depending upon the definition of adjacencies or the mode of identification of spatial relationships (e.g., areas vs. traffic flows). We restrict ourselves here to the most elemental of these combinations and the most naïve of definitions.

[2] Because we recognize that it is possible that people living within or immediately adjacent to target neighbourhoods are causing local problems, we also include variables related to the direct effects for each place variable. This allows us to account for those populations who travel greater distances to these places and contribute to local problems.

greater than expected levels of problem outcomes. This occurs when local and lagged (distal) populations meet in a central retail area and become involved in social interactions that lead to accelerated rates of problem outcomes. These population "mixing" effects, as they will be called here, are also of importance collectively with all the lagged variables, individually as well. They can be identified by statistically significant effects associated with specific place and population interactions.

Analyzing Spatial Data

Analyses of neighborhood data require more sophistication than analyses of other larger-scale ecological units (e.g., states or provinces). Within these small areas, rates of problem outcomes will tend to be Poisson rather than normally distributed and the movement of people through these areas may "smear" effects. Therefore, outcomes may be spatially autocorrelated between adjacent neighborhoods. Both problems render application of standard ordinary least squares models inappropriate. Consequently, a series of Poisson regression models were used to examine the contribution of social disorganization and routine activities theories in explaining each outcome measure. The models assume that conditional measurement errors are Poisson distributed. Residuals from these models were then subject to a test for spatial autocorrelated error (Moran Coefficient; Cliff and Ord, 1973, 1981). All analyses were weighted by population size within units to account for heteroscedasticity that arises in small area analyses (Greene, 1993).

Seven models were fit for each outcome measure. The first three models (presented in Table 5.6.2) assessed the separate contributions of measures of social organization and routine activities to the explanation of problem rates. Rao's likelihood chi-square tests are used to assess the separate contribution of person and place characteristics in each case (G^2; Fienberg, 1980). Tests for spatial autocorrelation are presented for the Combined Model (Model 3). The next four models examined the separate contributions of measures taken in local and lagged areas to the explanation of problem rates (Table 5.6.3). Again Rao's likelihood chi-square tests are used to assess the separate contribution of local and lagged characteristics in each case.

RESULTS

As shown in Table 5.6.2, the separate contributions of social disorganization (person) and routine activities (place) measures to explanations of distributions of alcohol- and drug-related problems in neighborhoods areas were nearly all significant and substantive. For each model in this table, G^2 and Pseudo-R^2 values are given. As shown, both the G^2 statistics and the Pseudo-R^2 values indicate that the fits of the Social Disorganization and Routine Activities models alone were poorer than those for the combined model. Differences between these reduced models and the Combined Model were significant ($p < .001$) in all but one case. The exception was the measure of MVC from hospital trauma data when examined with respect to Social Disorganization measures. This G^2 could only be considered, at best, marginally significant ($p = .057$). The final column shows that spatial autocorrelation of the residuals was a significant ($p < .05$) source of measurement error in only two of the eleven models, and in each case was of negligible size (i.e., not significant if tests were Bonferroni protected).

Table 5.6.3 shows separate tests of Social Disorganization and Routine Activities measures related to local and lagged areas. In a substantial majority of cases, there were

Table 5.6.2 Comparisons of fits for social disorganization, routine activities, and combined models (n = 304)

Injury/event by data source	Model 1 Social Disorganization Full model of person characteristics (df = 12)		Model 2 Routine Activities Full model of place characteristics (df = 24)		Model 3 Combined Model Person + place characteristics (df = 34)		Residual ρ_s	
	G^2	Pseudo-R^2	G^2	Pseudo-R^2	G^2	Pseudo-R^2	Moran	p
Alcohol-related indicators*								
Assaults (2000)								
Police Incidents	2204.75	.4972	2309.99	.4732	1516.69	.6541	.041	.190
Emergency Medical Services	1183.66	.3851	1217.29	.3676	842.21	.5625	.054	.091
Hospital Trauma Center	349.56	.2910	373.07	.2433	284.83	.4223	−.037	.312
Motor Vehicle Crashes (1998)								
SWITRS	2387.68	.2102	1857.33	.3856	1392.93	.5392	.027	.371
Emergency Medical Services	2017.60	.2202	1817.99	.2974	1300.48	.4974	−.014	.755
Hospital Trauma Center	76.20 **	.2990	60.66	.4419	42.86	.6057	−.039	.291
Night-time Motor Vehicle Crashes (1998)								
SWITRS	608.25	.1797	481.67	.3504	410.39	.4465	.047	.136
Emergency Medical Services	630.58	.1996	594.65	.2452	480.56	.3900	−.002	.966
Illicit drug indicators*								
Drug Possessions (2000)								
Police Incidents	2444.43	.4708	3040.30	.3418	1672.12	.6380	.074	.021
Drug Sales (2000)								
Police Incidents	694.73	.3827	1077.97	.0422	452.68	.5978	−.036	.329
Drug Overdose (2000)								
Emergency Medical Services	345.58	.2779	365.18	.2369	276.46	.4223	.068	.035

Notes:
* p < .001, comparison of person and place to combined models for all effects, except where noted.
** p = .057

Table 5.6.3 Tests of model fits assessing the contribution of local and lagged variable to the combined model (n = 304)

Injury/event by data source	Model 4 Local Social Disorganization (Δdf = 4)		Model 5 Lagged Social Disorganization (Δdf = 8)		Model 6 Local Routine Activities (Δdf = 11)		Model 7 Lagged Routine Activities (Δdf = 12)	
	ΔG^2	p	ΔG^2	p	ΔG^2	p	ΔG^2	p
Alcohol-related indicators								
Assaults (2000)								
Police Incidents	53.98	<.001	134.21	<.001	77.58	<.001	173.70	<.001
Emergency Medical Services	56.14	<.001	115.51	<.001	71.54	<.001	85.42	<.001
Hospital Trauma Center	11.27	.024	37.59	<.001	17.17	.103*	27.50	.007
Motor Vehicle Crashes (1998)								
SWITRS	122.32	<.001	313.38	<.001	153.37	<.001	271.82	<.001
Emergency Medical Services	230.95	<.001	291.68	<.001	76.95	<.001	121.57	<.001
Hospital Trauma Center	7.26	.123*	15.67	.047	3.96	.971*	19.07	.087*
Night-time Motor Vehicle Crashes (1998)								
SWITRS	31.42	<.001	51.85	<.001	50.00	<.001	60.24	<.001
Emergency Medical Services	61.40	<.001	65.55	<.001	15.82	.148*	24.68	.016
Illicit drug indicators								
Drug Possessions (2000)								
Police Incidents	197.75	<.001	301.96	<.001	123.28	<.001	192.03	<.001
Drug Sales (2000)								
Police Incidents	136.43	<.001	105.62	<.001	86.87	<.001	247.33	<.001
Drug Overdose (2000)								
Emergency Medical Services	20.63	<.001	40.86	<.001	18.90	.063*	38.69	<.001

Note: *not significant at p < .05.

significant and substantive effects related to measures from both local and lagged areas. Some 34 of the 44 G^2 tests were significant at p < .001. Four of the remaining ten were significant at p < .05. Hospital Trauma Center data counted for four of the non-significant effects indicating that the data source, not the substantive areas of specific local or lagged effects, may be the cause. For instance, injury severity or the relatively small numbers of these problems in this data source, due to the scarcity of the event or the low geocoding hit rate, may weaken relationships between person and place characteristics and problems related to MVC and assaults.

As mentioned, the "mixing" of local and distal (lagged) populations in local areas was also examined using G^2 block tests for each set of population mixing variables (see Table 5.6.4) to examine whether or not population mixing significantly contributed to the model for each outcome. All 33 G^2 tests were statistically significant at p < .01, supporting the idea that some local problems may result from interactions between individuals living locally and those living further away.

Finally, we present specific effects of the combined models for each outcome measure in Table 5.6.4. Since both local and lagged population and place characteristics are clearly important, individual effects measures within these groupings of variables are of interest. In order to simplify the presentation of the results, we only show the direction of effects related to significant blocks of variables (p < .05) identified in Table 5.6.4. Rather than try to interpret the findings from each individual model, we present three general trends that should be noted with regard to correlates of the problems outcomes.

First, the effects observed in the models are generally stable within types of outcomes (assaults, MVC, and drug possessions and sales). That is, the direction of the effects of any given variable remains the same across all measures of a single outcome. For example, effects for concentrated wealth of local populations were negatively related to assaults as measured by police incident reports, EMS workers, and hospital trauma centers.

Second, the direction of effects related to individual variables are not consistent across different types of outcomes. For example, while concentrated wealth was negatively related to assaults, it was positively associated with MVC. This challenges current thinking on risk and protective factors as some characteristics of neighborhood areas can simultaneously both create a "risk" for and "protection" from harmful behaviors.

Third, there are direct effects of place characteristics (e.g., Local Routine Activity bar variables) on many of the outcomes, indicating that measures of local and lagged populations are not sufficient to identify populations contributing to alcohol- and drug-related behaviors in these neighborhood areas. Specifically, certain kinds of places (e.g., bars and vacant housing) are positively related to drug sales, possessions, and/or overdoses, indicating that some populations must be traveling a certain amount of distance to obtain or use drugs.

CONCLUSION

The purpose of this chapter was to present an example of ecological approaches to examining drug use and related harm by showing that both population and place characteristics contribute to these problems, that models of these relationships must account for spatial interactions across neighborhood areas, and to examine the local vs. global consequences of control. By using five different outcomes of drug use and related problems, we show that incident-based ecological models can explain 39–65% of the variation in the distribution of these problems across neighborhood areas.

Table 5.6.4 Poisson regression results of combined models for assaults, motor vehicle accidents, night-time motor vehicle accidents, drug possessions, drug sales, and drug overdoses (n = 304)

		Assaults			MVC			Night-time MVC		Drug possession	Drug sales	Drug overdose
		Police	EMS	Trauma*	SWITRS	EMS	Trauma*	SWITRS	EMS*	Police	Police	EMS*
Base Model	Constant	+	−		+	+			−	+	−	
	Population	+	+		+	+			+	+		−
Local Social Disorganization	Concentrated wealth	−	−	−	+	+	▨				−	−
	Residential instability	−	+		+	+	▨	+	+	+	−	
	Poor education	+	+	+	+	+	▨			+	+	+
Lagged Social Disorganization	Population	+	+		−			+			+	
	Concentrated wealth		−	−						+	+	
	Residential instability									+	+	+
	Poor education	+	+			+		+		+	+	+
*Population Mixing***	Population					−		−	−	−		
	Concentrated wealth		+									
	Residential instability	+				+			+		+	
	Poor education	−	−			−			−	−	−	
Local Routine Activities	Population	−	+	▨	−	−	▨		▨	−	+	▨
	Bar		+	▨			▨	−	▨	+	+	▨
	Restaurant			▨			▨		▨	+		▨
	Off-premise			▨			▨		▨			▨
	Retail			▨	−		▨		▨	+	+	▨
	Vacant housing	+			+	+	+	+		+	+	

(*Continued*)

Table 5.6.4 Poisson regression results of combined models for assaults, motor vehicle accidents, night-time motor vehicle accidents, drug possessions, drug sales, and drug overdoses (n = 304) (*Continued*)

		Assaults			MVC			Night-time MVC		Drug possession	Drug sales	Drug overdose
		Police	EMS	Trauma*	SWITRS	EMS	Trauma*	SWITRS	EMS*	Police	Police	EMS*
*Population Mixing***	Bar	−		░	+		░	+	░		−	░
	Restaurant	+	−	░	+		░		░	−	+	░
	Off-premise	−	−	░	+	+	░		░	+	−	░
	Retail	−	+	░	−	−	░		░	−	−	−
	Vacant housing		+	░			░		░	−		−
Lagged Routine Activities	Lag population	−	−	−	−		░	−			−	
	Bar	−	−		+		░					
	Restaurant	−		+	+		░					
	Off-premise		+	+	+	+	░				+	
	Retail				−	−	░					
	Vacant housing	+	+		−	−	░	−				
*Population Mixing***	Bar	+	+	░			░		░	+	+	
	Restaurant	+	+	░	−		░		░	+	−	+
	Off-premise		+	░			░	−	░	+	+	
	Retail			░		+	░		+		+	
	Vacant housing	+		░	+	+	░	+	░		+	

Note: *Shaded areas indicate non-significant Rao's Likelihood Chi-Square Ratio.
**Population mixing variables represent population interactions for specific social disorganization or routine activities domain under which they are listed.

This study shows that theories of social disorganization (people) and routine activities (places) both contribute to explanations of alcohol- and drug-related harm. The significant contribution of spatial lag variables to these models show that residents are not solely responsible for concentrations of problems in their neighborhoods. Instead, the spatial intersection of at risk populations and places with low guardianship are responsible for rates of problems in different neighborhood areas. In fact, the significant effects representing direct effects related to Routine Activities measures suggest that some populations are traveling across multiple neighborhood areas to become involved in problem outcomes (e.g., illegal drug sales).

Finally, the contribution of population and place characteristics is not the same for all outcomes. As mentioned, some variables act as both a risk and protective factor, depending upon the outcome of interest (e.g., concentrated wealth), thus making it difficult to design large scale community interventions that are effective at reducing all alcohol- and drug-related problems. A salient example of the discrepancy between the apparent determinants of problem outcomes and direction of effect is observed in the contrast between the impacts of concentrated wealth upon assault versus motor vehicle crash rates. Fewer numbers of assaults occur in areas with greater concentrated wealth while significantly more motor vehicle crashes occur in areas with greater concentrated wealth. Can neighborhood areas regulate some aspects of community to minimize the occurrence of all problem outcomes? Or, will an individual neighborhood's attempt to regulate these problems shift those problems to other neighborhood areas within the same community? The difficulty for prevention programs is to determine how to regulate activity in these areas that minimizes harm across all areas for multiple problem outcomes.

Local and Global Effects

One question that communities often ask with regard to the implementation of prevention programs is "Will these efforts be rewarded by effective and/or substantive change in alcohol and drug problems?" As the outcomes of these analyses suggest, the scientifically appropriate answer is an uncomfortable, "Maybe." As indicated by these results, the local effects of prevention efforts will be conditional upon other global characteristics of community settings. Two examples will help frame this conclusion and point the way toward a better understanding of the effects of preventive interventions.

As shown in Table 5.6.4, two factors are dominant as ecological correlates of alcohol and drug problems across Census block groups in this city, population characteristics related to lower educational attainment and place characteristics related to the extent of vacant housing. In the case of lower educational attainment, assaults, MVC, and drug possessions, sales and overdoses are greater in areas within and adjacent to larger concentrations of these populations. In the case of vacant housing, greater numbers of assaults, MVC and drug sales and possession incidents occur in these areas, especially when accompanied by relatively low population densities (reflecting a further absence of guardianship). If these effects represent the stable long-run impacts of changes in these measures on rates of these problem outcomes, a relevant question to ask is whether local changes in educational attainment or housing characteristics will have substantive effects on reducing problems. Clearly, the results of these analyses suggest that, at least on a local basis, they will.

But what about the global basis? A more thorough examination of Table 5.6.4 reveals that both lower educational attainment and densities of vacant housing are also related to *reductions* in assaults, MVCs and drug possession and sales incidents. But these effects appear only in neighborhoods that are near to high population areas (those effects related to lagged populations). Greater amounts of vacant housing, and larger populations with lower educational attainment, are in this sense protective when located near to high population areas, as if adjacency to densely populated areas itself somehow moderated effects related to neighborhood disorganization. Local effects of population and place characteristics are not fixed, but functions of ecological context. Consequently, local effects of preventive interventions will be moderated by the larger social contexts of community settings.

Policy Implications

The departure of local effects from global effects related to specific population or place characteristics would not be of interest were it not the case that local preventive interventions (e.g., resistance skills training in schools, changes in enforcement patterns) take place in the larger social and regulatory contexts of communities. The departure of local and global effects between different problem outcomes (e.g., alcohol-related crashes vs. alcohol-related violence) would not be of interest were it not the case that regulations to ameliorate one problem (e.g., reducing outlet densities to reduce violence) may aggravate another (e.g., reduced outlet densities leading to increased crashes). These observations suggest that the adoption of community-wide policies or prevention strategies may not consistently reduce alcohol- and drug-related problems across all areas within communities. These observations also suggest that local educational prevention programs may exhibit differential effectiveness between community contexts, and, as an example, global regulations to reduce numbers of alcohol outlets may reshape the geographic distributions of problem outcomes but not, necessarily, reduce overall alcohol-related problems.

Communities are in the position of having to decide what problems they think are most important and what programs or policies will work to reduce these problems. Finding the right portfolio of programs and policies requires understanding their local and global impacts and their interaction with local social and economic conditions (see also Chapter 7.2). Although considerable further research will be required to understand the different community contexts in which different programs may be more-or-less effective, and the impacts of global policies upon local outcomes, it is certain that any calculation of risks and benefits to a community will have to be based upon a weighting of probable local and global outcomes.

The results of the current work suggest that three relatively global facets of populations and places are important to the reduction of alcohol and drug problems: (1) the concentrated wealth of populations is related to greater rates of MVC and lesser rates of violence and drug sales and use within community areas. Complementarily, greater impoverishment is related to lesser rates of MVC and greater rates of violence and drug sales and use; (2) lower educational attainment is related to substantially greater rates of problems of all sorts, violence, MVC and illegal drug sales and use; and (3) poor housing conditions, reflected in a predominance of vacant housing, is an attractor for problems of all sorts, violence, MVC, and drug sales. In general, these effects persist independent of particular local conditions. Other effects, on the other hand, are more local and particular: direct effects of bar densities upon local violent assaults appears in analyses of emergency medical systems data. But bars are also related to greater rates of MVC when located near to high population areas. Unstable neighborhoods are characteristically related to greater rates of assault (again using emergency medical systems data) and MVC. But residential instability also becomes important to the prediction of drug sales in neighborhoods near to high population areas and, very importantly, residential instability in neighboring areas affects rates of drug crimes and overdoses in local areas (spatial lag effects).

These observations suggest that continued global efforts to reduce poverty, improve education, and eliminate poor housing will generally act to reduce alcohol- and drug-related problems (with the obvious exception of likely increases in MVC). They also suggest that regulatory efforts to change rates of drug and alcohol problems using other mechanisms (i.e., reductions in outlet densities or modifications in conditions related to residential instability such as the amount of owner-occupied housing) would benefit from some local focus. Clearly, reductions in bar densities will have direct local impacts upon rates of assault and MVC, but these reductions will be most advantageous in places with larger numbers of individuals likely to use these outlets. Efforts to reduce residential instability will benefit local areas (for MVC) but also nearby areas (with regard to the amelioration of rates of drug crimes and overdoses). However, in neither case will global efforts have simple and consistent local effects. Reduced bar densities are also related to greater rates of night-time MVC and drug sales. Stable neighborhoods, on their own merits, encourage drug sales. Until the mechanisms that relate these aspects of regulation to problem outcomes across community areas are better understood, blanket regulation of these aspects of drug and alcohol markets will have to be undertaken with considerable care.

ACKNOWLEDGEMENTS

Research for and preparation of this manuscript were supported by NIAAA Research Center Grant P60-AA06282 and NIAAA Grants No. R37-AA12927 and R01-AA11968.

REFERENCES

Alaniz, M.A., Cartmill, R.S. and Parker, R.N. (1998) Immigrants and violence: the importance of neighborhood context. *Hispanic Journal of Behavioral Science*, **20**, 155–174.

Cliff, A.D. and Ord, J.K. (1973) *Spatial Autocorrelation*. London: Pion Limited.

Cliff, A.D. and Ord, J.K. (1981) *Spatial Processes Models and Applications*. London: Pion Limited.

Cohen, J., Gorr, W. and Singh, P. (2003) Estimating intervention effects in varying risk settings: do police raids reduce illegal drug dealing at nuisance bars? *Criminology*, **41**(2), 257–292.

Cohen, L.E. and Felson, M. (1979) Social change and crime rate trends: a routine activity approach. *American Sociological Review*, **44**, 588–608.

Coulton, C., Korbin, J.E., Su, M. and Chow, J. (1995) Community level factors and child maltreatment rates. *Child Development*, **66**, 1262–1276.

Eck, J.E. (1995) A general model of the geography of illicit retail marketplaces. In J.E. Eck and D. Weisburd (eds), *Crime and Place: Crime Prevention Studies*. Vol. 4. Washington, DC: Police Executive Research Forum.

Fell, J. and Nash, C. (1989) The nature of the alcohol problem in U.S. fatal crashes. *Health Education Quarterly*, **16**, 335–343.

Felson, M. (1987) Routine activities and crime prevention in the developing metropolis. *Criminology*, **25**, 911–931.

Fienberg, S.E. (1980) *The Analysis of Cross-Classified Data*. Cambridge, MA: MIT Press.

Freisthler, B. (2004) A spatial analysis of social disorganization, alcohol access, and rates of child maltreatment in neighborhoods. *Children and Youth Services Review*, **26**(9), 307–319.

Gorman, D., Speer, P.W., Gruenewald, P.J. and Labouvie, E.W. (2001) Spatial dynamics of alcohol availability, neighborhood structure and violent crime. *Journal of Studies on Alcohol*, **62**, 628–636.

Greene, W.H. (1993) *Econometric Analysis*. 2nd edn. New York: Macmillan Publishing.

Gruenewald, P.J. and Treno, A.J. (2000) Local and global alcohol supply: economic and geographic models of community systems. *Addiction*, **95**, S537–S549.

Gruenewald, P.J., Holder, H.D. and Treno, A.J. (2003) Environmental approaches to the prevention of alcohol, drug use and related problems. In A.W. Graham, T.K. Schultz, M.F. Mayo-Smith, R.K. Ries and B.B. Wilford (eds). *Principles of Addiction Medicine*, 3rd edn. Chevy Chase, MD: American Society of Addiction Medicine, pp. 383–394.

Gruenewald, P.J., Millar, A., Ponicki, W.R. and Brinkley, G. (2000) Physical and economic access to alcohol: the application of geostatistical methods to small area analysis in community settings. In R. Wilson and M. DuFour (eds). NIAAA Research Monograph 36, *Small Area Analysis and the Epidemiology of Alcohol Problems*, pp. 163–212.

Gruenewald, P.J., Freisthler, B., Remer, L., LaScala, E.A. and Treno, A.J. (2003) Ecological models of alcohol, drugs and violence crime: crime potentials, crime mapping and geospatial analysis. Paper presented at the International Research Symposium—Preventing Substance Use, Risky Use and Harm: What is Evidence Based Policy? 24–27 February, Perth, Western Australia.

Gruenewald, P.J., Millar, A., Treno, A.J., Ponicki, W.R., Yang, Z. and Roeper, P. (1996) The geography of availability and driving after drinking. *Addiction*, **91**, 967–983.

Holder, H.D. (1998) *Alcohol and the Community*: A Systems Approach to Prevention. New York: Cambridge University Press.

Kennedy, B.P., Isaac, N.E. and Graham, J.D. (1996) The role of heavy drinking in the risk of traffic fatalities. *Risk Analysis*, **16**, 565–569.

LaScala, E.A., Johnson, F. and Gruenewald, P.J. (2001) Neighborhood characteristics of alcohol-related pedestrian injury collisions: a geostatistical analysis. *Prevention Science*, **2**, 123–134.

Lipton, R. and Gruenewald, P.J. (2002) The spatial dynamics of violence and alcohol outlets. *Journal of Studies on Alcohol*, **63**, 187–195.

Pihl, R.O., Lau, M.L. and Assaad, J.-M. (1997) Aggressive disposition, alcohol, and aggression. *Aggressive Behavior*, **23**, 11–18.

Rice, K.J. and Smith, W.R. (2002) Socioecological models of automotive theft: integrating routine activity and social disorganization approaches. *Journal of Research in Crime and Delinquency*, **39**(3), 304–335.

Roncek, D.W. and Maier, P.A. (1991) Bars, blocks, and crimes revisited: linking the theory of routine activities to the empiricism of "hot spots". *Criminology*, **29**, 725–753.

Sampson, R.J., Raudenbush, S.W. and Earls, F. (1997) Neighborhoods and violent crime: a multilevel study of collective efficacy. *Science*, **277**, 918–924.

Scribner, R.A., MacKinnon, D.P. and Dwyer, J.H. (1995) The risk of assaultive violence and alcohol availability in Los Angeles County. *American Journal of Public Health*, **85**, 335–340.

Shaw, C.R. and McKay, H.D. (1947) *Juvenile Delinquency and Urban Areas*. Chicago: University of Chicago Press.

Smith, W.R., Frazee, S.G. and Davison, E.L. (2000) Furthering the integration of routine activity and social disorganization theories: small units of analysis and the study of street robbery as a diffusion process. *Criminology*, **38**(2), 489–523.

Treno, A.J., Grube, J.W. and Martin, S.E (2003) Alcohol availability as a predictor of youth drinking and driving: a hierarchical analysis of survey and archival data. *Alcoholism: Clinical and Experimental Research*, **27**(5), 835–840.

Zador, P. (1989) *Alcohol-Related Risk of Fatal Driver Injuries in Relation to Driver Age and Sex*. Washington, DC: Insurance Institute for Highway Safety.

Section 6 THE EVIDENCE BASE FOR PREVENTION IN BROAD PERSPECTIVE

EDITED BY PAUL J. GRUENEWALD

6.1 Introduction

PAUL J. GRUENEWALD
Prevention Research Center, Berkeley, CA, USA

"What works?" is the clarion question of prevention research. Answering that question is the goal of prevention researchers and prevention science. Ideally, prevention practitioners use the best information produced by prevention science to formulate politically and econom- ically successful programs. When they do so, effective and efficient prevention programs result (Sections 3 and 4). When they do not, ineffective programs proliferate and public funds are squandered. Thus, the extensive and costly US investment in project DARE (Drug Abuse Resistance Education), fielded in many schools throughout the USA while untested and unproven, has been rewarded with generally null effects (Ennett et al., 1994; Lyman et al., 1999). DARE remains a widely used program in public schools to reduce youth drug use. But DARE does not work. Whether DARE provides for other socially desirable effects (e.g., altering youth attitudes toward police or providing a sense of empowerment to parents) is an open question, but one that lies beyond the scope of a rigorously developed prevention science. The logic of prevention practice, particularly given the scarcity of re- sources available to local communities, is simple: Science-based prevention works. Invest in the science and effective programs will result. When this logic is followed, effective school-based preventive interventions can be developed (Chapter 3.3).

This seems obvious enough. But prevention practitioners do not always have ready access to information about what works, and prevention researchers are not always as forthcoming as they could be to make recommendations regarding likely effective programs. It is in the nature of science, and scientists, to be conservative about making recommendations. It is in the nature of prevention practice and practitioners, on the other hand, to try, despite a lack of information, to reduce drug and alcohol problems. Bridging this gap is a major goal of the current work. The chapters in this section provide summaries by leading researchers in the field of best approaches to science-based prevention.

Chapter 6.2, "What is 'evidence' and can we provide it?" (Saltz), gives the reader a look into the nature of "evidence" for effective programs from the perspective of prevention researchers. This chapter shows how "evidence" for effective programs can inform preven- tion practice, but also how "evidence" of ineffective programs may be just as informative to prevention research. So long as program failures are well documented, knowing what does not work is as valuable as knowing what does.

Chapter 6.3, "US Policy on Illegal Drugs: What We Don't Know Keeps Hurting Us— A Perspective on Future Research Needs" (Anthony), continues this examination of the nature of scientific evidence. This chapter presents an evidence-based assessment of the

Preventing Harmful Substance Use: The Evidence Base for Policy and Practice.
Edited by T. Stockwell, P. J. Gruenewald, J. W. Toumbourou and W. Loxley.
© 2005 John Wiley & Sons, Ltd. ISBN 0-470-09227-0 (hbk) 0-470-09228-9 (pbk).

effectiveness of efforts to reduce drug supply and demand through law enforcement and other prevention strategies in the USA. In general, it is suggested that evidence for the effectiveness of supply and demand reduction strategies is lacking, largely due to inadequacies in systems for measuring drug use and related problems. It is also concluded that much of what constitutes evidence of effectiveness may simply be a matter of "impulse-response thinking", the tendency to interpret ambiguous data in favor of intervention efforts. Our very limited knowledge of the dynamics of drug markets, drug use and drug dependence keeps hurting us. And the science base is not improved by continued investments in a war on drugs unguided by scientific expertise.

Chapter 6.4, "Preventing Tobacco Use and Harm: What is Evidence-Based Policy?" (Younie et al.), presents the first of a series of success stories with regard to prevention research and practice. The authors show that many decades of research investment to develop the science base for treatment, prevention, and tobacco control measures have paid off in successful knowledge-based programs. In addition to successful pharmacotherapies for treating tobacco use, population preventive interventions can reduce tobacco use among young people and adults. With the maintenance of tobacco use in subpopulations, and its growth among women in the USA, there is still a long way to go in these areas, but much progress has been made.

Chapter 6.5, "Moving Toward a Common Evidence-Base for Alcohol and Other Drug Prevention Policy" (Holder and Treno), presents a coordinated assessment of population level approaches to the reduction of problematic alcohol use and related problems, tobacco use, and illegal drug use. The goal of this chapter is to outline the common frameworks of economic and physical availability that shape substance use and harm across these drugs. Economic costs of drugs, and the locations in which they can be purchased and used, affect levels of use and related problems. Viewed across the different substances, some glaring inconsistencies can be found. Thus, in the USA, extensive tracking mechanisms are in-place in most states to identify retail outlets that sell alcohol, and punish outlets for sales to minors. Oddly, also in most states, no similar record exists with regard to tobacco products, arguably a more dangerous drug with clearly identifiable health consequences.

Chapter 6.6, "The Evidence-Base for Preventing the Spread of Blood-Borne Diseases within and from Populations of Injecting Drug Users" (Russell and Carruthers), presents an area of research with a checkered international political history, one in which some countries have supported obvious harm reduction strategies for the reduction of blood-borne diseases (such as human immunodeficiency virus, HIV) and others have not. The authors review evidence that supports the importance of providing access to clean drug injecting paraphernalia for intravenous drug injectors and tracking sexual networks for transmission of disease. Despite clear evidence that some strategies may work, lack of funding and political will continue to hamper prevention efforts.

Chapter 6.7, "The Evidence-Base for Responding to Substance Misuse in Indigenous Minority Populations" (Gray and Saggers), concludes this section with a discussion of the very great need for prevention services among indigenous minority populations. Reviewing research from Australia, Canada, New Zealand and the USA, the authors argue that the social histories of these minority communities (i.e., colonialism, dispossession, economic marginalization) all lead to greater than average rates of problems with substance use and, consequently, a broad variety of health problems. They review the successful, and unsuccessful, supply, demand and harm reduction efforts that have been tried among these groups, and conclude that, in the long-run, "structural inequalities that contribute to indigenous substance misuse and related harms" must be addressed.

REFERENCES

Ennett, S.T., Tobler, N.S., Ringwalt, C.L. and Flewelling, R.L. (1994) How effective is drug abuse resistance education? A meta-analysis of Project DARE outcome evaluations. *American Journal of Public Health*, **84**, 1394–1401.

Lyman, D.R., Milish, R., Zimmerman, R., Novak, S.P., Logan, T.K., Martin, C., Leukefeld, C. and Clayton, R. (1999) Project DARE: no effects at 10-year follow-up. *Journal of Consulting and Clinical Psychology*, **67**, 590–593.

6.2 What is "Evidence", and Can We Provide It?

ROBERT F. SALTZ

Prevention Research Center, Berkeley, CA, USA

SUMMARY

The recent accumulation of evaluation and research on the efficacy of prevention policies and programs has brought us to the point where it is now time to take stock of how far we have come and to critically evaluate what the next steps should be. There is a danger that one might prematurely and wrongly rule out potentially powerful prevention strategies because of misunderstanding as to how research findings should be evaluated, and the role of science in prevention policy research.

Evaluations of "responsible beverage service" are used to show that simply tallying those that have positive effects overlooks critical distinctions not only in the quality of implementation, but also blurs fundamental differences in the hypothesized mechanisms being tested. If prevention science is to develop, it must identify these sometimes implicit mechanisms, articulate the hypothesized links connecting intervention with desired outcome, and then evaluate the utility of these differing strategies in a variety of settings. In doing so, prevention policy research will develop a more coherent body of findings that will not only make better sense of what is now an eccentric, particularistic collection of research studies, but will better serve practitioners and policy-makers by providing guidance on robust and general principles of policy implementation as well as basic strategies.

INTRODUCTION

Over the past 20 years or more, researchers have accumulated results from a number of studies specifically directed toward alcohol control policies and interventions. Furthermore, the number of such studies has grown each year as researchers in the United States and elsewhere have been catching up to the countries that had pioneered this research, including Scandinavia, Canada, Australia, and New Zealand. This accumulation has brought us to the point where it is now time to take stock of how far we have come and to critically evaluate

Preventing Harmful Substance Use: The Evidence Base for Policy and Practice.
Edited by T. Stockwell, P. J. Gruenewald, J. W. Toumbourou and W. Loxley.
© 2005 John Wiley & Sons, Ltd. ISBN 0-470-09227-0 (hbk) 0-470-09228-9 (pbk).

what the next steps should be. It is the purpose of this chapter to encourage a dialog among researchers and those interested in the practical application of research about the utility of our research to date and how to improve the relevance of future research to alcohol policy.

I argue here that alongside the successes in broadening the scope and number of policy research studies, substance use policy research also suffers from some conceptual weaknesses that may threaten its ability to answer the needs of policy-makers and move beyond the loose and somewhat eccentric collection of studies that are now available to provide guidance. The weaknesses that should be addressed include:

- confusion or misunderstanding as to how to weigh current research findings or in drawing conclusions as to the efficacy of prevention strategies;
- diffuse understanding of the role and potential of science in prevention research;
- the need to more rigorously pursue a coherent line of enquiry in policy research.

I hope to illustrate these weaknesses or challenges to the field using examples from studies related to "responsible beverage service", not just because they are familiar to me, but because discussion with others on how to interpret this body of research was in large part the motivation for pursuing this chapter's themes.

WHAT SHOULD WE MAKE OF RESEARCH TO DATE?

Types of Policy-Relevant Research

Of course, it is a truism that any and all research can have policy implications. If certain types of drinking behavior were to be shown as directly predicted through inheritance, there is little doubt that policies regarding alcohol treatment and criminality would be affected. Likewise, basic psycho-social research may lay an important foundation for informed policy-making or for identifying potential prevention strategies yet conceived. This is perhaps why many prevention researchers engage in basic research as well as more applied or focused studies.

Here, however, I wish to limit attention to research overtly directed toward guiding policy making. In this regard, we may distinguish several approaches for estimating the impact of various intervention strategies. First, there are those that observe naturally-occurring variations in environmental forces thought to influence drinking behavior either over people, places, or time. Studies looking at the association between price and alcohol consumption and problems across states or over time, for example, fall into this category, as would a study looking at how variations in liability insurance may influence commercial serving policies and compliance with local law. A feature of this research is that the variations in these environments usually do not arise from a purposive policy effort to control alcohol. Price fluctuations, for instance, may have nothing to do with prevention strategy and instead result from local market forces.

Second would be a class of studies in which variations in these environmental forces are the result of specific policy decisions, even if the motivations for those policies are not directly related to the prevention of alcohol-related problems. Alcohol taxes may be increased, for example, as a strategy to raise revenue rather than to influence drinking behavior. Such studies are sometimes called "natural experiments" because while the intervention may be outside the influence or control of the researcher, it nevertheless mimics action that might have been taken as part of a prevention effort.

A third category of research would comprise evaluations of interventions that are directly or at least closely controlled by the investigator and designed to answer the question of whether a specific intervention strategy "works" or not. Following convention as summarized by Holder et al. (1995), this research refers to "efficacy" studies.

Finally, effectiveness research refers to studies in which the efficacy of a specific intervention is less an issue (presumably because efficacy has already been demonstrated) than how well it can be implemented "in the field" and outside the direct or close control of an investigator (interested readers are referred to the article by Holder and colleagues for a good review of these types of studies and how they may represent phases of intervention research).

Currently, prevention research encompasses findings from all these types of studies, and reviews of research results often move across these categories of studies without making much of their differences (see, for example, Saltz, 1997). As evidence accumulates, however, it is crucial to recognize the relative strengths and weaknesses of these different research designs. Observational studies can suggest the potential impact of various interventions (e.g., the impact of tax changes), but finding an association in natural variations does not rule out the possibility that the association is due to a third source of influence that affects price and consumption together (as cautioned in the classic text by Campbell and Stanley, 1963). Even so-called natural experiments, where effects may be observed of a direct policy change may be suspect if again, the new policy were timed at the peak of a problem that was historically bound to drop (as in Campbell and Stanley's example of the Connecticut "crackdown" on speeding), or if the adoption of policy reflected global normative changes that were the more direct influence on behavior (as Ross, 1975, 1984, argued in the case of Scandinavian drunk driving laws).

As we gather more findings, then, we must begin to put greater weight on the quality of evidence as well as the quantity of findings in support of a given intervention strategy. At the very least, it must be clear as to which kinds of research questions are best answered by these different designs.

Even an apparently "simple" review of research findings can and often does go awry, however, when the implicit assumption is made that evidence for or against an intervention's efficacy is a matter of tallying up the score. Sometimes, this tally is done with gross categories (e.g., evidence is "consistent" vs "mixed"), but my argument is that to do any kind of tally is a serious misunderstanding of the function of efficacy research. Yet doing so is conventional.

What Is the Problem?

The nature of every efficacy study or evaluation is that it is simultaneously an evaluation of an underlying strategy (hypothesis) as well as the specific implementation of that strategy. This, in itself, is not a novel observation, and modern evaluation designs will include process measures as a check on the quality of the intervention (e.g., the intensity or fidelity of the intervention, or the awareness of a new policy, etc.). However, this distinction is rarely carried through to its logical conclusion: even among interventions that are done "well", or with complete fidelity, the implementation still represents an entirely different set of hypotheses than the more fundamental hypothesis underlying the primary intervention strategy, an additional set of hypotheses connecting implementation of the intervention to the outcome. Thus, any evaluation or efficacy study is implicitly testing a *hierarchy of hypotheses* simultaneously that flow from the most general (e.g., restricting availability reduces alcohol consumption) to the most specific (e.g., closing a bar at 1 a.m. instead of 2 a.m. shortens the duration or amount of consumption). In between is a myriad of connecting strategies that themselves represent theories or at least hypotheses of human behavior (e.g., how passing a law requiring closing an hour earlier is translated to compliance or non-compliance).

In the relatively early stage of research that we are in with respect to alcohol control policy, we cannot hope nor expect to have sufficient research to address these often unarticulated hypotheses. In the idealized version of meta-analysis, of course, one hopes to identify these various sub-hypotheses, code each published study on those various dimensions, and then estimate their single and collective influence on effect size. It remains an open question as to whether the articulation of all these hypotheses and sub-hypotheses will ever become possible.

In the present real world of policy research, however, I argue that policy researchers must understand that, when summarizing evidence regarding any specific intervention, even a *single* study showing positive impact is sufficient to support the most fundamental evaluation question, "Can this policy or intervention have an impact?" Once such a result is reported, the question is rightfully re-cast as "Under what conditions does this intervention work?" As discussed below, although these two questions are apparently similar, they lead to fundamentally different research strategies.

Example: Responsible Beverage Service

So how do these issues arise in a concrete example? Let us take a closer look at the research base related to "responsible beverage service" or RBS. RBS refers to the steps that servers of alcoholic beverages may take to reduce the chances that their patrons or guests become intoxicated, or to their intervention to prevent harm due to someone becoming impaired. The main idea is that bars and restaurants can have a significant direct impact on the level of alcohol impairment of their customers and, consequently, an indirect impact on levels of deaths and injuries associated with drinking (e.g., alcohol-impaired driving). At a minimum, server intervention requires that servers of alcoholic beverages make sure that no intoxicated or impaired customer is left to drive away in that condition. In order to make our more general argument, we here give only a cursory summary of studies that have been more completely reviewed elsewhere (see, for instance, McKnight, 1993; Saltz, 1997; Graham, 2000).

The hope that those who serve alcohol might be in a position to prevent subsequent harm to drinkers and others stems from several observations. First, someone presumably not impaired by alcohol (the commercial server) is in a position to intervene when the drinker's own judgment may well be impaired. Second, there was a legal precedent (in the USA) for holding alcohol servers and establishments liable for monetary costs in the case where a customer known to be intoxicated was served alcohol that contributed to damages or injury to innocent third parties (Mosher, 1984). This, in turn, implies not only that there is a legal and cultural support for servers to take responsibility for their serving practices, but that a mechanism might already be in place to encourage them to do so.

Note that in this early period of formulating the rationale for RBS as an intervention, there were already a few working hypotheses in play: first, that there was potential for effective server intervention, in that a large proportion of impaired drivers were originating from licensed businesses (O'Donnell, 1985). Second, an implicit set of legal arguments regarding hypotheses about what legal actions might either (a) provide legal legitimacy to the intervention, or (b) provide a motivation for businesses and servers to adopt RBS as a house policy.

Naturally, at this juncture, the question arose as to what, specifically, was needed to get a business to adopt RBS. Rather than being addressed directly, this question was "resolved" by the development of early training programs created by various trainers, the most visible perhaps being the commercial TIPS (Training for Intervention Procedures by Servers of Alcohol) program (Chafetz, 1984). This program also formed the content of one of the first evaluations of RBS, conducted by Russ and Geller (1987), who reported findings supportive of a positive effect on sales to research assistants posing as intoxicated patrons (so-called "pseudopatrons"; see Saltz, 1997). At about the same time, another evaluation, by McKnight (1988), involved the development and delivery of a customized responsible beverage service training program to 100 establishments in eight different cities across the USA. The impact reported (again, using pseudopatrons) was small and not substantively meaningful, but here, too, RBS was a training program.

Shortly thereafter, more studies of server training were conducted. Gliksman and his colleagues (1993) report a design in which manager and complementary server training courses were given to four different establishments in Thunder Bay, Ontario, with four other sites used for comparison. Here, significantly improved scores of appropriate server behavior were observed in the intervention sites. Finally, among other similar studies done at this time, Howard-Pitney and others (1991) conducted a study in Park City, Utah, where a newly expanded state law required servers and managers to be trained every three years. Here, no differences in interventions were observed between the treatment and control servers.

Is "server training" effective?

Although there were other approaches to RBS evaluated during this same period, the commercial programs and these early evaluations more-or-less tended to identify RBS programs with "server training". Among this group of studies, however, the question arises as to what can be concluded. Many reviewers would simply conclude that the evidence is "mixed", and that, with the close similarity of these programs (a few hours' instruction to servers in nearly all cases), there is little to distinguish between those indicating some impact versus those that seemed to be ineffective. Even so, we *can* conclude that server training *can* have an effect, at least over a short term (which all these studies were limited to), and within a limited scope of server behavior (i.e., refusing service to intoxicated pseudopatrons). The effect is obviously not consistent in every case, so the question becomes not whether server training is effective, but rather, "What can produce consistent results?"

Other RBS models

But there were and are different models for RBS interventions as well, and they help us begin to distinguish different dimensions of the basic strategy and its implementation. Some programs, like Australia's Patron Care (Carvolth, 1988) trained servers to act as referral agents, recommending alcohol treatment programs to patrons whose chronic heavy drinking might indicate a need for treatment. Other programs combined training with changes in house policies and procedures. Saltz, for example, evaluated an RBS program that coupled server and manager training (20 hours) with a package of changes in serving procedures and serving sizes (eliminating pitchers) all directed at preventing intoxication and intervening when patrons were nearing the legal limit of intoxication (Saltz, 1987). Two similar Navy clubs for enlisted personnel were selected, with one serving as a program site and the other as a comparison. The program resulted in a fairly substantial reduction in the proportion of patrons over the legal limit of intoxication (from 33% to 15%), at least over the short run (i.e., two months after implementation).

Implicit assumptions of this intervention included the need to support server and manager training with comprehensive changes in serving practices (including standard serving sizes, changes in assigning staff to fixed stations to allow them to monitor patron consumption). The training itself differed from others in that it emphasized intervening with patrons *before* they reached intoxication rather than waiting until after they became visibly impaired.

An evaluation by Stockwell et al. (1993) of the "Freo Respects You" program was aimed at over 50 licensed establishments in Fremantle, Western Australia. The program planners started with the premise that server training alone would not be sufficient to change serving practices unless accompanied by management support and cooperation from law enforcement agencies. Having organized support from both the state Hotels and Hospitality Association and local public authorities, the program was launched with a media campaign and comprised two key components: conducting formal (and confidential) "risk assessments" for each licensee or manager; and organizing workshops for licensees, managers, and bar staff.

Researchers reported that participation in the voluntary program was disappointing with only ten of the 50 targeted businesses involved. Furthermore, while staff knowledge and attitudes regarding serving laws was improved, pseudopatrons feigning intoxication were only refused service in 8 out of 78 attempts. Surprisingly, then, exit breath tests with actual patrons showed a statistically significant drop in the proportion of them with breath alcohol levels in excess of .08 (in comparison with the control community). This difference seemed due to large decreases in three of the participating businesses, with the researchers suggesting that this could reflect different levels of implementation of the program and policies at the outlets. These results might have come from heavy drinkers going to other places to drink, but it also happened that the business with the most successful implementation and outcomes reported an increase in profits.

The variable quality of server training approaches sets up the expectation that mandated training may have little effect. It was surprising, then, to find that mandatory server training in the state of Oregon appeared to significantly lower alcohol-related crashes—by 23% net of other potential effects (Holder and Wagenaar, 1994).

In yet another model of implementation, one efficacy study is particularly intriguing in that it involved no training component at all but rather focused on compliance with serving laws already on the books. A study by McKnight and Streff (1993) evaluated the impact of increased enforcement of laws prohibiting service to obviously intoxicated patrons. Plain-clothes police officers visited bars and restaurants monitoring beverage service over the course of one year. Service to pseudo-patrons feigning intoxication declined from 84% to 47% while service in a comparison site showed declines of a much smaller magnitude. The proportion of DUI arrestees coming from licensed establishments declined from 32% to 23%, whereas the proportion increased slightly in the comparison site.

Similarly, civil lawsuits might serve as motivators for preventive server behavior. Wagenaar and Holder (1991) showed that two well-publicized successful dram shop liability lawsuits in Texas accounted for drops of 6.5% and 5.3% in alcohol-related crash rates.

Finally, a variation on RBS has developed that addresses whole neighborhoods or business districts in an attempt to generally exercise social control among businesses serving alcohol and the districts comprising them. The Surfers Paradise Safety Action Project was a demonstration project centering on the use of responsible beverage service practices to lower alcohol-related violence and disorder in the central business district of that tourist area on Australia's Gold Coast. The program comprised three major strategies: (1) the development of community-based task forces; (2) conducting risk assessments similar to those done in Fremantle, with subsequent implementation of a community "code of practice"; and (3) increased enforcement of license laws, particularly those tied to the prevention of assaults. Observed physical assaults in a sample of outlets declined from 9.8 per 100 hours of observation to 4.7 (Homel and Clark, 1994). Observations also found a significant reduction in binge drinking among men and in rates of intoxication.

Clearly, as this brief review shows, there is a wide diversity of RBS mechanisms that may be employed and evaluated and that set different conceptual perspectives in play. One should be able to appreciate, then, the difficulty of providing a quick answer to whether RBS "works" or not. I doubt the situation is much different for many other prevention strategies one might consider.

SO WHAT'S THE EVIDENCE?

One motivation for this chapter stemmed from the author's overhearing a reaction to an oral presentation that reported some differences across US states with different levels of incentives for server training, but that refusal to serve obviously-intoxicated pseudopatrons was very low in almost all cases (Dresser, 2000). One audience member took the report to mean that "RBS doesn't work." Apart from the mistake of assuming that one study's findings alone should settle the issue, it was also bothersome to realize that for this person, and likely for many others, conclusions were going to be drawn in the hopes of turning the presentation into a guide to action (e.g., "RBS isn't a viable strategy, so let's not put resources into it").

It may be, however, that the research community has not fully articulated the purposes of "efficacy" research, or how to evaluate a body of results (despite the efforts of Holder et al., 1995). One, perhaps unspoken, assumption of many may be that we simply tally the number of positive vs negative findings for any given intervention and let the relative numbers guide our enthusiasm for the strategy.

This is most certainly wrong. This approach is only plausible when the cases reviewers are tallying are identical implementations or replications of a highly standardized intervention. But even under these circumstances, a reasonable approach would be to first look for variations in application or setting that would account for differences between program outcomes. No, the point of efficacy research is to find whether ANY version of a general intervention strategy might "work". The question is, "Can this general strategy reduce alcohol consumption or problems in *any* combination of settings, implementation, or population?" If, based upon a well-designed study, the answer is "yes", *even in only one instance*, then the study has done its work.

With this understanding, then, it behooves us to have as diverse a set of efficacy studies as possible, given that they can conceivably fall under some recognizable heading, such as "responsible beverage service". Analogous to a search strategy, we would want efficacy studies to fan out, so to speak, across a wide territory so as to report back any successes. In the case of RBS studies, we have seen a fairly healthy mix of conventional (voluntary) server training alongside evaluations of state-wide mandatory training, major civil lawsuits, enforcement of serving laws, and generalized enforcement campaigns.

From this mix, we can begin to formulate hypotheses about the mechanisms by which bars and restaurants might begin to be significant sources of preventive action. The question moves from "what works" in some general way, to "HOW does it work?" In the case of the RBS studies here, we have built a collection of undeveloped hypotheses about mechanisms. Do bar staff just need to be informed of the laws regarding service (i.e., are they ignorant of the law)? Is it a case, rather, of their being motivated to perform an intervention? Do we need only to focus on management (information or motivation) and then assume that managers will gain staff compliance? Is enforcement of serving laws necessary—or sufficient?

Efficacy research is a necessary first step (1) to answer the question of whether there is any chance that the general strategy can be effective; and (2) to begin to frame questions of how the strategy achieves the desired result and thus how to maximize successful implementation. The *ad hoc* quality of the efficacy research should now be replaced by more systematic research on these "new" questions.

FROM EVALUATION TO SCIENCE

Terms such as "science-based prevention", "proven interventions", or "empirically-supported strategies", too often beg the question of what is meant by science in prevention research. It is generally understood to be linked with evaluations that use good measures and designed to minimize potential "threats to validity" in Campbell and Stanley's (1963) now classic sense.

Certainly, the use of good measures and rigorous evaluation designs is more common today than two decades ago, and an advance over prior practice, but we would argue that conducting an evaluation solely to answer the question of whether something "worked" or not is not particularly a scientific endeavor, and a collection of results generated by such evaluations is not what most knowledgeable practitioners would think of as "science", no matter how useful those results would be to prevention specialists and policy-makers.

No, the science is developed in studies designed to illuminate the underlying and general mechanisms that may operate across an entire class or set of prevention strategies. Indeed, the very notion of what forms a class of strategies will evolve as researchers gain better appreciation of their common mechanisms. Over time, we may consider RBS to be a subset of "deterrence" strategies (where managers are working to avoid fines or loss of license) rather than, say, of "educational" strategies. Building upon a deterrence mechanism, our research may join others to determine, for instance, the relative impact of the severity of punishment vs the celerity of punishment in this domain. Our research designs would likely involve experimental designs to compare the impact of differing deterrence strategies. Yes, it would resemble evaluations, but the purpose would extend beyond the simple "what works" to a better understanding of how deterrence operates via general mechanisms that cut across specific applications.

This is how science diverges from evaluation *per se*—the focus shifts from particularistic characteristics of specific interventions to those general mechanisms that allow us to better predict the success of an entire class of interventions, rather than having to try every possibility out in an unsystematic fashion. As we know better how deterrence, or education, economic incentives, or environmental "cueing" work in general, we are in a better position to know how they might be employed in novel situations and contexts. In the absence of scientific knowledge of this kind, evaluation *per se* is more likely to trap its practitioners into local backwaters of replicating trivial variants of a limited set of programs that have shown even a modicum of effects.

What's the Problem with Program Fidelity?

This general argument provides a corollary that addresses a rather unproductive debate among prevention researchers as to the relative merits of strict adherence to program fidelity vs allowing or even encouraging adaptation to different settings or populations. It is understandable that one might argue that a program shown to work in some setting should be reproduced exactly as was done in that setting, for we would have no basis for arguing that any departure would be an enhancement. On the other hand, experienced preventionists also "know" that a program can be enhanced by allowing the program personnel or the targets of the strategy to customize some elements and thus gain ownership. The fact that these camps often argue their points is testimony to our immaturity as a science, for the question is clearly one of being able to separate out superficial aspects of the program from the fundamental forces that give it whatever effectiveness it has been found to have. Without being able to discriminate, many program developers will insist that even seemingly trivial aspects of their program be replicated exactly.

The situation is even more muddled for those whose prevention targets are organizations or communities. Here, we have developed even fewer operative theories relevant to purposive change, and so, we find even more unsupported appeals to replicating practice rather than pursuing investigations into organizational change *per se*.

What about Basic Prevention Research?

As implied by the label, our field does engage in research that investigates some fundamental mechanisms (e.g., price effects), and such work should be pursued and will be helpful. The remarks above are directed more towards questions regarding purposive interventions—the kind of questions posed by policy-makers seeking guidance from research. The mechanisms most often pursued by basic prevention research often resemble epidemiology, in that it is usually observational in nature, passively observing those mechanisms as they occur outside of the control or direction of the researcher. Though this is important research, there may well be fundamentally different mechanisms at work when we turn to purposive interventions. Observing the relationship of price to alcohol consumption under naturally occurring conditions, for example, may or may not predict the outcome of a deliberate change in that tax rate, especially if the magnitude of change lies outside the range of "naturally-occurring" change.

CONCLUSION: HOW CAN PREVENTION RESEARCH BETTER SERVE POLICY-MAKERS?

When bringing research results to policy-making, researchers know both more and less than they think they do. If, in reviewing a collection of efficacy studies, we merely tally the number of wins and losses, we do ourselves and the policy-makers a disservice, for the efficacy studies will tell us at least whether success is possible, and, if they are sufficiently diverse in their design, will give us clues as to what mechanisms are likely to prove important in follow-up research.

That follow-up research, however, must be more than simple replication of a program or strategy that worked once before. Of course those replications can be useful, especially if they fail to reproduce the positive result, as we would then turn our attention to the factors that differed between attempts. This, however, is a highly inefficient practice in comparison to designing research to specifically illuminate those mechanisms. In the case of RBS studies, for example, we would want to specifically explore how deterrence, education, or economic incentive may affect the impact of a general strategy that has "worked" in some cases.

So, we "know" more than we acknowledge when we refer to "mixed results" for a given strategy, yet we have not, as a field, developed the kind of knowledge that would be truly generalized and useful for policy-makers, who today cannot be blamed for feeling frustrated by research that appears fractured, chaotic, and particularistic.

Those policy-makers have a role in this state of affairs, too, for if the research community is to work toward a science of prevention, it will benefit enormously by working closely with policy-makers, who are in a position to initiate policies in such a way as to facilitate the sort of research we are arguing for here. More than simply building research funds and personnel into any policy or strategy, the policy initiative could be designed to vary across jurisdictions or populations in order to more directly investigate how that general strategy evolves and how its impact may differ across settings and with differing components or mechanisms (e.g. enforcement vs voluntary compliance). Although such variation often carries political difficulties, there are many more opportunities for this option than are ever undertaken. Researchers represent an untapped resource in this regard, as they can help articulate the fundamental aspects of a given policy and help shape its implementation in order to facilitate learning more than simply whether it "worked" or not. Ideally, research and policy can work in true and proactive partnership.

REFERENCES

Campbell, D.T. and Stanley, J.C. (1963) *Experimental and Quasi-Experimental Designs for Research.* Chicago: Rand McNally College Publishing Company.

Carvolth, R. J. (1988) Patron care: initial process evaluation of hospitality industry interventions. *Australian Drug and Alcohol Review* 7(2), 157–161.

Chafetz, M.E. (1984) Training in intervention procedures: a prevention program. *Abstracts: Review of Alcohol and Driving*, **5**, 17–19.

Dresser, J. (2000) Comparing statewide alcohol server training systems. Paper presented at 15th International Conference on Alcohol, Drugs and Traffic Safety, Stockholm, Sweden, 22–26 September.

Gliksman, L., McKenzie, D., Single, E., Douglas, R., Brunet, S., and Moffatt, K. (1993) The role of alcohol providers in prevention: an evaluation of a server intervention program. *Addiction*, **88**, 1189–1197.

Graham, K. (2000) Preventive interventions for on-premise drinking: a promising but under-researched area for prevention. *Contemporary Drug Problems*, **27**(Fall), 593–668.

Holder, H. and Wagenaar, A. (1994) Mandated server training and reduced alcohol-involved traffic crashes: a time series analysis of the Oregon experience. *Accident Analysis and Prevention*, **26**(1), 89–97.

Holder, H., Boyd, G., Howard, J., Flay, B., Voas, R. and Grossman, M. (1995) Alcohol-problem prevention research policy: the need for a phases research model. *Journal of Public Health Policy*, **16**(3), 324–346.

Homel, R. and Clark, J. (1994) The prediction and prevention of violence in pubs and clubs. In R.V. Clarke (ed.), *Crime Prevention Studies*. Vol. 3. Monsey, NY: Criminal Justice Press.

Howard-Pitney, B., Johnson, M.D., Altman, D., Hopkins, R. and Hammond, N. (1991) Responsible alcohol service: a study of server, manager, and environmental impact. *American Journal of Public Health*, **81**, 197–199.

McKnight, A.J. (1988) *Development and Field Test of a Responsible Alcohol Service Program, Final Report* (Contract No. DTNH22-84-C-07170). Washington, DC: U.S. Department of Transportation, National Highway Traffic Safety Administration.

McKnight, A.J. (1993) Server intervention: accomplishments and needs. *Alcohol Health and Research World*, **17**(1), 76–83.

McKnight, A.J. and Streff, F.M. (1993) The effect of enforcement upon service of alcohol to intoxicated patrons of bars and restaurants. In *Alcohol, Drugs and Traffic Safety—T92. Proceedings of the 12th International Conference on Alcohol, Drugs, and Traffic Safety*. Cologne, Germany: Verlag TÜV Rheinland, pp. 1296–1302.

Mosher, J.M. (1984) The impact of legal provisions on barroom behavior: toward an alcohol-problems prevention policy. *Alcohol*, **1**, 205–211.

O'Donnell, M. (1985) Research on drinking locations of alcohol-impaired drivers: implication for prevention policies. *Journal of Public Health Policy*, **6**, 510–525.

Ross, H-L. (1975) Scandinavian myth: the effectiveness of drinking-and-driving legislation in Sweden and Norway, *Journal of Legal Studies*, **4**(2), 285–310.

Ross, H-L. (1984) *Deterring the Drinking Driver: Legal Policy and Social Control*. revised and updated edition. Lexington, MA: D.C. Heath and Company.

Russ, N.W. and Geller, E.S. (1987) Training bar personnel to prevent drunken driving: a field evaluation. *American Journal of Public Health*, **77**, 952–954.

Saltz, R.F. (1987) The roles of bars and restaurants in preventing alcohol-impaired driving: an evaluation of server intervention. *Evaluation and the Health Professions*, **10**(1), 5–27.

Saltz, R.F. (1997) Prevention where alcohol is sold and consumed: server intervention and responsible beverage service. In M. Plant, E. Single, and T. Stockwell (eds), *Alcohol: Minimising the Harm*. London: Free Association Books, Ltd.

Stockwell, T., Rydon, P., Lang, E. and Beel, A. (1993) *An Evaluation of the 'Freo Respects You' esponsible Alcohol Service Project*. Perth, Western Australia: National Centre for Research into the Prevention of Drug Abuse, Curtin University.

Wagenaar, A.C. and Holder, H.D. (1991) Effects of alcoholic beverage server liability on traffic crash injuries. *Alcoholism: Clinical and Experimental Research*, **15**(6), 942–947.

6.3 US Policy on Illegal Drugs: What We Don't Know Keeps Hurting us—A Perspective on Future Research Needs

JAMES C. ANTHONY

Johns Hopkins University, MD, USA

SUMMARY

In recent years, the US government has made illegal drug supply and demand reduction expenditures exceeding $10 billion per year, mainly allocated to supply reduction and law enforcement. With few exceptions, these measures have been embraced without benefit of good evidence that they will make a valued difference. Major investments are being made for epidemiological surveillance of drug-taking and its health or social casualties, but not for studies of dynamics of drug involvement and drug dependence, nor for studies of drug pricing and how drug users respond to prices—crucial evidence if we are to understand the sustained economic vitality of illegal drug markets. Some very good research on drug treatment and prevention programs has been completed, confirming patient benefits from some modalities, but often contradicting firmly held beliefs about the impact of globally popular programs. Still, for the most part, we remain in a "patent medicine" era for these programs, many of which can be marketed without a shred of definitive evidence about effect or safety. As for law enforcement and supply reduction programs, evaluation seems to be a dirty word; in the main, it just isn't done.

Observations along these lines were the subject matter of a recent report from the National Research Council of the National Academies of Science and Engineering in the USA, entitled "Informing America's Policy on Illegal Drugs: What We Don't Know Keeps Hurting Us" (Manski et al., 2002). This chapter will draw attention to selected NRC committee observations, as well as committee recommendations for improving drug control evaluation and filling current gaps in evidence about drug control policies. The complete text of the report is available on the Internet at http://www.nap.edu and from the National Academy Press.

Preventing Harmful Substance Use: The Evidence Base for Policy and Practice.
Edited by T. Stockwell, P. J. Gruenewald, J. W. Toumbourou and W. Loxley.
© 2005 John Wiley & Sons, Ltd. ISBN 0-470-09227-0 (hbk) 0-470-09228-9 (pbk).

INTRODUCTION

In the mid-1990s, General Barry McCaffrey, Director of the Office of National Drug Control Policy of the United States of America commissioned outside expert opinion on conflicting evaluative reports about the impact of governmental investments in drug control that indicated these investments both did and did not reduce access to and use of illegal drugs in the USA. He also requested a set of recommendations about the nation's needs for better drug policy research. In response, the National Research Council of the National Academies of Science and Engineering (NAS/NRC) mobilized a committee, chaired by Professor Charles Manski of Northwestern University. The committee issued two monographs. The first monograph challenged the findings of both of the conflicting evaluative reports on the impact of governmental investments in drug control. The second monograph, entitled "Informing America's Policy on Illegal Drugs: What We Don't Know Keeps Hurting Us," offered a more general perspective on drug policy research.

I was selected by the NAS/NRC to be one of 16 members of the Committee on Data and Research for Policy on Illegal Drugs. The names of all committee members and key staff for the final report are listed in Table 6.3.1. After a summary of the findings of the committee, this chapter will offer a personal perspective on the two monographs and the committee recommendations. In this regard, I will highlight just three points:

1. Definitive evidence about drug control policy instruments generally cannot come from simple impulse-response thinking.
2. We should not expect multivariable systems research to yield definitive evidence about the comparative impact of drug control policy instruments until we have improved the input data and until we gain mastery and understanding of how the data measurement characteristics change in response to the drug control actions.
3. To a large extent, we lack definitive evidence about the impact of alternative drug policy instruments because policy-makers and politicians do not work in tandem with scientists and policy analysts with the technical skills and expertise to conduct the evaluations. If definitive evidence about policy impact is a highly valued goal, there should be an alliance that increases the subset of problems where the art of politics intersects with the art of science.

These remarks reflect my own observations regarding the findings of the committee. They do not represent either a consensus view of the committee, nor of Johns Hopkins University, my academic home.

RECOMMENDATIONS OF THE COMMITTEE

The summary of recommendations from the committee all are summarized in the conclusions from seven different chapters: Chapter 3: Data Needs for Monitoring Drug Problems, Chapter 4: Drug Data Organization, Chapter 5: Supply Reduction Policy, Chapter 6: Sanctions Against Users of Illegal Drugs, Chapter 7: Preventing Drug Use, Chapter 8: Treatment of Drug Users, and Chapter 9: Final Thoughts. It is clear from these recommendations that the committee was skeptical about many claims drawn from current data and research on illegal drug monitoring, prevention and treatment programs. The committee recommendations included the development of much more extensive and transparent

Table 6.3.1 Committee on Data and Research for Policy on Illegal Drugs

Committee Chair	Charles F. Manski	Department of Economics and Institute for Policy Research	Northwestern University
Committee Members	James C. Anthony	Bloomberg School of Public Health	Johns Hopkins University
	Alfred Blumstein	H. John Heinz III School of Public Policy and Management	Carnegie-Mellon University
	Richard J. Bonnie	School of Law	University of Virginia
	Jeanette Covington	Department of Sociology	Rutgers, The State University of New Jersey
	Denise C. Gottfredson	Department of Criminology and Criminal Justice	University of Maryland
	Philip B. Heymann	Center for Criminal Justice	Harvard University
	Joel L. Horowitz	Department of Economics	The University of Iowa
	Robert J. MacCoun	School of Law and Richard and Rhoda Graduate School of Public Policy	University of California, Berkeley
	Mark H. Moore	Kennedy School of Government	Harvard University
	William Nordhaus	Department of Economics	Yale University
	Charles O'Brien	VA Medical Center	University of Pennsylvania
	Robert H. Porter	Department of Economics	Northwestern University
	Paul R. Rosenbaum	Department of Statistics	University of Pennsylvania
	James Q. Wilson	Anderson Graduate School of Management	University of California, Los Angeles
	Darnell F. Hawkins	Department of African American Studies	University of Illinois at Chicago
Study Director	Carol V. Petrie		
Consultant	John V. Pepper	Department of Economics	University of Virginia
Research Associate	Kathleen Frydl		
Senior Project Assistant	Ralph Patterson		

data collection, surveillance and monitoring programs (going so far as to specifically recommend better access to current standing data sources), greater emphasis upon understanding drug markets for the purpose of supply reduction, greater and more rigorous research on the effectiveness of sanctions to reduce and prevent drug use, a broadening of prevention research far beyond limited "social competency, skill development and normative educational" approaches, and greater focus upon randomized control trials for drug treatments (see Table 6.3.2). The committee placed greatest emphasis upon future research funding to "build the scientific infrastructure for research on illegal drug markets and the effects of drug control interventions".

Table 6.3.2 Recommendations of the committee in its Final Report

Under the heading of Data Needs for Monitoring Drug Problems (Chapter 3):

3.1   The committee recommends that the ONDCP and the granting agency (currently NIDA) establish an oversight committee of statisticians and other experts, knowledgeable in procedures for balancing the needs for public access with the goal of confidentiality, to establish guidelines for providing access and for monitoring whether access to the data is quickly and easily provided.

3.2   The committee recommends that the granting agency require that the contractors who gather data for Monitoring the Future move immediately to provide appropriate access to the longitudinal data. The committee recommends that if access is not provided in accordance with the guidelines of the oversight committee, the ONDCP and the granting agency consider whether the public interest requires relocating the grant in another organization that will provide the level of access necessary for the data to be most useful for purposes of informing public policy on illegal drugs.

3.3   The committee recommends that work be started to develop methods for acquiring consumption data [i.e., how much dosage units consumed per day].

3.4   The committee recommends that methods be developed to supplement the data collected in the National Household Survey on Drug Abuse and Monitoring the Future in order to obtain adequate coverage of subpopulations with high rates of drug use.

3.5   The committee recommends a systematic and rigorous research program (1) to understand and monitor [representative sample survey] nonresponse and (2) to develop methods to reduce nonresponse to the extent possible.

3.6   The committee strongly recommends a systematic and rigorous research program (1) to understand and monitor inaccurate response in the national use surveys and (2) to develop methods to reduce reporting errors to the extent possible.

3.7   The committee recommends that the ONDCP and the Centers for Disease Control and Prevention undertake to develop principles and procedures for information and surveillance systems on illegal drug-taking and its associated hazards.

3.8   The committee recommends that work be started to develop methods for improving existing data and acquiring more reliable drug price data.

3.9   The committee recommends that a major effort be devoted to 'importing' standard procedures on constructing price indices into the development of price indices for illegal drugs. This effort should take place in collaboration with federal statistical agencies that specialize in this area, particularly the Bureau of Labor Statistics.

3.10   The committee recommends that consideration be given to constructing a set of satellite accounts that track the flows in sectors comprising legal and illegal drugs. This set of accounts would be called the National Drug Accounts. These satellite accounts would not enter into the current core national income and product accounts.

Under the heading of Drug Data Organization (Chapter 4):

4.1   The committee recommends that public use files of all major statistical series should be deposited in a data library. On a broader level, every agency sponsoring the collection of population-based data related to illegal drugs should require in their contracts and grants the timely deposit of public use files in an appropriate data library or its dissemination in other ways.

4.2   The committee recommends the formation of an executive branch board to review proposed data collection protocols that might be used as a part of a research effort to design, collect, report, and validate statistical series on economic data, such as prices, expenditures, and consumption [of drugs]. It may be necessary to have rules or legislation enabling the board to exercise its functions in a manner that clearly separates law enforcement from this research enterprise.

Table 6.3.2   *(Continued)*

4.3	The committee recommends that the ONDCP place organizational improvements for data high on its agenda in the immediate future. If it does not move quickly to implement the changes required to improve the statistical data, the President and Congress should find other ways to ensure that the substantive and organizational changes are swiftly and effectively achieved.

Under the heading of Supply Reduction Policy (Chapter 5):

5.1	The committee recommends that the ONDCP should encourage research agencies to develop a sustained program of information and empirical research aiming to discover how drug production, transport, and distribution respond to interdiction and domestic enforcement activities. The committee strongly recommends that empirical research address three critical issues of geographical substitution, deterrence, and adaptation.
5.2	The committee recommends research on how illegal drug prices are determined. Much law enforcement activity is aimed, at least in part, at increasing the price of drugs. Without reliable knowledge of how retail prices are determined, one can only speculate about the effectiveness of such programs.
5.3	The committee recommends survey research on the labor supply of illegal drug dealers.
5.4	The committee recommends that state and local governments be encouraged to explore and assess alternative approaches to law enforcement, including decreases as well as increases in the intensity of enforcement. Organizational arrangements should be made to ensure that the resulting changes in law enforcement measures and policies are well designed and that the data needed to evaluate their consequences are acquired and analyzed.

Under the heading of Sanctions Against Users of Illegal Drugs (Chapter 6):

6.1	The committee recommends that the National Institute of Justice and the National Institute on Drug Abuse collaboratively undertake research on the declarative and deterrent effects, costs, and cost-effectiveness of sanctions against the use of illegal drugs. Particular attention should be paid to the relation between the severity of the prescribed sanctions and conditions of enforcement and the rates of initiation and termination of illegal drug use among different segments of the population.
6.2	The committee recommends that the NIH and NIDA collaborate in stimulating research on the effects of supplemental sanctions, including loss of welfare benefits, driver's licenses, and public housing, on the use of illegal drugs.
6.3	The committee recommends that the Bureau of Labor Statistics monitor the measures taken by employers to discourage use of illegal drugs by their employees, including drug testing, and that the NIDA support rigorous research on the preventive effects and cost-effectiveness of workplace drug testing.
6.4	The committee recommends that the NIDA and the Office of Educational Research and Improvement support rigorous research on the preventive effects, costs, and cost-effectiveness of drug testing in high schools, with a particular emphasis on the relationship between drug testing and other formal and informal mechanisms of social control.

Under the heading of Preventing Drug Use (Chapter 7):

7.1	The committee recommends additional research to assess the effectiveness of social competency skill development and normative education approaches, which emphasize conveying correct information about the prevalence of drug use and its harmful effects.
7.2	The committee recommends additional research on prevention practices implemented under conditions of normal practice so that variability in effects from study to study may be better understood. The committee recommends further research on alternative methods and targeting mechanisms for teaching social competency skills.

(Continued)

Table 6.3.2   Recommendations of the committee in its Final Report *(Continued)*

7.3	The committee recommends a major increase in current efforts to evaluate drug prevention efforts. Further research is needed to better understand (1) effects of the entire spectrum of plausible approaches to prevention proposed or in use, rather than those that are most easily evaluated; (2) effects of drug prevention programs implemented under conditions of normal practice, outside the boundaries of the initial tightly controlled experimental tests of program efficacy under optimal conditions; (3) effects of different combinations of prevention programs, for example, how they complement each other or detract from one another when used in combination, as they most often are; and (4) the extent to which experimentally induced delays in [first use of] tobacco, alcohol, and other illegal drugs yield reductions in later involvement with cocaine and other illegal drugs, specifically, and long-term effects of prevention programming generally.

Under the heading of Treatment of Drug Users (Chapter 8):

8.1	The committee recommends that priorities for the funding of treatment evaluation research should be changed; large-scale national treatment inventory studies should not be conducted at the expense of greater funding for randomized controlled clinical trials.
8.2	The committee recommends greater scientific attention to the now-missed opportunities to conduct randomized trials of drug treatments with no-treatment control conditions.
8.3	The committee recommends that treatment researchers should take greater advantage of possible opportunities for randomization to no-treatment control groups. For example, we strongly encourage studies of incarcerated and post-incarcerated prisoners as outlined in this report. The committee urges federal and state agencies and private institutions to minimize organizational obstacles to such studies, within ethical and legal bounds.
8.4	The committee strongly recommends that treatments intended to benefit people be evaluated in carefully conducted randomized controlled experiments.
8.5	The committee recommends broader use of meta-analytic techniques for cumulating and comparing findings across treatment outcome studies.

Under the heading of Final Thoughts (Chapter 9):

9.1	The committee recommends that the NIJ, the National Science Foundation, and the Bureau of Justice Statistics should be assigned joint responsibility and given the necessary funding to build the scientific infrastructure for research on illegal drug markets and the effects of drug control interventions.

Clearly, the committee expressed deep concern regarding the relatively uninformed thrust of drug control policy in the USA. But it is important to note that the USA is not unique in this respect. Uninformed drug control policy appears the rule, rather than the exception, among most developed countries of the world. This is not to be taken to mean, however, that US drug control policy does not work or is necessarily inappropriate. Rather the report of the committee is at some pains to point out that we simply do not know how well current drug control policy works, or what form a "best" or "optimal" drug control policy might take. The research base is simply inadequate to let us know very much at all.

Three Points of Emphasis

1. Definitive evidence about drug control policy instruments generally cannot come from simple impulse-response thinking.

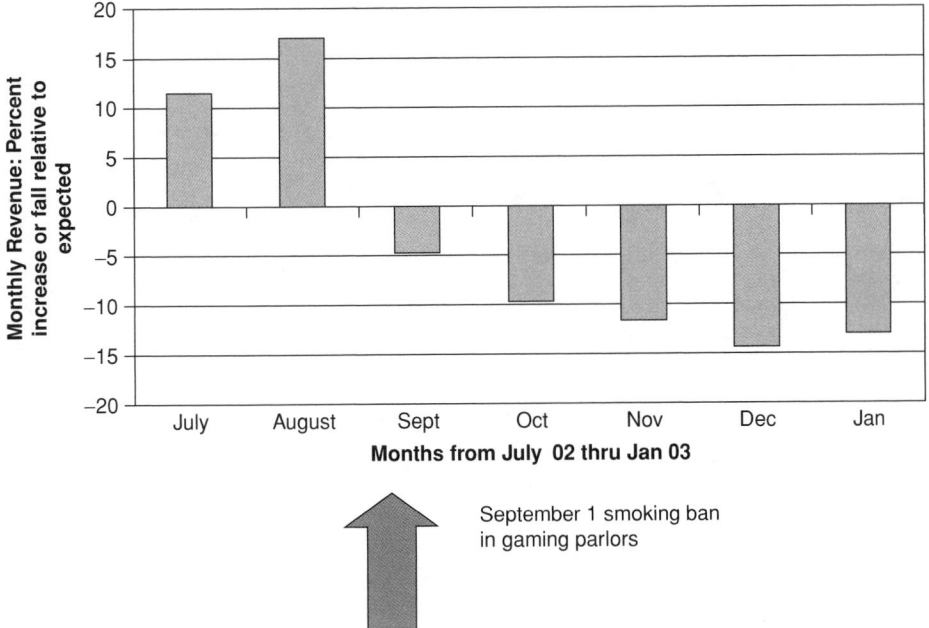

Figure 6.3.1 Example of impulse-response approach: tobacco ban and gambling revenue impact, 2002–2003, Tabcorp.

Figure 6.3.1 illustrates the approach of simple impulse-response thinking. The values shown in this figure recently were released by Tabcorp of Victoria State in Australia, which controls about half of the 30,000 poker machines in Victoria's gaming venues. In order to explain a recent dip in gambling industry revenues, Tabcorp noted a tobacco smoking ban in gaming parlors, imposed on the 1st of September 2002. Poker machine revenue growth had been up in July (+11%) and August 2002 (+17%). Starting with the month of the smoking ban, revenues dropped markedly relative to expected values. Compared to a year earlier, September 2002 revenues were down (5%). In October, they were down 10%; November (−12%); December (−14%); and January 2003 (−13%). If we can assume that all else was held constant, it would appear that the tobacco smoking ban was an effective policy instrument with respect to gambling behavior and gambling industry revenues.

The same type of impulse-response thinking guided America's massive and still disappointing investment in a recent mass media campaign to discourage illegal drug use. This type of thinking is illustrated in Figure 6.3.2, from one of our recent government publications. The data in Figure 6.3.2 show long-term time trends in the prevalence of recently active cannabis smoking as gauged by a nationally representative self-report sample survey of 8th graders in the US, along with concurrent trends in the 8th grade students' assertions about disapproval of cannabis use and their perceptions of the risks associated with cannabis use.

The word balloons represent the impulse-response thinking. In 1991–92, as disapproval and risk perceptions weaken, the figure depicts an upward turn in prevalence of cannabis use. The word balloon for 1996 says that "Attitudes about risk and approval began to harden after 1996", coincident with a leveling of use in that year.

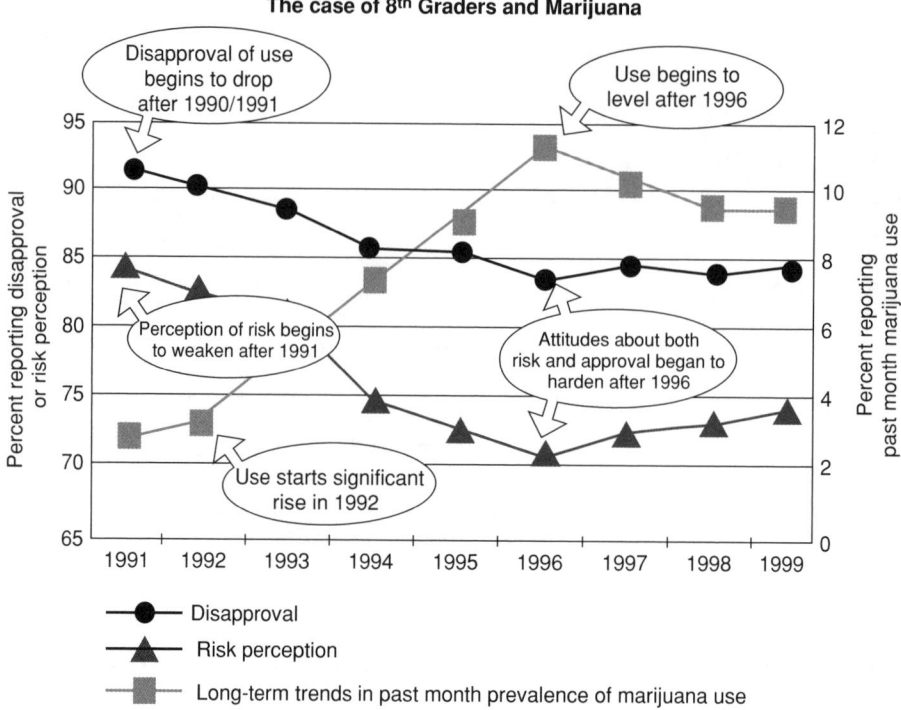

Figure 6.3.2 Time trends in survey estimates for recently active cannabis use by 8th graders, and for attitudes and beliefs about cannabis use.
Note: Data from the USA, 1991–1999.

According to this kind of impulse-response thinking now guiding our country's expensive mass media campaign, young people's levels of cannabis use are determined by their assertions of disapproval and perceptions about risks associated with cannabis use. However, as noted in our committee report and by others, it also is possible that the levels of cannabis use are determining the disapproval and risk perception levels. Or worse, for the policy analyst, the levels of disapproval may be determining the accuracy and completeness of reporting about cannabis use. That is, as disapproval levels increase, the young cannabis users may be less likely to report accurately and completely about their actual cannabis use.

Leaving aside current evidence that America's mass media campaign actually may be promoting onset of illegal drug use by our nation's young people, the drug policy analyst must face a thicket of reciprocal relationships in any effort to evaluate the impact of drug control instruments. In addition, the drug policy analyst must face the possibility that our indicators of youthful drug use are reactive when we take drug policy actions that express disapproval of drug use as part of the intended declarative or deterrent effects of drug control.

Clearly, in these circumstances, more than one variable is changing. All else is not being held constant as we focus on the one impulse-response relationship. Of special importance is the possibility of reactive measurement—the selection and deployment of drug policy instruments may alter measurement properties of the data used to evaluate the impact of each instrument.

2. We should not expect multivariable systems research to yield definitive evidence about the comparative impact of drug control policy instruments until we have improved the input data and until we gain mastery and understanding of how the data measurement characteristics change in response to the drug control actions.

Policy interventions into complex social issues generally require complex evaluation methods and measures, "systems" of such measures related to one another through networks of mathematical relationships. Consequently, I should add that when all is said and done, when sophisticated multivariable systems research appears to provide guidance, there is good reason to make a close inspection of more basic one-, two-, and three-variable system output before drawing firm conclusions.

Some excellent systems research developments have been made during the past 15 years. But systems research is not perfect. As an example, within the past fortnight (prior to November 2003), Australia received a report on the long-term economic impact of global warming and environmental change, with projections based upon a rather complex multivariable systems research model. Upon close inspection of one-, two-, and three-variable outputs from the systems research model, an independent referee found the model to depend upon generally implausible projections of economic growth in South Africa and other emerging market economies of the world relative to the now more established economies. So even well-founded models of relatively well-understood systems deserve skeptical scrutiny before application.

The recent excellent systems research on drug policy instruments also is vulnerable to errors in the complex modeling process. It has an additional special vulnerability because of the reactive measurement problems mentioned in relation to much simpler impulse-response models. Thus, in this particular regard, there was wisdom in General McCaffrey's request for outside expert opinions about the conflicting evaluative reports about the impact of governmental investments in drug control, even though one of the reports was the work of an excellent systems research team at Rand. As a general rule in any high stakes policy evaluation process, outside expert opinions always should be commissioned. The outside experts can shed light on the implicit decisions and assumptions made by the systems researchers, which may represent but a small subset of possible decisions and assumptions in this context.

3. To a large extent, we lack definitive evidence about the impact of alternative drug policy instruments because policy-makers and politicians do not work in tandem with scientists and policy-analysts with the technical skills and expertise to conduct the evaluations. If definitive evidence about policy impact is a highly valued goal, there should be an alliance that increases the subset of problems where the art of politics intersects with the art of science.

When I speak of the intersection of politics and science, I have in mind Aristotle's characterization of politics as "the art of the possible" and Sir Peter Medawar's characterization of science as "the art of the soluble". Drawing upon these ideas, it is reasonable to conceive of drug policies as representing entries into a two-by-two table of the "possible" and the "soluble" (Figure 6.3.3).

The main thrust of this final argument is that the best drug policy research of the future will require a new alliance of politicians, policy-makers, policy analysts, and scientists. As

The Problem Sets
of Science:

	What is Soluble	What is Not Soluble
The Problem Sets of Politics:		
What is Possible	Soluble and possible	Possible but not soluble
What is Not Possible	Soluble but not possible	Not soluble nor possible

Figure 6.3.3   The problem sets of science and the problem sets of politics

scientists, we can frame soluble research questions that now cannot be addressed because current politics do not make them possible. The challenge for this new alliance will be to create new opportunities for research on drug policy—that is, opportunities that do not exist at present.

My own favorite set of these new research opportunities is located within the domain of social experimentation, with an application of randomized field experiments and interrupted time series designs in order to firm up the current evidence on drug policy. Drug policies of the past, such as the international psychotropic conventions and national laws in many countries, have created a straitjacket for drug policy research. The result of this straitjacket is that we now know less than we could know. Ignorant of the effects of the individual drug policy instruments in the top schedules of the current psychotropic laws, we combine these instruments within a heterogeneous cocktail that keeps us in a state of extended ignorance. For example, when a drug is newly assigned to Schedule II of the convention, there is an ensemble of new restrictions. Some of these restrictions are directed toward channels of manufacture and wholesale supply. Other concurrently implemented restrictions are directed toward retail distributors such as physicians who prescribe and pharmacists who dispense Schedule II controlled drugs. Because these instruments of drug policy are engaged as an ensemble, all at once, we have no opportunity to inspect the impact of each restrictive instrument, individually.

If we wish to gauge the effect of each restrictive instrument with more definitive evidence, the political approach must be changed systematically so that the effects of different combinations can be evaluated. Or, if we wish to gauge the effect of the ensemble with more definitive evidence, the political approach must be one that would allow individual sub-national jurisdictions to ramp out the ensemble in a systematic series—not all at once at the national level, as is the present approach.

In my view, the most definitive evidence about drug policy impact will come only when policy-makers, politicians, and scientists join in an alliance to create a deliberate new type of systematic variation in the selection and deployment of drug policy instruments, strengthened when possible with the approach of randomized assignment in relation to time and place. If public health and public safety problems associated with drug use are truly important, we should use formal social experimentation to gain definitive evidence about the impact about what works as intended and what does not work.

Particularly in relation to drug control policy instruments, law enforcement, and drug supply reduction efforts, we now are in an era akin to the "patent medicine" era before the first pure food and drug legislation. Especially in the domain of law enforcement and criminal justice (but also in some domains of prevention and treatment research), actions are taken and programs are developed without clear evidence of benefit or safety. Especially with respect to law enforcement, criminal justice, prevention, and treatment, it is widely assumed that "more is better" and there is no evidence to the contrary because no one is probing these assumptions akin to the manner we probe for faulty assumptions about the safety and benefits of pharmaceutical products.

It was through randomized controlled trials of new drugs that we have emerged from the "patent medicine" era of the early twentieth century pharmaceutical research and development, and we now insist upon definitive evidence to substantiate claims that new medicines will be safe and effective. If we are brave and not faint-hearted, randomized controlled trials of competing drug policy instruments can help lead us out of the current "patent medicine" era of drug policy instruments. But brave politicians and policy-makers will have to join in alliance with brave policy analysts and scientists, working to increase the possibilities for social experimentation and action research, if we hope to gain more definitive evidence about the impact of alternative drug control policy instruments. If this kind of alliance can be forged, it should be possible to gain firm knowledge of what happens when the intensity of law enforcement and criminal justice activities is decreased systematically, in order to complement new knowledge on what happens when intensity of law enforcement and criminal justice activities are increased.

THE COMMITTEE'S FINAL RECOMMENDATIONS

With these three main points as backdrop, I'll now turn to the committee's final recommendations, which are presented as Table 6.3.2 in a chapter summary format. Understanding the composition of the committee (Table 6.3.1), you will not be surprised to see that a National Academy of Sciences and National Research Council committee is advocating a lot of new research. Indeed, we joked to ourselves that the only headlines from this effort would be in the "dog bites man" tenor: "NRC committee recommends new research". Nonetheless, we reviewed much good research and many good research initiatives, and we found reason to re-double these efforts and to advocate even more good and better work.

The committee voiced these recommendations in the hopes that they would give impetus to help forge the above-mentioned alliance of brave politicians, policy makers, policy analysts, and scientists—an alliance that is needed if we are to gain definitive evidence about the impact of drug control policy instruments. As noted at the end of the introduction to the report:

> It makes no sense to continue to argue about drug policy for additional decades, as we have so often in the past, in terms of plausible but unverified assumptions about the nature of drug production, distribution, and use. If society is to make wiser decisions in the years ahead, we must now decide on a strategy to identify the critical empirical questions for drug policy and take the steps needed to answer these questions. Initiating this process is the important task addressed in this report.

ACKNOWLEDGEMENTS

Preparation of this chapter was supported in part by the Johns Hopkins University, MD, and the National Institute on Drug Abuse. The views reflected herein are those of the author and are not necessarily those of the university or NIDA.

REFERENCES

Manski, C.E., Pepper, J.V. and Petrie, C.V. (2002) *Informing America's Policy on Illegal Drugs: What We Don't Know Keeps Hurting Us*. Washington, DC: National Academy Press.

6.4 Preventing Tobacco Use and Harm: What Is Evidence Based Policy?

SANDRA YOUNIE
Monash University, Vic, Australia

MICHELLE SCOLLO, RON BORLAND
VicHealth Centre for Tobacco Control, Vic, Australia

DAVID HILL
The Cancer Council Victoria, Australia

SUMMARY

The majority of tobacco users commence in early to mid-adolescence. Tobacco smoking can be characterised as a chronic, relapsing disorder. While risk increases with amount smoked, there is no safe level of use (i.e., all use is risky). Duration of use is the most important predictor of premature death with the majority of excess morbidity and mortality avoidable if people quit before middle age. Investment in initiatives that reduce smoking among pregnant women and those at risk of cardiovascular disease provide quickest returns in reduced health care episodes and expenditure. Measures that successfully reduce smoking among parents probably reduce smoking uptake by children, and high levels of smoking among both children and parents appear to be associated with higher levels of illicit drug use.

The evidence base for pharmcotherapies in the treatment of tobacco dependence is very strong. Population-level initiatives such as tax increases, mass media-led campaigns and smoke-free policies are all highly cost-effective in reducing population-smoking levels, including among children and young people.

Australian tobacco control initiatives have been based on "social ecology" conceptualisations of the problem, which acknowledge the pivotal role of the media in shaping social values, and public and political opinion.

Broad social change, as well as more focused prevention and cessation initiatives, has drawn heavily on research findings from the behavioural sciences. Considerable effort (mainly, in Australian, in the NGO sector) has gone into documenting policy inputs and monitoring impact and outcome measures.

Preventing Harmful Substance Use: The Evidence Base for Policy and Practice.
Edited by T. Stockwell, P. J. Gruenewald, J. W. Toumbourou and W. Loxley.
© 2005 John Wiley & Sons, Ltd. ISBN 0-470-09227-0 (hbk) 0-470-09228-9 (pbk).

This chapter discusses why conceptualising tobacco-related harm from legal, economic and social policy perspectives should also help build support for tobacco control policy among academic and practising economists and lawyers, and in the business, welfare and government sectors.

INTRODUCTION

Smoking is the largest single cause of preventable death and disease in Australia. In 1998, an estimated 19,019 Australians died from smoking caused disease, approximately 50 deaths per day (Ridolfo and Stevenson, 2001). Many of the diseases caused by smoking are chronic and disabling, affecting people in their most productive years. Smoking imposes costs on the individuals, the health care system, business and those closest to smokers. In the financial year 1998–99, it was estimated that smoking cost the community $21 billion (Collins and Lapsley, 2002).

Numerous authoritative, independent bodies have systematically reviewed the evidence on the impact of tobacco control interventions. These include the World Bank (World Bank, 1999); the World Health Organization (World Health Organization, 1998); the Cochrane Collaboration; the UK Association of Public Health (Reid, 1996); the US Centers for Disease Control (Centers for Disease Control and Prevention, 1999, 2000; Centers for Disease Control, 2001); the National Cancer Institute of the US National Institutes of Health and National Research Council (National Cancer Institute, 1991); and the US Surgeon General (AHCPR, 1996; US Department of Health and Human Services, 2000). All agree that realistically funded, comprehensive tobacco control programmes that include anti-smoking advertising as a major component do reduce tobacco consumption both among adult and teenage smokers (VCTC, 2001).

A comprehensive approach to tobacco control includes public education, health warnings, pricing policy, further controls on promotion, control of toxic ingredients, cessation support, reduction in passive smoking, research, special programmes for indigenous and other at-risk groups, implementation of current legislation (e.g., sales to minors), investigation of litigation, support for international activity (e.g., FCTC), consistency across government and appropriate funding.

INITIATING TOBACCO USE

The majority of tobacco users commence in early to mid-adolescence. Hill and Borland (1991) estimated that in Australia more than 90% who currently smoke took up the habit as teenagers. Most of the tobacco industry's new customers each year, as for the last 30 years, are young people, many as young as 12 years of age (Hill et al, 1999).

While tobacco companies disingenuously spend money on "soft-sell" strategies purporting to discourage children from what is alluringly described as an "adult" habit (Bates et al., 2000), hundreds of millions of dollars of future streams of income for the industry are assured as around 42,800 Australian schoolchildren each year continue to take up smoking, around 3,567 each month (White and Scollo, 2003).

Nicotine Addiction

Tobacco smoking can be characterised as a chronic, relapsing disorder. The US Surgeon General report (2000) describes tobacco dependence as a "chronic disease with remission and relapse". Smoking ten or more cigarettes a day was reported to result in tolerance and physical dependence, which in turn produce withdrawal symptoms (US Department of Health and Human Services, 2000).

More than 90% of smokers want to stop, and almost 80% of Australian smokers have tried in the past to quit (unsuccessfully) (Tan et al., 2000). On any single attempt to quit, unaided, more than 95% of smokers will fail (US Department of Health and Human Services, 1990). Most smokers will require multiple attempts before successfully quitting, especially if they are heavy smokers (Fiore et al., 1990; Cummings et al., 1997). Success rates for quitting can differ according to whether it is the first quit attempt or a subsequent one (Friend and Levy, 2001).

While risk increases with amount smoked, there is no safe level of use (all use is risky). Cigarette smoke contains more than 4,000 chemicals (IARC, 1986). Nicotine within tobacco is a psychoactive drug that affects mood and performance. Adolescent exposure to nicotine produces immediate and long-lasting changes in central nor-adrenaline and dopamine brain pathways. The effects of adolescent smoking and neuro-exposure to nicotine may underlie long-term behavioural changes (Trauth et al., 2001). Some of these changes appear to remain long after use ceases—the so-called "changed-brain syndrome".

Mortality and Morbidity Associated with Nicotine Dependence

Duration of smoking appears to be the most important predictor of premature death. Stopping smoking before middle age has been estimated to prevent more than 90% of the major health risks attributable to smoking (Peto et al., 2000).

In most years since 1964, the US Surgeon General has issued a report describing some aspect of the impact of tobacco on population health. In many of these reports, the Surgeon General included statements of the causal relationship between smoking and disease based on rigorous scientific reviews of all relevant studies published, internationally, to that time. Similar reports have been produced in relation to smoking and cancer by the International Agency for Research on Cancer (IARC) (1986, 2002). Cancers in which a causal relationship has been established include: lung, bladder, cervix, colorectal, oesophageal, kidney, leukemia, laryngeal, liver, oral, oropharynx and hypopharynx, pancreatic, urinary tract and vulva. Other major diseases (for which a causal relationship has been established) include coronary heart disease, peripheral vascular disease, stroke, chronic obstructive pulmonary disease (COPD) and eye disease.

Even stopping smoking after a major illness can confer benefits. Smokers who continue to smoke after an acute myocardial infarction (AMI) have a higher incidence of subsequent events than non-smokers or quitters (Cavender et al., 1992).

INVESTMENTS TARGETED AT POPULATION "SUB-GROUPS"

The costs of smoking to the government are greater than costs associated with any other drug use (Mathers et al., 1999; Ridolfo and Stevenson, 2001). It accounted for 142,500 hospital-isations and 940,000 patients days in Australia in 1998. Smoking is responsible for 10% of all disease treatment costs including a quarter of treatment costs for low-birth-weight infants and greater than 40% of heart disease treatment costs in those aged less than 65. Investment in initiatives that reduce smoking among pregnant women and those at risk of cardiovascular disease provide quickest returns in reduced health care episodes and expenditure.

Smoking has significant impact on maternal and reproductive outcomes. Smokers have a 10–40% lower probability of conception at each menstrual cycle and an increased risk for primary and secondary infertility. They are also at a higher or increased risk for ectopic pregnancies, spontaneous abortion, pre-term rupture of membranes, abruptio placentae and placenta previa. Consequences for their babies are also significant, with increased or higher risk of suffering low birth weight, small for their gestational age and of increased risk of mortality either in the period just before or after birth (perinatal), stillbirths, the first four weeks after birth (neonatal) and from sudden infant death syndrome (SIDS) (US Department of Health and Human Services, 2001). Benefits of interventions for pregnant women and their babies are significant and immediate. Significant cost savings are associated with averting pregnancy complications and low birth weight deliveries. The direct medical costs of a complicated birth are estimated to be 66% higher for a smoker than for non-smokers, a reflection of the greater severity of complications and the more intensive care required (Orleans et al., 2000).

Smoking causes cardiovascular disease (CVD) (US Department of Health and Human Services, 1983) and is a major factor in the rate of progression of cardiovascular disease (Marshall and Stevenson, 2001). In Australia, 13% of deaths from cardiovascular disease have been attributed to cigarette smoking (Ridolfo and Stevenson, 2001). Passive smoking has also been found to have a deleterious effect on cardiovascular health (Glantz and Parmley, 1991).

The benefits of smoking cessation accrue more rapidly for heart disease and stroke than for cancer and emphysema (US Department of Health and Human Services, 1990). Lightwood and Glantz (1997) estimated that a US national program, similar to California's Proposition 99, reducing smoking prevalence by 1% per year in the 35–64 year old age group would prevent $63,840\pm15,521$ (mean$\pm$SD) hospitalisations for heart attacks and $34,366\pm9261$ fewer hospitalisations for stroke. On a per thousand hospitalisation basis, this converts to 98 hospitalisations prevented (and 1,300 deaths from heart attacks outside the hospital) would realise potential cost savings of ~$US3.2 billion ($A5.4 billion) (undiscounted) from a program that reduced prevalence by 1% per year over a 7-year period. Even a one-time 1% reduction in absolute smoking prevalence was estimated to prevent 924 ± 679 heart attacks and 538 ± 508 strokes, resulting in potential cost savings of 44 ± 26 million (in 1995 US dollars). Only the direct costs of medical care, rehabilitation and follow-up costs are included (indirect and intangible costs are not included). The value of avoided costs per quitters varies by sex as women have a lower risk of AMI than men until after menopause. Therefore savings from avoided AMIs are much less for women aged 35 to 64. This study concluded that avoided short-term medical costs (7 year period) for AMI and stroke alone would almost pay for the entire Proposition 99 program.

Figure 6.4.1 shows the cooperative impact of cessation and prevention strategies over the next 50 years or so.

WHY NOT FOCUS ON CHILDREN?

While it is important to prevent children taking up smoking, the evidence shows that children's smoking habits are influenced by those of adults. Research shows that as adult

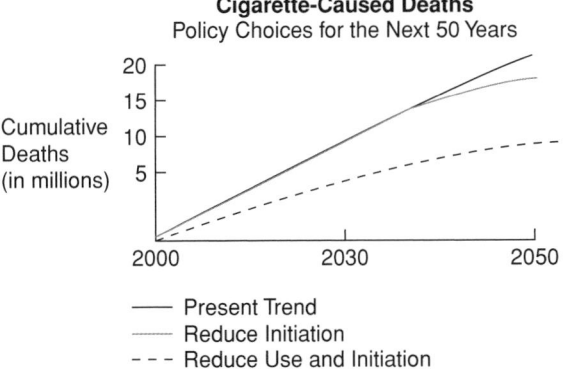

Figure 6.4.1 Comparative impact of cessation and prevention strategies.
Sources: Reproduced and adapted from J. Slade, personal communication, and Henningfield (2000) with permission of BMJ Publishing Group.

smoking prevalence increases, so does youth smoking. Mortality from tobacco in the first half of the twenty first century will be affected much more by the number of adult smokers who stop than by the number of adolescents who start (Peto et al., 2000).

Measures that successfully reduce smoking among parents probably reduce smoking uptake by children, and high levels of smoking among both children and parents appear to be associated with higher levels of illicit drug use.

The analysis of results from the 1997 "Australian National Survey of Mental Health and Well-being" show that current smokers had a 1.9 times greater chance of having a sedative, stimulant or opiate-use disorder, are more than 2.9 times likely to meet the criteria for an alcohol disorder and are 5.0 times more likely to meet the criteria for cannabis-use disorder. The survey found a strong relationship between substance use disorders, mental health disorders and tobacco, suggestive that people with these problems are more likely to start smoking and less likely to quit once they have started (Degenhardt et al., 2001).

The Factors that Influence Whether Children Smoke Are Similar to Those for Adults

A survey undertaken by the Centre for Behavioural Research in Cancer (unpublished) reported that, 12–17-year-old secondary school students had a 54% chance of "ever smoking" if neither parent smoked, increasing to 65% if one parent smoked and to 75% if both parents smoked. For smoking in the past week, the student had a 17% chance if neither parents smoked, increasing to 25% if one parent smoked and increasing again to 36% if both parents smoked.

A survey of American adolescents aged 15–17 years found that adolescents whose parents had quit were almost one-third less likely to be "ever smokers" (more than 100 cigarettes in their lifetime) than those with a parent who still smoked. Adolescents who had "ever smoked" were twice as likely to quit if parents had quit (see Figure 6.4.2). Parental influence on reducing smoking initiation in adolescents was found to be most effective if the parents had quit prior to the child reaching 9 years of age. The earlier parents quit, the less likely their child is to ever smoke (Farkas et al., 1999).

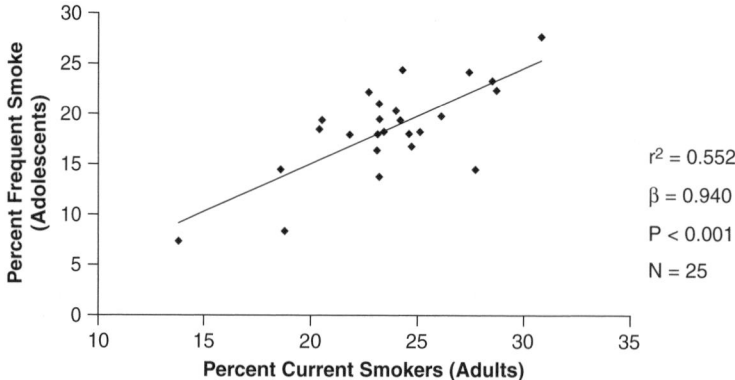

Figure 6.4.2   As adult smoking prevalence increases, so does youth smoking
Sources: 1997 Youth Risk Behavior Survey (14–18 year old public school students) and 1997
Behavioral Risk Factor Survey (adults 18+ years old). Reproduced from Tworek et al. (2003).
Notes: Frequent Smoking among youth = smoking on ≥ 20 days during the previous 30 days. Adult
current smoking = smoking every day or on some days.

ARE PHARMACOTHERAPIES SUCCESSFUL IN TREATING TOBACCO DEPENDENCE?

The evidence base for pharmacotherapies in the treatment of tobacco dependence is very strong. A Cochrane review of more than 90 trials found that nicotine replacement therapy (NRT) helps people to stop smoking. NRT increased the chances of quitting about one and a half to two times (OR 1.71, 95% CI 1.60–1.83), whatever the level of additional support and encouragement compared to no intervention or unassisted quitting (Lancaster et al., 2000). Similarly, a recent systematic review of all literature assessing clinical effectiveness, cost-effectiveness and adverse events of bupropion and nicotine, undertaken by York University, found that the evidence is unequivocable that NRT as an aid to smoking cessation is more effective than placebo. This study investigated both nicotine gum and the patch and did not find evidence supporting one form of NRT as being less efficacious. Nor did the study find any difference in response to NRT by population subgroup (Woolacott et al., 2002).

   Evidence from two large trials and two smaller unpublished trials suggests that bupropion (Zyban) is also effective as a smoking cessation intervention (OR 2.73 95% CI 1.90 to 3.94) (Lancaster et al., 2000). Zyban requiring a doctor's prescription and medical involvement may be important in increasing the cessation rates even though the quality and length of this involvement have not been examined (Friend and Levy, 2001). The systematic review, undertaken by York University, concluded that bupropion is more effective than placebo. No difference was found between subgroups suffering either COPD or CVD and the general smoking population nor for those who have failed in the past to cease smoking with bupropion.

   The incidence of adverse events with NRT therapy is low. The most significant issue with NRT use is its ability to delay the reversal of adverse effects of smoking that are achieved with smoking cessation, therefore use of NRT in patients with CVD is not recommended. Bupropion has several major side effects, the most significant being seizure. The risk is lower for slow release (SR) formulation, used in Australia, but still poses a problem even in populations screened to exclude those at risk. However, Woolacott et al. (2002) commented that no randomised controlled trial of bupropion in smoking cessation has reported any seizures, which they believe may be due to the strict screening of patients in clinical trials versus general practice.

There is evidence that when access barriers, particularly costs, are removed, consumers are interested in using NRT (Hughes et al., 1991; Curry et al., 1998). Schiffman et al. (1997) showed that NRT use increased 152% in the year when NRT was offered over the counter. Access policies may influence the effectiveness of treatment. It has been argued that easier access to NRT may increase effectiveness by encouraging people to use the treatments for the prescribed amount of time. However, it is also argued that the process of having to pay for treatment may screen out less committed and less well-informed smokers (Friend and Levy, 2001).

Drug therapy has been found to be most effective when combined with counselling or behavioural programmes to address the contextual and ritual elements around smoking (Silagy et al., 2001). It has been found that, in experimental settings, combined use of pharmacotherapy and behavioural therapy yielded quit rates approximately four times those of no intervention (Fiore et al., 1994; AHCPR, 1996).

Jha and Chaloupka (2000) estimated that the introduction of more liberal supply of nicotine replacement treatments worldwide would assist six million smokers to quit and avert one million deaths.

Assessing the cost-effectiveness of different smoking cessation interventions can be difficult due to differing methods and assumptions about costs used in the studies. Nevertheless, evaluated studies consistently show that smoking cessation interventions are relatively cost-effective in terms of life-years saved. NRT, when added to current practice, has been found to be cost-effective with an incremental cost per quitter of under £1,000 (Woolacott et al., 2002). In their systematic review, Woolacott et al. (2002) reported that there are no published studies evaluating the relative cost-effectiveness of bupropion SR for smoking. Results of this model found the incremental cost-effectiveness ratio of bupropion SR generally better than that of NRT, but as the adverse effects of bupropion were not considered and only limited available data on the relative efficacy of bupropion, it was recommended that these results be interpreted with caution.

Population-Level Initiatives

Population-level initiatives such as tax increases, mass media-led campaigns and smoke-free policies are all highly cost-effective in reducing population-smoking levels, including among children and young people.

Tax increases have been found to be the "single most effective intervention" in reducing demand for tobacco and especially among the young who are more sensitive to price changes (Jha and Chaloupka, 2000). A 10% rise in the price of tobacco has been found to reduce smoking by about 4% in high-income countries and about 8% in low and middle-income countries. This translates to approximately 42 million smokers in 1995 quitting and would prevent 10 million premature tobacco related deaths (Jha and Chaloupka, 2000). Tax increases are particularly cost effective because of the low cost associated with introducing this measure.

While Chaloupka (1998) acknowledges that higher tobacco taxes will significantly reduce cigarette smoking, and other tobacco use, he qualifies this finding. For a specific tax increase

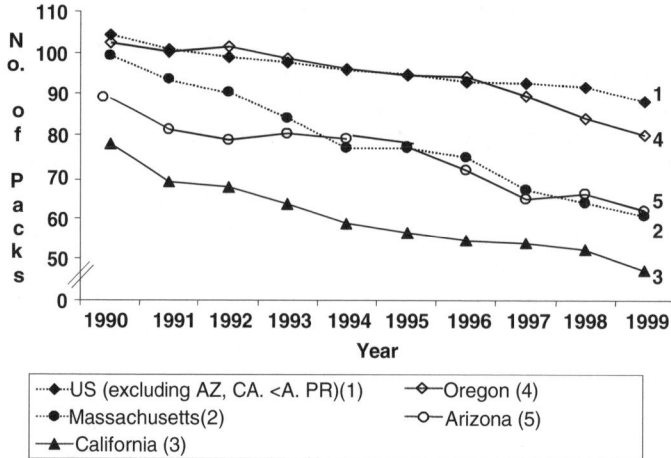

Figure 6.4.3   Changes in per capita cigarette sales in state with large, comprehensive tobacco control campaigns versus the rest of the US
Source: Reprinted from Farrelly et al. (2003) with permission from Elsevier.

to have maximum effect on reducing consumption, it must be a real, sustained increase, which is greater than the rate of inflation. The impact of the tobacco tax depends on the magnitude of the price increase (see Figure 6.4.3). The impact of tax increases can be partially compensated for if smokers substitute higher tar and nicotine cigarettes. Smuggling can reduce the effect on consumption of a tax increase.

Evidence from Australia and the USA shows that mass media campaigns are also effective in reducing smoking. In NSW the Quit For Life campaign, launched in 1983, produced a sharp and significant drop in adult smoking prevalence while figures for Victoria, which had no campaign, remained steady. The following year, Quit was launched in Victoria, and adult smoking prevalence fell sharply (Pierce et al., 1990) (Figure 6.4.4).

An economic evaluation of the first phase of the National Tobacco Campaign (May–December 1997), which was associated with a 1.4% reduction in smoking prevalence across the Australian community, concluded that it has resulted in both substantial savings and significant health improvements for the Commonwealth Government. For an outlay of $7 million by the Commonwealth government, 190,000 people were estimated to have quit smoking, a cost per quitter of between $37–47.

A study of the relative effects of taxation versus an anti-smoking campaign on cigarette consumption found that both were effective means of reducing cigarette consumption (Hu et al., 1995). Though this study found that the 25 cent per pack increase in State tax was more effective than the anti-smoking media campaign (expenditure of approximately $26 million), they concluded that the strength of the effects observed was influenced by the magnitude of the taxes and the amount of expenditure of the mass media campaign.

Increasing expenditure mirrors patterns of decline in smoking prevalence; when tobacco control expenditure has been reduced, smoking prevalence figures have levelled off (VCTC, 2001).

Well-funded campaigns in the United States have also been effective in reducing smoking. Following introduction of the California campaign, 1990 to 1993, there was an

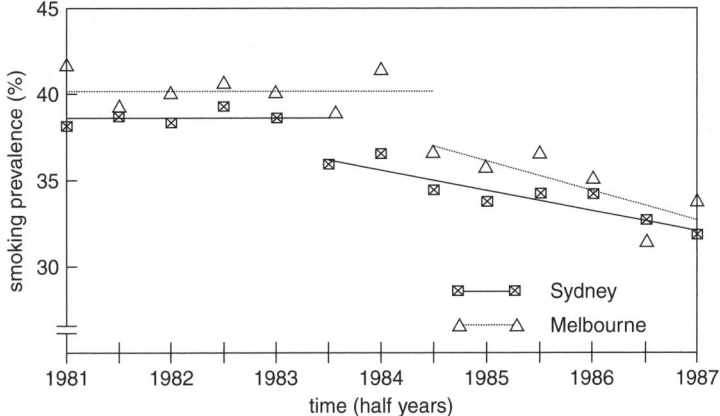

Figure 6.4.4 Age-standardized prevalence, males, Sydney and Melbourne, before and after launch of Quit Campaigns.
Source: Reproduced from Pierce et al. (1990) with permission of the American Public Health Association.

unprecedented and unparalleled decline in tobacco consumption in California, over 50% faster than the national average (Pierce et al., 1998). Evaluation of the Massachusetts campaign, 1993–99, showed a 25% decline in adult smoking prevalence compared to no detectable change in the rest of the USA, excluding California (Biener et al., 2000).

Policies to prevent smoking in public places and workplaces, if introduced in conjunction with strong social consensus against smoking in public places and therefore self-enforcement of restrictions, have been shown to significantly reduce cigarette consumption (Jha and Chaloupka, 2000). Preventing smoking in public places has not been found to impose costs on businesses; indeed, they are often associated with a positive impact.

The Policy Environment

Australian tobacco control initiatives have been based on "social ecology" conceptualisations of the problem, acknowledging the pivotal role of the media in shaping social values, and public and political opinion. Broad social change strategies as well as more focused prevention and cessation initiatives have drawn heavily on research findings from the behavioural sciences. Considerable effort (mainly, in Australia, in the NGO sector) has gone into documenting policy inputs and into monitoring impact and outcome measures.

Social ecology is used to describe how populations fit into a physical, economic, cultural and social environment (Lemyre and Orpana, 2002). A social ecological approach to tobacco prevention brings an appreciation of additional, more comprehensive social and environmental influences, aside from the individual (initiation of smoking and cessation). Health promotion programs are likely to be most effective when they contribute to the weight of influences for desired change and work to counteract influences resisting change and/or promoting undesired change (e.g., lobbying for advertising bans on cigarettes). While this multi-faceted approach can make programmes more effective, it makes evaluating the effects difficult. There is a complexity of forces affecting behaviour from the point of view of the individual being encouraged to change health behaviour (Borland, 1992).

The focus of evaluation should be on the overall program, and the role of the program within the broader social context. In doing this it is important to demonstrate, where possible, that component interventions are contributing at levels commensurate with their previously demonstrated potency. The most important data, however, are the trends in the prevalence of risk behaviours or health protective behaviours. It is from this data that a soundly based analysis of the effectiveness of programs must begin.

(Borland, 1992)

Conceptualising tobacco-related harm from legal, economic and social policy perspectives should also help to build support for tobacco control policy among academic and practising economists and lawyers, and in the business, welfare and government sectors.

Tobacco marketing raises many troubling legal questions. Tobacco companies have not only failed to warn consumers about the health risks of smoking but have deliberately sought to muddy the waters about these risks and the addictiveness of nicotine. While tobacco can be legally sold in Australia, the conduct of manufacturers and sellers of tobacco in the marketing of tobacco needs further exploration.

Governments should intervene in the tobacco market, as most smokers are addicted to nicotine before they are adults and therefore able to fully comprehend the risks and costs associated with smoking. Smoking imposes significant costs not just on the individual but also on society as a whole, including businesses, public infrastructure (litter, fires) and families. Collins and Lapsley (2002) have estimated the total tangible and intangible costs of past and present tobacco abuse at over $21 billion in 1998–99 (current prices), representing over 60% of the total social costs of drug use in Australia. These costs are resources which in this financial year are unavailable to the community for consumption or investment purposes as a result of the effects of past and present tobacco use, plus the costs such as pain and suffering imposed by this use.

Most of the social costs of smoking are borne by individuals, in the form of health and addictive spending and lost production in the home, estimated to be $9.3 billion in 1998–99 prices (Collins and Lapsley, 2002). Australian smokers currently contribute around $4.8476 billion per annum in government taxes on tobacco products (Costello, 2002–03), around $245 per capita (ABS, 2002). Barely half of 1% of this amount is devoted to anti-smoking education (around $25m per annum, Federal and State) (VCTC, 2001).

Further investment in tobacco control interventions, that reduce smoking prevalence, could provide significant cost savings to governments in the form of the avoidable future direct health care costs, both medical and pharmaceutical.

RECOMMENDATIONS

Governments should implement policies and programmes that have proven to be effective in reducing the harm from tobacco use. First, they should prevent cigarettes becoming affordable or available to children. This can be achieved by regular indexation of tobacco excise and customs duty, by ensuring that the duty increases regularly in line with average weekly earnings and estimates of children's average weekly disposable pocket money and by preventing evasion of customs and excise duty.

Second, they should ban all forms of advertising and enforce the laws banning sales to minors.

Third, they should inform consumers. Industry misconduct can be exposed though litigation and orders sought to prevent or address continuing or future misconduct. Smoking risks can be conveyed through strengthened product labelling requirements that disclose information about ingredients including toxic output of cigarettes when smoked and the potential addictiveness and overall health risks posed by cigarettes.

Fourth, governments should run at commercially realistic levels mass media campaigns encouraging people to quit and promoting services and treatments available.

Fifth, they should reduce the involuntary exposure to toxic tobacco by-products through mandated smoking bans in all workplaces and public places. Licence fees on cigarette manufacturers and importers would provide a funding sufficient to cover the cost of necessary regulation and information programmes.

A sixth overarching policy for governments is to re-orient the health care system towards greater investment in prevention. They need to fund a comprehensive evidence-based tobacco dependence treatment program that maximises the use of existing public health and health care infrastructure, irrespective of location or proficiency in English. Adequate financial support should be provided to support a National Quitline; promotion of Quitlines to health professionals; provide a level of "standard care" for smokers by health professionals; additional support for people whose smoking poses high immediate risk; improved access and quality use of NRT; and to smokers whose extreme social disadvantage warrants special effort, for example, indigenous Australians. Finally, governments need to fund ongoing research, evaluation and surveillance to ensure that policies and programmes are being implemented as intended, and to monitor smoking behaviour and the incidence of diseases and other social costs associated with smoking.

REFERENCES

Agency for Health Care Policy and Research (AHCPR) (USA) (1996) *Smoking Cessation: Clinical Guideline No 18.*

Australian Bureau of Statistics (ABS) (2002) *Australian Demographic Statistics*, June Qtr 2002, 3101.0. Canberra: Australian Bureau of Statistics.

Bates, C., Watkins, P. and McNeill, A. (2000) *PR in the Playground: Tobacco Company Youth Anti-Smoking Programs*. London: ASH UK; Cancer Research Fund; October.

Biener, L., Harris, J. and Hamilton, W. (2000) Impact of the Massachusetts tobacco control programme: population based trend analysis. *British Medical Journal*, **321**, 351–354.

Borland, R. (1992) Evaluating comprehensive health promotion programs. *Health Promotion Journal of Australia*, **2**(2), 16–21.

Cavender, J.B., Rogers, W.J., Fisher, L.D., Gersh, B.J., Coggin, C.J. and Myers, W.O. (1992) Effects of smoking on survival and morbidity in patients randomized to medical or surgical therapy in the Coronary Artery Surgery Study (CASS): 10-year follow-up. CASS Investigators. *Journal of the American College of Cardiology*, **20**, 287–294.

Centers for Disease Control (2001) *Investment in Tobacco Control: State Highlights 2001*. Atlanta, GA: US Department of Health and Humans Services.

Centers for Disease Control and Prevention (1999) *Best Practices for Comprehensive Tobacco Control Programs*. Atlanta, GA: US., Department of Health and Human Services, Centers for Disease Control and Prevention, National Center for Chronic Disease Prevention and Health Promotion, Office on Smoking and Health.

Centers for Disease Control and Prevention (2000) *Strategies for Reducing Exposure to Environmental Tobacco Smoke, Increasing Tobacco-Use Cessation, and Reducing Initiation in Communities and Health-Care Systems: A Report on Recommendations of the Task Force on Community Preventive Services.* Atlanta, GA: US Department of Health and Human Services; November 10 2000. MMWR 2000; 49 (No. RR-12).

Chaloupka, F. (1998) How effective are taxes in reducing tobacco consumption? In *The Social Cost of Smoking: 1998.* Lausanne, Switzerland.

Collins, D.J. and Lapsley, H.M. (2002) *Counting the Cost: Eestimates of the Social Costs of Drug Abuse in Australia in 1998–99.* Canberra: Commonwealth Department of Health and Aging.

Costello P. (2002–03) *Final Budget Outcome Part II: Government Finance Statistics Statements, Table 12.* Canberra: AGPS.

Cummings, K.M., Hyland, A., Ockene, J.K., Hymowitz, N. and Manley, M. (1997) Use of the nicotine skin patch by smokers in 20 communities in the United States, 1992–1993. *Tobacco Control*, **6**, S63–70.

Curry, S.J., Grothaus, L.C., McAfee, T. and Pabiniak, C. (1998) Use and cost effectiveness of smoking-cessation services under four insurance plans in a health maintenance organization. *The New England Journal of Medicine*, **339**, 673–679.

Degenhardt, L., Hall, W. and Lynskey, M. (2001) Alcohol, cannabis and tobacco use among Australians: a comparison of their associations with other drug use and use disorders, affective and anxiety disorders, and psychosis. *Addiction*, **96**, 1603–1614.

Farkas, A., Distefan, J., Choi, W., Gilpin, E., Pierce, J. (1999) Does parental smoking cessation discourage adolescent smoking? *Preventive Medicine*, **28**, 213–218.

Fiore, M.C., Smith, S.S., Jorenby, D.E. and Baker T. (1994) The effectiveness of the nicotine patch for smoking cessation: a meta-analysis. *JAMA*, **271**(24): 1940–1947.

Fiore, M.C., Novotny, T.E., Pierce, J.P., Giovino, G.A., Hatziandreu, E.J., Newcomb, P.A. et al. (1990) Methods used to quit smoking in the United States. Do cessation programs help? *JAMA*, **263**, 2760–2765.

Friend, K. and Levy, D.T. (2001) Smoking treatment interventions and policies to promote their use: a critical review. *Nicotine Tobacco Research*, **3**, 299–310.

Glantz, S. and Parmley, W. (1991) Passive smoking and heart disease epidemiology, physiology and biochemistry. *Circulation*, **83**, 1–12.

Hill, D. and Borland, R. (1991) Adults' accounts of onset of regular smoking: influences of school, work and other settings. *Public Health Reports*, **109**, 181–185.

Hill, D., White, V. and Letcher, T. (1999) Tobacco use among Australian secondary students in 1996. *Australian and New Zealand Journal of Public Health*, **23**, 252–259.

Hu, T.W., Sung, H.Y. and Keeler, T.E. (1995) Reducing cigarette consumption in California: tobacco taxes vs an anti-smoking media campaign. *American Journal of Public Health*, **85**, 1218–1222.

Hughes, J.R., Wadland, W., Fenwick, J.W., Lewis, J. and Bickel W. (1991) Effect of cost on the self-administration and efficacy of nicotine gum: a preliminary study. *Preventive Medicine*, **20**(4), 486–496.

International Agency for Research on Cancer (IARC) (1986) *Tobacco Smoking.* IARC Monographs on the Evaluation of Carcinogen Risk of Chemicals to Humans. Vol. 38. Lyon: World Health Organization.

International Agency for Research on Cancer (IARC) (2002)

Jha, P. and Chaloupka, F. (2000) The economics of global tobacco control. *British Medical Journal*, **7257**, 358–361.

Lancaster, T., Stead, L., Silagy, C. and Sowden, A. (2000) Regular review: effectiveness of interventions to help people stop smoking: findings from the Cochrane Library. *British Medical Journal*, **7257**, 355–357.

Lemyre, L. and Orpana, H. (2002) Hypothesis: the research page. Integrating population health into social ecology: role of family medicine researchers. *Canadian Family Physician*, **48**, 1349–1353.

Lightwood, K. and Glantz, S. (1997) Short term economic and health benefits of smoking cessation: myocardial infarction and stroke. *Circulation*, **96**, 1089–1096.

Marshall, R. and Stevenson, M. (2001) Smoking and cardiovascular disease. *West Virginia Medical Journal*, **97**, 17–20.

Mathers, C., Vos, T. and Stevenson, C. (1999) *The Burden of Disease and Injury in Australia*. Canberra: Australian Institute of Health and Welfare.

National Cancer Institute (1991) *Strategies to Control Tobacco Use in the United States: A Blueprint for Public Health Action in the 1990s. Smoking and Tobacco Control Monograph No. 1*. Bethesda, MD: US Department of Health and Human Services, Public Health Service, National Institutes of Health, National Cancer Institute.

Orleans, C.T., Barker, D.C., Kaufman, N.J. and Marx, J.F. (2000) Helping pregnant smokers quit: meeting the challenge in the next decade. *Tobacco Control*, **9**, III6–11.

Peto, R., Darby, S., Deo, H., Silcocks, P., Whitley, E. and Doll, R. (2000) Smoking, smoking cessation, and lung cancer in the UK since 1950: combination of statistics with two case-control studies. *British Medical Journal*, **321**, 323–329.

Pierce, J., Macaskill, A. and Hill, D. (1990) Long-term effectiveness of mass media led antismoking campaigns in Australia. *American Journal of Public Health*, **80**, 565–569.

Pierce, J., Gilpin, E., Emery, S., White, M., Rosbrook, B. and Berry, C. (1998) Has the California Tobacco Control Program reduced smoking? *JAMA*, **230**, 893–899.

Reid, D. (1996) Tobacco control: overview. *British Medical Bulletin*, **52(1)**: 108–120.

Ridolfo, B. and Stevenson, C. (2001) *Quantification of Drug-caused Mortality and Morbidity in Australia, 1998*. Canberra: Australian Institute of Health and Welfare.

Shiffman, S., Gitchell, J.G., Pinney, J.M., Burton, S.L., Kemper, K.E. and Ea, L. (1997) Public health benefit of over-the-counter nicotine medications. *Tobacco Control*, **6**: 306–310.

Silagy, C., Lancaster, T., Stead, L., Mant, D. and Fowler, G. (2001) *Nicotine Replacement Therapy for Smoking Cessation*. Cochrane Database Syst Rev, CD000146 www.cochrane.org/indexo.htm.

Tan, N., Wakefield, M. and Freeman, J. (2000) Changes associated with the National Tobacco Campaign: results of the second follow-up survey. In *Australia's National Tobacco Campaign: Evaluation Report*. Vol. 2. Canberra: Commonwealth Department of Health and Aged Care, pp. 21–76.

Trauth, J., Seidler, F., Ali, S. and Slotkin, T. (2001) Adolescent nicotine exposure produces immediate and long-term changes in CNS noradrenergic and dopaminergic function. *Brain Research*, **892**, 269–280.

Tworek, C., Giovino, G.A., Yang, J., Wakefield, M., Cummings, K.M. and Chaloupka, F. (2003) Exploring the relationship between cigarette smoking among adolescents and adults in the United States. ImpacTeen Research paper Series, No. 26. Available online: http://www.impacteen.org/ab_RPNo26_2003.htm.

US Department of Health and Human Services (1983) *The Health Consequences of Smoking: Cardiovascular Disease: A Report of the Surgeon General*. Rockville, MD: Public Health Service, Office on Smoking and Health.

US Department of Health and Human Services (1990) *The Health Benefits of Smoking Cessation: A Report of the Surgeon General*. Rockville, MD: US Department of Health and Human Services, Public Health Service Centers for Disease Control, Center for Chronic Disease Prevention and Health Promotion, Office on Smoking and Health.

US Department of Health and Human Services (2000) *Reducing Tobacco Use: A Report of the Surgeon General*. Atlanta, GA: US Department of Health and Human Services, Public Health Service, Centers for Disease Control and Prevention, National Center for Chronic Disease Prevention and Health Promotion, Office on Smoking and Health.

US Department of Health and Human Services (2001) *Women and Smoking: A Report of the Surgeon General*. Atlanta, GA: US Department of Health and Human Services, Centers for Disease

Control and Prevention, National Center for Chronic Disease Prevention and Health Promotion, Office on Smoking and Health.

Vichealth Centre for Tobacco Control (VCTC) (2001) *Tobacco Control: A Blue Chip Investment in Public Health*. Melbourne: The Cancer Council, Victoria.

White, V. and Scollo, M. (2003) How many children take up smoking each year in Australia? *Australian and New Zealand Journal of Public Health*, **27**(3): 359–360.

Woolacott, N.F., Jones, L., Forbes, C.A., Mather, L.C., Sowden, A.J., Song, F.J. et al. (2002) The clinical effectiveness and cost-effectiveness of bupropion and nicotine replacement therapy for smoking cessation: a systematic review and economic evaluation. *Health Technology Assessment*, **6**, 1–245.

World Bank (1999) *Curbing the Epidemic: Governments and the Economics of Tobacco Control*. Washington, DC: World Bank.

World Health Organization (1998) *Guidelines for Controlling and Monitoring the Tobacco Epidemic*. Geneva: WHO.

6.5 Moving Toward a Common Evidence Base for Alcohol and Other Drug Prevention Policy

HAROLD D. HOLDER AND ANDREW J. TRENO
Prevention Research Center, Berkeley, CA, USA

SUMMARY

The effectiveness of a program or prevention strategy remains an empirical question, separable from an evaluation of the program implementation. In the end, effective public health and safety policy concerning alcohol and other drugs must apply approaches that have demonstrated evidence of effectiveness.

As suggested by a review of the current prevention research literature, the development of common strategies to assess the relative contributions of different alcohol and drug prevention programs and strategies to the improvement of public health is indicated.

STANDARDS OF EVIDENCE FOR PREVENTION STRATEGIES

Solid empirical evidence should form the basis for the decisions about how to reduce the frequency and prevalence of substance abuse. At minimum, this evidence should; (1) indicate that the intervention can alter substance abuse problems; (2) be based upon methodologically strong research; and (3) have evidence of effectiveness in more than one setting.

PUBLIC POLICIES TO REDUCE SUBSTANCE USE AND ABUSE

Alcohol policies are generally designed to reduce risky drinking and risky drinking situations in the population and these policies can be broadly characterized to affect either the economic availability of alcohol (mainly retail price), the physical availability of alcohol (mainly through alcohol outlets), or law enforcement policies that affect risks related to drinking (e.g., drinking and driving).

Preventing Harmful Substance Use: The Evidence Base for Policy and Practice.
Edited by T. Stockwell, P. J. Gruenewald, J. W. Toumbourou and W. Loxley.
© 2005 John Wiley & Sons, Ltd. ISBN 0-470-09227-0 (hbk) 0-470-09228-9 (pbk).

Economic Availability

Like other retail products, sales of alcohol respond to costs to the consumer, i.e., retail price (Cook and Tauchen, 1982; Levy and Sheflin, 1983). Much of the work demonstrating these relationships has been recently summarized by Chaloupka et al. (2002). Since alcohol prices can affect drinking, prices in turn can also affect other problems related to use. Among adults, alcohol taxes and prices have been related to rates of cirrhosis mortality, single vehicle night-time crashes (crashes that often involve the use of alcohol), and violence (e.g., arrests for assault).

Importantly, several studies have also demonstrated that higher alcoholic beverage taxes or prices can affect alcohol use among young people (Grossman, et al., 1987; Grossman et al., 1998) and drinking and driving among youth and/or young adults (Chaloupka et al., 1993; Ruhm, 1996). Moreover, these beneficial effects would also appear to extend to rates of high school and college graduation (Cook and Moore, 1993), and engagement in physical fights among youth (Markowitz, 2000). As a preventive intervention, Laixuthai and Chaloupka (1993) estimated that indexing the price of beer to inflation would reduce overall youthful drinking by 9% and youthful heavy drinking by 20%.

Deliberate preventive interventions that increase beverage prices for the purpose of reducing problems are few and far between. One notable exception is a recent study of an increase in 5 cents per standard drink which began in April 1992 in the Northern Territory of Australia under the "Living with Alcohol Program" (LAP). Prior to the implementation of additional preventive strategies in 1996 (i.e., lowered legal blood alcohol content while driving and a special levy on case wine), there were statistically significant reductions in road deaths (34.5%) and other mortality (23.4%) as well as traffic crashes requiring hospitalization (28.3%) (Stockwell et al., 2001).

Physical Availability

Additional components of consumer costs for alcoholic beverages are their availability and convenience to obtain. Transportation costs involved in obtaining alcohol, the convenience of purchasing beverages at different places, and the general availability of alcohol in different locations (i.e., outlet densities, hours and days of sale) have all been argued to affect the full prices of these beverages, greater full prices being related to reductions in use (Stockwell and Gruenewald, 2001). Further, demographic proscriptions on purchases of alcohol through outlets are argued to affect use by different segments of the population (e.g., underage youth).

Minimum drinking age or alcohol purchase

Minimum purchase ages vary widely throughout the developed world, ranging from age 12 through age 21. In the 1980s, all US states adopted a uniform 21 minimum age, providing a natural test of the effectiveness of these laws in reducing youth alcohol use and problems. Substantial decreases in alcohol purchases among underage drinkers were demonstrated (Yu et al., 1997) with reductions in drinking and driving (Klepp et al., 1996) and fatal crashes (Voas et al., 1999). Conversely, decreasing the minimum legal drinking age, not surprisingly, has been found to increase drinking and related problems among youth including use (Smart and Fejer, 1975), and crashes (Bako et al., 1976).

In one summary of previous studies, Wagenaar and Toomey (2000) found that a higher legal drinking age was associated with reduced alcohol consumption among youth. Analyses of 24 published studies that assessed the effects of changes in the legal minimum drinking age on other health indicators also showed reductions in other problems such as suicide, homicide, or vandalism. These analyses led them to conclude that, compared to a wide range of other programs and efforts to reduce drinking among young people, increasing the legal age for purchase and consumption of alcohol to 21 appears to have been the most effective strategy. In agreement, the National Highway Traffic Safety Administration estimated that the drinking age of 21 reduced traffic fatalities by 846 deaths in 1997 and prevented a total of 17,359 deaths since 1975 (NHTSA 1998).

Even with these higher minimum drinking age laws, young people can and do purchase alcohol (e.g., Preusser and Williams, 1992; Forster et al., 1994; Grube, 1997). Such sales result from low and inconsistent levels of enforcement especially when there is little community support for underage alcohol sales laws (Wagenaar and Wolfson, 1994, 1995). However, even moderate increases in enforcement can reduce sales of alcohol to minors by as much as 35% to 40%, especially when combined with media and other community and policy activities (Grube, 1997; Wagenaar et al., 2000).

Outlet densities

The geographical concentration of alcohol outlets in neighborhoods and communities can either enhance or delay alcohol access. Gruenewald et al. (1993), for example, found a 10% reduction in the density of alcohol outlets would reduce consumption of spirits by from 1% to 3% and consumption of wine by 4%. Outlet densities have also been related to self-reported rates of drinking and driving (Gruenewald et al., 2002), alcohol-related crashes within neighborhoods (Scribner et al., 1994; Jewell and Brown, 1995) and in surrounding neighborhoods (Gruenewald et al., 1996), and have been demonstrated to have similar geographical relationships to pedestrian injury collisions (LaScala et al., 2001) and violent assaults (Scribner et al., 1995; Gorman et al., 2004).

Relatively little is known about the relationships of outlet densities to youth alcohol use and problems. However, one recent study indicates that greater outlet densities are related to greater rates of drinking and driving among licensed underage youth (Treno et al., 2003). This is the first solid evidence of a relationship between alcohol outlet densities and drinking-related risky behavior by youth.

Days and hours of retail sale

Limitations on days of sale may have mixed effects on overall problem rates (Nordlund, 1985), reducing problems on the particular day on which sales have been prohibited, but failing to reduce problems across the entire week. With this caveat, a large number of studies may be set aside. Turning to those that address this concern, in an early study of changes in permitted days of sale in Sweden in the 1980s, Olsson and Wikström (1982) found reduced days of sale related to rates of domestic violence and public drunkenness and Norström and Skog (2001) found a net 3% increase in alcohol sales with Saturday opening of liquor stores in Sweden.

Limitations on hours of sale may or may not affect use and related problems. This may depend upon the particular hours so regulated. In general, mixed results have been found from a number of analyses of the effects of extended tavern closing hours in Britain on health and drinking-driving statistics (Raistrick et al., 1999: 134–136). However, Chikritzhs et al., (1997) and Chikritzhs and Stockwell (2002) conducted a controlled study of extending training permits (ETP) which enable licensed establishment to have longer hours of alcohol sales, and found that hotels with ETPs had greater alcohol sales and twice the level of monthly assaults compared with their comparison hotels without ETPs, with no effect on the rate of traffic accidents associated with ETPs. Increases in alcohol sales were predominant among high alcohol content beers, wines and spirits. Similar reductions in high risk drinking among young people were observed to be related to earlier closing hours in one study in the USA (Baker et al., 2000).

Limitations on both hours and days of sale would also appear to be an effective way of reducing problems related to alcohol use. A study of an isolated Aboriginal community (Tennant's Creek) in Australia found that limiting take-away sales to the hours of noon to 9 p.m. on other days, and closing bars until noon on Thursday and Friday produced a 19.4% decrease in drinking over a two-year period, and a reduction in arrests, hospital admissions, and women's refuge admissions (Gray et al., 2000; Brady, 2000).

Responsible beverage service

Alcohol servers often encounter intoxicated patrons in bars and restaurants. However, service to such patrons is rarely refused. Consequently, actors are often called upon to feign severe levels of intoxication at licensed premises in order to establish estimates for service refusals. Using this technique, Toomey et al. (1999) found that over 60% of the time these persons were served alcohol. Greater levels of service have been observed in other similar studies (see Saltz and Stanghetta, 1997; Rydon and Stockwell, 1997). In response to these observations, responsible beverage service (RBS) programs have been initiated that help establishments create clear policies for alcohol sales (e.g., requiring clerks or servers to check identification for all customers appearing to be under the age of 30 years) and train servers in their implementation (e.g., teaching clerks and servers to recognize altered or false identification). See Rydon and Stockwell (1997) for a summary of RBS strategies for licensed establishments. RBS can be implemented at both on-premise (Saltz and Stanghetta, 1997) and off-premise establishments (Grube, 1997) and appears most effective when coupled with changes in serving policies (e.g., elimination of happy hours, Saltz and Hennessy, 1990a, b, and Saltz, 1988). RBS has been found to reduce the number of intoxicated patrons leaving a bar (e.g., Dresser and Gliksman, 1998) and to reduce the number of car crashes (e.g., Holder and Wagenaar, 1994).

Whether RBS interventions can reduce minors' use of alcohol is less clear. Establishments with firm and clear policies (e.g., checking ID for all patrons who appear under the age of 30) and a system for monitoring staff compliance are less likely to sell alcohol to minors (Wolfson et al., 1996). However, Grube (1997) found such training alone had a negligible effect beyond those related to increased enforcement (i.e., police stings for underage sales). In Australia, Lang et al. (1996, 1998) found that age was rarely checked in bars after training, although decreases in the number of intoxicated patrons were observed. Nevertheless, once established programs are in place, RBS training may increase checking of identification by servers for a period of up to four years (Buka and Birdthistle, 1999). In addition, the threat of liability for sales to underage youth and intoxicated patrons appears to affect self-reported heavy drinking and driving after drinking across states in the US (Stout et al., 2000).

Drinking and Driving

Policies that discourage drinking and driving can reduce alcohol-related crashes and related injuries and death (see Stewart, 1996; Shults et al., 2001). These strategies include increased and highly visible law enforcement such as random breath testing, sobriety checkpoints, and reductions in the level of legal blood alcohol concentration among drivers. They also may include specific legal sanctions for underage drivers who, despite legal sanctions, remain substantially at-risk for drinking and driving.

Random Breath Testing (RBT) involves extensive and continuous random stops of drivers who are required to take a breath test to establish their blood alcohol level (BAL). BALs over the legally established limit result in legal sanctions. RBT programs have been shown to consistently reduce car crashes (Homel, 1990; Ross 1988a, b; Shults et al., 2001).

Sobriety checkpoints are RBT programs that are implemented under proscribed circumstances that often involve pre-notification about when and where RBT stops will be implemented. Despite these restrictions, sobriety checkpoints have also been shown to reduce drinking and driving and related traffic crashes (Stuster and Blowers, 1995; Henstridge et al., 1997).

Legal blood alcohol concentrations (BAC) at which a driver is considered legally impaired are set in many places by specific *per se* laws. Over the past several decades, the *per se* level has been reduced in many countries in Europe, Canada, states in the USA, Australia and New Zealand. Reductions in *per se* limits are associated with reduced crash levels (Liben, et al., 1987; Zador et al., 1989). In this context, "administrative *per se*" laws also permit the withdrawal of driving privileges without court action, simply on the evidence as established by police subject to judicial review. These laws have been adopted by 38 states in the USA (Hingson et al., 1996) and have been associated with a 5–9% decline in night-time fatal crashes (Hingson, 1993; Zador et al., 1989).

Legal BALs for underage drinking drivers may be set lower then those for adults. Such zero tolerance laws also commonly invoke other penalties such as automatic license revocation. An analysis of the effect of zero-tolerance laws in 12 states found a 20% relative reduction in the proportion of single vehicle night-time fatal crashes (i.e., those most involving alcohol) among underage drivers when compared with nearby states that did not pass zero-tolerance laws (Hingson et al., 1994; Martin et al., 1996). A study of all 50 states and the District of Columbia in the USA found a net decrease of 24% in the number of young drivers with positive BACs after the implementation of zero tolerance laws (Voas et al., 1999).

Otherwise unrelated programs also have an effect upon drinking and driving among young people. Graduated licensing programs place special limits on new or young drivers such as restricting nighttime driving. One such program in Connecticut led to a 14% net reduction in crash involvement among the youngest drivers (Ulmer et al., 2000). Similar effects have been found in studies conducted in New Zealand (Langley et al., 1996) and Canada (Mann et al., 1997; Boase and Tasca, 1998).

TOBACCO POLICIES

Economic Availability

There is consistent evidence that increasing the price of cigarettes reduces smoking both by affecting initiation and consumption. The major means available to alter the price of cigarettes are excise taxes applied to the product by federal or state governments. While producers, wholesalers, and retail outlets can make adjustments in prices to accommodate increases in excise taxes, the net effect of any increase in excise taxes is an increase in the final retail price (Sweanor et al., 1992; Zimring and Nelson, 1995). Generally, as prices increase, demand, measured by sales of tobacco products, declines (Baltagi and Levin, 1986; Keeler et al., 1993). It appears that much of the elasticity related to use arises in the initial decision to smoke. Among older users there is a corresponding decline in price elasticity (Lewit and Coate, 1982). Consequently, there is strong evidence that increasing cigarette and smokeless tobacco taxes is an important method of reducing the prevalence of adolescent tobacco, and subsequently adult, tobacco use.

Physical Availability

There are a variety of mechanisms by which physical access to tobacco products may be restricted. Although scientific investigations into the efficacy of this regulatory approach are limited, several areas of investigation have shown promise. These include minimum age limits for purchases, bans on smoking in public areas, and restrictions on tobacco advertising.

Restrictions on cigarette sales

Like alcohol, one strategy for reducing rates of introduction to smoking and levels of smoking among cigarette users would be to restrict retail access to this product. Surprisingly, this strategy has seen limited application with regard to tobacco products, products that despite their obvious harm to the health of individuals go relatively unregulated at local and state levels. Thus, the state of California uses a licensing system to regulate the sale and distribution of alcohol, notifying the public of any change in ownership or location of every alcohol outlet, but has no similar licensing system for tobacco products. Because of their obvious harmful effects to young people, and the importance of limiting early onset of tobacco use, greater regulatory emphasis has been placed upon restricting ages at which tobacco products can be sold to youth. These policies have had mixed success.

In the USA, sales of cigarettes and smokeless tobacco are illegal to persons under 18 years of age in all 50 States and the District of Columbia. Nevertheless, data from young people indicate that purchases of tobacco products can be accomplished with the same relative ease as purchases of alcohol (Forster et al., 1992; Forster et al., 1997; O'Grady et al., 1999). Younger smokers are more likely than older smokers to cite vending machines as their primary source of cigarettes (Forster et al., 1997) and retail outlets with self-service displays are more likely to sell cigarettes to underage youth than outlets keeping tobacco behind the counter (Wildey et al., 1995). Attempts to change sales to youth by educating merchants about the public health benefits of underage sales laws have had limited impact (Feighery et al., 1991) and there is evidence that vendors who participate in voluntary industry-sponsored programs were as likely to make illegal sales as nonparticipants (DiFranza et al., 1996). On the other hand, increased enforcement of underage sales laws does appear to reduce sales to young people (Forster et al., 1998). Landrine et al. (2000) assessed sales to minors at 72 California tobacco outlets before and after the implementation of a California law increased enforcement. They reported a significant reduction in sales to minors associated with the increased level of law enforcement.

The crucial question, of course, is whether reducing sales actually contributes to reducing adolescent smoking (Lantz et al., 2000). In general, it appears that more restrictive tobacco control laws are related to lower rates of smoking among young people (grades 8 through 12, Chaloupka and Pacula, 1999; Wakefield and Chaloupka, 2000). A program that rewarded store clerks for not selling tobacco to youth (Biglan et al., 1995) found that prevalence of smoking was significantly lower one and five years after the start of the study. Despite this evidence, enforcement of laws restricting retail sales to adolescents has become controversial because of some inconsistencies in demonstrated effects (Fichtenberg and Glantz, 2002; Ling et al., 2002) and because such enforcement is seen as expensive and in competition with other more proven strategies for reducing youth smoking. The argument for such policies is based upon a limited number of controlled studies of retail restrictions that demonstrate changes in youth smoking (Forster and Wolfson, 1998) that have not adequately examined either enforcement actions or expense. Although restrictions on youth access to tobacco products do appear to reduce use, the costs and benefits of such programs are not well understood.

Restrictions on smoking locations

Restrictions or bans on smoking in public places are popular regulatory strategies for reducing harm related to smoking. However, evaluations of the effectiveness of such bans are very limited. Longo et al. (1996), for example demonstrated that quit rates among smokers in hospitals were higher than for the comparison workers after comparing for differences in socio-economic status and prior smoking rates. School policies that restrict smoking on school grounds have also been evaluated and, when applied in concert with other prevention strategies, appear to be related to lower rates of smoking (Pentz et al., 1989; Elder et al., 1996). Despite the many changes that have taken place at local levels with regard to permissible locations for public smoking, little other policy research has been conducted in this area.

ILLICIT DRUG POLICIES

Environmental approaches to the prevention of illicit drug use have been concentrated on restrictions in the supply of drugs, primarily interdiction of the supply both at the international and the local level. In most countries, such strategies have primarily been in the hands of law enforcement (police and drug agents, military, and customs officials). This interdiction approach to drug supply has a complementary emphasis on sanctions against those convicted of supplying drugs. However, in general, unlike alcohol and tobacco, there has been little, if any, scientific evaluation of alternative policies.

Economic Availability

Like alcohol and cigarettes, drug sales can be affected by retail price. However, since drugs are illegal, the only current means to increase price is by reducing available supply. This can be achieved, in principle, by reducing production in source countries, interdiction of distributions to the USA, or domestic enforcement of drug laws that constrain illegal market activities. Rydell and Everingham (1994) present a model-based policy analysis of these alternative methods of controlling cocaine use in the United States and conclude that money spent on supply control programs increases costs to producers (e.g., through replacement of supplies lost due to seizures) and costs of compensating drug traffickers for risks of arrest and imprisonment. Presumably, these costs are passed along to the consumer as price increases, which in turn decrease consumption. Data on drug prices themselves, often collected from police informants, are most notable for their extreme variability over time and space (Caulkins and Reuter, 1998). The degree to which such variations reflect changes in real prices versus measurement error is unknown given the questionable reliability of these price data. Nevertheless, there is limited evidence that illegal drug prices affect use (Desimone and Farrelly, 2003), problems (emergency department admissions, Caulkins, 2001), and crime (Desimone, 2001).

Physical Availability

While an environmental policy for reducing drug supply has received considerable attention in public discussion and debate, there have been few controlled studies of the relative effectiveness of these strategies in reducing drug use. Supporters of the enforcement emphasis claim that law enforcement activities in recent years have led to substantial drug seizures and to the arrest, prosecution, and punishment of many drug traffickers and users. They presume that these seizures and arrests have reduced the availability and use of illegal drugs, both directly and through deterrence. Research support for these claims, however, is not available. DiNardo (1993) found no indication that regional and time variation in DEA (Drug Enforcement Agency) seizures of cocaine were related to either the demand for or price of cocaine. These results concur with those of a study undertaken by the US Congress House Subcommittee on Crime (1994) which investigated the effectiveness of strategies to reduce the supply of drugs in the United States and the wisdom of readjusting the proportion of funds given to supply and demand efforts to combat illegal drug use. The study noted that interdiction programs have failed to prevent the rapid growth of cocaine imports in the 1980s. In the past few years, imports seem to have stabilized at historically high levels, despite significant growth in the late 1980s of interdiction expenditures. Generally, when one considers the existence of "backstop" technologies by which smugglers can avoid interdiction (e.g., smuggling small shipments over land), and the low costs incurred by smugglers as a fraction of all routes on which interdiction must take place, increased costs due to interdiction are small and effects on consumption minimal (Caulkins et al., 1993).

Community policing has also been proposed as a strategy to reduce drug availability. Such policies emphasize crime prevention based upon close cooperation between police and residents to reduce both crime and fear of crime (Fleissner and Heinzelmann, 1996). Uchida et al. (1992) used Oakland, California, and Birmingham, Alabama, as test sites for the effectiveness of several different policing models for controlling the problem of street-level drug trafficking. The findings showed that community policing had dramatic effects on citizen perceptions of quality of life, property crime, and satisfaction with police services. Further, violent crimes reported to the police declined substantially where police–citizen contacts occurred.

Punishment

It is often also claimed that the deterrent effects of drug enforcement can affect local drug distribution operations. Thus, greater punishment for violations of drug control laws may be related to reduced levels of distribution and use. Cavanagh (1993) analyzed the methods that are currently available in the United States for punishing and controlling criminal behavior and concluded that increasing the certainty, severity, and/or celerity of punishment for drug-related crimes would require large additional investments in all parts of the criminal justice system and corrections system. Even if it were possible to increase punishment levels, current research provides no clear answer as to whether this would ultimately reduce drug-related crime.

POLICY STRATEGIES

At this point, there is sufficient research available to guide decision-makers in selecting effective prevention policy strategies for alcohol and tobacco. For illicit drugs, the policy strategies that have received a great deal of attention are efforts to reduce availability, including blocking the delivery of drugs and deterring suppliers of drugs via harsh penalties. In general, such strategies for reducing illicit drug use have not received as much scientific evaluation as have strategies directed at alcohol problems and smoking.

Alcohol

Based on the available evidence, the most effective policies to reduce alcohol-involved problems appear to be (1) taxation or price increases; (2) minimum age; (3) random breath testing with associated public awareness of enforcement; (4) zero tolerance or graduated driving licenses for youth; (5) enforcement of sales of alcohol to underage persons; (6) restrictions on days and hours of sale; (7) responsible beverage server strategies; and (8) changes in alcohol outlet densities. Relatively large changes in the conditions of sale, however, such as moving from monopoly to privatization of alcohol retailing, can increase access to alcohol. Similarly, the introduction or legalization of specific beverage types appears to change beverage preferences and possibly increase consumption. No policy to reduce heavy drinking and alcohol-involved problems can be effective unless it is effectively enforced and there is community support and public awareness of both the policy and its enforcement.

Tobacco

Increasing the retail prices of cigarettes through taxation and reducing illegal sales of tobacco to young people are potentially effective strategies for reducing smoking initiation and overall smoking rates among youth. Evaluation of efforts to reduce retail access of cigarettes has shown reductions in purchases, but no studies have tested reductions in youth smoking as a result of reduced retail access. Some modest effects on youth smoking are attributed to specific types of school-based education, but not all. The effects of restrictions on smoking location seems promising based on current research knowledge.

Illicit Drugs

Illicit drugs represent a special challenge for prevention. There is some evidence that the use of illicit drugs responds to the economic rules of price and availability just like alcohol and cigarettes. However, since these are illegal commodities that operate outside the administrative regulation and control domains utilized for alcohol and tobacco, special problems for enforcement as well as scientific evaluation of effectiveness of environmental strategies exist. The illicit drug market is unregulated and as such can become (and often does) a free-wheeling economic system (almost a pure system of supply and demand, unaffected by government licensing or formal restrictions). More careful consideration of the unique features of this market is clearly indicated.

On the other hand, if interdiction strategies do reduce supply and demand is unchanged, then price will increase, thus providing economic disincentives like those achieved for alcohol and tobacco through excise taxes. High prices can provide barriers to experimental or occasional drug users. The policy dilemma for a supply strategy is that lowering the supply increases the cost for heavy (often dependent) users and stimulates other activities such as burglary or prostitution to obtain money to purchase illicit drugs. Thus, the scarcer the product (when there exists an unmet demand), the greater the potential profit for retail drug suppliers. In this situation, police and military interdiction of supplies can actually increase profit opportunities by making supplies scarce (see Levin et al., 1975; Rasmussen, 1999). Interdiction to physically confiscate illicit drug supplies is not the same as establishing very high sanctions and penalties for the possession, distribution, and sale of illicit drugs. There is no solid controlled evidence that such sanctions reduce supply. Experience from other environmental strategies to deter use or abuse suggests that certainty of detection (not necessarily severity of punishment) could be a more effective environmental approach.

CONCLUSION

Policies as prevention strategies to alter the environment do not usually target a specific risk group but rather alter existing structures to reduce the potential risk of harm or of a social problem. For example, setting a minimum drinking age for alcohol or purchase age for cigarettes is a policy to reduce access to alcohol or cigarettes by all persons below a certain age. In general, public policies for alcohol and smoking (which usually address environmental strategies) have scientific evidence of effectiveness. On average, policies, as they involve changes in rules and regulations or increased emphasis for existing activities, are likely to be lower in cost than specially funded local educational prevention programs which require an ongoing investment in staff, materials, and other resources. Policies directed at the environment have a longer potential effective life, once implemented, than prevention programs that must be maintained and thus funded each year.

Effective implementations of environmental strategies confront two major difficulties. First, they are often controversial and thus politically difficult to implement, especially for alcohol and tobacco, which have legal retail markets. There must be political will and public support for such strategies. Second, environmental strategies, especially those conducted at the community level, often do not provide the level of immediate public satisfaction and personal reward to program staff that educational or service strategies provide. This can mean that environmental strategies may not be as attractive to community members, especially volunteers. The policy strategies for reducing illicit drug use await more careful and dispassionate evaluation. In most cultures, there is a general ban on illegal drugs and thus enforcement of these laws is the major public policy response.

ACKNOWLEDGEMENTS

Chapter presented at NDRI International Research Symposium, "Preventing Substance Use, Risky Use, and Harm: What is Evidence-Based Policy?" Fremantle, Australia, 24–27 February, 2003. Research for and preparation of this chapter were supported by NIAAA Research Center Grant P60-AA06282 and NIAAA Grant No. R37-AA12927.

REFERENCES

Baker, T.K., Johnson, M.B., Voas, R.B. and Lange, J.E. (2000) Reduce youthful binge drinking: call an election in Mexico. *Journal of Safety Research,* **31**(2), 61–69.

Bako, G., MacKenzie, W.C. and Smith, E.S.O. (1976) The effect of legislated lowering of the drinking age on total highway accidents among young drivers in Alberta, 1970–1972. *Canadian Journal of Public Health,* **67**(2), 161–163.

Baltagi, B.H. and Levin, D. (1986) Estimating dynamic demand for cigarettes using panel data: the effects of bootlegging, taxation, and advertising reconsidered. *The Review of Economics and Statistics,* **68**, 148–155.

Biglan, A., Henderson, J., Humphreys, D., Yasui, M., Whisman, R., Black, C. and James, L. (1995) Mobilising positive reinforcement to reduce youth access to tobacco. *Tobacco Control,* **4**, 42–48.

Boase, P. and Tasca, L. (1998) *Graduated Licensing System Evaluation: Interim Report.* Toronto: Ministry of Transportation of Ontario.

Brady, M. (2000) Alcohol policy issues of indigenous people in the United States, Canada, Australia and New Zealand. *Contemporary Drug Problems,* **27**(3), 435–510.

Buka, S.L. and Birdthistle, I.J. (1999) Long-term effects of a community-wide alcohol server training intervention. *Journal of Studies on Alcohol,* **60**(1), 27–36.

Caulkins, J.P. (2001) Drug prices and emergency department mentions for cocaine and heroin. *American Journal of Public Health,* **91**, 1446–1448.

Caulkins, J.P. and Reuter, P. (1998) What price data tell us about drug markets. *Journal of Drug Issues,* **28**, 593–612.

Caulkins, J., Crawford, G. and Reuter, P. (1993) Simulation of adaptive response: a model of drug interdiction. *Mathematical and Computer Modelling,* **17**(2), 37–52.

Cavanagh, D.P. (1993) *Relations Between Increases in the Certainty, Severity, and Celerity of Punishment for Drug Crimes and Reductions in the Level of Crime, Drug Crime, and the Effects of Drug Abuse.* Cambridge, MA: BOTEC Analysis Corporation.

Chaloupka, F.J. and Pacula, R.L. (1999) Sex and race differences in young people's responsiveness to price and tobacco control policies. *Tobacco Control,* **8**(4), 373–377.

Chaloupka, F.J., Saffer, H. and Grossman, M. (1993) Alcohol control policies and motor vehicle fatalities. *Journal of Legal Studies,* **22**(1), 161–186.

Chikritzhs, T. and Stockwell, T. (2002) The impact of later trading hours for Australian public houses (hotels) on levels of violence. *Journal of Studies on Alcohol,* **63**, 591–599.

Chikritzhs, T., Stockwell, T. and Masters, L. (1997) *Evaluation of the Public Health and Safety Impact of Extended Training Permits for Perth Hotels and Night-Clubs.* Western Australia: National Centre for Research into the Prevention of Drug Abuse,

Cook, P.J. and Moore, M.J. (1993) Drinking and schooling. *Journal of Health Economics,* **12**, 411–429.

Cook, P.J. and Tauchen, G. (1982) The effect of liquor taxes on heavy drinking. *Bell Journal of Economics,* **13**(2), 379–390.

Desimone, J. (2001) The effect of cocaine prices on crime. *Economic Inquiry,* **39**, 627–643.

Desimone, J. and Farrelly, M.C. (2003) Price and enforcement effects on cocaine and marijuana demand. *Economic Inquiry,* **41**, 98–115.

DiFranza, J.R., Savageau, J.A. and Aisquith, B.F. (1996) Youth access to tobacco: the effects of age, gender, vending machine locks, and "it's the law" programs. *American Journal of Public Health,* **86**(2), 221–224.

DiNardo, J. (1993) Law enforcement, the price of cocaine and cocaine use. *Mathematical and Computer Modelling,* **17**(2), 53–64.

Dresser, J. and Gliksman, L. (1998) Comparing statewide alcohol server training systems. *Pharmacology, Biochemistry, and Behavior,* **61**, 150.

Elder, J.P., Perry, C.L., Stone, E.J., Johnson, C.C., Yang, M., Edmundson, E.W., Smyth, M.H., Galati, T., Feldman, H., Cribb, P. and Parcel, G.S. (1996) Tobacco use measurement, prediction, and intervention in elementary schools in four states: the CATCH study. *Preventive Medicine*, **25**(4), 486–494.

Feighery, E., Altman, D.G. and Shaffer, G. (1991) The effects of combining education and enforcement to reduce tobacco sales to minors. *Journal of the American Medical Association*, **266**(22), 3168–3171.

Fichtenberg, C.M. and Glantz, S.A. (2002) Youth access interventions do not affect youth smoking. *Pediatrics*, **109**, 1088–1092.

Fleissner, D. and Heinzelmann, F. (1996) *Crime Prevention Through Environmental Design and Community Policing*. Washington, DC: Bureau of Justice Assistance, Office of Justice Programs, US Department of Justice.

Forster, J.L. and Wolfson, M. (1998) Youth access to tobacco: policies and politics. *American Review of Public Health*, **19**, 203–235.

Forster, J.L., Hourigan, M. and McGovern, P. (1992) Availability of cigarettes to underage youth in three communities. *Preventive Medicine*, **21**(3), 320–328.

Forster, J.L., McGovern, P.G., Wagenaar, A.C., Wolfson, M., Perry, C.L. and Anstine, P.S. (1994) The ability of young people to purchase alcohol without age identification in northeastern Minnesota, USA. *Addiction*, **89**, 699–705.

Forster, J.L., Murray, D.M., Wolfson, M., Blaine, T.M., Wagenaar, A.C. and Hennrikus, D.J. (1998) The effects of community policies to reduce youth access to tobacco. *American Journal of Public Health*, **88**(8), 1193–1198.

Forster, J.L., Wolfson, M., Murray, D.M., Wagenaar, A.C. and Claxton, A.J. (1997) Perceived and measured availability of tobacco in 14 Minnesota communities: the TPOP Study. *American Journal of Preventive Medicine*, **13**(3), 167–174.

Gorman, D.M., Gruenewald, P.J., Hanlon, P.J., Mezic, I., Waller, L.A., Castillo-Chavez, C., Bradley, E. and Mezic, J. (in press) Implications of systems dynamic models and control theory for environmental approaches to the prevention of alcohol- and other drug-related problems. *Substance Use and Misuse*, September, 2003.

Gray, D., Saggers, S., Atkinson, D., Sputore, B. and Bourbon, D. (2000) Beating the grog: evaluation of the Tennant Creek liquor licensing restrictions. *Australian and New Zealand Journal of Public Health*, **24**(1), 39–44.

Grossman, M., Chaloupka, F.J. and Sirtalan, I. (1998) An empirical analysis of alcohol addiction: results from Monitoring the Future panels. *Economic Inquiry*, **36**, 39–48.

Grossman, M., Coate, D. and Arluck, G.M. (1987) Price sensitivity of alcoholic beverages in the United States: youth alcohol consumption. In H.D. Holder, (ed.), *Control Issues in Alcohol Abuse Prevention: Strategies for States and Communities*. Greenwich, CT: JAI Press, Inc., pp. 169–198.

Grube, J.W. (1997) Preventing sales of alcohol to minors: results from a community trial. *Addiction*, **92**(Suppl. 2), S251–S260.

Gruenewald, P.J., Johnson, F. and Treno, A.J. (2002) Outlets, drinking and driving: a multilevel analysis of availability. *Journal of Studies on Alcohol*, **63**, 460–468.

Gruenewald, P.J., Ponicki, W.B. and Holder, H.D. (1993) The relationship of outlet densities to alcohol consumption: a time series cross-sectional analysis. *Alcoholism: Clinical and Experimental Research*, **17**(1), 38–47.

Gruenewald, P.J., Millar, A., Treno, A.J., Ponicki, W.R., Yang, Z. and Roeper, P. (1996) The geography of availability and driving after drinking. *Addiction*, **91**, 967–983.

Henstridge, J., Homel, R. and Mackay, P. (1997) *The Long-Term Effects of Random Breath Testing in Four Australian States: A Time Series Analysis*. Queensland, Australia: Data Analysis Australia, Griffith University, School of Justice Administration.

Hingson, R. (1993) Prevention of alcohol-impaired driving. *Alcohol Health and Research World*, **17**(1), 28–34.

Hingson, R.W., Heeren, T. and Winter, M. (1994) Effects of lower legal blood alcohol limits for young and adult drivers. *Alcohol, Drugs and Driving*, **10**, 243–252.

Hingson, R.W., McGovern, T., Howland, J., Heeren, T., Winter, M. and Zakocs, R. (1996) Reducing alcohol-impaired driving in Massachusetts: the Saving Lives Program. *American Journal of Public Health*, **86**(6), 791–797.

Holder, H.D. and Wagenaar, A.C. (1994) Mandated server training and reduced alcohol-involved traffic crashes: a time series analysis of the Oregon experience. *Accident Analysis and Prevention*, **26**(1), 89–97.

Homel, R. (1990) Random breath testing and random stopping programs in Australia. In R.J. Wilson and R.E. Mann (eds), *Drinking and Driving: Advances in Research and Prevention*. New York: Guilford Publications.

Jewell, R.T. and Brown, R.W. (1995) Alcohol availability and alcohol-related motor vehicle accidents. *Applied Economics*, **27**, 759–765.

Keeler, T.E., Hu, T.W., Barnett, P.G. and Manning, W.G. (1993) Taxation, regulation, and addiction: a demand function for cigarettes based on time-series evidence. *Journal of Health Economics*, **12**, 1–18.

Klepp, K.I., Schmid, L.A. and Murray, D.M. (1996) Effects of the increased minimum drinking age law on drinking and driving behavior among adolescents. *Addiction Research*, **4**(3), 237–244.

Laixuthai, A. and Chaloupka, F.J. (1993) Youth alcohol use and public policy. *Contemporary Policy Issues*, **11**(4), 70–81.

Landrine, H., Klonoff, E.A. and Reina-Patton, A. (2000) Minors' access to tobacco before and after the California STAKE Act. *Tobacco Control*, **9** (Suppl. 2), ii15–ii17.

Lang, E., Stockwell, T., Rydon, P. and Beel, A. (1996) Use of pseudo-patrons to assess compliance with laws regarding underage drinking. *Australian and New Zealand Journal of Public Health*, **20**(3), 296–300.

Lang, E., Stockwell, T., Rydon, P. and Beel, A. (1998) Can training bar staff in responsible serving practices reduce alcohol-related harm? *Drug and Alcohol Review*, **17**(1), 39–50.

Langley, J.D, Wagenaar, A.C. and Begg, D.J. (1996) An evaluation of the New Zealand graduated driver licensing system. *Accident Analysis and Prevention*, **28**(2), 139–146.

Lantz, P.M., Jacobson, P.D., Warner, K.E., Wasserman, J., Pollack, H.A., Berson, J. and Ahstrom, A. (2000) Investing in youth tobacco control: a review of smoking prevention and control strategies. *Tobacco Control*, **9**, 47–63.

LaScala, E.A., Gruenewald, P.J. and Johnson, F. (2001) Neighborhood characteristics of alcohol-related pedestrian injury collisions: a geostatistical analysis. *Prevention Science*, **2**, 123–134.

Levin, G., Roberts, E. and Hirsh, G. (1975) *The Persistent Poppy: A Computer Aided Search for Heroin Policy*. New York: Ballinger Publishing Company.

Levy, D. and Sheflin, N. (1983) New evidence on controlling alcohol use through price. *Journal of Studies on Alcohol*, **44**, 920–937.

Lewit, E.M. and Coate, D. (1982) The potential for using excise taxes to reduce smoking. *Journal of Health Economics*, **1**, 121–145.

Liben, C.B., Vingilis, E.R. and Blefgen, H. (1987) The Canadian drinking-driving countermeasure experience. *Accident Analysis and Prevention*, **19**(3), 159–181.

Ling, P.M., Landman, A. and Glantz, S.A. (2002) It is time to abandon youth access tobacco programs. *Tobacco Control,* **11**, 3–16.

Longo, D.R., Brownson, R.C., Johnson, J.C., Hewett, J.E., Kruse, R.L., Novotny, T.E. and Logan, R.A. (1996) Hospital smoking bans and employee smoking behavior: results of a national survey. *Journal of the American Medical Association*, **275**(16), 1252–1257.

Mann, R.E., Stoduto, G., Anglin, L., Pavic, B., Fallon, F., Lauzon, R. and Amitay, O.A. (1997) Graduated licensing in Ontario: impact of the 0 BAL provision on adolescents' drinking-driving. In C. Mercier-Guyon (ed.), *Alcohol, Drugs, and Traffic Safety*, Vol. 3. Annecy, France: Centre d'Etudes et de Recherches en Médecine du Trafic, pp. 1055–1060.

Markowitz, S. (2000) *The Role of Alcohol and Drug Consumption in Determining Physical Fights and Weapon Carrying by Teenagers*. Cambridge, MA: National Bureau of Economic Research Working Paper No. 7500.

Martin, S.E., Grube, J.W., Voas, R.V., Baker, J. and Hingson, R. (1996) Zero tolerance laws: effective public policy? *Alcoholism: Clinical and Experimental Research*, **20**(Suppl. 8), 147A–150A.

National Highway Traffic Safety Administration. (1998) *Traffic Safety Facts 1997: Alcohol*. Washington, DC: Department of Transportation, National Center for Statistics and Analysis.

Nordlund, S. (1985) *Effects of Saturday Closing of Wine and Spirits Shops in Norway*. National Institute for Alcohol Research, SIFA Mimeograph No. 5/85, Oslo, presented at the 31st International Institute on the Prevention and Treatment of Alcoholism, Rome, Italy, 2–7 June.

Norström, T. and Skog, O.J. (2001) Alcohol and mortality: Methodological and analytical issues in aggregates analyses. *Addiction*, **96**(Suppl. 1), 5–18.

O'Grady, B., Ashbridge, M. and Abernathy, T. (1999) Analysis of factors related to illegal tobacco sales to young people in Ontario. *Tobacco Control*, **8**(3), 301–305.

Olsson, O. and Wikström, P-O.H. (1982) Effects of the experimental Saturday closing of liquor retail stores in Sweden. *Contemporary Drug Problems*, **XI**(3), 325–353.

Pentz, M.A., Dwyer, J.H., MacKinnon, D.P., Flay, B.R., Hansen, W.B., Wang, E.Y. and Johnson, C.A. (1989) A multi-community trial for primary prevention of adolescent drug abuse: effects on drug use prevalence. *Journal of the American Medical Association*, **261**, 3259–3266.

Preusser, D.F. and Williams, A.F. (1992) Sales of alcohol to underage purchasers in three New York counties and Washimgton DC. *Journal of Public Health Policy*, **13**, 306–317.

Raistrick, D., Hodgson, R. and Ritson, B. (eds) (1999) *Tackling Alcohol Together*. London: Free Association Books.

Rasmussen, D. (1999) Reducing the harms of drug policy: an economic perspective. *Substance Use and Abuse*, **34**(1), 49–67.

Ross, H.L. (1988a) Deterrence-based policies in Britain, Canada and Australia. In M.D. Laurence, J.R. Snortum, and F.E. Zimring (eds), *The Social Control of Drinking and Driving*. Chicago: University of Chicago Press, pp. 64–78.

Ross, H.L. (1988b) British drink-driving policy. *British Journal of Addiction*, **83**(8), 863–865.

Ruhm, C.J. (1996) Alcohol policies and highway vehicle fatalities. *Journal of Health Economics*, **15**, 435–454.

Rydell, C.P. and Everingham, S.S. (1994) *Controlling Cocaine: Supply Versus Demand Programs*. Santa Barbara, CA: Rand Corporation.

Rydon, P. and Stockwell, T. (1997) Local regulation and enforcement strategies for licensed premises. In M. Plant, E. Single, and T. Stockwell (eds), *Alcohol: Minimising the Harm. What Works?* New York: Free Association Books, Ltd, pp. 211–229.

Saltz, R.F. (1988) Server intervention and responsible beverage service programs. In *Surgeon General's Workshop on Drunk Driving: Background Papers*. U.S. Department of Health and Human Services, Office of the Surgeon General, Rockville, MD, pp. 169–179.

Saltz, R.F. and Hennessy, M. (1990a) *The Efficacy of "Responsible Beverage Service" Programs in Reducing Intoxication*. Working Paper. Berkeley, CA: Prevention Research Center.

Saltz, R.F. and Hennessy, M. (1990b) *Reducing Intoxication in Commercial Establishments: An Evaluation of Responsible Beverage Service Practices*. Working Paper. Berkeley, CA: Prevention Research Center.

Saltz, R.F. and Stanghetta, P. (1997) A community-wide responsible beverage service program in three communities: early findings. *Addiction*, **92**(Suppl. 2), S237–S249.

Scribner, R.A., MacKinnon, D.P. and Dwyer, J.H. (1994) Alcohol outlet density and motor vehicle crashes in Los Angeles County cities. *Journal of Studies on Alcohol*, **55**, 447–453.

Scribner, R.A., MacKinnon, D.P. and Dwyer, J.H. (1995) The risk of assaultive violence and alcohol availability in Los Angeles County. *American Journal of Public Health*, **85**, 335–340.

Shults, R.A., Elder, R.W., Sleet, D.A., Nichols, J.L., Alao, M.O., Garande-Kulis, V.G., Zaza, S., Sosin, D.M., Thompson, R.S. and the Task Force on Community Preventive Services (2001) Review of evidence regarding interventions to reduce alcohol-impaired driving. *American Journal of Preventive Medicine*, **31**(Suppl. 4), 66–88.

Smart, R.G. and Fejer, D. (1975) Six years of cross-sectional surveys of student drug use in Toronto. *Bulletin on Narcotics*, **XXVII**(2), 11–22.

Stewart. K. (1996) Alcohol and drugs: The nature of and reasons for the decline in drinking and driving in the United States. An update. In *Proceedings of the Conference: Road Safety in Europe and Strategic Highway Research Program*. VTI Konferens No. 4A, Part 3. Swedish National Road and Transport Research Institute, Linköping, Sweden, pp. 1–12.

Stockwell, T. and Gruenewald, P.J. (2001) Controls on the physical availability of alcohol. In N. Heather, T.J. Peters and T. Stockwell (eds), *Handbook on Alcohol Dependence and Alcohol Related Problems*. New York: Wiley, pp. 699–720.

Stockwell, T., Chikritzhs, T., Hendrie, D., Fordham, R., Ying, F., Phillips, M., Cronin, J. and O'Reilly, B. (2001) The public health and safety benefits of the Northern Territory's Living with Alcohol Programme. *Drug and Alcohol Review*, **20**, 167–180.

Stout, E., Sloan, F.A., Liang, L. and Davies, H.H. (2000) Reducing harmful alcohol-related behaviors: effective regulatory methods. *Journal of Studies on Alcohol*, **61**, 402–412.

Stuster, J.W. and Blowers, P.A. (1995) *Experimental Evaluation of Sobriety Checkpoint Programs*. Washington, DC: National Highway Traffic Safety Administration.

Sweanor, D., Ballin, S., Corcoran, R.D., Davis, A., Deasy, K., Ferrence, R.G., Lahey, R., Lucido, S., Nethery, W.J. and Wasserman, J. (1992) Report of the tobacco policy research study group on tobacco pricing and taxation in the United States. *Tobacco Control*, **1**(Suppl.), 531–536.

Toomey, T.L., Wagenaar, A.C., Kilian, G., Fitch, O., Rothstein, C. and Fletcher, L. (1999) Alcohol sales to pseudo-intoxicated bar patrons. *Public Health Reports*, **114**, 337–342.

Treno, A. J., Grube, J.W. and Martin, S.E (2003) Alcohol availability as a predictor of youth drinking and driving: a hierarchical analysis of survey and archival data. *Alcoholism: Clinical and Experimental Research*, **27**(5), 835–840.

Uchida, C., Forst, B. and Annan, S. (1992) *Controlling Street-Level Drug Trafficking: Evidence from Oakland and Birmingham*. Washington, DC: Bureau of Justice Assistance, Office of Justice Programs, US Department of Justice.

Ulmer, R.G., Ferguson, S.A., Williams, A.F. and Preusser, D.F. (2000) *Teenage Crash Reduction Associated with Delayed Licensure in Connecticut*. Arlington, VA.

U.S. Congress House Subcommittee on Crime (1994) *International Drug Supply, Control, and Interdiction: Hearing Before the U.S. House Subcommittee on Crime and Criminal Justice of the Committee on the Judiciary, July 15, 1993*, Washington, DC: U.S. Congress.

Voas, R.B., Tippetts, A.S. and Fell, J. (1999) United States limits drinking by youth under age 21: does this reduce fatal crash involvements? Paper presented at the annual meeting of the Association for the Advancement of Automotive Medicine, Barcelona, Spain, September.

Wagenaar, A.C. and Toomey, T.L. (2000) *Effects of Minimum Drinking Age Laws: Review and Analyses of the Literature*. Prepared for Advisory Council Subcommittee, Rockville, MD.

Wagenaar, A.C. and Wolfson, M. (1994) Enforcement of the legal minimum drinking age in the United States. *Journal of Public Health Policy*, **15**, 37–53.

Wagenaar, A.C. and Wolfson, M. (1995) Deterring sales and provision of alcohol to minors: a study of enforcement in 295 counties in four states. *Public Health Reports*, **110**, 419–427.

Wagenaar, A.C., Murray, D.M. and Toomey, T.L. (2000) Communities mobilizing for change on alcohol (CMCA): effects of a randomized trial on arrests and traffic crashes. *Addiction*, **95**(2), 209–217.

Wakefield, M. and Chaloupka, F. (2000) Effectiveness of comprehensive tobacco control programmes in reducing teenage smoking in the USA. *Tobacco Control*, **9**(2), 177–186.

Wildey, M.B., Woodruff, S.I., Pampalone, S.Z. and Conway, T.L. (1995) Self-service sale of tobacco: how it contributes to youth access. *Tobacco Control*, **4**, 355–361.

Wolfson, M., Toomey, T.L., Murray, D.M., Forster, J.L., Short, B.J. and Wagenaar, A.C. (1996) Alcohol outlet policies and practices concerning sales to underage people. *Addiction*, **91**(4), 589–602.

Yu, J., Varone, R. and Shacket, R.W. (1997) *Fifteen-Year Review of Drinking Age Laws: Preliminary Findings of the 1996 New York State Youth Alcohol Survey*. New York: Office of Alcoholism and Substance Abuse.

Zador, P., Lund, A., Fields, M. and Weinberg, K. (1989) Fatal crash involvement and laws against alcohol-impaired driving. *Journal of Public Health Policy*, **10**, 467–485.

Zimring, F.E. and Nelson, W. (1995) Cigarette taxes as cigarette policy. *Tobacco Control*, **4**, 525–533.

6.6 The Evidence Base for Preventing the Spread of Blood-Borne Diseases within and from Populations of Injecting Drug Users

MARCIA RUSSELL

Prevention Research Center, Berkeley, CA, USA

SUSAN CARRUTHERS

National Drug Research Institute, Curtin University of Technology, Perth, WA, Australia

SUMMARY

The efficacy of drug treatment and harm reduction programs in reducing the transmission of HIV among IDUs via contaminated drug paraphernalia has been repeatedly demonstrated, but currently available interventions have been less successful in preventing the transmission of HCV and HBV. New cases of HIV and HBV are more likely to be associated with high-risk sexual behavior than with exposure to contaminated drug paraphernalia. Current research is concerned with understanding dynamic relations between IDU and sex networks in order to prevent the emergence of new epidemics. Although IDU does not appear to be a major factor in the transmission of HIV and HBV in countries with high national prevalence rates, prevalence among IDUs in these countries is higher than it is among the non-drug using population, and a comprehensive effort to reduce the spread of HIV and HBV should include prevention programs targeting IDUs. A comprehensive approach that combines drug treatment, ready access to sterile needles and syringes, counseling regarding safe injection and sexual practices, HBV vaccination, and community outreach is most highly recommended; such programs should specifically target the special needs of high-risk populations such as prisoners, prostitutes, and the homeless. Despite evidence that these interventions can substantially reduce the incidence of blood-borne viruses (BBVs) associated with IDU, they are frequently not implemented in a widespread or consistent manner. Lack of funding and political discomfort with harm reduction approaches are major obstacles.

Preventing Harmful Substance Use: The Evidence Base for Policy and Practice.
Edited by T. Stockwell, P. J. Gruenewald, J. W. Toumbourou and W. Loxley.
© 2005 John Wiley & Sons, Ltd. ISBN 0-470-09227-0 (hbk) 0-470-09228-9 (pbk).

INTRODUCTION

There are three viral infections to which injecting drug users (IDUs) are particularly vulnerable: the human immune-deficiency virus (HIV), the hepatitis B virus (HBV) and the hepatitis C virus (HCV). Because all three viruses are efficiently transmitted by parenteral means, they are frequently grouped together under the umbrella of blood-borne viruses (BBVs). Two decades of research have identified behaviors which put IDUs at risk of exposure to these viruses; these include the sharing of needles and syringes, the sharing of other injecting equipment (i.e., cookers, cotton, or water), and blood-to-blood contact involved in giving or receiving injections. More recently, video film of injecting events clearly demonstrates the multiple opportunities within the injection process which can result in exposure to foreign and potentially infected blood (Carruthers, 2003; Flynn et al., 1996). It would seem logical to assume that BBV prevention strategies that address these common risk factors would be effective in preventing transmission of all three BBVs. However, the viruses differ in their prevalence and incidence among IDUs, their characteristics, natural histories, and routes of transmission in ways that render generic prevention strategies inadequate (see Table 6.6.1).

Briefly, hepatitis B and C are more easily transmitted than HIV by exposure to contaminated blood via needle stick injuries (Gerberding, 1995). Once a person is infected, infection is chronic in all HIV cases, in 75 to 85% of HCV cases, and in only 2 to 6% of HBV cases that occur in older children or adults. HIV infection rates among IDUs are quite variable, whereas HCV and HBV infection rates tend to be uniformly high (Hagan and Des Jarlais, 2000). Despite similarities in HCV and HBV infection rates, the fact that a substantially higher proportion of HCV infections become chronic means that IDUs who share injecting equipment are much more likely to come into contact with an active case of hepatitis C than B. The likelihood of contracting HBV is increased by the fact that it is efficiently transmitted sexually, as well as via blood-to-blood exposure, a characteristic it shares with

Table 6.6.1 Characteristics of viruses

	HIV	HCV	HBV
Infectivity[a]	0.2–0.5%	3–10%	2–40%
Chronicity	100%	75%–85%	2–6% in older children and adults
Prevalence in IDUs[b]	1%–76%	50%–90%	50%–90%
Sexual transmission	Yes	Rare	Yes
Vaccination	No	No	Yes
Percentage of new BBVs associated with IDU in the United States	28%	60%	17%
Percentage of new BBVs associated with IDU in Australia	4.3%	85%	Not available
Worldwide prevalence of chronic infection	40M	170M	350M[c]

Notes:
[a] Likelihood of infections via percutaneous injury inflicted by a contaminated sharp object.
[b] Evidence of past or chronic infection.
[c] An estimated two billion people are estimated to have been infected by HBV, one-third of the world population.

HIV. In contrast, HCV is rarely transmitted sexually (Terrault, 2002). Because unprotected sexual behavior is so prevalent, new cases of HIV and HBV are much more likely than HCV to be contracted via sexual rather than IDU transmission. HBV is the only BBV of the three for which there is an effective vaccine, and vaccination is a critical component of efforts to prevent its transmission.

The three BBVs also differ in their effects on the individual. HIV is the most feared of the infections. Until the advent of highly active antiretroviral therapy (HAART) in 1996, infection with HIV gradually suppressed the immune system, increasing susceptibility to life-threatening opportunistic diseases, such as pneumonia and cancer. HAART inhibits replication of the HIV virus, which improves health dramatically and extends life, but it does not eliminate the virus. Accordingly, this demanding and expensive treatment regimen must be maintained for life, and complications of long-term therapy are beginning to emerge, such as abnormalities of lipid metabolism, the development of drug intolerance and drug-resistant strains, and liver toxicity, exacerbated by co-infections with HCV and HBV (Powderly, 2002). HCV/HIV co-morbidity rates are as high as 80–90% in IDUs, and liver disease progresses more rapidly because HIV suppresses the immune system, facilitating the replication of HCV (Sullivan and Fiellin, 2004).

Although acute HCV infections are mild and typically go undiagnosed, serious liver disease develops over a period of 20 to 30 years in approximately 30% of those infected (Alter and Seeff, 2000). HCV treatment has improved substantially in recent years. Using a combination of pegylated interferon and ribavirin, sustained viral response rates (an absence of HCV RNA six months after the end of treatment) are 40–45% in patients with genotype 1 (the most common in the United States) and 80% in those with genotypes 2 or 3 (Di Bisceglie and Hoofnagle 2002). Past policy was to require six months' abstinence before treating HCV in alcohol or drug users (Centers for Disease Control and Prevention, 1998). Substance abusers were excluded from treatment because of concerns regarding their ability to comply with treatment, their proneness to severe psychiatric side effects caused by interferon, and their risk of re-infection. Policy change was influenced by emerging evidence indicating that with careful management, substantial numbers of IDUs can achieve a sustained viral response and avoid re-infection even if they relapse to active drug use, plus recognition that in many countries IDUs constitute the largest group of persons infected with HCV and most new infections occur in drug users (Edlin, 2004).

Acute HBV infections are rarely fatal, but in chronically infected persons mortality rates related to long-term liver disease range from 15–25% (Centers for Disease Control and Prevention, 2003 a, b). There are substantial geographic differences in the epidemiology of HBV (Alter, 2003). Worldwide, it is the most prevalent of the three BBVs considered here. Over two billion people have been infected, and infection is chronic in 350 million. Some 45% of the world's population lives in countries having high HBV endemicity, with over 8% chronically infected. Primary routes of transmission in these countries are perinatal, exposure to HBV on household surfaces, and nosocomial infection (i.e., exposure via non-sterile medical procedures). Risk of infection is 70 to 90% in infants born to chronically infected mothers, and 90% of these infections become chronic; risk of chronicity is also considerably higher among young children than it is among older children and adults. WHO recommends vaccination at birth to reduce HBV transmission in countries of high or intermediate endemicity, but as of 2000 only 31% of the world's births were in countries that had adopted this policy. In low endemicity countries (i.e., those having chronic infection rates of 1 to 2%), IDU, sexual, and occupational exposure are primary routes of transmission.

In time, routine vaccination of infants and adolescents will virtually eliminate HBV in these countries. Meanwhile it is important to vaccinate adults at high risk, such as IDUs, men who have sex with men, persons seeking treatment for a sexually transmitted disease, clients of substance abuse programs, prisoners, psychiatric patients, the mentally retarded, homeless persons, and health care workers at risk of occupational exposure.

Much of the variability in prevalence of HIV in IDUs is related to differences in the implementation and timing of harm reduction strategies to prevent its transmission. In countries where little or nothing is done to prevent HIV transmission in IDU populations, it spreads readily, resulting in high prevalence rates (Joseph et al., 2000). However, implementation of harm reduction strategies such as drug treatment, needle and syringe exchange programs, and promoting safer injection and sexual practices, have been successful in reducing the numbers of new HIV cases in high-prevalence populations, and they have prevented the establishment of HIV in IDU populations when they have been implemented in a timely fashion (Loxley, 2000).

Harm reduction strategies that have been effective in preventing the transmission of HIV among IDUs have been less successful in preventing the transmission of HCV, although they may have reduced its incidence somewhat (Crofts et al., 1997a). Based on surveillance of acute hepatitis cases in sentinel countries, it is estimated that the incidence of HCV in the United States declined from 180,000 in 1984 to 28,000 in 1995 and has remained low since then (Alter and Moyer, 1998). Much of this decline occurred among IDUs; however, IDUs continue to acquire HCV infections relatively rapidly after beginning to inject (Garfein et al., 1996). Two factors may contribute to this apparent inconsistency. The advent of HIV greatly reduced casual experimentation with injecting drugs, and this would have reduced HCV incidence. A more negative possibility is that surveillance based on reporting of acute cases may underestimate the current incidence of HCV among IDUs. Evidence that this may be so came from a study of acute hepatitis B and C in a cohort of IDUs conducted in one of the sentinel counties (Hagan et al., 2002); acute symptoms of HCV infection occurred rarely and were not reported when they did occur.

STRATEGIES TO PREVENT TRANSMISSION OF BBVs IN IDUs

A comprehensive approach that includes community-based outreach, drug treatment and sterile syringe access programs is recommended as the most effective strategy for preventing the transmission of HIV and other blood-borne infections in IDUs and their communities (National Institute on Drug Abuse, 2002). Each of these strategies should include programs for BBV testing, prevention and education counseling, and referral to other health and social services. Research in many countries and in many settings has proven the efficacy of these programs.

Drug Treatment/Methadone Maintenance

Drug treatment restricts the spread of BBVs by reducing the frequency of injections. Peer-reviewed, empirical studies published between 1988 and 1998 were recently reviewed to examine the evidence for drug treatment's effectiveness in reducing HIV-risk behaviors and sero-conversion rates (Sorensen and Copeland, 2000). Of 33 that met criteria for inclusion in the review, 28 were based on methadone maintenance treatment (MMT) programs, and 26 of the 28 showed positive results in reducing HIV infection and risk behaviors.

Methadone is a long-acting opiate agonist that relieves narcotic craving, suppresses the abstinence syndrome, and blocks the euphoric effects associated with heroin (Joseph et al., 2000). It has been used since the 1960s for the long-term treatment of heroin addiction. It is thought that studies in MMT programs are more likely to yield positive HIV prevention effects because virtually all patients were engaging in high-risk needle use prior to treatment, treatment directly affects high-risk needle use, and treatment lasts long enough to have an effect not only on high-risk behaviors, but also on HIV sero-conversion rates, the most convincing evidence of effective prevention. The evidence for reducing HIV-related risk was more convincing for drug use than sexual behavior, but where reductions in high-risk sexual behavior occurred they were related to quitting prostitution and enhancing self-efficacy for practicing safer sex.

Sorensen and Copeland (2000) discussed a number of limitations in the methodologies employed in the studies they reviewed. Longitudinal studies in behavior change during the course of drug treatment had no control groups, so it was not possible to assess the extent to which behavior might have changed without treatment. Whereas, in studies that did employ out-of-treatment control groups, there were often significant differences in the characteristics of IDUs who were in treatment compared to those who were not, (e.g., IDUs in treatment tended to be older, had been injecting drugs for longer periods of time, and were less likely to be Black or Hispanic in some studies). The more rigorous studies controlled for differences such as these statistically in their analyses and still found significant reductions in HIV risk, but drop-out and attrition were high in the studies reviewed, introducing the potential for bias in the retention in treatment of patients who were more conscientious about reducing HIV risk behaviors. Nonetheless, it was concluded that the literature offered extremely powerful evidence that MMT prevents HIV infection.

There is less evidence that MMT is effective in reducing the risk of transmission of hepatitis C (Crofts et al., 1997b). For one thing, Crofts and his colleagues found that 67% of the MMT patients who had been tested at least once were found to be already positive for HCV antibodies. Thus, for many IDUs entry into an MMT program comes too late in their injecting careers to prevent HCV. Another important factor is that substance abuse is a chronic relapsing condition, and it is estimated that as many as 80% of the IDUs in MMT relapse at some point during the course of their treatment. As indicated earlier, the likelihood of being exposed to HCV during such a relapse is high because chronic cases are so prevalent among IDUs, and it is highly infective. This is one compelling reason to include counseling to reduce unsafe injecting practices as an important part of drug treatment programs.

Counseling to Reduce Unsafe Injecting And Sexual Practices

Teaching IDUs how to protect themselves and others from BBVs in the event of a relapse is a necessary part of drug treatment, as well as other prevention programs. In addition, drug treatment programs need to provide testing for BBVs, educate patients who test positive about proactive steps they can take to deal with their infection, provide needed referrals for care and follow-up, and provide counseling to avoid transmitting infection to others. A national survey of 246 MMT and drug-free treatment programs in the United

States compared the content and comprehensiveness of HCV education by each (Strauss et al., 2004). All the programs provided HCV education to at least some of their patients. However, compared to drug-free programs, MMT programs covered a significantly greater number of HCV-related topics. MMT programs also covered a significantly greater proportion of specific topics (e.g., how to avoid transmitting HCV, the importance of testing for HCV, treatment options if HCV positive). Of special concern was that fewer than three-quarters of the drug-free programs addressed what to do if co-infected with HIV and HCV and how to maintain health if HCV positive, and only about half of the drug-free and methadone maintenance treatment programs educated HCV-positive patients about the importance of obtaining vaccinations for hepatitis A and B. Not only are MMT programs providing more HCV services to their patients, but a greater proportion of MMT program managers are dissatisfied with their current level of HCV service provision (Strauss et al., 2003).

Counseling to reduce sexual risk behaviors associated with the transmission of HIV and HBV in IDUs is needed to complement efforts to reduce injection frequency and teach safer injecting practices. As part of an HIV/AIDS Prevention Research Synthesis Project, a series of meta-analyses were performed on interventions of various types (Des Jarlais and Semaan, 2002). It was concluded that meta-analysis revealed a strong and significant effect of HIV prevention interventions on sex behaviors of drug users (Semaan et al., 2002). Extrapolation of their results indicated that, in a population with a 72% prevalence of risk behavior, the proportion of users who would reduce their risk behaviors would be 12.6% greater in the intervention group than in a comparison group. Thus, interventions can lead to sexual risk reduction among IDUs, and this justifies their continued implementation. However, developing interventions with stronger effects remains a high priority. In industrialized countries, epidemics of sexually transmitted HIV occurred among men having sex with men, whereas in developing countries heterosexual transmission is more prevalent. A disturbing trend observed in the United States is a growing prevalence of heterosexually-transmitted HIV among minorities, especially affecting young females (Wingood, 2003).

Needle and Syringe Exchange Programs (NSEPs)

NSEPs complement drug treatment intervention programs by preventing the transmission of BBVs in several ways. They provide IDUs with access to sterile injection equipment if they have a treatment lapse; they provide a link to treatment for IDUs who want to quit using drugs; and they provide prevention services to IDUs who are not yet ready to seek treatment. The latter is particularly important in view of the fact that the vast majority of IDUs are not in treatment, and those who do enter treatment generally present after an extended period of drug use during which infection may already have taken place. This is especially true for HCV, which is typically contracted early in the injecting career of a drug user (Carruthers et al., 1997; Garfein et al., 1996).

In areas where they are widely available, NSEPs have been highly effective in preventing HIV; but, as in the case of MMT, they have been less successful in preventing the spread of HCV (Crofts et al., 1997a). The majority of IDUs who use NSEPs regularly report occasional sharing, and over time even occasional sharing is very likely to result in exposure to HCV. Procedures for sterilizing injection paraphernalia that are effective in reducing risk of HIV transmission do not protect against transmission of HCV, and the risk of contact with a HCV positive injector is far more likely than contact with an HIV positive person.

Sharing of cooker and cotton has been implicated in the transmission of HCV in IDUs who denied sharing syringes (Hagan et al., 2001). Despite evidence that positive outcomes associated with needle and syringe programs far outweigh negative outcomes, access to sterile injection equipment in many communities is limited by lack of funding and legal and regulatory barriers (Vlahov and Junge, 1998; Taussig et al., 2000).

Community-Based Outreach

The most effective strategy for preventing transmission of BBVs among IDUs is to prevent the initiation of injecting drug use. Persuading prospective IDUs not to start injecting drugs is one of the goals of community-based outreach programs. They also interface with the other components of a comprehensive prevention program by trying to persuade IDUs who want to quit using drugs to go into treatment, and to persuade IDUs who do not want to quit using drugs to use safer methods of injecting. Findings from observational research evaluating the effects of outreach-based HIV interventions on post-intervention behavior changes were recently integrated across 36 studies (Coyle et al., 1998). In two-thirds of the studies it was found that participation in street-based outreach interventions was followed with office-based HIV testing and counselling. Criteria employed to study results of controlled studies included the plausibility of cause and effect, correct temporal sequence, consistency of findings across reports, strength of associations observed, specificity of associations, and dose–response relationships between interventions and observed outcomes.

The majority of the published evaluations showed that IDUs in a variety of places and time periods changed their baseline drug-related and sex-related risk behaviors following their participation in an outreach-based HIV risk reduction intervention (i.e., IDUs regularly reported significant follow-up reductions in drug injection, multi-person reuse of syringes and needles, multi-person reuse of other injection equipment (cookers, cotton, rinse water), and crack use (Coyle et al., 1998). Also observed were significant intervention effects in promoting entry into drug treatment and increasing needle disinfection. Although drug users significantly reduced sex-related risks and increased condom use, the majority still practiced unsafe sex. One quasi-experimental study found that reductions in injection risk led to significantly reduced HIV seroincidence among outreach participants. Few investigators looked at dosage effects, but two reports suggested that the longer the exposure to outreach-based interventions, the greater the reductions in drug injection frequency. Coyle and her colleagues (1998) concluded that the accumulated evidence supported the effectiveness of outreach-based interventions in reaching out-of-treatment IDUs, providing the means for behavior changes, and inducing behavior change in the desired direction. The findings provide sound evidence that participation in outreach-based prevention programs can lead to lower HIV incidence rates among program participants.

HIGH-RISK SUB-POPULATIONS

Criminal Justice Populations

Because injecting drug use is illegal, and illegal activities are often undertaken to support a drug habit, a history of IDU is common among prisoners, and the prevalence of BBVs is higher than in the general population. For example, it was estimated that between 20% and

26% of all people living with HIV in the United States and between 29% and 43% of the HCV cases passed through a correctional facility in 1997 (Hammett et al., 2002). Continued IDU in prisons and other risk factors for virus transmission, such as unprotected sex, violence, and rape, lend urgency to recommendations that interventions that have proven effective in preventing the transmission of BBVs in the community be implemented in prisons (WHO, 1993; Dolan et al., 2003). In Europe, 19 small needle and syringe exchange programs have been pilot tested, and six have been evaluated (Dolan et al., 2003). Findings indicate that these programs are likely to prevent the transmission of BBVs, as rates of syringe sharing fell sharply. There were no new cases of HIV, HCV, or HBV, and other health measures improved (i.e., rates of drug overdose fell, and there were fewer abscesses). Rates of drug use were stable or decreased; there were no cases in which needles were used as weapons, and no indication that new users were initiated into injecting. Accordingly, results in these small pilot intervention programs were promising, and studies are now needed in larger prisons.

MMT programs are available in relatively few prison settings, (e.g., New South Wales, Australia (Byrne and Dolan, 1998); the Netherlands (Langendam et al., 1998); Canada (Anonymous, 2002); and New York City (Tomasino et al., 2001). The Key Extended Entry Program (KEEP) was established in New York City in 1987; it performs over 18,000 detoxifications for opiate-dependent inmates and 4,000 admissions for MMT per year. An evaluation of its effectiveness was conducted among inmates who were not enrolled in MMT at arrest (Magura et al., 1993). Some 80% were injecting drug users who admitted committing an average of 117 property crimes and 19 violent crimes in the six months before entering jail. Methadone program participants were compared to a control group of similar addicts who received seven-day heroin detoxification in jail. Those who had received MMT were more likely than controls to apply for MMT or other drug treatment after release and to be in treatment at follow-up 6.5 months later. Moreover, being in treatment at follow-up was associated with lower drug use and crime, but rates of retention in community treatment after release were modest. Process evaluation revealed that KEEP participants had more chronic and severe social and personal deficits than other addicts applying for MMT, and they needed more support to stay in treatment.

A randomized clinical trial of methadone maintenance in an Australian prison found at follow-up that heroin use was significantly lower among treated than control subjects, and treated subjects had lower levels of drug injecting and syringe sharing; however, there was no difference in HIV or hepatitis C incidence (Dolan et al., 2003). Further studies are needed, but promising findings suggest that prison-based methadone maintenance programs should be introduced or expanded in those communities that have MMT programs available for prisoners' continued support after leaving prison.

Recommendations for the prevention and control of infections with hepatitis viruses in correctional settings have recently been published and rated according to whether they are strongly recommended (on the basis of > 2 consistent, well-conceived, well-executed studies with control groups or longitudinal measurements); recommended (on the basis of > 1 well-conceived, well-executed, controlled, or time-series study; or > 3 studies with more limited execution); indicated (on the basis of previous scientific observation and theoretic rationale, but case-controlled or prospective studies do not exist); or not recommended (on the basis of published literature recommending against a practice) (Centers for Disease Control and Prevention, 2003a). Detailed recommendations are provided as they pertain to correctional staff and prisoners (pregnant juveniles, juveniles, pregnant women, and adults). They cover a wide variety of topics, including pre-exposure vaccination for HAV and HBV, pre-vaccination and post-vaccination testing, HBV vaccination as post-exposure prophylaxis, serologic testing for HBV and HCV infection, post-exposure management for HCV, chronic HBV and HCV treatment, health education and release planning. Implementation of these recommendations is hampered by short-term prison stays, lack of resources, and prisoners' unwillingness to participate. However, barriers to treatment adherence can be eliminated or minimized in prison settings (Allen et al., 2003).

IDU and Sex Networks: Commercial Sex Workers/Men who Have Sex with Men

Understanding the dynamics of sexual transmission of HIV among drug-using populations was the topic of a recent meeting to discuss future prevention research that would integrate biological, behavioral, and environmental perspectives (Normand et al., 2003). Rapid transmission of HIV and HBV occurs when networks of persons who share drug paraphernalia or persons who have unprotected sex with multiple partners include an infected person. As discussed, rates of BBVs are high in IDUs, and a number of factors increase the likelihood that IDU networks will overlap with risky sex networks. IDUs are likely to be sexually active, partners of IDUs are unlikely to consistently use condoms, rates of prostitution are high among partners of IDUs and female IDUs, and drug use and heavy alcohol use are associated with risky sexual behavior. The end result is often that infected IDUs transmit HIV or HBV to their sexual partners, who then transmit it to their sexual networks, and members of their sexual networks transmit the infection to their partners. The ways and extent to which IDU and sex networks overlap and contribute to HIV and HBV epidemics vary in different regions of the world, at different times in a given region, and in different subpopulations of a region. Poverty has been defined as a major contributor to the spread of HIV, operating through such socio-economic forces as gender inequality, prostitution, drug use in poor populations, imprisonment, economic conditions that disrupt families, and cultural attitudes (Fournier and Carmichael, 1998).

During 1994–98, the most commonly reported risk factor for HBV infection in the United States was high-risk heterosexual activity (39.8%) followed by men who have sex with men (MSM) activity (14.6%) and IDU (13.8%) (Goldstein et al., 2002). Over half of all patients (55.5%) reported treatment for a sexually transmitted disease (STD) or incarceration in a prison or jail prior to their illness, suggesting that more than half of the acute hepatitis B cases might have been prevented through routine hepatitis B immunization in STD clinics and correctional health care programs.

In developed countries, HIV has spread mainly through sex networks comprised of men who have sex with men (MSM) (Clatts et al., 2003; Patterson and Semple, 2003), although that may be changing in the United States (Wingood, 2003). Clatts and colleagues (2003) recommended that increased attention be given to social factors that are associated with early sexual activity among young MSM, and Patterson and Semple (2003) proposed safer sex programs targeting HIV-positive drug-using MSM, particularly methamphetamine users.

Global HIV epidemics: the example of Thailand

Worldwide, the vast majority of HIV infections have occurred in the most impoverished regions, principally Sub-Saharan Africa and parts of Asia. It is estimated that approximately

90% to 95% of these cases are attributable to unprotected sex (Celentano, 2003). The predominance of sexually transmitted disease in these epidemics has resulted in little attention being given to prevention initiatives that focus on drug abuse. A case in point is Thailand (Ainsworth et al., 2003; Celentano, 2003). In 1988, an explosive increase in HIV infection was observed among Bangkok IDUs. However, little was done to prevent HIV transmission until it began spreading rapidly through the military, other patrons of brothels, and their wives and girlfriends. The Thai government then launched the 100 Percent Condom Campaign, a four-pronged effort that targeted sex workers in brothels for health education, mandated STD examinations, and mandated condom use plus free condoms. The general public received health education explaining the consequences of HIV and encouraging condom use. The effectiveness of this campaign in halting HIV spread in the military and other brothel customers received international acclaim. However, drug use in Thailand is treated as a legal, rather than a public health problem, and the prevalence of HIV remains high, a particular concern since IDU has increased in recent years. Of further concern is that funding for the 100 Percent Condom Campaign is threatened by an economic downturn and diversion of prevention funds to providing treatment for the large infected population. The potential for sexually transmitted HIV to increase in the wake of sub-optimal enforcement of government prevention policy is exacerbated by a wave of desperately poor immigrants from neighboring countries who trade sex for money outside brothels supervised by the Thai government. These factors may fuel future HIV epidemics in Thailand, despite initial success in reducing incidence rates.

CONCLUSION

The research reviewed here clearly indicates that there is no single strategy that can prevent the spread of blood-borne diseases within and from IDUs. Vaccination is the best way to prevent HBV, but vaccines are lacking for HIV and HCV. Transmission of all three BBVs, especially HIV, can be reduced by combining primary prevention with harm reduction techniques that target IDUs at all stages of their injecting careers, prior to initiation of injecting, prior to treatment seeking, in treatment, and in recovery. Primary prevention includes both outreach programs to prevent the initiation of IDU and drug treatment to reduce IDU; harm reduction programs, such as needle and syringe exchange programs and instruction on safe injection techniques, minimize the likelihood of BBV transmission among IDUs who are not seeking treatment or have relapsed. However, research is needed to develop more effective methods to prevent the transmission of HCV among IDUs and more effective methods to reduce sexual transmission of HIV and HBV by IDUs and their partners. A troubling finding of this review is that funding and implementation of primary prevention and harm reduction programs lag far behind demonstration of their effectiveness. Stigmatization of IDUs, commercial sex workers, and MSMs together with current legal sanctions against IDU and prostitution set the stage for punitive, rather than public health approaches to prevention of BBV transmission. Research is needed to determine whether current legal sanctions complement or undermine public health prevention efforts, whether a paradigm shift would be cost-effective, and how public opinion and the political will might be generated to support such a shift, should research findings warrant it.

REFERENCES

Ainsworth, M., Beyrer, C., et al. (2003) AIDS and public policy: the lessons and challenges of "success" in Thailand. *Health Policy*, **64**(1), 13–37.

Allen, S.A., Spaulding, A.C. et al. (2003) Treatment of chronic hepatitis C in a state correctional facility. *Annals of Internal Medicine*, **138**(3): 187–90.

Alter, H.J. and Seeff, L.B. (2000) Recovery, persistence, and sequelae in hepatitis C virus infection: a perspective on long-term outcome. *Seminars in Liver Disease*, **20**(1), 17–35.

Alter, M.J. (2003) Epidemiology and prevention of hepatitis B. *Seminars in Liver Disease*, **23**(1): 39–46.

Alter, M.J. and Moyer, L.A. (1998) The importance of preventing hepatitis C virus infection among injection drug users in the United States. *Journal of Acquired Immune Deficiency Syndrome and Human Retrovirol*, **18** (Suppl. 1), S6–10.

Anonymous (2002) Canada: federal prison system expands access to methadone. *Can HIV AIDS Policy Law Review*, **7**(1), 15–17, 20.

Byrne, A. and Dolan, K. (1998) Methadone treatment is widely accepted in prisons in New South Wales. *British Medical Journal*, **316**(7146), 1744–1745.

Carruthers, S. (2003) *Hepatitis C and Novice Injecting Drug Users*. Monograph No 4. National Drug Research Institute. Perth, Western Australia: Curtin University of Technology.

Carruthers, S., Loxley, W. et al. (1997) The Australian study of HIV and injecting drug use part II: predicting exposure to hepatitis C and hepatitis B. *Drug and Alcohol Review*, **16**(3), 215–221.

Celentano, D.D. (2003) HIV prevention among drug users: an international perspective from Thailand. *Journal of Urban Health*, **80**(4 Suppl. 3), iii97–iii105.

Centers for Disease Control and Prevention (1998) Recommendations for prevention and control of hepatitis C virus (HCV) infection and HCV-related chronic disease. *Morbidity and Mortality Weekly Report*, **47**(RR-19), 1–39.

Centers for Disease Control and Prevention (2003a) Prevention and control of infections with hepatitis viruses in correctional settings. *Morbidity and Mortality Weekly Report*, **52**(RR-1), 36.

Centers for Disease Control and Prevention (2003b) *Hepatitis B Fact Sheet*. Available online: www.cdc.gov/hepatitis, (accessed 1 April 2004).

Clatts, M.C., Goldsamt, L. et al. (2003) The social course of drug injection and sexual activity among YMSM and other high-risk youth: an agenda for future research. *Journal of Urban Health*, **80**(4 Suppl. 3), iii26–39.

Coyle, S.L., Needle, R.H. et al. (1998) Outreach-based HIV prevention for injecting drug users: a review of published outcome data. *Public Health Report*, **113**(Suppl. 1), 19–30.

Crofts, N., Jolley, D. et al. (1997a) Epidemiology of hepatitis C virus infection among injecting drug users in Australia. *Journal of Epidemiology and Community Health*, **51**(6), 692–697.

Crofts, N., Nigro, L. et al. (1997b) Methadone maintenance and hepatitis C virus infection among injecting drug users. *Addiction*, **92**(8), 999–1005.

Des Jarlais, D.C. and Semaan, S. (2002) HIV prevention research: cumulative knowledge or accumulating studies? An introduction to the HIV/AIDS prevention research synthesis project supplement. *Journal of Acquired Immune Deficiency Syndrome*, **30**(Suppl. 1), S1–7.

Di Bisceglie, A.M. and Hoofnagle, J.H. (2002) Optimal therapy of hepatitis C. *Hepatology*, **36**(5 Suppl. 1), S121–127.

Dolan, K., Rutter, S. et al. (2003) Prison-based syringe exchange programmes: a review of international research and development. *Addiction*, **98**(2), 153–158.

Dolan, K.A., Shearer, J. et al. (2003) A randomised controlled trial of methadone maintenance treatment versus wait list control in an Australian prison system. *Drug and Alcohol Dependence*, **72**(1), 59–65.

Edlin, B.R. (2004) Hepatitis C prevention and treatment for substance users in the United States: acknowledging the elephant in the living room. *International Journal of Drug Policy*, **15**, 81–91.

Flynn, N.M., Anderson, R. et al. (1996) Seeing is believing: Videotaped high-risk injection behaviour. Paper presented at Seventh International Conference on the Reduction of Drug Related Harm, Hobart, Australia.

Fournier, A.M. and Carmichael, C. (1998) Socioeconomic influences on the transmission of human immunodeficiency virus infection: the hidden risk. *Archives of Family Medicine*, **7**(3), 214–217.

Garfein, R.S., Vlahov, D. et al. (1996) Viral infections in short-term injection drug users: the prevalence of the hepatitis C, hepatitis B, human immunodeficiency, and human T-lymphotropic viruses. *American Journal of Public Health*, **86**(5), 655–661.

Gerberding, J.L. (1995) Drug therapy: management of occupational exposures to blood-borne viruses. *New England Journal of Medicine*, **332**(7), 444–451.

Goldstein, S.T., Alter, M.J. et al. (2002) Incidence and risk factors for acute hepatitis B in the United States, 1982–1998: implications for vaccination programs. *Journal of Infectious Diseases*, **185**(6), 713–719.

Hagan, H. and Des Jarlais, D.C. (2000) HIV and HCV infection among injecting drug users. *Mount Sinai Journal of Medicine*, **67**(5–6), 423–428.

Hagan, H., Snyder, N. et al. (2002) Case-reporting of acute hepatitis B and C among injection drug users. *Journal of Urban Health* **79**(4), 579–585.

Hagan, H., Thiede, H. et al. (2001) Sharing of drug preparation equipment as a risk factor for hepatitis C. *American Journal of Public Health*, **91**(1), 42–46.

Hammett, T.M., Harmon, M.P. et al. (2002) The burden of infectious disease among inmates of and releasees from US correctional facilities, 1997. *American Journal of Public Health*, **92**(11), 1789–1794.

Joseph, H., Stancliff, S. et al. (2000) Methadone maintenance treatment (MMT): a review of historical and clinical issues. *Mount Sinai Journal of Medicine*, **67**(5–6), 347–364.

Langendam, M.W., van Haastrecht, H.J. et al. (1998) Differentiation in the Amsterdam methadone dispensing circuit: determinants of methadone dosage and site of methadone prescription. *Addiction*, **93**(1), 61–72.

Loxley, W. (2000) Doing the possible: harm reduction, injecting drug use and blood borne viral infections in Australia. *International Journal of Drug Policy*, **11**(6), 407–416.

Magura, S., Rosenblum, A. et al. (1993) The effectiveness of in-jail methadone maintenance. *Journal of Drug Issues*, **23**(1), 75–100.

National Institute on Drug Abuse (2002) *Principles of HIV Prevention in Drug-Using Populations: A Research-Based Guide*. Bethesda, MD: National Institute on Drug Abuse, p. 32.

Normand, J.L., Lambert, E.Y. et al. (2003) Understanding the dynamics of sexual transmission of HIV among drug-using populations: an integration of biological, behavioral, and environmental perspectives. *Journal of Urban Health*, **80**(4 Suppl. 3), iii1–6.

Patterson, T.L. and Semple, S.J. (2003) Sexual risk reduction among HIV-positive drug-using men who have sex with men. *Journal of Urban Health*, **80**(4 Suppl. 3), iii77–87.

Powderly, W.G. (2002) Long-term exposure to lifelong therapies. *Journal of Acquired Immune Deficiency Syndrome*, **29**(Suppl. 1), S28–40.

Semaan, S., Des Jarlais, D.C. et al. (2002) A meta-analysis of the effect of HIV prevention interventions on the sex behaviors of drug users in the United States. *Journal of Acquired Immune Deficiency Syndrome*, **30** (Suppl. 1), S73–93.

Sorensen, J. and Copeland, A. (2000) Drug abuse treatment as an HIV prevention strategy: a review. *Drug and Alcohol Dependence*, **59**(1), 17–31.

Strauss, S. M., Astone, J. et al. (2003) Gaps in the drug-free and methadone treatment program response to Hepatitis C. *Journal of Substance Abuse Treatment*, **24**(4), 291–297.

Strauss, S.M., Astone, J.M. et al. (2004) The content and comprehensiveness of hepatitis C education in methadone maintenance and drug-free treatment units. *Journal of Urban Health*, **81**(1), 38–47.

Sullivan, L.E. and Fiellin, D.A. (2004) Hepatitis C and HIV infections: implications for clinical care in injection drug users. *American Journal of Addiction*, **13**(1), 1–20.

Taussig, J.A., Weinstein, B. et al. (2000) Syringe laws and pharmacy regulations are structural constraints on HIV prevention in the US. *Aids*, **14** (Suppl. 1), S47–51.

Terrault, N.A. (2002) Sexual activity as a risk factor for hepatitis C. *Hepatology*, **36**(5, Suppl. 1), S99–105.

Tomasino, V., Swanson, A.J. et al. (2001) The Key Extended Entry Program (KEEP): a methadone treatment program for opiate-dependent inmates. *Mount Sinai Journal of Medicine*, **68**(1), 14–20.

Vlahov, D. and Junge, B. (1998) The role of needle exchange programs in HIV prevention. *Public Health Report*, **113** (Suppl. 1), 75–80.

Wingood, G.M. (2003) Feminization of the HIV epidemic in the United States: major research findings and future research needs. *Journal of Urban Health*, **80**(4 Suppl. 3), iii67–76.

World Health Organization (1993) *WHO Guidelines on HIV Infection and AIDS in Prisons*. Geneva: World Health Organization.

6.7 The Evidence Base for Responding to Substance Misuse in Indigenous Minority Populations

DENNIS GRAY

National Drug Research Institute, Curtin University of Technology, Perth, WA, Australia

SHERRY SAGGERS

Centre for Social Research, Edith Cowan University; National Drug Research Institute, Curtin University of Technology, Perth, WA, Australia

SUMMARY

This chapter provides a review of the effectiveness of measures to prevent psychoactive substance misuse in indigenous minority populations in Australia, New Zealand, Canada and the United States of America. Despite considerable heterogeneity between and within these populations, there are also important commonalities. Generally, levels of substance misuse are significantly higher among them than among the non-indigenous majority populations of those countries and this results in commensurately high rates of substance caused health and social problems

These levels of misuse and harm are socially determined. They are a consequence of a complex hierarchy of social relationships—including common histories of colonialism and dispossession and economic and social marginalisation—that influence both demand for and supply of various substances. As well as focusing on interventions to address the obvious manifestations of substance misuse, strategies to prevent the elevated levels of substance misuse among indigenous peoples must address the underlying social determinants.

Interventions aimed *specifically* at indigenous populations usually seek: to make interventions for general populations more culturally appropriate for indigenous populations; to address those factors that exacerbate levels of substance misuse and related harm among indigenous populations; or to employ elements of indigenous cultures to address misuse and related harm. Such interventions—which generally focus on the individual, family or community levels—are considered under the headings: supply reduction, demand reduction and harm reduction. Rigorous evaluations of these interventions are relatively few but point to some successes and to the factors that contribute to them.

Preventing Harmful Substance Use: The Evidence Base for Policy and Practice.
Edited by T. Stockwell, P. J. Gruenewald, J. W. Toumbourou and W. Loxley.
© 2005 John Wiley & Sons, Ltd. ISBN 0-470-09227-0 (hbk) 0-470-09228-9 (pbk).

Nevertheless, overall, such interventions have had limited success in reducing indigenous substance misuse. This and the limited impact of large-scale programmes aimed at ameliorating the status of indigenous peoples—as attested by the social inequalities they continue to face—indicate the need for greater efforts to address the structural inequalities that contribute to indigenous substance misuse and related harm.

INTRODUCTION

In this chapter, we aim to provide an overview of the effectiveness of measures to prevent psychoactive substance misuse in indigenous minority populations in Australia, New Zealand, Canada and the United States of America. These indigenous populations are ethnically, culturally and historically diverse—both inter- and intra-nationally. The systems of government and the policy regimes under which they live also vary considerably. Nevertheless, there are some commonalities between them and it is possible to make some generalisations—although they must be treated with caution.

At the outset it must be made clear that the "evidence base" for responding to substance misuse in indigenous minority populations is limited. There are several reasons for this:

- There are no publications that comprehensively document the range of interventions at national levels.
- Publications that describe particular interventions, or types of interventions, do not provide a representative picture of the range of interventions that are being, or have been, undertaken in any country.
- Of the interventions for which descriptive publications are available, few have been formally evaluated.
- The evaluations that have been undertaken are extremely variable in quality—for a number of methodological, political and cultural reasons (Gray et al., 1995).

It is also important to note that the heterogeneity of indigenous communities means that uniform intervention strategies cannot easily be applied and this in itself makes it difficult to generalise evaluation results.

These problems are compounded by the variety of publication types in which evaluation reports on indigenous intervention projects appear. Searches of the major scholarly publication databases (which focus on refereed journals) return limited numbers of publications. Most evaluation reports are published in what is known as the "grey literature"—including publications by government and non-government agencies and technical reports. However, there are no comprehensive databases that facilitate easy access to such reports, and searches such as the one conducted for this review are unlikely to identify all of what has been written—especially if searches are being conducted from an overseas base without the benefit of "local knowledge". For the purpose of this chapter, we have relied primarily on review articles published since 1995 (some of which summarise earlier research findings) and a small number of primary research reports that add to findings from those reviews.

SUBSTANCE MISUSE AND RELATED HARM

It is not the purpose of this chapter to review the epidemiology of substance use and related harms among indigenous minority populations in Australia, New Zealand, Canada and the USA. However, generally speaking, levels of substance misuse (although, in the case of alcohol, not use) among these populations are significantly higher than among the non-indigenous majority populations of those countries. However, even within countries there are significant variations in levels of use and misuse. The most commonly used substances are tobacco, alcohol and cannabis, with relatively smaller but significant use of various illicit drugs and inhalants; and, importantly, many people are poly-drug users (Saggers and Gray 1998; French 2000; Gray and Saggers 2003).

These elevated levels of misuse result in commensurately high rates of substance caused mortality, hospital and special treatment facility admissions, and primary health care presentations for both physical and mental problems. They are also associated with higher levels of social disruption, job loss, family violence and breakdown, assaults and other crime, motor vehicle crashes, suicides and homicides.

Social Determinants of Indigenous Substance Misuse

What are the causes of these higher levels of substance misuse among indigenous peoples and what can be done to prevent them? First, it is important to point out that abstention from use, or misuse, of particular substances is not simply a function of the personal characteristics of individuals. It is also a consequence of a complex web of social relationships—including factors that influence both demand for and supply of various substances. Epidemiological explanations of health and illness (including substance misuse) are increasingly emphasizing what are known as the "social determinants of health".

The social determinants of health are part of geographically located, interactional hierarchies including international, national, state/provincial, regional, local, familial and individual levels. In turn, these geographic hierarchies are cross-cut by various formal and informal economic, governmental, class, ethnic and gender relationships. Furthermore, relationships within these cross-cutting hierarchies are culturally mediated. Within this complex web there are factors that render individuals vulnerable and resistant to particular health problems—including substance misuse—and these act differentially over the life-courses of individuals. In the case of substance misuse, these relationships are complicated by the fact that dependence itself feeds back and becomes a causal factor in its own right. Lynch (2000) among others has provided a graphic depiction of the relationships between the social determinants of health status (see Figure 6.7.1). Effective strategies to prevent health problems require focusing not only upon individuals but on ameliorating those structural factors that render people vulnerable, or amplifying those that render them resistant (Loxley et al., 2004).

In the case of indigenous peoples, much substance misuse is a consequence of the same factors that determine substance misuse patterns among the non-indigenous populations that surround them. Clearly, however, there are some factors associated with their status as minority populations that account for the elevated levels of misuse and harm observed among them. Various psychological, social, cultural, historical, economic and political factors have been identified as contributing to such high levels of indigenous substance misuse. Undoubtedly, these all play some role. However, given the ethnic and cultural

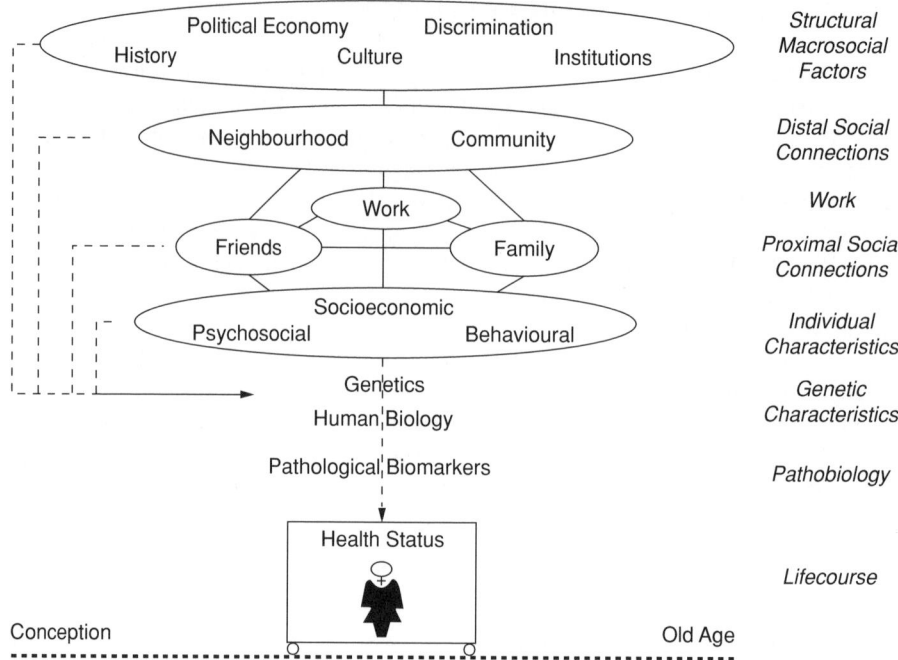

Figure 6.7.1   A multi-level and multi-time point approach to social epidemiology
Source: Reproduced from Lynch (2000) with permission of the Australasian Epidemiological Association.

diversity of indigenous peoples the common patterns of misuse and harm cannot be attributed to uniformity along those dimensions. What these populations do share, however, is a common history of colonialism and dispossession and economic and social marginalisation—which impact differentially on groups and individuals within them. This has resulted in widespread poverty, unemployment, reduced access to and opportunity for education, physical and mental ill-health and alienation (Saggers and Gray 1998). As well as focusing on essential interventions to address the obvious manifestations of substance misuse, strategies to prevent the elevated levels of substance misuse among indigenous peoples must address the underlying social determinants (Frank et al., 2000).

PREVENTION

While there are gaps in our knowledge—and while our knowledge is often not translated into policy and practice—we know a great deal about what is effective in preventing substance misuse in the general populations of the countries under consideration (Loxley et al., 2004). In general, the interventions directed at those wider population groups are also directed towards indigenous peoples as part of those populations. However, interventions aimed *specifically* at indigenous populations usually seek: to make interventions for general populations more culturally appropriate for indigenous populations; to address those factors that exacerbate levels of substance misuse and related harm among indigenous populations; or to employ elements of indigenous cultures to address misuse and related harm.

Strategies to prevent substance misuse and related harm can usefully be considered in three categories: supply reduction, demand reduction and harm reduction. However, there are different emphases on these categories of intervention between the countries under consideration, between state/provincial jurisdictions within them, and at local levels (May and Moran, 1995; Health Canada, 1998; Australia, Ministerial Council on Drugs Strategy, 2003). Additionally, there are different emphases on the strategies depending upon types of substances under consideration and their legal status.

Supply Reduction

International evidence demonstrates that reducing the supply of psychoactive substances leads to reductions in consumption, and hence to reduced substance-related health and social harms (Loxley et al., 2004). In each of the countries under consideration, there are regulatory and law enforcement strategies to either limit or prohibit the use of various categories of psychoactive substances. In addition to the application of these wider strategies, indigenous communities—either alone or in coalitions with non-indigenous communities—have brought to bear additional controls over the supply of such substances, particularly alcohol.

In Australia—using various pieces of state/territory legislation—remote indigenous communities have prohibited the consumption of alcohol or declared themselves "dry". There have been no recent studies of the impact of such measures. However, a 1990 review by d'Abbs found that this strategy was generally successful but that its benefits were not found in all communities that had adopted the approach and that in some areas there were difficulties in enforcing bans. He also noted that there had been three earlier reviews all of which concluded that, although there were shortcomings, on balance the benefits outweighed the cost of those bans (d'Abbs, 1990).

Results of similar bans in the United States are equivocal. May and Moran (1995) report that alcohol is prohibited on a significant proportion of Native American reservations, and note claims that this measure "has not been effective. Boot-legging and off-reservation purchasing of alcohol has (*sic*) largely circumvented this policy" (1995: 295–296).

However, two more recent studies from Alaska show that alcohol-related injury mortality among Alaska Natives from "wet" villages was 2.7 times that among those from "dry" villages (Landen et al., 1997); and in an isolated locality there was a statistically significant decrease in the number of alcohol-related hospital outpatient visits when a ban on possession and importation of alcohol was imposed (Chui et al., 1997).

Brady notes that local prohibitions have been employed in Canada where, as in the United States, there has been considerable debate about their merits (2000: 475–476). She also notes that because Māori do not live in discrete reserves or settlements, the option of local prohibitions is not open to them (2000: 477–478). The limited evidence suggests that such prohibitions can be effective, particularly in remote communities, but need community support and the means to enforce them.

Despite the effectiveness of bans on alcohol in remote communities in Australia, some mostly non-indigenous people have argued that the bans simply transfer problem drinking from the communities to towns. To address this perceived problem they proposed that indigenous communities take up the option of establishing "wet canteens" which it was claimed would encourage indigenous people to drink more moderately. For seven of eight Northern Territory communities that had taken up this option, d'Abbs estimated per capita consumption of pure alcohol for the 1994–95 financial year. Rather than moderating consumption, he found that consumption among males and females respectively in those communities was 76% and 183% higher than the Northern Territory average. Furthermore, he identified several negative social and political consequences of the establishment of the clubs (d'Abbs, 1998).

In small town environments, Indigenous Australians have used provisions of state/territory liquor licensing legislation that include harm minimisation provisions to have additional restrictions imposed on the supply of alcohol. The type of restrictions that have been imposed vary by location but include some combination of measures including: banning sales of wine in casks of > 2 litres (essentially an indirect price control measure as this is the cheapest form of beverage per standard drink in Australia); restricting pre-midday sales to low alcohol content beverages only; restrictions on trading hours, for both on- and off-premise sales; and restriction of takeaway sales on particular days of the week. d'Abbs and Togni reviewed the efficacy of these packages of restrictions (but not individual measures) in five locations. They reported that: "Restrictions were found to have a modest but real impact on alcohol consumption, and a significant impact on indicators of alcohol-related harm, especially violence" (2000: 45).

Such strategies are more likely to succeed when initiated by indigenous people themselves as part of diverse complementary measures tackling demand and supply issues. Community support is also important, and evidence suggests that while alcohol restrictions are often contentious when introduced, they can enjoy broad community support after a trial period (Saggers and Gray, 1998; d'Abbs and Togni, 2000).

While they have been successful in a limited number of rural locations, the piecemeal introduction of such restrictions has meant that they have not had a significant impact on state or territory-wide patterns of consumption and related harm and they fly in the face of wider pressures to further liberalise controls on the availability of alcohol in Australia. Furthermore, indirect price control measures such as banning particular beverages can be undermined by retailers who substitute other cheaply priced beverages for those prohibited.

In Australia, supply reduction strategies have also been employed to reduce petrol sniffing and its associated harms in the remote communities where such sniffing is most prevalent. In two large reserve areas, the sniffing and the supply of petrol for sniffing have been declared illegal. Although these measures have not been formally evaluated, anecdotal evidence indicates that they have had limited effect. This has been attributed to the easy availability of petrol, and the ineffectiveness of the sanctions as a deterrent (MacLean and d'Abbs, 2002).

A more successful strategy has been the prohibition of petrol and the substitution of aviation fuel (avgas), which lacks the psychoactive effects of petrol. This measure was being employed in 30 remote communities in 2003 and an evaluation of the programme found that it was "safe, effective and popular in reducing petrol sniffing" (Aboriginal Drug and Alcohol Council, 2003: 8). It was also found to be more successful than attempts to lock up petrol supplies, especially when combined with other strategies such as diversionary activities (MacLean and d'Abbs, 2002).

Demand Reduction

Drug and alcohol education programmes—many school-based—are among the most ubiquitous interventions for indigenous peoples, and are either based on the assumption that substance misuse is due to ignorance of the deleterious effects of alcohol and other drugs, or are directed to changing risky use behaviours. Generally, evaluations have focused on programme processes or short-term outcomes (Gray et al., 2000). For instance, an evaluation of a drug education programme for indigenous children on Palm Island in Queensland, Australia, which sought to help children identify reasons for and peer pressures towards drinking, found that children became more aware of peer pressure to drink and that fewer children may have taken up drinking because of the program (Gray et al., 2000).

In the USA many such programmes have addressed the effects and consequences of substance misuse among indigenous communities both on and off reservations. Objectives of these programmes include: increasing self-esteem, resistance to peer pressure, and perceptions of the risk of using alcohol and other drugs; and building bicultural competence (May and Moran, 1995). Few of these programmes have been evaluated, but the etiologic literature suggests that a combination of emphases on self-esteem, belief and value systems, practical life skills and social supports have demonstrated efficacy (May and Moran, 1995).

The latter two factors—life skills and social supports—are part of a suite of social determinants including education and employment that are associated with less destructive patterns of substance use, although the precise mechanisms by which this occurs is still unclear (Loxley et al., 2004). In Canada and Australia, Royal Commissions conducted in the 1990s focused on the association between economic conditions and the health and well-being of indigenous people. Certainly indigenous peoples throughout the world continue to stress the links between their colonial histories and marginalisation from mainstream economic opportunities and the persistence of poor health and substance misuse in their populations (Saggers and Gray, 1998; Brady, 2000).

More recent research on the impact of social cohesion on health has directed attention to broad community development strategies, in addition to interventions focused on factors such as education and employment. In New Zealand, for instance, policies of cultural affirmation which utilise indigenous organisations to develop and conduct substance misuse programmes are creating meaningful employment for Māori while specifically addressing alcohol and other drug use (Durie 2001).

There are also many general programmes in Australia, Canada, New Zealand and the United States designed to revitalise and maintain secure cultural identities for indigenous peoples. The rationale for these approaches attributes substance misuse to the declining influence of traditional culture following colonisation. Many interventions employ a combination of traditional culture and western modalities to address substance problems. This makes the role of traditional cultural elements very difficult to evaluate (Saggers and Gray, 1998; Brady, 2000). However, while there is limited evidence of the efficacy of the role of cultural approaches, a review of the Australian literature demonstrates that structural factors such as remaining at school, and having a job are generally protective against tobacco smoking, alcohol and other drug misuse among indigenous people (Loxley et al., 2004).

Sport and recreation, too, have been widely used to promote substance-free or harm minimisation messages among indigenous people. These strategies are based on notions that lack of meaningful activities promotes misuse, and take advantage of the high levels of interest in sport and recreation among many indigenous communities. In New Zealand, for example, an urban Māori campaign has been directed at encouraging a wide range of sporting organisations—netball and various football codes—to adopt policies promoting moderate alcohol use (in Durie, 2001:140). In Australia, too, sport and recreation have been an important part of strategies to prevent substance misuse. Again, evaluations of these approaches are rare, or not systematic, and frequently concerned only with their acceptability to the target population (Gray et al., 2000). However, evaluation of a fitness training programme among young native Canadians claimed that alcohol and drug use had stabilised as a consequence of the intervention (May and Moran, 1995).

From local through to national levels, use of the mass media has become an important tool for health promotion activities aimed at reducing the demand for alcohol and other substances. This includes everything from poster campaigns designed by school children, alcohol-free pow-wows, discos and concerts, and television advertisements (May and Moran, 1995; Brady, 2000). For instance, the Australian government funded a territory-based bush tour by the indigenous rock group Yothu Yindi and an associated television commercial targeting adolescent alcohol abuse. An evaluation claimed the campaign was effective, but that interpretations of the message varied and that more supporting information was required to extend its promotional appeal (Gray et al., 2000).

Some communities have also banned alcohol advertising at indigenous events such as pow-wows or sports events (May and Moran, 1995). At a national level some countries have mounted advertising campaigns to counteract attempts by the liquor industry to recruit more indigenous drinkers (May and Moran, 1995; Durie, 2001). According to researchers in New Zealand, advertising messages about moderate drinking were viewed positively by both urban and rural Māori, particularly among younger people (in Durie, 2001: 42). However, it is not known how this influenced drinking behaviours *per se*.

While there is a paucity of rigorous evaluation of demand reduction strategies in all countries, a promising trend has been the use of research conducted among the non-indigenous populations in each country to inform policy and practice among indigenous peoples (May and Moran, 1995; Saggers and Gray, 1998). With attention to issues such as cultural and contextual appropriateness, those programmes with proven efficacy may be adapted for use among indigenous populations.

TREATMENT

Among non-indigenous populations, treatment has been shown to be an effective means of reducing demand and preventing substance misuse (Loxley et al., 2004). In Australia in 1999–2000, community-based residential and non-residential treatment services comprised about 40% of 277 intervention projects targeted specifically at indigenous people and accounted for about 60% of expenditure on intervention projects (Gray et al., 2002).

Historically, in each of the countries under consideration, most treatment programs for indigenous people have focused on treatment for alcohol dependence (rather than dependence on other drugs) and have been based on the 12-steps model (Sellman et al., 1997; Brady, 2000; Thomason, 2000; Health Canada, n.d.;). This has been identified as a limitation on the effectiveness of treatment programs, and there have been calls to broaden the base of treatment approaches (Brady, 1995)—a call that is being increasingly heeded in both Australia and Canada (Brady, 2000; Health Canada, n.d.). As well as providing treatment based on the 12-steps model and other modalities such as cognitive behavioural therapy, treatment programmes provide a variety of skills enhancement and personal development programmes.

Again in Australia, Canada and the United States, the proportions of treatment programmes for indigenous people conducted in residential settings are significantly greater than those among non-indigenous people. In Australia, at least, there are two reasons for this.

First, there are few treatment programmes of any kind in the rural and remote communities in which many indigenous people reside, and to obtain treatment people must move to regional centres where they require accommodation. Second, many clients need to get out of their communities to escape the pressures associated with high levels of consumption there. Despite this emphasis, however, there are also numerous non-residential programmes and in Canada a mobile treatment programme has been implemented in some remote communities to overcome barriers to participation in residential programmes (Weibe and Huebert 1996).

A key difference between treatment services provided by indigenous community-controlled organisations and those conducted by non-indigenous agencies is the incorporation of indigenous cultural elements. Such incorporation varies across a broad continuum. At one end it involves the employment of indigenous staff members who are familiar with the ways of clients through to the inclusion of indigenous healing ceremonies at the other (Sellman et al., 1997; Berkowitz, 1998; Brady, 2000; French, 2000; Health Canada, n.d.;). A particularly important focus in many programmes is upon treating families—recognising the importance of family in indigenous social organisation and the social context in which substance misuse is embedded.

It is apparent through the preparation of this chapter, that few Aboriginal substance abuse programmes have been formally evaluated, although it is generally recognised that there are good programmes in existence reporting successes in both drug and alcohol abuse treatment (Health Canada, n.d.: 13). This finding is echoed in reviews or papers from Australia, New Zealand and the United States (Sellman et al., 1997; Gray et al., 2000; Thomason, 2000; Strempel et al., 2004).

Harm Reduction

Harm reduction strategies are those which focus on minimising the harm associated with substance misuse. In some contexts, the harms associated with use are regarded as greater than the substance misuse itself (for example, HIV transmitted by sharing of injecting equipment) and the priority is on reducing that harm without *necessarily* seeking to reduce substance use. In other contexts and policy environments the emphasis might be upon both.

Night patrols

In Australia a number of communities have introduced "night patrols"—sometimes referred to as "mobile assistance patrols" or "warden schemes". These mobile patrols often work cooperatively with other service providers such as the police and ambulance services. They seek to prevent intoxicated persons from harming themselves and others by removing them from public to safe locations and to reduce the number of indigenous people in police custody. In the 1999–2000 financial year there were 69 night patrols operating in both indigenous communities and towns.

There are no published outcome evaluations of night patrols. However, a review of nine patrols in the Northern Territory (Mosey, 1994) and two reports that include information on individual patrols in Western Australia (Sputore et al., 1998) and the Northern Territory (Strempel et al., 2004) provide some data on process measures. Each of the patrols reviewed enjoyed wide-spread community support in large part derived from community control and the employment of indigenous personnel. Anecdotal evidence from both community members and the police suggested that the patrols were effective in reducing alcohol-related anti-social behaviour and freeing the police to deal with more serious matters. Night patrols are generally seen to be more effective where they work in conjunction with sobering-up shelters.

Sobering-up shelters

In Australia in 1999–2000, there were 23 sobering-up shelters; the main role of which was to provide temporary haven for, and supervision of, people at risk of causing harm to themselves or others and to divert intoxicated people from police custody. As well as providing these basic services, some also provide direct links or referrals to treatment programmes (Sputore et al., 1998; Strempel et al., 2004). One study has shown a significant reduction in police detentions associated with the operation of a sobering-up shelter (Sputore et al., 1998). As with night patrols, the limited available qualitative evidence available indicates that such shelters enjoy wide-spread support from indigenous people and the police.

Needle exchange

In both Australia and Canada, needle exchange programmes have been a key strategy to reduce the harms associated with injecting drug use—particularly the spread of blood-borne viruses. However, such a strategy is opposed by the US Government. In Australia, needle exchange programmes have been shown to be cost-effective and to have played a major role in containing the HIV/AIDS epidemic (Loxley et al., 2004) and a Health Canada paper reports that these programs have not led to an increase in drug use (Health Canada, 2001). In Canada, indigenous people are over-represented among the clients of syringe exchange services (Health Canada, 2001). In Australia, in 1999–2000, there were six exchange programmes specifically for indigenous people, an unknown number of indigenous community-controlled health services provided needle exchange services, and indigenous people also accessed mainstream services (Loxley et al., 2004). However, we were unable to identify any evaluations of the impact of such programmes on indigenous peoples.

ELEMENTS OF SUCCESSFUL PROGRAMMES

It is sometimes observed that many indigenous intervention projects are less than optimally successful because key elements of process are not in place or are inadequate. Two qualitative studies have identified such elements. The first reviewed a non-residential solvent abuse community intervention in Canada (Round Lake Treatment Centre, cited in Health Canada, nd). The other reviewed five indigenous Australian projects, including a night patrol, a health promotion project, and residential and non-residential treatment programmes (Strempel et al., 2004). In summary, the elements identified in these studies are:

- indigenous community control, good governance and social accountability, commitment by chief and council;
- a clear set of principles, plan, and strategy, including a realistic time-frame;
- clearly defined management structures, strong managerial leadership and support;
- recruitment of appropriate staff (including native language speakers where appropriate) and staff development and support;
- holistic, multi-strategy, flexible interventions;

- intra- and inter-agency collaboration;
- adequate resourcing;
- reporting, monitoring and evaluation procedures.

Together, these key elements provide a guide for the development of measures for the process evaluation of indigenous intervention projects.

CONCLUSION

In addition to interventions aimed at general populations, a wide range of interventions specifically targeting indigenous peoples have been introduced by both governments and indigenous community organisations. As this review highlights, there have been relatively few evaluations of such interventions and there is clearly a need for more research in this area. However, the paucity of formal evaluations should not be interpreted as meaning that the various interventions are ineffective. The limited evidence we have presented indicates that interventions targeting communities, families and individuals can be effective providing that they are developed in response to local needs and circumstances in accord with elements that have been identified as contributing to such effectiveness.

In our introduction we highlighted the web of social factors that determine the higher levels of substance misuse and related harm reported among indigenous populations and the need for interventions that address these determinants at all levels. However, as the material we have reviewed indicates, most interventions directed explicitly at substance misuse focus on the individual, family or community levels. Moreover, as the continuing high levels of substance misuse attest, the overall impact of interventions at these levels has been limited. We identified no interventions at the macro-level targeted *specifically* at substance misuse. It was beyond the scope of this chapter to review large-scale programmes aimed at ameliorating the status of indigenous peoples. Nevertheless, the continuing social inequalities faced by indigenous peoples indicates the limited impact of these latter programmes and the need for greater efforts to address the structural inequalities that contribute to indigenous substance misuse.

ACKNOWLEDGEMENTS

The National Drug Research Institute is funded by the Australian Government Department of Health and Ageing.

REFERENCES

Aboriginal Drug and Alcohol Council (2003) *"They Sniffed and They Sniffed and It Just Wasn't There"*: *An Evaluation of the Comgas Scheme.* Report prepared for the Comgas Evaluation Working Group. Canberra: Department of Health and Ageing.

Australia, Ministerial Council on Drugs Strategy (2003) *National Drug Strategy: Aboriginal and Torres Strait Islander Peoples Complementary Action Plan 2003–2006.* Canberra: National Drug Strategy Unit, Department of Health and Aging.

Berkowitz G., Peterson, S., Smith, E.M., Taylor, T. and Brindis, C. (1998) Community and treat-
    ment program challenges for chemically dependent American Indian and Alaska Native women.
    Contemporary Drug Problems, **25**(Fall), 347–371.
Brady, M. (1995) *Broadening the Base of Treatment for Aboriginal People with Alcohol Problems.*
    Technical paper no. 29. Sydney: National Drug and Alcohol Research Centre, University of New
    South Wales.
Brady, M. (2000) Alcohol policy issues for indigenous people in the United States, Canada, Australia
    and New Zealand. *Contemporary Drug Problems*, **27**(Fall): 435–509.
Chiu, A.Y., Perez, P.E. and Parker, N. (1997) Impact of banning alcohol on outpatient visits in Barrow,
    Alaska. *Journal of the American Medical Association*, **278**(21), 1775–1777.
d'Abbs, P. (1990) *Dry Areas, Alcohol and Aboriginal Communities: A Review of the Northern Territory
    Restricted Areas Legislation*. Darwin: Drug and Alcohol Bureau, Northern Territory Department
    of Health and Community Services and Racing, Gaming and Liquor Commission.
d'Abbs, P. (1998) Out of sight, out of mind? Licensed clubs in remote Aboriginal communities.
    Australian and New Zealand Journal of Public Health, **22**(6), 679–684.
d'Abbs, P. and Togni, S. (2000) Liquor licensing and community action in regional and remote
    Australia: a review of recent initiatives. *Australian and New Zealand Journal of Public Health*,
    24(1), 45–53.
Durie, M. (2001) *Mauri Ora: The Dynamics of Māori Health*. Auckland: Oxford University Press.
Frank, J.W., Moore, R.S. and Ames, G.M. (2000) Historical and cultural roots of drinking problems
    among American Indians. *American Journal of Public Health*, **90**(3), 344–351.
French, L.A. (2000) *Addictions and Native Americans*. Westport, CT: Praeger.
Gray, D. and Saggers, S. (2003). Substance misuse. In N. Thomson (ed.), *The Health of Indigenous
    Australians*. Melbourne: Oxford University Press.
Gray, D., Saggers, S., Drandich, M., Wallam, D. and Plowright, P. (1995) Evaluating government
    health and substance abuse programs for indigenous peoples: a comparative review. *Australian
    Journal of Public Health*, **19**(6), 567–572.
Gray, D., Saggers, S., Sputore, B. and Bourbon, D. (2000). What works? A review of evaluated alcohol
    misuse interventions among Aboriginal Australians. *Addiction*, **95**(1), 11–22.
Gray, D., Sputore, B., Stearne, A. et al. (2002) *Indigenous Drug and Alcohol Projects: 1999–2000*.
    ANCD Research Paper 4. Canberra: Australian National Council on Drugs.
Health Canada (n.d.) *Literature Review. Evaluation Strategies in Aboriginal Substance Abuse Pro-
    grams: A Discussion Paper*. Available online: http://www.hc-sc.gc.ca/fnihb-dgspni/fnihb/cp/
    nnadap/publications/literary_review_abuse_prgs.pdf (accessed 27th April 2004).
Health Canada (1998) National Native Alcohol and Drug Abuse Program: General Review 1998.
    Available online: http://www.hc-sc.gc.ca/fnihb-dgspni/fnihb/cp/nnadap/publications/nnadap
    general_review.pdf (accessed 27th April 2004).
Health Canada (2001) *Reducing the Harm Associated with Injection Drug Use in Canada*. Ottawa:
    Health Canada.
Landen, M.G., Beller, M., Funk, E. et al. (1997) Alcohol-related injury death and alcohol availability
    in remote Alaska. *Journal of the American Medical Association*, **278**(21), 1755–1758.
Loxley, W., Toumbourou, J.W., Stockwell, T. et al. (2004) *The Prevention of Substance Use, Risk and
    Harm in Australia: A Review of the Evidence*. Canberra: Population Health Division, Australian
    Government Department of Health and Ageing.
Lynch, J. (2000) Social epidemiology: some observations about the past, present and future.
    Australasian Epidemiologist, **7**(3), 7–15.
MacLean, S.J. and d'Abbs P.H.N. (2002) Petrol sniffing in Aboriginal communities: a review of
    interventions. *Drug and Alcohol Review* **21**(1), 65–72.
May, P.A. and Moran, J.R. (1995) Prevention of alcohol misuse: a review of health promotion efforts
    among American Indians. *Journal of American Health Promotion*, **9**(4), 288–299.

Mosey, A. (1994) *Central Australian Night Patrols: A Review*. Alice Springs: Drug and Alcohol Services Association.

Saggers, S. and Gray, D. (1998) *Dealing with Alcohol: Indigenous Usage in Australia, New Zealand and Canada*. Melbourne: Cambridge University Press.

Sellman, J.D., Huriwai, T.T. and Deering, D.E. (1997) Cultural linkage: treating Māori with alcohol and drug problems in dedicated Māori treatment programs. *Substance Use and Misuse*, **32**(4), 415–424.

Sputore, B., Gray, D., Bourbon, D. and Baird, K. (1998) *Evaluation of the Kununurra-Waringarri Aboriginal Corporation and Ngnowar-Aerwah Aboriginal Corporation's Alcohol Projects*. Perth, WA: National Centre for Research into the Prevention of Drug Abuse, Curtin University of Technology.

Strempel, P., Saggers, S., Gray, D. and Stearne, A. (2004) *Indigenous Drug and Alcohol Projects: Elements of Best Practice*. ANCD Research Paper 8. Canberra: Australian National Council on Drugs.

Thomason, T.C. (2000) Issues in the treatment of Native Americans with alcohol problems. *Journal of Multicultural Counselling and Development*, **October**: 243–252.

Weibe, J. and Huebert K.M. (1996) Community mobile treatment: what it is and how it works. *Journal of Substance Abuse Treatment*, **13**(1), 23–31.

Section 7   FUTURE DIRECTIONS FOR PREVENTION POLICY AND RESEARCH

EDITED BY TIM STOCKWELL

7.1 Introduction

TIM STOCKWELL

Centre for Addictions Research of BC, Victoria, Canada

In this final section, a series of broad perspectives is provided on the significance of the evidence base for what works in prevention. It is intended that these chapters provide the most specific and succinct guidance for policy-makers concerned to prevent drug-related harm at the population level. Thus, Chapter 7.2 provides a how-to-do-it guide for maximising returns from investment in competing prevention programmes with different estimates of cost-effectiveness and reach. Chapter 7.3 provides specific, evidence-based estimates, not previously published, of the cost–benefit ratios of 84 interventions covering harm reduction, treatment and "prevention". Chapter 7.5 provides global ratings of the strength of the evidence in support of 70 preventive interventions, using "prevention" in the broad sense outlined in Chapter 1.1, using a scale designed to give summary advice to policy-makers. A conceptual model summarising the ways in which different elements of effective prevention can work in synergy with each other is also provided in Chapter 7.5 along with a number of specific policy and research recommendations regarding future directions for investment of the prevention dollar/euro/pound etc. No further recommendations will be specified in this Section introduction, the chapters will speak for themselves.

Attempts to implement policies, even those with the strongest evidence base, quickly encounter social, economic and political realities that must be negotiated with care and skill. Chapter 7.4 provides an introduction to the contributions that have been made, and still need to be made, from ethnographic studies of drug users to understanding the social realities in which drug use and related harm can occur. Such studies are necessarily local and culture-specific whereas much of the evidence considered in this book is intended to be cross-cultural. The model in Chapter 7.5 of preventive interventions across the life-course identifies the critical role of local communities in terms of both mediating the impact of prevention strategies as well as shaping their implementation. Ethnographic research can be a valuable tool for guiding local implementation and, more generally, for informing the understanding of the social contexts in which risky drug use and harm occurs.

With increasing accountability for government expenditures, negotiating economic realities around the prevention of drug-related harm is a requirement that all policy-makers will be aware of. The tools and data provided on cost-effectiveness and cost–benefits in the next two chapters of this section should prove particularly useful here. It is interesting that Miller and Hendrie (Chapter 7.3) identify environmental harm reduction strategies for the prevention of substance use related harms to have the highest cost–benefit ratios:

Preventing Harmful Substance Use: The Evidence Base for Policy and Practice.
Edited by T. Stockwell, P. J. Gruenewald, J.W. Toumbourou and W. Loxley.
© 2005 John Wiley & Sons, Ltd. ISBN 0-470-09227-0 (hbk) 0-470-09228-9 (pbk).

the introduction of less porous cigarette papers and the use of "floatable" winter coats in native Alaskan communities are striking examples promising particularly high yields from investments.

Some of the most evidence-based preventive interventions considered in this book have not only zero cost but, under some circumstances, can even generate revenue for governments. Varieties of taxation strategies are pre-eminent here, e.g., maintaining high prices per unit of legal drug (cigarette sticks or "standard drinks") and/or special levies for harm reduction purposes. However, these interventions immediately raise the toughest reality of all to negotiate: political reality. It is not sufficient for a prevention strategy to be proven effective and cost-effective—it must also be the case that political decision-makers feel safe enough, or brave enough, that its introduction will not threaten (1) their personal interests or (2) their political viability. A recent discussion of alcohol policy in the UK (see Room, 2004) has highlighted how political viability is directly affected by powerful commercial vested-interest groups that can compromise the potential for public health and safety benefits through government policy reforms. These powerful commercial influences on political viability expose flaws in democratic structures as for the most part they operate separately from considerations of public opinion and voter intentions. National opinion data (e.g., AIHW, 2002) shows that highly effective strategies often enjoy public support but are not necessarily implemented—and nor are the benefits of implementation fully explained to the voting public.

In relation to the prevention of harms associated with illicit drugs, official and police corruption can be seen as the direct equivalent to the adverse influence of commercial vested interests. While parrying with vested interest, political reality must also account for the central role of public opinion and this can be a major influence in the implementation of effective policy. The negotiation of cannabis law reforms has been assisted by studies of public opinion (e.g., Lenton et al., 2000). The Swiss government proceeded with the widespread implementation of heroin prescription programmes following a referendum (as is frequently the case with Swiss public policy) (Klingemann, 1998). The fear of the spread of dangerous infectious diseases in the general public at the outset of the AIDS/HIV epidemic swung public opinion and enabled courageous political decisions to be made in the interests of both illicit drug users and the community at large.

The skill and resolve to negotiate social, economic and political realities become more critical when the policy task involves large-scale system change. This challenge is evident when attempting to influence by all available means the developmental pathways through which children and young people become introduced to drug use and go on to experience drug-related harms. A knowledge base is emerging from longitudinal research indicating the modifiable influences that can encourage healthy child development. These child development research findings have been supplemented and extended by a number of evaluation studies that have demonstrated the possibility of reducing drug use and improving developmental outcomes through preventative interventions. By supporting vulnerable families through the parenting task there exists the possibility of reducing the likelihood that both they and their children will engage in heavy drug use (Catalano et al., 1999; Olds et al., 1999). An important finding emerging from developmental prevention studies is that there can be benefits for all children by improving key developmental environments such as families, pre-schools, schools and community services. However, a striking finding emerging from a number of studies is that the greatest benefits of these initiatives often fall to the most vulnerable and disadvantaged children and young people (Eddy et al., 2000;

Hawkins et al., 2001). As developmental prevention programmes may involve many years of implementation before benefits become evident, the challenge of encouraging investment in this area is likely to be considerable. The rewards for political leadership in this area are, however, also likely to be very great. A very good case can be made for the economic and social benefits of prevention programmes and when their benefits are understood they tend to be well supported. The diversity in the settings and the age-ranges targeted by developmental prevention programmes means that selectivity will need to be exercised in deciding the right programme mix for a specific community. Once again political leadership will be required as many prevention programmes have only been newly developed and are unknown while community members may advocate better known programmes that may be ineffective or worse.

We conclude that there is a great and wide need for improved accountability in public policy on substance use issues so that it is more in step with the evidence for what will have most community benefit. Present patterns of investment in prevention programmes and policies are often unrelated and even opposed to the existing and growing evidence base. Advocacy and education of the community about effective public policy are needed to ensure that elected leaders support more effective strategies to ensure the massive toll of health, social and legal problems from risky substance use is reduced.

REFERENCES

Australian Institute of Health and Welfare (2002) *2001 National Drug Strategy Household Survey: First Results.* Canberra: Australian Institute of Health and Welfare.

Catalano, R.F., Gainey, R.R., Fleming, C.B., Haggerty, K.P. and Johnson, N.O. (1999) An experimental intervention with families of substance abusers one-year follow-up of the focus on families project. *Addiction*, **94**, 241–254.

Eddy, J.M., Reid, J.B. and Fetrow, R.A. (2000) An elementary school-based prevention program targeting modifiable antecedents of youth delinquency and violence: linking the interests of families and teachers (LIFT). *Journal of Emotional and Behavioral Disorders*, **8**(3), 165–176.

Hawkins, J.D., Guo, J., Hill, K., Battin-Pearson, S. and Abbott, R. (2001) Long term effects of the Seattle Social Development intervention on school bonding trajectories. In J. Maggs and J. Schulenberg (eds), *Applied Developmental Science Special issue Prevention as Altering the Course of Development*, 5 edn, pp. 225–236.

Klingemann, H.H. (1998) Politics, public opinion and the Swiss Heroin Trial. In T. Stockwell (ed.), *Drug Trials and Tribulations: Lessons for Australian Drug Policy, Proceedings of an International Symposium.* Perth, WA National Centre for Research into the Prevention of Drug Abuse.

Lenton, S., Heale, P., Erickson, P., Single, E., Lang, E. and Hawks, D.V. (2000) *The Regulation of Cannabis Possession, Use and Supply: A Discussion Document Prepared for the Drugs and Crime Prevention Committee of The Parliament of Victoria. Monograph No. 3.* National Drug Research Institute, Perth, Western Australia.

Olds, D.L., Henderson, C.R., Kitzman, H.J., Eckenrode, J.J., Cole, R.E. and Tatelbaum, R.C. (1999) Prenatal and infancy home visitation by nurses: recent findings. *The Future of Children*, **9**(1), 44–65.

Room, R. (2004) Disabling the public interest: alcohol strategies and policies for England. *Addiction*, **99**, 1083–1089.

7.2 Investing for Cost-Effectiveness in the Face of Uncertainty: Applying Financial Portfolio Optimization to Prevention Programming

JONATHAN P. CAULKINS

Carnegie Mellon University, H. John Heinz III School of Public Policy and Management; RAND Drug Policy Research Center, Pittsburgh, USA

SUMMARY

There is widespread agreement that government spending ought to be driven by considerations of cost-effectiveness or other similar performance measures. Yet programme cost-effectiveness estimates are often highly uncertain; that is clearly the case with prevention interventions. Hence, investing exclusively in the programme with the highest point estimate of cost-effectiveness is risky. It puts all of the taxpayers' eggs in one basket, and that basket might end up performing below expectations. Elementary portfolio optimization theory from finance suggests how to diversify risky investments. Methods are presented for adapting this theory to the problem of government investment in prevention programmes.

INTRODUCTION

There has been increasing emphasis in government generally (e.g., through the Government Performance and Results Act in the USA), and in the prevention field specifically, on quantifying the benefits and costs of alternative interventions. The goal is to "invest" scarce resources in the interventions yielding the greatest "return". The use of business jargon such as "investing" and "return" by academics and practitioners alike is self-conscious. It is driven by the belief that government policies ought to benefit from the rigorous management practices that are presumed to characterize private sector decision-making and to account for the greater efficiency and performance of the private sector.

This chapter takes no position on the overall wisdom of modeling government practices on private sector operations, but does argue that if one is going to base resource allocation

Preventing Harmful Substance Use: The Evidence Base for Policy and Practice.
Edited by T. Stockwell, P. J. Gruenewald, J.W. Toumbourou and W. Loxley.
© 2005 John Wiley & Sons, Ltd. ISBN 0-470-09227-0 (hbk) 0-470-09228-9 (pbk).

on quantitative estimates of cost and performance, those estimates ought to be viewed as uncertain. Particularly for prevention programmes, there is considerable uncertainty surrounding these estimates, so basing decisions only on point estimates is unwise.

Fortunately, performance uncertainty can be estimated and accounted for with simple spreadsheet analysis on a laptop. In particular, this chapter shows how elementary ideas from portfolio optimization in finance can be used to inform strategies for diversifying investments over a portfolio of prevention interventions.

Most of this discussion will be couched in terms of cost-effectiveness. Some see cost-effectiveness as inferior to or a preliminary step toward a cost–benefit analysis, which is sometimes viewed as the only "correct" framework for quantitative policy analysis. Indeed, some examples below will work with monetized outcomes. However, often the policy context within which prevention's performance is considered is more accurately characterized as allocating a fixed budget across scalable programmes (which invites cost-effectiveness analysis) rather than making go/no-go funding decisions based on whether benefits exceed costs and without regard to budget constraints (the classical framing of decisions in benefit–cost analysis). At any rate, this is an expositional issue; the ideas in this chapter can be used in conjunction with benefit–cost analysis, cost-effectiveness analysis, or any other form of quantitative policy analysis.

Having estimates of the cost-effectiveness of various programmes can inform the decision of how to spend the next dollar: It should be spent on the programme with the most favorable cost–effectiveness ratio if the objective is to get the most "bang for the buck". Naturally, policy-makers are not interested in how to spend the next dollar but rather the next million or hundred million dollars. It is assumed here that the cost-effectiveness results apply on this larger scale. The assumption that benefits increase linearly with investment can be a fairly strong one, but expanding prevention programmes often means giving the same programme to more individuals, not increasing programme intensity. Expanding an intervention currently operating in one school district by implementing it in another district is more likely to double the effect than is doubling the intensity of the intervention in the first district.

If programme effects scale linearly in programme expenditures, the prescription for spending more than one dollar is simple when there is no uncertainty:[1]

1. Rank programmes in order of cost-effectiveness, from best to worst.
2. Move down the list, funding each programme in succession to the fullest extent possible.
3. Stop when you run out of money.

This algorithm maximizes the *expected* benefit per dollar spent. However, many factors underlying cost-effectiveness estimates are uncertain. Programmes could perform better or worse than expected so decision-makers may have a second objective: ensuring that a prevention investment strategy achieves at least some minimum cost-effectiveness.

The preceding algorithm could concentrate resources in one or a few programmes. If those programmes turn out to perform much worse than expected, the entire investment may yield a low cost-effectiveness. "Hedging one's bet" by investing in an array of programmes reduces the *expected* cost-effectiveness, but the risk that the entire investment would fail

---

[1] This algorithm assumes programmes can be funded at any level between zero and some maximum. If each programme must be funded fully or not at all, them the problem becomes a "knapsack problem" which can be solved as an integer programming problem.

would be less. The aphorism "Don't put all your eggs in one basket" is a reminder that in an uncertain world, it is sometimes wise to give up a little efficiency (effectiveness per dollar) to insure against the worst outcomes (i.e., to reduce variance in performance).

Folk wisdom does not provide concrete guidance for how to manage investments, but finance theory does. The problem of optimally trading off expected cost-effectiveness and reductions in downside risk strongly parallels the classic portfolio management problem in which an investor decides how to distribute funds across a range of financial instruments (e.g., stocks) that have different expected returns and levels of risk. The next section summarizes the classic framing of this portfolio optimization problem.

"OPTIMAL" INVESTMENT PORTFOLIOS: THE RISK–RETURN TRADEOFF

A fundamental problem in portfolio management studied by Markowitz (1959) is deciding what proportion of scarce funds to invest in each possible instrument or, in the present context, in each prevention programme. Let p_j denote the proportion of funds invested in programme j. Then the goal is to find the "optimal" vector of proportions $\mathbf{p}^T = (p_1, p_2, \ldots, p_n)$.[2] For example, if there were four programmes that each received one-quarter of the available funding, one would write $\mathbf{p}^T = (0.25, 0.25, 0.25, 0.25)$. Naturally these proportions must be non-negative and sum to unity.

The performance of each programme is unknown and thus should be modeled as a random variable with an expectation, a variance, and a covariance with the random variables representing the cost-effectiveness of each of the other programmes under consideration.

The expected cost-effectiveness from a portfolio of investments in linearly scalable prevention programmes is just the pairwise product of the funding proportion invested in each programme times the expected cost-effectiveness of that programme. If the expected benefit per dollar invested in the four programmes were $\mathbf{e}^T = (1, 3, 2, 2)$, then the expected cost-effectiveness from an equally apportioned portfolio would be

$$\mathbf{p}^T\mathbf{e} = 0.25 * 1 + 0.25 * 3 + 0.25 * 2 + 0.25 * 2 = 2.$$

The variance of the cost-effectiveness of this portfolio would be $\mathbf{p}^T\mathbf{C}\,\mathbf{p}$, where $\mathbf{C}$ is the covariance matrix. Specifically, element c_{ij} of matrix $\mathbf{C}$ is the covariance of the two random variables representing the cost-effectiveness of programmes i and j. The square root of the variance, i.e., the standard deviation, is an equally valid measure of risk and is more intuitive inasmuch as it is measured in the same units as cost-effectiveness. The variance is expressed in those units squared. Explaining metrics such as kilograms of marijuana use averted per million taxpayer dollars spent is hard enough without also having to explain what (kilograms/million dollars)^2 means.

Typically one seeks to maximize the expected outcome subject to a constraint that risk (measured in terms of the variance or standard deviation) be less than or equal to some upper bound or one seeks to minimize risk subject to a constraint that the expected outcome meet some lower bound. These are nonlinear optimization problems, but because of their quadratic form (concave quadratic objective with linear constraints or vice versa), they can

---

[2] The superscript T denotes the "transpose" operator. The custom is to think of vectors as being a column of numbers. To write them as a row, we must turn them on their side or "transpose" the vector into a row.

easily be solved in a spreadsheet with Excel's built-in Solver function or with an add-in. Most modern introductory textbooks in Management Science explain how to do this.[3]

Repeatedly solving the problem with different bounds allows one to trace out a risk–return tradeoff curve. This curve represents a collection of risk–return combinations that are (1) feasible and (2) not dominated in the sense that there is no way of obtaining the same return with less risk or the same risk with a greater return.

In general, there is no objective way to label any point on this curve as being superior to any other point. Different decision-makers in different contexts would be willing to give up more or less expected return in exchange for a given reduction in risk. Thus, the curve represents a menu of options that are all "candidates" for being selected, in the sense that they are feasible and non-dominated. However, this menu of candidate solutions is much smaller than the total number of feasible funding options, so creating this efficient risk–return tradeoff curve greatly simplifies the final decision. Also, a fundamental insight is that decision makers should invest in programmes whose returns are not strongly correlated or, better yet, are negatively correlated. Otherwise, if one of the funded programmes does badly, it is likely that all will.

PROGRAMMES WHOSE PERFORMANCE IS UNCORRELATED

When the uncertainty surrounding the performance of each programme is uncorrelated, the portfolio optimization calculations are particularly simple. Lack of correlation might be the case when the programmes are unrelated or operate through distinct causal mechanisms.

In this case, the covariance matrix, C, is a diagonal matrix (i.e., all off diagonal elements are zero), and the variance of the portfolio's performance is just the weighted sum of the programme-specific variances, weighting by the square of the proportion of funding allocated to that programme. That is,

$$\text{portfolio variance} = \sum_i p_i^2 \sigma_i^2,$$

where σ_i^2 is the variance of the cost-effectiveness estimate for programme i. The optimization problem can then be written as:

$$\begin{aligned}
\text{Max} \quad & \sum_i p_i x_i \\
\text{subject to} \quad & \sum_i p_i^2 \sigma_i^2 \leq M \\
& \sum_i p_i = 1 \\
& p_i \geq 0 \quad \forall i.
\end{aligned}$$

There would be one p_i for each of the N programmes, but since those p_is must sum to unity, there are effectively only $N-1$ choice variables. For $N > 3$, the feasible region characterizing all possible options cannot be drawn. However, when there are just two programmes, the feasible region is one-dimensional, specifically it is the scalar variable $0 \leq p_1 \leq 1$. (Given p_1, the other variable p_2 is fully determined by the constraint $p_1 + p_2 = 1$.)

---

[3] My favorite is Cliff Ragsdale's *Spreadsheet Modeling and Decision Analysis* (2004, Southwestern) because it gives such clear, step-by-step instruction on how to use Excel, but there are a number of excellent alternatives.

Hence, for two programmes one can literally see the risk–return performance for every possible portfolio in one graph. Such a graph helps solidify intuition about the fundamental concepts involved in portfolio diversification, so it is explored with a numerical example.

The two programmes considered here are mandatory minimum sentence for high-level dealers and model school-based drug prevention programmes. Both affect drug use and there is considerable uncertainty concerning their cost-effectiveness, but they operate through such distinct mechanisms that it is not an unreasonable simplification to assume that uncertainty about their performance is essentially uncorrelated.

Caulkins et al., modeled the cost-effectiveness of mandatory minimum sentences. For sentences given to high-level dealers, such as those prosecuted at the federal level, their best estimate of cost-effectiveness was 36 kilograms of cocaine consumption averted per million programme dollars spent (1997: 48). Through Monte Carlo simulation of uncertainty in parameter estimates, they estimated a variance on this cost-effectiveness estimate of 373.7 (1997: 143), implying a standard deviation of $\sqrt{373.7} = 19.3$.[4]

Caulkins et al. (2002) likewise estimate that a present value of $1000 in social benefits accrue from sending one youth through a model school-based drug prevention programme as a result of reduced use of all substances, licit and illicit, assuming that effects on illicit drugs not studied explicitly (notably heroin and methamphetamine) are similar to those estimated for cocaine. Parallel Monte Carlo simulations with respect to parametric uncertainty suggest a standard deviation around this estimate of $219 (result not previously reported in this form). Dividing by the estimated $150 in social cost to administer the prevention programme suggests a point estimate for model prevention's cost-effectiveness of $1000 / $150 = $6.67, with a standard deviation of $219 / $150 = $1.46.[5]

To express the cost-effectiveness of mandatory minimum sentences in common units, the social benefit per gram of cocaine use averted is assumed to be $215 (Caulkins et al., 2002), yielding a corresponding mean and standard deviation in social benefits per programme dollar spent of $7.74 and $4.16, respectively.[6]

If one ignored uncertainty and sought merely to maximize expected cost-effectiveness, one would allocate all funds to mandatory sentencing because its point estimate of cost-effectiveness ($7.74) exceeds the corresponding estimate for prevention ($6.67). Increasing from zero the proportion of funding going to prevention, p, and decreasing the corresponding proportion of funding going to mandatory minimum sentences to $1 - p$, reduces the expected value of the portfolio's cost-effectiveness to

$$\$6.67\,p \; + \; \$7.74\,(1-p) \; = \; \$7.74 - \$1.07\,p.$$

However, the variance of the estimated cost-effectiveness:

$$p^2 * \$1.46 * \$1.46 \; + \; (1-p)^2 * \$4.16 * \$4.16$$

decreases in p until p reaches about 89%.

---

[4] The mean cost-effectiveness in the simulation was a bit higher, 39 kilograms per million dollars, but the 36 kilogram per million dollar figure is still the best point estimate of cost-effectiveness.

[5] Even though both the numerator and denominator of this ratio are expressed in dollars, I still prefer to think about this as a cost–effectiveness ratio not a benefit–cost ratio because the two types of dollars are not fungible. The dollars in the denominator represent programme costs, including the opportunity cost of using class time to teach drug prevention not traditional academic subjects; those in the numerator represent a monetization of benefits accruing from reduced drug use. One cannot trade the former for the latter in any market. The monetization in the numerator represents nothing more than a convenient way of aggregating benefits from the reduced use of several different kinds of substances.

[6] 36 kilograms * 1000 grams/kilogram * $215 / gram divided by $1,000,000 = $7.74. Similarly, 19.3 kilograms * 1000 grams/kilogram * $215 / gram divided by $1,000,000 = $4.16.

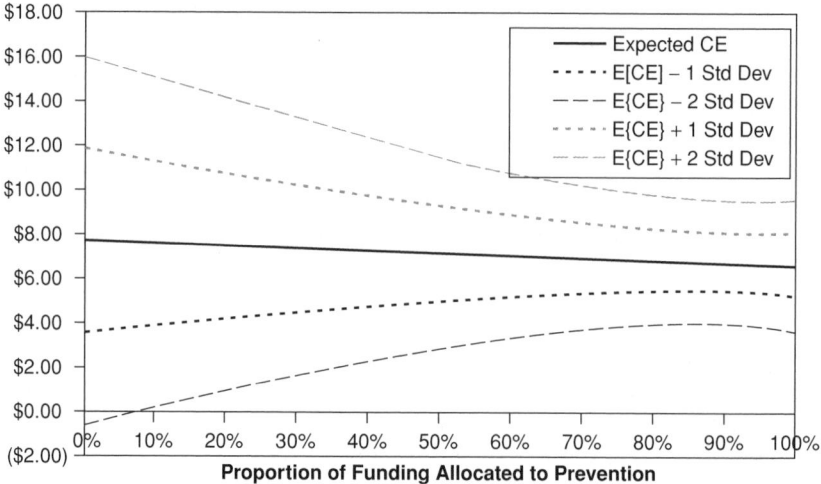

Figure 7.2.1 Expected CE ratio with $+/-$ and 2 Std Dev Bands, as a function of proportion of funding allocated to prevention

This trade-off is illustrated graphically in Figure 7.2.1, which plots the expected cost-effectiveness, as well as the expected value plus and minus one and two standard deviations, as a function of the proportion of funding allocated to prevention. Note that the portfolio uncertainty approximately follows a normal distribution because the distributions of simulation results for both mandatory sentencing and prevention were unimodal, approximately symmetric, and characterized by small tails in either direction. Given that approximation, when all resources are invested in mandatory sentencing, there is about a 5% chance that the actual cost-effectiveness will be below 1, even though the expected value is $7.44. In contrast, as long as at least 70% of funding is invested in prevention, that outcome is very unlikely to occur because of parametric uncertainty (less than one chance in 10,000). Likewise, to maximize the chance of doing at least as well as some cost-effectiveness target less than $7.44, one ought to invest in prevention as well as incarceration. For example, putting about 85% of available funding in prevention maximizes the chance of averting at least $6 in social cost from reduced drug use per $1 in social cost incurred by the intervention.

GENERAL CASE OF PROGRAMMES WHOSE PERFORMANCE IS CORRELATED

The optimization part of portfolio optimization is not really any different when the random variables representing the program's performance are correlated. The only difference is that the covariance matrix, **C**, is no longer diagonal. The challenge is estimating the problem parameters, specifically the off-diagonal elements of that covariance matrix.

In conventional financial applications the covariance matrix is typically estimated empirically by examining a historical record of asset performance. For stocks, one might literally compute the covariance of the daily or weekly returns of each pair of stocks over the last few months.

When allocating dollars to investments that are not traded in markets there is no such historical record. Instead one can model each program's cost-effectiveness as a function of more elemental uncertain factors whose correlations across programmes might be known or are sufficiently elementary that it is possible for form judgments about them. Then the cost-effectiveness of all programmes can be jointly simulated, via Monte Carlo simulation, to construct an artificial history of their performance. Covariances can then be estimated from this artificial history, and the portfolio optimization can proceed just as in conventional finance applications. This approach is simple, but is perhaps worth illustrating with an example that considers three hypothetical prevention programmes.

Caulkins et al. (2002) modeled the cost-effectiveness of school-based prevention programmes as the product of ten independent factors, as is explained succinctly in Caulkins et al. 2004. Since prevention effectiveness is usually expressed as a percentage reduction in use, the model begins by estimating how much the average student would use over the course of a lifetime in the absence of prevention. Multiplying by the percentage reduction in use achieved by prevention gives the reduction in use (e.g., grams of cocaine) per person. Multiplying by the social costs averted per unit of drug not used yields total social value per person exposed to the programme. Thus, the model combines three estimates: amount of use, percentage reduction in use, and social value per unit of drug not used. The first two are in turn the product of two or three factors, and four adjustments must be made, yielding a ten-factor model. These calculations are carried through for four substances (tobacco, heavy drinking, marijuana, and cocaine) and the results summed.

Caulkins et al. (2002, 2004) studied a single, composite, model prevention programme. Table 7.2.1 lists the base case estimates of the ten factors for this idealized composite

Table 7.2.1 Ten-factor model for estimating prevention's effect on social costs of use over a lifetime, filled in with "best guess" estimates of prevention's impact

	Cocaine	Marijuana	Cigarettes	Alcohol
Units of Use	Grams	Grams	Packs	Self-reported instances of drunkenness[a]
F1: Baseline Use per Initiate	350	560	8900	640
F2: Baseline Proportion of Cohort Initiating	18%	62%	78%	58%
F3: Discount Factor	0.53	0.58	0.42	0.49
F4: Prevention's Short-term Effectiveness	10.9%	16.0%	16.8%	12.8%
F5: Reduction in Lifetime Use per Unit of Short-Term Effectiveness	27.6%	19.4%	14.0%	17.3%
F6: Correlation–Causation Ratio	0.9	0.9	0.9	0.9
F7: Scale-Up Factor	0.6	0.6	0.6	0.6
F8: Social Multiplier	2.0	1.0	1.0	1.0
F9: Market Multiplier	1.3	1.0	1.0	1.0
F10: Social Cost per Unit of Use	$215	$12	$8	$98
Social Benefit per Prevention Participant	$300	$20	$300	$210
Total	$840 per participant			

Note: [a] The model focuses on drunkenness because alcohol consumption per se is not well linked to social costs. Self-reports are cited because there is no way of converting self-reports of drunkenness into actual occurrences. This is not a problem because the social cost per unit of "use" for alcohol is per *self-reported* instance of drunkenness, so the self-reported "adjustment" occurs in both the numerator and denominator of the cost-effectiveness ratio and so cancels out.

programme, their product, and, hence, the resulting social benefit estimate. Associated with each factor was an uncertainty range (Caulkins et al., 2002, Table A.1, pp. 114–115).

Since Caulkins et al. (2002) considered just one composite programme, there was no portfolio problem to be solved. Nor were parameter estimates generated for multiple different programmes in this format. For illustrative purposes here, three hypothetical programmes will be considered. The first will be assumed to be particularly effective at controlling illicit drugs, but somewhat less effective at controlling tobacco use and heavy drinking. The second will be particularly effective against tobacco use, the last, against heavy drinking. In each case, simulation sample estimates for Factors F4 and F5 are assumed to be equally likely to take on any value between Caulkins et al.'s (2002) point-estimate and maximum value for the substance(s) the programme was particularly effective at controlling and between the point-estimate and minimum value for the other substances.

It is not important that the reader understands each of the factors in detail, let alone how they are estimated. For present purposes only three things are of concern: (1) understanding how these factors are combined to estimate social benefit per programme participant; (2) how the various factor estimates can be replaced with random variables to simulate uncertainty; and (3) how those various factors might be correlated.

Concerning how these ten factors are combined, Table 7.2.1 is essentially just a formatted extract of a spreadsheet. The ten factors (rows 1–10) are initially just constants. Social benefit per prevention participant by drug is just the product of the ten factors. Literally, the Excel formula behind the \$300 for cocaine is just =PRODUCT(. . .) where the arguments of the PRODUCT function are just the cell references of the ten factor estimates in the cocaine column. Likewise, the total social benefit is just the sum of the social benefits across drugs. In Excel, the formula is =SUM(. . .) where the argument is the cell references for the drug-specific totals. In short, the factors are combined algebraically, and that is a trivial calculation in a spreadsheet.

The next question is how to turn the 40 parameter estimates per programme (10 factors times 4 drugs = 40 parameters) into random variables to reflect uncertainty concerning those parameters. With an appropriate Excel add-in, such as Crystal Ball, that is literally just a matter of pointing and clicking. Point to each cell in turn, click on the icon to define that parameter as a random variable (called the "Define Assumptions" button in Crystal Ball) and fill in the dialogue boxes to indicate the type of random variable that best models its uncertainty (Normal, Beta, Uniform, etc.) and the associated distributional parameters. For example, most parameters in the present exercise were modeled as having a triangular distribution, so minimum, mode, and maximum values were specified. Specifically, those values were taken from Caulkins et al. (2002, Table A.1). The exceptions were Factors F4 and F5, which were modeled as uniform random variables, as described above.

The final issue is how to specify correlations among these random parameters. Essentially one just creates a copy of the spreadsheet for each programme under consideration and customizes the parameters governing the random factors to reflect the programme specific characteristics. For example, in the example here, programme #1 is imagined to be particularly effective at preventing use of illicit drugs, so the distribution parameters for its factors F4 and F5 are larger than for the other hypothetical programmes. Then specifying correlations among these random variables is essentially just a matter of filling in dialogue boxes in Crystal Ball. Realistically there are some spreadsheet tricks and short-cuts one can use to make this process a bit more elegant, but those are spreadsheet technicalities and not of concern here.

Conceptually the bigger question is understanding how to think about what factors are likely to be highly correlated. The details depend on the model (what factors overall cost-effectiveness is built up from) and the programmes under consideration. The general thinking process can be illustrated, however, with regard to the key factors in Caulkins et al.'s (2002, 2004) ten-factor model.

Factors may be correlated across substances and/or across programmes. For example, Factors F1 and F2 are clearly perfectly correlated across prevention programmes because they describe what use would be in the absence of these programmes. Consider Factor F2 in particular. When estimating the cost-effectiveness of a single programme, one source of uncertainty is what proportion of youth would have initiated in the absence of prevention because the cost-effectiveness of a programme that cuts drug use by a given percentage will scale linearly in the level of use. Furthermore, the lifetime prevalence for a birth cohort that is now in, say, 7th grade is clearly an uncertain quantity. It might not be unreasonable to forecast that they will use at rates comparable to their forebears, but that is only a forecast. The future may be different than the past. In particular, if the baseline cost-effectiveness estimate assumed use rates like those in the past, but baseline use turned out to be twice as great, then the cost-effectivenss would also be twice as great as forecast, holding all else equal. However, if baseline use is twice as high for Program #1, then it will also be exactly twice as high for Program #2 because both would be applied to the same cohort of individuals. So, the correlation across programmes for Factors F1 and F2 is perfect. The correlation across drugs may or may not be high. That depends on whether one views variation in drug use over time as reflecting drug-specific epidemics (low correlation) or some underlying predilection for intoxication or deviant behavior (high correlation). Indeed, if the substances were perceived of as substitutes, even a negative correlation could be defended. The calculations reported below presumed no inter-drug correlations, but they could just as easily have been done with some other assumption.

The scale-up factor (Factor F7) has the opposite behavior. The scale-up factor captures degradation in programme quality as it moves from the small-scale, intensively moni-tored format typical of the randomized control trial (RCT) experiments upon which cost-effectiveness estimates are based to the bureaucratic "mass production" mode. In medical jargon, it might be called the ratio of effectiveness to efficacy. Again there is uncertainty about its exact value for any given programme, but there is not much reason to think the uncertainty about the extent of degradation for one programme is highly correlated with that of another programme. If it turns out that Program #1 scaled up badly, that does not necessarily tell one much about whether a completely different intervention will scale up well or badly. On the other hand, if scaling up eroded substantially Program #1's ability to prevent marijuana use, that may say a lot about how scaling up likely affected its ability to prevent alcohol or tobacco use. So for the scale-up factor one would expect a high corre-lation across drugs within a programme, but a low correlation between programmes. For simplicity it is assumed here there is perfect correlation across drugs and zero correlation across programmes for the scale-up factor and also for the correlation-causation multiplier (Factor F6). The latter takes longer to define and explain, but ultimately the considerations are parallel.

Consider next a program's effectiveness in terms of percentage reduction in risk factors at first follow up (Factor F4) and the extent to which those reductions translate into reduc-tions in lifetime use (Factor F5). These uncertainties stem from uncertainty concerning the performance of the evaluated research intervention, not how that RCT intervention scales

Table 7.2.2   Simulation results for three hypothetical prevention programmes

	Program #1	Program #2	Program #3
Expected benefit per programme participant			
Drug targetted by programme	Illicit Drugs	Tobacco	Alcohol
Average cost-effectiveness	$839.25	$737.02	$870.96
Covariance table: empirical estimate of covariance matrix C			
Program #1	51,842	18,085	20,013
Program #2	18,085	30,173	10,148
Program #3	20,013	10,148	49,233

up. The most concrete example would be sampling variability in the reported effectiveness estimates, but it could also come from non-response, ambiguity from aggregating related but not-identical outcomes measures, etc. Again, there is little reason to expect correlation across programmes. There is also, however, not much reason to expect strong correlations across drugs within a programme. Just because random variation meant that published estimates of programme #1's ability to reduce cigarette use were high does not mean that corresponding estimates of the program's impact on alcohol use necessarily are also too high. So uncertainty for these factors is modeled as uncorrelated across drugs as well as across programmes.

Again, the general points are three-fold. First, programme cost-effectiveness should be modeled as a function of underlying factors whose correlations across programmes and programme benefits is easy to think about. Second, having modeled cost-effectiveness as a function of parameter point estimates in a spreadsheet, replacing point estimates with random variables is a simple point and click exercise with a spreadsheet simulation add-in. Third, mechanically, specifying correlations between factors is similarly trivial. Conceptually one needs to think about how these factors are correlated, but if the multi-factor model is crafted elegantly, this can be a fairly intuitive process.

Once all factor correlations have been specified, one runs the simulation many times, saving the cost-effectiveness results for each programme on each trial. The covariance in programme performance observed over this simulated history can be used as the covariance matrix C. Table 7.2.2 shows the results of such a simulation run for the example considered here.

Repeatedly solving the portfolio optimization problem with these parameters computes the risk–return frontier (see Figure 7.2.2). It shows how much additional "return" (increase in expected portfolio cost-effectiveness) one can achieve by taking on additional risk. (The horizontal axis is risk, specifically the standard deviation in the portfolio's return, because with more than two programmes the portfolio allocation **p** is a vector, not a scalar, and so cannot be graphed.) Typically one sees on the right-hand side of the curve that substantial increases in risk must be accepted to squeeze out additional increments in expected cost-effectiveness. Conversely, relatively little has to be given up in terms of expected cost-effectiveness in order to reduce substantially uncertainty concerning the portfolio's performance.

For each point on this curve, the optimization finds the corresponding portfolio. Figure 7.2.3 illustrates these for each point in Figure 7.2.2 indicated by a square block. Naturally, the block on the far right, yielding the highest expected cost-effectiveness, corresponds to investing all funds in the single programme with the highest point estimate of cost-effectiveness, which, in this hypothetical example, was Program #3. That is indicated by the furthest right bar in Figure 7.2.3 having 100% of the funding allocated to Program #3. If one

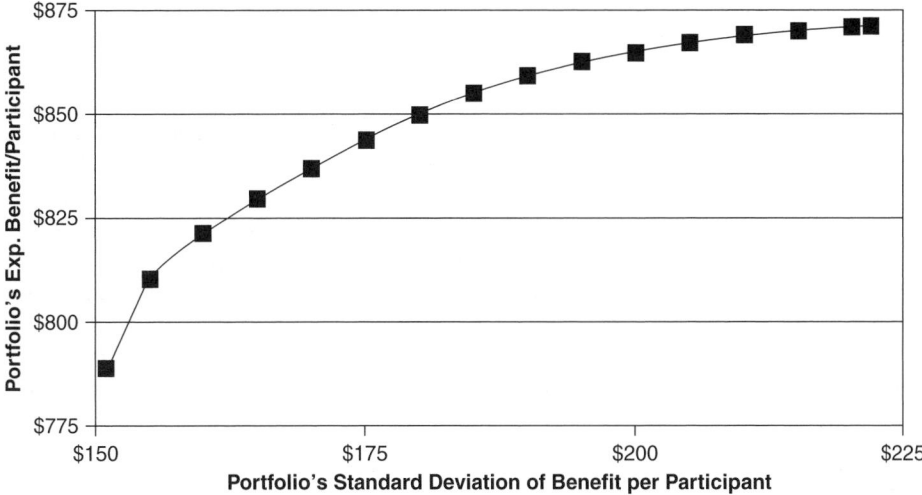

Figure 7.2.2 Risk–return trade-off curve for hypothetical three-programme example: portfolio's expected benefit per programme participant plotted vs. corresponding standard deviation

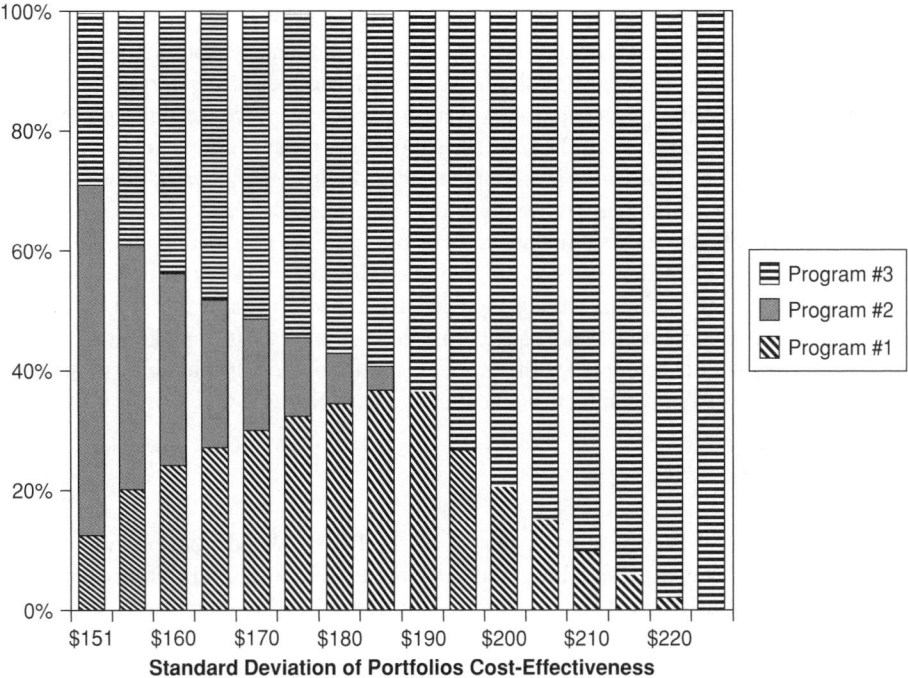

Figure 7.2.3 Prevention portfolios corresponding to different points on the risk–return frontier

were willing to trade off a little expected cost-effectiveness to reduce risk, i.e., to move to the left on the risk–return curve, then one begins to shift some of the funding into Program #1, in the proportions indicated by the bars in Figure 7.2.3. A funding mix of roughly one-third to Program #1 and two-thirds to Program #3 (8th bar from the right) reduces risk, measured by the standard deviation, by 14% (from 222 to 190) while reducing the expected cost-effectiveness by only 1.3% (from 871 to 860).

If further reductions in risk are desired, then it becomes optimal to allocate funding to Program #2 as well. Thus the bars still further to the left in Figure 7.2.3 have regions corresponding to the color shading of all three programmes. Indeed, the minimum variance portfolio (the bar furthest to the left in Figure 7.2.3) allocates more than 50% of the available funding to Program #2. Even though it had the smallest point estimate of cost-effectiveness, Program #2's estimate also had the smallest variance (See Table 7.2.2) and the smallest co-variance with the other programmes, so Program #2 has a role to play in a balanced portfolio.

CONCLUSION

The impulse to maximize the cost-effectiveness of government programmes such as prevention interventions is understandable. Usually, however, there is uncertainty surrounding the estimated cost-effectiveness of programmes, so the actual cost-effectiveness of a particular set of investments may differ from that forecast at the time of the investment. Hence, cost-effectiveness is better thought of as a random variable, not a known constant. Furthermore it can be risky to maximize expected cost-effectiveness by investing solely in the programmes with the highest point estimates of cost-effectiveness for the same reasons that putting all of one's money in a single stock can be risky, however well that stock has performed in the past.

Elementary portfolio optimization theory from finance provides a simple prescription for diversifying investment portfolios, whether those investments are in stocks or prevention programmes. The mechanics involve repeatedly solving a simple risk–return tradeoff optimization problem, which is easy to do in any spreadsheet.

The biggest challenge for investments in social programmes is estimating the covariance in the performance of various pairs of programmes. However, this can be done via Monte Carlo simulation if cost-effectiveness is modeled as a random variable that is a function of other, more elemental random factors and correlations of those factors are known or can be estimated. The result is a simple set of steps one can follow to allocate dollars efficiently across programmes even when there is uncertainty about cost-effectiveness.

ACKNOWLEDGEMENTS

This chapter is based in part on work funded by the Robert Wood Johnson Foundation's Substance Abuse Policy Research Program. I am grateful for the helpful comments of many colleagues, particularly David Boyum, Susan Everingham, Peter Greenwood, and Rosalie Pacula.

REFERENCES

Caulkins, J.P., Pacula, R., Paddock, S. and Chiesa, J. (2004) What we can—and can't—expect from school-based drug prevention. *Drug and Alcohol Review.* vol 23(1), pp. 79–87.

Caulkins, J.P., Paddock, S., Pacula, R. and Chiesa, J. (2002) *School-Based Drug Prevention: What Kind of Drug Use Does it Prevent?* Research Report No. MR-1459-RWJ. Santa Monica, CA: RAND Drug Policy Research Center.

Caulkins, J.P., Rydell, C.P., Schwabe, W.L. and Chiesa, J. (1997) *Mandatory Minimum Drug Sentences: Throwing Away the Key or the Taxpayers' Money?* Santa Monica, CA: RAND Drug Policy Research Center, MR-827-DPRC.

Markowitz, H. (1959) *Portfolio Selection: Efficient Diversification of Investments.* New York: Wiley.

Ragsdale, C. (2004) *Spreadsheet Modeling and Decision Analysis.* Southwestern.

7.3 How Should Governments Spend the Drug Prevention Dollar?: A Buyer's Guide

TED R. MILLER

Pacific Institute for Research and Evaluation, Calverton, MD, USA

DELIA HENDRIE

The University of Western Australia, School of Population Health, Australia

SUMMARY

This chapter compares 84 estimates of the return on investment in substance abuse prevention, treatment, and harm reduction. More than half of the $682 billion annual bill for alcohol and drug abuse in the United States results from crimes, injuries, and poisonings. Accordingly, many of the interventions address those risks. The catalogue of proven interventions is large. We provide unit costs, medical cost savings, benefit–cost ratios, and cost per quality-adjusted life year (QALY) for 75 substance abuse prevention or harm reduction measures and nine treatment measures. Among these, 53 offer net cost savings; only 14 are of questionable value. The measures often cover different domains, e.g., impaired driving and violence, making it easier to package a complementary set. Massing multiple interventions against the same harms will shrink problem size and reduce the return on added interventions below the levels shown here. Benefit–cost ratios and aggregate cost savings estimates can guide selection of an optimal intervention package within the available resources. Political feasibility and local priorities also must be considered. Measures that may shift drinking to residential settings should be embraced cautiously; their impacts on domestic violence and maximum blood alcohol levels are unexplored. In contrast, selected consumption-related, violence, and impaired driving interventions are especially appealing to implement because conceptually they address multiple problem behaviours even though their impacts on only a subset have been measured. Future evaluations should routinely assess these broader impacts.

Preventing Harmful Substance Use: The Evidence Base for Policy and Practice.
Edited by T. Stockwell, P. J. Gruenewald, J.W. Toumbourou and W. Loxley.
© 2005 John Wiley & Sons, Ltd. ISBN 0-470-09227-0 (hbk) 0-470-09228-9 (pbk).

INTRODUCTION

This chapter does the following: (1) presents the costs used in computing the return on preventive investments; (2) defines terms and summarises methods; (3) explains where the estimates came from; (4) summarises the return on investment in interventions addressing substance abuse or associated harms; and (5) describes ways to structure a cost-effective, multi-pronged intervention approach.

The Costs of Substance Abuse

Crime and injury are the primary harms of substance abuse. Of the $501 billion US alcohol abuse bill and $181 billion drug abuse bill in 2002, crime accounted for 20% (Table 7.3.1). Impaired driving accounted for another 19% of alcohol costs; other injuries—pedalcyclist injuries, falls, burns, drownings, and suicides—accounted for 26%. Consequently, intervening in the harms resulting from substance abuse must concentrate heavily on preventing crime and injury or improving their outcomes.

METHODS

Benefit Definitions

Table 7.3.1 breaks the costs of substance abuse, which become the savings from prevention, into four components (see Miller and Levy, 2000, for details). *Medical costs* include averted acute care, rehabilitation, long-term medical care, institutional care, and ancillary expenses. *Other resource costs* include police, fire services, criminal adjudication and sanctioning, property damage/loss, and travel delay. *Work loss costs* value wage and household work lost by substance abusers, their victims, and their supervisors/co-workers. Insurance claims processing and tort litigation costs are included with medical savings for health-care claims and with work-loss savings for work-loss claims. (*Other monetary costs* sum work loss and other resource costs; *economic costs* add medical costs to them.) *Quality of life savings* place a dollar value on intangibles, the pain, suffering, and lost enjoyment of life that victims and their families avoid.

Miller and Levy (2000) measure quality of life savings in quality-adjusted life years (QALYs). A QALY is a health outcome measure that assigns a value of 1 to a year of perfect health and 0 to death (Gold et al., 1996). Fatal risk reduction—loss of a lifetime of QALYs—is valued based on what people are willing to pay for it (Kenkel, 1998). All benefit–cost estimates were computed with a conservative $3.6 million value per "statistical life"; the value per QALY is $102 300.

Substance Abuse Cost Estimation

Table 7.3.1 starts from widely cited economic cost estimates for substance abuse in the US (Harwood et al., 1998). It substitutes crime costs including QALY losses attributable to drugs and alcohol from Miller et al. (2004) and alcohol-attributable road crash costs from Blincoe et al. (2002). Applying methods and data from Miller et al. (2000), it computes the economic costs and QALY losses from other injuries, then combines them with alcohol attribution estimates (Miller et al., 2004). Finally, it computes QALY

Table 7.3.1 Costs of alcohol and drug abuse, United States, 2000 (in millions of 2002 dollars)

Cost category	Alcohol abuse					Drug abuse				
	Medical	Other Resource	Work	Quality of Life	Total	Medical	Other Resource	Work	Quality of Life	Total
Violent crime	3,396	13,126	7,794	67,664	91,980	885	4,740	4,260	20,260	30,145
Property crime	3	1,384	7	62	1,456	32	10,872	54	413	11,371
Impaired driving	6,354	13,518	22,906	54,464	97,242					
Other injury	12,514	2,039	18,815	124,605	157,973					
Illness and poisoning	25,908	974	25,084	100,392	136,347	13,534	436	25,023	100,148	139,141
Total	48,175	31,041	74,606	347,187	501,009	14,451	16,048	29,337	120,821	180,657

losses for the chronic and acute illnesses associated with substance abuse by subtracting the injury losses from estimated aggregate disability-adjusted life years lost to substance abuse (Murray and Lopez, 1996). Miller and Levy's (2000) league table of injury prevention estimates used benefit values compatible with Table 7.3.1.

Including impacts on quality of life is the key improvement of Table 7.3.1 over Harwood et al.'s estimates. These impacts are critical components of return on investment. The largest US injury problems differ when identified using economic costs versus QALYs (Hendrie and Miller 2004a). Thus ignoring the impact on either measure risks serious resource misallocation.

Cost–Outcome Analysis Computations

We followed the methods and used the reporting framework from our prior review (Miller and Levy, 2000). That means we recomputed benefits and costs where possible to make the estimates more consistent, discounted future costs and benefits back to the current year using a 2.5% discount rate, and adopted a societal viewpoint that incorporates costs and savings to abusers, victims and the public. Thereby, benefit–cost ratios and costs per QALY saved can be compared between interventions. We reduced benefits by 25% when the underlying effectiveness estimates were for a demonstration because effectiveness is generally reduced when scaling up and replicating.

To compute cost per QALY saved, we first computed the net cost of the intervention—the intervention cost minus the medical care, other resource, litigation, and claims processing cost savings. When these savings exceed the intervention cost, the intervention offers net cost savings. Otherwise the cost per QALY saved equals the net cost divided by the number of QALYs saved. We also estimated benefit–cost ratios that show the savings per dollar invested or return on investment.

SOURCE OF THE ESTIMATES

This chapter reports cost–outcome estimates for 84 substance abuse prevention and harm reduction measures. Sixty-three come from Miller and Levy (2000), Miller (2001), or Zaloshnja et al. (2003).

- *Adjusted estimates.* For compatibility with the benefit–cost ratios for other personal protective safety devices, we excluded purchase and installation time from Miller and Levy's (1997) smoke alarm estimate. We recomputed savings from the Iowa Strengthening Families Program (ISFP) and Preparing for the Drug-Free Years (PDFY) (Spoth et al., 2002), substituting benefit estimates from Table 7.3.1.
- *Original estimates.* We developed eight new estimates for this chapter. One was for an unsuccessful substance abuse education programme (Ennet et al., 1994). We made estimates for four family-centred or school-based life skills programmes with the model and programme-specific effectiveness estimates in Caulkins et al. (2002) rather than include Caulkins' hypothetical composite programme. Benefits came from Table 7.3.1 and, for smoking, from Biglan et al. (2004). We dropped Caulkins' benefit-raising multipliers for cocaine and shifted to our 25% reduction in effectiveness for demonstrations. We estimated Project Northland and the Midwest Prevention

Programme (MPP) cost \$800/participant, the average for the similar ISFP and PDFY programmes. Costs of Project Alert and Life Skills Training came from Caulkins et al. (1999) with teacher salaries adjusted to account for fringe benefits and non-facilities overhead including supervision. (Estimating ISFP and PDFY benefit–cost ratios with the Caulkins model would change them minimally.)

The remaining ratios—for laws mandating use of smoke alarms, booster seats, and child bicycle helmets—derived from analyses of private purchase of these devices. To derive them, we applied the empirically based rule of thumb (Miller, 2001) that legislative mandates impose passage, implementation, publicity, and enforcement costs averaging 9.4% of device costs per new user.

- *Excluded estimates.* We omitted a 'preliminary' benefit–cost ratio of 2.9 for coordinated community environmental programmes including media campaigns, responsible server training, and impaired-driving enforcement (Holder et al., 2000). This estimate excludes costs for police and volunteer time and savings from documented violence reduction.

RESULTS

Because interventions with diversified impacts are desirable, the measures considered include directly targeted interventions and broader crime prevention, highway safety, injury prevention, and trauma systems interventions. This section examines the interventions by problem area, probing which measures might merit adoption. Then it re-examines them based on the approach adopted (e.g., legislative, behavioural), seeking insight into the approaches most likely to succeed and merit evaluation.

Table 7.3.2 organises the 84 cost–outcome analyses by approach (space precludes a parallel table by problem area). Some injury prevention measures in Table 7.3.2 may seem remotely related to substance abuse. They are not. Our analysis of alcohol-and-drug attributable injuries drove their selection. Bicycle helmets are included, for example, because alcohol causes almost 40% of pedalcyclist hospitalisations and deaths; median barriers are included because they prevent cross-median crashes that are strongly associated with driving when impaired.

Many measures in Table 7.3.2 offer an excellent return on investment. With limited resources, wariness of marginal interventions seems prudent since return will vary around the mean estimates shown. Therefore, measures with benefit–cost ratios less than 2.0 or costs per QALY above \$51 000 are dubious implementation candidates.

Measures Targeting Consumption

Sixteen interventions directly target reducing consumption or over-the-limit consumption of alcohol or drugs. The interventions reduce consumption in varied ways, including raising price, inducing servers to discontinue service for the intoxicated, combining workplace peer pressure with random drug and alcohol testing (from Miller et al., 2004, evaluated from the employer's perspective), intervening medically, and strengthening families or adolescents. Eight of them offer net cost savings (cost/QALY < \$0 in Table 7.3.2), meaning their costs are less than their resource cost savings. One (the original Drug Abuse Resistance Education or DARE programme) is ineffective.

Table 7.3.2 Costs, benefits, benefit–cost ratios and costs/QALY for selected alcohol and drug interventions (in 2002 dollars)

Intervention by approach	Unit cost	Medical	Other monetary	Quality of Life	Total benefits[a]	Benefit–cost ratio	Cost/QALY	% DWI deaths reduced
PHYSICAL ENVIRONMENT MODIFICATION								
Streetlights at Bars, Native America	$365/light	$880	$660	$1,500	$3,000	8.4	<$0	
Install Bridge-End Guardrail	$9,000/bridge	$4,700	$85,000	$255,000	$345,000	38	<$0	1
Install Median Barrier (1–12 foot median)	$190,000/mile	$20,000	$147,000	$322,000	$489,000	2.6	$46,000	6
Install Median Barrier (≥13 foot median)	$190,000/mile	$4,300	$32,000	$71,000	$108,000	0.6	$253,000	2
Less Porous Cigarette Paper	$.0001/pack	$0.004	$0.007	$0.05	$0.06	607	<$0	
Driver Airbag	$345/bag	$110	$460	$970	$1,500	4.5	$8,600	13
Passenger Airbag	$180/bag	$29	$110	$230	$360	2.0	$67,000	4
PERSONAL PROTECTIVE DEVICES								
Monitored Burglar and Fire Alarms	$740/home/year	$1.30	$400	$400	$790	1.1	$98,000	
Battery-Operated Smoke Alarm	$30/home[b]	$19	$220	$640	$870	29	<$0	
Child Safety Seat Distribution, Ages 0–4	$45/seat provided	$120	$430	$1,200	$1,800	40	<$0	>1
Booster Seat, Ages 4–7	$30/seat	$280	$640	$1,100	$2,000	67	<$0	>1
Winter Coats that Float Drowning Prevention, Native Alaska	$0.10/person	$0	$52	$150	$200	2,045	<$0	
Motorcycle Helmet	$210/helmet	$190	$1,400	$2,300	$3,900	18	<$0	2.5
Child's Bicycle Helmet	$10/helmet	$43	$130	$350	$530	53	<$0	>1
All-Terrain Vehicle Helmet	$120/helmet	$9	$110	$350	$470	4.0	$33,000	
SOCIAL ENVIRONMENT MODIFICATION								
Mandatory Server Training	$40/driver	$9	$56	$95	$160	3.8	$16,000	17
Big Brothers/Big Sisters Mentoring	$1,100/child	$150	$3,900	$2,900	$6,900	6.5	<$0	
Graduation Incentives	$19,400/child	$310	$4,000	$5,400	$9,700	0.5	$315,000	
Financial Assistance @ Release	$2,900/client	$250	$4,400	$4,500	$9,200	3.2	<$0	
Subsidized Jobs, Age < 27	$10,600/client	$0	$0	$0	$0	0	Infinite	
Subsidized Jobs, Age > + 27	$10,600/client	$820	$14,000	$15,000	$30,000	2.8	<$0	

Work-Release Programs	GT $0/client	$0	$0	$0	$0	0	Infinite	
In-Prison Vocational Education	$2,000/client	$520	$9,200	$9,400	$19,000	9.6	<$0	
In-Prison Adult Basic Education	$2,000/client	$390	$6,800	$7,000	$14,000	7.2	<$0	
In-Prison Life Skills Programs	$850/client	$0	$0	$0	$0	0	Infinite	
INFORMATIONAL ONLY								
DARE (police lecture at school)	>$0/child	$0	$0	$0	$0	0	Infinite	
Scaring Young Offenders Straight	>$0	$0	$0	$0	$0	0	Infinite	
BEHAVIOURAL MODIFICATION								
Iowa Strengthening Families Programme	$880/family	$1,500	$3,500	$11,000	$16,000	18	<$0	
Preparing for the Drug-Free Years	$710/family	$750	$1,700	$5,600	$8,000	11	<$0	
Midwest Prevention Programme	$800/family	$320	$1,500	$4,600	$6,500	8.1	$6,200	
Project Northland	$800/family	$200	$1,400	$4,200	$5,800	7.2	$11,000	
Project Alert	$100/student	$31	$300	$270	$1,200	12	$5,200	
Life Skills Training	$240/student	$23	$560	$1,600	$2,200	8.4	$14,000	
Perry Preschool & Home Visits	$14,700/child	$1,400	$40,000	$39,000	$80,000	5.5	<$0	
Rochester 2-Yr Nurse Home Visits	$7,800/child	$1,100	$19,000	$22,000	$42,000	5.4	<$0	
Syracuse 5-Yr Home Visits	$47,900/child	$850	$25,000	$23,000	$49,000	1.02	$150,000	
Parent Training	$3,400/child	$500	$3,000	$11,000	$15,000	4.4	$23,000	
Seattle Parent/Teacher Training	$3,200/child	$600	$7,600	$11,000	$19,000	5.9	<$0	
Job Search/Counselling @Release	$570/client	$190	$3,200	$3,300	$6,800	12	<$0	
Youth Offender Aggression Replacement Training	$420/client	$1,100	$23,000	$19,000	$43,000	101	<$0	
Lansing Adolescent Diversion	$1,600/client	$1,500	$38,000	$30,000	$69,000	44	<$0	
Moral Reconation Therapy	$300/client	$280	$4,900	$5,000	$10,000	34	<$0	
Reasoning and Rehabilitation	$310/client	$80	$1,800	$1,400	$3,300	10.5	<$0	
Behavioural Sex Offender Treatment	$6,800/client	$800	$2,600	$12,000	$16,000	2.3	$27,000	
LEGISLATION								
20% Alcohol Tax	$9/drinker/year	$4	$30	$50	$84	9.3	<$0	4
30% Alcohol Tax	$17/drinker/year	$5	$38	$66	$110	6.4	$6,800	6
21 Minimum Legal Drinking Age	$160/youth 18–20	$34	$190	$360	$590	3.6	$18,000	4
.08% Driver Blood Alcohol Limit	$2.90/driver	$3	$16	$26	$44	15	<$0	7
Zero Alcohol Tolerance, Drivers Under 21	$31/driver	$48	$250	$480	$780	25	<$0	4
Administrative License Revocation (ALR)	$2,850/ALR	$2,900	$13,000	$33,000	$49,000	17	<$0	5.5

Continued

Table 7.3.2 Costs, benefits, benefit-cost ratios and costs/QALY for selected alcohol and drug interventions (in 2002 dollars) (*Continued*)

Intervention by Approach	Unit cost	Medical	Other monetary	Quality of Life	Total benefits (a)	Benefit–cost ratio	Cost/QALY	% DWI deaths reduced
ALR with Per Se Law	$2,700/ALR	$3,500	$16,000	$39,000	$58,000	22	<$0	6.5
Pass Child Safety Seat Law, Ages 0–4	$49/new user	$120	$430	$1,200	$1,800	37	<$0	>1
Pass Booster Seat Law, Ages 4–7	$33/new user	$280	$640	$1,100	$2,000	61	<$0	>1
Pass/Upgrade Safety Belt Law	$275/new user	$220	$1,500	$3,200	$4,900	18	<$0	10
Pass Motorcycle Helmet Law	$1,200/new user	$190	$1,400	$2,300	$3,900	3.2	$29,000	2.5
Pass Child Bicycle Helmet Law	$11/new user	$43	$130	$350	$530	48	<$0	>1
Provisional Licensing + Midnight Driving Curfew	$68/driver	$34	$200	$320	$550	8.1	<$0	2
Change Driving Curfew to 10 PM	$130/driver	$20	$120	$190	$330	2.6	$31,000	1
Pass Smoke Alarm Law	$33/new user[d]	$19	$220	$640	$870	26	<$0	
ENFORCEMENT								
Enforce Serving Intoxicated Patron Law	$.30/driver	$3	$10	$13	$25	84	<$0	11
Add Alcohol Testing to Peer Support[c]	$10/employee				$628	63	<$0	
Sobriety Checkpoints	$8,800/checkpoint	$4,200	$18,000	$44,000	$67,000	7.6	<$0	15
Enhanced Belt Law Enforcement	$260/new user	$180	$1,200	$2,600	$4,000	15	<$0	10
SANCTIONING								
Optimised Sentencing	$13,400/crime	$1,100	$4,600	$24,000	$29,000	2.2	$50,000	
3 Strikes and You're Out	$18,000/crime	$1,100	$4,600	$24,000	$29,000	1.6	$70,000	
Intensive Probation Supervision, Youth	$1,600/client	$200	$4,000	$3,600	$7,800	5.0	<$0	
Intensive Probation Supervision, Adult	$3,500/client	$130	$3,000	$2,200	$5,300	1.5	$46,000	
Young Offender Boot Camp	–$2,100/client	–$630	–$13,000	–$11,000	–$25,000	0.08	Infinite	
Alcohol-Testing Ignition Interlock	$1,000/vehicle	$230	$2,200	$3,900	$6,400	6.5	<$0	7
DWI Offender Auto Impoundment	$850/vehicle	$320	$1,500	$2,600	$4,500	5.3	$190	4
DWI Offender Electronic House Arrest	$1,500/arrestee	$190	$930	$1,600	$2,700	1.8	<$0	3

CLINICAL								
Brief Alcohol Intervention	$79/lecture	$180	$580	$2,200	$2,900	37	<$0	6
Substance Abuse Treatment	$10,100/abuser	$37,000	$118,000	$444,000	$599,000	59	<$0	
Drug Courts	$2,100/client	$200	$5,600	$3,800	$9,600	4.6	<$0	
In-Prison Substance Abuse Therapy	$5,800/client	$510	$8,900	$9,100	$19,000	3.2	<$0	
Post-release Substance Abuse Treatment	$2,300/client	$0	$0	$0	$0	0	Infinite	
DWI Intensive Probation + Treatment	$1,250/arrestee	$370	$1,400	$2,500	$4,300	3.4	<$0	4
Multi-Systemic Therapy	$4,800/client	$5,100	$109,000	$93,000	$206,000	43	<$0	
Functional Family Therapy	$2,200/client	$1,900	$40,000	$34,000	$77,000	35	<$0	
Treatment Foster Care	$2,000/client	$3,700	$78,000	$66,000	$148,000	73	<$0	
OTHER								
Poison Control Centre Services	$36/call	$250	$0	$0	$250	6.9	<$0	
Triaged Regional Trauma System Services	$1,450/admit	$1,800	$420	$1,900	$4,100	2.9	<$0	14
Workplace Peer Support + Drug Testing[c]	$61/employee				$1,500	24	<$0	
Youth Suicide Prevention, Native America	$160/youth	$34	$900	$5,300	$6,200	39	$850	

Notes: (*a*) Numbers do not correspond exactly to prior columns due to rounding. All numbers were computed, then rounded.
(*b*) Includes 2 alarms per home.
(*c*) Cost savings from this programme were evaluated from the employer's perspective. Societal savings would be larger.
(*d*) In 2002 US dollars. Blank cells are unknown/not applicable.

Several of these interventions warrant widespread implementation: raising alcohol excise taxes to 20% of the pre-tax selling price; a minimum legal drinking age of 21; screening adults for heavy alcohol use, then treating dependent drinkers and delivering a stiff physician lecture to other heavy drinkers that says "You drink more than most people, you need to cut back, and I am confident that you can." Brief intervention and dependency treatment offer especially large returns on investment. Passing and enforcing laws against serving intoxicated patrons and training servers to recognise impairment and terminate service without excessive confrontation seem very promising but need wider evaluation before moving to national implementation. In workplaces with endemic substance abuse, coupling a peer support and workplace culture change programme, management support for substance abuser rehabilitation, and drug and alcohol testing is quite promising and merits broader evaluation.

Family-centred interventions with a school component are more costly than school-based life skills training but also offer larger returns. The most effective programmes strengthen youth bonds to family, school, and community. These include the ISFP, PDFY, MPP, Project Northland, and the Seattle Social Development Program (SDP). ISFP, PDFY, and SDP performance is especially impressive as impact of these programmes on drug and tobacco use has not been evaluated, as it has for the other programmes. Although family-centred programmes will achieve more, the narrower Life Skills Training and Project Alert offer solid returns. With a limited budget, they let a school system reach the most children, but the same money would yield greater benefits if spent targeting the broader family-centred programmes and related mentoring to the schools at highest risk.

Systemic Crime Prevention Measures

Aos et al. (2001) more fully describe the crime prevention measures. Systemic measures get at the root causes of crime. They potentially could reduce multiple risky behaviours including binge drinking and drug abuse. Except for home visitation programmes for infants and toddlers, however, these measures have been evaluated solely in terms of their impact on violence or crime more broadly. That makes their benefit–cost ratios conservative. Sixteen of the 25 programmes offer net cost savings, but six others have costs that exceed their benefits. To better understand complementarity, we segmented the measures into programmes for youth who have not yet offended and programmes targeting youth and adult offenders.

Among non-offender programmes, intensive home visitation programmes, possibly coupled with pre-school enrichment programmes, can reduce child abuse and a range of problems as targeted low-income toddlers reach adolescence and adulthood. But the return on these costly investments takes decades and has not always appeared. That makes it difficult to recommend them when resources are tight. Better values for the money are: (1) Parent–Teacher Training—bonding and behavioural training programmes that target students ages 6–12 and their parents such as the SDP or the Good Behaviour Game; and (2) Big Brothers/Big Sisters Mentoring, where an adult volunteer spends 12 contact hours per month with an at-risk youth and also identifies substance abuse and medical problems, which the programme refers for treatment.

The three youth offender programmes identified all targeted ages 12–17 and yielded net cost savings. These interventions address the causes of delinquency and related substance abuse. They seek to improve family and school/community functioning. Multi-systemic therapy costs more per youth than functional family therapy or treatment foster care but also has a greater impact on problem behaviours and is recommended if resources permit. Treatment foster care requires trained, dedicated foster parents for each child; foster parent scarcity constrains this approach to situations where the child must be removed from home.

Three adult programmes involuntarily treat offender substance abuse problems, which in some cases reduces crime. Measures we recommend adopting are drug courts that case-manage substance abuse treatment, in-prison vocational and basic education, job and financial assistance at release to help offenders transition back into society, and cognitive–behavioural moral reconation therapy to raise moral development and treat moral reasoning disorders of treatment-resistant populations. These programmes address different aspects of the underlying problem and should work well in concert.

Narrowly Targeted Crime Prevention Measures

Eight measures are intended exclusively to reduce crime. Since 67% of violent crimes and 58% of property crimes in the USA involve alcohol or drugs (Miller et al., 2004), effective measures should reduce crime related to substance abuse. Two strong candidates for widespread implementation emerge: cognitive–behavioural therapy for sex offenders and diversion of low-risk first offenders from juvenile court to a service-oriented system. Intensive probation supervision for young offenders yields net cost savings primarily because it is less expensive than incarceration, not because it improves outcomes. Three measures are not cost-effective.

Impaired Driving Measures

Nine highly beneficial measures directly reduce harm from drinking by reducing impaired driving frequency. They have specific and general deterrence effects. Sobriety checkpoints, for example, apprehend impaired drivers who would otherwise have crashed; fear of getting caught in checkpoints deters other driving after drinking.

Driver blood alcohol limits and driving curfews may reduce consumption and associated harms including crime and high-risk sex. Only their impact on impaired driving has been evaluated.

Reasonable ways to prevent reoffending couple case-managed treatment with alcohol-testing interlocks that prevent auto use by impaired drivers, impoundment of offenders' vehicles, or electronic house arrest (Taylor et al., 2002). The best choice depends on local feasibility and judicial preference.

Sixteen general highway safety measures reduce the harm that impaired driving causes as well as other injuries on the highway. These measures may be implemented by the impaired or occupants of vehicles they might collide with. Eight offer net cost savings and only one is not cost-effective. Individuals generally will benefit from adopting personal protective devices like child booster seats (Hendrie and Miller, 2004b). Governments should pass and enforce usage laws. Typically, laws induce about 40% of the population to use these devices, yielding broad savings and incidental protection against impaired driving.

The estimates for road improvements are illustrations from a large list. Return on these improvements varies with road speed, location-specific crash experience, and expected traffic volume. The listed measures are particularly effective against impaired driving crashes, but the measures to implement should be based on overall impact, not impaired driving impact.

Fire Prevention Measures

Less porous cigarette paper will self-extinguish if left to smoulder, thus reducing the chance of cigarette fires, which often also involve alcohol. Smoke alarm laws and voluntary smoke alarm purchases address these and broader fire risks. Both a mandated shift to less porous paper and an alarm law are recommended.

Health Services Interventions

Health services reduce harm by improving outcomes of trauma from substance abuse. Two measures warrant implementation: establishing regional hospital specialties in trauma care, then triaging serious injuries to these hospitals, and a 24-hour regional or national phone-in poison control centre that advises the public and health providers about and supervises home treatment of illicit drug overdoses (a frequent type of call) and other poisonings.

Other Measures

The remaining four measures are diverse. Driving curfews for youth may force them to curtail their drinking and does reduce impaired driving. A midnight curfew offers a higher return than a 10 p.m. curfew and is recommended. Two interventions offered net cost savings in Native American settings but need further evaluation before widespread implementation. One, a youth suicide prevention programme combined counselling, peer support, and prevention of alcohol abuse, child abuse, and domestic violence. The second located winter coats that float and convinced local residents who use small boat transport to buy them, thus aiding both sober and intoxicated boaters who fall overboard.

APPROACHES UNDERLYING THE PREVENTIVE MEASURES

The preventive measures analysed address diverse problems. Their approaches to intervention range widely from simple education to legislative change to clinical care. Table 7.3.2 classifies the measures into ten categories adapted from the US Task Force on Community Preventive Services framework (Zaza et al., 2000).

- *Physical Environment Modification.* Six of the seven physical environment modifications are broad highway safety measures. The seventh is a self-extinguishing cigarette redesign. These measures tend to be either very beneficial or marginal and expensive. Usage rates critically impact the return on the larger capital investments. A driver airbag that provides protection whenever someone is driving is a better investment than a passenger airbag that often protects an empty seat. The return on airbags also declines as safety belt use increases.
- *Personal Protective Devices.* The eight measures in this category reduce harm from hazardous events, including ones caused by substance abuse, if people buy and use them. They reduce the harm that substance abusers do themselves and limit the harm they can inflict on others. Devices like child seats and smoke alarms that address daily hazards yielded net cost savings. Devices like all-terrain vehicle helmets that are only used occasionally offer weaker returns. The return on burglar alarms would be larger in a high-crime area than in the isolated, rich suburb where they were evaluated.

- *Social Environment Modification.* Nine of ten social environment changes aimed at violence, with server training the sole exception. The violence interventions either were strong successes or failed. Although successful interventions warranting widespread adoption have used the social environmental change model, successful social change interventions are difficult to design and require rigorous evaluation.
- *Informational Only.* Both interventions that relied strictly on educating youth about proper and hazardous behaviour were ineffective. We recommend against adopting or testing strictly informational interventions.
- *Behavioural Modification.* The 17 behavioural measures were divided between substance use, early childhood, and violence prevention measures. This approach is recommended for treating the root causes of multi-risk behaviour. Measures applied to people with problems, including three cognitive–behavioural therapies, were quite successful. Family-centred and to a lesser extent school-based behavioural youth substance use prevention programmes offered an excellent return too. Home visitation programmes, however, were costly, risky, and slow in producing results.
- *Legislation.* The 15 measures in this group targeted alcohol price, youth alcohol consumption, impaired driving, use of personal protective devices, or youth driving curfews. Perhaps because strong evidence underlies many laws or the cost of legislative intervention is modest, legislation-based investments were extremely sound. Alcohol taxes and driver curfews had optimal levels that maximised return on investment. More stringent measures imposed more of their costs on lower-risk people and thus offered lower returns. Still, they offered additional benefits at a price that was not prohibitive.
- *Enforcement.* Stricter and more visible enforcement of four effective laws was quite successful and directly impacted the physical and social environment. Critically, threshold enforcement levels are required to achieve the advertised return.
- *Sanctioning.* The eight sanctioning measures included five relatively unattractive crime reduction measures. Three targeted measures aimed at reducing impaired driving recidivism, however, yielded solid returns.
- *Clinical.* Six clinical measures aimed at treating substance abuse and three at treating violent offenders. These measures generally were quite successful, although violent individuals with substance abuse problems were much more effectively treated in prison than in the community.
- *Other.* The two health systems and two comprehensive multi-pronged approaches yielded excellent returns.

SELECTING INTERVENTION PACKAGES

Substance abuse causes a wide range of harm. There is no miracle cure. No one measure will reduce the problem so dramatically that no further public action is desirable. Rather, a range of preventive and palliative measures need to be implemented in concert to reduce consumption and the harm caused by residual consumption. Given the number and diversity of proven interventions, optimal resource allocation requires selecting the most complementary and politically feasible set. The objective is to maximise return on investment within the funding available. The focus is on identifying a sensible package of interventions that supplement existing measures.

Benefit–cost ratios and cost per QALY saved are helpful guides, but other factors—aggregate benefits obtained, overlapping effects, spillover costs and benefits, and government cost—become relevant when selecting a package that yields the maximum gains at the lowest possible price. Political feasibility is important too; a less cost-effective programme can be superior if the alternative with the higher return has a lower chance of widespread implementation or involves a long implementation delay.

Aggregate Benefits

In a resource-constrained world, the best alternative may not have the highest benefit–cost ratio or lowest cost per QALY saved. Another alternative may yield larger benefits but at a slightly higher cost per unit of safety. Choosing interventions to address a problem requires weighing the overall impact on the problem and the benefits per dollar invested. Zero alcohol tolerance for drivers under 21 and child safety seat laws, for example, have much higher benefit–cost ratios than most impaired driving interventions. But drivers under 21 account for only 18% of impaired driving deaths in the USA, young child occupants 1%, motorcyclists 7%, and hardcore recidivists 10%. Interventions targeted on these groups leave 64% of the problem untouched. Less cost-effective interventions address broader aspects of the problem and can prevent many more impaired driving deaths.

Thus, aggregate benefit and return on investment can suggest different intervention priorities. The last column in Table 7.3.2 shows the estimated impacts of selected interventions on impaired driving deaths. The largest mortality reductions will come from sobriety checkpoints, server interventions, improved trauma care, and increased occupant protection. In contrast, the largest return on investments in public interventions will come from laws mandating child occupant protection, child bicycle helmet use, and zero alcohol tolerance for drivers under 21. With constrained resources, the greatest percentage reduction might come from these non-overlapping, high-return interventions, not those with the greatest impact on the problem.

Intervention Overlap

No single intervention will reduce the impaired driving problem by more than 17%. The question is not the best single intervention to implement, but the best package of interventions. Understanding intervention overlap is key to selecting that package. Interventions targeting different aspects of the problem are good candidates for combined implementation. For example, if one intervention reduces the risk of drivers below the minimum legal drinking age while a second reduces the risk of repeat impaired-driving offenders whose licences previously were revoked, implementing both together will yield the full benefits of both. But if graduated licensing with a midnight driving curfew for new drivers offers an 11% reduction in impaired driving crashes in this age group and zero tolerance for alcohol for drivers under 21 offers a 40% reduction, combined, the two interventions offer only a 46.6% (40% + 11% * (100% − 40%)) reduction in the youth portion of the problem.

Unevaluated Spillover Effects

Another concern is the potential for unevaluated spillover effects on other problems. A designated driver programme, for example, might reduce impaired driving but cause drinkers to arrive home at higher blood alcohol levels, potentially raising the risk of alcohol poisoning, of domestic violence upon arrival, and of chronic illness. In contrast, enforcing laws against serving intoxicated patrons reduces public consumption and the broad array of associated harms. An offsetting drinking shift to domestic settings may raise domestic violence risk. Unfortunately, effectiveness studies almost never evaluate spillover effects.

This chapter differentiated harm reduction efforts that target a focused problem from ones that reduce substance use or treat the underlying causes of substance abuse. For example, one violence reduction approach may address the causes of multi-risk behaviour while another simply reduces the opportunity to behave violently. Typical evaluations only measure impacts on targeted harms, even when spillover reductions in other harms seem likely. All else equal, it seems advisable to give preference to the interventions that conceptually should reduce multiple harms.

Government's Perspective

Resource-scarce governments need to consider costs and benefits from their own perspective as well as society's. The intervention costs in Table 7.3.2 are a mix. Some would be government-funded. Others would be borne by private citizens (e.g., to buy mandated safety equipment) or by volunteers. Legislation often imposes discomfort and inconvenience costs for new safety device users, mobility loss costs when legal driving conditions are restricted, or delay costs at enforcement checkpoints.

The governmental return on investment is likely to vary much more between countries than the societal return. The New Zealand government, for example, picks up far more of the work-loss bill for injury victims than the US government. Similarly, universal government health care coverage would cause many governments to receive far more of the medical savings than the US government would. Although 63% of the interventions offer net societal cost savings, we suspect far fewer will yield net government cost savings. For example, only 22 of the 84 measures (26%) yield medical cost savings that exceed their costs, with medical cost savings of 4 additional impaired driving measures (5%) exceeding intervention costs net of discomfort, inconvenience, mobility loss, and delay.

CONCLUSION

Policy-makers need to broaden substance abuse research. Abuse is symptomatic of multi-risk behaviour. Evaluations should be comprehensive, exploring any plausible effects on alcohol, tobacco, and other drug abuse, crime, and risky sex. Sound assessments of substance abuse burden and the return on intervention must consider impacts on quality of life.

Policy-makers selecting substance abuse interventions should apply a series of filters. The estimates in this chapter provide the first filter, allowing elimination of interventions that offer a questionable return on investment. This financial information also should be used to guide choices between interventions that score comparably on other criteria. Additional filters that policy-makers should use in selecting interventions are political feasibility, local priorities, appropriateness for the target population, aggregate impact, affordability, unmeasured spillover benefits, immediacy of the impacts (weeks versus years), and reductions in effectiveness due to prior or planned implementation of measures with overlapping impacts.

The most effective interventions only reduce the substance abuse problem by 10% to 15%. Therefore multiple interventions should be packaged. Eight impaired driving measures, for example, were needed to reduce the US problem by 35%.

With more than 20% of adults in countries like the USA and the Netherlands already drinking heavily and 5% of adults worldwide abusing illicit drugs (McVay, 2004), it is too late for prevention and treatment alone to solve the problem. Interventions targeting harm reduction are essential. The maximum return will result from focusing resources on a mix of abuse prevention, harm reduction, and treatment.

ACKNOWLEDGEMENTS

The US National Institute on Alcohol Abuse and Alcoholism grant AA09812-02 partially supported this work.

REFERENCES

Aos, S., Phipps, P., Barnoski, R. and Lieb, R. (2001) *The Comparative Costs and Benefits of Programs to Reduce Crime, Version 4.0.* Research Report No. 01-05-1201, Olympia, Washington: Washington State Institute for Public Policy.

Biglan, A., Brennan, P.A., Foster, S.L., Holder, H.D., Miller, T.R., Cunningham, P.B., Derzon, J.H., Fishbein, D.H., Flay, B.R., Goeders, N.E., Kelder, S.H., Kenkel, D., Meyer, R. and Zucker, R.A. (2004) *Multiproblem Youth: Prevention, Intervention, and Treatment.* New York: Guilford Press.

Blincoe, L., Seay, A., Zaloshnja, E., Miller, T.R., Romano, E.O., Luchter, S. and Spicer, R.S. (2002) *The Economic Impact of Motor Vehicle Crashes,* 2000. Research Report No. DOT HS 809 446, Washington, DC: US Department of Transportation, NHTSA.

Caulkins, J.P., Pacula, R., Paddock, S. and Chiesa, J.R. (2002) *School-Based Drug Prevention: What Kind of Drug Use Does It Prevent?* Research Report No. MR-1459-RWJ, Santa Monica, CA: RAND, Drug Policy Research Center.

Caulkins, J.P., Rydell, C.P., Everingham, S.S., Chiesa, J.R. and Bushway, S. (1999) *An Ounce of Prevention, a Pound of Uncertainty: The Cost-Effectiveness of School-Based Drug Prevention Programs.* Research Report No. MR-923-RWJ, Santa Monica, CA: RAND.

Ennett, S.T., Tobler, N.S., Ringwalt, C.L. and Flewelling, R.L. (1994) How effective is Drug Abuse Resistance Education? A meta-analysis of project DARE outcome evaluations. *American Journal of Public Health,* **84**, 1394–1401.

Gold, M.R., Siegel, J.E., Russell, L.B. and Weinstein, M.C. (eds), (1996) *Cost-Effectiveness in Health and Medicine.* New York: Oxford University Press.

Harwood, H.J., Fountain, D. and Livermore, G. (1998) The economic cost of alcohol and drug abuse in the United States, 1992. National Institute on Drug Abuse and National Institute on Alcohol Abuse and Alcoholism. Available online <http://165.112.78.61/economiccosts/Index.html> (accessed February 2004).

Hendrie, D. and Miller, T.R. (2004a, in press) Assessing the burden of injuries: competing measures. *Injury Control and Safety Promotion.*

Hendrie, D. and Miller, T.R. (2004b) Economic evaluation of injury prevention and control programs. In R. McClure, M. Stevenson and S. McEvoy (eds), *The Scientific Basis of Injury Prevention and Control.* Sydney, Australia: IP Communications, pp. 372–390.

Holder, H.D., Gruenewald, P.J., Ponicki, W.R., Treno, A.J., Grube, J.W., Saltz, R.F., Voas, R.B., Reynolds, R., Davis, J., Sanchez, L., Gaumont, G. and Roeper, P. (2000) Effect of community-based interventions of high-risk drinking and alcohol-related injuries. *The Journal of the American Medical Association*, **284**, 2341–2347.

Kenkel, D. (1998) A guide to cost-benefit analysis of drunk-driving policies. *Journal of Drug Issues*, **28**, 795–812.

McVay, D. (2004) Drug war facts. Available online: <www.drugwarfacts.org/druguse.htm>. (accessed February 2004).

Miller, T.R. (2001) The effectiveness review trials of Hercules and some economic estimates for the stables: commentary. *American Journal of Preventive Medicine,* **21**(4S), 9–12.

Miller, T.R. and Levy, D.T. (1997) Cost-outcome analysis in injury prevention and control: a primer on methods. *Injury Prevention*, **3**, 288–293.

Miller, T.R. and Levy, D.T. (2000) Cost-outcome analysis in injury prevention and control: eighty-four recent estimates for the United States. *Medical Care*, **38**, 562–582.

Miller, T.R., Romano, E.D. and Spicer, R.S. (2000) The cost of childhood unintentional injuries and the value of prevention. *The Future of Children*, **10**, 137–163.

Miller, T.R., Spicer, R.S. and Smith, G. (2004) *Does Alcohol Cause Injury?: The Bottle's Fingerprints on the Victims*. Working Paper, Calverton, MD: Pacific Institute for Research and Evaluation.

Miller, T.R., Zaloshnja, E. and Spicer, R.S. (2004) *Effectiveness and Benefit-Cost Ratios of Peer-Based Workplace Substance Abuse Prevention Coupled with Random Testing*. Working Paper, Calverton, MD: Pacific Institute for Research and Evaluation.

Miller, T.R., Levy, D.T., Cohen, M.A. and Cox, K.L. (2004, in press) The costs of alcohol and drug-involved crime. *Prevention Science*.

Murray, C. and Lopez, A. (1996) *The Global Burden of Disease*. Cambridge, MA: Harvard University Press.

Spoth, R.L., Guyll, M. and Day, S.X. (2002) Universal family-focused interventions in alcohol-use disorder prevention: cost-effectiveness and cost-benefit analyses of two interventions. *Journal of Studies on Alcohol*, **63**, 219–228.

Taylor, D., Miller, T.R. and Cox, K.L. (2002) *Impaired Driving in the United States: State Cost Fact Sheets*. Research Report No. DTNH22-98-D-35079, Task Order 7, Calverton, MD: Pacific Institute for Research and Evaluation.

Zaloshnja, E., Miller, T.R., Galbraith, M.S., Lawrence, B.A., DeBruyn, L.M., Bill, N., Hicks, K.R., Keiffer, M. and Perkins, R. (2003) Reducing injuries among Native Americans: five cost-outcome analyses. *Accident Analysis and Prevention*, **35**, 631–639.

Zaza, S., Wright-De Aguero, L.K., Briss, P.A., Truman, B.I., Hopkins, D.P., Hennessy, M.H., Sosin, D.M., Anderson, L., Carande-Kulis, V.G., Teutsch, S.M. and Pappaioanou, M. (2000) Data collection instrument and procedure for systematic reviews in the Guide to Community Preventive Services. Task Force on Community Preventive Services. *American Journal of Preventive Medicine*, **18**, 44–74.

7.4 Key Moments in the Ethnography of Drug-Related Harm: Reality Checks for Policy-Makers?

DAVID MOORE

National Drug Research Institute, Curtin University of Technology, Perth, WA, Australia

SUMMARY

As the various chapters in this book demonstrate, drug research, policy and practice encompass a broad field that includes many different approaches—such as psychology, epidemiology and public health. While these approaches provide invaluable insights into drug use, they sometimes neglect a dimension that is crucial to policy and practice—the meaning of drug use for drug users themselves. The ethnography of drug use, with its focus on everyday, lived experience, vividly conveys the "cultural logics" constructed by drug users and the complex interweavings of these cultural logics with wider social, economic and cultural structures. While "ethnography" shares many of the methods of qualitative research more generally (e.g., in-depth interviews), it is distinguished by its principal reliance on interaction with drug users as they go about their everyday activities.

Ethnography has a long history in the drug field that has produced many important studies. This chapter reviews several key moments in drug ethnography and is organised around six overlapping themes. First, ethnography has played an important role in explicating drug-related behaviour that may, at first glance, seem "irrational" or incomprehensible to policy-makers and practitioners. From the perspective of drug users, there may be compelling reasons for engaging in harmful drug use. Second, ethnography has documented the negative impact of poorly-designed policy and practice on drug-related harm. In particular, ethnographic research has demonstrated how saturation policing may exacerbate, rather than reduce, drug-related harm. Third, ethnography has provided important data on "hidden populations", including the sometimes "hidden" assumptions that inform drug research, policy and practice. Fourth, ethnography has challenged conventional policy and practice, such as public health orthodoxy regarding the dangers of sharing injecting paraphernalia. Fifth, ethnography has, in multidisciplinary combination with other approaches, particularly drug epidemiology, produced innovative

Preventing Harmful Substance Use: The Evidence Base for Policy and Practice.
Edited by T. Stockwell, P. J. Gruenewald, J.W. Toumbourou and W. Loxley.
© 2005 John Wiley & Sons, Ltd. ISBN 0-470-09227-0 (hbk) 0-470-09228-9 (pbk).

explanations for patterns of HIV/AIDS infection. Finally, ethnography has played a key role in assisting in the design of specific prevention programmes, particularly in relation to injecting drug use and the prevention of HIV/AIDS, that target the cultural and social dimensions of drug-related harm.

INTRODUCTION

Scan the pages of this book: "prevention portfolios"; "economic costs"; "social determinants"; "multiple levels of intervention"; "regulation and enforcement"; "developmental predictors and pathways"; "government control of sale, distribution and marketing". All invaluable perspectives within the eclectic field that is drug research, policy and practice, but all conform to what anthropologist Clifford Geertz (1976) has called "experience-far" concepts—understandings of human behaviour far removed from the cultural frameworks of the people ("experience-near" concepts in Geertz's scheme) whose use of drugs has resulted, or is deemed in danger of resulting, in harm. The ethnography of drug use, with its focus on everyday, lived experience, vividly conveys these experience-near concepts by consistently prioritising the accounts—the "cultural logics"—constructed by drug users. Furthermore, drug ethnography has revealed the complex interweavings of cultural logics and wider social, economic and cultural structures. As McKeganey (2003) has argued, the human "stories" produced by ethnographic research have yet-to-be-appreciated power in the "largely evidence-free zone of drug policy".

By "ethnography" I refer to those studies that are primarily reliant on extended and extensive participant observation conducted in and around drug scenes and subcultures, aiming for organic immersion in the field, negotiating and maintaining relationships with drug users and their associates, *in situ*, complemented, where appropriate, by other methods such as conducting in-depth, repeat interviews, reviewing census data and generating socio-demographic profiles. The methodological focus on drug use in natural social settings distinguishes ethnography from other approaches and enables it to produce unique insights into drug-related harm.

When compared to many other areas of drug research and policy, ethnography is relatively old, with a tradition of recognisably ethnographic drug research stretching back to the 1930s. With a policy-maker and practitioner readership in mind, this is not a detailed review of drug ethnography (see, e.g., Feldman and Aldrich, 1990; Singer, 1999; Rhodes and Moore, 2001) but a reminder of just some of its many key moments and a plea for policy-makers to acknowledge, amidst the various knowledge claims made in "evidence-based" drug policy and practice, the unique value of ethnographic insights. While my focus here is ethnography that has particular relevance to drug policy and practice, I also note its crucial, and possibly less recognised, role in challenging orthodox, and potentially limiting, views of the interaction between humans and drugs (e.g., in noting the diversity and variety of human experience with drugs), and in posing powerful epistemological, theoretical and methodological challenges to drug research, policy and practice.

UNDERSTANDING "IRRATIONAL" BEHAVIOUR

Recently, the author of a review of the international literature on amphetamine use made the claim that potential users of amphetamines would be deterred from using them once their deleterious effects became visible. Yet, in 1968, Harvey Feldman published a paper in which he explained why this is not always the case. Drawing on his observations of the spread of heroin use through disadvantaged areas in New York, he attempted to answer two questions: (1) who are the "eager recruits" and how are they drawn into experimentation with heroin?; and (2) why do they continue to experiment when evidence of the negative consequences of heroin addiction, in the form of older "neighbourhood addicts", is "pathetically visible"?

In the marginalised neighbourhoods in which Feldman worked, adolescent boys and young men were expected to live up to gendered ideals of "toughness, strength, daring, and the willingness to challenge the bleak fate of being poor", which were personified in the "ideal type" of the "stand-up cat". Failure to embrace this cultural orientation meant being labelled a "punk" or "square". He noted that when heroin entered these neighbourhoods, it was the older, established stand-up cats who first experimented with it. They played a crucial role in these emerging markets by linking adult criminals involved in drug production and distribution to potential customers, and driving demand for heroin through their association with it. Their reputations and access to multiple networks allowed heroin use to spread fast. Within six months, Feldman observes, non-users had begun to develop negative attitudes to heroin use, built largely on their own observations of, and experiences with, older heroin users. They witnessed the negative impact of sustained heavy use—withdrawal symptoms, overdoses, decreased interest and prowess in street fighting, drug debts and imprisonment. Despite this, some continued to experiment with heroin. Why? Feldman's answer focuses on the important role of the stand-up cat ideology. Mastery of one's heroin use became the ultimate test of reputation. "His challenge is to triumph in a situation where previous heroes have failed." The heavy odds against success, daily evident in his observations of others, made heroin use that much more of a challenge. The test of toughness became one's ability to start using heroin, but then to control or cease use.

In hindsight, we might note the relative absence of political economy in Feldman's account but it refocused attention away from psychological predispositions and the social-structural weaknesses of "slums" to the *processes* involved in becoming a heroin user—the social interactions, identities and ideologies of those involved, seeing them not as the product of "anomie" but as new ways of enhancing status and prestige (see also Lindesmith, 1947; Finestone, 1957). Its wider importance is that knowledge of the negative effects of drug use is not, in itself, sufficient to prevent drug use that is potentially harmful and that the cultural logics of drug users must always be considered in formulating policy responses.

DOCUMENTING THE EFFECTS OF BAD POLICY

Given that the use of drugs such as heroin, cocaine and the amphetamines is illegal in most parts of the world, what has drug ethnography had to say about policy responses involving policing? Lisa Maher and David Dixon (1999) investigated the consequences of saturation, or zero-tolerance, policing for the Cabramatta area of Sydney, Australia's "principal heroin market", on the basis of extensive ethnographic research among the Indo-Chinese community. They argued that, despite a policy commitment to harm minimisation, law enforcement considerations had assumed priority in drug policing. The climate of uncertainty and fear generated by such policing strategies among participants in the street-based heroin market led to several harmful consequences for public health, mainly increased risk of blood-borne virus transmission and other drug-related harm (e.g., overdose, vascular damage). In addition, the disruptions to the street heroin market that occurred as a result of policing strategies dispersed drug users from their usual injecting locations, which increased the risk of overdose and needlestick injuries from discarded syringes, and increased the difficulty of establishing long-term relationships between health and other service providers and street-based injectors. It *may* also have led to increased availability of drugs in areas where they were previously scarce and to increased drug-related property crime. Social displacement also led to "functional specialisation" and "hierarchical differentiation" among some sectors of the drug market (which may, in the long term, lead to the development of more organised, professional and enduring styles of criminality) and to increased volatility and violence. Finally, the displacement of heroin led to increased use of benzodiazepines (and therefore increased risk of overdose) and methadone, and to increased rates of transition from smoking to injecting heroin.

The harmful consequences of saturation policing were not confined to public health, with damaging effects on police–public relations. Maher and Dixon noted that cultural insensitivity and improper behaviour on the part of police officers led to strained relations between the Indo-Chinese community and the NSW police force. With respect to harm reduction policy, they noted the serious disjunction between senior and operational police in their commitment to harm reduction, with the latter displaying a poor understanding of harm reduction. Police definitions of, and responses to, "drug problems" overshadowed those of their "partners" (e.g., drug and health agencies) in supposedly interagency harm-reduction initiatives.

Maher and Dixon concluded that there was a need to develop alternative strategies to saturation policing to improve the quality of life in central business districts; that drug markets should be contained in locations which caused least harm; that a policy commitment to target higher-level dealers should not translate into an operational focus on street-level dealers and users; that police should avoid contact at the point of injecting because of the health risks to police and drug users; that police should not confiscate or destroy injecting equipment; and that police should receive better training with regard to harm minimisation and its aims. Using police to harass drug users into treatment, with accompanying "tough on drugs" publicity, was, at worst, politically expedient, at best, misguided, if there was no corresponding commitment to increased funding for treatment to adequate levels. What actually happened was that drug users ended up in prison because of inadequate treatment provision. The policy implication is that policing can never be *the* answer (see also Aitken et al., 2002; Rhodes et al., 2003).

FOCUSING ON "HIDDEN POPULATIONS"

The term "hidden populations" is frequently used to refer to those drug users who do not come into contact with official agencies and who are therefore "invisible" in drug statistics. However, one may also see the term as indicative of the general orientation of the drug field—that people who might be hidden to drug agencies and standard methods of data collection are often perfectly visible if one visits a nightclub or scrutinises one's own social networks. Another possible way of looking at the issue of (in)visibility is to draw attention to another "hidden" aspect of drug policy and practice—the assumptions and concepts that guide, and therefore also limit, these activities (e.g., Moore, 2004).

One study that has dealt with this issue at length is Gusfield's (1981) *The Culture of Public Problems: Drinking-Driving and the Symbolic Order*. The book grew out of Gusfield's involvement in a study of drink-driving in California in the 1970s, in which he interviewed and observed those involved in the drink-driving process—drink-drivers, police, judges and other court officials, social workers, researchers and policy makers. He realised that it might be profitable to bring to bear on drink-driving research an ethnographic and sociological perspective similar to that normally applied to the study of drinking.

Put simply, Gusfield's thesis was that the "problem of drinking-driving" in the USA was constructed in certain ways—as a "drama of individualism" centring on the "killer drunk"—rather than as, say, a problem in transportation (e.g., how do we prevent drunken people from crashing, or why do we build drinking establishments near busy roads?): "Every perspective is a way of *not* seeing as well as a way of seeing" (Gusfield, 1981: 187). The "culture" of drink-driving research emphasised alcohol as the problem and located the source of motor-vehicle accidents in the moral failings of the individual motorist, rather than in the social institutions in which the motorist was enmeshed or in the physical environment through which the motorist drove.

CONTRADICTING PUBLIC HEALTH ORTHODOXY

The sharing of needles and syringes (and other injecting paraphernalia), identified as the main transmission route for HIV infection, has been a main focus of policy and practice. Stephen Koester (1994) drew on five years of ethnographic research amongst injecting drug users (IDUs) in Denver, Colorado, in order to understand this phenomenon in context. In contrast to earlier research explaining needle sharing as a form of ritual, as a means of establishing trust and social bonds with other IDUs or as a substitute for sexual intimacy, Koester argued that needle sharing occurred because needles "are scarce, and they are scarce because they are illegal to possess without medical justification". In Denver, IDUs preferred not to share needles and syringes because of (1) equipment deterioration or failure; (2) delays in consuming drugs; and (3) the implied subordination of the syringe recipient to the donor. Yet, despite these strong disincentives, needle sharing remained common. One pressing reason was the artificial scarcity of needles and syringes created by US drug laws. Because of their rigorous enforcement by police, IDUs were reluctant to carry syringes. The threat of arrest was perceived as more immediate than that of HIV infection (see also Connors, 1992). The direct consequences of the laws appeared relatively minor but being identified as an IDU to police and the courts had more serious consequences in the future.

The economic marginalisation of street-based IDUs forced them to regularly engage in highly visible strategies in order to obtain drugs. There were two main strategies: being involved in various forms of partnership with other IDUs, and acting as a "runner", a liaison role between dealers and those buyers who lacked direct contacts. IDUs did not want to further increase their chances of arrest by carrying syringes, until the point at which they had secured drugs. This led to high-risk behaviour because IDUs consumed their drugs as quickly as possible in order to minimise the risk of arrest and to relieve withdrawal symptoms. The first available syringe had often been used. Given that sharing could thus be seen as a pragmatic response to the legal situation, Koester's main conclusion was that the laws governing possession of needles and syringes required urgent revision.

Philippe Bourgois also provided a critique of "oversimplified" understandings of needle sharing and HIV infection (Bourgois, 1998), based on three years of participant observation with homeless heroin injectors in San Francisco. His central message was that while needle sharing was viewed as "bad behaviour" by public health, in street drug settings it was viewed as "good, generous behaviour". He argued that, contrary to the findings of epidemiological surveys and self-report studies, the sharing of injecting paraphernalia amongst homeless injectors was endemic but that these risk practices were mandated by the complex logics of precarious income-generation, the moral economy of social relationships and the "biological imperatives" of heroin addiction. Homeless injectors, marshalling their meagre resources to avoid becoming "dopesick" in a competitive and dangerous street environment, had little choice but to routinely engage in a range of practices that put them at risk of HIV infection. Echoing Koester, these practices, he stressed, emerged from the political economy of survival in extremely marginalised communities, the ways in which street injectors prioritised the daily risks they faced and the restricted circulation of sterile injecting equipment in the US context.

Where Bourgois differed from Koester was in his attention to prevention. The harm-reduction messages disseminated to homeless injectors by local (and, he adds, "sensitive") outreach workers revolved around an absolutist and hypersanitary message: never share needles and syringes or injecting paraphernalia. In addition to the impossibility of conforming to such public health messages, there was the "symbolic violence" involved in insulting "dope fiends" and pushing them into "defensive denial" of their risk practices. These unrealistic messages merely perpetuated their marginalisation. Instead he proposed that outreach programmes flood shooting encampments/galleries with sterile injecting equipment, thereby reducing the market value of needles and syringes.

SOLVING NUMBER GAMES

A long-standing epidemiological puzzle in the United States has been how to explain divergent HIV prevalence among IDUs in different parts of the country. An important first step in seeking an ethnographically informed understanding of this phenomenon was a study that combined ethnography with laboratory-based research (Clatts et al., 1999). Clatts and his colleagues embarked on a multidisciplinary project that involved two main steps. First, ethnographic research was conducted in two sites: New York and Denver. Standardised observations of drug preparation and injection were recorded. Most drug solutions were heroin-based, almost 50% of them were heated to aid in dissolution, three types of "cookers" were used and the drug form dictated the length of heating. The temperatures achieved in heating drug solutions were also measured.

The second step involved laboratory work that simulated the field conditions described in the ethnographic data through experimenting with various combinations of heat source, cooker type, volume of water and temperature. The temperature of drug solutions was determined by the heating source, the thickness of the cooker and the volume of drug solution. By heating contaminated drug solutions, HIV was inactivated rapidly, with no viral matter recoverable after 15 seconds of heating by which time the drug solutions had reached 65° Celsius.

These findings suggested a number of things. First, while HIV prevention had focused on lowering the prevalence of needle-sharing, less attention had been paid to reducing the sharing of drug-injecting paraphernalia. Yet paraphernalia-sharing was also widespread. Heating inactivated HIV and for some IDUs was a part of common routines for preparing drugs for injection, especially where less soluble forms of heroin predominated. Therefore,

IDUs should be encouraged: (1) to incorporate heating into their drug preparation routines, ensuring that they heated the solution for at least 15 seconds or until bubbles appeared in the solution (indicating that boiling point was being approached); and (2) to use thinner cookers in order to allow more rapid heating to the desired temperature.

Ciccarone and Bourgois (2003) conducted another study that combined ethnography with laboratory-based and clinical research, in order to further understanding of the HIV epidemiological puzzle. The authors noted previous explanations for the HIV prevalence divergence, with none being definitive or empirically satisfactory: different interfaces between the men who have sex with men (MSM) and IDU populations; the absence of shooting galleries on the west coast early in the epidemic; different public health and law enforcement responses affecting needle availability; and different drugs of choice amongst IDUs in different parts of the country. Their thesis was that "black tar" heroin (BTH) may have retarded the spread of HIV in cities where it was the dominant form of heroin.

They compared DEA data from 20 cities with HIV prevalence data for MSM and IDUs. The cities in which BTH was the dominant form had lower HIV prevalence, whilst those where powder heroin was the dominant form had high prevalence. Cities with mixes of the two heroin forms had low- to mid-range HIV prevalence. Perhaps the most interesting finding was that Seattle, a BTH city, had an HIV prevalence of 2.4%, while Vancouver, a powder heroin city only 225 kms away, had an HIV prevalence of 23.2%. The only city that did not conform to this clear pattern was San Francisco, and this may have been because the IDU and MSM populations had been oversampled by epidemiological studies and because of the "epidemic" of cocaine injection in the late 1980s.

Ciccarone and Bourgois triangulated ethnography, laboratory and clinical data in order to show that the chemical properties of BTH produced certain kinds of injecting behaviour that may reduce HIV transmission. BTH forced IDUs to rinse vigorously and frequently—before injecting in order to test syringe function and following injection to preserve function. This reduced the blood, and consequently the HIV load, in the syringe. They also hypothesised that rinsing with water had not appeared as a protective factor because IDUs had so routinised the practice that they failed to report it in surveys, and possibly also because "intensity of rinsing" had not been examined as a factor. The ethnography also supported the earlier finding of Clatts and colleagues that IDUs heated BTH in order to dissolve it, thereby reducing transmission via cookers. They suggested that one very effective way of reducing HIV spread would be to promote vigorous and frequent rinsing of syringes with water, a pragmatic, inexpensive and effective response relevant to those IDUs lacking resources.

IMPLEMENTING POLICY AND PRACTICE

Ethnography has arguably achieved its greatest policy impact in HIV/AIDS prevention. Building on the "Chicago model" of "community epidemiology" (Hughes, 1977), Wayne Weibel (1988) described a "staged educational sequence" for HIV/AIDS prevention among IDUs that comprised five components. First, the relevant target population was identified through prevalence and other quantitative data, and accessed through indigenous fieldworkers, usually former or current high-status members of the target group. They delivered culturally appropriate prevention at local sites, using their personal contacts and common frames of reference. Second, the prevention programmes established the relevance and credibility of their messages to the target groups. Third, the prevention programme provided an interpretive framework within which to assess high-risk behaviours and which also provided the means to formulate alternatives. The members of the target population were empowered as active partners in the assessment of their own behaviour and in seeking an understanding of the factors contributing to high-risk behaviours. The alternatives offered were practical and appealing, compatible with the social norms and values of the group, and subject to ongoing review. He noted that this element of the programme—which relied on the interpretive framework of "addicts"—was well received. The fourth component was the need to maintain high levels of awareness and to reinforce behaviour change, through ongoing revision and review in order to prevent inertia and complacency. Finally, those involved were encouraged to assess and change not only their own behaviour but also to support these processes among their friends and associates, so that there was an "indirect" intervention process that complemented the direct intervention of indigenous field-workers.

This "prevention advocacy" emphasised empowerment of, and ownership by, the targeted social groups. Weibel's finding that "addicts" assumed social responsibility that could be channelled into HIV prevention was borne out by later research showing that IDUs changed their behaviour in response to HIV prevention (e.g., Broadhead and Heckathorn, 1994; Power, 1995).

In a paper published six years later, Singer and Weeks (1994) took up many of the themes raised by Weibel but broadened the discussion to include a more explicit focus on the political-economic dimensions of injecting drug use and HIV/AIDS, and to introduce the idea of "social prevention". Singer and Weeks were more critical of HIV/AIDS prevention, arguing that the assumptions driving research and prevention were a "prison" from which we had to escape if prevention was to be more targeted and therefore more successful. Although the article did not report on a specific ethnographic project, it drew on the authors' many years of conducting such research with IDUs.

Research and prevention were driven by standard epidemiological categories that were linked to routes of transmission, but were then treated as if they labelled naturally occurring social groups that shared cohesive behaviour patterns, sociocultural identities and normative attitudes and values. Dramatic variations within these categories were ignored as was the fact that the categories made little sense to members of affected populations, e.g., being the "sex partner of an IDU" did not, in itself, create a shared identity. Standard and uniform prevention programmes ignored such variation.

The second assumption that they targeted was the individual focus of much prevention, which was dominated by psychological or psychosocial models of human thought and action. These downplayed or ignored the social and structural factors that shaped human behaviour and led to reductionist explanations for complex behaviours, e.g., that needle sharing was a bonding ritual among marginalised IDUs. IDUs engaged in risk because there were often few real alternatives.

Singer and Weeks accepted that HIV/AIDS prevention had been driven by good intentions but argued that its shortcomings were many: little targeting of subgroups with high infection rates; little recognition of social influences; failure to identify high-risk hidden subgroups and the social factors that placed them at risk; little attention to social groups with shared identities and values; little attention to developing prevention programmes for unique patterns of risk in specific populations; little acknowledgement of the lack of shared identity in being infected with HIV; and failure to target indirect sharing among low-income populations. They advocated an approach that emphasised: peer education; a focus on the problems accompanying HIV (e.g., poverty); the role of those who reduced their risk; availability and accessibility of services; and community involvement. In summary, they called for a form of prevention that was much more cognisant of social and economic contexts through a focus on social networks, neighbourhood-level issues (e.g., street sex work) and social groups that were relevant to their members.

CONCLUSION

The works I have selected for review reveal the central elements of an ethnographic perspective on drug-related harm. They offer sustained descriptions and analyses of the cultural logics of drug users, the wider contexts in which drug use occurs and the frequent irrelevance of prevention programmes that are driven by flawed assumptions or political expediency, and focused on individual behaviour change. What they show is that drug users often engage in harmful drug use because there are few alternatives. Expecting them to respond positively to prevention programmes that do not address the contexts in which harmful drug use occurs is a chimera. Ethnography, drawing on theories in anthropology, sociology and related disciplines, provides a set of insights into the contexts of drug-related harm that should inform policy and practice.

ACKNOWLEDGMENTS

I thank Tim Stockwell for helpful comments on an earlier draft of this chapter. The National Drug Research Institute receives core funding from the Australian Government Department of Health and Ageing.

REFERENCES

Aitken, C. et al. (2002) The impact of a police crackdown on a street drug scene: evidence from the street. *International Journal of Drug Policy*, **13**(3), 189–198.

Bourgois, P. (1998) The moral economies of homeless heroin addicts: confronting ethnography, HIV risk, and everyday violence in San Francisco shooting encampments. *Substance Use and Misuse*, **33**(11), 2323–2351.

Broadhead, R.S and Heckathorn, D.D. (1994) AIDS prevention among injection drug users: agency problems and new approaches. *Social Problems*, **41**(3), 473–496.

Ciccarone, D. and Bourgois, P. (2003) Explaining the geographical variation of HIV among injection drug users in the United States. *Substance Use and Misuse*, **38**(14), 2049–2063.

Clatts, M.C. et al. (1999) HIV-1 transmission in injection paraphernalia: heating drug solutions may inactivate HIV-1. *Journal of Aquired Immune Deficiency Syndromes*, **22**, 194–99.

Connors, M.M. (1992) Risk perception, risk taking and risk management among intravenous drug users: implications for AIDS prevention. *Social Science and Medicine*, **34**(6), 591–601.

Feldman, H.W. (1968) Ideological supports to becoming and remaining a heroin addict. *Journal of Health and Social Behavior*, **9**(2), 131–139.

Feldman, H.W. and Aldrich, M. (1990) The role of ethnography in substance abuse research and public policy: historical precedent and future prospects. In E. Lambert (ed.), *The Collection and Interpretation of Data from Hidden Populations*. Rockville, MD: National Institute on Drug Abuse.

Finestone, H. (1957) Cats, kicks and color. *Social Problems*, **5**, 3–13.

Geertz, C. (1976) "From the native's point of view": On the nature of anthropological understanding. In K.H Basso and H.A. Selby (eds), *Meaning in Anthropology*. Albuquerque, NM: University of New Mexico Press.

Gusfield, J.R. (1981) *The Culture of Public Problems: Drinking-Driving and the Symbolic Order*. Chicago: University of Chicago Press.

Hughes, P. (1977) *Behind the Wall of Respect: Community Experiments in Heroin Addiction Control*. Chicago: University of Chicago Press.

Koester, S.K. (1994) Copping, running, and paraphernalia laws: contextual variables and needle risk behavior among injection drug users in Denver. *Human Organization*, **53**(3), 287–295.

Lindesmith, A. (1947) *Opiate Addiction*. Bloomington, IN: Principia Press.

Maher, L. and Dixon, D. (1999) Policing and public health: law enforcement and harm minimization in a street-level drug market. *British Journal of Criminology*, **39**(4), 488–512.

McKeganey, N. (2003) The bitter sweet of ethnographic research. *International Journal of Drug Policy* **14**(1), 123–125.

Moore, D. (2004) Governing street-based injecting drug users: a critique of heroin overdose prevention in Australia. *Social Science and Medicine* 59(7), pp. 1547–1557.

Power, R. (1995) A model for qualitative action research amongst illicit drug users. *Addiction Research*, **3**(3), 165–181.

Rhodes, T. and Moore, D. (2001) On the qualitative in drugs research: Part one. *Addiction Research and Theory*, **9**(4), 279–299.

Rhodes, T. et al. (2003) Situational factors influencing drug injecting, risk reduction and syringe exchange in Togliatti City, Russian Federation: a qualitative study of micro risk environment. *Social Science and Medicine*, **57**(1), 9–54.

Singer, M. (1999) The ethnography of street drug use before AIDS: a historical review. In P.L. Marshall, M. Singer and M.C. Clatts (eds), *Integrating Cultural, Observational, and Epidemiological Approaches in the Prevention of Drug Abuse and HIV/AIDS*. Bethesda, MD: National Institute on Drug Abuse.

Singer, M. and Weeks, M.R. (1994) Preventing AIDS in communities of color: anthropology and social prevention. *Human Organization*, **55**(4), 488–492.

Weibel, W.W. (1988) Combining ethnographic and epidemiological methods in targeted AIDS interventions: the Chicago model. In R.J. Battjes and R.W. Pickens (eds), *Needle Sharing among Intravenous Drug Abusers: National and Interdisciplinary Perspectives*. Rockville, MD: National Institute on Drug Abuse.

7.5 Recommendations for New Directions in the Prevention of Risky Substance Use and Related Harms

TIM STOCKWELL
Centre for Addictions Research of BC, Victoria, Canada

PAUL J. GRUENEWALD
Prevention Research Center, Berkeley, CA, USA

JOHN W. TOUMBOUROU
Centre for Adolescent Health, Vic, Australia

WENDY LOXLEY
National Drug Research Institute, Perth, WA, Australia

SUMMARY

This chapter presents recommendations for future investments in policy, practice and research. Ratings of the strength of the evidence base for a range of preventive interventions are provided. Investment is especially recommended in four broad areas.

1. *Universal interventions to prevent tobacco use and risky alcohol use* are recommended as these drugs generate the most health, economic and social drug problems globally. The bulk of these problems are found within mainstream society among persons with average levels of social disadvantage and developmental risk. Regulation of physical and economic availability has the strongest evidence of effectiveness and cost-effectiveness. Parental and community role models strongly influence patterns of use among young people, hence prevention strategies must address adult substance use.

2. *Greater accountability for law enforcement to reduce population-level harms.* There is a great need for quality research and monitoring of the effectiveness of law enforcement strategies and their over-arching policy frameworks, both for legal and illegal drugs. There is some evidence that making a substance illegal reinforces community values against use of drugs and greatly increases their cost. There may

Preventing Harmful Substance Use: The Evidence Base for Policy and Practice.
Edited by T. Stockwell, P. J. Gruenewald, J.W. Toumbourou and W. Loxley.
© 2005 John Wiley & Sons, Ltd. ISBN 0-470-09227-0 (hbk) 0-470-09228-9 (pbk).

be benefits in reducing overall harms through a number of law enforcement strategies including better enforcement of liquor licensing laws, through moving to civil rather than criminal penalties for cannabis use and through greater diversion of offenders to treatment. Legal sanctions should not, however, unduly exacerbate problems with excessive criminal sanctions or disrupt treatment and harm reduction services.

3. *Broad developmental interventions and targeted interventions with vulnerable and disadvantaged groups*. These strategies can enhance the overall development of children and young people, while also delaying the onset of drug use and reducing drug-related harm. Broad-spectrum and targeted interventions should be delivered to support families at key developmental stages: infancy, preparation for primary school and also during the early school years. Targeted interventions are also required to build resilience in children and young people from disadvantaged backgrounds, such as some indigenous communities. There is evidence that these strategies may have particular benefits for the prevention of illicit drug use but more research is required.

4. *Brief intervention, treatment and harm reduction approaches for adolescents and adults with emerging or established risky drug use*. Significant investment in brief screening and counselling interventions and in proven treatment methods, whether abstinence-oriented or harm-reducing, can reduce drug-related harm *at the population level*. Family members, particularly children, need to be involved in treatment programmes to help break inter-generational patterns of substance use and related harm. Greater investment is needed in the delivery and evaluation of harm reduction programmes for the full range of legal and illegal drugs. *Recommendations* are made for future research investments to improve the targeting and effectiveness of a broad suite of complementary prevention measures. Strong political leadership can be required to introduce some effective drug policies, both to take on commercial vested interest groups and, sometimes, to lead public opinion.

A COMMUNITY SYSTEMS MODEL FOR PREVENTION OF RISKY SUBSTANCE USE AND HARM ACROSS THE LIFE COURSE: PUTTING IT ALL TOGETHER

Many perspectives, issues and prevention strategies have been reviewed in the foregoing chapters with an overall community systems perspective introduced in Chapter 4.2. We will attempt in this final chapter to provide some synthesis and suggest overall directions for future investment of human and financial resources into the important task of reducing population level harms caused by drug use. We will also provide summaries of the evidence base using a rating system described by Loxley et al. (2004) in a more detailed summary and review of the evidence.

Figure 7.5.1 provides a summary of the main opportunities for continued and enhanced investment to prevent drug-related harms. Figure 7.5.1 depicts an integrated relationship between children's drug use and the patterns of drug use modelled more broadly by adults. A carefully coordinated mix of investment, rather than any single service strategy, has

Table 7.5.1 Overview of recommended patterns of investment in prevention of risky substance use and harm across the whole community

Substance type	Risk patterns	Main risk populations	Harm prevalence	Recommended supply reduction strategies	Recommended demand reduction strategies	Recommended harm reduction strategies	Main recommended level of application
Tobacco	Regular use and dependence	General	Leading cause of drug-related harm overall	Taxation*** Government Monopoly 🖰	Brief intervention*** School drug education** Enforcement of minimum purchase age laws** Treatment*	Restrictions on smoking in public places*** Smoke-free alternatives*	Universal
Alcohol	Intoxication and regular use	General, males	2nd leading cause of harm, 1st in some regions	Taxation*** Controls on hours and density of outlets** Minimum drinking age of 21 years***	Brief intervention*** Treatment*** Community action on local policy**	Random breath testing of drivers*** Safe glassware* Thiamine-fortification of drinks and flour***	Universal
Cannabis	Regular use and dependence	General, males	Low for health related harms, high for criminal justice costs	Prohibition with civil penalties*	Brief intervention*** Treatment***	Use of civil penalties to reduce social harms with criminal penalties*	Universal and targeted
Other illicit substances	Overdose, intoxication, dependence	Socially and developmentally disadvantaged, males	Lower than legal drugs for health and social costs, high for law enforcement costs	Control of precursor chemicals 🖰	Treatment*** Developmental prevention** Diversion from criminal justice system*	Needle exchanges*** Hepatitis B vaccination for users*** Prescribed heroin** Safe injecting rooms*	Targeted
All substances	Intoxication, regular use, dependence	General, young people, males, disadvantaged	Substantial: 12.4% of all deaths	Legal structures and practices to promote health and safety	Early life interventions: Post-natal home visits** Pre-school preparation**	Public education about the care of intoxicated persons at risk of fatal overdose*	Universal and targeted

Source: Adapted from Loxley, Toumbourou, Stockwell, et. al., 2004.
Note: *** Strong evidence for wide implementation; ** Strong evidence for implementation with evaluation; * Promising, needs further research to define best practice. 🖰 Strong rationale, further research recommended.

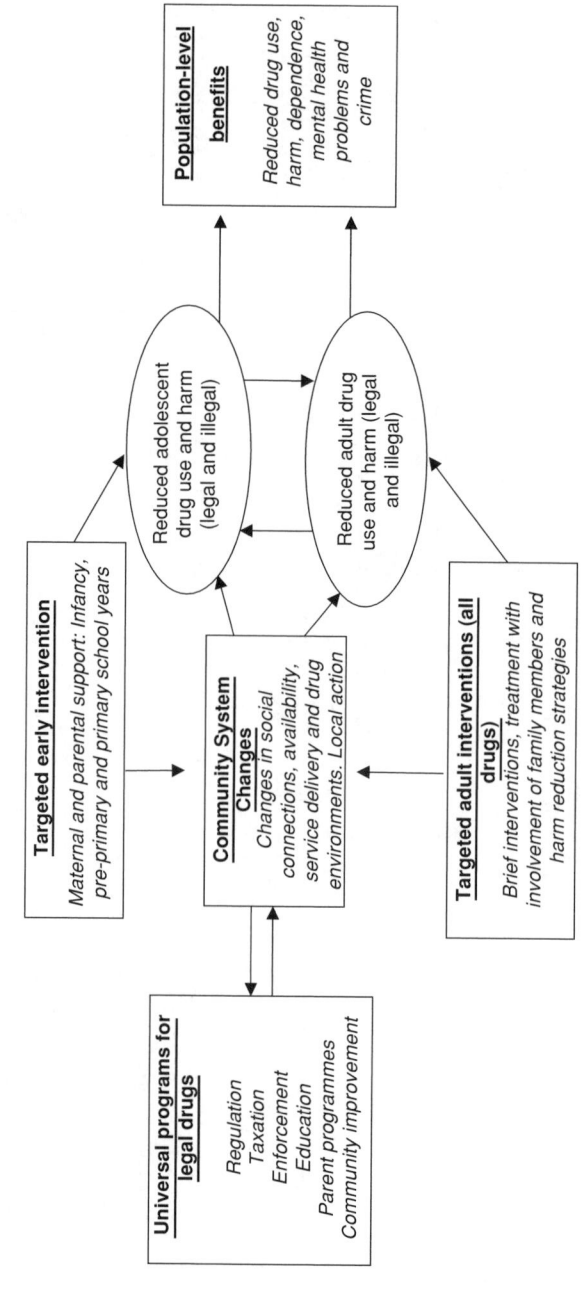

Figure 7.5.1 A summary of recommended interventions for future investment

the greatest chance of success. The programme complexity once again suggests the importance of tailoring the mix of investment to the specific and distinct needs of particular communities.

The Need to Redirect Investment in Prevention

Patterns of government investment in prevention in many countries are inconsistent with the evidence base presented in the foregoing pages. A prime example is the disparity between the UK Government's 2004 Alcohol Harm Reduction Strategy (UK Cabinet Office, 2004) and the evidence expertly summarised in *Alcohol, No Ordinary Commodity* (Babor et al., 2003; Room, 2004). The overall cost-effectiveness of government investment can be maximised by (1) directing resources towards prevention of the underlying patterns of drug use responsible for the most prevalent and serious harms; (2) taking account of the extent to which patterns of risk are concentrated in particular social groups or more evenly distributed across the whole population; (3) emphasising investment in interventions that have evidence of effectiveness at the population level in controlled studies; (4) funding research designed to fill gaps in the evidence base; and (5) comprehensive epidemiological monitoring to maintain appropriate targeting of funding and quality in delivery of funded programmes. Against these multiple criteria, the main patterns of inconsistency are as listed below.

1. An excessive focus on illegal compared with legal drugs. One example is the 2004/2005 Australian federal budget in which AU$470 million was allocated to a National Illicit Drug Strategy, mostly for law enforcement, and only $4 million was specifically allocated to an alcohol harm reduction strategy. Another is US expenditure on drug research in 2002: the National Institute on Drug Abuse received US$900 million while the National Institute on Alcohol Abuse and Alcoholism received US$400 million. The total US National Drug Control Policy had a budget of US$11.5 billion in 2002 of which US$6 billion was for law enforcement and border control, the rest for treatment and prevention activities. A proportion of US$300 million allocated to the Center for Substance Abuse Treatment and US$200 million allocated to the Center for Substance Abuse Prevention would have been directed towards alcohol and tobacco.
2. An excessive reliance on public education and persuasion rather than effective regulation of the physical and economic availability of legal drugs. There is recent evidence that school-based education regarding alcohol and tobacco can have benefits with relatively low expenditure, however, regulatory approaches are far more cost-effective.
3. The widespread use of expensive and punitive criminal sanctions against cannabis, a drug with harmful effects no doubt but for which it is hard to identify many deaths or hospital admissions caused by its use (e.g., Ridolfo and Stevenson, 2001). Many jurisdictions are now experimenting with the replacement of criminal with civil penalties for use and possession of cannabis while still actively deterring use.
4. The use of expensive and punitive criminal justice processes of unknown effectiveness for people with drug offences associated with substance dependence instead of diversion to early intervention and treatment programmes. Australia, the UK and some American states have introduced and are evaluating a range of police and court diversion programmes.

5. The duplication of efforts across many areas of government in relation to interventions in the early years. Investment in interventions in the early years can yield social and economic benefits in the areas of crime, mental health, health care and substance use problems, but must be well coordinated at a community level.
6. Insufficient investment in evidence-based strategies for the reduction of harm in people who continue to use legal and/or illegal drugs.

Specific applications of these main conclusions are summarised in Table 7.5.1 by substance type and with main recommended interventions categorised into supply, demand and harm reduction. More detailed ratings of the strength of the evidence base for specific prevention strategies are also provided in Tables 7.5.2 to 7.5.6. There are often both real and perceived political impediments to the implementation of effective policies as will be discussed further.

Table 7.5.2 Evidence base for judicial and law enforcement strategies for illegal drugs

Intervention	Target population	Comments and qualifications	Source
★ **Evidence for implementation**			
Civil penalties only for cannabis use and possession	General population	Reduces adverse effects of criminal penalties without increasing levels of use	Chapter 5.4
Intensive local policing targeting street drug markets	Illegal drug dealers	Evidence of reductions in dealing and little displacement. Need to be mindful of unintended consequences	Loxley et al., 2004
Local enforcement supported by community development	Illegal drug producers and suppliers	One large multi-site US study shows short-term benefits	Loxley et al., 2004
Diversion away from criminal justice for illicit drug using offenders	Illegal drug users	Promising results from trials but need stronger designs	Chapter 5.5
Drug Courts	Illegal drug users	Promising results from early evaluations, stronger evaluation designs needed	Chapter 5.5
Methadone programmes in prisons	Prisoners	Strong evidence for methadone programmes in community, early promising results in prisons. Potential to reduce spread of blood-borne viruses.	Loxley et al., 2004
ꙮ **Warrants further research**			
Legal prohibition as a support to social norms unfavourable to illicit drug use	General population	Theoretical support and indirect evidence for general deterrent effect but not for deterring re-offending	Loxley et al., 2004
Law enforcement as a trigger for treatment entry	Problem drug users	Indirect evidence, worthy of investigation	Loxley et al., 2004
Border protection by police and customs	Drug suppliers	Basic data unavailable, no published evaluations	Manski et al., 2001; Loxley et al., 2004

THE EVIDENCE BASE FOR PREVENTION: A SUMMARY

On the basis of the material reviewed elsewhere in this book and major systematic reviews (principally Loxley et al., 2004; Babor et al., 2003) we have applied ratings of the strength of the evidence for 70 major varieties of prevention strategy. A rating system first developed by Patton and Toumbourou (Toumbourou et al., 2000) and applied systematically by Loxley et al. (2004) was followed. It is designed to give concise advice for future directions for investment in prevention programmes and policies. In some instances we have updated the ratings provided both by Loxley et al. (2004) and Babor et al. (2003) in light of more recently published research evidence. The starting point for most of the ratings below was those in the Australian Government-funded review by Loxley et al. (2004) with some updating from new material in the present book. Application of the following rating system was agreed between the editors alone and does not imply the support of other contributing authors to the present book. The agreed ratings are summarised under four main headings each reflecting important broad recommendations about future directions for investment in prevention programs and policies:

O Limited investigation. No relevant effectiveness studies identified and no empirical or theoretical rationale. OR the limited evidence available is inconsistent or contradictory.

☒ Evidence is negative for the use of this strategy to prevent the targeted outcome. This rating required consistent null or negative findings in well-controlled evaluation studies.

⌐ Warrants further research. Strategies with a strong rationale and promising evidence for their implementation or outcome, but key elements not clearly resolved or evaluated only in small scale or inadequately controlled studies. Policies and programmes utilising these strategies are priority targets for future research funding.

★ Evidence for implementation. Published studies provide a sound theoretical rationale, a clearly specified service delivery format, acceptance within service delivery organisations, target population recruitment on a scale sufficient to usefully contribute to population health impacts, and adequate consumer approval measured using indicators such as programme retention. Policies and programmes utilising these strategies might be supported for implementation where there are few costs and obvious benefits. In other cases wider implementation may await rigorously controlled outcome evaluation to better establish benefits.

★★ Evidence for outcomes. This rating was applied where positive outcomes were consistently published in well-controlled interventions. Interventions were required to be of sufficient scale to ensure outcomes within the constraints imposed by large-scale population health frameworks. Policies and programmes utilising these strategies should be carefully monitored for their impacts while being supported for jurisdiction-wide dissemination.

★★★ Evidence for broad implementation and dissemination. This rating requires published reports of impacts where programmes were delivered on a large scale, not by research teams, but rather by government auspice bodies or other service delivery agents. Evidence for dissemination was only sought for strategies demonstrating evidence for outcomes. Monitoring for effective delivery recommended.

Table 7.5.3 Evidence base for regulatory and law enforcement strategies for alcohol and tobacco

Intervention	Target population	Comments and qualifications	Chapters
★★★ *Evidence for effective dissemination/implementation*			
Taxation	General population, especially young adults	Strongest level of evidence. Need to maintain high price per unit of alcohol and per cigarette, indexed to inflation	Chapters 3.4 and 6.5
Introduction of 21 years as minimum legal drinking age	Adolescents, young adults	Strong evidence from US experience, limited public support in many countries	Chapters 3.2, 3.4, 6.5
Enforcement of purchase age laws	Adolescents	Use of children to test willingness to sell and/or police decoys recommended	Chapters 3.2, 3.4, 6.5
Restrictions on smoking in public places	General population	Systematic reviews show reductions in environmental tobacco smoke	Chapters 6.4 and 6.5
Random breath-testing of drivers	People who drink before driving	Maximum benefit with high visibility and frequent testing	Chapters 3.4 and 6.5
★★ *Evidence for outcome efficacy*			
Community action on alcohol for structural policy change	Local community	Strategies to mobilise community to ensure effective local regulation and law enforcement	Chapters 3.2, 3.4, 4.2 and 4.4
Restrictions on late trading hours	General population, especially young adults	Late night trading associated with increased violence	Chapters 3.4 and 6.5
Enforcement of liquor laws not to serve intoxicated customers	General population, especially young adults	Rarely enforced but shown to reduce violence and road trauma	Chapters 3.4, 4.6, 6.5
Responsible alcohol service with liquor law enforcement	General population, especially young adults	Without credible deterrence against over-service there is no benefit	Chapters 3.4, 4.6, 6.2 and 6.5

★★ *Evidence for outcome efficacy (continued)*

Licensee codes of conduct with liquor law enforcement	General population, especially young adults	Without liquor law enforcement can be a "look good" only measure	Chapter 4.3
Local liquor restrictions	Local communities with identified problems	Evidence strong for remote communities with significant indigenous population	Chapter 6.7
Restrictions on price discounting	General population, especially young adults	While effective these increasingly run counter to free trade and competition policies	Chapter 6.5
Restrictions on tobacco advertising and sponsorship	General population	Cochrane reviews support impact at population level	Chapter 6.4
Ignition interlocks	Repeat drink-drivers	Highly effective while fitted ie can only drive if have zero BAC	Chapter 7.3
Lower BAC limits for young drivers	Young drivers	Strong rationale, some positive outcomes	Chapter 3.4
★ *Evidence for implementation*			
Dram Shop laws	General population	These deter service to intoxicated customers with threat of legal action	Chapter 3.4
Breath-testing in high injury risk workplaces	Workers in high injury risk occupations	Routine breath-testing in some occupations essential e.g airline pilots	Chapter 4.5
⌂ *Warrants further research*			
Restrictions on liquor outlet density	General population	Strong evidence for an association with levels of population harm, need intervention studies and models for community level application	Chapters 2.5 and 6.5

Greater Investment is Needed in Universal Interventions to Prevent Tobacco Use and Risky Alcohol Use

These drugs generate the most health, economic and social drug problems. In Chapter 2.2 it was shown that globally over 90% of drug-caused deaths and/or disability is due to tobacco and alcohol while less than 10% is attributable to illicit drugs. While tobacco use (e.g., Suahpush, 2004) and, to a lesser extent, risky alcohol use (Bloomfield, 2004) are more frequently found in lower socio-economic groups, the bulk of these problems are still usually found within mainstream society among persons with average levels of social disadvantage and developmental risk (Stockwell et al., 2004). A summary of the evidence base for alcohol and tobacco interventions is shown in Tables 7.5.3 and 7.5.4. The universal regulation of physical and economic availability of legal drugs has the strongest evidence for both effectiveness and cost-effectiveness. Parental and community role models also strongly influence patterns of use among adolescents and young adults, hence prevention strategies must address all age groups. Universal social marketing programmes have some evidence of limited effectiveness, especially when they support regulatory and community action strategies. Unlike Babor et al. (2003), some forms of educational intervention are recommended here. Recent evidence of sustained benefits from well-designed school-based interventions targeting legal drugs has influenced these ratings (see Chapter 3.3). There is a possible tension between the objective of delaying onset of alcohol use, for example by raising the legal drinking age to 21 years, and new evidence that a harm reduction approach to school alcohol education can reduce alcohol intake and related risk behaviours (McBride et al., 2004). A future research direction might be to resolve whether these strategies can be used in a complementary fashion or whether they are incompatible.

In general, universal regulatory strategies are highly cost-effective but can carry political risks if their introduction is not managed well. Alcohol and tobacco industry lobby groups continuously struggle, by all means at their disposal, to weaken regulations that are in the interests of public health and safety (e.g., Room, 2004). However, public opinion is often very supportive of effective regulatory strategies such as random breath testing, restrictions on smoking in public places and even alcohol taxation (AIHW, 2002; Stockwell, 2004). There are political risks but there are also examples where these have been overcome with courage and sound preparation such as the *Living With Alcohol* programme in the Northern Territory, Australia (Stockwell et al., 2001). Public opinion will often follow when a strong lead is taken by politicians to implement an evidence-based policy.

Greater Accountability for the Reduction of Population-Level Harms through Law Enforcement

Law enforcement strategies can reduce public health, safety and order problems associated with both legal and illegal substances. As summarised above, the evidence is stronger for the enforcement of laws regarding the supply of alcohol and tobacco than for illicit drugs, though absence of evidence in the latter case should not be taken to necessarily mean ineffectiveness. There is evidence that law enforcement may play a role in prevention by reinforcing community values against use and supply of illegal drugs (Loxley et al., 2004). However, the important US Academy of Sciences report summarised in Chapter 6.3 found that the massive investment in the US War Against Drugs had only a flimsy evidence base to support it and that while border protection may reduce the flow of dangerous substances into countries and significantly raise prices, there is a need for improved data collection

Table 7.5.4 Evidence base for universal demand reduction strategies for substance use problems among adolescents, young adults and older age groups

Intervention	Target population	Comments and qualifications	Source
★★ *Evidence for outcome efficacy*			
Quit smoking campaigns	Smokers	National campaigns can reduce smoking rates but need to be maintained. Most effective in combination with regulatory strategies	Chapter 6.4
School alcohol and tobacco education programmes	12 to 15 year old school children	Recent evidence of sustained benefits for alcohol programmes, method of implementation critical. Strong evidence for tobacco. Need not be costly	Chapter 3.2, 3.3
★ *Evidence for implementation*			
National low risk drinking guidelines and standard drink labelling	General population	Consistent with and support brief interventions and road safety campaigns	Loxley et al., 2004
Community mobilisation	General population	Evidence of modest benefits for reduced use of tobacco, alcohol and cannabis. Strongest effects when involve restrictions on youth access. Additional benefit unclear	Chapter 6.5
Social marketing using mass media	Adolescents	Some studies have found evidence of short-term impacts on tobacco, alcohol and cannabis use among adolescents	Chapter 3.5
⊡ *Warrants further research*			
Parent education programmes	Parents of adolescents	Some evidence of positive benefits for all main drug types, few studies	Chapter 3.2
School improvement programmes	Children and adolescents	Some evidence of positive benefits for a variety of outcomes, need more research	Chapter 3.2
Peer intervention and peer education	Adolescents	Good rationale, need more research	Chapter 3.2

on drug use patterns, drug purity, and enforcement activity to properly evaluate and direct this effort. The lack of published literature, particularly relating to the cost-effectiveness of illicit drug law enforcement strategies, is a general concern (Chapter 6.3; Loxley et al., 2004) and is an area in which research should be undertaken as a matter of priority so that public investment in illicit drug supply reduction can be justified.

Enforcement should not, however, exacerbate problems with excessive criminal sanctions or disrupt treatment and harm reduction services—which police "crackdowns" have the capacity to do (Loxley et al., 2004). A profitable future direction for research investment would be how to avoid unintended consequences or "harm maximisation" from law enforcement efforts for both legal and illegal drugs (see Chapter 4.7). In the meantime, far greater investment is needed in the enforcement of laws regarding availability of legal drugs which, together with the use of civil rather than criminal penalties for cannabis use (Chapter 5.4) and the diversion of offenders to treatment (Chapter 5.5), is known to contribute to reductions in drug-related harm.

Broad Developmental Interventions and Targeted Interventions with Vulnerable and Disadvantaged Groups

Broad-spectrum and targeted interventions should be delivered to support families and young people at key developmental stages: infancy, preparation for primary school and also during the primary school years (see Section 3). Evidence reviewed in Chapter 3.2 suggests that social and developmental risk factors are highly predictive of both problem drug use and any use of illicit substances (e.g., Stockwell et al., 2004). The ratings in Table 7.5.5 relate to evidence for "broad spectrum" benefits in reducing social developmental risk factors that have been shown to lead children to subsequently become involved in drug use and harms. Targeting these factors is likely to lead to other benefits in reducing mental health problems, conduct disorders, delinquency, violence, educational failure and other health risk behaviours. Long-term follow-up studies are required in order to establish causal links between exposure to these interventions (e.g., pre-natal and ante-natal care) and the distal outcomes of reductions in problematic drug use. Investment in broad spectrum interventions has the potential to benefit many sectors of society in multiple ways but should not detract from investment in substance-use specific interventions with proven ability to reduce risky use and/or harm. There is a need for future longitudinal and controlled intervention research to clarify the extent of benefits for the prevention of substance use and related harm.

Brief Intervention, Treatment and Harm Reduction Approaches for Adolescents and Adults with Emerging or Developed Risky Drug Use Patterns

Brief screening and counselling interventions can be highly cost-effective and are specially recommended for wide application in primary health care and community settings. Much has been written about the difficulties with implementing brief interventions on a sufficient scale to impact upon community level harms (e.g., Roche and Freeman, 2004). There is also evidence that significant investment in proven treatment methods, whether abstinence-oriented or harm-reducing, can reduce drug-related harm at the population level. Examples include reductions in crime as a result of treatment for opiate dependence (Gossop et al., 1998) and possible reductions in road trauma in regions with a well-resourced alcohol treatment sector (Smart and Mann, 2000). Family members, particularly parents with young children, need to be involved in treatment programmes to help break inter-generational patterns of substance use and related harm.

There has been strengthening evidence for a wide range of pure harm reduction initiatives for legal as well as illegal drugs. These seek to reduce the significant harms experienced by individuals who continue to use drugs in risky ways. When applied to illicit drugs these strategies are particularly controversial when new strategies are first considered. It is usually feared by some that helping drug users sends the wrong message to impressionable young people in particular and society in general, e.g., by the creation of safe injecting sites in Australia, Canada and Europe (Stoever, 2002; Bullington and Maier-Katkin 2002) and the conduct of trials of prescribed heroin in Europe (Haemmig and Tschacher, 2001). Noting the growing evidence for the effectiveness of these programmes, it is recommended that future research explores this issue empirically to establish whether or not harm reduction programmes do increase young people's interest in risky drug use.

Strong political leadership is usually required for the introduction of new harm reduction initiatives. Examples of this include the rapid introduction of needle and syringe exchange programmes in Australia to prevent the spread of AIDS among injecting drug users in

Table 7.5.5 Evidence base for broad spectrum benefits (not specific to substance use problems) from interventions targeting children and adolescents

Intervention	Target population	Comments and qualifications	Source
★★ *Evidence for outcome efficacy*			
Antenatal home visits by nurses	At risk mothers	Broad spectrum benefits in later childhood	Chapter 3.2
Family home visiting (children age 0 to 4 years)	At risk families	Broad spectrum benefits for later adolescence	Chapter 3.2
Education programmes for parents with young children	At risk families	Short-term benefits demonstrated	Chapter 3.2
Pre-primary school preparation programmes	Children age 5 to 6 years	Short-term benefits demonstrated. Longer term benefits in small studies	Chapter 3.2
Family interventions	Families with children aged 5 to 10 years	Broad spectrum benefits, need to resolve optimal components and target group	Chapter 3.2
School organisation and behaviour management	Primary/elementary and middle schools	Broad spectrum developmental improvements together with greater benefits for more disadvantaged youth	Chapter 3.2
★★ **Evidence for implementation**			
Early school drug education	Primary schools	Inconsistent results with this age group, need new process and outcome studies	Chapter 3.2
▷ **Warrants further research**			
Programs to prevent or delay pregnancy	Young and vulnerable mothers	Need longer term studies including follow-up of next generation	Chapter 3.2
Health Service re-orientation	Pregnant women and new mothers	Encouraging evidence from targeted studies with at-risk women, need universal studies	Chapter 3.2
Youth sport and recreation programmes	Adolescents	Good rationale, need more research	Chapter 3.2
Mentorship	Adolescents	Good rationale, need more research	Chapter 3.2
Secondary school organisation and behaviour management	Secondary school children	Evidence for success in primary schools and evidence for feasibility in secondary schools	Chapter 3.2
Employment and training programmes	School leavers, young adults	Pre-employment assistance, work experience and post-school training. Need evidence of benefit from an intervention study	Loxley et al., 2004

Table 7.5.6 Evidence base for treatment, brief intervention and harm reduction strategies for legal and illegal substances

Intervention	Target population	Comments and qualifications	Source
★★★ *Evidence for effective dissemination/implementation*			
Hepatitis B vaccination	General population and injecting drug users	Highly effective, can be delivered population wide, need to increase uptake among drug users	Loxley et al., 2004
Needle and syringe distribution	Injecting drug users	Systematic reviews and economic evaluations provide very strong support, widely implemented	Loxley et al., 2004
Brief interventions	Smokers, at risk drinkers	Strong supporting evidence for screening, brief advice and follow-up by GPs and community nurses	Loxley et al., 2004
Treatment for alcohol and nicotine dependence	Problem drinkers and cigarette smokers	Stronger evidence for some treatment than others, some evidence that community level benefits obtained	Loxley et al., 2004
★★ *Evidence for outcome efficacy*			
Smoking cessation programmes during pregnancy	Pregnant women, unborn infants	Can reduce smoking and low birth weight	Loxley et al., 2004
Thiamine supplementation of flour and of alcoholic drinks	High risk and dependent alcohol drinkers	Strong rationale, national implementation, evidence of reduction in Wernicke-Korsakoff Syndrome	Loxley et al., 2004
Prescribed heroin	Heroin dependent IDUs	European trials show very high retainment, major health and social benefits	e.g. Haemmig and Tschacher, 2001
Violence prevention on licensed premises	People who attend bars and nightclubs	Evidence from well-controlled studies of reduced violence, city-wide implementation	Chapter 4.3
★ *Evidence for implementation*			
Plastic or tempered glassware for licensed premises	People who attend bars and nightclubs	Strong rationale, limited formal evaluation	Loxley et al., 2004
Harm reduction alcohol education in schools	School children aged 12 to 15 years	Evidence of reduced risky behaviours in well-controlled study	Chapter 3.3
Harm reduction components in liquor licensee codes of conduct	People who attend bars and nightclubs	Provision of food, low alcohol drinks and measures to reduce "bar-hopping" part of successful programmes	Chapter 4.3
Supervised injecting centres	Injecting drug users	Strong rationale, evidence of acceptability and successful implementation	Loxley et al., 2004

Intervention	Target group	Comments	Reference
Education to prevent opiate overdoses	Injecting opiate drug users	Strong rationale, evidence of acceptability and successful implementation	Loxley et al., 2004
Overdose prevention protocols for police and emergency service personnel	Injecting opiate drug users	Designed to encourage drug users to seek medical help for overdoses	Loxley et al., 2004
□ Warrants further research			
Alternative nicotine delivery systems	Cigarette smokers	Apparently successful national experiment in Sweden—need evaluation of population-wide impacts on lung cancer rates	Chapter 5.2
Night patrols and sobering up shelters to care for drunk people	Communities with public drunkenness	No outcome studies, process studies show well-received and implemented. Strong rationale	Loxley et al., 2004; Chapter 6.7
Provision of Naloxone for peer administration by injecting drug users	Injecting drug users	Strong rationale. Promising international experience, very few unintended consequences	Loxley et al., 2004
Harm reduction school drug education	School children aged 12 to 15 years	Evidence for effectiveness with alcohol, could be expanded to cannabis and party drugs	Chapter 3.3
Guidelines for safe dance clubs and parties	Party and nightclub-goers	Environmental characteristics contribute to drug-related harm (e.g. crowding, temperature, provision of water). Need outcome studies	Loxley et al., 2004
Pill-testing at dance venues	Party and nightclub-goers	Sound rationale, widely implemented, well-accepted, not evaluated	Loxley et al., 2004
O Limited investigation			
Low tar cigarettes	Cigarette smokers	Evidence that smokers compensate by inhaling harder, may maintain smoking habits	Chapter 5.2
☒ Evidence is negative			
"Staggered" closing times for late night liquor outlets	Party and nightclub-goers	Where this leads to an overall increase in late trading hours evidence of increased violence	Loxley et al., 2004
Retractable syringes	Injecting drug users and general community	No evidence of spread of HIV from discarded needles, will not prevent needle-sharing	Loxley et al., 2004

Australia while Dr Neal Blewett was Minister for Health (Blewett, 1986). Another concerns the role of Swiss politicians during the introduction of heroin by prescription to long-term addicts (Klingemann, 1998). Strong supply reduction and harm reduction can go hand in hand—but can also be in conflict. Special protocols and procedures need to be developed and evaluated for law enforcement agencies to determine how both supply and harm reduction can be maximised (see Table 7.5.6).

CONCLUSION, RESEARCH AND POLICY IMPLICATIONS

The major aim of this book has been to summarise the existing evidence base regarding "what works" in the prevention of substance use problems in the hope that this might assist the development of a comprehensive prevention agenda that can be implemented with synergistic actions across multiple government departments and sectors of society. Such an agenda would need to identify opportunities for remedying risk and increasing protection across all sectors of government so as to contribute to a national effort to reduce drug-related harm.

It is clear that there is a great disparity between the broad evidence base for prevention programmes and policies and the patterns of investment usually displayed by governments. The greatest expenditure is generally directed towards the deterrence or prevention of those risky patterns of drug use which generate the least harm and for which there is the least impressive evidence of effectiveness. A number of effective prevention strategies have been identified here for which there is already significant public support but are not as widely implemented as they could be. In some cases, such as the strict regulation of late night drinking venues, politicians are sometimes more inclined to listen to the concerns of commercial vested interest groups than they are to public opinion or public health advocates (e.g., Room, 2004). In other cases, and a few have been identified, strong political leadership can overcome these impediments and bring public opinion with them with lasting benefits to public health, safety and order.

A small number of summary recommendations for policy and future research are listed below.

Policy Recommendation 1 **Prevention Policy Must Be Securely Based on High Quality Social, Epidemiological, Biomedical and Intervention Research**

It is a generally accepted truism that effective policy in any area must be evidence-based. Much lip service is paid to this principle without necessarily considering the full range of essential evidence. While the present volume has attempted to summarise the key evidence, the authors recognise the need for the evidence base to be continuously refreshed and updated as new understandings and data relevant to protection and risk reduction come to light. In particular, prevention policy must be explicitly informed by the following four kinds of evidence:

1. evidence regarding what are the major *patterns of risk and harm* at the *population level* using sophisticated indicators of harm, sensitive to social, legal as well as health dimensions of drug-related harm (e.g., injecting drugs, becoming intoxicated, smoking cigarettes);

2. evidence regarding what are the main direct *mechanisms* that would, in principle, achieve increased protection and reduced risk if effectively implemented (e.g., delaying onset of use of drugs, adding thiamine to alcohol, providing clean needles);

3. evidence from intervention studies regarding *optimal programmes and methods* for ensuring such mechanisms are effectively implemented (e.g., supporting parents of primary school children; providing harm and risk reduction classroom-based programmes; limiting late night trading hours of licensed premises) again relying on population level health and safety outcomes as the gold standard in evaluation;

4. evidence-based principles regarding *optimal processes* for implementing interventions across a range of key domains (e.g., media, schools, licensed premises, community coalitions).

It is important to maintain a broad conceptualisation in attempting to monitor success in reducing drug-related harm. Measures of success need to encompass not only estimates of drug-caused deaths but also be sensitive to years of life lost, disability and the extent of social harms.

Policy Recommendation 2 Existing Tobacco Control Strategies Should Be Maintained, with an Increased Emphasis on Youth

It is clear that prevention strategies for tobacco have been highly successful in economically developed countries over recent decades and need to be continued. The negotiation of an international Framework Convention on Tobacco Control should reinforce these gains and facilitate progress in developing countries in the future. Universal programmes that combine the best elements of regulation, taxation and enforcement should be enhanced and supported by well-designed and appealing mass media campaigns. Continuation of the effort to reduce smoking rates for adults is warranted both for the benefit to adults, but also as a means of breaking the causal nexus with youth smoking. A greater focus on children and youth is also warranted. There appear to be very good prospects for reducing both early age tobacco use and progression to regular use. A universal, community-based focus on reducing developmental risk factors and enhancing protective factors has the potential to further enhance the existing successes in tobacco control. The possibility of instigating greater government control of the production and marketing of tobacco products should also be explored.

Policy Recommendation 3 The Prevention of Alcohol-Related Harm Should Receive Greater Priority

There are markedly high levels of alcohol misuse in many countries, particularly among young people. Harm reduction approaches have demonstrated success in reducing alcohol-related harm, including alcohol involvements in vehicle accidents and in violence in and around licensed premises. However, the application of evidence-based strategies to regulate alcohol marketing, distribution and use remains poorly coordinated and uneven across communities. There are substantial benefits achievable through the application of universal regulatory and enforcement strategies supported by public education campaigns focussing on alcohol. It is strongly recommended that the World Health Organization prompts work on the development of an international Framework Convention on Alcohol Regulation to help raise the profile of this issue and coordinate international efforts (see Chapter 2.2).

The global impact of risky alcohol use on disability adjusted life-years is roughly the same as that of tobacco and international leadership is required to respond appropriately to this major issue for public health, safety and order.

Policy Recommendation 4 Harm Reduction Strategies Should Be a Significant Aspect of National Drug Policies

Such approaches should be supported and further research conducted to ascertain their effectiveness. Particular attention should be given to stabilising the hepatitis C epidemic by ensuring that needle distribution programmes are expanded to ensure that every injector can use a new needle for each injection. The international experiences with safe injecting rooms and heroin trials recommend their uptake in other countries.

Policy Recommendation 5 Policy Should Be Developed to Enable a Coordinated Prevention Response within Local Communities

Many of the interventions reviewed in this book require a local level of implementation and coordination. There is a strong case for early intervention programmes targeted at disadvantaged groups in society to support families with young children in providing effective parenting and in preparing children for school. There is growing evidence that the most severe and entrenched drug problems have their origins in developmental pathways characterised by early deficits and the accumulation of a high number of risk factors. One priority area here is to increase investment in parent education and family support in drug treatment programmes with a view to breaking inter-generational cycles of problematic drug use. Primary schools also provide opportunities to improve developmental outcomes for children with a high number of risk factors through universal prevention focused on enhancing social environments. Such programmes are most effective if coordinated and integrated within local communities so as to ensure they can be sustained over time. In addition, community action initiatives are needed to reduce the harmful consequences of alcohol and other drug use. Local policing and enforcement efforts can reduce inappropriate marketing and distribution practices for legal drugs such as sales to intoxicated patrons and minors. Community harms can also be reduced through a number of other measures including better management of environments where alcohol is sold, alcohol server training, policing to reduce drink driving and efforts to reduce potentially violent drinking contexts. These strategies are also likely to contribute to improved social environments for children and young people.

RESEARCH RECOMMENDATIONS

Research Recommendation 1 Regular, Timely and Reliable Indicators of Risk, Protection and Harm Need to Be Reported Nationally, Regionally and Locally

In most countries major improvements can be made to existing drug monitoring systems. There are usually few data collected on levels of risk and harm as they affect vulnerable and disadvantaged groups such as indigenous populations. Consistent reporting of levels of risk and harm between different jurisdictions has only rarely been achieved. Mechanisms for translating data to the local level and disseminating to communities are also only rarely achieved but are important undertakings for supporting local action. Investment should also be made in the development of well-validated models of the political, economic, social and psychological mechanisms that link substance use to related harms, enabling better targeted preventive interventions. It is suggested that comprehensive national models for monitoring risk, protection and harm should be developed across all drug types utilising data from multiple sources including crime and health data, sales data and self-report data. It is often the case that a number of different bodies collect these data hence there is a need to reduce duplication through greater coordination of the process. The World Health Organization has published guides to epidemiological monitoring for tobacco (WHO 1998), illicit drugs (WHO, 2000a) and alcohol (WHO, 2000b).

Research Recommendation 2 The Increased Application of Sophisticated New Analytic Methods to Evaluate Community, State and Nation-Wide Interventions

Despite considerable consensus as to the desirability of achieving "evidence-based policy" there tend to be hard operational boundaries separating the areas of funding allocation, service delivery and research. Although there are good grounds for communities to be given a greater role for the coordination and delivery of prevention programmes, innovation in this area needs to be carefully monitored and evaluated. Many seemingly common-sense prevention programmes have been shown through evaluation to ultimately have minimal or negative effects. Controlled trials to evaluate community interventions are often an unrealisable ideal in policy evaluation and pose particular difficulties where interventions impact the largest population aggregations involving states or nations. In effect, this means that interventions that have the most profound potential for population impacts have the lowest potential to be subjected to controlled evaluation trials. Fortunately, new community evaluation models and approaches have been developed that use quasi-experimental designs (see Chapter 3.5), time series analysis and spatial mapping (see Chapter 6.2). The application of sophisticated approaches to evaluation will be required in order to monitor and evaluate important community investments such as the local impacts of new regulatory policies and their enforcement (e.g., Young et al., 2004), the effects of social marketing and the influence of community mobilisation campaigns. By geographically and temporally phasing funding for the implementation of new community interventions programme managers can increase the potential for controlled evaluation. However, the central requirement for community evaluation is the application and modelling of valid temporal indicators of community risk, protection and harm that can be associated with accurate details of community programme delivery. This reinforces again the importance of investing in adequate data collection (Policy Recommendation 1).

Research Recommendation 3 Community-Level Investigations into the Relative Benefits of Different Prevention Approaches, e.g., Preventing Drug Use Versus Reducing Drug-Related Harm

A more deliberate attempt to phase the introduction of community programme funding and temporally sequenced systems of data collection could enhance the prospects for community-level evaluation. The introduction of more sophisticated approaches to evaluating community interventions can ensure accountability for state and national funding while enhancing opportunities for local innovation around different approaches to community prevention. Currently, there are important unanswered questions regarding the relative merits of different community prevention approaches. For example, there is evidence for longitudinal relationships between an early onset of alcohol use and the subsequent development of high level alcohol use and related harms. Would delaying onset of drinking reduce the likelihood of later problems? More specifically, given that what we know about prevention effectiveness is almost entirely grounded in work with alcohol and tobacco (Manski et al., 2001), would delaying the use and risky use of legal drugs delay or prevent the uptake of illegal drugs? There is indicative longitudinal data to suggest this may be the case (Loxley et al., 2004), but there is also evidence that the developmental pathways to illegal drug use may be somewhat segmented (Stockwell et al., 2004). There is evidence that drug education programmes can have positive impacts on drug use and harms where their focus is more directly based on harm reduction (e.g., McBride et al., 2004). Despite promising early indications, it remains unclear whether the broader application of harm reduction approaches could undermine efforts to make drug use less fashionable to young people. Behind these considerations lie important policy questions regarding the potential benefits of different community prevention approaches. Well-conducted community interventions accompanied by effective evaluation will be important in helping to advance understanding of both the impacts of different community prevention approaches and also the processes by which these interventions lead to impacts.

Research Recommendation 4 **The Feasibility of Alternative Options for Government Control Over the Marketing and Distribution of Tobacco Should Be Investigated**

To further advance tobacco control, the additional application of universal regulatory and enforcement strategies supported by public education campaigns should be considered (see Chapter 5.2). To encourage a consistent approach to regulation, legislation for specific drugs needs to be based on evidence for their harm. As tobacco contributes the highest level of harm, it is fitting that regulatory strategies be adjusted accordingly. Building on international successes in tobacco control, it is timely for new regulatory approaches to tobacco marketing and distribution to be considered. Limiting tobacco distribution to pharmaceutical prescriptions subject to a diagnosis of tobacco dependence should be investigated as one option. Phasing the introduction of this type of policy innovation would enhance the potential for its evaluation.

REFERENCES

Australian Institute of Health and Welfare (2002) *2001 National Drug Strategy Household Survey: First Results.* Canberra: Australian Institute of Health and Welfare.

Babor, T., Caetano, R., Casswell, S., Edwards, G., Giesbrecht, N., Graham, K., Grube, J., Gruenewald, P., Hill, L., Holder, H., Homel, R., Österberg, E., Rehm, J., Room, R. and Rossow, I. (2003) *Alcohol, No Ordinary Commodity: Research and Public Policy.* Oxford: Oxford University Press.

Blewett, N. (1986) Media—servicing medicine or community? Paper presented at Australian Medical Writers Association, Adelaide, 18 September, 1986.

Bloomfield, K., Gmel, G., Grittner, U., Kramer, S. and Eckloff, J. (2004) Social inequalities in alcohol consumption and alcohol-related problems in the study countries of the EU concerted action "Gender, culture and alcohol problems: A multi-national study". Plenary presentation at the 30th annual alcohol epidemiology symposium of the Kettil Bruun Society for social and epidemiological research on alcohol, Helsinki, Finland, 31 May–4 June.

Bullington, B. and Maier-Katkin, D. (2002) Introduction: German drug policy in the 21st century. *Journal of Drug Issues*, **32**(2), 357–362.

Gossop, M., Marsden, J. and Stewart, D. (1998) *NTORS at One Year: Changes in Substance Use, Health and Criminal Behaviour One Year after Intake.* London: Department of Health.

Haemmig, R.B. and Tschacher, W. (2001) Effects of high-dose heroin versus morphine in intravenous drug users: a randomised double-blind crossover study. *Journal of Psychoactive Drugs*, **33**(2), 104–110.

Klingemann, H. (1998) Politics, public opinion and the Swiss Heroin Trial. In T. Stockwell (ed.), *Drug Trials and Tribulations: Lessons for Australian Drug Policy, Proceedings of an International Symposium.* Perth, Western Australia: National Centre for Research into the Prevention of Drug Abuse.

McBride, N. (2004) School drug education: a developing field and one element in a community approach to drugs and young people. *Addiction*, **99**, 292–298.

Loxley, W., Toumbourou, J., Stockwell, T.R., Haines, B., Scott, K., Godfrey, C., Waters, E. and Patton, G. (2004) *The Prevention of Substance Use, Risk and Harm in Australia: A Review of the Evidence.* A report prepared for the Australian Government Department of Health and Ageing. National Drug Research Institute and the Centre for Adolescent Health. Canberra: AGPS.

Manski, C.F., Pepper, J.V. and Petrie, C.V. (2001) *Informing America's Policy on Illegal Drugs: What We Don't Know Keeps Hurting Us.* Washington, DC: National Academy Press.

McBride, N., Farringdon, F., Midford, R., Meuleners, L., and Phillips, M. (2004) Harm minimisation in schools: final results of the School Health and Alcohol Harm Reduction Project (SHAHRP). *Addiction*, **99**, 278–291.

Ridolfo, B. and Stevenson, C. (2001) *The Quantification of Drug-Caused Mortality and Morbidity in Australia, 1998.* Canberra: Australian Institute of Health and Welfare.

Roche, A. and Freeman, T. (2004) Brief interventions: good in theory but weak in practice. *Drug and Alcohol Review*, **23**, 11–18.

Room, R. (2004) Disabling the public interest: alcohol strategies and policies for England. *Addiction.* (In Press)

Smart, R.G. and Mann, R.E. (2000) The impact of programs for high-risk drinkers on population levels of alcohol problems. *Addiction*, **95**(1), 37–52.

Stockwell, T.R. (2004) Harm reduction: the drugification of alcohol policies and the alcoholisation of drug policies. In H. Klingemann and R. Muller (eds), *From Science to Action? 100 Years Later—Alcohol Policies Revisited.* Dordrecht: Kluwer Academic Publishers. pp. 49–59.

Stockwell, T.R., Chikritzhs, T., Hendrie, D., Fordham, R.J., Ying, F., Phillips, M., Cronin, J. and O'Reilly, B. (2001) The public health and safety benefits of the Northern Territory's Living With Alcohol programme. *Drug and Alcohol Review*, **20**(2), 167–180.

Stockwell, T.R., Toumbourou, J., Letcher, P., Smart, D., Sanson, A. and Bond, L. (2004) Risk and protection factors for different intensities of adolescent substance use: when does the Prevention Paradox apply? *Drug and Alcohol Review*, **23**(1), 67–77.

Stoever, H. (2002) Consumption rooms: a middle ground between health and public order concerns. *Journal of Drug Issues*, **32**(2), 597–606.

Suahpush, M. (2004) Smoking and social inequality. Letter to the editor. *Australian and New Zealand Journal of Public Health*, **28**(3), 297.

Toumbourou, J.W., Patton, G., Sawyer, S., Olsson, C., Web-Pullman, J., Catalano, R., and Godfrey, C. (2000) *Evidence-Based Interventions for Promoting Adolescent Health.* Melbourne: Centre for Adolescent Health,

UK Cabinet Office (2004) *Alcohol Harm Reduction Strategy for England.* London: Prime Minister's Strategy Unit. Available online: http://www. strategy.gov.uk/files/pdf/al04SU.pdf

World Health Organization (1998) *Guidelines for Controlling and Monitoring the Tobacco Epidemic.* Geneva: World Health Organization.

World Health Organization (2000a) *Guide to Drug Abuse Epidemiology.* Geneva: World Health Organization.

World Health Organization (2000b) *International Guide for Monitoring Alcohol Consumption and Related Harm.* Geneva: World Health Organization.

Young, D.J., Stockwell, T.R., Cherpitel, C., Ye, Y., MacDonald, S., Borges, G. and Giesbrecht, N. (in press) Emergency room injury presentations as an indicator of alcohol-related problems in the community: A multilevel analysis of an international study. *Journal of Studies on Alcohol.*

Index